WEB DEVELOPMENT WITH DJANGO

Learn to build modern web applications with a Python-based framework

Ben Shaw, Saurabh Badhwar, Andrew Bird, Bharath Chandra K S, and Chris Guest

WEB DEVELOPMENT WITH DJANGO

Authors: Ben Shaw, Saurabh Badhwar, Andrew Bird, Bharath Chandra K S, and Chris Guest

Reviewers: Bidhan Mondal and Subhash Sundaravadivelu

Managing Editors: Abhishek Rane and Saumya Jha

Acquisitions Editors: Sneha Shinde, Anindya Sil, and Alicia Wooding

Production Editor: Shantanu Zagade

Editorial Board: Megan Carlisle, Samuel Christa, Mahesh Dhyani, Heather Gopsill, Manasa Kumar, Alex Mazonowicz, Monesh Mirpuri, Bridget Neale, Dominic Pereira, Shiny Poojary, Abhishek Rane, Brendan Rodrigues, Erol Staveley, Ankita Thakur, Nitesh Thakur, and Jonathan Wray

First published: February 2021

Production reference: 2250521

ISBN: 978-1-83921-250-5

Published by Packt Publishing Ltd.

Livery Place, 35 Livery Street

Birmingham B3 2PB, UK

Table of Contents

Chapter 2: Models and Migrations   69

Chapter 3: URL Mapping, Views, and Templates   129

Chapter 4: Introduction to Django Admin   155

Chapter 5: Serving Static Files

Chapter 6: Forms   273

Chapter 7: Advanced Form Validation and Model Forms   339

Chapter 8: Media Serving and File Uploads   389

Chapter 10: Advanced Django Admin and Customizations 501

Chapter 11: Advanced Templating and Class-Based Views

529

Chapter 16: Using a Frontend JavaScript Library with Django   733

Index   777

PREFACE

ABOUT THE BOOK

Do you want to develop reliable and secure applications that stand out from the crowd, rather than spending hours on boilerplate code? If so, the Django framework is where you should begin. Often referred to as a "batteries included" web development framework, Django comes with all the core features needed to build a standalone application.

Web Development with Django takes this philosophy and equips you with the knowledge and confidence to build real-world applications using Python.

Starting with the essential concepts of Django, you'll cover its major features by building a website called Bookr – a repository for book reviews. This end-to-end case study is split into a series of bitesize projects that are presented as exercises and activities, allowing you to challenge yourself in an enjoyable and attainable way.

As you progress, you'll learn various practical skills, including how to serve static files to add CSS, JavaScript, and images to your application, how to implement forms to accept user input, and how to manage sessions to ensure a reliable user experience. Throughout this book, you'll cover key daily tasks that are part of the development cycle of a real-world web application.

By the end of this book, you'll have the skills and confidence to creatively tackle your own ambitious projects with Django.

ABOUT THE AUTHORS

Ben Shaw is a software engineer based in Auckland, New Zealand. He has worked as a developer for over 14 years and has been building websites with Django since 2007. In that time, his experience has helped many different types of companies, ranging in size from start-ups to large enterprises. He is also interested in machine learning, data science, automating deployments, and DevOps. When not programming, Ben enjoys outdoor sports and spending time with his partner and son.

Saurabh Badhwar is an infrastructure engineer who works on building tools and frameworks that enhance developer productivity. A major part of his work involves using Python to develop services that scale to thousands of concurrent users. He is currently employed at LinkedIn and works on infrastructure performance tools and services.

Andrew Bird is the data and analytics manager of Vesparum Capital. He leads the software and data science teams at Vesparum, overseeing full-stack web development in Django/React. He is an Australian actuary (FIAA, CERA) who has previously worked with Deloitte Consulting in financial services. Andrew also currently works as a full-stack developer for Draftable Pvt. Ltd. He manages ongoing development of the donation portal for the Effective Altruism Australia website on a voluntary basis. Andrew has also co-written one of our bestselling titles, "The Python Workshop".

Bharath Chandra K S lives in Sydney, Australia, and has over 10 years of software industry experience. He is very passionate about software development on the Python stack, including frameworks such as Flask and Django. He has experience of working with both monolithic and microservice architectures and has built various public-facing applications and data processing backend systems. When not cooking up software applications, he likes to cook food.

Chris Guest started programming in Python 20 years ago, when it was an obscure academic language. He has since used his Python knowledge in the publishing, hospitality, medical, and academic sectors. Throughout his career, he has worked with many Python web development frameworks, including Zope, TurboGears, web2py, and Flask, although he still prefers Django.

WHO THIS BOOK IS FOR

Web Development with Django is designed for programmers who want to gain web development skills with the Django framework. To fully understand the concepts explained in this book, you should have basic knowledge of Python programming, as well as familiarity with JavaScript, HTML, and CSS.

ABOUT THE CHAPTERS

Chapter 1, Introduction to Django, starts by getting a Django project set up almost immediately. You'll learn how to bootstrap a Django project, respond to web requests, and use HTML templates.

Chapter 2, Models and Migrations, introduces Django data models, the method of persisting data to a SQL database.

Chapter 3, URL Mapping, Views, and Templates, builds on the techniques that were introduced in *Chapter 1, Introduction to Django*, and explains in greater depth how to route web requests to Python code and render HTML templates.

Chapter 4, Introduction to Django Admin, shows how to use Django's built-in Admin GUI to create, update, and delete data stored by your models.

Chapter 5, Serving Static Files, explains how to enhance your website with styles and images, and how Django makes managing these files easier.

Chapter 6, Forms, shows you how to collect user input through your website by using Django's Forms module.

Chapter 7, Advanced Form Validation and Model Forms, builds upon *Chapter 6, Forms*, by adding more advanced validation logic to make your forms more powerful.

Chapter 8, Media Serving and File Uploads, shows how to further enhance sites by allowing your users to upload files and serve them with Django.

Chapter 9, Sessions and Authentication, introduces the Django session and shows you how to use it to store user data and authenticate users.

Chapter 10, Advanced Django Admin and Customization, continues on from *Chapter 4, Introduction to Django Admin*. Now that you know more about Django, you can customize the Django admin with advanced features.

Chapter 11, Advanced Templating and Class-Based Views, lets you see how to reduce the amount of code you need to write by using some of Django's advanced templating features and classes.

Chapter 12, Building a REST API, gives you a look at how to add a REST API to Django, to allow programmatic access to your data from different applications.

Chapter 13, Generating CSV, PDF, and Other Binary Files, further expands the capabilities of Django by showing how you can use it to generate more than just HTML.

Chapter 14, Testing, is an important part of real-world development. This chapter shows how to use the Django and Python testing frameworks to validate your code.

Chapter 15, Django Third-Party Libraries, exposes you to some of the many community-built Django libraries, showing how to use existing third-party code to quickly add functionality to your project.

Chapter 16, Using a Frontend JavaScript Library with Django, brings interactivity to your website by integrating with React and the REST API that was created in *Chapter 12, Building a REST API*.

Chapter 17, Deployment of a Django Application (Part 1 – Server Setup), begins the process of deploying the application by setting up your own server. This is a bonus chapter and is downloadable from the GitHub repository for this book.

Chapter 18, Deploying a Django Application (Part 2 – Configuration and Code Deployment), finishes up the project by showing you how to deploy your project to a virtual server. This is also a bonus chapter and is downloadable from the GitHub repository for this book.

CONVENTIONS

Code words in text, database table names, folder names, filenames, file extensions, pathnames, dummy URLs, and user input are shown as follows: "It is created and scaffolded by running the **django-admin.py** command on the command line with the **startproject** argument."

Words that you see on screen, for example, in menus or dialog boxes, also appear in the text like this: "In the **Preferences List** pane on the left, open the **Project: Bookr** item and then click **Project Interpreter**."

A block of code is set as follows:

```
urlpatterns = [path('admin/', admin.site.urls),\
               path('', reviews.views.index)]
```

In cases where inputting and executing some code gives an immediate output, this is shown as follows:

```
>>> qd.getlist("k")
['a', 'b', 'c']
```

In the preceding example, the code entered is **qd.getlist("k")** and the output is **['a', 'b', 'c']**.

New terms and important words are shown like this: "Django models define the data for your application and provide an abstraction layer to SQL database access through an **Object Relational Mapper (ORM)**."

Lines of code that span multiple lines are split using a backslash (\ ). When the code is executed, Python will ignore the backslash, and treat the code on the next line as a direct continuation of the current line.

For example:

```
urlpatterns = [path('admin/', admin.site.urls), \
               path('', reviews.views.index)]
```

Long code snippets are truncated and the corresponding names of the code files on GitHub are placed at the top of the truncated code. The permalinks to the entire code are placed beneath the code snippet. It should look as follows:

settings.py

```
INSTALLED_APPS = ['django.contrib.admin',\
                  'django.contrib.auth',\
                  'django.contrib.contenttypes',\
                  'django.contrib.sessions',\
                  'django.contrib.messages',\
                  'django.contrib.staticfiles',\
                  'reviews']
```

The full code can be found at http://packt.live/2Kh58RE.

BEFORE YOU BEGIN

Each great journey begins with a humble step. Before we can do awesome things with Django, we need to be prepared with a productive environment. In this section, we will see how to do that.

INSTALLING PYTHON

Before using Django version 3 or later, you will need Python 3 installed on your computer. Mac and Linux operating systems usually have some version of Python installed, but it's best to make sure you're running the latest version. On Mac, for Homebrew users, you can just type the following:

```
$ brew install python
```

On Debian-based Linux distributions, you can check which version is available by typing the following:

```
$ apt search python3
```

Depending on the output, you can then type something along the lines of the following:

```
$ sudo apt install python3 python3-pip
```

For Windows, you can download the Python 3 installer here: https://www.python.org/downloads/windows/. Once you have the installer, click on it to run, and then follow the instructions. Be sure to select the **Add Python 3.x to PATH** option.

Once installed, from Command Prompt, you can run **python** to launch a Python interpreter.

Note that on macOS and Linux, depending on your configuration, the **python** command might launch Python version 2 or Python version 3. To be sure, make sure to specify **python3**. On Windows, you should just run **python** as this will always launch Python version 3.

Similarly with the **pip** command. On macOS and Linux, specify **pip3**; on Windows, just **pip**.

INSTALLING PYCHARM COMMUNITY EDITION

In *Web Development with Django*, we will be using PyCharm **Continuity Edition (CE)** as our **Integrated Development Environment (IDE)** for editing our code as well as running and debugging it. It can be downloaded from https://www.jetbrains.com/pycharm/download/. Once you have the installer, follow the instructions to install it in the usual way for your operating system.

You can find detailed installation instructions for macOS, Linux, and Windows at this link: https://www.jetbrains.com/help/pycharm/installation-guide.html#standalone. The system requirements for PyCharm can be found here: https://www.jetbrains.com/help/pycharm/installation-guide.html#requirements. For more information on accessing PyCharm after installation, you can follow this link: https://www.jetbrains.com/help/pycharm/run-for-the-first-time.html.

VIRTUALENV

Though not required, we recommend using a Python virtual environment, which will keep the Python packages for *Web Development with Django* separate from your system packages.

First, we'll look at how to set up a virtual environment on macOS and Linux. The **virtualenv** Python package needs to be installed, and this can be done with **pip3**:

```
$ pip3 install virtualenv
```

Then we can create a virtual environment in the current directory:

```
$ python3 -m virtualenv <virtualenvname>
```

Once the virtual environment has been created, we need to source it so that the current terminal knows to use that environment's Python and packages. This is done like this:

```
$ source <virtualenvname>/bin/activate
```

On Windows, we can use the built-in **venv** library, which works in a similar manner. We don't need to install anything. To create a virtual environment in the current directory, we can run the following command:

```
> python -m venv <virtualenvname>
```

Once it has been created, activate it with the activate script inside the **Scripts** directory, which is inside the new virtual environment:

```
> <virtualenvname>\Scripts\activate
```

In macOS, Linux, and Windows, you will know that the virtual environment has been activated because its name, in brackets, will precede the prompt. For example:

```
(virtualenvname) $
```

INSTALLING DJANGO

After activating your virtual environment, you can install Django using **pip3** or **pip** (depending on your operating system). At the time of writing this book, the latest version of Django was 3.1. All the code used in this book is compatible with both Django 3.0 and 3.1. More information on these two different versions is given in the next section. To install Django 3.1, use the following command:

```
(virtualenvname)$ pip3 install django==3.1
```

If you want to install Django 3.0, use the following command:

```
(virtualenvname)$ pip3 install django==3.0
```

As long as your virtual environment has been activated, it will use the version of **pip** in that environment and install packages in that environment too.

DJANGO 3.0 AND DJANGO 3.1

From Django 3.1 onward, the authors of Django changed the method by which paths are joined together in the Django settings file. We'll explain the settings file in depth in *Chapter 1, Introduction to Django*, but for now you just need to know that this file is called **settings.py**.

In earlier versions, the **BASE_DIR** setting variable (the path to your project on disk) was created as a string, like this:

```
BASE_DIR = os.path.dirname(os.path.dirname(os.path.abspath(__file__)))
```

The **os** package was imported into **settings.py**, and paths joined with the **os.path.join** function. For example:

```
STATIC_ROOT = os.path.join(BASE_DIR, "static")  # Django 3.0 and earlier
```

In Django 3.1, **BASE_DIR** is now a **pathlib.Path** object. It is assigned like this:

```
BASE_DIR = Path(__file__).resolve().parent.parent
```

Path objects and strings can be joined using the **/** (divide) operator that **pathlib. Path** overloads:

```
STATIC_ROOT = BASE_DIR / "static"  # Django 3.1+
```

The **os.path.join** function can also be used to join **pathlib.Path** objects, provided that it has been imported into **settings.py** first.

Since most Django projects in production today use versions of Django prior to 3.1, we've chosen to use the **os.path.join** function to join paths throughout this book. If you're using Django 3.1, then you just need to make sure that you add a line to import the **os** module at the start of **settings.py**, like so:

```
import os
```

Once added, you can follow the instructions throughout the book without modification. We'll remind you to make this change when you start working with **settings.py**, too.

Apart from this minor addition, no modifications need to be done to the code examples, exercises, and activities throughout this book to support Django 3.0 or 3.1. We cannot guarantee that all the code examples in this book will be 100% compatible with later versions of Django, and so we strongly recommend that you use either version 3.0 or 3.1 as you work your way through the book.

DB BROWSER FOR SQLITE

This book uses SQLite as an on-disk database when developing your projects. Django provides a command-line interface for accessing its data using the text command, but GUI applications are also available to make data browsing friendlier.

The tool we recommend is **DB Browser for SQLite**, or just **DB Browser** for short. It is a cross-platform (Windows, macOS, and Linux) GUI application.

INSTALLING ON WINDOWS

1. Download the installer for the correct architecture of Windows (32-bit or 64-bit) from https://sqlitebrowser.org/dl/.

2. Run the downloaded installer and follow the Setup Wizard instructions:

Figure 0.1: Setup Wizard page

3. After accepting **End-User License Agreement**, you'll be asked to select shortcuts for the application. It is recommended that you enable **Desktop** and **Program Menu** shortcuts for DB Browser so that once installed, the application is easier to find:

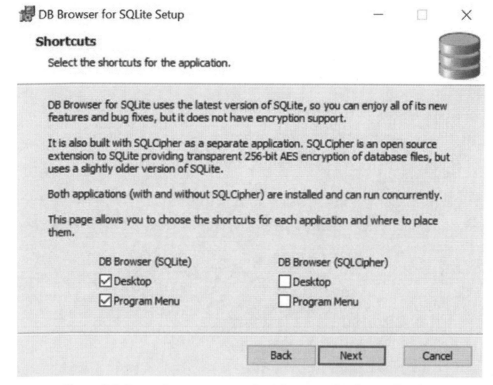

Figure 0.2: Page where you can select shortcuts for the application

4. You should be fine to follow the defaults by just clicking **Next** at each screen throughout the installation.

5. If you didn't add **Program Menu** or **Desktop** shortcuts in *step 3*, then you'll need to find DB Browser in `C:\Program Files\DB Browser for SQLite`.

INSTALLING ON MACOS

1. Download the application disk image for macOS from https://sqlitebrowser.org/dl/.

2. Once the download has finished, open the disk image. You'll see a window like this:

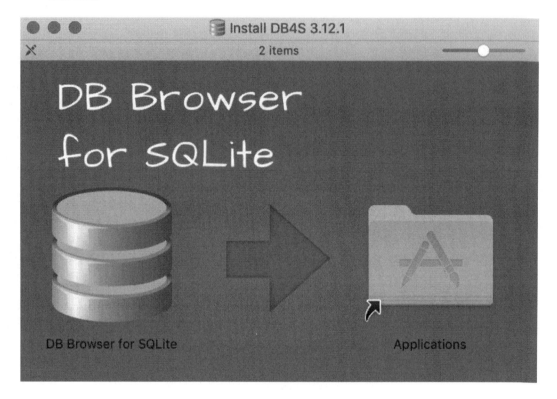

Figure 0.3: Disk image

Drag and drop the **DB Browser for SQLite** application to the **Applications** folder to install it.

3. Once installed, you can launch **DB Browser for SQLite** from inside your **Applications** folder.

INSTALLING ON LINUX

The installation instructions for Linux will depend on which distribution you're using. You can find the instructions at https://sqlitebrowser.org/dl/.

USING DB BROWSER

Here are a few screenshots illustrating a couple of the features of DB Browser. The screenshots were taken on macOS, but the behavior is similar on all platforms. The first step after opening is to select your SQLite database file:

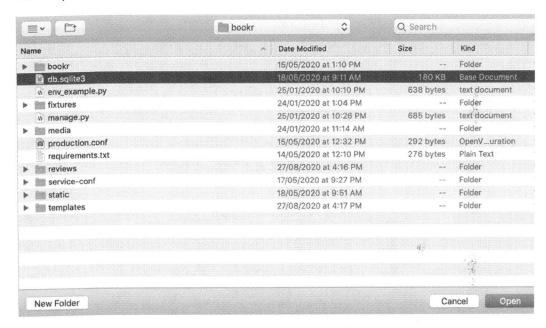

Figure 0.4: Database open dialogue

Once a database file is open, we can explore its structure in the **Database Structure** tab. *Figure 0.5* demonstrates this:

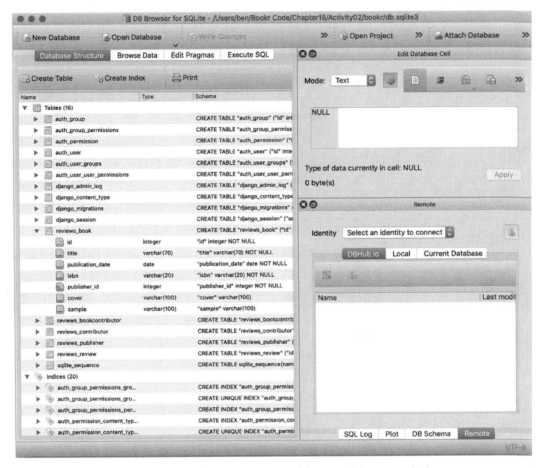

Figure 0.5: Database Structure with one table expanded

The **reviews_book** table has been expanded in the preceding screenshot so that we can see its table structure. We can also browse the data inside tables by switching to the **Browse Data** tab:

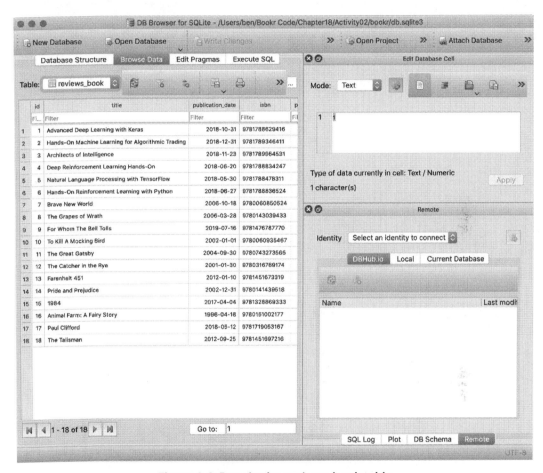

Figure 0.6: Data in the reviews_book table

The final thing we might want to do is execute SQL commands (you'll learn about these in *Chapter 2, Models and Migrations*). This is done inside the **Execute SQL** tab:

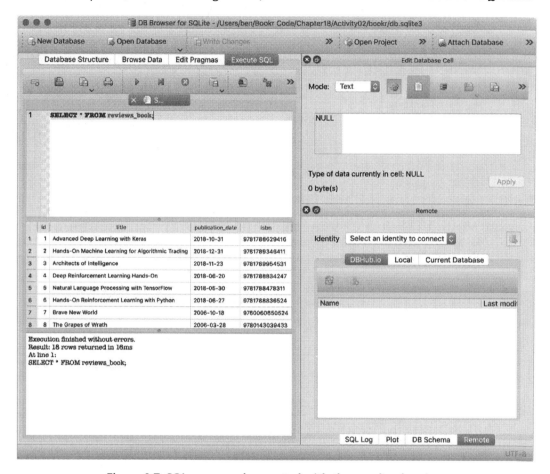

Figure 0.7: SQL command executed with the results showing

Figure 0.7 shows the results of executing the SQL statement **SELECT * FROM reviews_book**.

Don't worry if you're not sure what this all means yet (at this point you don't even have an SQLite file to try this out on). It will make more sense once you start learning about Django models, databases, and SQL queries as you progress through the book. *Chapter 2, Models and Migrations*, is where you'll start working with DB Browser.

THE BOOKR PROJECT

Throughout this book, you'll be progressively building an app called **Bookr**. It is designed to let users browse and add book reviews (and books as well). As you complete the exercises and activities in each chapter, you'll be adding more features to the application. The GitHub repository for this book contains individual folders for the exercises and activities. These folders will usually include the files where the code of the app has changed.

THE FINAL DIRECTORY

Each chapter's code will also have a directory called **final**. This directory will include all the code written for the app through to the end of that chapter. So, for example, the **final** folder for *Chapter 5*, *Serving Static Files*, will contain the full code for the Bookr app until the end of that chapter. That way, if you lose progress, you can use the code in the **final** folder of, say, **Chapter 5**, to start **Chapter 6**.

The following screenshot shows how the directory structure would appear for a chapter after downloading the code from the GitHub repo to disk (refer to the *Installing the Code Bundle* section for more details on how to download the code from the repo):

Name	Date modified	Type
Activity7.01	20-12-2020 16:32	File folder
Activity7.02	20-12-2020 16:32	File folder
Exercise7.01	20-12-2020 16:32	File folder
Exercise7.02	20-12-2020 16:32	File folder
Exercise7.03	20-12-2020 16:32	File folder
final	20-12-2020 16:32	File folder

Figure 0.8: Chapter-level directory structure for Bookr

POPULATING THE DATA

When you reach *Chapter 2*, *Models and Migrations*, it is recommended that you populate your database with the list of sample books we have provided so that your end result remains more or less similar to ours. Make sure you don't skip the section entitled *Populating the Bookr Database* in *Chapter 2*, *Models and Migrations*, wherein we have provided a tiny script that lets you quickly populate the database.

INSTALLING THE CODE BUNDLE

Download the code files from GitHub at http://packt.live/3nIWPvB. Refer to these code files for the complete code bundle. The files here contain the exercises, activities, activity solutions, bonus chapters, and some intermediate code for each chapter.

On the GitHub repo's page, you can click the green **Code** button and then click the **Download ZIP** option to download the complete code as a ZIP file to your disk (refer to *Figure 0.9*). You can then extract these code files to a folder of your choice, for example, **C:\Code**:

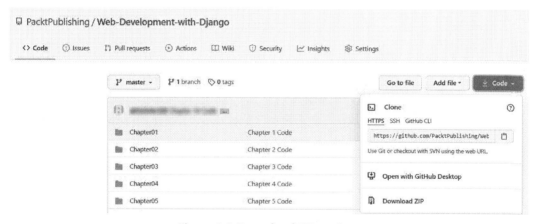

Figure 0.9: Download ZIP option

GET IN TOUCH

Feedback from our readers is always welcome.

General feedback: If you have any questions about this book, please mention the book title in the subject of your message and email us at **customercare@ packtpub.com**.

Errata: Although we have taken every care to ensure the accuracy of our content, mistakes do happen. If you have found a mistake in this book, we would be grateful if you could report this to us. Please visit www.packtpub.com/support/errata and complete the form.

Piracy: If you come across any illegal copies of our works in any form on the internet, we would be grateful if you could provide us with the location address or website name. Please contact us at **copyright@packt.com** with a link to the material.

If you are interested in becoming an author: If there is a topic that you have expertise in, and you are interested in either writing or contributing to a book, please visit authors.packtpub.com.

PLEASE LEAVE A REVIEW

Let us know what you think by leaving a detailed, impartial review on Amazon. We appreciate all feedback – it helps us continue to make great products and help aspiring developers build their skills. Please spare a few minutes to give your thoughts – it makes a big difference to us. You can leave a review by clicking the following link: https://packt.link/r/9781839212505.

1

INTRODUCTION TO DJANGO

OVERVIEW

This chapter introduces you to Django and its role in web development. You will begin by learning how the **Model View Template** (**MVT**) paradigm works and how Django processes HTTP **requests** and **responses**. Equipped with the basic concepts, you'll create your first Django project, called **Bookr**, an application for adding, viewing, and managing book reviews. It's an application you'll keep enhancing and adding features to throughout this book. You will then learn about the `manage.py` command (used to orchestrate Django actions). You will use this command to start the Django development server and test whether the code you've written works as expected. You will also learn how to work with **PyCharm**, a popular Python IDE that you'll be using throughout this book. You will use it to write code that returns a **response** to your web browser. Finally, you'll learn how to use PyCharm's debugger to troubleshoot problems with your code. By the end of this chapter, you'll have the necessary skills to start creating projects using Django.

INTRODUCTION

"The web framework for perfectionists with deadlines." It's a tagline that aptly describes Django, a framework that has been around for over 10 years now. It is battle-tested and widely used, with more and more people using it every day. All this might make you think that Django is old and no longer relevant. On the contrary, its longevity has proved that its Application Programming Interface (API) is reliable and consistent, and even those who learned Django v1.0 in 2007 can mostly write the same code for Django 3 today. Django is still in active development, with bugfixes and security patches being released monthly.

Like Python, the language in which it is written, Django is easy to learn, yet powerful and flexible enough to grow with your needs. It is a "batteries-included" framework, which is to say that you do not have to find and install many other libraries or components to get your application up and running. Other frameworks, such as **Flask** or **Pylons**, require manually installing third-party frameworks for database connections or template rendering. Instead, Django has built-in support for database querying, URL mapping, and template rendering (we'll go into detail on what these mean soon). But just because Django is easy to use doesn't mean it is limited. Django is used by many large sites, including Disqus (https://disqus.com/), Instagram (https://www.instagram.com/), Mozilla (https://www.mozilla.org/), Pinterest (https://www.pinterest.com/), Open Stack (https://www.openstack.org/), and National Geographic (http://www.nationalgeographic.com/).

Where does Django fit into the web? When talking about web frameworks, you might think of frontend JavaScript frameworks such as ReactJS, Angular, or Vue. These frameworks are used to enhance or add interactivity to already-generated web pages. Django sits in the layer beneath these tools and instead is responsible for routing a URL, fetching data from databases, rendering templates, and handling form input from users. However, this does not mean you must pick one or the other; JavaScript frameworks can be used to enhance the output from Django, or to interact with a REST API generated by Django.

In this book, we will build a Django project using the methods that professional Django developers use every day. The application is called **Bookr**, and it allows browsing and adding books and book reviews. This book is divided into four sections. In the first section, we'll start with the basics of scaffolding a Django app and quickly build some pages and serve them with the Django development server. You'll be able to add data to the database using the Django admin site.

The next section focuses on adding enhancements to Bookr. You'll serve static files to add styles and images to the site. By using Django's **form** library, you'll add interactivity, and by using file uploads, you will be able to upload book covers and other files. You'll then implement user login and learn how to store information about the current user in the session.

In section three, you'll build on your existing knowledge and move to the next level of development. You'll customize the Django admin site and then learn about advanced templating. Next, you'll learn how to build a **REST API** and generate non-HTML data (such as CSVs and PDFs), and you'll finish the section by learning about testing Django.

Many third-party libraries are available to add functionality to Django and to make development easier and thus save time. In the final section, you'll learn about some of the useful ones and how to integrate them into your application. Applying this knowledge, you'll integrate a JavaScript library to communicate with the REST framework you built in the previous section. Finally, you'll learn how to deploy your Django application to a virtual server.

By the end of the book, you will have enough experience to design and build your own Django project from start to finish.

SCAFFOLDING A DJANGO PROJECT AND APP

Before diving deep into the theory behind Django paradigms and HTTP requests, we'll show you how easy it is to get a Django project up and running. After this first section and exercise, you will have created a Django project, made a request to it with your browser, and seen the response.

A Django project is a directory that contains all the data for your project: code, settings, templates, and assets. It is created and scaffolded by running the **django-admin.py** command on the command line with the **startproject** argument and providing the project name. For example, to create a Django project with the name **myproject**, the command that is run is this:

```
django-admin.py startproject myproject
```

This will create the **myproject** directory, which Django populates with the necessary files to run the project. Inside the **myproject** directory are two files (shown in *Figure 1.1*):

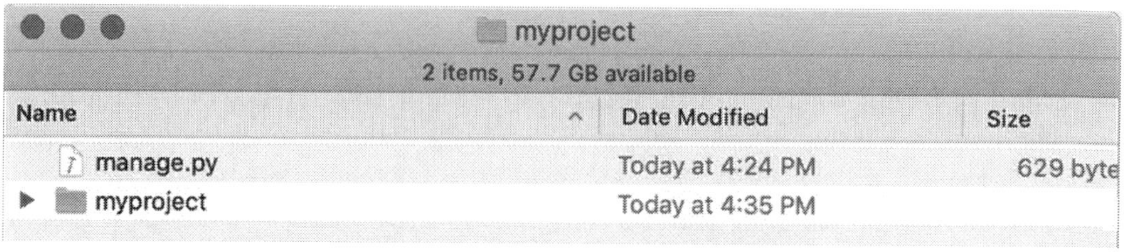

Figure 1.1: Project directory for myproject

manage.py is a Python script that is executed at the command line to interact with your project. We will use it to start the **Django dev server**, a development web server you will use to interact with your Django project on your local computer. Like **django-admin.py**, commands are passed in on the command line. Unlike **django-admin.py**, this script is not mapped in your system path, so we must execute it using Python. We will need to use the command line to do that. For example, inside the project directory, run the following command:

```
python3 manage.py runserver
```

This passes the **runserver** command to the **manage.py** script, which starts the Django dev server. We will examine more of the commands that **manage.py** accepts in the *Django Project* section. When interacting with **manage.py** in this way, we call these management commands. For example, we might say that we are *"executing the runserver management command."*

The **startproject** command also created a directory with the same name as the project, in this case, **myproject** (*Figure 1.1*). This is a Python package that contains settings and some other configuration files that your project needs to run. We will examine its contents in the *Django Project* section.

After starting the Django project, the next thing to do is to start a Django app. We should try to segregate our Django project into different apps, grouped by functionality. For example, with Bookr, we will have a **reviews** app. This will hold all the code, HTML, assets, and database classes specific to working with book reviews. If we decided to expand Bookr to sell books as well, we might add a **store** application, containing the files for the bookstore. Apps are created with the **startapp** management command, passing in the application name. For example:

```
python3 manage.py startapp myapp
```

This creates the app directory (**myapp**) inside the project directory. Django automatically populates this with files for the app that are ready to be filled in when you start developing. We'll examine these files and discuss what makes a good app in the *Django Apps* section.

Now that we've introduced the basic commands to scaffold a Django project and application, let's put them into practice by starting the Bookr project in the first exercise of this book.

EXERCISE 1.01: CREATING A PROJECT AND APP, AND STARTING THE DEV SERVER

Throughout this book, we will be building a book review website named Bookr. It will allow you to add fields for publishers, contributors, books, and reviews. A publisher will publish one or more books, and each book will have one or more contributors (author, editor, co-author, and so on). Only admin users will be allowed to modify these fields. Once a user has signed up for an account on the site, they will be able to start adding reviews to a book.

In this exercise, you will scaffold the **bookr** Django project, test that Django is working by running the dev server, then create the **reviews** Django app.

You should already have a virtual environment set up with Django installed. To learn how to do that, you can refer to the *Preface*. Once you're ready, let's start by creating the Bookr project:

1. Open a Terminal and run the following command to create the **bookr** project directory and the default subfolders:

```
django-admin startproject bookr
```

This command does not generate any output but will create a folder called **bookr** inside the directory in which you ran the command. You can look inside this directory and see the items we described before for the **myproject** example: the **bookr** package directory and **manage.py** file.

2. We can now test that the project and Django are set up correctly by running the Django dev server. Starting the server is done with the **manage.py** script.

   In your Terminal (or Command Prompt), change into the **bookr** project directory (using the **cd** command), then run the **manage.py runserver** command.

```
python3 manage.py runserver
```

> **NOTE**
>
> On Windows, you may need to run replace **python3** (highlighted) with just **python** to make the command work every time you run it.

This command starts the Django dev server. You should get output similar to the following:

```
Watching for file changes with StatReloader
Performing system checks...

System check identified no issues (0 silenced).

You have 17 unapplied migration(s). Your project may not work
properly until you apply the migrations for app(s): admin, auth,
contenttypes, sessions.
Run 'python manage.py migrate' to apply them.

September 14, 2019 - 09:40:45
Django version 3.0a1, using settings 'bookr.settings'
Starting development server at http://127.0.0.1:8000/
Quit the server with CONTROL-C.
```

You will probably have some warnings about unapplied migrations, but that's okay for now.

3. Open up a web browser and go to `http://127.0.0.1:8000/`, which will show you the Django welcome screen (*Figure 1.2*). If you see this, you know your Django project was created successfully and it all is working fine for now:

The install worked successfully! Congratulations!

You are seeing this page because DEBUG=True is in your settings file and you have not configured any URLs.

⚪ **Django Documentation**
Topics, references, & how-to's

‹› **Tutorial: A Polling App**
Get started with Django

Figure 1.2: Django welcome screen

4. Go back to your Terminal and stop the development server running using the *Ctrl + C* key combination.

5. We'll now create the **reviews** app for the **bookr** project. In your Terminal, make sure you are in the **bookr** project directory, then execute the following command to create the **reviews** app:

```
python3 manage.py startapp reviews
```

> **NOTE**
>
> After creating the **reviews** app, the files in your **bookr** project directory would look like this: http://packt.live/3nZGy5D.

There is no output if the command was successful, but a **reviews** app directory has been created. You can look inside this directory to see the files that were created: the **migrations** directory, **admin.py**, **models.py**, and so on. We'll examine these in detail in the *Django Apps* section.

In this exercise, we created the **bookr** project, tested that the project was working by starting the Django dev server, then created the **reviews** app for the project. Now that we've had some hands-on time with a Django project, we'll return to some of the theory behind Django's design and HTTP requests and responses.

MODEL VIEW TEMPLATE

A common design pattern in application design is **Model View Controller** (**MVC**), where the model of the application (its data) is displayed in one or more views and a controller marshals interaction between the model and view. Django follows a somewhat similar paradigm called **Model View Template** (**MVT**).

Like MVC, MVT also uses models for storing data. However, with MVT, a view will query a model and then render it with a template. Usually, with MVC languages, all three components need to be developed with the same language. With MVT, the template can be in a different language. In the case of Django, the models and views are written in Python and the Template in HTML. This means that a Python developer could work on the models and views, while a specialist HTML developer works on the HTML. We'll first explain models, views, and templates in more detail, and then look at some example scenarios where they are used.

MODELS

Django models define the data for your application and provide an abstraction layer to SQL database access through an **Object Relational Mapper** (**ORM**). An ORM lets you define your data schema (classes, fields, and their relationships) using Python code, without needing an understanding of the underlying database. This means you can define your database layer in Python code and Django will take care of generating SQL queries for you. ORMs will be discussed in detail in *Chapter 2, Models and Migrations*.

> **NOTE**
>
> **SQL** stands for **Structured Query Language** and is a way of describing a type of database that stores its data in tables, with each table having several rows. Think of each table being like an individual spreadsheet. Unlike a spreadsheet, though, relationships can be defined between the data in each table. You can interact with data by executing SQL queries (often referred to as just queries when talking about databases). Queries allow you to retrieve data (**SELECT**), add or change data (**INSERT** and **UPDATE** respectively), and remove data (**DELETE**). There are many SQL database servers to choose from, such as SQLite, PostgreSQL, MySQL, or Microsoft SQL Server. Much of the SQL syntax is similar between databases, but there can be some differences in dialect. Django's ORM takes care of these differences for you: when we start coding, we will use the SQLite database to store data on disk, but later when we deploy to a server, we will switch to PostgreSQL but won't need to make any code changes.

Normally, when querying a database, the results come back as primitive Python objects, (for example, lists of strings, integers, floats, or bytes). When using the ORM, results are automatically converted into instances of the model classes you have defined. Using an ORM means that you are automatically protected from a type of vulnerability known as a SQL injection attack.

If you're more familiar with databases and SQL, you always have the option of writing your own queries too.

VIEWS

A Django view is where most of the logic for your application is defined. When a user visits your site, their web browser will send a request to retrieve data from your site (in the next section, we will go into more detail on what an HTTP request is and what information it contains). A view is a function that you write that will receive this request in the form of a Python object (specifically, a Django **HttpRequest** object). It is up to your view to decide how it should respond to the request and what it should send back to the user. Your view must return an **HttpResponse** object that encapsulates all the information being provided to the client: content, HTTP status, and other headers.

The view can also optionally receive information from the URL of the request, for example, an ID number. A common design pattern of a view is to query a database via the Django ORM using an ID that is passed into your view. Then the view can render a template (more on this in a moment) by providing it with data from the model retrieved from the database. The rendered template becomes the content of **HttpResponse** and is returned from the view function. Django takes care of the communication of the data back to the browser.

TEMPLATES

A template is a **HyperText Markup Language** (**HTML**) file (usually – any text file can be a template) that contains special placeholders that are replaced by variables your application provides. For example, your application could render a list of items in either a gallery layout or a table layout. Your view would fetch the same models for either one but would be able to render a different HTML file with the same information to present the data differently. Django emphasizes safety, so it will take care of automatically escaping variables for you. For example, the < and > symbols (among others) are special characters in HTML. If you try to use them in a variable, then Django automatically encodes them so they render correctly in a browser.

MVT IN PRACTICE

We'll now look at some examples to illustrate how MVT works in practice. In the examples, we have a **Book** model that stores information about different books, and a **Review** model that stores information about different reviews of the books.

In the first example, we want to be able to edit the information about a book or review. Take the first scenario, editing a book's details. We would have a view to fetch the **Book** data from the database and provide the **Book** model. Then, we would pass context information containing the **Book** object (and other data) to a template that would show a form to capture the new information. The second scenario (editing a review) is similar: fetch a **Review** model from the database, then pass the **Review** object and other data to a template to display an edit form. These scenarios might be so similar that we can reuse the same template for both. Refer to *Figure 1.3*.

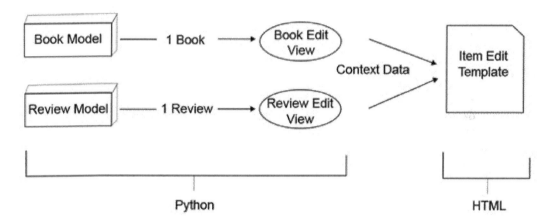

Figure 1.3: Editing a single book or review

You can see here that we use two models, two views, and one template. Each view fetches a single instance of its associated model, but they can both use the same template, which is a generic HTML page to display a form. The views can provide extra context data to slightly alter the display of the template for each model type. Also illustrated in the diagram are the parts of the code that are written in Python and those that are written in HTML.

In the second example, we want to be able to show the user a list of the books or reviews that are stored in the application. Furthermore, we want to allow the user to search for books and get a list of all that match their criteria. We will use the same two models as the previous example (**Book** and **Review**), but we will create new views and templates. Since there are three scenarios, we'll use three views this time: the first fetches all books, the second fetches all reviews, and the last searches for books based on some search criteria. Once again, if we write a template well, we might be able to just use a single HTML template again. Refer to *Figure 1.4*:

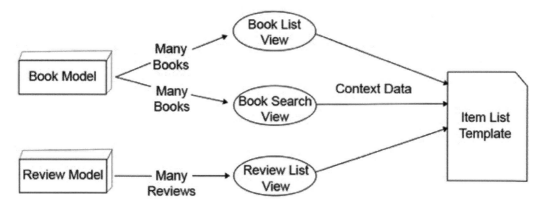

Figure 1.4: Viewing multiple books or reviews

The **Book** and **Review** models remain unchanged from the previous example. The three views will fetch many (zero or more) books or reviews. Then, each view can use the same template, which is a generic HTML file that iterates over a list of objects that it is given and renders them. Once again, the views can send extra data in the context to alter how the template behaves, but the majority of the template will be as generic as possible.

In Django, a model does not always need to be used to render an HTML template. A view can generate the context data itself and render a template with it, without requiring any model data. See *Figure 1.5* for a view sending data straight to a template:

Figure 1.5: From view to template without a model

In this example, there is a welcome view to welcome a user to the site. It doesn't need any information from the database, so it can just generate the context data itself. The context data depends on the type of information you want to display; for example, you could pass the user information to greet them by name if they are logged in. It is also possible for a view to render a template without any context data. This can be useful if you have static information in an HTML file that you want to serve.

INTRODUCTION TO HTTP

Now that you have been introduced to MVT in Django, we can look at how Django processes an HTTP request and generates an HTTP response. But first, we need to explain in more detail what HTTP requests and responses are, and what information they contain.

Let's say someone wants to visit your web page. They type in its URL or click a link to your site from a page they are already on. Their web browser creates an HTTP request, which is sent to the server hosting your website. Once a web server receives the HTTP request from your browser, it can interpret it and then send back a response. The response that the server sends might be simple, such as just reading an HTML or image file from disk and sending it. Or, the response might be more complex, maybe using server-side software (such as Django) to dynamically generate the content before sending it:

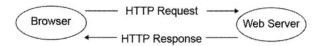

Figure 1.6: HTTP request and HTTP response

The request is made up of four main parts: the method, path, headers, and body. Some types of requests don't have a body. If you just visit a web page, your browser will not send a body, whereas if you are submitting a form (for example, by logging into a site or performing a search), then your request will have a body containing the data you're submitting. We'll look at two example requests now to illustrate this.

The first request will be to an example page with the URL **https://www.example. com/page**. When your browser visits that page, behind the scenes, this is what it's sending:

```
GET /page HTTP/1.1
Host: www.example.com
User-Agent: Mozilla/5.0 (X11; Ubuntu; Linux x86_64; rv:15.0)
Firefox/15.0.1
Cookie: sessid=abc123def456
```

The first line contains the method (**GET**) and the path (**/page**). It also contains the HTTP version, in this case, **1.1**, although you don't have to worry about this. Many different HTTP methods can be used, depending on how you want to interact with the remote page. Some common ones are **GET** (retrieve the remote page), **POST** (send data to the remote page), **PUT** (create a remote page), and **DELETE** (delete the remote page). Note that the descriptions of the actions are somewhat simplified—the remote server can choose how it responds to different methods, and even experienced developers can disagree on the correct method to implement for a particular action. It's also important to note that even if a server supports a particular method, you will probably need the correct permissions to perform that action—you can't just use **DELETE** on a web page you don't like, for example.

When writing a web application, the vast majority of the time, you will only deal with **GET** requests. When you start accepting forms, you'll also have to use **POST** requests. It is only when you are working with advanced features such as creating REST APIs that you will have to worry about **PUT**, **DELETE**, and other methods.

Referring back to the example request again, from line 2 onward are the headers of the request. The headers contain extra metadata about the request. Each header is on its own line, with the header name and its value separated by a colon. Most are optional (except for **Host**—more on that soon). Header names are not case sensitive. For the sake of the example, we're only showing three common headers here. Let's look at the example headers in order:

- **Host**: As mentioned, this is the only header that is required (for HTTP 1.1 or later). It is needed for the webserver to know which website or application should respond to the request, in case there are multiple sites hosted on a single server.

- **User-Agent**: Your browser usually sends to the server a string identifying its version and operating system. Your server application could use this to serve different pages to different devices (for example, a mobile-specific page for smartphones).

- **Cookie**: You have probably seen a message when visiting a web page that lets you know that it is storing a cookie in the browser. These are small pieces of information that a website can store in your browser that can be used to identify you or save settings for when you return to the site. If you were wondering about how your browser sends these cookies back to the server, it is through this header.

There are many other standard headers defined and it would take up too much space to list them all. They can be used to authenticate to the server (**Authorization**), tell the server what kind of data you can receive (**Accept**), or even state what language you'd like for the page (**Accept-Language**, although this will only work if the page creator has made the content available in the particular language you request). You can even define your own headers that only your application knows how to respond to.

Now let's look at a slightly more advanced request: one that sends some information to a server, and thus (unlike the previous example) contains a body. In this example, we are logging into a web page by sending a username and password. For example, you visit **https://www.example.com/login** and it displays a form to enter username and password. After you click the **Login** button, this is the request that is sent to the server:

```
POST /login HTTP/1.1
Host: www.example.com
Content-Type: application/x-www-form-urlencoded
Content-Length: 32

username=user1&password=password1
```

As you can see, this looks similar to the first example, but there are a few differences. The method is now **POST**, and two new headers have been introduced (you can assume your browser would still be sending the other headers that were in the previous example too):

- **Content-Type** : This tells the server the type of data that is included in the body. In the case of **application/x-www-form-urlencoded**, the body is a set of key-value pairs. An HTTP client could set this header to tell the server if it was sending other types of data, such as JSON or XML, for example.

- **Content-Length**: For the server to know how much data to read, the client must tell it how much data is being sent. The **Content-Length** header contains the length of the body. If you count the length of the body in this example, you'll see it's 32 characters.

The headers are always separated from the body by a blank line. By looking at the example, you should be able to tell how the form data is encoded in the body: **username** has the value **user1** and **password** the value **password1**.

These requests were quite simple, but most requests don't get much more complicated. They might have different methods and headers but should follow the same format. Now that you've seen requests, we'll take a look at the HTTP responses that come back from the server.

An HTTP response looks similar to a request and consists of three main parts: a status, headers, and a body. Like a request, though, depending on the type of response, it might not have a body. The first response example is a simple successful response:

```
HTTP/1.1 200 OK
Server: nginx
Content-Length: 18132
Content-Type: text/html
Set-Cookie: sessid=abc123def46


<!DOCTYPE html><html><head>…
```

The first line contains the HTTP version, a numeric status code (**200**), and then a text description of what the code means (**OK**—the request was a success). We'll show some more statuses after the next example. Lines 2 to 5 contain headers, similar to a request. Some headers you have seen before; we will explain them all in this context:

- **Server**: This is similar to but the opposite of the **User-Agent** header: this is the server telling the client what software it is running.

- **Content-Length**: The client uses this value to determine how much data to read from the server to get the body.

- **Content-Type**: The server uses this header to indicate to the client what type of data it is sending. The client can then choose how it will display the data—an image must be displayed differently to HTML, for example.

- **Set-Cookie**: We saw in the first request example how a client sends a cookie to the server. This is the corresponding header that a server sends to set that cookie in the browser.

After the headers is a blank line, and then the body of the response. We haven't shown it all here, just the first few characters of the HTML that is being received, out of the 18,132 that the server has sent.

Next, we'll show an example of a response that is returned if a requested page is not found:

```
HTTP/1.1 404 Not Found
Server: nginx
Content-Length: 55
Content-Type: text/html

<!DOCTYPE html><html><body>Page Not Found</body></html>
```

It is similar to the previous example, but the status is now **404 Not Found**. If you've ever been browsing the internet and received a **404** error, this is the type of response your browser received. The various status codes are grouped by the type of success or failure they indicate:

- **100-199**: The server sends codes in this range to indicate protocol changes or that more data is required. You don't have to worry about these.

- **200-299**: A status code in this range indicates the successful handling of a response. The most common one you will deal with is **200 OK**.

- **300-399**: A status code in this range means the page you are requesting has moved to another address. An example of this is a URL shortening service that would redirect you from the short URL to the full one when you visit it. Common responses are **301 Moved Permanently** or **302 Found**. When sending a redirect response, the server will also include a **Location** header that contains the URL that should be redirected to.

- **400-499**: A status code in this range means that the request could not be handled because there was a problem with what the client sent. This is in contrast to a request not being able to be handled due to a problem on the server (we will discuss those soon). We've already seen a *404 Not Found* response; this is due to a bad request because the client is requesting a document that does not exist. Some other common responses are **401 Unauthorized** (the client should log in) and **403 Forbidden** (the client is not allowed to access the specific resource). Both problems could be avoided by having the client login, hence them being considered client-side (request) problems.

- **500-599**: Status codes in this range indicate an error on the server's side. The client shouldn't expect to be able to adjust the request to fix the problem. When working with Django, the most common server error status you will see is **500 Internal Server Error**. This will be generated if your code raises an exception. Another common one is **504 Gateway Timeout**, which might occur if your code is taking too long to run. The other variants that are common to see are **502 Bad Gateway** and **503 Service Unavailable**, which generally mean there is a problem with your application's hosting in some way.

These are only some of the most common HTTP statuses. You can find a more complete list at https://developer.mozilla.org/en-US/docs/Web/HTTP/Status. Like HTTP headers, though, statuses are arbitrary, and an application can return custom statuses. It is up to the server and clients to decide what these custom statuses and codes mean.

If this is your first time being introduced to the HTTP protocol, there's quite a lot of information to take in. Luckily, Django does all the hard work and encapsulates the incoming data into an **HttpRequest** object. Most of the time, you don't need to know about most of the information coming in, but it's available if you need it. Likewise, when sending a response, Django encapsulates your data in an **HttpResponse** object. Normally you just set the content to return, but you also have the freedom to set HTTP status codes and headers. We will discuss how to access and set the information in **HttpRequest** and **HttpResponse** later in this chapter.

PROCESSING A REQUEST

This is a basic timeline of the request and response flows, so you can get an idea of what the code you'll be writing does at each stage. In terms of writing code, the first part you will write is your view. The view you create will perform some actions, such as querying the database for data. Then the view will pass this data to another function to render a template, finally returning the **HttpResponse** object encompassing the data you want to send back to the client.

Next, Django needs to know how to map a specific URL to your view, so that it can load the correct view for the URL it receives as part of a request. You will write this URL mapping in a URL configuration Python file.

When Django receives a request, it parses the URL config file, then finds the corresponding view. It calls the view, passing in an **HttpRequest** object representing the request. Your view will return its **HttpResponse**, then Django takes over again to send this data to its host web server and back out to the client that requested it:

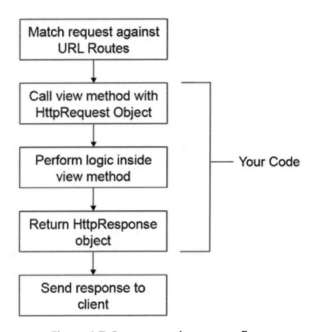

Figure 1.7: Request and response flow

The request-response flow is illustrated in *Figure 1.7*; the sections indicated as *Your Code* are code that you write—the first and last steps are taken care of by Django. Django does the URL matching for you, calls your view code, then handles passing the response back to the client.

DJANGO PROJECT

We already introduced Django projects in a previous section. To remind ourselves of what happens when we run **startproject** (for a project named **myproject**): the command creates a **myproject** directory with a file called **manage.py**, and a directory called **myproject** (this matches the project name, in *Exercise 1.01, Creating a Project and App, and Starting the Dev Server*; this folder was called **bookr**, the same as the project). The directory layout is shown in *Figure 1.8*. We'll now examine the **manage.py** file and the **myproject** package contents in more detail:

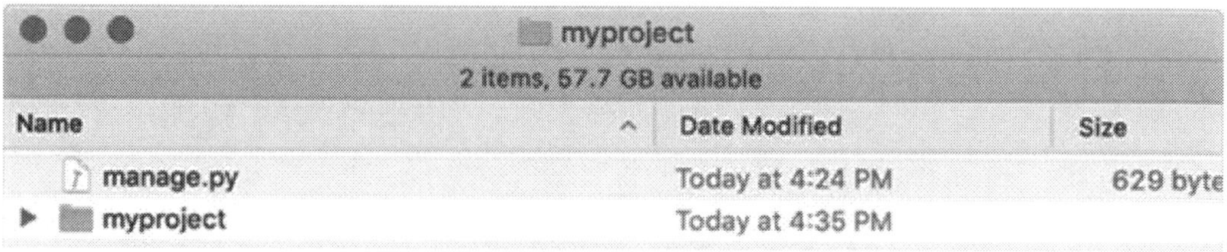

Name	Date Modified	Size
manage.py	Today at 4:24 PM	629 byte
▶ myproject	Today at 4:35 PM	

myproject
2 items, 57.7 GB available

Figure 1.8: Project directory for myproject

manage.py

As the name suggests, this is a script that is used to manage your Django project. Most of the commands that are used to interact with your project will be supplied to this script on the command line. The commands are supplied as an argument to this script; for example, if we say to run the **manage.py runserver** command, we would mean running the **manage.py** script like this:

```
python3 manage.py runserver
```

There are a number of useful commands that **manage.py** provides. You will be introduced to them in more detail throughout the book; some of the more common ones are listed here:

- **runserver**: Starts the Django development HTTP server, to serve your Django app on your local computer.

- **startapp**: Creates a new Django app in your project. We'll talk about what apps are in more depth soon.

- **shell**: Starts a Python interpreter with the Django settings pre-loaded. This is useful for interacting with your application without having to manually load in your Django settings.

- **dbshell**: Starts an interactive shell connected to your database, using the default parameters from your Django settings. You can run manual SQL queries in this way.

- **makemigrations**: Generate database change instructions from your model definitions. You will learn what this means and how to use this command in *Chapter 2, Models and Migrations*.

- **migrate**: Applies migrations generated by the **makemigrations** command. You will use this in *Chapter 2, Models and Migrations*, as well.

- **test**: Run automated tests that you have written. You'll use this command in *Chapter 14, Testing*.

A full list of all commands is available at https://docs.djangoproject.com/en/3.0/ref/django-admin/.

THE MYPROJECT DIRECTORY

Moving on from the **manage.py** file, the other file item created by **startproject** is the **myproject** directory. This is the actual Python package for your project. It contains settings for the project, some configuration files for your web server, and the global URL maps. Inside the **myproject** directory are five files:

- **__init__.py**

- **asgi.py**

- **settings.py**

- **urls.py**

- **wsgi.py**

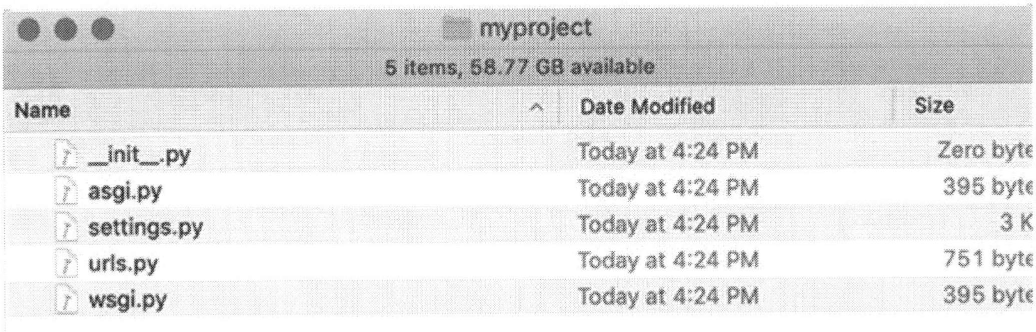

Name	Date Modified	Size
__init__.py	Today at 4:24 PM	Zero byte
asgi.py	Today at 4:24 PM	395 byte
settings.py	Today at 4:24 PM	3 K
urls.py	Today at 4:24 PM	751 byte
wsgi.py	Today at 4:24 PM	395 byte

myproject
5 items, 58.77 GB available

Figure 1.9: The myproject package (inside the myproject project directory)

__init__.py

An empty file that lets Python know that the **myproject** directory is a Python module. You'll be familiar with these files if you've worked with Python before.

settings.py

This contains all the Django settings for your application. We will explain the contents soon.

urls.py

This has the global URL mappings that Django will initially use to locate views or other child URL mappings. You will add a URL map to this file soon.

asgi.py and wsgi.py

These files are what ASGI or WSGI web servers use to communicate with your Django app when you deploy it to a production web server. You normally don't need to edit these at all, and they aren't used in day-to-day development. Their use will be discussed more in *Chapter 17, Deployment of a Django Application*.

DJANGO DEVELOPMENT SERVER

You have already started the Django dev server in *Exercise 1.01, Creating a Project and App, and Starting the Dev Server*. As we mentioned previously, it is a web server intended to only be run on the developer's machine during development. It is not intended for use in production.

By default, the server listens on port **8000** on **localhost (127.0.0.1)**, but this can be changed by adding a port number or address and port number after the **runserver** argument:

```
python3 manage.py runserver 8001
```

This will have the server listen on port **8001** on **localhost (127.0.0.1)**.

You can also have it listen on a specific address if your computer has more than one, or **0.0.0.0** for all addresses:

```
python3 manage.py runserver 0.0.0.0:8000
```

This will have the server listen on all your computer's addresses on port **8000**, which can be useful if you want to test your application from another computer or your smartphone.

The development server watches your Django project directory and will restart automatically every time you save a file so that any code changes you make are automatically reloaded into the server. You still have to manually refresh your browser to see changes there, though.

When you want to stop the **runserver** command, it can be done in the usual way for stopping processes in the Terminal: by using the *Ctrl + C* key combination.

DJANGO APPS

Now that we've covered a bit of theory about apps, we can be more specific about their purpose. An app directory contains all the models, views, and templates (and more) that they need to provide application functionality. A Django project will contain at least one app (unless it has been heavily customized to not rely on a lot of Django functionality). If well designed, an app should be able to be removed from a project and moved to another project without modification. Usually, an app will contain models for a single design domain, and this can be a useful way of determining whether your app should be split into multiple apps.

Your app can have any name as long as it is a valid Python module name (that is, using only letters, numbers, and underscores) and does not conflict with other files in your project directory. For example, as we have seen, there is already a directory called **myproject** in the project directory (containing the **settings.py** file), so you could not have an app called **myproject**. As we saw in *Exercise 1.01, Creating a Project and App, and Starting the Dev Server*, creating an app uses the **manage.py startapp appname** command. For example:

```
python3 manage.py startapp myapp
```

The **startapp** command creates a directory within your project with the name of the app specified. It also scaffolds files for the app. Inside the **app** directory are several files and a folder, as shown in *Figure 1.10*:

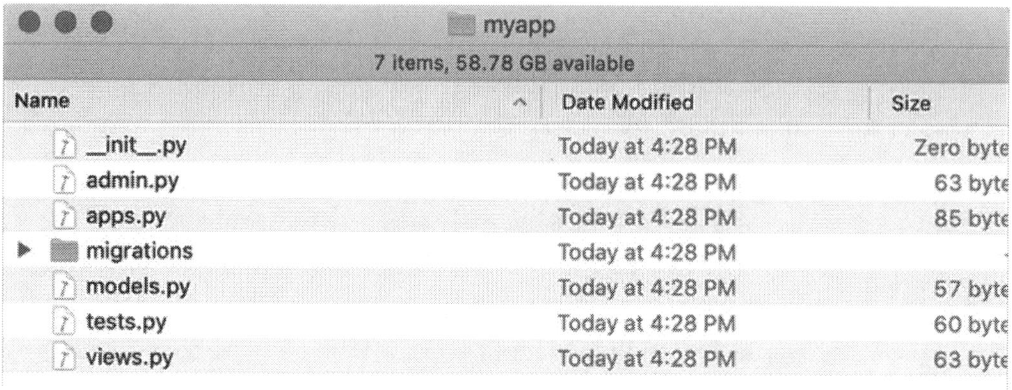

Figure 1.10: The contents of the myapp app directory

- **__init.py__**: An empty file indicating that this directory is a Python module.

- **admin.py**: Django has a built-in admin site for viewing and editing data with a Graphical User Interface (GUI). In this file, you will define how your app's models are exposed in the Django admin site. We'll cover this in more detail in *Chapter 4, Introduction to Django Admin*.

- **apps.py**: This contains some configuration for the metadata of your app. You won't need to edit this file.

- **models.py**: This is where you will define the models for your application. You'll read about this in more detail in *Chapter 2, Models and Migrations*.

- **migrations**: Django uses migration files to automatically record changes to your underlying database as the models change. They are generated by Django when you run the **manage.py makemigrations** command and are stored in this directory. They do not get applied to the database until you run **manage.py migrate**. They will be also be covered in *Chapter 2, Models and Migrations*.

- **tests.py**: To test that your code is behaving correctly, Django supports writing tests (unit, functional, or integration) and will look for them inside this file. We will write some tests throughout this book and cover testing in detail in *Chapter 14, Testing*.

- **views.py**: Your Django views (the code that responds to HTTP requests) will go in here. You will create a basic view soon, and views will be covered in more detail in *Chapter 3, URL Mapping, Views, and Templates*.

We will examine the contents of these files more later, but for now, we'll get Django up and running in our second exercise.

PYCHARM SETUP

We confirmed in *Exercise 1.01, Creating a Project and App, and Starting the Dev Server*, that the Bookr project has been set up properly (since the dev server runs successfully), so we can now start using **PyCharm** to run and edit our project. PyCharm is an IDE for Python development, and it includes features such as code completion, automatic style formatting, and a built-in debugger. We will then use PyCharm to start writing our URL maps, views, and templates. It will also be used to start and stop the development server, which will allow the debugging of our code by setting breakpoints.

EXERCISE 1.02: PROJECT SETUP IN PYCHARM

In this exercise, we will open the Bookr project in PyCharm and set up the project interpreter so that PyCharm can run and debug the project:

1. Open PyCharm. When you first open PyCharm, you will be shown the **Welcome to PyCharm** screen, which asks you what you want to do:

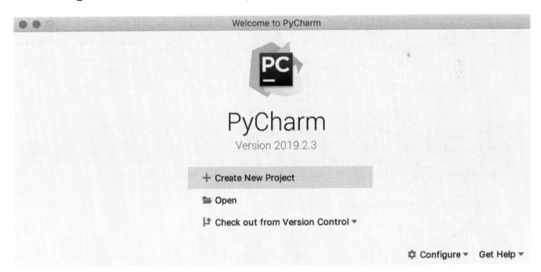

Figure 1.11: PyCharm welcome screen

2. Click **Open**, then browse to the **bookr** project you just created, then open it. Make sure you are opening the **bookr** project directory and not the **bookr** package directory inside.

If you haven't used PyCharm before, it will ask you about what settings and themes you want to use, and once you have answered all those questions, you will see your **bookr** project structure open in the **Project** pane on the left of the window:

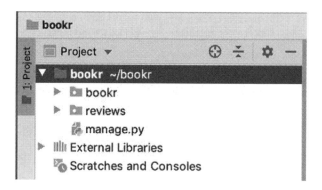

Figure 1.12: PyCharm Project pane

Your **Project** pane should look like *Figure 1.12* and show the **bookr** and **reviews** directories, and the **manage.py** file. If you do not see these and instead see **asgi.py**, **settings.py**, **urls.py**, and **wsgi.py**, then you have opened the **bookr** package directory instead. Select **File** -> **Open**, then browse and open the **bookr** project directory.

Before PyCharm knows how to execute your project to start the Django dev server, the interpreter must be set to the Python binary inside your virtual environment. This is done first by adding the interpreter to the global interpreter settings.

3. Open the **Preferences** (macOS) or **Settings** (Windows/Linux) window inside PyCharm.

    macOS:

    PyCharm Menu -> **Preferences**

    Windows and Linux:

    File -> **Settings**

4. In the preferences list pane on the left, open the **Project: bookr** item, then click **Project Interpreter**:

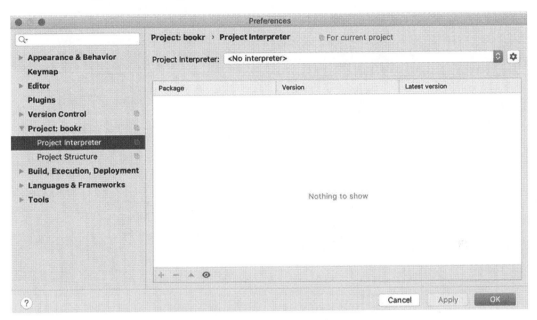

Figure 1.13: Project interpreter settings

5. Sometimes PyCharm can automatically determine virtual environments, so in this case, **Project Interpreter** may already be populated with the correct interpreter. If it is, and you see Django in the list of packages, you can click **OK** to close the window and complete this exercise.

In most cases, though, the Python interpreter must be set manually. Click the cog icon next to the **Project Interpreter** dropdown, then click **Add**....

6. The **Add Python Interpreter** window is now displayed. Select the **Existing environment** radio button and then click the ellipses (...) next to the **Interpreter** dropdown. You should then browse and select the Python interpreter for your virtual environment:

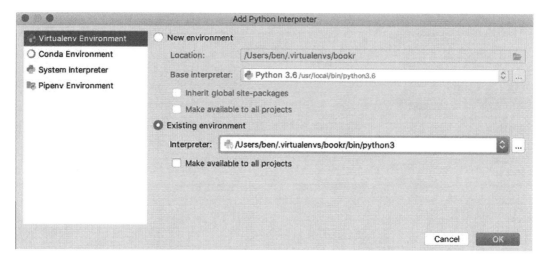

Figure 1.14: The Add Python Interpreter window

7. On macOS (assuming you called the virtual environment **bookr**), the path is usually **/Users/<yourusername>/.virtualenvs/bookr/bin/python3**. Similarly, in Linux, it should be **/home/<yourusername>/.virtualenvs/bookr/bin/python3**.

   If you're unsure, you can run the **which python3** command in the Terminal where you previously ran the **python manage.py** command and it will tell you the path to the Python interpreter:

```
which python3
/Users/ben/.virtualenvs/bookr/bin/python3
```

   On Windows, it will be wherever you created your virtual environment with the **virtualenv** command.

   After selecting the interpreter, your **Add Python Interpreter** window should look like *Figure 1.14*.

8. Click **OK** to close the **Add Python interpreter** window.

9. You should now see the main preferences window, and Django (and other packages in your virtual environment) will be listed (see *Figure 1.15*):

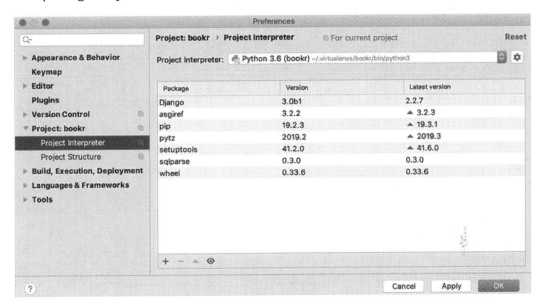

Figure 1.15: Packages in the virtual environment are listed

10. Click **OK** in the main **Preferences** window to close it. PyCharm will now take a few seconds to index your environment and the libraries installed. You can see the process in its bottom-right status bar. Wait for this process to finish and the progress bar will disappear.

11. To run the Django dev server, Python needs to be configured with a run configuration. You will set this up now.

    Click **Add Configuration**... in the top right of the PyCharm project window, to open the **Run/Debug Configuration** window:

Figure 1.16: The Add Configuration... button in the top right of the PyCharm window

12. Click the **+** button in the top left of this window and select **Python** from the dropdown menu:

Figure 1.17: Adding a new Python configuration in the Run/Debug Configuration window

13. A new configuration panel with fields regarding how to run your project will display on the right of the window. You should fill out the fields as follows.

    The **Name** field can be anything but should be understandable. Enter **Django Dev Server**.

    Script Path is the path to your **manage.py** file. If you click the folder icon in this field, you can browse your filesystem to select the **manage.py** file inside the **bookr** project directory.

    Parameters are the arguments that come after the **manage.py** script, the same as if running it from the command line. We will use the same argument here to start the server, so enter **runserver**.

> **NOTE**
>
> As mentioned earlier, the **runserver** command can also accept an argument for the port or address to listen to. If you want to, you can add this argument after **runserver** in the same **Parameters** field.

The **Python interpreter** setting should have been automatically set to the one that was set in *steps 5* to *8*. If not, you can click the arrow dropdown on the right to select it.

Working directory should be set to the **bookr** project directory. This has probably already been set correctly.

Add content roots to PYTHONPATH and **Add source roots to PYTHONPATH** should both be checked. This will ensure that PyCharm adds your **bookr** project directory to **PYTHONPATH** (the list of paths that the Python interpreter searches when loading a module). Without those checked, the imports from your project will not work correctly:

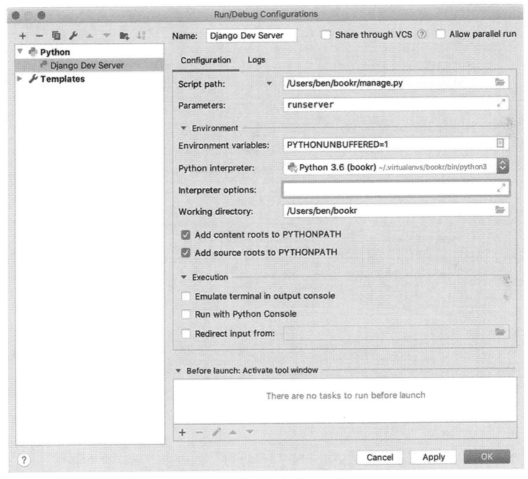

Figure 1.18: Configuration settings

Ensure that your **Run/Debug configurations** window looks similar to *Figure 1.18*, then click **OK** to save the configuration.

14. Now, instead of starting the Django dev server in a Terminal, you can click the play icon in the top right of the **Project** window to start it (see *Figure 1.19*):

Figure 1.19: Django dev server configuration with play, debug, and stop buttons

15. Click the play icon to start the Django dev server.

> **NOTE**
>
> Make sure you stop any other instances of the Django dev server that are running (such as in a Terminal) otherwise the one you are starting will not be able to bind to port **8000** and will fail to start.

16. A console will open at the bottom of the PyCharm window, which will show output indicating that the dev server has started (*Figure 1.20*):

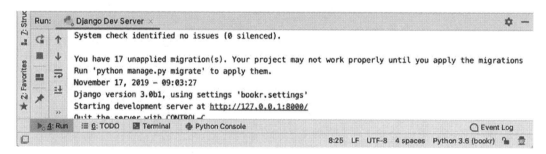

Figure 1.20: Console with the Django dev server running

17. Open a web browser and navigate to **http://127.0.0.1:8000**. You should see the same Django example screen as you did earlier, in *Exercise 1.01, Creating a Project and App, and Starting the Dev Server* (*Figure 1.2*), which will confirm that once again everything is set up correctly.

In this exercise, we opened the Bookr project in PyCharm, then set the Python interpreter for our project. We then added a run configuration in PyCharm, which allows us to start and stop the Django dev server from within PyCharm. We will also be able to debug our project later by running it inside PyCharm's debugger.

VIEW DETAILS

You now have everything set up to start writing your own Django views and configure the URLs that will map to them. As we saw earlier in this chapter, a view is simply a function that takes an **HttpRequest** instance (built by Django) and (optionally) some parameters from the URL. It will then do some operations, such as fetching data from a database. Finally, it returns **HttpResponse**.

To use our Bookr app as an example, we might have a view that receives a request for a certain book. It queries the database for this book, then returns a response containing an HTML page showing information about the book. Another view could receive a request to list all the books, then return a response with another HTML page containing this list. Views can also create or modify data: another view could receive a request to create a new book; it would then add the book to the database and return a response with HTML that displays the new book's information.

In this chapter, we will only be using functions as views, but Django also supports class-based views, which allow you to leverage object-oriented paradigms (such as inheritance). This allows you to simplify code used in multiple views that have the same business logic. For example, you might want to show all books or just books by a certain publisher. Both views need to query a list of books from the database and render them to a book list template. One view class could inherit from the other and just implement the data fetching differently and leave the rest of the functionality (such as rendering) identical. Class-based views can be more powerful but also harder to learn. They will be introduced later, in *Chapter 11, Advanced Templates and Class-Based Views*, when you have more experience with Django.

The **HttpRequest** instance that is passed to the view contains all the data related to the request, with attributes such as these:

- **method**: A string containing the HTTP method the browser used to request the page; usually this is **GET**, but it will be **POST** if the user has submitted a form. You can use this to change the flow of the view, for example, show an empty form on **GET**, or validate and process a form submission on **POST**.

- **GET**: A **QueryDict** instance containing the parameters used in the URL query string. This is the part of the URL after the **?**, if it contains one. We go further into **QueryDict** soon. Note that this attribute is always available even if the request was not **GET**.

- **POST**: Another **QueryDict** containing the parameters sent to the view in a **POST** request, like from a form submission. Usually, you would use this in conjunction with a Django form, which will be covered in *Chapter 6, Forms*.

- **headers**: A case-insensitive key dictionary with the HTTP headers from the request. For example, you could vary the response with different content for different browsers based on the **User-Agent** header. We discussed some HTTP headers that are sent by the client earlier in this chapter.

- **path**: This is the path used in the request. Normally, you don't need to examine this because Django will automatically parse the path and pass it to view function as parameters, but it can be useful in some instances.

We won't be using all these attributes yet, and others will be introduced later, but you can now see what role the **HttpRequest** argument plays in your view.

URL MAPPING DETAIL

We briefly mentioned URL maps earlier in the *Processing a Request* section. Django does not automatically know which view function should be executed when it receives a request for a particular URL. The role of a URL mapping to build this link between a URL and a view. For example, in Bookr, you might want to map the URL **/books/** to a **books_list** view that you have created.

The URL-to-view mapping is defined in the file that Django automatically created called **urls.py**, inside the **bookr** package directory (although a different file can be set in **settings.py**; more on that later).

This file contains a variable, **urlpatterns**, which is a list of paths that Django evaluates in turn until it finds a match for the URL being requested. The match will either resolve to a view function, or to another **urls.py** file also containing a **urlpatterns** variable, which will be resolved in the same manner. URL files can be chained in this manner for as long as you want. In this way, you can split URL maps into separate files (such as one or more per app) so that they don't become too large. Once a view has been found, Django calls it with an **HttpRequest** instance and any parameters parsed from the URL.

Rules are set by calling the **path** function, which takes the path of the URL as the first argument. The path can contain named parameters that will be passed to a view as function parameters. Its second argument is either a view or another file also containing **urlpatterns**.

There is also the **re_path** function, which is similar to **path** except it takes a regular expression as the first argument for a more advanced configuration. There is much more to URL mapping; however, and it will be covered in *Chapter 3, URL Mapping, Views, and Templates*.

```
from django.contrib import admin
from django.urls import path

urlpatterns = [
    path('admin/', admin.site.urls),
]
```

Figure 1.21: The default urls.py file

To illustrate these concepts, *Figure 1.21* shows the default **urls.py** file that Django generates. You can see the **urlpatterns** variable, which lists all the URLs that are set up. Currently, there is only one rule set up, which maps any path starting with **admin/** to the admin URL maps (the **admin.site.urls** module). This is not a mapping to a view; instead, it is an example of chaining URL maps together—the **admin.site.urls** module will define the remainder of the paths (after **admin/**) that map to the admin views. We will cover the Django admin site in *Chapter 4, Introduction to Django Admin*.

We will now write a view and set up a URL map to it to see these concepts in action.

EXERCISE 1.03: WRITING A VIEW AND MAPPING A URL TO IT

Our first view will be very simple and will just return some static text content. In this exercise, we will see how to write a view, and how to set up a URL map to resolve to a view:

> **NOTE**
>
> As you make changes to files in your project and save them, you might see the Django development server automatically restarting in the Terminal or console in which it is running. This is normal; it automatically restarts to load any code changes that you make. Please also note that it won't automatically apply changes to the database if you edit models or migrations—more on this in *Chapter 2, Models and Migrations*.

1. In PyCharm, expand the **reviews** folder in the project browser on the left, then double-click the **views.py** file inside to open it. In the right (editor) pane in PyCharm, you should see the Django automatically generated placeholder text:

```
from django.shortcuts import render


# Create your views here.
```

It should look like this in the editor pane:

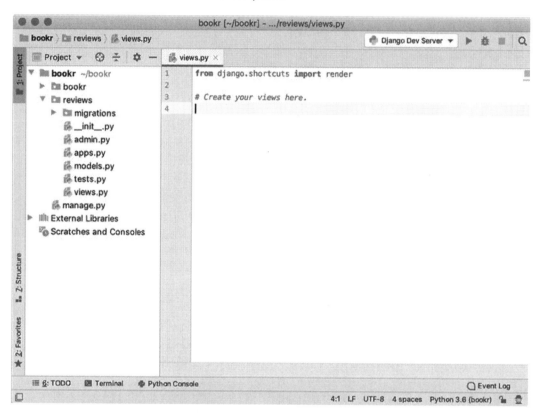

Figure 1.22: views.py default content

2. Remove this placeholder text from **views.py** and instead insert this content:

```
from django.http import HttpResponse

def index(request):
    return HttpResponse("Hello, world!")
```

First, the **HttpResponse** class needs to be imported from **django.http**. This is what is used to create the response that goes back to the web browser. You can also use it to control things such as the HTTP headers or status code. For now, it will just use the default headers and **200 Success** status code. Its first argument is the string content to send as the body of the response.

Then, the view function returns an **HttpResponse** instance with the content we defined (**Hello, world!**):

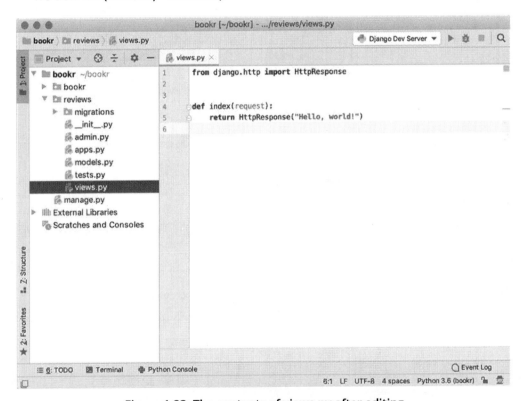

Figure 1.23: The contents of views.py after editing

3. We will now set up a URL map to the **index** view. This will be very simple and won't contain any parameters. Expand the **bookr** directory in the **Project** pane, then open **urls.py**. Django has automatically generated this file.

    For now, we'll just add a simple URL to replace the default index that Django provides.

4. Import your views into the **urls.py** file, by adding this line after the other existing imports:

```
import reviews.views
```

5. Add a map to the index view to the **urlpatterns** list by adding a call to the **path** function with an empty string and a reference to the **index** function:

```
urlpatterns = [path('admin/', admin.site.urls),\
                path('', reviews.views.index)]
```

> **NOTE**
>
> The preceding code snippet uses a backslash (\ ) to split the logic across multiple lines. When the code is executed, Python will ignore the backslash, and treat the code on the next line as a direct continuation of the current line.

Make sure you don't add brackets after the **index** function (that is, it should be **reviews.views.index** and not **reviews.views.index()**) as we are passing a reference to a function rather than calling it. When you're finished, your **urls.py** file should like *Figure 1.24*:

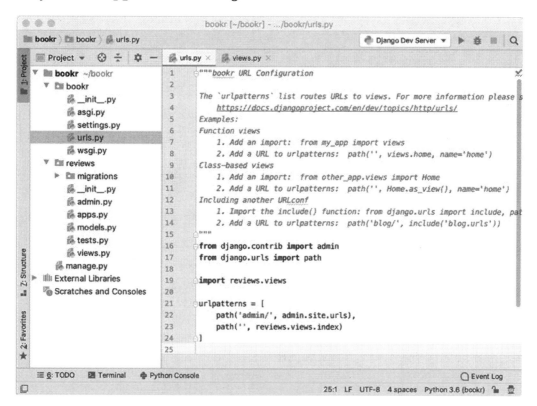

Figure 1.24: urls.py after editing

6. Switch back to your web browser and refresh. The Django default welcome screen should be replaced with the text defined in the view, **Hello, world!**:

Figure 1.25: The web browser should now display the Hello, world! message

We just saw how to write a view function and map a URL to it. We then tested the view by loading it in a web browser.

GET, POST, AND QUERYDICT OBJECTS

Data can come through an HTTP request as parameters on a URL or inside the body of a **POST** request. You might have noticed parameters in a URL when browsing the web—the text after a **?**—for example, **http://www.example. com/?parameter1=value1&parameter2=value2**. We also saw earlier in this chapter an example of form data in a **POST** request, for logging in a user (the request body was **username=user1&password=password1**).

Django automatically parses these parameter strings into **QueryDict** objects. The data is then available on the **HttpRequest** object that is passed to your view—specifically, in the **HttpRequest.GET** and **HttpRequest.POST** attributes, for URL parameters and body parameters respectively. **QueryDict** objects are objects that mostly behave like dictionaries, except that they can contain multiple values for a key.

To show different methods of accessing items, we'll use a simple **QueryDict** named **qd** with only one key (**k**) as an example. The **k** item has three values in a list: the strings **a**, **b**, and **c**. The following code snippets show output from a Python interpreter.

First, the **QueryDict qd** is constructed from a parameter string:

```
>>> qd = QueryDict("k=a&k=b&k=c")
```

When accessing items with square bracket notation or the **get** method, the last value for that key is returned:

```
>>> qd["k"]
'c'
>>> qd.get("k")
'c'
```

To access all the values for a key, the **getlist** method should be used:

```
>>> qd.getlist("k")
['a', 'b', 'c']
```

getlist will always return a list—it will be empty if the key does not exist:

```
>>> qd.getlist("bad key")
[]
```

While **getlist** does not raise an exception for keys that do not exist, accessing a key that does not exist with square bracket notation will raise **KeyError**, like a normal dictionary. Use the **get** method to avoid this error.

The **QueryDict** objects for **GET** and **POST** are immutable (they cannot be changed), so the **copy** method should be used to get a mutable copy if you need to change its values:

```
>>> qd["k"] = "d"
AttributeError: This QueryDict instance is immutable
>>> qd2 = qd.copy()
>>> qd2
<QueryDict: {'k': ['a', 'b', 'c']}>
>>> qd2["k"] = "d"
>>> qd2["k"]
"d"
```

To give an example of how **QueryDict** is populated from a URL, imagine an example URL: **http://127.0.0.1:8000?val1=a&val2=b&val2=c&val3**.

Behind the scenes, Django passes the query from the URL (everything after the **?**) to instantiate a **QueryDict** object and attach it to the **request** instance that is passed to the view function. Something like this:

```
request.GET = QueryDict("val1=a&val2=b&val2=c&val3")
```

Remember, this is done to the **request** instance before you receive it inside your view function; you do not need to do this.

In the case of our example URL, we could access the parameters inside the view function as follows:

```
request.GET["val1"]
```

Using standard dictionary access, it would return the value **a**:

```
request.GET["val2"]
```

Again, using standard dictionary access, there are two values set for the **val2** key, so it would return the last value, **c**:

```
request.GET.getlist("val2")
```

This would return a list of all the values for **val2**: **["b", "c"]**:

```
request.GET["val3"]
```

This key is in the query string but has no value set, so this returns an empty string:

```
request.GET["val4"]
```

This key is not set, so **KeyError** will be raised. Use **request.GET.get("val4")** instead, which will return **None**:

```
request.GET.getlist("val4")
```

Since this key is not set, an empty list (**[]**) will be returned.

We will now look at **QueryDict** in action using the **GET** parameters. You will examine **POST** parameters further in *Chapter 6, Forms*.

EXERCISE 1.04: EXPLORING GET VALUES AND QUERYDICT

We will now make some changes to our **index** view from the previous exercise to read values from the URL in the **GET** attribute, and then we will experiment with passing different parameters to see the result:

1. Open the **views.py** file in PyCharm. Add a new variable called **name** that reads the user's name from the **GET** parameters. Add this line after the **index** function definition:

```
name = request.GET.get("name") or "world"
```

2. Change the return value so the name is used as part of the content that is returned:

```
return HttpResponse("Hello, {}!".format(name))
```

In PyCharm, the changed code will look like this:

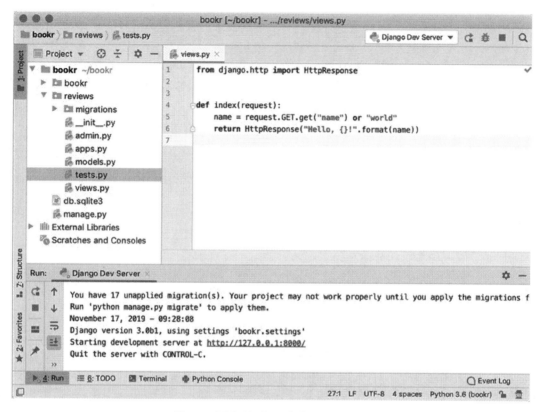

Figure 1.26: Updated views.py file

3. Visit **http://127.0.0.1:8000** in your browser. You should notice that the page still says **Hello, world!** This is because we have not supplied a **name** parameter. You can add your name into the URL, for example, **http://127.0.0.1:8000?name=Ben**:

Figure 1.27: Setting the name in the URL

4. Try adding two names, for example, **http://127.0.0.1:8000?name=Ben&name=John**. As we mentioned, the last value for the parameter is retrieved with the **get** function, so you should see **Hello, John!**:

Hello, John!

Figure 1.28: Setting multiple names in the URL

5. Try setting no name, like this: `http://127.0.0.1:8000?name=`. The page should go back to displaying **Hello, world!**:

Hello, world!

Figure 1.29: No name set in the URL

> **NOTE**
>
> You might wonder why we set **name** to the default **world** by using **or** instead of passing **'world'** as the default value to **get**. Consider what happened in *step 5* when we passed in a blank value for the **name** parameter. If we had passed **'world'** as a default value for **get**, then the **get** function would still have returned an empty string. This is because a value **is** set for **name**, it's just that it's blank. Keep this in mind when developing your views, as there is a difference between no value being set, and a blank value being set. Depending on your use case, you might choose to pass the default value for **get**.

In this exercise, we retrieved values from the URL in our view using the **GET** attribute of the incoming request. We saw how to set default values and which value is retrieved if multiple values are set for the same parameter.

EXPLORING DJANGO SETTINGS

We haven't yet looked at how Django stores its settings. Now that we've seen the different parts of Django, it is a good time to examine the **settings.py** file. This file contains many settings that can be used to customize Django. A default **settings.py** file was created for you when you started the Bookr project.

We will discuss some of the more important settings in the file now, and a few others that might be useful as you become more fluent with Django. You should open your **settings.py** file in PyCharm and follow along so you can see where and what the values are for your project.

Each setting in this file is just a file-global variable. The order in which we will discuss the settings is the same order in which they appear in this file, although we may skip over some—for example, there is the **ALLOWED_HOSTS** setting between **DEBUG** and **INSTALLED_APPS**, which we won't cover in this part of the book (you'll see it in *Chapter 17, Deployment of a Django Application (Part 1 – Server Setup)*):

```
SECRET_KEY = '…'
```

This is an automatically generated value that shouldn't be shared with anyone. It is used for hashing, tokens, and other cryptographic functions. If you had existing sessions in a cookie and changed this value, the sessions would no longer be valid.

```
DEBUG = True
```

With this value set to **True**, Django will automatically display exceptions to the browser to allow you to debug any problems you encounter. It should be set to **False** when deploying your app to production:

```
INSTALLED_APPS = […]
```

As you write your own Django apps (such as the **reviews** app) or install third-party applications (which will be covered in *Chapter 15, Django Third-Party Libraries*), they should be added to this list. As we've seen, it is not strictly necessary to add them here (our **index** view worked without our **reviews** app being in this list). However, for Django to be able to automatically find the app's templates, static files, migrations, and other configuration, it must be listed here:

```
ROOT_URLCONF = 'bookr.urls'
```

This is the Python module that Django will load first to find URLs. Note that it is the file we added our index view URL map to previously:

```
TEMPLATES = […]
```

Right now, it's not too important to understand everything in this setting as you won't be changing it; the important line to point out is this one:

```
'APP_DIRS': True,
```

This tells Django it should look in a **templates** directory inside each **INSTALLED_APP** when loading a template to render. We don't have a **templates** directory for **reviews** yet, but we will add one in the next exercise.

Django has more settings available that aren't listed in the **settings.py** file, and so it will use its built-in defaults in these cases. You can also use the file to set arbitrary settings that you make up for your application. Third-party applications might want settings to be added here as well. In later chapters, we will add settings here for other applications. You can find a list of all settings, and their defaults, at https://docs. djangoproject.com/en/3.0/ref/settings/.

USING SETTINGS IN YOUR CODE

It can sometimes be useful to refer to settings from **settings.py** in your own code, whether they be Django's built-in settings or ones you have defined yourself. You might be tempted to write code like this to do it:

```
from bookr import settings

if settings.DEBUG:  # check if running in DEBUG mode
    do_some_logging()
```

> **NOTE**
>
> The # symbol in the preceding code snippet denotes a code comment. Comments are added into code to help explain specific bits of logic.

This method is incorrect, for a number of reasons:

- It is possible to run Django and specify a different settings file to read from, in which case the previous code would cause an error as it would not be able to find that particular file. Or, if the file exists, the import would succeed but would contain the wrong settings.

- Django has settings that might not be listed in the **settings.py** file, and if they aren't, it will use its own internal defaults. For example, if you removed the **DEBUG = True** line from your **settings.py** file, Django would fall back to using its internal value for **DEBUG** (which is **False**). You would get an error if you tried to access it using **settings.DEBUG** directly, though.

- Third-party libraries can change how your settings are defined, so your **settings.py** file would look completely different. None of the expected variables may exist at all. The behavior of all these applications is beyond the scope of this book, but it is something to be aware of.

The preferred way is to use **django.conf** module instead, like this:

```
from django.conf import settings  # import settings from here instead

if settings.DEBUG:
    do_some_logging()
```

When importing **settings** from **django.conf**, Django mitigates the three issues we just discussed:

- Settings are read from whatever Django settings file has been specified.

- Any default settings values are interpolated.

- Django takes care of parsing any settings defined by a third-party library.

In our new short example code snippet, even if **DEBUG** is missing from the **settings.py** file, it will fall back to the default value that Django has internally (which is **False**). The same is true for all other settings that Django defines; however, if you define your own custom settings in this file, Django will not have internal values for them, so in your code, you should have some provision for them not existing—how your code behaves is your choice and beyond the scope of this book.

FINDING HTML TEMPLATES IN APP DIRECTORIES

Many options are available to tell Django how to find templates, which can be set in the **TEMPLATES** setting of **settings.py**, but the easiest one (for now) is to create a **templates** directory inside the **reviews** directory. Django will look in this (and in other apps' **templates** directories) because of **APP_DIRS** being **True** in the **settings.py** file, as we saw in the previous section.

EXERCISE 1.05: CREATING A TEMPLATES DIRECTORY AND A BASE TEMPLATE

In this exercise, you will create a **templates** directory for the **reviews** app. Then, you will add an HTML template file that Django will be able to render to an HTTP response:

1. We discussed **settings.py** and its **INSTALLED_APPS** setting in the previous section (*Exploring Django Settings*). We need to add the **reviews** app to **INSTALLED_APPS** for Django to be able to find templates. Open **settings. py** in PyCharm. Update the **INSTALLED_APPS** setting and add **reviews** to the end. It should look like this:

```
INSTALLED_APPS = ['django.contrib.admin',\
                  'django.contrib.auth',\
```

```
'django.contrib.contenttypes',\
'django.contrib.sessions',\
'django.contrib.messages',\
'django.contrib.staticfiles',\
'reviews']
```

In PyCharm, the file should look like this now:

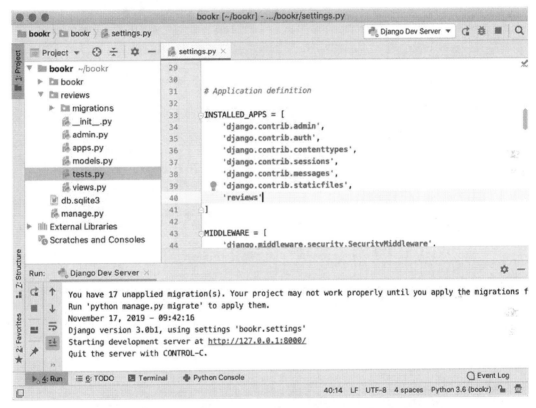

Figure 1.30: The reviews app added to settings.py

2. Save and close **settings.py**.

3. In the PyCharm Project browser, right-click the **reviews** directory and select **New** -> **Directory**:

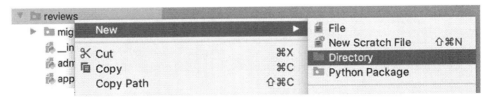

Figure 1.31: Creating a new directory inside the reviews directory

4. Enter the name **templates** and click **OK** to create it:

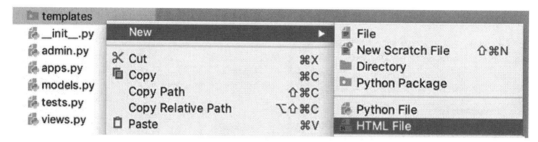

Figure 1.32: Name the directory templates

5. Right-click the newly created **templates** directory and select **New -> HTML File**:

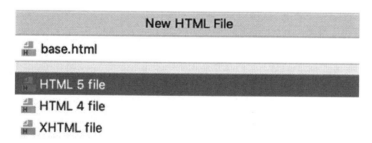

Figure 1.33: Creating a new HTML file in the templates directory

6. In the window that appears, enter the name **base.html**, leave **HTML 5 file** selected, and then press **Enter** to create the file:

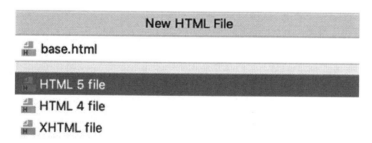

Figure 1.34: The New HTML File window

7. After PyCharm creates the file, it will automatically open it too. It will have this content:

```
<!DOCTYPE html>
<html lang="en">
<head>
    <meta charset="UTF-8">
    <title>Title</title>
```

```
</head>
<body>

</body>
</html>
```

8. Between the **<body>**...**</body>** tags, add a short message to verify that the template is being rendered:

```
<body>
    Hello from a template!
</body>
```

Here is how it will look like in PyCharm:

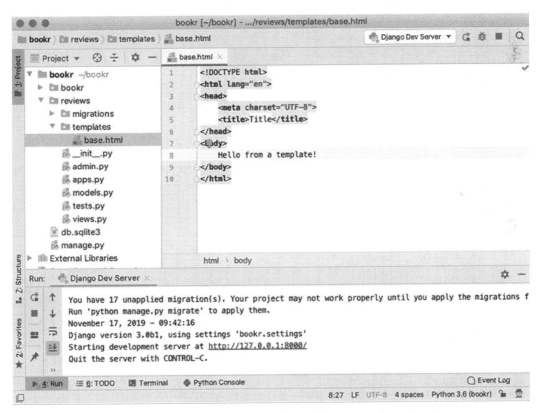

Figure 1.35: The base.html template with some example text

In this exercise, we created a **templates** directory for the **reviews** app and added an HTML template to it. The HTML template will be rendered once we implement the use of the **render** function on our view.

RENDERING A TEMPLATE WITH THE RENDER FUNCTION

We now have a template to use, but we need to update our **index** view so that it renders the template instead of returning the **Hello (name)!** text that it is currently displaying (refer to *Figure 1.29* for how it currently looks). We will do this by using the **render** function and providing the name of the template. **render** is a shortcut function that returns an **HttpResponse** instance. There are other ways to render a template to provide more control over how it is rendered, but for now, this function is fine for our needs. **render** takes at least two arguments: the first is always the request that was passed to the view, and the second is the name/relative path of the template being rendered. We will also call it with a third argument, the render context that contains all the variables that will be available in the template— more on this in *Exercise 1.07, Using Variables in Templates*.

EXERCISE 1.06: RENDERING A TEMPLATE IN A VIEW

In this exercise, you will update your **index** view function to render the HTML template you created in *Exercise 1.05, Creating a Templates Directory and a Base Template*. You will make use of the **render** function, which loads your template from disk, renders it, and sends it to the browser. This will replace the static text you are currently returning from the **index** view function:

1. In PyCharm, open **views.py** in the **reviews** directory.

2. We no longer manually create an **HttpResponse** instance, so remove the **HttpResponse** import line:

```
from django.http import HttpResponse
```

3. Replace it with an import of the **render** function from **django.shortcuts**:

```
from django.shortcuts import render
```

4. Update the **index** function so that instead of returning **HttpResponse**, it's returning a call to **render**, passing in the **request** instance and template name:

```
def index(request):
    return render(request, "base.html")
```

Here is how it will look like in PyCharm:

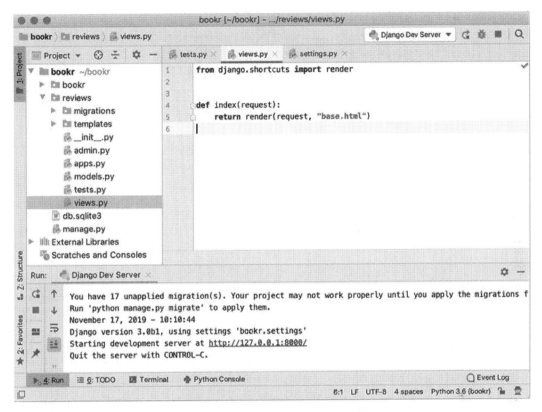

Figure 1.36: Completed views.py file

5. Start the dev server if it's not already running. Then, open your web browser and refresh **http://127.0.0.1:8000**. You should see the **Hello from a template!** message rendered, as in *Figure 1.37*:

Figure 1.37: Your first rendered HTML template

RENDERING VARIABLES IN TEMPLATES

Templates aren't just static HTML. Most of the time, they will contain variables that are interpolated as part of the rendering process. These variables are passed from the view to the template using a context: a dictionary (or dictionary-like object) that contains names for all the variables a template can use. We'll take Bookr again as an example. Without variables in your template, you would need a different HTML file for each book you wanted to display. Instead, we use a variable such as **book_name** inside the template, and then the view provides the template with a **book_name** variable set to the title of the book model it has loaded. When displaying a different book, the HTML does not need to change; the view just passes a different book to it. You can see how model, view, and template are all now coming together.

Unlike some other languages, such as PHP, variables must be explicitly passed to the template, and variables in the view aren't automatically available to the template. This is for security as well as to avoid accidentally polluting the template's namespace (we don't want any unexpected variables in the template).

Inside a template, variables are denoted by double braces, **{{ }}**. While not strictly a standard, this style is quite common and used in other templating tools such as Vue.js and Mustache. Symfony (a PHP framework) also uses double braces in its Twig templating language, so you might have seen them used similarly there.

To render a variable in a template, simply wrap it with braces: **{{ book_name }}**. Django will automatically escape HTML in output so that you can include special characters (such as **<** or **>**) in your variable without worrying about it garbling your output. If a variable is not passed to a template, Django will simply render nothing at that location, instead of throwing an exception.

There are many more ways to render a variable differently using filters, but these will be covered in *Chapter 3, URL Routers, Views, and Templates*.

EXERCISE 1.07: USING VARIABLES IN TEMPLATES

We'll put a simple variable inside the **base.html** file to demonstrate how Django's variable interpolation works:

1. In PyCharm, open **base.html**.

2. Update the **<body>** element so it contains a place to render the **name** variable:

```
<body>
Hello, {{ name }}!
</body>
```

3. Go back to your web browser and refresh (you should still be at **http://127.0.0.1:8000**). You will see that the page now displays **Hello, !**. This is because we have not set the **name** variable in the rendering context:

Hello, !

Figure 1.38: No value rendered in the template because no context was set

4. Open **views.py** and add a variable called **name**, set to the value **"world"**, inside the **index** function:

```
def index(request):
    name = "world"
    return render(request, "base.html")
```

5. Refresh your browser again. You should notice that nothing has changed: anything we want to render must be explicitly passed to the **render** function as **context**. This is the dictionary of variables that are made available when rendering.

6. Add the **context** dictionary as the third argument to the **render** function. Change your **render** line to this:

```
return render(request, "base.html", {"name": name})
```

In PyCharm, this should appear as follows:

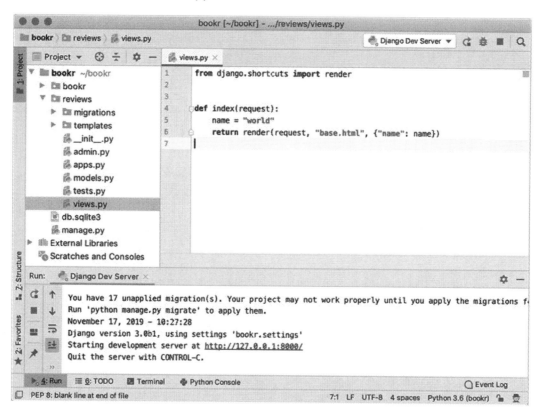

Figure 1.39: views.py with the name variable sent in the render context

7. Refresh your browser again and you'll see it now says **Hello, world!**:

Figure 1.40: A template rendered with a variable

In this exercise, we combined the template we created in the previous exercise with the **render** function, to render an HTML page with the **name** variable that was passed to it inside a **context** dictionary.

DEBUGGING AND DEALING WITH ERRORS

When programming, unless you're the perfect programmer who never makes mistakes, you'll probably have to deal with errors or debug your code at some point. When there is an error in your program, there are usually two ways to tell: either your code will raise an exception, or you will get an unexpected output or results when viewing the page. Exceptions you will probably see more often, as there are many accidental ways to cause them. If your code is generating unexpected output, but not raising any exceptions, you will probably want to use the PyCharm debugger to find out why.

EXCEPTIONS

If you have worked with Python or other programming languages before, you have probably come across exceptions. If not, here's a quick introduction. Exceptions are raised (or thrown in other languages) when an error occurs. The execution of the program stops at that point in the code, and the exception travels back up the function call chain until it is caught. If it is not caught, then the program will crash, sometimes with an error message describing the exception and where it occurred. There are exceptions that are raised by Python itself, and your code can raise exceptions to quickly stop execution at any point. Some common exceptions that you might see when programming Python are listed here:

- **`IndentationError`**

  Python will raise this if your code is not correctly indented or has mixed tabs and spaces.

- **`SyntaxError`**

  Python raises this error if your code has invalid syntax:

```
>>> a === 1
  File "<stdin>", line 1
    a === 1
        ^
SyntaxError: invalid syntax
```

- **ImportError**

    This is raised when an import fails, for example, if trying to import from a file that does not exist or trying to import a name that is not set in a file:

    ```
    >>> import missing_file
    Traceback (most recent call last):
      File "<stdin>", line 1, in <module>
    ImportError: No module named missing_file
    ```

- **NameError**

    This is raised when trying to access a variable that has not yet been set:

    ```
    >>> a = b + 5
    Traceback (most recent call last):
      File "<stdin>", line 1, in <module>
    NameError: name 'b' is not defined
    ```

- **KeyError**

    This is raised when accessing a key that is not set in a dictionary (or dictionary-like object):

    ```
    >>> d = {'a': 1}
    >>> d['b']
    Traceback (most recent call last):
      File "<stdin>", line 1, in <module>
    KeyError: 'b'
    ```

- **IndexError**

    This is raised when accessing an index outside the length of a list:

    ```
    >>> l = ['a', 'b']
    >>> l[3]
    Traceback (most recent call last):
      File "<stdin>", line 1, in <module>
    IndexError: list index out of range
    ```

- **TypeError**

  This is raised when trying to perform an operation on an object that does not support it, or when using two objects of the wrong type—for example, trying to add a string to an integer:

```
>>> 1 + '1'
Traceback (most recent call last):
  File "<stdin>", line 1, in <module>
TypeError: unsupported operand type(s) for +: 'int' and 'str'
```

Django also raises its own custom exceptions, and you will be introduced to them throughout the book.

When running the Django development server with **DEBUG = True** in your **settings.py** file, Django will automatically capture exceptions that occur in your code (instead of crashing). It will then generate an HTTP response showing you a stack trace and other information to help you debug the problem. When running in production, **DEBUG** should be set to **False**. Django will then return a standard internal server error page, without any sensitive information. You also have the option to display a custom error page.

EXERCISE 1.08: GENERATING AND VIEWING EXCEPTIONS

Let's create a simple exception in our view so you are familiar with how Django displays them. In this case, we'll try to use a variable that doesn't exist, which will raise **NameError**:

1. In PyCharm, open **views.py**. In the **index** view function, change the context being sent to the **render** function so that it's using a variable that doesn't exist. We'll try to send **invalid_name** in the context dictionary, instead of **name**. Don't change the context dictionary key, just its value:

```
return render(request, "base.html", {"name": invalid_name})
```

2. Go back to your browser and refresh the page. You should see a screen like *Figure 1.41*:

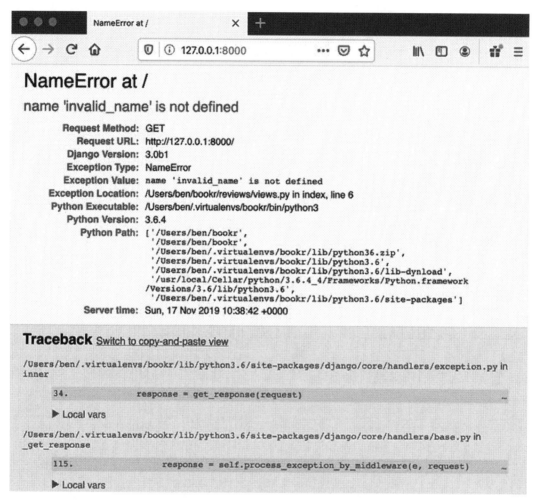

Figure 1.41: A Django exception screen

3. The first couple of header lines on the page tell you the error that occurred:

```
NameError at /
name 'invalid_name' is not defined
```

4. Below the header is a traceback to where the exception occurred. You can click on the various lines of code to expand them and see the surrounding code or click **Local vars** for each frame to expand them and see what the values of the variables are:

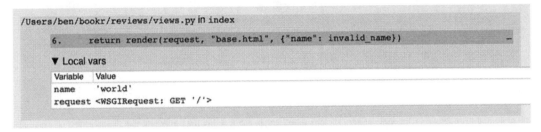

Figure 1.42: The line that causes the exception

5. In our case, we can see the exception was raised on *line 6* of our **views.py** file and, expanding **Local vars**, we see **name** has the value **world** and the only other variable is the incoming **request** (*Figure 1.42*).

6. Go back to **views.py** and fix your **NameError** by renaming **invalid_name** back to **name**.

7. Save the file and refresh your browser and **Hello World** should be displayed again (as in *Figure 1.40*).

In this exercise, we made our Django code raise an exception (**NameError**) by trying to use a variable that had not been set. We saw that Django automatically sent details of this exception and a stack trace to the browser to help us find the cause of the error. We then reverted our code change to make sure our view worked properly.

DEBUGGING

When you're trying to find problems in your code, it can help to use a debugger. This is a tool that lets you go through your code line by line, rather than executing it all at once. Each time the debugger is paused on a particular line of code, you can see the values of all the current variables. This is very useful for finding out errors in your code that don't raise exceptions.

For example, in Bookr, we have talked about having a view that fetches a list of books from the database and renders them in an HTML template. If you view the page in the browser, you might see only one book when you expect several. You could have the execution pause inside your view function and see what values were fetched from the database. If your view is only receiving one book from the database, you know there is a problem with your database querying somewhere. If your view is successfully fetching multiple books but only one is being rendered, then it's probably a problem with the template. Debugging helps you narrow down faults like this.

PyCharm has a built-in debugger to make it easy to step through your code and see what is happening on each line. To tell the debugger where to stop the execution of the code, you need to set a *breakpoint* on one or more lines of code. They are named as such because the execution of the code will *break* (stop) at that *point*.

For breakpoints to be activated, PyCharm needs to be set to run your project in its debugger. There is a small performance penalty but it usually is not noticeable, so you might choose to always run your code inside the debugger so that you can quickly set a breakpoint without having to stop and restart the Django dev server.

Running the Django dev server inside the debugger is as simple as clicking the debug icon instead of the play icon (see *Figure 1.19*) to start it.

EXERCISE 1.09: DEBUGGING YOUR CODE

In this exercise, you will learn the basics of the PyCharm debugger. You will run the Django dev server in the debugger and then set a breakpoint in your view function to pause execution so you can examine the variables:

1. If the Django dev server is running, stop it by clicking the *stop* button in the top-right corner of the PyCharm window:

Figure 1.43: Stop button in the top-right corner of the PyCharm window

2. Start the Django dev server again inside the debugger by clicking the debug icon just to the left of the stop button (*Figure 1.43*).

3. The server will take a few seconds to start, then you should be able to refresh the page in your browser to make sure it's still loading—you shouldn't notice any changes; all the code is executed the same as before.

4. Now we can set a breakpoint that will cause execution to stop so we can see the state of the program. In PyCharm, click just to the right of the line numbers, on line 5, in the gutter on the left of the editor pane. A red circle will appear to indicate the breakpoint is now active:

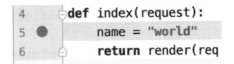

Figure 1.44: A breakpoint on line 5

5. Go back to your browser and refresh the page. Your browser will not display any content; instead, it will just continue to try to load the page. Depending on your operating system, PyCharm should become active again; if not, bring it to the foreground. You should see that line 5 is highlighted and at the bottom of the window, the debugger is shown. The stack frames (the chain of functions that were called to get to the current line) are on the left and current variables of the function are on the right:

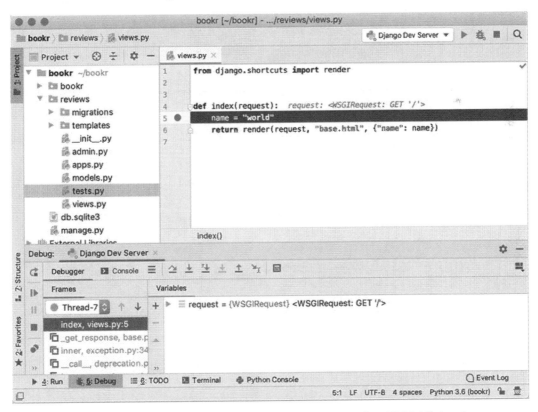

Figure 1.45: The debugger paused with the current line (5) highlighted

6.   There is currently one variable in scope, **request**. If you click the toggle triangle to the left of its name, you can show or hide the attributes it has set:

> ▼ ≣ request = {WSGIRequest} <WSGIRequest: GET '/'>
> ▶ ≣ COOKIES = {dict} <class 'dict'>: {'csrftoken': 'a3GEX
> ▶ ≣ FILES = {MultiValueDict} <MultiValueDict: {}>
> ▶ ≣ GET = {QueryDict} <QueryDict: {}>
> ▶ ≣ META = {dict} <class 'dict'>: {'PATH': '/Users/ben/.vi
> ▶ ≣ POST = {QueryDict} <QueryDict: {}>
> 🔢 _current_scheme_host = {str} 'http://127.0.0.1:8000
> 🔢 _encoding = {NoneType} None
> ▶ ≣ _messages = {FallbackStorage} <django.contrib.me
> 🔢 _read_started = {bool} False
> ▶ ≣ _stream = {LimitedStream} <_io.BytesIO object at 0x
> ▶ ≣ _upload_handlers = {list} <class 'list'>: [<django.cor
> ▶ ≣ body = {bytes} b"
> ▶ ≣ content_params = {dict} <class 'dict'>: {}
> 🔢 content_type = {str} 'text/plain'
> 🔢 csrf_cookie_needs_reset = {bool} True
> 🔢 csrf_processing_done = {bool} True
> 🔢 encoding = {NoneType} None
> ▶ ≣ environ = {dict} <class 'dict'>: {'PATH': '/Users/ben/.

Figure 1.46: The attributes of the request variable

For example, if you scroll down through the list of attributes, you can see that the method is **GET** and the path is **/**.

7.   The actions bar, shown in *Figure 1.47*, is above the stack frames and variables. Its buttons (from left to right) are as follows:

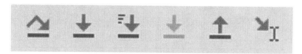

Figure 1.47: The actions bar

•   *Step Over*

Execute the current line of code and continue to the next line.

- *Step Into*

  Step into the current line. For example, if the line contained a function, it would continue with the debugger inside this function.

- *Step Into My Code*

  Step into the line being executed but continue until it finds code you have written. For example, if you're stepping into a third-party library code that later calls your code, it will not show you the third-party code, instead of continuing through until it returns to the code that you have written.

- *Force Step Into*

  Step into code that would normally not be stepped into, such as Python standard library code. This is only available in some rare cases and is normally not used.

- *Step Out*

  Return back out of the current code to the function or method that called it. The opposite of the *Step In* action.

- *Run To Cursor*

  If you have a line of code further along from where currently are that you want to execute without having to click *Step Over* for all the lines in between, click to put your cursor on that line. Then, click *Run To Cursor*, and execution will continue until that line.

  Note that not all buttons are useful all the time. For example, it can be easy to step out of your view and end up confusing Django library code.

8. Click the *Step Over* button once to execute line 5.

9. You can see the **name** variable has been added to the list of variables in the debugger view, and its value is **world**:

```
01 name = {str} 'world'
   request = {WSGIRequest} <WSGIRequest: GET '/'>
```

Figure 1.48: The new name variable is now in scope, with the value world

10. We are now at the end of our **`index`** view function, and if we were to step over this line of code, it would jump to Django library code, which we don't want to see. To continue executing and send the response back to your browser, click the **`Resume Program`** button on the left of the window (*Figure 1.49*). You should see that your browser has now loaded the page again:

Deb
2: Favorites
7: Structure

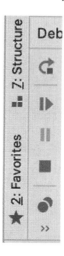

Figure 1.49: Actions to control execution—the green play icon is the Resume Program button

There are more buttons in *Figure 1.49*; from the top, they are **`Rerun`** (stops the program and restarts it), **`Resume Program`** (continues running until the next breakpoint), **`Pause Program`** (breaks the program at its current execution point), **`Stop`** (stops the debugger), **`View Breakpoints`** (opens a window to see all breakpoints you have set), and **`Mute Breakpoints`** (which will toggle all breakpoints on or off, but not remove them).

11. For now, turn off the breakpoint in PyCharm by clicking it (the red circle next to line 5):

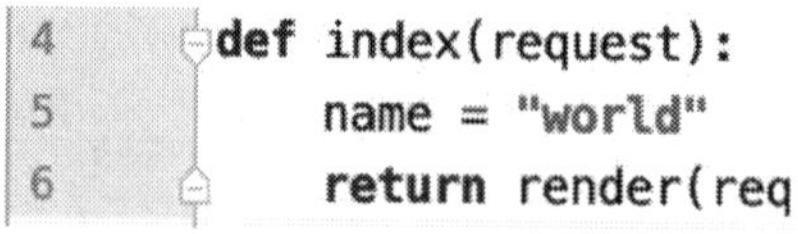
4 def index(request):
5 name = "world"
6 return render(req

Figure 1.50: Clicking the breakpoint that was on line 5 disables it

This is just a quick introduction to how to set breakpoints in PyCharm. If you have used debugging features in other IDEs, then you should be familiar with the concepts—you can step through code, step in and out of functions, or evaluate expressions. Once you have set a breakpoint, you can right-click on it to change options. For example, you can make the breakpoint conditional so that execution stops only under certain circumstances. All this is beyond the scope of this book but it's useful to know about when trying to solve problems in your code.

ACTIVITY 1.01: CREATING A SITE WELCOME SCREEN

The Bookr website that we are building needs to have a splash page that welcomes users and lets them know what site they are on. It will also contain links to other parts of the site, but these will be added in later chapters. For now, you will create a page with a welcome message.

These steps will help you complete the activity:

1. In your **index** view, render the **base.html** template.

2. Update the **base.html** template to contain the welcome message. It should be in both the **<title>** tag in **<head>** and in a new **<h1>** tag in the body.

    After completing the activity, you should be able to see something like this:

Figure 1.51: Bookr welcome page

> **NOTE**
>
> The solution to this activity can be found at http://packt.live/2Nh1NTJ.

ACTIVITY 1.02: BOOK SEARCH SCAFFOLD

A useful feature for a site like Bookr is the ability to search through the data to find something on the site quickly. Bookr will implement book searching, to allow users to find a particular book by part of its title. While we don't have any books to find yet, we can still implement a page that shows the text the user searched for. The user enters the search string as part of the URL parameters. We will implement the searching and a form for easy text entry in *Chapter 6, Forms*.

These steps will help you complete the activity:

1. Create a search result HTML template. It should include a variable placeholder to show the search word(s) that were passed in through the render context. Show the passed-in variable in the `<title>` and `<h1>` tags. Use an `<em>` tag around the search text in the body to make it italic.

2. Add a search view function in `views.py`. The view should read a search string from the URL parameters (in the request's **GET** attribute). It should then render the template you created in the previous step, passing in the search value to be substituted, using the context dictionary.

3. Add a URL mapping to your new view to `urls.py`. The URL can be something like `/book-search`.

After completing this activity, you should be able to pass in a search value through the URL's parameters and see it rendered on the resulting page. It should look like this:

Search Results for *Web Development with Django*

Figure 1.52: Searching for Web Development with Django

You should also be able to pass in special HTML characters such as **<** and **>** to see how Django automatically escapes them in the template:

Search Results for </html>

Figure 1.53: Notice how HTML characters are escaped so we are protected from tag injection

> **NOTE**
>
> The solution to this activity can be found at http://packt.live/2Nh1NTJ.

You have scaffolded the book search view and can demonstrate how variables are read from the **GET** parameters. You can also use this view to test how Django escapes special HTML characters automatically in a template. The search view does not actually search or show results yet, as there are no books in the database, but this will be added in *Chapter 6, Forms*.

SUMMARY

This chapter was a quick introduction to Django. You first got up to speed on the HTTP protocol and the structure of HTTP requests and responses. We then saw how Django uses the MVT paradigm, and then how it parses a URL, generates an HTTP request, and sends it to a view to get an HTTP response. We scaffolded the Bookr project and then created the **reviews** app for it. We then built two example views to illustrate how to get data from a request and use it when rendering templates. You should have experimented to see how Django escapes output in HTML when rendering a template.

You did all this with the PyCharm IDE, and you learned how to set it up to debug your application. The debugger will help you find out why things aren't working as they should. In the next chapter, you will start to learn about Django's database integration and its model system, so you can start storing and retrieving real data for your application.

2

MODELS AND MIGRATIONS

OVERVIEW

This chapter introduces you to the concept of databases and their importance in building web applications. You will start by creating a database using an open-source database visualization tool called **SQLite DB Browser**. You will then perform some basic **Create Read Update Delete** (**CRUD**) database operations using SQL commands. Then, you will learn about Django's **Object Relational Mapping** (**ORM**), using which your application can interact and seamlessly work with a relational database using simple Python code, eliminating the need to run complex SQL queries. You will learn about **models** and **migrations**, which are a part of Django's ORM, that are used to propagate database schematic changes from the application to the database, and also perform database CRUD operations. Toward the end of the chapter, you will study the various types of database relationships and use that knowledge to perform queries across related records.

INTRODUCTION

Data is at the core of most web applications. Unless we're talking about a very simple application such as a calculator, in most cases we need to store data, process it, and display it to the user on a page. Since most operations in user-facing web applications involve data, there is a need to store data in places that are secure, easily accessible, and readily available. This is where databases come in handy. Imagine a library operational before the advent of computers. The librarian would have to maintain records of book inventories, records of book lending, returns from students, and so on. All of these would have been maintained in physical records. The librarian, while carrying out their day-to-day activities, would modify these records for each operation, for example, when lending a book to someone or when the book was returned.

Today, we have databases to help us with such administrative tasks. A database looks like a spreadsheet or an Excel sheet containing records, with each table consisting of multiple rows and columns. An application can have many such tables. Here is an example table of a book inventory in a library:

Book Number	Author	Title	Number of Copies
Howto4563	Adam Chappel	How to Build a house	4
Travel5327	Charlie Hunt	How to holiday in Switzerland	5
Fiction3453	Evan Stark	The Mystery Cat	2
Howto4453	Bruce Williams	Sailing Guide	7

Figure 2.1: Table of a book inventory for a library

In the preceding table, we can see that there are columns with details about various attributes of the books in the library, while the rows contain entries for each book. To manage a library, there can be many such tables working together as a system. For example, along with an inventory, we may have other tables such as student information, book lending records, and so on. Databases are built with the same logic, where software applications can easily manage data.

In the previous chapter, we had a brief introduction to Django and its use in developing web applications. Then we learned about the Model-View-Template (MVT) concept. Later, we created a Django project and started the Django development server. We also had a brief discussion about Django's views, URLs, and templates.

In this chapter, we will start by learning about the types of databases and a few basic database operations using SQL. After that, we will move on to the concept of models and migrations in Django, which assist in faster development by providing a layer of abstraction to facilitate database operations using Python objects.

DATABASES

A database is a structured collection of data that helps manage information easily. A software layer called the Database Management System (DBMS) is used to store, maintain, and perform operations on the data. Databases are of two types, relational databases and non-relational databases.

RELATIONAL DATABASES

Relational databases or Structured Query Language (SQL) databases store data in a pre-determined structure of rows and columns called tables. A database can be made up of more than one such table, and these tables have a fixed structure of attributes, data types, and relations with other tables. For example, as we just saw in *Figure 2.1*, the book inventory table has a fixed structure of columns comprising **Book Number**, **Author**, **Title**, and **Number of Copies**, and the entries form the rows in the table. There could be other tables as well, such as **Student Information** and **Lending Records**, which could be related to the inventory table. Also, whenever a book is lent to a student, the records will be stored per the relationships between multiple tables (say, the **Student Information** and the **Book Inventory** tables).

This pre-determined structure of rules defining the data types, tabular structures, and relationships across different tables acts like scaffolding or a blueprint for a database. This blueprint is collectively called a database schema. When applied to a database, it will prepare the database to store application data. To manage and maintain these databases, there is a common language for relational databases called SQL. Some examples of relational databases are SQLite, PostgreSQL, MySQL, and OracleDB.

NON-RELATIONAL DATABASES

Non-relational databases or NoSQL (Not Only SQL) databases are designed to store unstructured data. They are well suited to large amounts of generated data that does not follow rigid rules, as is the case with relational databases. Some examples of non-relational databases are Cassandra, MongoDB, CouchDB, and Redis.

For example, imagine that you need to store the stock value of companies in a database using Redis. Here, the company name will be stored as the key and the stock value as the value. Using the key-value type NoSQL database in this use case is appropriate because it stores the desired value for a unique key and is faster to access.

For the scope of this book, we will be dealing only with relational databases as Django does not officially support non-relational databases. However, if you wish to explore, there are many forked projects, such as Django non-rel, that support NoSQL databases.

DATABASE OPERATIONS USING SQL

SQL uses a set of commands to perform a variety of database operations, such as creating an entry, reading values, updating an entry, and deleting an entry. These operations are collectively called **CRUD operations**, which stands for Create, Read, Update, and Delete. To understand database operations in detail, let's first get some hands-on experience with SQL commands. Most relational databases share a similar SQL syntax; however, some operations will differ.

For the scope of this chapter, we will use SQLite as the database. SQLite is a lightweight relational database that is a part of Python standard libraries. That's why Django uses SQLite as its default database configuration. However, we will also learn more about how to perform configuration changes to use other databases in *Chapter 17, Deployment of a Django Application (Part 1 – Server Setup)*. This chapter can be downloaded from the GitHub repository of this book, from http://packt.live/2Kx6FmR.

DATA TYPES IN RELATIONAL DATABASES

Databases provide us with a way to restrict the type of data that can be stored in a given column. These are called data types. Some examples of data types for a relational database such as SQLite3 are given here:

- **INTEGER** is used for storing integers.

- **TEXT** can store text.

- **REAL** is used for floating-point values.

For example, you would want the title of a book to have **TEXT** as the data type. So, the database will enforce a rule that no type of data, other than text data, can be stored in that column. Similarly, the book's price can have a **REAL** data type, and so on.

EXERCISE 2.01: CREATING A BOOK DATABASE

In this exercise, you will create a book database for a book review application. For better visualization of the data in the SQLite database, you will install an open-source tool called **DB Browser** for SQLite. This tool helps visualize the data and provides a shell to execute the SQL commands.

If you haven't done so already, visit the URL https://sqlitebrowser.org and from the *downloads* section, install the application as per your operating system and launch it. Detailed instructions for DB Browser installation can be found in the *Preface*.

> **NOTE**
>
> Database operations can be performed using a command-line shell as well.

1. After launching the application, create a new database by clicking **New Database** in the top-left corner of the application. Create a database named **bookr**, as you are working on a book review application:

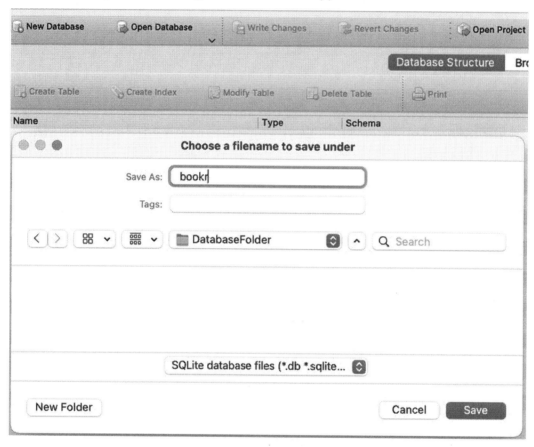

Figure 2.2: Creating a database named bookr

2. Next, click the **Create Table** button in the top-left corner and enter **book** as the table name.

> **NOTE**
>
> After clicking the **Save** button, you may find that the window for creating a table opens up automatically. In that case, you won't have to click the **Create Table** button; simply proceed with the creation of the book table as specified in the preceding step.

3. Now, click the **Add field** button, enter the field name as **title**, and select the type as **TEXT** from the dropdown. Here **TEXT** is the data type for the **title** field in the database:

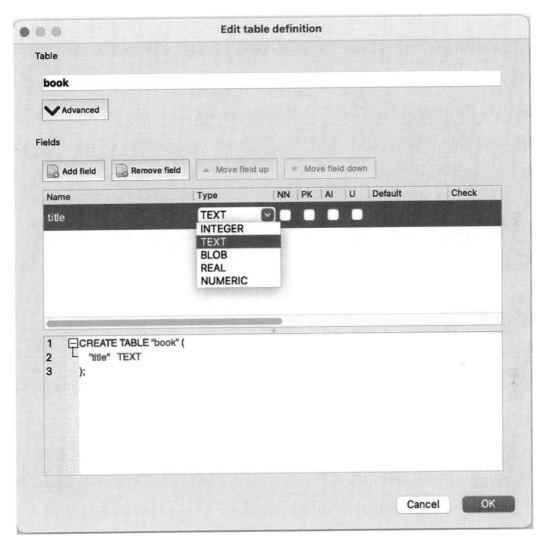

Figure 2.3: Adding a TEXT field named title

4. Similarly, add two more fields for the table named **publisher** and **author** and select **TEXT** as the type for both the fields. Then, click the **OK** button:

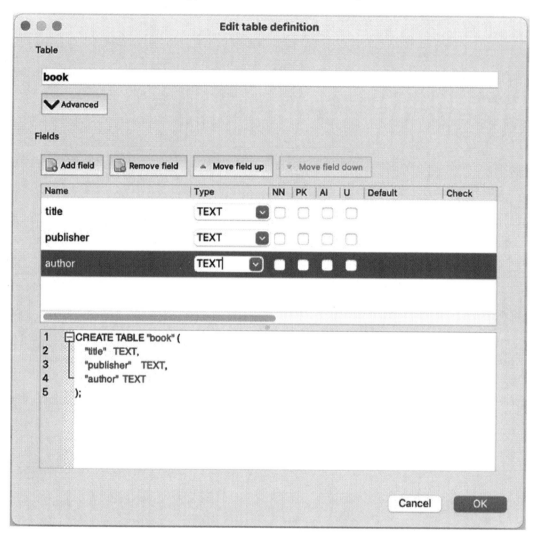

Figure 2.4: Creating TEXT fields named publisher and author

This creates a database table called **book** in the **bookr** database with the fields title, publisher, and **author**. This can be seen as follows:

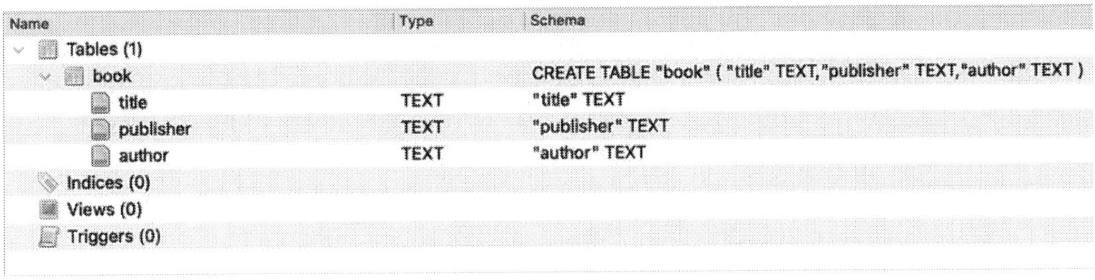

Figure 2.5: Database with the fields title, publisher, and author

In this exercise, we used an open-source tool called DB Browser (SQLite) to create our first database called **bookr**, and in it, we created our first table named **book**.

SQL CRUD OPERATIONS

Let's assume that the editors or the users of our book review application want to make some modifications to the book inventory, such as adding a few books to the database, updating an entry in the database, and so on. SQL provides various ways to perform such CRUD operations. Before we dive into the world of Django models and migrations, let's explore these basic SQL operations first.

For the CRUD operations that follow, you will be running a few SQL queries. To run them, navigate to the **Execute SQL** tab in DB Browser. You can type in or paste the SQL queries we've listed in the sections that follow in the **SQL 1** window. You can spend some time modifying your queries, and understanding them, before you execute them. When you're ready, click the icon that looks like a **Play** button or press the F5 key to execute the command. The results will show up in the window below the **SQL 1** window:

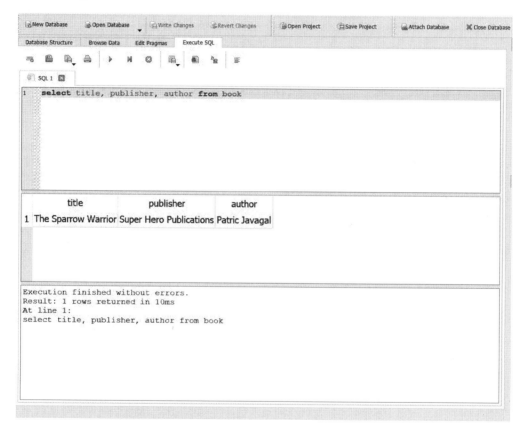

Figure 2.6: Executing SQL queries in DB Browser

SQL CREATE OPERATIONS

The **Create** operation in SQL is performed using the **insert** command, which, as the name implies, lets us insert data into the database. Let's go back to our **bookr** example. Since we have already created the database and the **book** table, we can now create or insert an entry in the database by executing the following command:

```
insert into book values ('The Sparrow Warrior', 'Super Hero
  Publications', 'Patric Javagal');
```

This inserts into the table named **book** the values defined in the command. Here, **The Sparrow Warrior** is the title, **Super Hero Publications** is the publisher, and **Patric Javagal** is the author of the book. Note that the order of insertion corresponds with the way we have created our table; that is, the values are inserted into the columns representing title, publisher, and author respectively. Similarly, let's execute two more inserts to populate the **book** table:

```
insert into book values ('Ninja Warrior', 'East Hill Publications',
   'Edward Smith');
insert into book values ('The European History', 'Northside
   Publications', 'Eric Robbins');
```

The three inserts executed so far will insert three rows into the **book** table. But how do we verify that? How would we know whether those three entries we inserted were entered into the database correctly? Let's learn how to do that in the next section.

SQL READ OPERATIONS

We can read from the database using the **select** SQL operation. For example, the following SQL **select** command retrieves the selected entries created in the **book** table:

```
select title, publisher, author from book;
```

You should see the following output:

	title	publisher	author
1	The Sparrow Warrior	Super Hero Publications	Patric Javagal
2	Ninja Warrior	East Hill Publications	Edward Smith
3	The European History	Northside Publications	Eric Robbins

Figure 2.7: Output after using the select command

Here, **select** is the command that reads from the database, and the fields **title**, **publisher**, and **author** are the columns that we intend to select from the book table. Since these are all the columns the database has, the select statement has returned all the values present in the database. The select statement is also called a SQL query. An alternate way to get all the fields in the database is by using the wildcard ***** in the select query instead of specifying all the column names explicitly:

```
select * from book;
```

This will return the same output as shown in the preceding figure. Now, suppose we want to get the author name for the book titled **The Sparrow Warrior**; in this case, the **select** query would be as follows:

```
select author from book where title="The Sparrow Warrior";
```

Here, we have added a special SQL keyword called **where** so that the **select** query returns only the entries that match the condition. The result of the query, of course, will be **Patric Javagal**. Now, what if we wanted to change the name of the book's publisher?

SQL UPDATE OPERATIONS

In SQL, the way to update a record in the database is by using the **update** command:

```
update book set publisher = 'Northside Publications' where
   title='The Sparrow Warrior';
```

Here, we are setting the value of publisher to **Northside Publications** if the value of the title is **The Sparrow Warrior**. We can then run the **select** query we ran in the SQL Read Operations section to see how the updated table looks after running the **update** command:

	title	publisher	author
	Filter	Filter	Filter
1	The Sparrow Warrior	Northside Publications	Patric Javagal
2	Ninja Warrior	East Hill Publications	Edward Smith
3	The European History	Northside Publications	Eric Robbins

Figure 2.8: Updating the value of publisher for the title The Sparrow Warrior

Next, what if we wanted to delete the title of the record we just updated?

SQL DELETE OPERATIONS

Here is an example of how to delete a record from the database using the **delete** command:

```
delete from book where title='The Sparrow Warrior';
```

delete is the SQL keyword for delete operations. Here, this operation will be performed only if the title is **The Sparrow Warrior**. Here is how the book table will look after the delete operation:

	title	publisher	author
1	Ninja Warrior	East Hill Publications	Edward Smith
2	The European History	Northside Publications	Eric Robbins

Figure 2.9: Output after performing the delete operation

These are the basic operations of SQL. We will not go very deep into all the SQL commands and syntax, but feel free to explore more about database base operations using SQL.

> **NOTE**
>
> For further reading, you can start by exploring some advanced SQL **select** operations with **join** statements, which are used to query data across multiple tables. For a detailed course on SQL, you can refer to *The SQL Workshop* (https://www.packtpub.com/product/the-sql-workshop/9781838642358).

DJANGO ORM

Web applications constantly interact with databases, and one of the ways to do so is using SQL. If you decide to write a web application without a web framework like Django and instead use Python alone, Python libraries such as **psycopg2** could be used to interact directly with the databases using SQL commands. But while developing a web application with multiple tables and fields, SQL commands can easily become overly complex and thus difficult to maintain. For this reason, popular web frameworks such as Django provide a level of abstraction using which we can easily work with databases. The part of Django that helps us do this is called **ORM**, which stands for **Object Relational Mapping**.

Django ORM converts object-oriented Python code into actual database constructs such as database tables with data type definitions and facilitates all the database operations via simple Python code. Because of this, we do not have to deal with SQL commands while performing database operations. This helps in faster application development and ease in maintaining the application source code.

Django supports relational databases such as SQLite, PostgreSQL, Oracle Database, and MySQL. Django's database abstraction layer ensures that the same Python/Django source code can be used across any of the above relational databases with very little modification to the project settings. Since SQLite is part of the Python libraries and Django is configured by default to SQLite, for the scope of this chapter, we shall use SQLite while we learn about Django models and migrations.

DATABASE CONFIGURATION AND CREATING DJANGO APPLICATIONS

As we have already seen in *Chapter 1, Introduction to Django*, when we create a Django project and run the Django server, the default database configuration is of SQLite3. The database configuration will be present in the project directory, in the **settings.py** file.

> **NOTE**
>
> Make sure you go through the **settings.py** file for the **bookr** app. Going through the entire file once will help you understand the concepts that follow. You can find the file at this link: http://packt.live/2KEdaUM.

So, for our example project, the database configuration will be present at the following location: **bookr/settings.py**. The default database configuration present in this file, when a Django project is created, is as follows:

```
DATABASES = {\
        'default': {\
                'ENGINE': 'django.db.backends.sqlite3',\
                'NAME': os.path.join\
                        (BASE_DIR, 'db.sqlite3'),}}
```

> **NOTE**
>
> The preceding code snippet uses a backslash (\ ) to split the logic
> across multiple lines. When the code is executed, Python will ignore the
> backslash, and treat the code on the next line as a direct continuation of the
> current line.

The DATABASES variable is assigned with a dictionary containing the database details
for the project. Inside the dictionary, there is a nested dictionary with a key as default.
This holds the configuration of a default database for the Django project. The reason
we have a nested dictionary with **default** as a key is that a Django project could
potentially interact with multiple databases, and the default database is the one used
by Django for all operations unless explicitly specified. The ENGINE key represents
which database engine is being used; in this case, it is **sqlite3**.

The **NAME** key defines the name of the database, which can have any value. But for
SQLite3, since the database is created as a file, **NAME** can have the full path of the
directory where the file needs to be created. The full path of the **db** file is processed
by joining (or concatenating) the previously defined path in **BASE_DIR** with
db.sqlite3. Note that **BASE_DIR** is the project directory as already defined in the
settings.py file.

If you are using other databases, such as PostgreSQL, MySQL, and so on, changes will
have to be made in the preceding database settings as shown here:

```
DATABASES = {\
        'default': {\
                'ENGINE': 'django.db\
                        .backends.postgresql',\
                'NAME': 'bookr',\
                'USER': <username>,\
                'PASSWORD': <password>,\
                'HOST': <host-IP-address>,\
                'PORT': '5432',}}
```

Here, changes have been made to **ENGINE** to use PostgreSQL. The host IP address and port number of the server need to be provided for **HOST** and **PORT** respectively. As the names suggest, **USER** is the database username and **PASSWORD** is the database password. In addition to changes in the configuration, we will have to install the database drivers or bindings along with the database host and credentials. This will be covered in detail in later chapters, but for now, since we are using SQLite3, the default configuration will be sufficient. Note that the above is just an example to show the changes you'll need to make to use a different database such as PostgreSQL, but since we are using SQLite, we shall use the database configuration that exists already, and there is no need to make any modifications to the database settings.

DJANGO APPS

A Django project can have multiple apps that often act as discrete entities. That's why, whenever required, an app can be plugged into a different Django project as well. For example, if we are developing an e-commerce web application, the web application can have multiple apps, such as a chatbot for customer support or a payment gateway to accept payments as users purchase goods from the application. These apps, if needed, can also be plugged into or reused in a different project.

Django comes with the following apps enabled by default. The following is a snippet from a project's **settings.py** file:

```
INSTALLED_APPS = ['django.contrib.admin',\
                  'django.contrib.auth',\
                  'django.contrib.contenttypes',\
                  'django.contrib.sessions',\
                  'django.contrib.messages',\
                  'django.contrib.staticfiles',]
```

These are a set of installed or default apps used for the admin site, authentication, content types, sessions, messaging, and an application to collect and manage static files. In the upcoming chapters, we shall study this in-depth. For the scope of this chapter, though, we shall understand why Django migration is needed for these installed apps.

DJANGO MIGRATION

As we have learned before, Django's ORM helps make database operations simpler. A major part of the operation is to transform the Python code into database structures such as database fields with stated data types and tables. In other words, the transformation of Python code into database structures is known as **migration**. Instead of creating dozens of tables by running SQL queries, you would write models for them in Python, something you'll learn to do in an upcoming section titled *Creating Models and Migrations*. These models will have **fields**, which form the blueprints of database tables. The fields, in turn, will have different field types giving us more information about the type of data stored there (recall how we specified the data type of our field as **TEXT** in *step 4* of *Exercise 2.01, Creating a Book Database*).

Since we have a Django project set up, let's perform our first migration. Although we have not added any code yet to our project, we can migrate the applications listed in **INSTALLED_APPS**. This is necessary because Django's installed apps need to store the relevant data in the database for their operations, and migration will create the required database tables to store the data in the database. The following command should be entered in the terminal or shell to do this:

```
python manage.py migrate
```

> **NOTE**
>
> For macOS, you can use **python3** instead of **python** in the preceding command.

Here, **manage.py** is a script that was automatically created when the project was created. It is used for carrying out managerial or administrative tasks. By executing this command, we create all the database structures required by the installed apps.

As we are using DB Browser for SQLite to browse the database, let's take a look at the database for which changes have been made after executing the **migrate** command.

The database file will have been created in the project directory under the name **db.sqlite3**. Open DB Browser, click **Open Database**, navigate until you find the **db.sqlite3** file, and open it. You should see a set of newly created tables created by the Django migration. It will look as follows in DB Browser:

Name	Type	Schema
∨ 🗔 Tables (11)		
> 🗔 auth_group		CREATE TABLE "auth_group" ("id" integer NOT NULL PRIMARY KEY
> 🗔 auth_group_permissions		CREATE TABLE "auth_group_permissions" ("id" integer NOT NULL
> 🗔 auth_permission		CREATE TABLE "auth_permission" ("id" integer NOT NULL PRIMAR
> 🗔 auth_user		CREATE TABLE "auth_user" ("id" integer NOT NULL PRIMARY KEY
> 🗔 auth_user_groups		CREATE TABLE "auth_user_groups" ("id" integer NOT NULL PRIMA
> 🗔 auth_user_user_permissions		CREATE TABLE "auth_user_user_permissions" ("id" integer NOT N
> 🗔 django_admin_log		CREATE TABLE "django_admin_log" ("id" integer NOT NULL PRIMA
> 🗔 django_content_type		CREATE TABLE "django_content_type" ("id" integer NOT NULL PRI
> 🗔 django_migrations		CREATE TABLE "django_migrations" ("id" integer NOT NULL PRIMA
> 🗔 django_session		CREATE TABLE "django_session" ("session_key" varchar(40) NOT
> 🗔 sqlite_sequence		CREATE TABLE sqlite_sequence(name,seq)
> 🗞 indices (15)		
🗔 Views (0)		
🗔 Triggers (0)		

Figure 2.10: Contents of the db.sqlite3 file

Now, if we browse through the newly created database structure by clicking the database tables, we see the following:

Name	Type	Schema
∨ 🗔 Tables (11)		
∨ 🗔 auth_group		CREATE TABLE "auth_group" ("id" integer NOT NULL PRIMA
🗋 id	integer	"id" integer NOT NULL PRIMARY KEY AUTOINCREMENT
🗋 name	varchar(150)	"name" varchar(150) NOT NULL UNIQUE
∨ 🗔 auth_group_permissions		CREATE TABLE "auth_group_permissions" ("id" integer NOT
🗋 id	integer	"id" integer NOT NULL PRIMARY KEY AUTOINCREMENT
🗋 group_id	integer	"group_id" integer NOT NULL
🗋 permission_id	integer	"permission_id" integer NOT NULL
∨ 🗔 auth_permission		CREATE TABLE "auth_permission" ("id" integer NOT NULL
🗋 id	integer	"id" integer NOT NULL PRIMARY KEY AUTOINCREMENT
🗋 content_type_id	integer	"content_type_id" integer NOT NULL
🗋 codename	varchar(100)	"codename" varchar(100) NOT NULL
🗋 name	varchar(255)	"name" varchar(255) NOT NULL

Figure 2.11: Browsing through the newly created database structure

Notice that the database tables created have different fields, each with their respective data types. Click the **Browse data** tab in DB Browser and select a table from the dropdown. For instance, after clicking the **auth_group_permissions** table, you should see something like this:

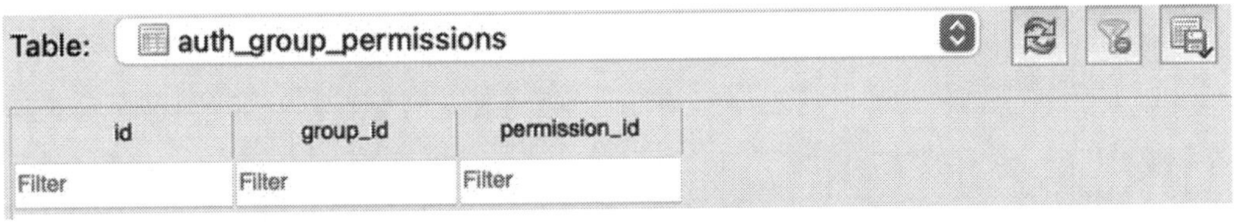

Figure 2.12: Viewing the auth_group_permissions table

You will see that there is no data available for these tables yet because Django migration only creates the database structure or the blueprint, and the actual data in the database is stored during the operation of the application. Now since we have migrated the built-in or default Django apps, let's try to create an app and perform a Django migration.

CREATING DJANGO MODELS AND MIGRATIONS

A Django model is essentially a Python class that holds the blueprint for creating a table in a database. The **models.py** file can have many such models, and each model transforms into a database table. The attributes of the class form the fields and relationships of the database table as per the model definitions.

For our reviews application, we need to create the following models and their database tables consequently:

- Book: This should store information about books.

- Contributor: This should store information about the person(s) who contributed to writing the book, such as author, co-author, or editor.

- Publisher: As the name implies, this refers to the book publisher.

- Review: This should store all the books' reviews written by the users of the application.

Every book in our application will need to have a publisher, so let's create **Publisher** as our first model. Enter the following code in **reviews/models.py**:

```python
from django.db import models

class Publisher(models.Model):
    """A company that publishes books."""
    name = models.CharField\
            (max_length=50, \
            help_text="The name of the Publisher.")
    website = models.URLField\
```

```
                    (help_text="The Publisher's website.")
    email = models.EmailField\
            (help_text="The Publisher's email address.")
```

> **NOTE**
>
> You can take a look at the complete models.py file for the bookr app by
> clicking the following link: http://packt.live/3hmFQxn.

The first line of code imports the Django's **models** module. While this line will be
autogenerated at the time of the creation of the Django app, do make sure you add it
if it is not present. Following the import, the rest of the code is defining a class named
Publisher, which will be a subclass of Django's **models.Model**. Furthermore, this
class will have attributes or fields such as name, website, and email.

FIELD TYPES

As we can see, each of these fields is defined to have the following types:

- **CharField**: This field type is used to store shorter string fields, for example,
  Packt Publishing. For very large strings, we use **TextField**.

- **EmailField**: This is similar to **CharField**, but validates whether the string
  represents a valid email address, for example, customersupport@packtpub.com.

- **URLField**: This is again similar to **CharField**, but validates whether the string
  represents a valid URL, for example, https://www.packtpub.com.

FIELD OPTIONS

Django provides a way to define field options to a model's field. These field options
are used to set a value or a constraint, and so on. For example, we can set a
default value for a field using **default=<value>**, to ensure that every time a
record is created in the database for the field, it is set to a default value specified
by us. Following are the two field options that we have used while defining the
Publisher model:

- **help_text**: This is a field option that helps us add descriptive text for a field
  that gets automatically included for Django forms.

- **max_length**: This option is provided to **CharField** where it defines the
  maximum length of the field in terms of the number of characters.

Django has many more field types and field options that can be explored from the extensive official Django documentation. As we go about developing our sample book review application, we shall learn about those types and fields that are used for the project. Now let's migrate the Django models into the database. Execute the following command in the shell or terminal to do that (run it from the folder where your **manage.py** file is stored):

```
python manage.py makemigrations reviews
```

The output of the command looks like this:

```
Migrations for 'reviews':
  reviews/migrations/0001_initial.py
    - Create model Publisher
```

The **makemigrations <appname>** command creates the migration scripts for the given app; in this case, for the reviews app. Notice that after running makemigrations, there is a new file created under the **migrations** folder:

Figure 2.13: New file under the migrations folder

This is the migration script created by Django. When we run **makemigrations** without the app name, the migration scripts will be created for all the apps in the project. Next, let's list the project migration status. Remember that earlier, we applied migrations to Django's installed apps and now we have created a new app, reviews. The following command, when run in the shell or terminal, will show the status of model migrations throughout the project (run it from the folder where your **manage. py** file is stored):

```
python manage.py showmigrations
```

The output for the preceding command is as follows:

```
admin
  [X]  0001_initial
  [X]  0002_logentry_remove_auto_add
  [X]  0003_logentry_add_action_flag_choices
auth
  [X]  0001_initial
  [X]  0002_alter_permission_name_max_length
  [X]  0003_alter_user_email_max_length
  [X]  0004_alter_user_username_opts
  [X]  0005_alter_user_last_login_null
  [X]  0006_require_contenttypes_0002
  [X]  0007_alter_validators_add_error_messages
  [X]  0008_alter_user_username_max_length
  [X]  0009_alter_user_last_name_max_length
  [X]  0010_alter_group_name_max_length
  [X]  0011_update_proxy_permissions
contenttypes
  [X]  0001_initial
  [X]  0002_remove_content_type_name
reviews
  [ ]  0001_initial
sessions
  [X]  0001_initial
```

Here, the **[X]** mark indicates that the migrations have been applied. Notice the difference that all the other apps' migrations have applied except that of reviews. The **showmigrations** command can be executed to understand the migration status, but this is not a mandatory step while performing model migrations.

Next, let's understand how Django transforms a model into an actual database table. This can be understood by running the **sqlmigrate** command:

```
python manage.py sqlmigrate reviews 0001_initial
```

We should see the following output:

```
BEGIN;
--
-- Create model Publisher
--
CREATE TABLE "reviews_publisher" ("id" integer \
    NOT NULL PRIMARY KEY AUTOINCREMENT, "name" \
    varchar(50) NOT NULL, "website" varchar(200) \
    NOT NULL, "email" varchar(254) NOT NULL);
COMMIT;
```

The preceding snippet shows the SQL command equivalent used when Django migrates the database. In this case, we are creating the **reviews_publisher** table with the fields name, website, and email with the defined field types. Furthermore, all these fields are defined to be **NOT NULL**, implying that the entries for these fields cannot be null and should have some value. The **sqlmigrate** command is not a mandatory step while doing the model migrations.

PRIMARY KEYS

Let's assume that a database table called users, as its name suggests, stores information about users. Let's say it has more than 1,000 records and there are at least 3 users with the same name, Joe Burns. How do we uniquely identify these users from the application? The solution is to have a way to uniquely identify each record in the database. This is done using **Primary Keys**. A primary key is unique for a database table, and as a rule, a table cannot have two rows with the same primary key. In Django, when the primary key is not explicitly mentioned in the database models, Django automatically creates **id** as the primary key (of type integer), which auto increments as new records are created.

In the previous section, notice the output of the **python manage.py sqlmigrate** command. While creating the **Publisher** table, the **SQL CREATE TABLE** command was adding one more field called **id** to the table. **id** is defined to be **PRIMARY KEY AUTOINCREMENT**. In relational databases, a primary key is used to uniquely identify an entry in the database. For example, the book table has **id** as the primary key, which has numbers starting from 1. This value increments by 1 as new records are created. The integer value of **id** is always unique across the book table. Since the migration script has already been created by executing makemigrations, let's now migrate the newly created model in the reviews app by executing the following command:

```
python manage.py migrate reviews
```

You should get the following output:

```
Operations to perform:
    Apply all migrations: reviews
Running migrations:
    Applying reviews.0001_initial... OK
```

This operation creates the database table for the reviews app. The following is a snippet from DB Browser indicating the new table **reviews_publisher** has been created in the database:

reviews_publisher		CREATE TABLE "reviews_publisher" ("id" integer NOT N(
id	integer	"id" integer NOT NULL PRIMARY KEY AUTOINCREMENT
name	varchar(50)	"name" varchar(50) NOT NULL
website	varchar(200)	"website" varchar(200) NOT NULL
email	varchar(254)	"email" varchar(254) NOT NULL

Figure 2.14: reviews_publisher table created after executing the migration command

So far, we have explored how to create a model and migrate it into the database. Let's now work on creating the rest of the models for our book review application. As we've already seen, the application will have the following database tables:

- **Book**: This is the database table that holds the information about the book itself. We have already created a **Book** model and have migrated this to the database.

- **Publisher**: This table holds information about the book publisher.

- **Contributor**: This table holds information about the contributor, that is, the author, co-author, or editor.

- **Review**: This table holds information about the review comments posted by the reviewers.

Let's add the **Book** and **Contributor** models, as shown in the following code snippet, into **reviews/models.py**:

```
class Book(models.Model):
    """A published book."""
    title = models.CharField\
            (max_length=70, \
             help_text="The title of the book.")
    publication_date = models.DateField\
                       (verbose_name=\
                        "Date the book was published.")
    isbn = models.CharField\
           (max_length=20, \
            verbose_name="ISBN number of the book.")


class Contributor(models.Model):
    """
A contributor to a Book, e.g. author, editor, \
co-author.
    """
    first_names = models.CharField\
                  (max_length=50, \
                   help_text=\
                   "The contributor's first name or names.")
    last_names = models.CharField\
                 (max_length=50, \
                  help_text=\
                  "The contributor's last name or names.")
    email = models.EmailField\
            (help_text="The contact email for the contributor.")
```

The code is self-explanatory. The **Book** model has the fields title, publication_date, and isbn. The **Contributor** model has the fields **first_names** and **last_names** fields and the email ID of the contributor. There are some newly added models as well, apart from the ones we have seen in the Publisher model. They have **DateField** as a new field type, which, as the name suggests, is used to store a date. A new field option called **verbose_name** is also used. It provides a descriptive name for the field.

RELATIONSHIPS

One of the powers of relational databases is the ability to establish relationships between data stored across database tables. Relationships help maintain data integrity by establishing the correct references across tables, which in turn helps maintain the database. Relationship rules, on the other hand, ensure data consistency and prevent duplicates.

In a relational database, there can be the following types of relations:

- Many to one
- Many to many
- One to one

Let's explore each relationship in detail.

MANY TO ONE

In this relationship, many records (rows/entries) from one table can refer to one record (row/entry) in another table. For example, there can be many books produced by one publisher. This is a case of a many-to-one relationship. To establish this relationship, we need to use the database's foreign keys. A foreign key in a relational database establishes the relationship between a field from one table and a primary key from a different table.

For example, say you have data about employees belonging to different departments stored in a table called **employee_info** with their employee ID as the primary key alongside a column that stores their department name; this table also contains a column that stores that department's department ID. Now, there's another table called **departments_info**, which has department ID as the primary key. In this case, then, the department ID is a foreign key in the **employee_info** table.

In our **bookr** app, the **Book** model can have a foreign key referring to the primary key of the **Publisher** table. Since we have already created the models for **Book**, **Contributor**, and **Publisher**, now let's establish a many-to-one relationship across the **Book** and **Publisher** models. For the **Book** model, add the last line:

```
class Book(models.Model):
    """A published book."""
    title = models.CharField\
            (max_length=70, \
             help_text="The title of the book.")
    publication_date = models.DateField\
```

```
                      (verbose_name=\
                       "Date the book was published.")
    isbn = models.CharField\
            (max_length=20, \
             verbose_name="ISBN number of the book.")
    publisher = models.ForeignKey\
              (Publisher, on_delete=models.CASCADE)
```

Now the newly added **publisher** field is establishing a many-to-one relationship between **Book** and **Publisher** using a foreign key. This relationship ensures the nature of a many-to-one relationship, which is that many books can have one publisher:

- **models.ForeignKey**: This is the field option to establish a many-to-one relationship.

- **Publisher**: When we establish relationships with different tables in Django, we refer to the model that creates the table; in this case, the **Publisher** table is created by the **Publisher** model (or the Python class Publisher).

- **on_delete**: This is a field option that determines the action to be taken upon the deletion of the referenced object. In this case, the **on_delete** option is set to **CASCADE (models.CASCADE)**, which deletes the referenced objects.

For example, assume a publisher has published a set of books. For some reason, if the publisher has to be deleted from the application, the next action is CASCADE, which means delete all the referenced books from the application. There are many more **on_delete** actions, such as the following:

- **PROTECT**: This prevents the deletion of the record unless all the referenced objects are deleted.

- **SET_NULL**: This sets a null value if the database field has been previously configured to store null values.

- **SET_DEFAULT**: Sets to a default value on the deletion of the referenced object.

For our book review application, we will be using only the CASCADE option.

MANY TO MANY

In this relationship, multiple records in a table can have a relationship with multiple records in a different table. For example, a book can have multiple co-authors and each author (contributor) could have written multiple books. So, this forms a many-to-many relationship between the **Book** and **Contributor** tables:

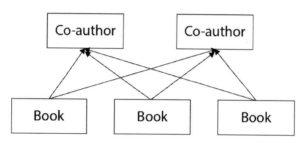

Figure 2.15: Many-to-many relationship between books and co-authors

In **models.py**, for the Book model, add the last line as shown here:

```
class Book(models.Model):
    """A published book."""
    title = models.CharField\
            (max_length=70, \
            help_text="The title of the book.")
    publication_date = models.DateField\
                       (verbose_name=\
                       "Date the book was published.")
    isbn = models.CharField\
           (max_length=20, \
           verbose_name="ISBN number of the book.")
    publisher = models.ForeignKey\
               (Publisher, on_delete=models.CASCADE)
    contributors = models.ManyToManyField\
                  ('Contributor', through="BookContributor")
```

The newly added contributors field establishes a many-to-many relationship with Book and Contributor using the ManyToManyField field type:

- **models.ManyToManyField**: This is the field type to establish a many-to-many relationship.

- **through**: This is a special field option for many-to-many relationships. When we have a many-to-many relationship across two tables, if we want to store some extra information about the relationship, then we can use this to establish the relationship via an intermediary table.

For example, we have two tables, namely **Book** and **Contributor**, where we need to store the information on the type of contributor for the book, such as Author, Co-author, or Editor. Then the type of contributor is stored in an intermediary table called **BookContributor**. Here is how the **BookContributor** table/model looks. Make sure you include this model in **reviews/models.py**:

```
class BookContributor(models.Model):
    class ContributionRole(models.TextChoices):
        AUTHOR = "AUTHOR", "Author"
        CO_AUTHOR = "CO_AUTHOR", "Co-Author"
        EDITOR = "EDITOR", "Editor"

    book = models.ForeignKey\
            (Book, on_delete=models.CASCADE)
    contributor = models.ForeignKey\
                (Contributor, \
                 on_delete=models.CASCADE)
    role = models.CharField\
            (verbose_name=\
            "The role this contributor had in the book.", \
            choices=ContributionRole.choices, max_length=20)
```

> **NOTE**
>
> The complete **models.py** file can be viewed at this link:
> http://packt.live/3hmFQxn.

An intermediary table such as **BookContributor** establishes relationships by using foreign keys to both the **Book** and **Contributor** tables. It can also have extra fields that can store information about the relationship the **BookContributor** model has with the following fields:

- **book**: This is a foreign key to the **Book** model. As we saw previously, **on_delete=models.CASCADE** will delete an entry from the relationship table when the relevant book is deleted from the application.

- **Contributor**: This is again a foreign key to the **Contributor** model/table. This is also defined as **CASCADE** upon deletion.

- **role**: This is the field of the intermediary model, which stores the extra information about the relationship between **Book** and **Contributor**.

- **class ContributionRole(models.TextChoices)**: This can be used to define a set of choices by creating a subclass of **models.TextChoices**. For example, **ContributionRole** is a subclass created out of **TextChoices**, which is used by the roles field to define Author, Co-Author, and Editor as a set of choices.

- **choices**: This refers to a set of choices defined in the models, and they are useful when creating Django **Forms** using the models.

> **NOTE**
>
> When the through field option is not provided while establishing a many-to-many relationship, Django automatically creates an intermediary table to manage the relationship.

ONE-TO-ONE RELATIONSHIPS

In this relationship, one record in a table will have a reference to only one record in a different table. For example, a person can have only one driver's license, so a person to their driver's license could form a one-to-one relationship:

Figure 2.16: Example of a one-to-one relationship

The OneToOneField can be used to establish a one-to-one relationship, as shown here:

```
class DriverLicence(models.Model):
    person = models.OneToOneField\
            (Person, on_delete=models.CASCADE)
    licence_number = models.CharField(max_length=50)
```

Now that we have explored database relationships, let's come back to our bookr application and add one more model there.

ADDING THE REVIEW MODEL

We've already added the **Book** and **Publisher** models to the **reviews/models. py** file. The last model that we are going to add is the **Review** model. The following code snippet should help us do this:

```
from django.contrib import auth

class Review(models.Model):
    content = models.TextField\
            (help_text="The Review text.")
    rating = models.IntegerField\
            (help_text="The rating the reviewer has given.")
    date_created = models.DateTimeField\
                (auto_now_add=True, \
                help_text=\
                "The date and time the review was created.")
    date_edited = models.DateTimeField\
                (null=True, \
                help_text=\
                "The date and time the review was last edited.")
    creator = models.ForeignKey\
            (auth.get_user_model(), on_delete=models.CASCADE)
    book = models.ForeignKey\
            (Book, on_delete=models.CASCADE, \
            help_text="The Book that this review is for.")
```

> **NOTE**
>
> The complete **models.py** file can be viewed at this link:
> http://packt.live/3hmFQxn.

The **review** model/table will be used to store user-provided review comments and ratings for books. It has the following fields:

- **content**: This field stores the text for a book review, hence the field type used is **TextField** as this can store a large amount of text.

- **rating**: This field stores the review rating of a book. Since the rating is going to be an integer, the field type used is **IntegerField**.

- **date_created**: This field stores the time and date when the review was written, hence the field type is **DateTimeField**.

- **date_edited**: This field stores the date and time whenever a review is edited. The field type is again **DateTimeField**.

- **Creator**: This field specifies the review creator or the person who writes the book review. Notice that this is a foreign key to **auth.get_user_model()**, which is referring to the **User** model from Django's built-in authentication module. It has a field option **on_delete=models.CASCADE**. This explains that when a user is deleted from the database, all the reviews written by that user will be deleted.

- **Book**: Reviews have a field called **book**, which is a foreign key to the **Book** model. This is because for a book review application, reviews have to be written, and a book can have many reviews, so this is a many-to-one relationship. This is also defined with a field option, **on_delete=models.CASCADE**, because once the book is deleted, there is no point in retaining the reviews in the application. So, when a book is deleted, all the reviews referring to the book will also get deleted.

MODEL METHODS

In Django, we can write methods inside a model class. These are called **model methods** and they can be custom methods or special methods that override the default methods of Django models. One such method is __str__(). This method returns the string representation of the **Model** instances and can be especially useful while using the Django shell. In the following example, where the __str__() method is added to the **Publisher** model, the string representation of the **Publisher** object will be the publisher's name:

```
class Publisher(models.Model):
    """A company that publishes books."""
    name = models.CharField\
        (max_length=50, \
```

```
            help_text="The name of the Publisher.")
    website = models.URLField\
            (help_text="The Publisher's website.")
    email = models.EmailField\
            (help_text="The Publisher's email address.")


    def __str__(self):
        return self.name
```

Add the **_str_()** methods to **Contributor** and **Book** as well, as follows:

```
class Book(models.Model):
    """A published book."""
    title = models.CharField\
            (max_length=70, \
            help_text="The title of the book.")
    publication_date = models.DateField\
                    (verbose_name=\
                    "Date the book was published.")
    isbn = models.CharField\
            (max_length=20, \
            verbose_name="ISBN number of the book.")
    publisher = models.ForeignKey\
            (Publisher, \
            on_delete=models.CASCADE)
    contributors = models.ManyToManyField\
                ('Contributor', through="BookContributor")


    def __str__(self):
        return self.title



class Contributor(models.Model):
    """
A contributor to a Book, e.g. author, editor, \
co-author.
    """

    first_names = models.CharField\
                (max_length=50, \
                help_text=\
                "The contributor's first name or names.")
```

```
    last_names = models.CharField\
              (max_length=50, \
               help_text=\
               "The contributor's last name or names.")
    email = models.EmailField\
            (help_text=\
             "The contact email for the contributor.")

    def __str__(self):
        return self.first_names
```

MIGRATING THE REVIEWS APP

Since we have the entire model file ready, let's now migrate the models into the database, similar to what we did before with the installed apps. Since the reviews app has a set of models created by us, before running the migration, it is important to create the migration scripts. Migration scripts help in identifying any changes to the models and will propagate these changes into the database while running the migration. Execute the following command to create the migration scripts:

```
python manage.py makemigrations reviews
```

You should get an output similar to this:

```
reviews/migrations/0002_auto_20191007_0112.py
  - Create model Book
  - Create model Contributor
  - Create model Review
  - Create model BookContributor
  - Add field contributors to book
  - Add field publisher to book
```

Migration scripts will be created in a folder named **migrations** in the application folder. Next, migrate all the models into the database using the **migrate** command:

```
python manage.py migrate reviews
```

You should see the following output:

```
Operations to perform:
  Apply all migrations: reviews
Running migrations:
  Applying reviews.0002_auto_20191007_0112... OK
```

After executing this command, we have successfully created the database tables defined in the **reviews** app. You may use DB Browser for SQLite to explore the tables you have just created after the migration. To do so, open DB Browser for SQLite, click the **Open Database** button (*Figure 2.17*), and navigate to your project directory:

Figure 2.17: Click the Open Database button

Figure 2.18: Locating db.sqlite3 in the bookr directory

You should now be able to browse the new sets of tables created. The following figure shows the database tables defined in the **reviews** app:

∨ ▦ reviews_book		CREATE TABLE "reviews_book" ("id" integer NOT NULL PRIMARY KE
id	integer	"id" integer NOT NULL PRIMARY KEY AUTOINCREMENT
title	varchar(70)	"title" varchar(70) NOT NULL
publication_date	date	"publication_date" date NOT NULL
isbn	varchar(20)	"isbn" varchar(20) NOT NULL
publisher_id	integer	"publisher_id" integer NOT NULL
∨ ▦ reviews_bookcontributor		CREATE TABLE "reviews_bookcontributor" ("id" integer NOT NULL F
id	integer	"id" integer NOT NULL PRIMARY KEY AUTOINCREMENT
role	varchar(20)	"role" varchar(20) NOT NULL
book_id	integer	"book_id" integer NOT NULL
contributor_id	integer	"contributor_id" integer NOT NULL
∨ ▦ reviews_contributor		CREATE TABLE "reviews_contributor" ("id" integer NOT NULL PRIM/
id	integer	"id" integer NOT NULL PRIMARY KEY AUTOINCREMENT
first_names	varchar(50)	"first_names" varchar(50) NOT NULL
last_names	varchar(50)	"last_names" varchar(50) NOT NULL
email	varchar(254)	"email" varchar(254) NOT NULL
∨ ▦ reviews_publisher		CREATE TABLE "reviews_publisher" ("id" integer NOT NULL PRIMAF
id	integer	"id" integer NOT NULL PRIMARY KEY AUTOINCREMENT
name	varchar(50)	"name" varchar(50) NOT NULL
website	varchar(200)	"website" varchar(200) NOT NULL
email	varchar(254)	"email" varchar(254) NOT NULL
∨ ▦ reviews_review		CREATE TABLE "reviews_review" ("id" integer NOT NULL PRIMARY I
id	integer	"id" integer NOT NULL PRIMARY KEY AUTOINCREMENT
content	text	"content" text NOT NULL
rating	integer	"rating" integer NOT NULL
date_created	datetime	"date_created" datetime NOT NULL
date_edited	datetime	"date_edited" datetime
book_id	integer	"book_id" integer NOT NULL
creator_id	integer	"creator_id" integer NOT NULL

Figure 2.19: Database tables as defined in the reviews app

DJANGO'S DATABASE CRUD OPERATIONS

As we have created the necessary database tables for the book review application, let's work on understanding the basic database operations with Django.

We've already briefly touched on database operations using SQL statements in the section titled *SQL CRUD Operations*. We tried creating an entry into the database using the **Insert** statement, read from the database using the **select** statement, updated an entry using the **update** statement, and deleted an entry from the database using the **delete** statement.

Django's ORM provides the same functionality without having to deal with the SQL statements. Django's database operations are simple Python code, hence we overcome the hassle of maintaining SQL statements among the Python code. Let's take a look at how these are performed.

To execute the CRUD operations, we will enter Django's command-line shell by executing the following command:

```
python manage.py shell
```

> **NOTE**
>
> For this chapter, we will designate Django shell commands using the **>>>** notation (highlighted) at the start of the code block. While pasting the query into DB Browser, make sure you exclude this notation every time.

When the interactive console starts, it looks as follows:

```
Type "help", "copyright", "credits" or "license" for more information.
(InteractiveConsole)
>>>
```

EXERCISE 2.02: CREATING AN ENTRY IN THE BOOKR DATABASE

In this exercise, you will create a new entry in the database by saving a model instance. In other words, you will create an entry in a database table without explicitly running a SQL query:

1. First, import the **Publisher** class/model from **reviews.models**:

   ```
   >>>from reviews.models import Publisher
   ```

2. Create an object or an instance of the **Publisher** class by passing all the field values (name, website, and email) required by the **Publisher** model:

   ```
   >>>publisher = Publisher(name='Packt Publishing', website='https://
   www.packtpub.com', email='info@packtpub.com')
   ```

3. Next, to write the object into the database, it is important to call the **save()** method, because until this is called there will not be an entry created in the database:

   ```
   >>>publisher.save()
   ```

Now you can see a new entry created in the database using DB Browser:

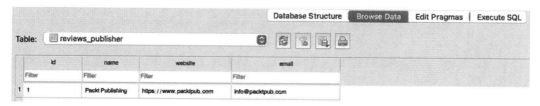

Figure 2.20: Entry created in the database

4. Use the object attributes to make any further changes to the object and save the changes to the database:

```
>>>publisher.email
'info@packtpub.com'
>>> publisher.email = 'customersupport@packtpub.com'
>>> publisher.save()
```

You can see the changes using DB Browser as follows:

Figure 2.21: Entry with the updated email field

In this exercise, you created an entry in the database by creating an instance of the model object and used the **save()** method to write the model object into the database.

Note that by following the preceding method, the changes to the class instance are not saved until the **save()** method is called. However, if we use the **create()** method, Django saves the changes to the database in a single step. We'll use this method in the exercise that follows.

EXERCISE 2.03: USING THE CREATE() METHOD TO CREATE AN ENTRY

Here, you will create a record in the **contributor** table using the **create()** method in a single step:

1. First, import the Contributor class as before:

```
>>> from reviews.models import Contributor
```

2. Invoke the **create()** method to create an object in the database in a single step. Ensure that you pass all the required parameters (**first_names**, **last_names**, and **email**):

```
>>> contributor =
  Contributor.objects.create(first_names="Rowel",
    last_names="Atienza", email="RowelAtienza@example.com")
```

3. Use DB Browser to verify that the contributor record has been created in the database. If your DB Browser is not already open, open the database file **db.sqlite3** as we just did in the previous section. Click **Browse Data** and select the desired table – in this case, the **reviews_contributor** table from the **Table** dropdown, as shown in the screenshot – and verify the newly created database record:

Figure 2.22: Verifying the creation of the record in DB Browser

In this exercise, we learned that using the **create()** method, we can create a record for a model in a database in a single step.

CREATING AN OBJECT WITH A FOREIGN KEY

Similar to how we created a record in the **Publisher** and **Contributor** tables, let's now create one for the **Book** table. If you recall, the **Book** model has a foreign key to **Publisher** that cannot have a null value. So, a way to populate the publisher's foreign key is by providing the created **publisher** object in the book's **publisher** field as shown in the following exercise.

EXERCISE 2.04: CREATING RECORDS FOR A MANY-TO-ONE RELATIONSHIP

In this exercise, you will create a record in the **Book** table including a foreign key to the **Publisher** model. As you already know, the relationship between **Book** and **Publisher** is a many-to-one relationship, so you have to first fetch the **Publisher** object and then use it while creating the book record:

1. First, import the **Publisher** class:

```
>>>from reviews.models import Book, Publisher
```

2. Retrieve the **publisher** object from the database using the following command. The **get()** method is used to retrieve an object from the database. We still haven't explored database read operations. For now, use the following command; we will go deeper into database read/retrieve in the next section:

```
>>>publisher = Publisher.objects.get(name='Packt Publishing')
```

3. When creating a book, we need to supply a **date** object as publication_date is a date field in the **Book** model. So, import **date** from datetime so that a date object can be supplied when creating the **book** object as shown in the following code:

```
>>>from datetime import date
```

4. Use the **create()** method to create a record of the book in the database. Ensure that you pass all the fields, namely **title**, **publication_ date**, **isbn**, and the **publisher** object:

```
>>>book = Book.objects.create(title="Advanced Deep Learning
  with Keras", publication_date=date(2018, 10, 31),
    isbn="9781788629416", publisher=publisher)
```

Note that since **publisher** is a foreign key and it is not nullable (cannot hold a **null** value), it is mandatory to pass a **publisher** object. When the mandatory foreign key object publisher is not provided, the database will throw an integrity error.

Figure 2.23 shows the **Book** table where the first entry is created. Notice that the foreign key field (**publisher_id**) points to the id (primary key) of the **Publisher** table. The entry **publisher_id** in the book's record is pointing to a **Publisher** record that has **id** (primary key) **1** as shown in the following two screenshots:

Figure 2.23: Foreign key pointing to the primary key for reviews_book

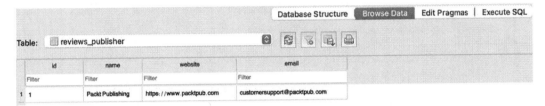

Figure 2.24: Foreign key pointing to the primary key for reviews_publisher

In this exercise, we learned that while creating a database record, an object can be assigned to a field if it is a foreign key. We know that the **Book** model also has a many-to-many relationship with the Contributor model. Let's now explore the ways to establish many-to-many relations as we create records in the database.

EXERCISE 2.05: CREATING RECORDS WITH MANY-TO-MANY RELATIONSHIPS

In this exercise, you will create a many-to-many relationship between **Book** and **Contributor** using the relationship model **BookContributor**:

1. In case you have restarted the shell and lost the **publisher** and the **book** objects, retrieve them from the database by using the following set of Python statements:

```
>>>from reviews.models import Book
>>>from reviews.models import Contributor
>>>contributor = Contributor.objects.get(first_names='Rowel')
book = Book.objects.get(title="Advanced Deep Learning with Keras")
```

2. The way to establish a many-to-many relationship is by storing the information about the relationship in the intermediary model or the relationship model; in this case, it is **BookContributor**. Since we have already fetched the book and the contributor records from the database, let's use these objects while creating a record for the **BookContributor** relationship model. To do so, first, create an instance of the **BookContributor** relationship class and then save the object to the database. While doing so, ensure you pass the required fields, namely the **book** object, **contributor** object, and **role**:

```
>>>from reviews.models import BookContributor
>>>book_contributor = BookContributor(book=book,
   contributor=contributor, role='AUTHOR')
>>> book_contributor.save()
```

Notice that we specified the role as **AUTHOR** while creating the **book_contributor** object. This is a classic example of storing relationship data while establishing a many-to-many relationship. The role can be **AUTHOR, CO_AUTHOR**, or **EDITOR**.

This established the relationship between the book *Advanced Deep Learning with Keras* and the contributor Rowel (Rowel being the author of the book).

In this exercise, we established a many-to-many relationship between **Book** and **Contributor** using the **BookContributor** relationship model. With regards to the verification of the many-to-many relationship that we just created, we will see this in detail in a few exercises later on in this chapter.

EXERCISE 2.06: A MANY-TO-MANY RELATIONSHIP USING THE ADD() METHOD

In this exercise, you will establish a many-to-many relationship using the **add()** method. When we don't use the relationship to create the objects, we can use **through_default** to pass in a dictionary with the parameters defining the required fields. Continuing from the previous exercise, let's add one more contributor to the book titled *Advanced Deep Learning with Keras*. This time, the contributor is an editor of the book:

1. If you have restarted the shell, run the following two commands to import and fetch the desired book instance:

```
>>>from reviews.models import Book, Contributor
>>>book = Book.objects.get(title="Advanced Deep Learning with
   Keras")
```

2. Use the **create()** method to create a contributor as shown here:

```
>>>contributor = Contributor.objects.create(first_names='Packt',
   last_names='Example Editor',
      email='PacktEditor@example.com')
```

3. Add the newly created contributor to the book using the **add()** method. Ensure you provide the relationship parameter **role** as **dict**. Enter the following code:

```
>>>book.contributors.add(contributor,
   through_defaults={'role': 'EDITOR'})
```

Thus, we used the **add()** method to establish a many-to-many relationship between the book and contributor while storing the relationship data role as **Editor**. Let's now take a look at other ways of doing this.

USING CREATE() AND SET() METHODS FOR MANY-TO-MANY RELATIONSHIPS

Assume the book *Advanced Deep Learning with Keras* has a total of two editors. Let's use the following method to add another editor to the book. If the contributor is not already present in the database, then we can use the **create()** method to simultaneously create an entry as well as to establish the relation with the book:

```
>>>book.contributors.create(first_names='Packtp', last_names=
   'Editor Example', email='PacktEditor2@example.com',
      through_defaults={'role': 'EDITOR'})
```

Similarly, we can also use the **set()** method to add a list of contributors for a book. Let's create a publisher, a set of two contributors who are the co-authors, and a **book** object. First, import the **Publisher** model, if not already imported, using the following code:

```
>>>from reviews.models import Publisher
```

The following code will help us do so:

```
>>> publisher = Publisher.objects.create(name='Pocket Books',
   website='https://pocketbookssampleurl.com', email='pocketbook@example.
com')
>>> contributor1 = Contributor.objects.create(first_names=
   'Stephen', last_names='Stephen', email='StephenKing@example.com')
>>> contributor2 = Contributor.objects.create(first_names=
   'Peter', last_names='Straub', email='PeterStraub@example.com')

>>> book = Book.objects.create(title='The Talisman',
   publication_date=date(2012, 9, 25), isbn='9781451697216',
      publisher=publisher)
```

Since this is a many-to-many relationship, we can add a list of objects in just one go, using the **set()** method. We can use through_defaults to specify the role of the contributors; in this case, they are co-authors:

```
>>> book.contributors.set([contributor1, contributor2],
    through_defaults={'role': 'CO_AUTHOR'})
```

READ OPERATIONS

Django provides us with methods that allow us to read/retrieve from the database. We can retrieve a single object from the database using the **get()** method. We have already created a few records in the previous sections, so let's use the **get()** method to retrieve an object.

EXERCISE 2.07: USING THE GET() METHOD TO RETRIEVE AN OBJECT

In this exercise, you will retrieve an object from the database using the **get()** method:

1. Fetch a **Publisher** object that has a **name** field with the value **Pocket Books**:

```
>>>from reviews.models import Publisher
>>> publisher = Publisher.objects.get(name='Pocket Books')
```

2. Re-enter the retrieved **publisher** object and press *Enter*:

```
>>> publisher
<Publisher: Pocket Books>
```

Notice that the output is displayed in the shell. This is called a string representation of an object. It is the result of adding the model method **__str__()** as we did in the *Model Methods* section for the **Publisher** class.

3. Upon retrieving the object, you have access to all the object's attributes. Since this is a Python object, the attributes of the object can be accessed by using . followed by the attribute name. So, you can retrieve the publisher's name with the following command:

```
>>> publisher.name
'Pocket Books'
```

4. Similarly, retrieve the publisher's website:

```
>>> publisher.website
'https://pocketbookssampleurl.com'
```

The publisher's email address can be retrieved as well:

```
>>> publisher.email
'pocketbook@example.com'
```

In this exercise, we learned how to fetch a single object using the **get()** method. There are several disadvantages to using this method, though. Let's find out why.

RETURNING AN OBJECT USING THE GET() METHOD

It is important to note that the **get()** method can only fetch one object. If there is another object carrying the same value as the field mentioned, then we can expect a *"returned more than one"* error message. For example, if there are two entries in the **Publisher** table with the same value for the name field, we can expect an error. In such cases, there are alternate ways to retrieve those objects, which we will be exploring in the subsequent sections.

We can also get a *"matching query does not exist"* error message when there are no objects returned from the **get()** query. The **get()** method can be used with any of the object's fields to retrieve a record. In the following case, we are using the **website** field:

```
>>> publisher = Publisher.objects.get(website='https://
pocketbookssampleurl.com')
```

After retrieving the object, we can still get the publisher's name, as shown here:

```
>>> publisher.name
'Pocket Books'
```

Another way to retrieve an object is by using its primary key – **pk**, as can be seen here:

```
>>> Publisher.objects.get(pk=2)
<Publisher: Pocket Books>
```

Using pk for the primary key is a more generic way of using the primary key field. But for the **Publisher** table, since we know that **id** is the primary key, we can simply use the field name **id** to create our **get()** query:

```
>>> Publisher.objects.get(id=2)
<Publisher: Pocket Books>
```

> **NOTE**
>
> For **Publisher** and all the other tables, the primary key is **id**, which was automatically created by Django. This happens when a primary key field is not mentioned at the time of the creation of the table. But there can be instances where a field can be explicitly declared as a primary key.

EXERCISE 2.08: USING THE ALL() METHOD TO RETRIEVE A SET OF OBJECTS

We can use the **all()** method to retrieve a set of objects. In this exercise, you will use this method to retrieve the names of all contributors:

1. Add the following code to retrieve all the objects from the **Contributor** table:

```
>>>from reviews.models import Contributor


>>> Contributor.objects.all()
<QuerySet [<Contributor: Rowel>, <Contributor: Packt>, <Contributor:
Packtp>, <Contributor: Stephen>, <Contributor:
  Peter>]>
```

Upon execution, you will get a **QuerySet** of all the objects.

2. We can use list indexing to look up a specific object or to iterate over the list using a loop to do any other operation:

```
>>> contributors = Contributor.objects.all()
```

3. Since **Contributor** is a list of objects, you can use indexing to access any element in the list as shown in the following command:

```
>>> contributors[0]
<Contributor: Rowel>
```

In this case, the first element in the list is a contributor with a **first_names** value of **'Rowel'** and a **last_names** value of **'Atienza'**, as you can see from the following code:

```
>>> contributors[0].first_names
'Rowel'
>>> contributors[0].last_names
'Atienza'
```

In this exercise, we learned how to retrieve all the objects using the **all()** method and we also learned how to use the retrieved set of objects as a list.

RETRIEVING OBJECTS BY FILTERING

If we have more than one object for a field value, then we cannot use the **get()** method since the **get()** method can return only one object. For such cases, we have the **filter()** method, which can retrieve all the objects that match a specified condition.

EXERCISE 2.09: USING THE FILTER() METHOD TO RETRIEVE OBJECTS

In this exercise, you will use the **filter()** method to get a specific set of objects for a certain condition. Specifically, you will retrieve all the contributors' names who have their first name as **Peter**:

1. First, create two more contributors:

```
>>>from reviews.models import Contributor
>>> Contributor.objects.create(first_names='Peter', last_
names='Wharton', email='PeterWharton@example.com')
>>> Contributor.objects.create(first_names='Peter', last_
names='Tyrrell', email='PeterTyrrell@example.com')
```

2. To retrieve those contributors who have the value of **first_names** as **Peter**, add the following code:

```
>>> Contributor.objects.filter(first_names='Peter')
<QuerySet [<Contributor: Peter>, <Contributor: Peter>,
   <Contributor: Peter>]>
```

3. The **filter()** method returns the object even if there is only one. You can see this here:

```
>>>Contributor.objects.filter(first_names='Rowel')
<QuerySet [<Contributor: Rowel>]>
```

4. Furthermore, the **filter()** method returns an empty **QuerySet** if there is none matching the query. This can be seen here:

```
>>>Contributor.objects.filter(first_names='Nobody')
<QuerySet []>
```

In this exercise, we saw the use of filters to retrieve a set of a few objects filtered by a certain condition.

FILTERING BY FIELD LOOKUPS

Now, let's suppose we want to filter and query a set of objects using the object's fields by providing certain conditions. In such a case, we can use what is called a double-underscore lookup. For example, the **Book** object has a field named **publication_date**; let's say we want to filter and fetch all the books that were published after 01-01-2014. We can easily look these up by using the double-underscore method. To do this, we will first import the **Book** model:

```
>>>from reviews.models import Book
>>>book = Book.objects.filter(publication_date__gt=date(2014, 1, 1))
```

Here, **publication_date__gt** indicates the publication date, which is greater than (**gt**) a certain specified date – in this case, 01-01-2014. Similar to this, we have the following abbreviations:

- **lt**: Less than

- **lte**: Less than or equal to

- **gte**: Greater than or equal to

The result after filtering can be seen here:

```
>>> book
<QuerySet [<Book: Advanced Deep Learning with Keras>]>
```

Here is the publication date of the book that is part of the query set, which confirms that the publication date was after 01-01-2014:

```
>>> book[0].publication_date
datetime.date(2018, 10, 31)
```

USING PATTERN MATCHING FOR FILTERING OPERATIONS

For filtered results, we can also look up whether the parameter contains a part of the string we are looking for:

```
>>> book = Book.objects.filter(title__contains=
    'Deep learning')
```

Here, **title__contains** looks for all those objects with titles containing **'Deep learning'** as a part of the string:

```
>>> book
<QuerySet [<Book: Advanced Deep Learning with Keras>]>

>>> book[0].title
'Advanced Deep Learning with Keras'
```

Similarly, we can use **icontains** if the string match needs to be case-insensitive. Using **startswith** matches any string starting with the specified string.

RETRIEVING OBJECTS BY EXCLUDING

In the previous section, we learned about fetching a set of objects by matching a certain condition. Now, suppose we want to do the opposite; that is, we want to fetch all those objects that do not match a certain condition. In such cases, we can use the **exclude()** method to exclude a certain condition and fetch all the required objects. This will be clearer with an example. The following is a list of all contributors:

```
>>> Contributor.objects.all()
<QuerySet [<Contributor: Rowel>, <Contributor: Packt>,
  <Contributor: Packtp>, <Contributor: Stephen>,
    <Contributor: Peter>, <Contributor: Peter>,
      <Contributor: Peter>]>
```

Now, from this list, we will exclude all those contributors who have the value of **first_names** as **Peter**:

```
>>> Contributor.objects.exclude(first_names='Peter')
<QuerySet [<Contributor: Rowel>, <Contributor: Packt>,
  <Contributor: Packtp>, <Contributor: Stephen>]>
```

We see here that the query returned all those contributors whose first name is not Peter.

RETRIEVING OBJECTS USING THE ORDER_BY() METHOD

We can retrieve a list of objects while ordering by a specified field, using the **order_by()** method. For example, in the following code snippet, we order the books by their publication date:

```
>>> books = Book.objects.order_by("publication_date")
>>> books
<QuerySet [<Book: The Talisman>, <Book: Advanced Deep Learning
   with Keras>]>
```

Let's examine the order of the query. Since the query set is a list, we can use indexing to check the publication date of each book:

```
>>> books[0].publication_date
datetime.date(2012, 9, 25)
>>> books[1].publication_date
datetime.date(2018, 10, 31)
```

Notice that the publication date of the first book with index **0** is older than the publication date of the second book with index **1**. So, this confirms that the queried list of books has been properly ordered as per their publication dates. We can also use a prefix with the negative sign for the field parameter to order results in descending order. This can be seen from the following code snippet:

```
>>> books = Book.objects.order_by("-publication_date")
>>> books

<QuerySet [<Book: Advanced Deep Learning with Keras>,
   <Book: The Talisman>]>
```

Since we have prefixed a negative sign to the publication date, notice that the queried set of books has now been returned in the opposite order, where the first book object with index **0** has a more recent date than the second book:

```
>>> books[0].publication_date
datetime.date(2018, 10, 31)

>>> books[1].publication_date
datetime.date(2012, 9, 25)
```

We can also order by using a string field or a numerical. For example, the following code can be used to order books by their primary key or **id**:

```
>>>books = Book.objects.order_by('id')
<QuerySet [<Book: Advanced Deep Learning with Keras>,
  <Book: The Talisman>]>
```

The queried set of books has been ordered as per book **id** in ascending order:

```
>>> books[0].id
1
>>> books[1].id
2
```

Again, to order in descending order, the negative sign can be used as a prefix, as follows:

```
>>> Book.objects.order_by('-id')
<QuerySet [<Book: The Talisman>, <Book: Advanced Deep Learning
  with Keras>]>
```

Now, the queried set of books has been ordered per book **id** in descending order:

```
>>> books[0].id
2
>>> books[1].id
1
```

To order by a string field in alphabetical order, we can do something like this:

```
>>>Book.objects.order_by('title')
<QuerySet [<Book: Advanced Deep Learning with Keras>, <Book:
  The Talisman>]>
```

Since we have used the title of the book to order by, the query set has been ordered in alphabetical order. We can see this as follows:

```
>>> books[0]
<Book: Advanced Deep Learning with Keras>
>>> books[1]
<Book: The Talisman>
```

Similar to what we've seen for the previous ordering types, the negative sign prefix can help us sort in reverse alphabetical order, as we can see here:

```
>>> Book.objects.order_by('-title')
<QuerySet [<Book: The Talisman>, <Book: Advanced Deep Learning
   with Keras>]>
```

This will lead to the following output:

```
>>> books[0]
<Book: The Talisman>
>>> books[1]
<Book: Advanced Deep Learning with Keras>
```

Yet another useful method offered by Django is **values()**. It helps us get a query set of dictionaries instead of objects. In the following code snippet, we're using this for a **Publisher** object:

```
>>> publishers = Publisher.objects.all().values()

>>> publishers
<QuerySet [{'id': 1, 'name': 'Packt Publishing', 'website':
   'https://www.packtpub.com', 'email':
      'customersupport@packtpub.com'}, {'id': 2, 'name':
         'Pocket Books', 'website': 'https://pocketbookssampleurl.com',
            'email': 'pocketbook@example.com'}]>
>>> publishers[0]
{'id': 1, 'name': 'Packt Publishing', 'website':
   'https://www.packtpub.com', 'email':
      'customersupport@packtpub.com'}

>>> publishers[0]
{'id': 1, 'name': 'Packt Publishing', 'website':
   'https://www.packtpub.com', 'email':
      'customersupport@packtpub.com'}
```

QUERYING ACROSS RELATIONSHIPS

As we have studied in this chapter, the **reviews** app has two kinds of relationships – many-to-one and many-to-many. So far, we have learned various ways of making queries using **get()**, filters, field lookups, and so on. Now let's study how to perform queries across relationships. There are several ways to go about this – we could use foreign keys, object instances, and more. Let's explore these with the help of some examples.

QUERYING USING FOREIGN KEYS

When we have relationships across two models/tables, Django provides a way to perform a query using the relationship. The command shown in this section will retrieve all the books published by **Packt Publishing** by performing a query using model relationships. Similar to what we've seen previously, this is done using the double-underscore lookup. For example, the **Book** model has a foreign key of **publisher** pointing to the **Publisher** model. Using this foreign key, we can perform a query using double underscores and the field **name** in the **Publisher** model. This can be seen from the following code:

```
>>> Book.objects.filter(publisher__name='Packt Publishing')
<QuerySet [<Book: Advanced Deep Learning with Keras>]>
```

QUERYING USING MODEL NAME

Another way of querying is where we can use a relationship to do the query backward, using the model name in lowercase. For instance, let's say we want to query the publisher who published the book *Advanced Deep Learning with Keras* using model relationships in the query. For this, we can execute the following statement to retrieve the **Publisher** information object:

```
>>> Publisher.objects.get(book__title='Advanced Deep Learning
  with Keras')
<Publisher: Packt Publishing>
```

Here, **book** is the model name in lowercase. As we already know, the **Book** model has a **publisher** foreign key with the value of **name** as Packt Publishing.

QUERYING ACROSS FOREIGN KEY RELATIONSHIPS USING THE OBJECT INSTANCE

We can also retrieve the information using the object's foreign key. Suppose we want to query the publisher's name for the title *The Talisman*:

```
>>> book = Book.objects.get(title='The Talisman')
>>> book.publisher
<Publisher: Pocket Books>
```

Using the object here is an example where we use the reverse direction to get all the books published by a publisher by using the **set.all()** method:

```
>>> publisher = Publisher.objects.get(name='Pocket Books')

>>> publisher.book_set.all()
<QuerySet [<Book: The Talisman>]>
```

We can also create queries using chains of queries:

```
>>> Book.objects.filter(publisher__name='Pocket Books').filter(title='The
Talisman')
<QuerySet [<Book: The Talisman>]>
```

Let's perform some more exercises to shore up our knowledge of the various kinds of queries we have learned about so far.

EXERCISE 2.10: QUERYING ACROSS A MANY-TO-MANY RELATIONSHIP USING FIELD LOOKUP

We know that **Book** and **Contributor** have a many-to-many relationship. In this exercise, without creating an object, you will perform a query to retrieve all the contributors who contributed to writing the book titled *The Talisman*:

1. First, import the **Contributor** class:

    ```
    >>> from reviews.models import Contributor
    ```

2. Now, add the following code to query for the set of contributors on *The Talisman*:

    ```
    >>>Contributor.objects.filter(book__title='The Talisman')
    ```

    You should see the following:

    ```
    <QuerySet [<Contributor: Stephen>, <Contributor: Peter>]>
    ```

From the preceding output, we can see that Stephen and Peter are the contributors who contributed to writing the book *The Talisman*. The query uses the **book** model (written in lowercase) and does a field lookup for the **title** field using the double underscore as shown in the command.

In this exercise, we learned how to perform queries across many-to-many relationships using field lookup. Let's now look at using another method to carry out the same task.

EXERCISE 2.11: A MANY-TO-MANY QUERY USING OBJECTS

In this exercise, using a **Book** object, search for all the contributors who contributed to writing the book with the title *The Talisman*. The following steps will help you do that:

1. Import the Book model:

    ```
    >>> from reviews.models import Book
    ```

2. Retrieve a book object with the title *The Talisman*, by adding the following line of code:

```
>>> book = Book.objects.get(title='The Talisman')
```

3. Then retrieve all the contributors who worked on the book The Talisman using the **book** object. Add the following code to do so:

```
>>>book.contributors.all()
<QuerySet [<Contributor: Stephen>, <Contributor: Peter>]>
```

Again, we can see that Stephen and Peter are the contributors who worked on the book *The Talisman*. Since the book has a many-to-many relationship with contributors, we have used the **contributors.all()** method to get a query set of all those contributors who worked on the book. Now, let's try using the **set** method to perform a similar task.

EXERCISE 2.12: A MANY-TO-MANY QUERY USING THE SET() METHOD

In this exercise, you will use a **contributor** object to fetch all the books written by the contributor named **Rowel**:

1. Import the **Contributor** model:

```
>>> from reviews.models import Contributor
```

2. Fetch a **contributor** object whose **first_names** is **'Rowel'** using the **get()** method:

```
>>> contributor = Contributor.objects.get(first_names='Rowel')
```

3. Using the **contributor** object and the **book_set()** method, get all those books written by the contributor:

```
>>> contributor.book_set.all()
<QuerySet [<Book: Advanced Deep Learning with Keras>]>
```

Since **Book** and **Contributor** have a many-to-many relationship, we can use the **set()** method to query a set of objects associated with the model. In this case, **contributor.book_set.all()** returned all the books written by the contributor.

EXERCISE 2.13: USING THE UPDATE() METHOD

In this exercise, you will use the **update()** method to update an existing record:

1. Change **first_names** for a contributor who has the last name **Tyrrell**:

```
>>> from reviews.models import Contributor
>>> Contributor.objects.filter(last_names='Tyrrell').
  update(first_names='Mike')
1
```

The return value shows the number of records that have been updated. In this case, one record has been updated.

2. Fetch the contributor that was just modified using the **get()** method and verify that the first name has been changed to **Mike**:

```
>>> Contributor.objects.get(last_names='Tyrrell').first_names
'Mike'
```

> **NOTE**
>
> If the filter operation has more than one record, then the **update()** method will update the specified field in all the records returned by the filter.

In this exercise, we learned how to use the **update()** method to update a record in the database. Now, finally, let's try deleting a record from the database using the **delete()** method.

EXERCISE 2.14: USING THE DELETE() METHOD

An existing record in the database can be deleted using the **delete()** method. In this exercise, you will delete a record from the **contributors** table that has the value of **last_name** as **Wharton**:

1. Fetch the object using the **get** method and use the **delete** method as shown here:

```
>>> from reviews.models import Contributor
>>> Contributor.objects.get(last_names='Wharton').delete()
(1, {'reviews.BookContributor': 0, 'reviews.Contributor': 1})
```

Notice that you called the **delete()** method without assigning the **contributor** object to a variable. Since the **get()** method returns a single object, you can access the object's method without actually creating a variable for it.

2. Verify the **contributor** object with **last_name** as **'Wharton'** has been deleted:

```
>>> Contributor.objects.get(last_names='Wharton')
Traceback (most recent call last):
    File "<console>", line 1, in <module>
    File "/../site-packages/django/db/models/manager.py",
  line 82, in manager_method
    return getattr(self.get_queryset(), name)(*args, **kwargs)
    File "/../site-packages/django/db/models/query.py",
  line 417, in get
    self.model._meta.object_name
reviews.models.Contributor.DoesNotExist: Contributor
  matching query does not exist.
```

As you can see upon running the query, we got an *object does not exist* error. This is expected since the record has been deleted. In this exercise, we learned how to use the **delete** method to delete a record from the database.

ACTIVITY 2.01: CREATE MODELS FOR A PROJECT MANAGEMENT APPLICATION

Imagine you are developing a project management application called **Juggler**. Juggler is an application that can track multiple projects, and each project can have multiple tasks associated with it. The following steps will help you complete this activity:

1. Using the techniques we have learned so far, create a Django project called **juggler**.

2. Create a Django app called **projectp**.

3. Add the app projects in the **juggler/settings.py** file.

4. Create two related model classes called **Project** and **Task** in **projectp/models.py**.

5. Create migration scripts and migrate the models' definitions to the database.

6. Open the Django shell now and import the models.

7. Populate the database with an example and write a query displaying the list of tasks associated with a given project.

> **NOTE**
>
> The solution to this activity can be found at http://packt.live/2Nh1NTJ.

POPULATING THE BOOKR PROJECT'S DATABASE

Although we know how to create database records for the project, in the next few chapters, we will have to create a lot of records to work with the project. For that reason, we have created a script that can make things easy for us. This script populates the database by reading a **.csv** (**Comma-Separated Values**) file consisting of many records. Follow the next few steps to populate the project's database:

1. Create the following folder structure inside the project directory:

```
bookr/reviews/management/commands/
```

2. Copy the **loadcsv.py** file from the following location and **WebDevWithDjangoData.csv** into the folder created. This can be found on the GitHub repository for this book at http://packt.live/3pvbCLM.

   Because **loadcsv.py** is placed inside the **management/commands** folder, now it works like a Django custom management command. You can go through the **loadcsv.py** file and read more about writing Django custom management commands at this link: https://docs.djangoproject.com/en/3.0/howto/custom-management-commands/.

3. Now let's recreate a fresh database. Delete your SQL database file present in the project folder:

```
rm reviews/db.sqlite3
```

4. To create a fresh database again, execute the Django **migrate** command:

```
python manage.py migrate
```

   Now you can see the newly created **db.sqlite3** file under the **reviews** folder.

5. Execute the custom management command **loadcsv** to populate the database:

```
python manage.py loadcsv --csv reviews/management/commands/
WebDevWithDjangoData.csv
```

6. Using DB Browser for SQLite, verify that all the tables created by the **bookr** project are populated.

SUMMARY

In this chapter, we learned about some basic database concepts and their importance in application development. We used a free database visualization tool, DB Browser for SQLite, to understand what database tables and fields are, how records are stored in a database, and further performed some basic CRUD operations on the database using simple SQL queries.

We then learned how Django provides a valuable abstraction layer called ORM that helps us interact seamlessly with relational databases using simple Python code, without having to compose SQL commands. As a part of ORM, we learned about Django models, migrations, and how they help propagate the changes to the Django models in the database.

We shored up our knowledge of databases by learning about database relationships, and their key types, in relational databases. We also worked with the Django shell, where we used Python code to perform the same CRUD queries we performed earlier using SQL. Later, we learned how to retrieve our data in a more refined manner using pattern matching and field lookups. As we learned these concepts, we made considerable progress on our Bookr application as well. We created models for our **reviews** app and gained all the skills we need to interact with the data stored inside the app's database. In the next chapter, we will learn how to create Django views, URL routing, and templates.

3

URL MAPPING, VIEWS, AND TEMPLATES

OVERVIEW

This chapter introduces you to three core concepts of Django: **views**, **templates**, and **URL mapping**. You will start by exploring the two main types of views in Django: **function-based views** and **class-based views**. Next, you will learn the basics of Django template language and template inheritance. Using these concepts, you will create a page to display the list of all the books in the **Bookr** application. You will also create another page to display the details, review comments, and ratings of books.

INTRODUCTION

In the previous chapter, we were introduced to databases, and we learned how to store, retrieve, update, and delete records from a database. We also learned how to create Django models and apply database migrations.

However, these database operations alone cannot display the application's data to a user. We need a way to display all the stored information in a meaningful way to the user; for example, displaying all the books present in our Bookr application's database, in a browser, in a presentable format. This is where Django views, templates, and URL mapping come into play. Views are the part of a Django application that takes in a web request and provides a web response. For example, a web request could be a user trying to view a website by entering the website address, and a web response could be the web site's home page loading in the user's browser. Views are one of the most important parts of a Django application, where the application logic is written. This application logic controls interactions with the database, such as creating, reading, updating, or deleting records from the database. It also controls how the data can be displayed to the user. This is done with the help of Django HTML templates, which we will explore in detail in a later section.

Django views can be broadly classified into two types, **function-based views** and **class-based views**. In this chapter, we will learn about function-based views in Django.

> **NOTE**
>
> In this chapter, we will learn only about function-based views. Class-based views, which is a more advanced topic, will be discussed in detail in *Chapter 11*, *Advanced Templating and Class-Based Views*.

FUNCTION-BASED VIEWS

As the name implies, function-based views are implemented as Python functions. To understand how they work, consider the following snippet, which shows a simple view function named **home_page**:

```python
from django.http import HttpResponse


def home_page(request):
    message = "<html><h1>Welcome to my Website</h1></html>"
    return HttpResponse(message)
```

The view function defined here, named **home_page**, takes a **request** object as an argument and returns an **HttpResponse** object having the **Welcome to my Website** message. The advantage of using function-based views is that, since they are implemented as simple Python functions, they are easier to learn and also easily readable for other programmers. The major disadvantage of function-based views is that the code cannot be re-used and made as concise as class-based views for generic use cases.

CLASS-BASED VIEWS

As the name implies, class-based views are implemented as Python classes. Using the principles of class inheritance, these classes are implemented as subclasses of Django's generic view classes. Unlike function-based views, where all the view logic is expressed explicitly in a function, Django's generic view classes come with various pre-built properties and methods that can provide shortcuts to writing clean, reusable views. This property comes in handy quite often during web development; for example, developers often need to render an HTML page without needing any data inserted from the database, or any customization specific to the user. In this case, it is possible to simply inherit from Django's **TemplateView**, and specify the path of the HTML file. The following is an example of a class-based view that can display the same message as in the function-based view example:

```
from django.views.generic import TemplateView


class HomePage(TemplateView):
    template_name = 'home_page.html'
```

In the preceding code snippet, **HomePage** is a class-based view inheriting Django's **TemplateView** from the **django.views.generic** module. The class attribute **template_name** defines the template to render when the view is invoked. For the template, we add an HTML file to our **templates** folder with the following content:

```
<html><h1>Welcome to my Website</h1></html>
```

This is a very basic example of class-based views, which will be explored further in *Chapter 11, Advanced Templating and Class-Based Views*. The major advantage of using class-based views is that fewer lines of code need to be used to implement the same functionality as compared to function-based views. Also, by inheriting Django's generic views, we can keep the code concise and avoid the duplication of code. However, a disadvantage of class-based views is that the code is often less readable for someone new to Django, which means that learning about it is usually a longer process, as compared to function-based views.

URL CONFIGURATION

Django views cannot work on their own in a web application. When a web request is made to the application, Django's URL configuration takes care of routing the request to the appropriate view function to process the request. A typical URL configuration in the **urls.py** file in Django looks like this:

```
from . import views


urlpatterns = [path('url-path/' views.my_view, name='my-view'),]
```

Here, **urlpatterns** is the variable defining the list of URL paths, and **'url-path/'** defines the path to match.

views.my_view is the view function to invoke when there is a URL match, and **name='my-view'** is the name of the view function used to refer to the view. There may be a situation wherein, elsewhere in the application, we want to get the URL of this view. We wouldn't want to hardcode the value, as it would then have to be specified twice in the codebase. Instead, we can access the URL by using the name of the view, as follows:

```
from django.urls import reverse


url = reverse('my-view')
```

If needed, we can also use a regular expression in a URL path to match string patterns using **re_path()**:

```
urlpatterns = [re_path\
               (r'^url-path/(?P<name>pattern)/$', views.my_view, \
                name='my-view')]
```

Here, **name** refers to the pattern name, which can be any Python regular expression pattern, and this needs to be matched before calling the defined view function. You can also pass parameters from the URL into the view itself, for example:

```
urlpatterns = [path(r'^url-path/<int:id>/', views.my_view, \
               name='my-view')]
```

In the preceding example, **<int:id>** tells Django to look for URLs that contain an integer at this position in the string, and to assign the value of that integer to the **id** argument. This means that if the user navigates to **/url-path/14/**, the id=14 keyword argument is passed to the view. This is often useful when a view needs to look up a specific object in the database and return corresponding data. For example, suppose we had a **User** model, and we wanted the view to display the user's name.

The view could be written as follows:

```
def my_view(request, id):
    user = User.objects.get(id=id)
    return HttpResponse(f"This user's name is \
    { user.first_name } { user.last_name }")
```

When the user accesses **/url-path/14/**, the preceding view is called, and the argument **id=14** is passed into the function.

Here is the typical workflow when a URL such as **http://0.0.0.0:8000/ url-path/** is invoked using a web browser:

1. An HTTP request would be made to the running application for the URL path. Upon receiving the request, it reaches for the **ROOT_URLCONF** setting present in the **settings.py** file:

```
ROOT_URLCONF = 'project_name.urls'
```

    This determines the URL configuration file to be used first. In this case, it is the URL file present in the project directory **project_name/urls.py**.

2. Next, Django goes through the list named **urlpatterns**, and once it matches the **url-path/** with the path present in the URL **http://0.0.0.0:8000/ url-path/**, it invokes the corresponding view function.

URL configuration is sometimes also referred to as URL conf or URL mapping, and these terms are often used interchangeably. To understand views and URL mapping better, let's start with a simple exercise.

EXERCISE 3.01: IMPLEMENTING A SIMPLE FUNCTION-BASED VIEW

In this exercise, we will write a very basic function-based view and use the associated URL configuration to display the message **Welcome to Bookr!** in a web browser. We will also tell the user how many books we have in the database:

1. First, ensure that **ROOT_URLCONF** in **bookr/settings.py** is pointing to the project's URL file by adding in the following command:

```
ROOT_URLCONF = 'bookr.urls'
```

2. Open the **bookr/reviews/views.py** file and add the following code snippet:

```
from django.http import HttpResponse
from .models import Book
```

```
def welcome_view(request):
    message = f"<html><h1>Welcome to Bookr!</h1> "\
"<p>{Book.objects.count()} books and counting!</p></html>"
    return HttpResponse(message)
```

First, we import the **HttpResponse** class from the **django.http** module.
Next, we define the **welcome_view** function, which can display the message
Welcome to Bookr! in a web browser. The request object is a function
parameter that carries the HTTP **request** object. The next line defines the
message variable, which contains HTML that displays the header, followed by a
line that counts the number of books available in the database.

In the last line, we return an **HttpResponse** object with the string associated
with the message variable. When the **welcome_view** view function is called, it
will display the message **Welcome to Bookr!   2 Books and counting**
in the web browser.

3. Now, create the URL mapping to call the newly created view function. Open the
    project URL file, **bookr/urls.py**, and add the list of **urlpatterns** as follows:

```
from django.contrib import admin
from django.urls import include, path

urlpatterns = [path('admin/', admin.site.urls),\
               path('', include('reviews.urls'))]
```

The first line in the list of **urlpatterns**, that is, **path('admin/', admin.
site.urls)** routes to the admin URLs if **admin/** is present in the URL path
(for example, **http://0.0.0.0:8000/admin**).

Similarly, consider the second line, **path('', include('reviews.
urls'))**. Here, the path mentioned is an empty string, **''**. If the URL does
not have any specific path after **http://hostname:port-number/** (for
example, **http://0.0.0.0:8000/**), it includes the **urlpatterns** present in
review.urls.

The **include** function is a shortcut that allows you to combine URL
configurations. It is common to keep one URL configuration per application in
your Django project. Here, we've created a separate URL configuration for the
reviews app and have added it to our project-level URL configuration.

4. Since we do not have the URL module **reviews.urls** yet, create a file called **bookr/reviews/urls.py**, and add the following lines of code:

```
from django.contrib import admin
from django.urls import path
from . import views


urlpatterns = [path('', views.welcome_view, \
                    name='welcome_view'),]
```

5. Here, we have used an empty string again for the URL path. So, when the URL **http://0.0.0.0:8000/** is invoked, after getting routed from **bookr/urls.py** into **bookr/reviews/urls.py**, this pattern invokes the **welcome_view** view function.

6. After making changes to the two files, we have the necessary URL configuration ready to call the **welcome_view** view. Now, start the Django server with **python manage.py runserver** and type in **http://0.0.0.0:8000** or **http://127.0.0.1:8000** in your web browser. You should be able to see the message **Welcome to Bookr!**:

Welcome to Bookr!

2 books and counting!

Figure 3.1: Displaying "Welcome to Bookr!" and the number of books on the home page

> **NOTE**
>
> If there is no URL match, Django invokes error handling, such as displaying a **404 Page not found** message or something similar.

In this exercise, we learned how to write a basic view function and do the associated URL mapping. We have created a web page that displays a simple message to the user and reports how many books are currently in our database.

However, the astute reader will have noticed that it doesn't look very nice to have HTML code sitting inside our Python function as in the preceding example. As our views get bigger, this will become even more unsustainable. Therefore, we now turn our attention to where our HTML code is supposed to be – inside templates.

TEMPLATES

In *Exercise 3.01, Implementing a Simple Function-Based View*, we saw how to create a view, do the URL mapping, and display a message in the browser. But if you recall, we hardcoded the HTML message **Welcome to Bookr!** in the view function itself and returned an **HttpResponse** object, as follows:

```
message = f"<html><h1>Welcome to Bookr!</h1> "\
"<p>{Book.objects.count()} books and counting!</p></html>"
return HttpResponse(message)
```

Hardcoding of HTML inside Python modules is not a good practice, because as the content to be rendered in a web page increases, so does the amount of HTML code we need to write for it. Having a lot of HTML code among Python code can make the code hard to read and maintain in the long run.

For this reason, Django templates provide us with a better way to write and manage HTML templates. Django's templates not only work with static HTML content but also dynamic HTML templates.

Django's template configuration is done in the **TEMPLATES** variable present in the **settings.py** file. This is how the default configuration looks:

```
TEMPLATES = \
[{'BACKEND': 'django.template.backends.django.DjangoTemplates',\
  'DIRS': [],
  'APP_DIRS': True,
  'OPTIONS': {'context_processors': \
             ['django.template.context_processors.debug',\
              'django.template.context_processors.request',\
              'django.contrib.auth.context_processors.auth',\
              'django.contrib.messages.context_processors\
               .messages',\
          ],\
      },\
   },\
]
```

Let's go through each keyword present in the preceding snippet:

- **'BACKEND'**: **'django.template.backends.django.DjangoTemplates'**: This refers to the template engine to be used. A template engine is an API used by Django to work with HTML templates. Django is built with Jinja2 and the **DjangoTemplates** engine. The default configuration is the **DjangoTemplates** engine and Django template language. However, this can be changed to use a different one if required, such as Jinja2 or any other third-party template engine. For our Bookr application though, we will leave this configuration as it is.

- **'DIRS'**: **[]**: This refers to the list of directories where Django searches for the templates in the given order.

- **'APP_DIRS'**: **True**: This tells the Django template engine whether it should look for templates in the installed apps defined under **INSTALLED_APPS** in the **settings.py** file. The default option for this is **True**.

- **'OPTIONS'**: This is a dictionary containing template engine-specific settings. Inside this dictionary, there is a default list of context processors, which helps the Python code to interact with templates to create and render dynamic HTML templates.

The current default settings are mostly fine for our purposes. However, in the next exercise, we will create a new directory for our templates, and we will need to specify the location of this folder. For example, if we have a directory called **my_templates**, we need to specify its location by adding it to the **TEMPLATES** settings as follows:

```
TEMPLATES = \
[{'BACKEND': 'django.template.backends.django.DjangoTemplates',\
  'DIRS': [os.path.join(BASE_DIR, 'my_templates')],\
  'APP_DIRS': True,\
  'OPTIONS': {'context_processors': \
              ['django.template.context_processors.debug',\
               'django.template.context_processors.request',\
               'django.contrib.auth.context_processors.auth',\
               'django.contrib.messages.context_processors\
                .messages',\
          ],\
      },\
   },
```

BASE_DIR is the directory path to the project folder. This is defined in the **settings.py** file. The **os.path.join()** method joins the project directory with the **templates** directory, returning the full path for the templates directory.

EXERCISE 3.02: USING TEMPLATES TO DISPLAY A GREETING MESSAGE

In this exercise, we will create our first Django template, and, just as we did in the previous exercise, we will display the **Welcome to Bookr!** message using the templates:

1. Create a directory called **templates** in the **bookr** project directory and inside it, create a file called **base.html**. The directory structure should look like *Figure 3.2*:

Figure 3.2: Directory structure for bookr

> **NOTE**
>
> When the default configuration is used, that is when **DIRS** is an empty list, Django searches for templates present only in the app folders' **template** directory (the **reviews/templates** folder in the case of a book review application). Since we included the new template directory in the main project directory, Django's template engine would not be able to find the directory unless the directory is included in the **'DIRS'** list.

2. Add the folder to the **TEMPLATES** settings:

```
TEMPLATES = \
[{'BACKEND': 'django.template.backends.django.DjangoTemplates',\
  'DIRS': [os.path.join(BASE_DIR, 'templates')],
  'APP_DIRS': True,
```

```
    'OPTIONS': {'context_processors': \
            ['django.template.context_processors.debug',\
             'django.template.context_processors.request',\
             'django.contrib.auth.context_processors.auth',\
             'django.contrib.messages.context_processors\
             .messages',\
        ],\
      },\
    },\
        ]
```

3. Add the following lines of code into the **base.html** file:

```
<!doctype html>
<html lang="en">
<head>
    <meta charset=»utf-8»>
    <title>Home Page</title>
</head>
    <body>
        <h1>Welcome to Bookr!</h1>
    </body>
</html>
```

This is simple HTML that displays the message **Welcome to Bookr!** in the header.

4. Modify the code inside **bookr/reviews/views.py** so that it looks as follows:

```
from django.shortcuts import render

def welcome_view (request):
    return render(request, 'base.html')
```

Since we have already configured the **'templates'** directory in the **TEMPLATES** configuration, **base.html** is available for use for the template engine. The code renders the file **base.html** using the imported **render** method from the **django.shortcuts** module.

5. Save the files, run **python manage.py runserver**, and open the **http://0.0.0.0:8000/** or **http://127.0.0.1:8000/** URL to check the newly added template loading in the browser:

Figure 3.3: Displaying "Welcome to Bookr!" on the home page

In this exercise, we created an HTML template and used Django templates and views to return the message **Welcome to Bookr!**. Next, we will learn about the Django template language, which can be used to render the application's data along with HTML templates.

DJANGO TEMPLATE LANGUAGE

Django templates not only return static HTML templates but can also add dynamic application data while generating the templates. Along with data, we can also include some programmatic elements in the templates. All of these put together form the basics of **Django's template language**. This section looks at some of the basic parts of the Django template language.

TEMPLATE VARIABLES

A template variable is represented in between two curly braces, as shown here:

```
{{ variable }}
```

When this is present in the template, the value carried by the variables will be replaced in the template. Template variables help in adding the application's data into the templates:

```
template_variable = "I am a template variable."

<body>
        {{ template_variable }}
    </body>
```

TEMPLATE TAGS

A tag is similar to a programmatic control flow, such as an **if** condition or a **for** loop. A tag is represented between two curly braces and percentage signs, as shown. Here is an example of a **for** loop iterating over a list using template tags:

```
{% for element in element_list %}

{% endfor %}
```

Unlike Python programming, we also add the end of the control flow by adding the **end** tag, such as **{% endfor %}**. This can be used along with template variables to display the elements in the list, as shown here:

```
<ul>
    {% for element in element_list %}
        <li>{{ element.title }}</li>
    {% endfor %}
</ul>
```

COMMENTS

Comments in the Django template language can be written as shown here; anything in-between **{% comment %}** and **{% endcomment %}** will be commented out:

```
{% comment %}
    <p>This text has been commented out</p>
{% endcomment %}
```

FILTERS

Filters can be used to modify a variable to represent it in a different format. The syntax for a filter is a variable separated from the filter name using a pipe (|) symbol:

```
{{ variable|filter }}
```

Here are some examples of built-in filters:

- **{{ variable|lower }}**: This converts the variable string into lowercase.

- **{{ variable|title}}**: This converts the first letter of every word into uppercase.

Let's use the concepts we have learned up till now to develop the book review application.

EXERCISE 3.03: DISPLAYING A LIST OF BOOKS AND REVIEWS

In this exercise, we will create a web page that can display a list of all books, their ratings, and the number of reviews present in the book review application. For this, we will be using some features of the Django template language such as variables and template tags to pass the book review application data into the templates to display meaningful data on the web page:

1. Create a file called **utils.py** under **bookr/reviews/utils.py** and add the following code:

```python
def average_rating(rating_list):
    if not rating_list:
        return 0

    return round(sum(rating_list) / len(rating_list))
```

This is a helper method that will be used to calculate the average rating of a book.

2. Remove all the code present inside **bookr/reviews/views.py** and add the following code to it:

```python
from django.shortcuts import render

from .models import Book, Review
from .utils import average_rating

def book_list(request):
    books = Book.objects.all()
    book_list = []
    for book in books:
        reviews = book.review_set.all()
        if reviews:
            book_rating = average_rating([review.rating for \
                                         review in reviews])
            number_of_reviews = len(reviews)
        else:
            book_rating = None
            number_of_reviews = 0
        book_list.append({'book': book,\
                         'book_rating': book_rating,\
                         'number_of_reviews': number_of_reviews})
```

```
context = {
    'book_list': book_list
}
return render(request, 'reviews/books_list.html', context)
```

This is a view to display the list of books for the book review application. The first three lines import Django modules, model classes, and the helper method we just added.

Here, **books_list** is the view method. In this method, we start by querying the list of all books. Next, for every book, we calculate the average rating and the number of reviews posted. All this information for each book is appended to a list called **book_list** as a list of dictionaries. This list is then added to a dictionary named context and is passed to the render function.

The render function takes three parameters, the first one being the request object that was passed into the view, the second being the HTML template **books_list.html**, which will display the list of books, and the third is context, which we pass to the template.

Since we have passed **book_list** as a part of the context, the template will be using this to render the list of books using template tags and template variables.

3. Create the **book_list.html** file in the path **bookr/reviews/templates/reviews/books_list.html** and add the following HTML code in the file:

reviews/templates/reviews/books_list.html

```
1   <!doctype html>
2   <html lang="en">
3   <head>
4       <meta charset="utf-8">
5       <title>Bookr</title>
6   </head>
7       <body>
8           <h1>Book Review application</h1>
9           <hr>
```

You can find the complete code at http://packt.live/3hnB4Qr.

This is a simple HTML template with template tags and variables iterating over **book_list** to display the list of books.

4. In **bookr/reviews/urls.py**, add the following URL pattern to invoke the **books_list** view:

```
from django.urls import path
from . import views
```

```
urlpatterns = [path('books/', views.book_list, \
                    name='book_list'),]
```

This does the URL mapping for the **books_list** view function.

5. Save all the modified files and wait for the Django service to restart. Open **http://0.0.0.0:8000/books/** in the browser, and you should see something similar to *Figure 3.4*:

Book Review application

- Title: Advanced Deep Learning with Keras
  Publisher: Packt Publishing
  Publication Date: Oct. 31, 2018
  Rating: 4
  Number of reviews: 2

- Title: Hands-On Machine Learning for Algorithmic Trading
  Publisher: Packt Publishing
  Publication Date: Dec. 31, 2018
  Rating: None
  Number of reviews: 0
  Provide a rating and write the first review for this book.

- Title: Architects of Intelligence
  Publisher: Packt Publishing
  Publication Date: Nov. 23, 2018
  Rating: None
  Number of reviews: 0
  Provide a rating and write the first review for this book.

- Title: Deep Reinforcement Learning Hands-On
  Publisher: Packt Publishing
  Publication Date: June 20, 2018
  Rating: None
  Number of reviews: 0
  Provide a rating and write the first review for this book.

- Title: Natural Language Processing with TensorFlow
  Publisher: Packt Publishing
  Publication Date: May 30, 2018
  Rating: None
  Number of reviews: 0
  Provide a rating and write the first review for this book.

Figure 3.4: List of books present in the book review application

In this exercise, we created a view function, created templates, and also did the URL mapping, which can display a list of all books present in the application. Although we were able to display a list of books using a single template, next, let's explore a bit about how to work with multiple templates in an application that has common or similar code.

TEMPLATE INHERITANCE

As we build the project, the number of templates will increase. It is highly probable that when we design the application, some of the pages will look similar and have common HTML code for certain features. Using template inheritance, we can inherit the common HTML code into other HTML files. This is similar to class inheritance in Python, where the parent class has all the common code, and the child class has those extras that are unique to the child's requirement.

For example, let's consider the following to be a parent template that is named **base.html**:

```
<!doctype html>
<html lang="en">
<head>
    <meta charset="utf-8">
    <title>Hello World</title>
</head>
    <body>
        <h1>Hello World using Django templates!</h1>
        {% block content %}
        {% endblock %}
    </body>
</html>
```

The following is an example of a child template:

```
{% extends 'base.html' %}
{% block content %}
<h1>How are you doing?</h1>
{% endblock %}
```

In the preceding snippet, the line {% extends 'base.html' %} extends the template from base.html, which is the parent template. After extending from the parent template, any HTML code in-between the block content will be displayed along with the parent template. Once the child template is rendered, here is how it looks in the browser:

Hello World using Django templates!

How are you doing?

Figure 3.5: Greeting message after extending the base.html template

TEMPLATE STYLING WITH BOOTSTRAP

We have seen how to display all the books using views, templates, and URL mapping. Although we were able to display all the information in the browser, it would be even better if we could add some styling and make the web page look better. For this, we can add a few elements of **Bootstrap**. Bootstrap is an open-source **Cascading Style Sheets (CSS)** framework that is particularly good for designing responsive pages that work across desktop and mobile browsers.

Using Bootstrap is simple. First, you need to add the Bootstrap CSS to your HTML. You can experiment yourself by creating a new file called **example.html**. Populate it with the following code and open it in a browser:

```
<!doctype html>
<html lang="en">
  <head>
    <!-- Required meta tags -->
    <meta charset="utf-8">
    <meta name="viewport" content="width=device-width,
      initial-scale=1, shrink-to-fit=no">

    <!-- Bootstrap CSS -->
    <link rel="stylesheet"
      href="https://stackpath.bootstrapcdn.com/bootstrap/4.4.1/
      css/bootstrap.min.css" integrity="sha384-
      Vkoo8x4CGsO3+Hhxv8T/Q5PaXtkKtu6ug5TOeNV6gBiFeWPGFN9MuhOf23Q
      9Ifjh" crossorigin="anonymous">
```

```
  </head>
  <body>
    Content goes here

  </body>
</html>
```

The Bootstrap CSS link in the preceding code adds the bootstrap CSS library to your page. This means that certain HTML element types and classes will inherit their styles from Bootstrap. For example, if you add the **btn-primary** class to the class of a button, the button will be rendered as blue with white text. Try adding the following between **<body>** and **</body>**:

```
<h1>Welcome to my Site</h1>
<button type="button" class="btn btn-primary">Checkout my
  Blog!</button>
```

You will see that the title and button are both styled nicely, using Bootstrap's default styles:

Figure 3.6: Display after applying Bootstrap

This is because in the Bootstrap CSS code, it specifies the color of the **btn-primary** class with the following code:

```
.btn-primary {
    color: #fff;
    background-color: #007bff;
    border-color: #007bff
}
```

You can see that using third-party CSS libraries such as Bootstrap allows you to quickly create nicely styled components without needing to write too much CSS.

> **NOTE**
>
> We recommend that you explore Bootstrap further with their tutorial here: https://getbootstrap.com/docs/4.4/getting-started/introduction/.

EXERCISE 3.04: ADDING TEMPLATE INHERITANCE AND A BOOTSTRAP NAVIGATION BAR

In this exercise, we will use template inheritance to inherit the template elements from a base template and re-use them in the **book_list** template to display the list of books. We will also use certain elements of Bootstrap in the base HTML file to add a navigation bar to the top of our page. The bootstrap code for **base.html** was taken from https://getbootstrap.com/docs/4.4/getting-started/introduction/ and https://getbootstrap.com/docs/4.4/components/navbar/:

1. Open the **base.html** file from the location **bookr/templates/base.html**. Remove any existing code and replace it with the following code:

bookr/templates/base_html

```
1   <!doctype html>
2   {% load static %}
3   <html lang="en">
4     <head>
5       <!-- Required meta tags -->
6       <meta charset="utf-8">
7       <meta name="viewport" content="width=device-width,
          initial-scale=1, shrink-to-fit=no">
8
9       <!-- Bootstrap CSS -->
```

You can view the entire code for this file at http://packt.live/3mTjlBn.

This is a **base.html** file with all the Bootstrap elements for styling and the navigation bar.

2. Next, open the template at **bookr/reviews/templates/reviews/books_list.html**, remove all the existing code, and replace it with the following code:

reviews/templates/reviews/books_list.html

```
1   {% extends 'base.html' %}
2
3   {% block content %}
4   <ul class="list-group">
5     {% for item in book_list %}
6     <li class="list-group-item">
7        <span class="text-info">Title: </span> <span>{{
          item.book.title }}</span>
8        <br>
9        <span class="text-info">Publisher: </span><span>{{
          item.book.publisher }}</span>
```

You can view the complete code for this file at http://packt.live/3aPJv5O.

This template has been configured to inherit the **base.html** file and it has also been added with a few styling elements to display the list of books. The part of the template that helps in inheriting the **base.html** file is as follows:

```
{% extends 'base.html' %}


{% block content %}
{% endblock %}
```

3. After adding the two new templates, open either of the URLs `http://0.0.0.0:8000/books/` or `http://127.0.0.1:8000/books/` in your web browser to see the books list page, which should now look neatly formatted:

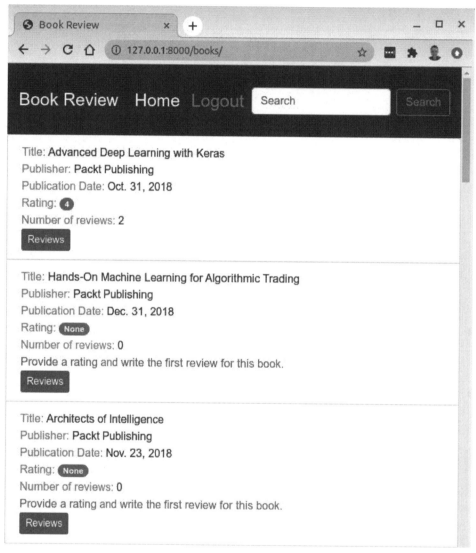

Figure 3.7: Neatly formatted book list page

In this exercise, we added some styling into the application using Bootstrap and we also used template inheritance while we displayed the list of books from the book review application. So far, we have worked extensively on displaying all the books present in the application. In the next activity, you will display details and reviews of an individual book.

ACTIVITY 3.01: IMPLEMENT THE BOOK DETAILS VIEW

In this activity, you will implement a new view, template, and URL mapping, to display these details of a book: title, publisher, publication date, and overall rating. In addition to these details, the page should also display all the review comments, specifying the name of the commenter and the dates on which the comments were written and (if applicable) modified. The following steps will help you complete this activity:

1. Create a book details endpoint that extends the base template.

2. Create a book details view that takes a specific book's primary key as the argument and returns an HTML page listing the book's details and any associated reviews.

3. Do the required URL mapping in **urls.py**. The book details view URL should be **http://0.0.0.0:8000/books/1/** (where **1** will represent the **ID** of the book being accessed). You can use the **get_object_or_404** method to retrieve the book with the given primary key.

> **NOTE**
>
> The **get_object_or_404** function is a useful shortcut for retrieving an instance based on its primary key. You could also do this using the .**get()** method described in *Chapter 2, Models and Migrations*, **Book. objects.get(pk=pk)**. However, **get_object_or_404** has the added advantage of returning an **HTTP 404 Not Found** response if the object does not exist. If we simply use **get()** and someone attempts to access an object that does not exist, our Python code will hit an exception and return an **HTTP 500 Server Error** response. This is undesirable because it looks as though our server has failed to handle the request correctly.

4. At the end of the activity, you should be able to click the **Reviews** button on the book list page and get the detail view of the book. The detail view should have all the details displayed in the following screenshot:

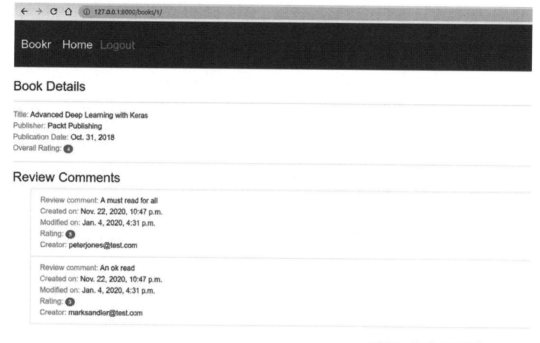

Figure 3.8: Page displaying the book details

SUMMARY

This chapter covered the core infrastructure required to handle an HTTP request to our website. The request is first mapped via URL patterns to an appropriate view. Parameters from the URL are also passed into the view to specify the object displayed on the page. The view is responsible for compiling any necessary information to display on the website, and then passes this dictionary through to a template that renders the information as HTML code that can be returned as a response to the user. We covered both class- and function-based views and learned about the Django template language and template inheritance. We created two new pages for the book review application, one displaying all the books present and the other being the book details view page. In the next chapter, we will learn about Django admin and superuser, registering models, and performing CRUD operations using the admin site.

4

INTRODUCTION TO DJANGO ADMIN

OVERVIEW

This chapter introduces you to the basic functionality of the Django admin app. You will start by creating superuser accounts for the Bookr app, before moving on to executing **Create Read Update Delete** (**CRUD**) operations with the admin app. You will learn how to integrate your Django app with the admin app and you'll also look at the behavior of `ForeignKeys` in the admin app. At the end of this chapter, you will see how you can customize the admin app according to a unique set of preferences by sub-classing the `AdminSite` and `ModelAdmin` classes, to make its interface more intuitive and user-friendly.

INTRODUCTION

When developing an app, there is often a need to populate it with data and then alter that data. We have already seen in *Chapter 2, Models and Migrations*, how this can be done on the command line using the Python **manage.py** shell. In *Chapter 3, URL Mapping, Views, and Templates*, we learned how to develop a web form interface to our model using Django's views and templates. But neither of these approaches is ideal for administering the data from the classes in **reviews/models.py**. Using the shell to manage data is too technical for non-programmers and building individual web pages would be a laborious process as it would see us repeating the same view logic and very similar template features for each table in the model. Fortunately, a solution to this problem was devised in the early days of Django when it was still being developed.

Django admin is actually written as a Django app. It offers an intuitively rendered web interface to give administrative access to the model data. The admin interface is designed to be used by the administrators of the website. It is not intended to be used by non-privileged users who interact with the site. In our case of a book review system, the general population of book reviewers will never encounter the admin app. They will see the app pages, like those that we built with views and templates in *Chapter 3, URL Mapping, Views, and Templates*, and will write their reviews on the pages.

Also, while developers put in a lot of effort to create a simple and inviting web interface for general users, the admin interface, being aimed at administrative users, maintains a utilitarian feel that typically displays the intricacies of the model. It may have escaped your attention, but you already have an admin app in your Bookr project. Look at the list of installed apps in **bookr/settings.py**:

```
INSTALLED_APPS = [
    'django.contrib.admin',
    ...
]
```

Now, look at the URL patterns in **bookr/urls.py**:

```
urlpatterns = [
    path('admin/', admin.site.urls),
    ...
]
```

If we put this path into our browser, we can see the link to the admin app on the development server is **http://127.0.0.1:8000/admin/**. Before we make use of it though, we need to create a superuser through the command line.

CREATING A SUPERUSER ACCOUNT

Our Bookr application has just found a new user. Her name is Alice, and she wants to start adding her reviews right away. Bob, who is already using Bookr, has just informed us that his profile seems incomplete and needs to be updated. David no longer wants to use the application and wants his account to be deleted. For security reasons, we do not want just any user performing these tasks for us. That's why we need to create a **superuser** with elevated privileges. Let's start by doing just that.

In Django's authorization model, a superuser is one with the **Staff** attribute set. We will examine this later in the chapter and learn more about this authorization model in *Chapter 9, Sessions and Authentication*.

We can create a superuser by using the **manage.py** script that we have explored in earlier chapters. Again, we need to be in the project directory when we enter it. We will use the **createsuperuser** subcommand by entering the following command in the command line (you will need to write **python** instead of **python3** if you're using Windows):

```
python3 manage.py createsuperuser
```

Let's go ahead and create our superuser.

> **NOTE**
>
> In this chapter, we will use email addresses that fall under the *example.com* domain. This follows an established convention to use this reserved domain for testing and documentation. You could use your own email addresses if you prefer.

EXERCISE 4.01: CREATING A SUPERUSER ACCOUNT

In this exercise, you will create a superuser account that lets the user log into the admin site. This functionality will be used in the upcoming exercises as well, to implement changes that only a superuser can. The following steps will help you complete this exercise:

1. Enter the following command to create a superuser:

```
python manage.py createsuperuser
```

   On executing this command, you will be prompted to create a superuser. This command will prompt you for a superuser name, an optional email address, and a password.

2. Add the username and email for the superuser as follows. Here, we are entering **bookradmin** (highlighted) at the prompt and pressing the *Enter* key. Similarly, at the next prompt, which asks you to enter your email address, you can add **bookradmin@example.com** (highlighted). Press the *Enter* key to continue:

```
Username (leave blank to use 'django'): bookradmin
Email address: bookradmin@example.com
Password:
```

   This will assign the name **bookradmin** to the superuser. Note that you won't see any output immediately.

3. The next prompt in the shell is for your password. Add a strong password and press the *Enter* key to confirm it once again:

```
Password:
Password (again):
```

   You should see the following message on your screen:

```
Superuser created successfully.
```

   Note that the password is validated according to the following criteria:

   It cannot be among the 20,000 most common passwords.

   It should have a minimum of eight characters.

   It cannot be only numerical characters.

   It cannot be derived from the username, first name, last name, or email address of the user.

With this, you have created a superuser named **bookradmin** who can log in to the admin app. *Figure 4.1* shows how this looks in the shell:

```
> python manage.py createsuperuser
Username (leave blank to use 'django'): bookradmin
Email address: bookradmin@example.com
Password:
Password (again):
Superuser created successfully.
>
```

Figure 4.1: Creating a superuser

4. Visit the admin app at **http://127.0.0.1:8000/admin** and log in with the superuser account that you have created:

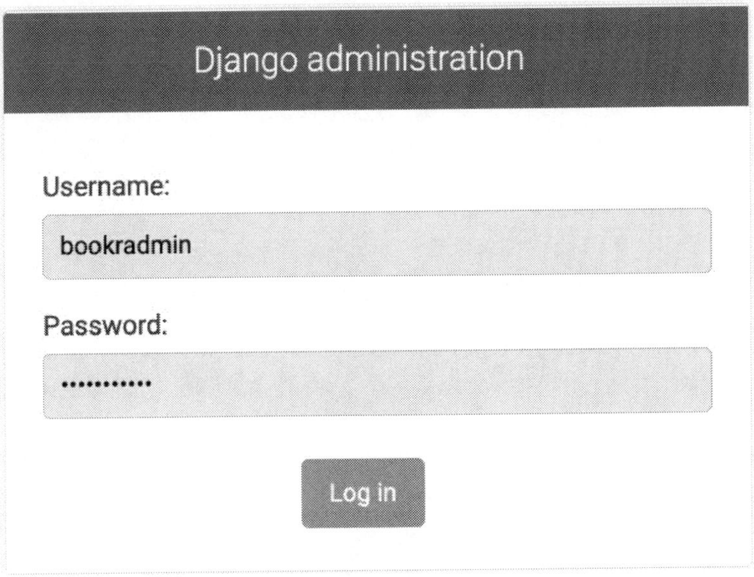

Figure 4.2 The Django administration login form

In this exercise, you created a superuser account that we will be using for the rest of this chapter, to assign or remove privileges as needed.

> **NOTE**
>
> The codes for all the exercises and activities used in this chapter can be found on the book's GitHub repository at http://packt.live/3pC5CRr.

CRUD OPERATIONS USING THE DJANGO ADMIN APP

Let's get back to the requests we got from Bob, Alice, and David. As a superuser, your tasks will involve creating, updating, retrieving, and deleting various user accounts, reviews, and title names. This set of activities is collectively termed CRUD. CRUD operations are central to the behavior of the admin app. It turns out that the admin app is already aware of the models from another Django app, **Authentication and Authorization** – referenced in **INSTALLED_APPS** as **'django. contrib.auth'**. When logging into **http://127.0.0.1:8000/admin/**, we are presented with the models from the authorization application, as shown in *Figure 4.3*:

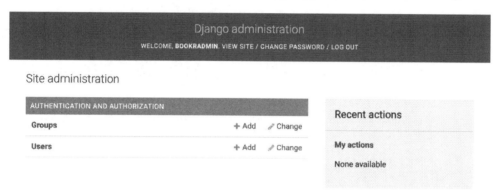

Figure 4.3: The Django administration window

When the admin app is initialized, it calls its **autodiscover()** method to detect whether any other installed apps contain an admin module. If so, these admin models are imported. In our case, it has discovered **'django.contrib.auth. admin'**. Now that the modules are imported and our superuser account is ready, let's start by working on the requests from Bob, Alice, and David.

CREATE

Before Alice starts writing her reviews, we need to create an account for her through the admin app. Once that is done, we can then look at the levels of administrative access that we can assign to her. To **Create** a user, we need only click the **+ Add** link next to **Users** (refer to *Figure 4.3*), and fill out the form, as shown in *Figure 4.4*.

> **NOTE**
>
> We don't want any random user to have access to the Bookr users' accounts. Therefore, it is imperative that we choose strong, secure passwords.

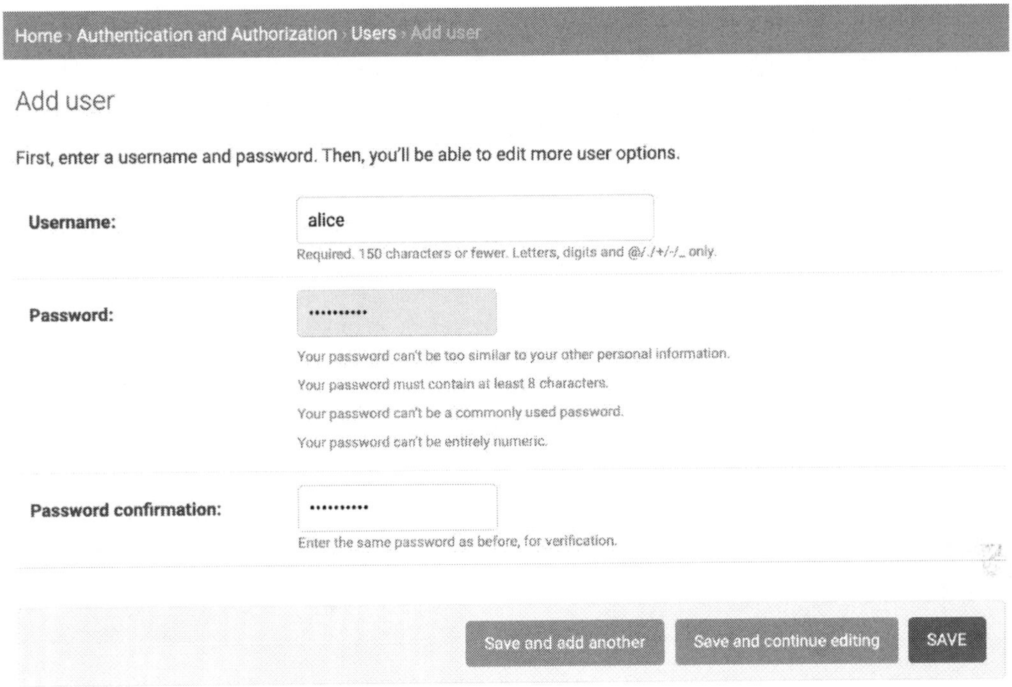

Figure 4.4: The Add user page

There are three buttons at the bottom of the form:

- **Save and add another** creates the user and renders the same **Add user** page again, with blank fields.

- **Save and continue editing** creates the user and loads the **Change user** page. The **Change user** page lets you add additional information that wasn't present on the **Add user** page, such as **First name**, **Last name**, and more (see *Figure 4.5*). Note that **Password** does not have an editable field on the form. Instead, it shows information about the hashing technique that it is stored with, in addition to a link to a separate *change password* form.

- **SAVE** creates the user and lets the user navigate to the **Select user to change** list page, as depicted in *Figure 4.6*.

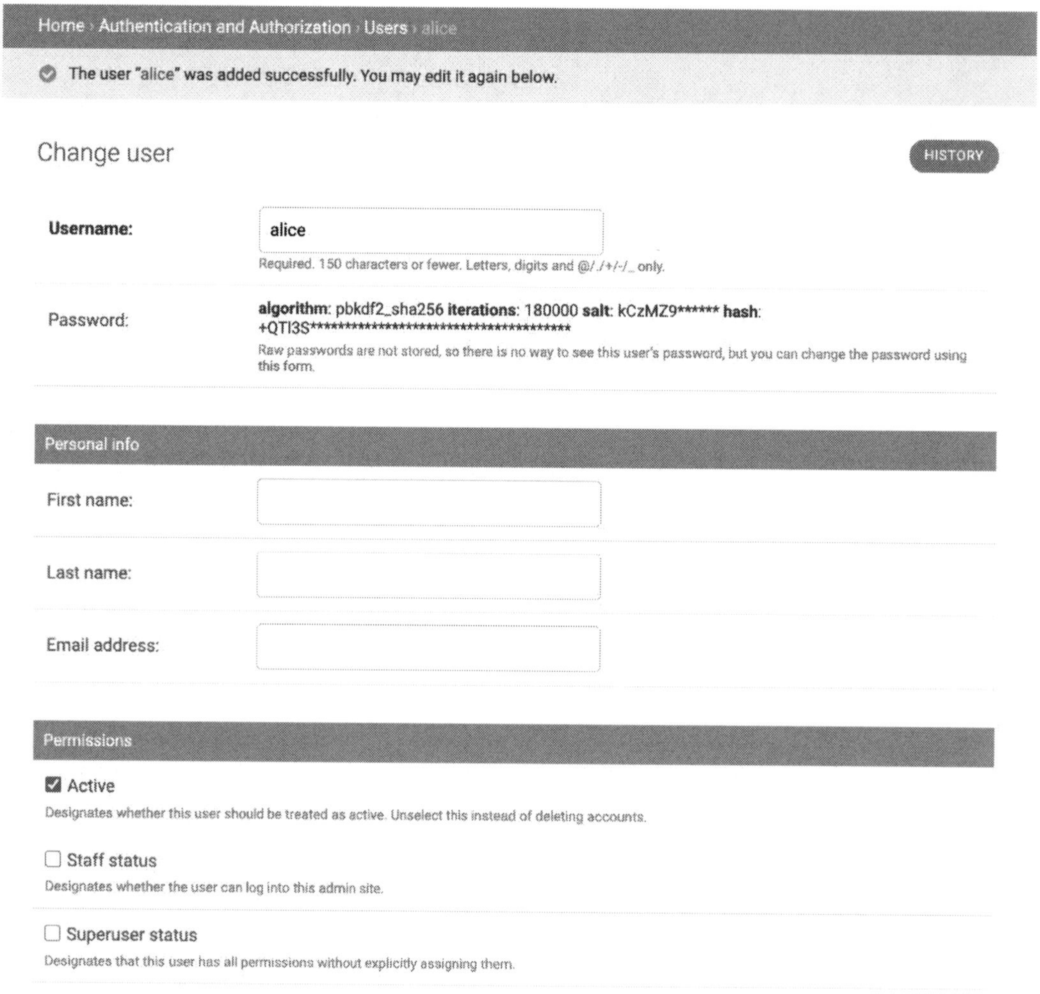

Home › Authentication and Authorization › Users › alice

✔ The user "alice" was added successfully. You may edit it again below.

Change user

HISTORY

Username:

alice

Required. 150 characters or fewer. Letters, digits and @/./+/-/_ only.

Password:

algorithm: pbkdf2_sha256 **iterations**: 180000 **salt**: kCzMZ9****** **hash**: +QTI3S***********************************

Raw passwords are not stored, so there is no way to see this user's password, but you can change the password using this form.

Personal info

First name:

Last name:

Email address:

Permissions

☑ Active
Designates whether this user should be treated as active. Unselect this instead of deleting accounts.

☐ Staff status
Designates whether the user can log into this admin site.

☐ Superuser status
Designates that this user has all permissions without explicitly assigning them.

Figure 4.5: The Change user page presented after clicking Save and continue editing

RETRIEVE

The administrative tasks need to be divided among some users, and for this, the admin (the person with the superuser account) would like to view those users whose email addresses end with *n@example.com* and assign the tasks to these users. This is where the **Retrieve** functionality can come in handy. After we have clicked the **SAVE** button on the **Add user** page (refer to *Figure 4.4*), we are taken to the **Select user to change** list page (as shown in *Figure 4.6*), which carries out the **Retrieve** operation. Note that the **Create** form is also reachable by clicking on the **ADD USER** button on the **Select user to change** list page. So, after we have added a few more users, the change list will look something like this:

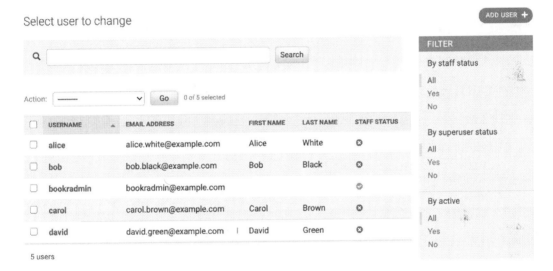

Figure 4.6: The Select user to change page

At the top of the form is a **Search** bar that searches the contents of the username, email address, and first and last names of users. On the right-hand side is a **FILTER** panel that narrows down the selection based on the values of **staff status**, **superuser status**, and **active**. In *Figure 4.7*, we will see what happens when we search the string **n@example.com** and see the results. This will return only the names of the users whose email addresses consist of a username ending in *n* and a domain starting with *example.com*. We will only see three users with email addresses matching this requirement – **bookradmin@example.com**, **carol.brown@example.com**, and **david.green@example.com**:

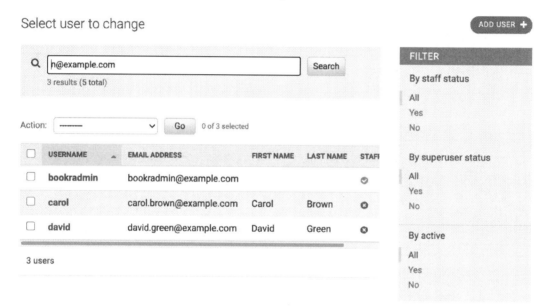

Figure 4.7: Searching for users by a portion of their email address

UPDATE

Remember that Bob wanted his profile to be updated. Let's **Update** Bob's unfinished profile by clicking the **bob** username link in the **Select user to change** list:

Select user to change

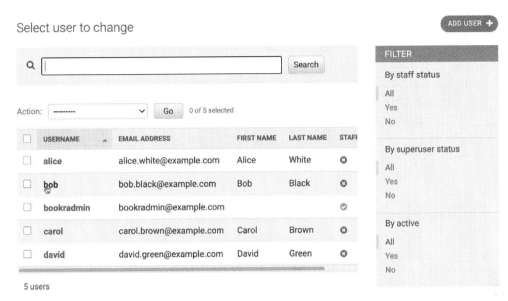

Figure 4.8: Selecting bob from the Select user to change list

This will take us back to the **Change user** form where the values for **First name**, **Last name**, and **Email address** can be entered:

Django administration

WELCOME, **BOOKRADMIN**. VIEW SITE / CHANGE PASSWORD / LOG OUT

Home › Authentication and Authorization › Users › bob

Change user   HISTORY

Username: bob

                       Required. 150 characters or fewer. Letters, digits and @/./+/-/_ only.

Password: **algorithm**: pbkdf2_sha256 **iterations**: 180000 **salt**: uC2Obk****** **hash**:
                      4vvlTw************************************

                      Raw passwords are not stored, so there is no way to see this user's password, but you can change the password using
                      this form.

Personal info

First name: Bob

Last name: Black

Email address: bob.black@example.com

Figure 4.9: Adding personal info

As can be seen from *Figure 4.9*, we are adding personal information about Bob here – his name, surname, and email address, specifically.

Another type of update operation is "soft deleting." The `Active` Boolean property allows us to deactivate a user rather than deleting the entire record and losing all the data that has dependencies on the account. This practice of using a Boolean flag to denote a record as inactive or removed (and subsequently filtering these flagged records out of queries) is referred to as a **Soft Delete**. Similarly, we can upgrade the user to `Staff status` or `Superuser status` by ticking the respective checkboxes for those:

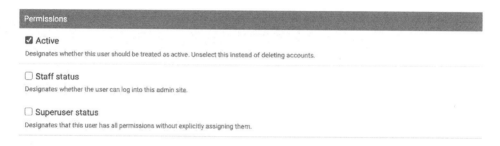

Figure 4.10: Active, Staff status, and Superuser status Booleans

DELETE

David no longer wants to use the Bookr application and has requested that we delete his account. The auth admin caters to this too. Select a user or user records on the `Select user to change` list page and choose the `Delete selected users` option from the `Action` dropdown. Then hit the **Go** button (*Figure 4.11*):

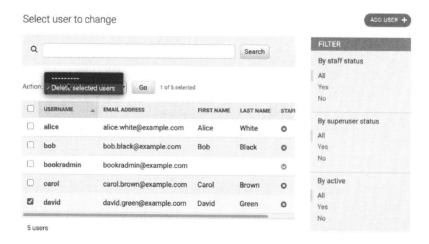

Figure 4.11: Deleting from the Select user to change list page

You will be presented with a confirmation screen and taken back to the **Select user to change** list once you have deleted the object:

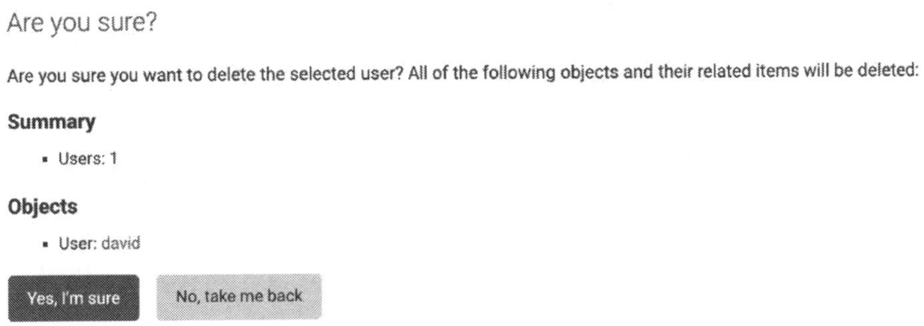

Are you sure?

Are you sure you want to delete the selected user? All of the following objects and their related items will be deleted:

Summary

- Users: 1

Objects

- User: david

Yes, I'm sure   No, take me back

Figure 4.12: User deletion confirmation

You will see the following message once the user is deleted:

Successfully deleted 1 user.

Figure 4.13: User deletion notification

After that confirmation, you will find that David's account no longer exists.

So far, we have learned how we can add a new user, get the details of another user, make changes to the data for a user, and delete a user. These skills helped us cater to Alice, Bob, and David's requests. As the number of users of our app grows, managing requests from hundreds of users will eventually become quite difficult. One way around this problem would be to delegate some of the administrative responsibilities to a selected set of users. We'll learn how to do that in the section that follows.

USERS AND GROUPS

Django's authentication model consists of users, groups, and permissions. Users can belong to many groups and this is a way of categorizing users. It also streamlines the implementation of permissions by allowing permissions to be assigned to collections of users as well as individuals.

In *Exercise 4.01, Creating a Superuser Account*, we saw how we could cater to Alice, David, and Bob's requests to make modifications to their profiles. It was quite easy to do and our application seems well-equipped to handle their requests.

What will happen when the number of users grows? Will the admin user be able to manage 100 or 150 users at once? As you can imagine, this can be quite a complicated task. To overcome this, we can give elevated permissions to a certain set of users and they can help ease the admin's tasks. And that's where groups come in handy. Though we'll learn more about users, groups, and permissions in *Chapter 9, Sessions and Authentication*, we can start understanding groups and their functionality by creating a `Help Desk user group` that contains accounts having access to the admin interface but lacking many powerful features, such as the ability to add, edit, or delete groups or to add or delete users.

EXERCISE 4.02: ADDING AND MODIFYING USERS AND GROUPS THROUGH THE ADMIN APP

In this exercise, we will grant a certain level of administrative access to one of our Bookr users, Carol. First, we will define the level of access for a group, and then we will add Carol to the group. This will allow Carol to update user profiles and check user logs. The following steps will help you implement this exercise:

1. Visit the admin interface at `http://127.0.0.1:8000/admin/` and log in as `bookradmin` using the account set up with the superuser command.

2. In the admin interface, follow the links to **Home › Authentication and Authorization › Groups**:

Site administration

AUTHENTICATION AND AUTHORIZATION		
Groups	✛ Add	✏ Change
Users	✛ Add	✏ Change

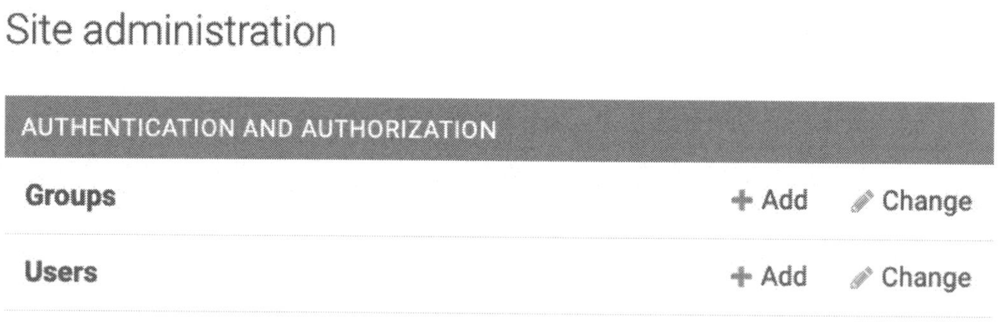

Figure 4.14: The Groups and Users options on the Authentication AND Authorization page

3. Use **ADD GROUP +** in the top right-hand corner to add a new group:

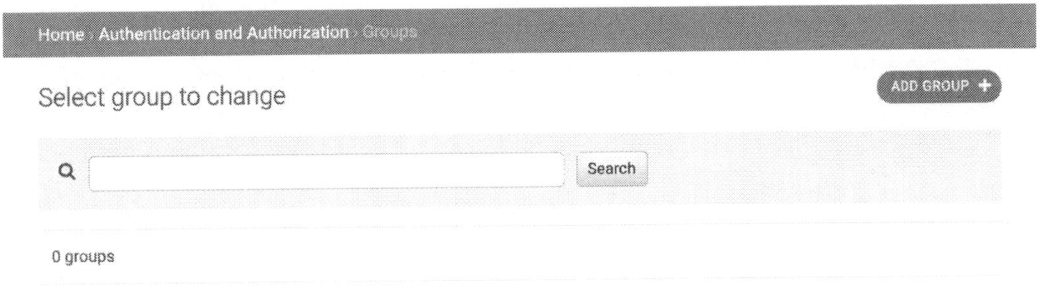

Figure 4.15: Adding a new group

4. Name the group **Help Desk User** and give it the following permissions, as shown in *Figure 4.16*:

Can view log entry

Can view permission

Can change user

Can view user

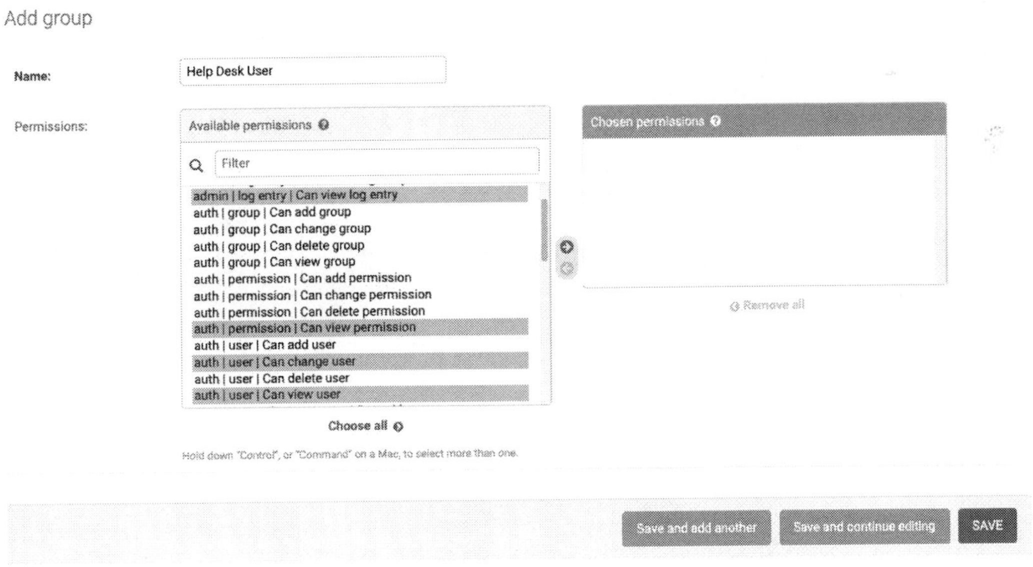

Figure 4.16: Selecting the permissions

This can be done by selecting the permissions from **Available permissions** and clicking the right arrow in the middle so that they appear under **Chosen permissions**. Note that to add multiple permissions at a time, you can hold down the *Ctrl* key (or *Command* for Mac) to select more than one:

Figure 4.17: Adding selected permissions into Chosen permissions

Once you click the **SAVE** button, you will see a confirmation message, stating that the group **Help Desk User** was added successfully:

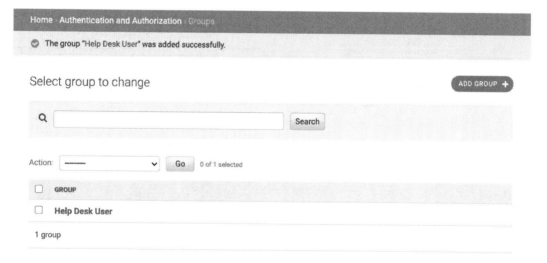

Figure 4.18: Message confirming that the group Help Desk User was added

5. Now, navigate to **Home** › **Authentication and Authorization** › **Users** and click the link of the user with the first name **carol**:

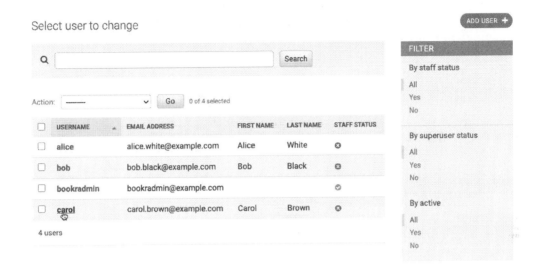

Figure 4.19: Clicking on the username carol

6. Scroll down to the **Permissions** fields set and select the **Staff status** checkbox. This is required for Carol to be able to log in to the admin app:

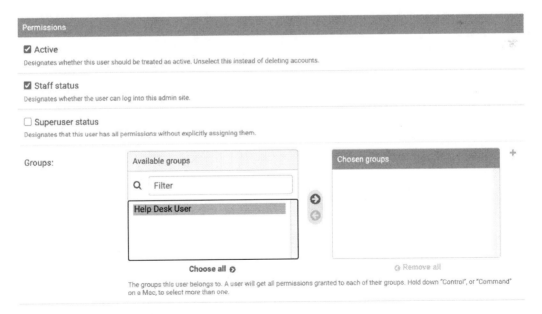

Figure 4.20: Clicking the Staff status checkbox

7. Add Carol to the **Help Desk User** group that we created in the previous steps by selecting it from the **Available groups** selection box (refer *Figure 4.20*) and clicking the right arrow to shift it into her list of **Chosen groups** (as shown in *Figure 4.21*). Note that unless you do this, Carol won't be able to log in to the admin interface using her credentials:

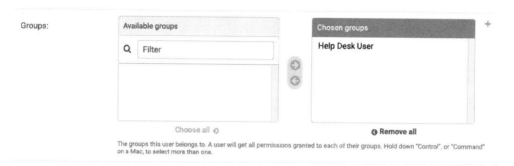

Figure 4.21: Shifting the Help Desk User group into the list of Chosen groups for Carol

8. Let's test whether what we've done up till now has yielded the right outcome. To do this, log out of the admin site and log in again as **carol**. Upon logging out, you should see the following on your screen:

Logged out

Thanks for spending some quality time with the Web site today.

Log in again

Figure 4.22: Logout screen

> **NOTE**
>
> If you don't recall the password that you initially gave her, you can change the password at the command line by typing `python3 manage.py changepassword carol`.

Upon successful login, on the admin dashboard, you can see that there is no link to **Groups**:

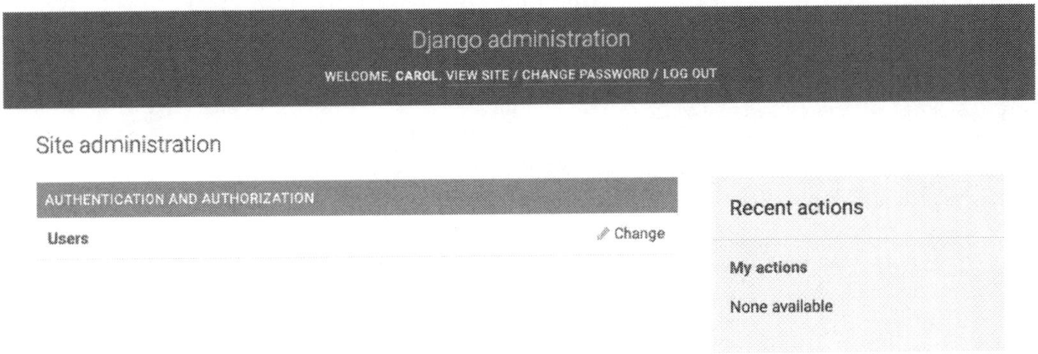

Figure 4.23: Admin dashboard

As we did not assign any group permissions, not even **auth | group | Can view group**, to the **Help Desk User** group, when Carol logs in, the **Groups** admin interface is not available to her. Similarly, navigate to **Home** › **Authentication and Authorization** › **Users**. Clicking a user link, you will see that there are no options to edit or delete the user. This is because of the permissions that were granted to the Help Desk User group, of which Carol is a member. The members of the group can view and edit users but cannot add or delete any user.

In this exercise, we learned how we can grant a certain amount of administrative privileges to users of our Django app.

REGISTERING THE REVIEWS MODEL

Let's say that Carol is tasked with improving the Reviews section in Bookr; that is, only the most relevant and comprehensive reviews should be shown, and duplicate or spammy entries should be removed. For this, she will need access to the **reviews** model. As we have seen above with our investigation of groups and users, the admin app already contains admin pages for the models from the authentication and authorization app, but it does not yet reference the models in our Reviews app.

To make the admin app aware of the models, we need to explicitly register them with the admin app. Fortunately, we don't need to modify the admin app's code to do so as we can instead import the admin app into our project and use its API to register our models. This has already been done in the authentication and authorization app, so let's try it with our Reviews app. Our aim is to be able to use the admin app to edit the data in our **reviews** model.

Take a look at the **reviews/admin.py** file. It is a placeholder file that was generated with the **startapp** subcommand that we used in *Chapter 1, Introduction to Django*, and currently contains these lines:

```
from django.contrib import admin


# Register your models here.
```

Now we can try to expand this. To make the admin app aware of our models, we can modify the **reviews/admin.py** file and import the models. Then we could register the models with the **AdminSite** object, **admin.site**. The **AdminSite** object contains the instance of the Django admin application (later, we will learn how to subclass this **AdminSite** and override many of its properties). Then, our **reviews/admin.py** will look as follows:

```
from django.contrib import admin

from reviews.models import Publisher, Contributor, \
Book, BookContributor, Review

# Register your models here.
admin.site.register(Publisher)
admin.site.register(Contributor)
admin.site.register(Book)
admin.site.register(BookContributor)
admin.site.register(Review)
```

The **admin.site.register** method makes the models available to the admin app by adding it to a registry of classes contained in **admin.site._registry**. If we chose not to make a model accessible through the admin interface, we would simply not register it. When you reload **http://127.0.0.1:8000/admin/** in your browser, you will see the following on the admin app landing page. Note the change in the appearance of the admin page after the **reviews** model has been imported:

Site administration

AUTHENTICATION AND AUTHORIZATION		
Groups	+ Add	Change
Users	+ Add	Change

REVIEWS		
Book contributors	+ Add	Change
Books	+ Add	Change
Contributors	+ Add	Change
Publishers	+ Add	Change
Reviews	+ Add	Change

Figure 4.24: Admin app landing page

CHANGE LISTS

We now have change lists populated for our models. If we click the **Publishers** link, we will be taken to **http://127.0.0.1:8000/admin/reviews/publisher** and see a change list containing links to the publishers. These links are designated by the **id** field of the **Publisher** objects.

If your database has been populated with the script in *Chapter 3, URL Mapping, Views, and Templates*, you will see a list with seven publishers that looks like *Figure 4.25*:

> **NOTE**
>
> Depending on the state of your database and based on the activities you have completed, the object IDs, URLs, and links in these examples may be numbered differently from those listed here.

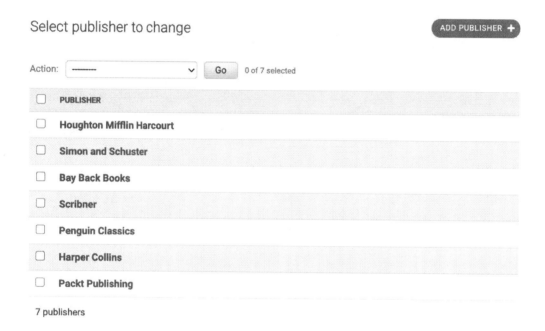

Select publisher to change

ADD PUBLISHER +

Action: ———— ▼ Go   0 of 7 selected

	PUBLISHER
☐	Houghton Mifflin Harcourt
☐	Simon and Schuster
☐	Bay Back Books
☐	Scribner
☐	Penguin Classics
☐	Harper Collins
☐	Packt Publishing

7 publishers

Figure 4.25: Select publisher to change list

THE PUBLISHER CHANGE PAGE

The publisher change page at `http://127.0.0.1:8000/admin/reviews/publisher/1` contains what we might expect (see *Figure 4.26*). There is a form for editing the publisher's details. These details have been derived from the `reviews.models.Publisher` class:

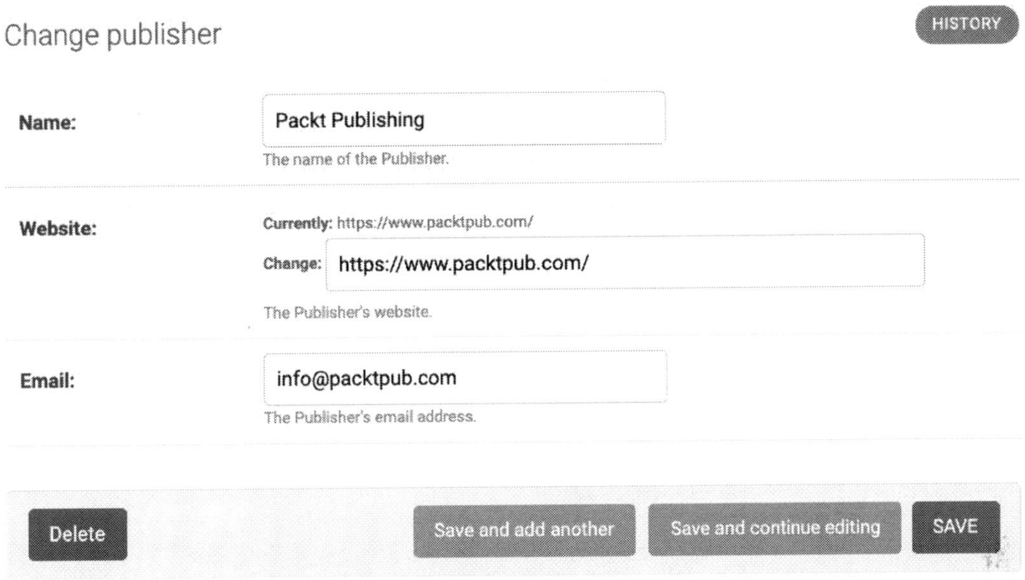

Change publisher

HISTORY

Name: Packt Publishing

The name of the Publisher.

Website: Currently: https://www.packtpub.com/

Change: https://www.packtpub.com/

The Publisher's website.

Email: info@packtpub.com

The Publisher's email address.

Delete   Save and add another   Save and continue editing   SAVE

Figure 4.26: Publisher change page

If we had clicked the **ADD PUBLISHER** button, the admin app would have returned a similar form for adding a publisher. The beauty of the admin app is that it gives us all of this CRUD functionality with just one line of coding – **admin.site.register(Publisher)** – using the definition of the **reviews.models.Publisher** attributes as a schema for the page content:

```
class Publisher(models.Model):
    """A company that publishes books."""
    name = models.CharField\
            (help_text="The name of the Publisher.",\
            max_length=50)
    website = models.URLField\
            (help_text="The Publisher's website.")
    email = models.EmailField\
            (help_text="The Publisher's email address.")
```

The publisher **Name** field is constrained to 50 characters as specified in the model. The help text that appears in gray below each field is derived from the **help_text** attributes specified on the model. We can see that **models.CharField**, **models.URLField**, and **models.EmailField** are rendered in HTML as input elements of type **text**, **url**, and **email** respectively.

The fields in the form come with validation where appropriate. Unless model fields are set to **blank=True** or **null=True**, the form will throw an error if the field is left blank, as is the case for the **Publisher.name** field. Similarly, as **Publisher.website** and **Publisher.email** are respectively defined as instances of **models.URLField** and **models.EmailField**, they are validated accordingly. In *Figure 4.27*, we can see validation of **Name** as a required field, validation of **Website** as a URL, and validation of **Email** as an email address:

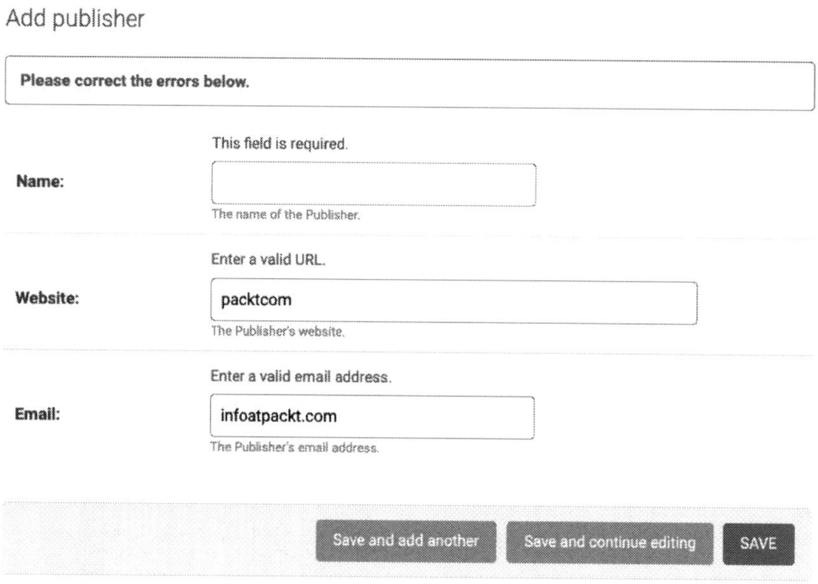

Add publisher

> Please correct the errors below.

This field is required.

Name:

The name of the Publisher.

Enter a valid URL.

Website:

packtcom

The Publisher's website.

Enter a valid email address.

Email:

infoatpackt.com

The Publisher's email address.

Save and add another   Save and continue editing   SAVE

Figure 4.27: Field validation

It is useful to examine how the admin app renders elements of the models to understand how it functions. In your browser, right-click **View Page Source** and examine the HTML that has been rendered for this form. You will see a browser tab displaying something like this:

```
<fieldset class="module aligned ">
    <div class="form-row errors field-name">
        <ul class="errorlist"><li>This field is required.</li></ul>
            <div>
                    <label class="required" for="id_name">Name:</label>
                        <input type="text" name="name" class="vTextField"
                        maxlength="50" required id="id_name">
                    <div class="help">The name of the Publisher.</div>
            </div>
    </div>
</div>
```

```
    <div class="form-row errors field-website">
        <ul class="errorlist"><li>Enter a valid URL.</li></ul>
            <div>
                    <label class="required" for="id_website">Website:</
label>
                        <input type="url" name="website" value="packtcom"
                        class="vURLField" maxlength="200" required
                        id="id_website">
                    <div class="help">The Publisher's website.</div>
            </div>
    </div>
    <div class="form-row errors field-email">
        <ul class="errorlist"><li>Enter a valid email address.</li></ul>
            <div>
                    <label class="required" for="id_email">Email:</label>
                        <input type="email" name="email"
value="infoatpackt.com"
                        class="vTextField" maxlength="254" required
                        id="id_email">
                    <div class="help">The Publisher's email address.</
div>
            </div>
    </div>
</fieldset>
```

The form has an ID of **publisher_form** and it contains a fieldset with HTML elements corresponding to the data structure of the **Publisher** model in **reviews/models.py**, shown as follows:

```
class Publisher(models.Model):
    """A company that publishes books."""
    name = models.CharField\
            (max_length=50,
            help_text="The name of the Publisher.")
    website = models.URLField\
            (help_text="The Publisher's website.")
    email = models.EmailField\
            (help_text="The Publisher's email address.")
```

Note that for the name, the input field is rendered like this:

```
<input type="text" name="name" value="Packt Publishing"
                class="vTextField" maxlength="50" required="" id="id_
name">
```

It is a required field, and it has a type of **text** and a **maxlength** of 50, as defined by the **max_length** parameter in the model definition:

```
name = models.CharField\
        (help_text="The name of the Publisher.",\
        max_length=50)
```

Similarly, we can see the website and email being defined in the model as **URLField** and **EmailField** are rendered in HTML as input elements of type **url** and **email** respectively:

```
<input type="url" name="website" value="https://www.packtpub.com/"
                class="vURLField" maxlength="200" required=""
                id="id_website">
<input type="email" name="email" value="info@packtpub.com"
                class="vTextField" maxlength="254" required=""
                id="id_email">
```

We have learned that this Django admin app derives sensible HTML representations of Django models based on the model definitions that we have provided.

THE BOOK CHANGE PAGE

Similarly, there is a change page that can be reached by selecting **Books** from the **Site administration** page and then selecting a specific book in the change list:

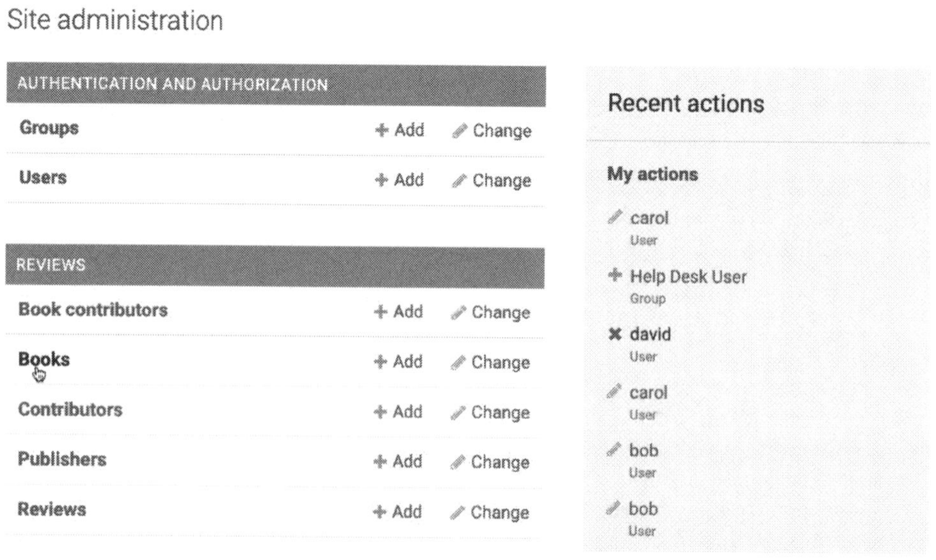

Site administration

AUTHENTICATION AND AUTHORIZATION		
Groups	+ Add	Change
Users	+ Add	Change

REVIEWS		
Book contributors	+ Add	Change
Books	+ Add	Change
Contributors	+ Add	Change
Publishers	+ Add	Change
Reviews	+ Add	Change

Recent actions

My actions

- carol
  User
- + Help Desk User
  Group
- ✖ david
  User
- carol
  User
- bob
  User
- bob
  User

Figure 4.28: Selecting Books from the Site administration page

After clicking **Books** as shown in the preceding screenshot, you will see the following on your screen:

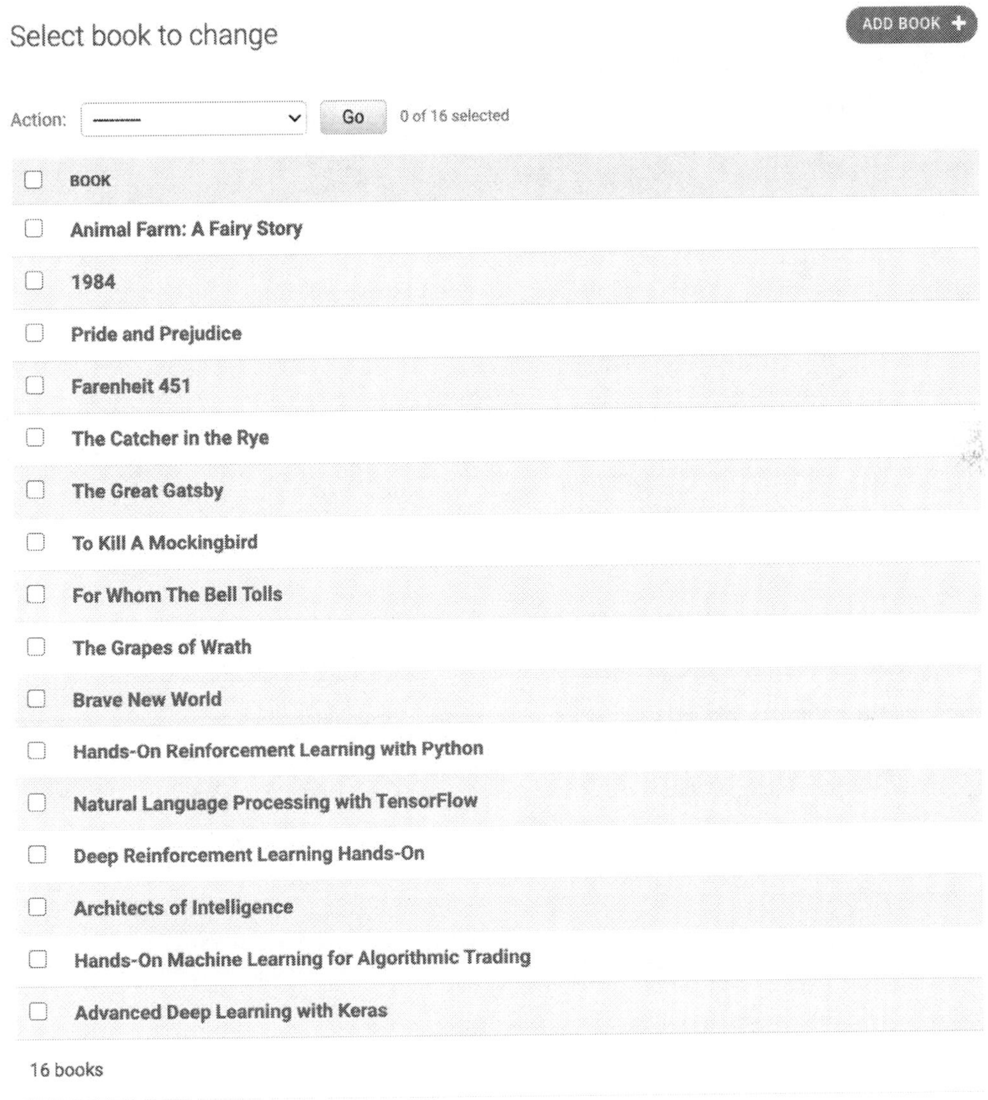

Select book to change

ADD BOOK +

Action: [_____ ▾] [Go] 0 of 16 selected

	BOOK
☐	Animal Farm: A Fairy Story
☐	1984
☐	Pride and Prejudice
☐	Farenheit 451
☐	The Catcher in the Rye
☐	The Great Gatsby
☐	To Kill A Mockingbird
☐	For Whom The Bell Tolls
☐	The Grapes of Wrath
☐	Brave New World
☐	Hands-On Reinforcement Learning with Python
☐	Natural Language Processing with TensorFlow
☐	Deep Reinforcement Learning Hands-On
☐	Architects of Intelligence
☐	Hands-On Machine Learning for Algorithmic Trading
☐	Advanced Deep Learning with Keras

16 books

Figure 4.29: The book change page

In this instance, selecting the book *Architects of Intelligence* will take us to the URL `http://127.0.0.1:8000/admin/reviews/book/3/change/`. In the previous example, all the model fields were rendered as simple HTML text widgets. The rendering of some other subclasses of `django.db.models.Field` used in `models.Book` are worthy of closer examination:

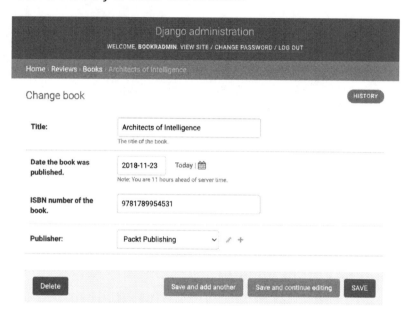

Figure 4.30: The Change book page

Here, `publication_date` is defined using `models.DateField`. It is rendered using a date selection widget. The visual representation of the widgets will vary amongst operating systems and choice of browser:

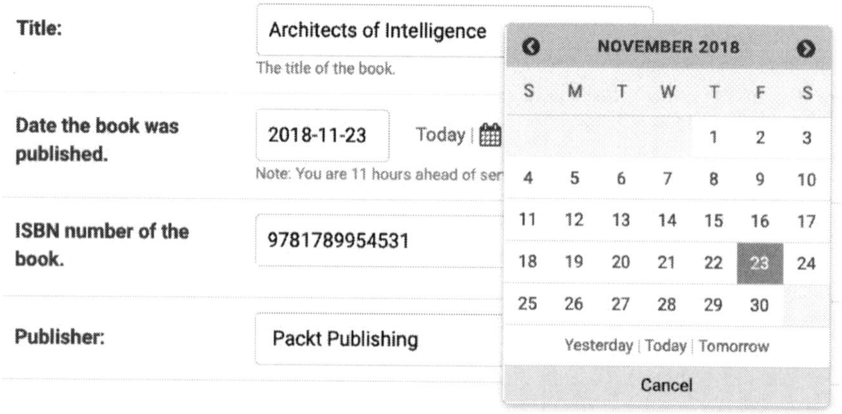

Figure 4.31: Date selection widget

As **Publisher** is defined as a foreign key relation, it is rendered by a **Publisher** dropdown with a list of **Publisher** objects:

Figure 4.32: Publisher dropdown

This brings us to how the admin app handles deletion. The admin app takes its cue from the models' foreign key constraints when determining how to implement deletion functionality. In the **BookContributor** model, **Contributor** is defined as a foreign key. The code in **reviews/models.py** looks as follows:

```
contributor = models.ForeignKey(Contributor, on_delete=models.CASCADE)
```

By setting **on_delete=CASCADE** on a foreign key, the model is specifying the database behavior required when a record is deleted; the deletion is cascaded to other objects that are referenced by the foreign key.

EXERCISE 4.03: FOREIGN KEYS AND DELETION BEHAVIOR IN THE ADMIN APP

At present, all **ForeignKey** relations in the **reviews** models are defined with an **on_delete=CASCADE** behavior. For instance, think of a case wherein an admin deletes one of the publishers. This would delete all the books that are associated with the publisher. We do not want that to happen, and that is precisely the behavior that we will be changing in this exercise:

1. Visit the **Contributors** change list at **http://127.0.0.1:8000/admin/ reviews/contributor/** and select a contributor to delete. Make sure that the contributor is the author of a book.

2. Click the **Delete** button, but don't click **Yes, I'm sure** on the confirmation dialog. You will see a message like the one in *Figure 4.33*:

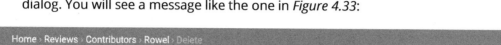

Home › Reviews › Contributors › Rowel › Delete

Are you sure?

Are you sure you want to delete the contributor "Rowel"? All of the following related items will be deleted:

Summary

- Contributors: 1
- Book contributors: 1

Objects

- Contributor: Rowel
  - Book contributor: BookContributor object (19)

Yes, I'm sure   No, take me back

Figure 4.33: Cascading delete confirmation dialog

In accordance with the **on_delete=CASCADE** argument to the foreign key, we are warned that deleting this Contributor object will have a cascading effect on a **BookContributor** object.

3. In the **reviews/models.py** file, modify the **Contributor** attribute of **BookContributor** to the following and save the file:

```
contributor = models.ForeignKey(Contributor, \
                        on_delete=models.PROTECT)
```

4. Now, try deleting the **Contributor** object again. You will see a message similar to the one in *Figure 4.34*:

Home › Reviews › Contributors › Rowel › Delete

Cannot delete contributor

Deleting the contributor 'Rowel' would require deleting the following protected related objects:

- Book contributor: BookContributor object (19)

Figure 4.34: Foreign key protection error

Because the **on_delete** argument is **PROTECT**, our attempt to delete the object with dependencies will throw an error. If we used this approach in our model, we would need to delete objects in the **ForeignKey** relation before we deleted the original object. In this case, it would mean deleting the **BookContributor** object before deleting the **Contributor** object.

5. Now that we have learned about how the admin app handles **ForeignKey** relations, let's revert the **ForeignKey** definition in the **BookContributor** class to this:

```
contributor = models.ForeignKey(Contributor, \
                        on_delete=models.CASCADE)
```

We have examined how the admin app's behavior adapts to the **ForeignKey** constraints that are expressed in model definitions. If the **on_delete** behavior is set to **models.PROTECT**, the admin app returns an error explaining why a protected object is blocking the deletion. This functionality can come in handy while building real-world apps, as there is often a chance of a manual error inadvertently leading to the deletion of important records. In the next section, we will look at how we can customize our admin app interface for a smoother user experience.

CUSTOMIZING THE ADMIN INTERFACE

When first developing an application, the convenience of the default admin interface is excellent for building a rapid prototype of the app. Indeed, for many simpler applications or projects that require minimal data maintenance, this default admin interface may be entirely adequate. However, as the application matures to the point of release, the admin interface will generally need to be customized to facilitate more intuitive use and to robustly control data, subject to user permissions. You might want to retain certain aspects of the default admin interface, and at the same time, make some tweaks to certain features to better suit your purposes. For example, you would want the publisher list to show the complete names of the publishing houses, instead of "**Publisher(1)**, **Publisher(2)** ..." and so on. In addition to the aesthetic appeal, this makes it easier to use and navigate through the app.

SITE-WIDE DJANGO ADMIN CUSTOMIZATIONS

We have seen a page titled **Log in | Django site admin** containing a
Django Administration form. However, an administrative user of the Bookr
application may be somewhat perplexed by all this Django jargon, and it would be
very confusing and a recipe for error if they had to deal with multiple Django apps
that all had identical admin apps. As a developer of an intuitive and user-friendly
application, you would want to customize this. Global properties like these are
specified as attributes of the **AdminSite** object. The following table details some of
the simplest customizations to improve the usability of your app's admin interface:

AdminSite Attribute	Base Value	Description
site_title	"Django site admin"	Populates the `<title>` tag on each page of the admin interface.
site_header	"Django administration"	Sets the header on the login form.
index_title	"Site administration"	Sets the heading on the admin index page (where the models are listed).
index_template	None	Path to find the admin index template. If unset, the `admin/index.html` template is used.
app_index_template	None	Path to find the app admin index template. If unset, the `admin/app_index.html` template is used.
login_template	None	Path to find the login template. If unset, the `admin/login.html` template is used.
logout_template	None	Path to find the logout template. If unset, the `registration/logged_out.html` template is used.
password_change_template	None	Path to find the password change template. If unset, the `registration/password_change_form.html` template is used.
password_change_done_template	None	Path to find the password change done template. If unset, the `registration/password_change_done.html` template is used.

Figure 4.35: Important AdminSite attributes

EXAMINING THE ADMINSITE OBJECT FROM THE PYTHON SHELL

Let's take a deeper look at the **AdminSite** class. We have already encountered
an object of class **AdminSite**. It is the **admin.site** object that we used in the
previous section, *Registering the Reviews Model*. If the development server is not
running, start it now with the **runserver** subcommand, as follows (use **python**
instead of **python3** for Windows):

```
python3 manage.py runserver
```

We can examine the **admin.site** object by importing the admin app in the Django shell, using the **manage.py** script again:

```
python3 manage.py shell
>>>from django.contrib import admin
```

We can interactively examine the default values of **site_title**, **site_header**, and **index_title** and see that they match the expected values of **'Django site admin'**, **'Django administration'**, and **'Site administration'** that we have already observed on the rendered web pages of the Django admin app:

```
>>> admin.site.site_title
'Django site admin'
>>> admin.site.site_header
'Django administration'
>>> admin.site.index_title
'Site administration'
```

The **AdminSite** class also specifies which forms and views are used to render the admin interface and determine its global behavior.

SUBCLASSING ADMINSITE

We can make some modifications to the **reviews/admin.py** file. Instead of importing the **django.contrib.admin** module and using its site object, we will import **AdminSite**, subclass it, and instantiate our customized **admin_site** object. Consider the following code snippet. Here, **BookrAdminSite** is a subclass of **AdminSite** that contains custom values for **site_title**, **site_header**, and **index_title**; **admin_site** is an instance of **BookrAdminSite**; and we can use this instead of the default **admin.site** object, to register our models. The **reviews/admin.py** file will look as follows:

```
from django.contrib.admin import AdminSite
from reviews.models import (Publisher, Contributor, Book,\
    BookContributor, Review)


class BookrAdminSite(AdminSite):
    title_header = 'Bookr Admin'
    site_header = 'Bookr administration'
    index_title = 'Bookr site admin'
```

```
admin_site = BookrAdminSite(name='bookr')


# Register your models here.
admin_site.register(Publisher)
admin_site.register(Contributor)
admin_site.register(Book)
admin_site.register(BookContributor)
admin_site.register(Review)
```

As we have now created our own **admin_site** object that overrides the behavior of the **admin.site** object, we need to remove the existing references in our code to the **admin.site** object. In **bookr/urls.py**, we need to point admin to the new **admin_site** object and update our URL patterns. Otherwise, we would still be using the default admin site and our customizations would be ignored. The change will look as follows:

```
from reviews.admin import admin_site
from django.urls import include, path
import reviews.views


urlpatterns = [path('admin/', admin_site.urls),\
               path('', reviews.views.index),\
               path('book-search/', reviews.views.book_search, \
                   name='book_search'),\
               path('', include('reviews.urls'))]
```

This produces the expected results on the login screen:

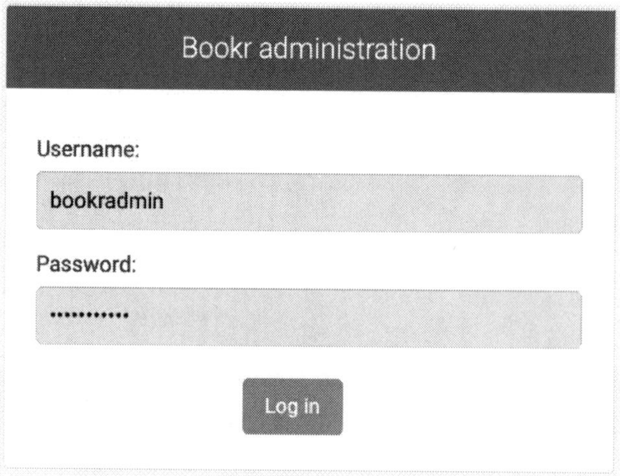

Figure 4.36: Customizing the login screen

However, now there is a problem; that is, we have lost the interface for auth objects. Previously, the admin app was discovering the models registered in **reviews/ admin.py** and in **django.contrib.auth.admin** through the auto-discovery process, but now we have overridden this behavior by creating a new **AdminSite**:

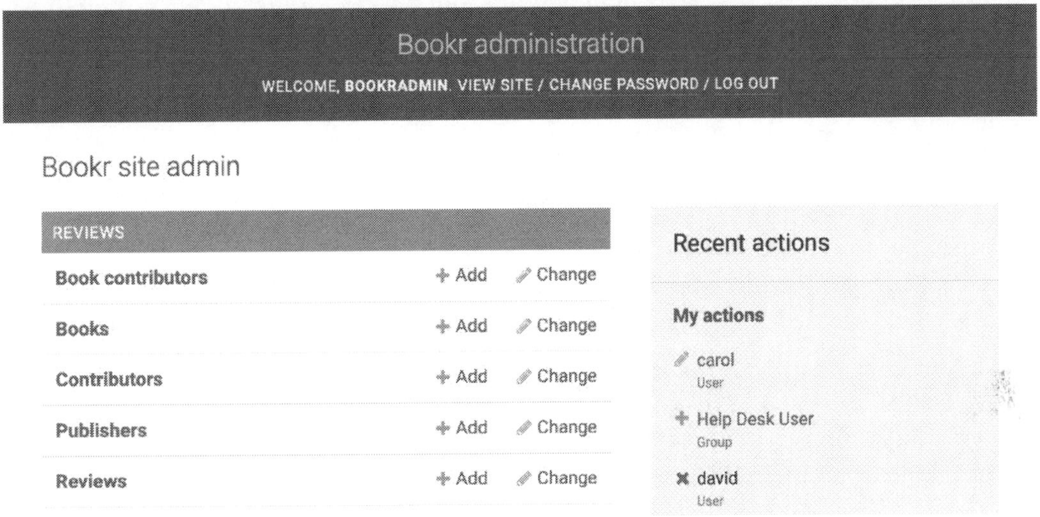

Bookr administration

WELCOME, **BOOKRADMIN**. VIEW SITE / CHANGE PASSWORD / LOG OUT

Bookr site admin

REVIEWS		
Book contributors	+ Add	Change
Books	+ Add	Change
Contributors	+ Add	Change
Publishers	+ Add	Change
Reviews	+ Add	Change

Recent actions

My actions

carol
User

+ Help Desk User
Group

✖ david
User

Figure 4.37: Customized AdminSite is missing Authentication and Authorization

We could go down the path of referencing both **AdminSite** objects to URL patterns in **bookr/urls.py**, but this approach would mean that we would end up with two separate admin apps for authentication and reviews. So, the URL **http://127.0.0.1:8000/admin** will take you to the original admin app derived from the **admin.site** object, while **http://127.0.0.1:8000/bookradmin** will take you to our **BookrAdminSite admin_site**. This is not what we want to do, as we are still left with the admin app without the customizations that we added when we sub-classed **BookrAdminSite**:

```
from django.contrib import admin
from reviews.admin import admin_site
from django.urls import path
urlpatterns = [path('admin/', admin.site.urls),\
               path('bookradmin/', admin_site.urls),]
```

This has been a clumsy problem with the Django admin interface that has led to a lot of ad hoc solutions in earlier versions. Since Django 2.1 came out, there is a simple way of integrating a customized interface for the admin app without breaking auto-discovery or any of its other default features. As **BookrAdminSite** is project-specific, the code does not really belong under our **reviews** folder. We should move **BookrAdminSite** to a new file called **admin.py** at the top level of the **Bookr** project directory:

```
from django.contrib import admin

class BookrAdminSite(admin.AdminSite):
    title_header = 'Bookr Admin'
    site_header = 'Bookr administration'
    index_title = 'Bookr site admin'
```

The URL settings path in **bookr/urls.py** changes to **path('admin/', admin.site.urls)** and we define our **ReviewsAdminConfig**. The **reviews/apps.py** file will contain these additional lines:

```
from django.contrib.admin.apps import AdminConfig
class ReviewsAdminConfig(AdminConfig):
    default_site = 'admin.BookrAdminSite'
```

Replace **django.contrib.admin** with **reviews.apps.ReviewsAdminConfig**, so that **INSTALLED_APPS** in the **bookr/settings.py** file will look as follows:

```
INSTALLED_APPS = ['reviews.apps.ReviewsAdminConfig',\
                  'django.contrib.auth',\
                  'django.contrib.contenttypes',\
                  'django.contrib.sessions',\
                  'django.contrib.messages',\
                  'django.contrib.staticfiles',\
                  'reviews']
```

With the **ReviewsAdminConfig** specification of **default_site**, we no longer need to replace references to **admin.site** with a custom **AdminSite** object, **admin_site**. We can replace those **admin_site** calls with the **admin.site** calls that we had originally. Now, **reviews/admin.py** reverts to the following:

```
from django.contrib import admin
from reviews.models import (Publisher, Contributor, Book,\
    BookContributor, Review)
```

```
# Register your models here.
admin.site.register(Publisher)
admin.site.register(Contributor)
admin.site.register(Book, BookAdmin)
admin.site.register(BookContributor)
admin.site.register(Review)
```

There are other aspects of **AdminSite** that we can customize, but we will revisit these in *Chapter 9, Sessions and Authentication* once we have a fuller understanding of Django's templates and forms.

ACTIVITY 4.01: CUSTOMIZING THE SITEADMIN

You have learned how to modify attributes of the **AdminSite** object in a Django project. This activity will challenge you to use these skills to customize a new project and override its site title, site header, and index header. Also, you will replace the logout message by creating a project-specific template and setting it in our custom **SiteAdmin** object. You are developing a Django project that implements a message board, called *Comment8or*. *Comment8or* is geared toward a technical demographic, so you need to make the phraseology succinct and abbreviated:

1. The *Comment8or* admin site will be referred to as **c8admin**. This will appear on the site header and index title.

2. For the title header, it will say **c8 site admin**.

3. The default Django admin logout message is **Thanks for spending some quality time with the Web site today**. In Comment8or, it will say **Bye from c8admin**.

These are the steps that you need to follow to complete this activity:

1. Following the process that you learned in *Chapter 1, Introduction to Django*, create a new Django project called **comment8or**, an app called **messageboard**, and run the migrations. Create a superuser called **c8admin**.

2. In the Django source code, there is a template for the logout page located in **django/contrib/admin/templates/registration/logged_out. html**.

3. Make a copy of it in your project's directory under **comment8or/templates/comment8or**. Modify the message in the template following the requirements.

4. Inside the project, create an **admin.py** file that implements a custom **SiteAdmin** object. Set the appropriate values for the attributes **index_title**, **title_header**, **site_header**, and **logout_template**, based on the requirements.

5. Add a custom **AdminConfig** subclass to **messageboard/apps.py**.

6. Replace the admin app with the custom **AdminConfig** subclass in **comment8or/settings.py**.

7. Configure the **TEMPLATES** setting so that the project's template is discoverable.

   When the project is first created, the login, app index, and logout pages will look as follows:

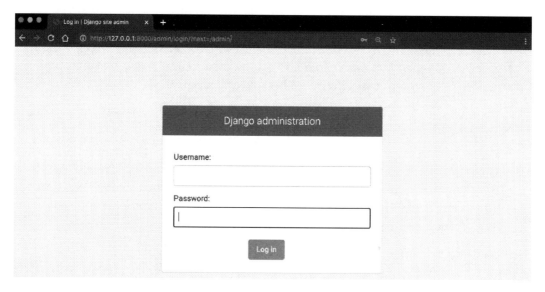

Figure 4.38: Login page for the project

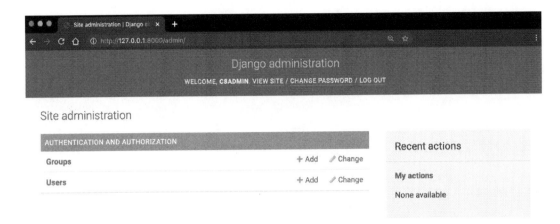

Figure 4.39: App index page for the project

Figure 4.40: Logout page for the project

After you have completed this activity, the login, app index, and logout pages will appear with the following customizations:

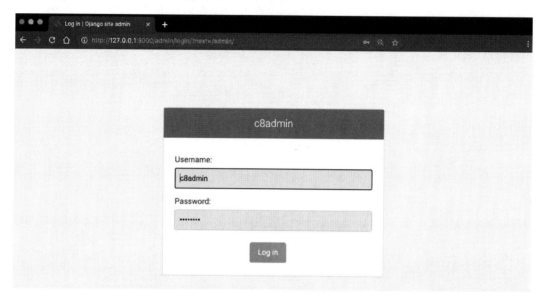

Figure 4.41: Login page after customization

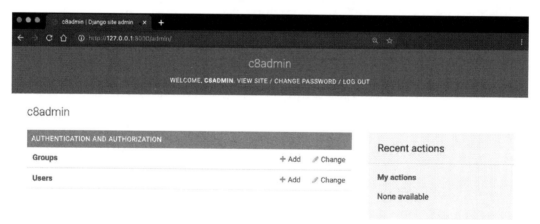

Figure 4.42: App index page after customization

Figure 4.43: Logout page after customization

You have successfully customized the admin app by sub-classing **AdminSite**.

> **NOTE**
>
> The solution to this activity can be found at http://packt.live/2Nh1NTJ.

CUSTOMIZING THE MODELADMIN CLASSES

Now that we've learned how a sub-classed **AdminSite** can be used to customize the global appearance of the admin app, we will look at how to customize the admin app's interface to individual models. Owing to the admin interface being generated automatically from the models' structure, it has an overly generic appearance and needs to be customized for the sake of aesthetics and usability. Click one of the **Books** links in the admin app and compare it to the **Users** link. Both links take you to change list pages. These are the pages that a Bookr administrator visits when they want to add new books or add or alter the privileges of a user. As explained above, a change list page presents a list of model objects with the option of selecting a group of them for bulk deletion (or other bulk activity), examining an individual object with a view to editing it, or adding a new object. Notice the difference between the two change list pages with a view to making our vanilla **Books** page as fully featured as the **Users** page.

The following screenshot from the **Authentication and Authorization** app contains useful features such as a search bar, sortable column headers for important user fields, and a result filter:

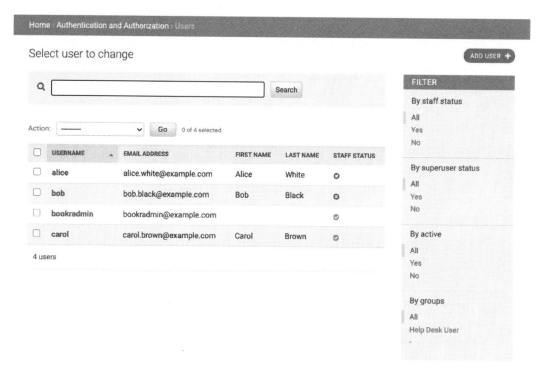

Figure 4.44: The Users change list contains customized ModelAdmin features

THE LIST DISPLAY FIELDS

On the **Users** change list page, you will see the following:

- There is a list of user objects presented, summarized by their **USERNAME, EMAIL ADDRESS, FIRST NAME, LAST NAME**, and **STAFF STATUS** attributes.

- These individual attributes are sortable. The sorting order can be changed by clicking the headers.

- There is a search bar at the top of the page.

- In the right-hand column, there is a selection filter that allows the selection of several user fields, including some not appearing in the list display.

However, the behavior for the **Books** change list page is a lot less helpful. The books are listed by their titles but not in alphabetical order. The title column is not sortable and there are no filter or search options present:

Figure 4.45: The Books change list

Recall from *Chapter 2, Models and Migrations*, that we defined **__str__** methods on the **Publisher**, **Book**, and **Contributor** classes. In the case of the **Book** class, it had a **__str__()** representation that returns the book object's title:

```
class Book(models.Model):

    ...

    def __str__(self):
        return "{} ({})".format(self.title, self.isbn)
```

If we had not defined the **__str__()** method on the **Book** class, it would have inherited it from the base **Model** class, **django.db.models.Model**.

This base class provides an abstract way to give a string representation of an object. When we have **Book** with a primary key, in this case, the **id** field, with a value of **17**, then we will end up with a string representation of **Book object (17)**:

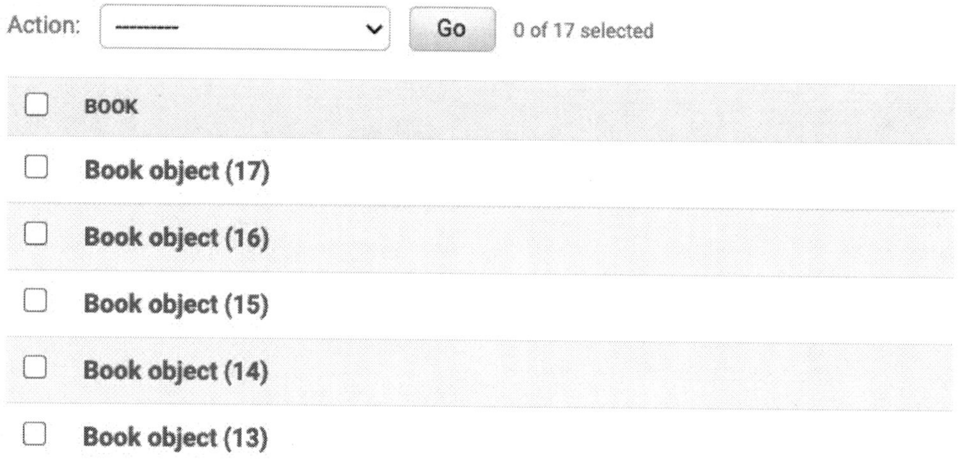

Action: [---------- ⌄] [Go] 0 of 17 selected

☐ **BOOK**

☐ **Book object (17)**

☐ **Book object (16)**

☐ **Book object (15)**

☐ **Book object (14)**

☐ **Book object (13)**

Figure 4.46: The Books change list using the Model __str__ representation

It could be useful in our application to represent a **Book** object as a composite of several fields. For example, if we wanted the books to be represented as **Title (ISBN)**, the following code snippet would produce the desired results:

```
class Book(models.Model):

    ...

    def __str__(self):
        return "{} ({})".format(self.title, self.isbn)
```

This is a useful change in and of itself as it makes the representation of the object more intuitive in the app:

Figure 4.47: A portion of the Books change list with the custom string representation

We are not limited to using the **__str__** representation of the object in the **list_display** field. The columns that appear in the list display are determined by the **ModelAdmin** class of the Django admin app. At the Django shell, we can import the **ModelAdmin** class and examine its **list_display** attribute:

```
python manage.py shell
>>> from django.contrib.admin import ModelAdmin
>>> ModelAdmin.list_display
('__str__',)
```

This explains why the default behavior of **list_display** is to display a single-columned table of the objects' **__str__** representations, so that we can customize the list display by overriding this value. The best practice is to subclass **ModelAdmin** for each object. If we wanted the **Book** list display to contain two separate columns for **Title** and **ISBN**, rather than having a single column containing both values as in *Figure 4.47*, we would subclass **ModelAdmin** as **BookAdmin** and specify the custom **list_display**. The benefit of doing this is that we are now able to sort books by **Title** and by **ISBN**. We can add this class to **reviews/admin.py**:

```
class BookAdmin(admin.ModelAdmin):
    list_display = ('title', 'isbn')
```

Now that we've created a **BookAdmin** class, we should reference it when we register our **reviews.models.Book** class with the admin site. In the same file, we also need to modify the model registration to use **BookAdmin** instead of the default value of **admin.ModelAdmin**, so the **admin.site.register** call now becomes the following:

```
admin.site.register(Book, BookAdmin)
```

Once these two changes have been made to the **reviews/admin.py** file, we will get a **Books** change list page that looks like this:

Action:	▼	Go	0 of 17 selected	
☐	**TITLE**			**ISBN NUMBER OF THE BOOK.**
☐	Paul Clifford			9781719053167
☐	Animal Farm: A Fairy Story			9780151002177
☐	1984			9781328869333
☐	Pride and Prejudice			9780141439518
☐	Farenheit 451			9781451673319

Figure 4.48: A portion of the Books change list with a two-column list display

This gives us a hint as to how flexible **list_display** is. It can take four types of values:

- It takes field names from the model, such as **title** or **isbn**.

- It takes a function that takes the model instance as an argument, such as this function that gives an initialized version of a person's name:

```
def initialled_name(obj):
    """ obj.first_names='Jerome David', obj.last_names='Salinger'
        => 'Salinger, JD' """
    initials = ''.join([name[0] for name in \
                        obj.first_names.split(' ')])
    return "{}, {}".format(obj.last_names, initials)


class ContributorAdmin(admin.ModelAdmin):
    list_display = (initialled_name,)
```

- It takes a method from the **ModelAdmin** subclass that takes the model object as a single argument. Note that this needs to be specified as a string argument as it would be out of scope and undefined within the class:

```
class BookAdmin(admin.ModelAdmin):

    list_display = ('title', 'isbn13')
    def isbn13(self, obj):
        """ '9780316769174' => '978-0-31-676917-4' """
        return "{}-{}-{}-{}-{}".format\
                            (obj.isbn[0:3], obj.isbn[3:4],\
                                obj.isbn[4:6], obj.isbn[6:12],\
                                obj.isbn[12:13])
```

- It takes a method (or a non-field attribute) of the model class, such as **__str__**, as long as it accepts the model object as an argument. For example, we could convert **isbn13** to a method on the **Book** model class:

```
class Book(models.Model):

    def isbn13(self):
        """ '9780316769174' => '978-0-31-676917-4' """
        return "{}-{}-{}-{}-{}".format\
                            (self.isbn[0:3], self.isbn[3:4],\
                                self.isbn[4:6], self.isbn[6:12],\
                                self.isbn[12:13])
```

Now when viewing the **Books** change list at **http://127.0.0.1:8000/admin/reviews/book**, we can see the hyphenated **ISBN13** field:

TITLE	ISBN13
☐ Paul Clifford	978-1-71-905316-7
☐ Animal Farm: A Fairy Story	978-0-15-100217-7
☐ 1984	978-1-32-886933-3
☐ Pride and Prejudice	978-0-14-143951-8
☐ Farenheit 451	978-1-45-167331-9

Figure 4.49: A portion of the Books change list with the hyphenated ISBN13

It is worth noting that computed fields such as **__str__** or our **isbn13** methods do not make for sortable fields on the summary page. Also, we cannot include fields of type **ManyToManyField** in **display_list**.

THE FILTER

Once the admin interface needs to deal with a significant number of records, it is convenient to narrow down the results that appear on change list pages. The simplest filters select individual values. For example, the user filter depicted in *Figure 4.6* allows the selection of users by **staff status**, by **superuser status**, and **active**. We've seen on the user filter that **BooleanField** can be used as a filter. We can also implement filters on **CharField**, **DateField**, **DateTimeField**, **IntegerField**, **ForeignKey**, and **ManyToManyField**. In this case, adding **publisher** as a **ForeignKey** of **Book**, it is defined on the **Book** class as follows:

```
publisher = models.ForeignKey(Publisher, \
                    on_delete=models.CASCADE)
```

Filters are implemented using the **list_filter** attribute of a **ModelAdmin** subclass. In our Bookr app, filtering by book title or ISBN would be impractical as it would produce a large list of filter options that return only one record. The filter that would occupy the right-hand side of the page would take up more space than the actual change list. A practical option would be to filter books by publisher. We defined a custom **__str__** method for the **Publisher** model that returns the publisher's **name** attribute, so our filter options will be listed as publisher names.

We can specify our change list filter in **reviews/admin.py** in the **BookAdmin** class:

```
    list_filter = ('publisher',)
```

Here is how the **Books** change page should look now:

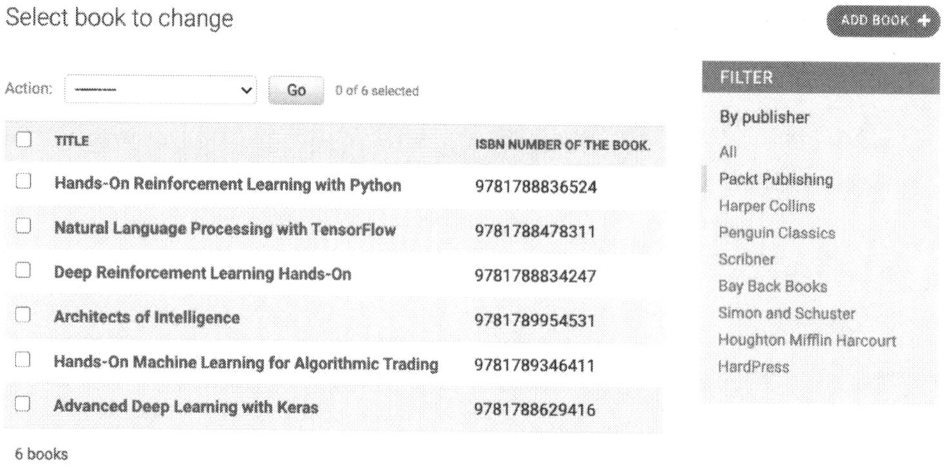

Figure 4.50: The Books change page with the publisher filter

With that line of code, we have implemented a useful publisher filter on the **Books** change list page.

EXERCISE 4.04: ADDING A DATE LIST_FILTER AND DATE_HIERARCHY

We have seen that the **admin.ModelAdmin** class provides useful attributes to customize filters on change list pages. For example, filtering by date is crucial functionality for many applications and can also help us make our app more user-friendly. In this exercise, we will examine how date filtering can be implemented by including a date field in the filter and look at the **date_hierarchy** filter:

1. Edit the **reviews/admin.py** file and modify the **list_filter** attribute in the **BookAdmin** class to include **'publication_date'**:

```
class BookAdmin(admin.ModelAdmin):
    list_display = ('title', 'isbn')
    list_filter = ('publisher', 'publication_date')
```

2. Reload the **Books** change page and confirm that the filter now includes date settings:

Figure 4.51: Confirming that the Books change page includes date settings

This publication date filter would be convenient if the Bookr project was receiving a lot of new releases, and we wanted to filter books by what was published in the last 7 days or a month. Sometimes though, we might like to filter by a specific year or a specific month in a specific year. Fortunately, the **admin.ModelAdmin** class comes with a custom filter attribute that is geared towards navigating hierarchies of temporal information. It is called **date_hierarchy**.

3. Add a **date_hierarchy** attribute to **BookAdmin** and set its value to **publication_date**:

```
class BookAdmin(admin.ModelAdmin):
    date_hierarchy = 'publication_date'
    list_display = ('title', 'isbn')
    list_filter = ('publisher', 'publication_date')
```

4. Reload the **Books** change page and confirm that the date hierarchy appears above the **Action** dropdown:

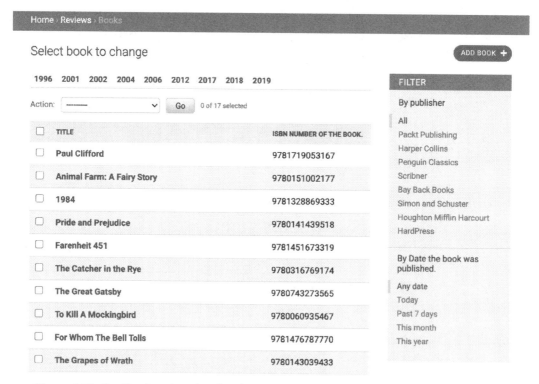

Figure 4.52: Confirming that the date hierarchy appears above the Action dropdown

5. Select a year from the date hierarchy and confirm that it contains a list of months in that year containing book titles and a total list of books:

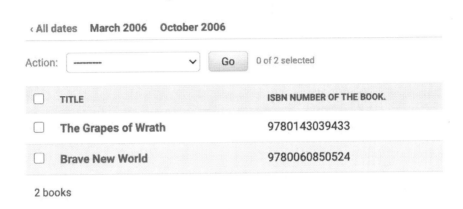

Figure 4.53: Confirming that the selection of a year from the date hierarchy shows the books published that year

6. Confirm that selecting one of these months further filters down to days in the month:

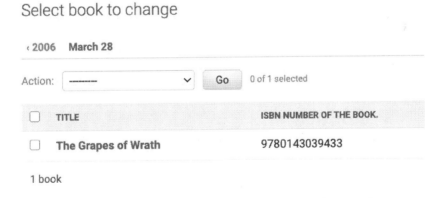

Figure 4.54: Filtering months down to days in the month

The **date_hierarchy** filter is a convenient way of customizing a change list that contains a large set of time-sortable data in order to facilitate faster record selection, as we saw in this exercise. Let's now look at the implementation of a search bar in our app.

THE SEARCH BAR

This brings us to the remaining piece of functionality that we wanted to implement – the search bar. Like filters, a basic search bar is quite simple to implement. We only need to add the **search_fields** attribute to the **ModelAdmin** class. The obvious character fields in our **Book** class to search on are **title** and **isbn**. At present, the **Books** change list appears with a date hierarchy across the top of the change list. The search bar will appear above this:

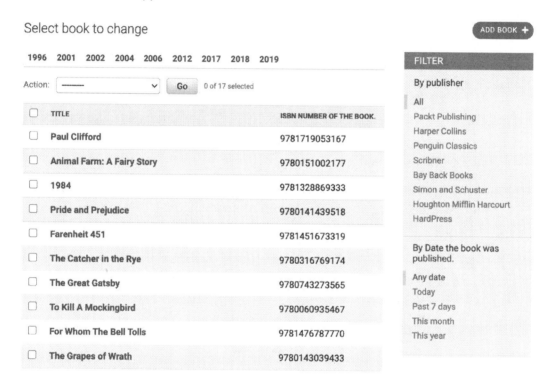

Figure 4.55: Books change list before the search bar is added

We can start by adding this attribute to **BookAdmin** in **reviews/admin.py** and examine the result:

```
search_fields = ('title', 'isbn')
```

The result would look like this:

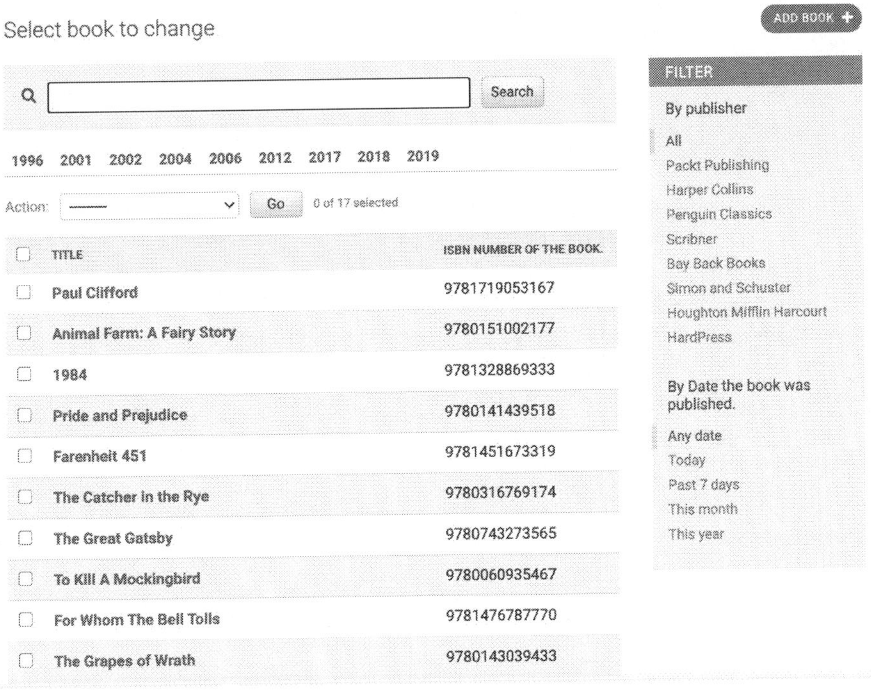

Figure 4.56: Books change list with the search bar

Now we can perform a simple text search on fields that match the title field or ISBN. This search requires precise string matches, so "color" won't match "colour." It also lacks the deep semantic processing that we expect from more sophisticated search facilities such as **Elasticsearch**. ISBN lookup is a very good feature if you happen to have a barcode scanner. Limiting our search to fields on the **Books** model is quite restrictive. We might want to search by publisher name too. Fortunately, **search_ fields** is flexible enough to accomplish this. To search on **ForeignKeyField** or **ManyToManyField**, we just need to specify the field name on the current model and the field on the related model separated by two underscores. In this case, **Book** has a foreign key, **publisher**, and we want to search on the **Publisher.name** field so it can be specified as **'publisher__name'** on **BookAdmin.search_ fields**:

```
search_fields = ('title', 'isbn', 'publisher__name')
```

If we wanted to restrict a search field to an exact match rather than return results that contain the search string, then the field can be suffixed with **'__exact'**. So, replacing **'isbn'** with **'isbn__exact'** will require the complete ISBN to be matched, and we won't be able to get a match using a portion of the ISBN.

Similarly, we constrain the search field to only return results that start with the search string by using the `'__startswith'` suffix. Qualifying the publisher name search field as `'publisher__name__startswith'` means that we will get results searching for "pack" but not for "ackt."

EXCLUDING AND GROUPING FIELDS

There are occasions when it is appropriate to restrict the visibility of some of the fields in the model in the admin interface. This can be achieved with the **exclude** attribute.

This is the review form screen with the **Date edited** field visible. Note that the **Date created** field does not appear – it is already a hidden view because **date_created** is defined on the model with the **auto_now_add** parameter:

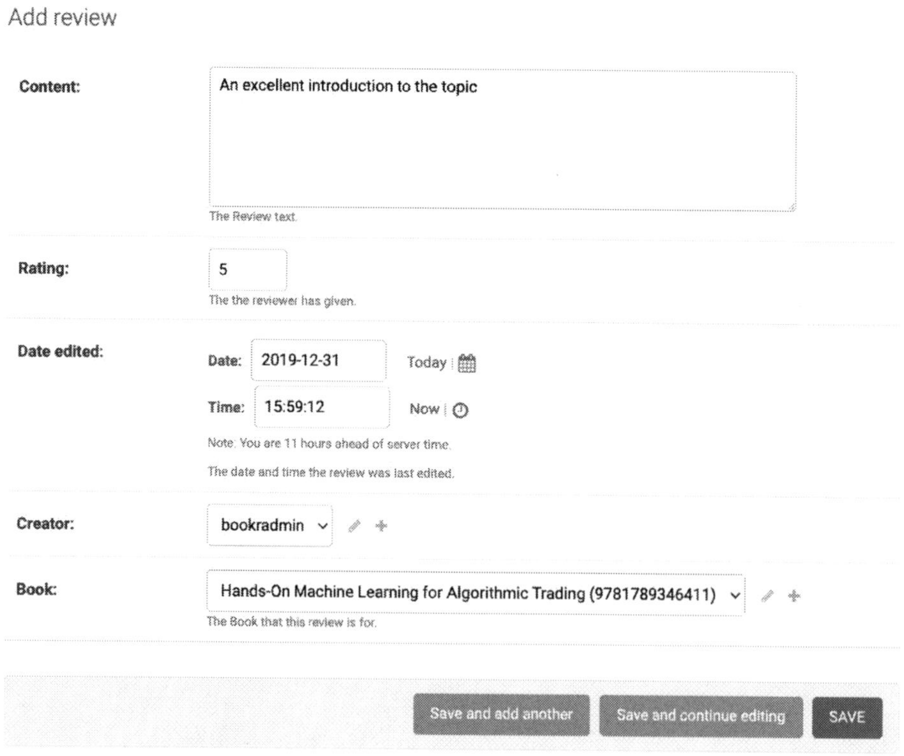

Add review

Content:	An excellent introduction to the topic
	The Review text.
Rating:	5
	The the reviewer has given.
Date edited:	Date: 2019-12-31 Today
	Time: 15:59:12 Now
	Note. You are 11 hours ahead of server time.
	The date and time the review was last edited.
Creator:	bookradmin
Book:	Hands-On Machine Learning for Algorithmic Trading (9781789346411)
	The Book that this review is for.

Save and add another   Save and continue editing   SAVE

Figure 4.57: The review form

If we wanted to exclude the **Date edited** field from the review form, we would do this in the **ReviewAdmin** class:

```
exclude = ('date_edited')
```

Then the review form would appear without **Date edited**:

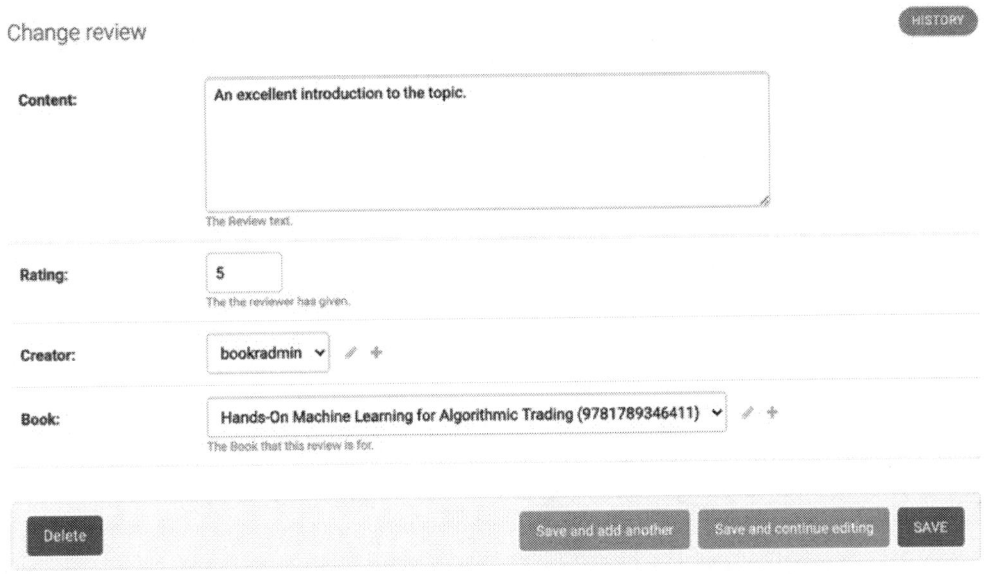

Figure 4.58: The review form with the Date edited field excluded

Conversely, it might be more prudent to restrict the admin fields to those that have been explicitly permitted. This is achieved with the **fields** attribute. The advantage of this approach is that if new fields are added in the model, they won't be available in the admin form unless they have been added to the **fields** tuple in the **ModelAdmin** subclass:

```
fields = ('content', 'rating', 'creator', 'book')
```

This will give us the same result that we saw earlier.

Another option is to use the **fieldsets** attribute of the **ModelAdmin** subclass to specify the form layout as a series of grouped fields. Each grouping in **fieldsets** consists of a title followed by a dictionary containing a **'fields'** key pointing to a list of field name strings:

```
fieldsets = (('Linkage', {'fields': ('creator', 'book')}),\
            ('Review content', \
                {'fields': ('content', 'rating')}))
```

The review form should look as follows:

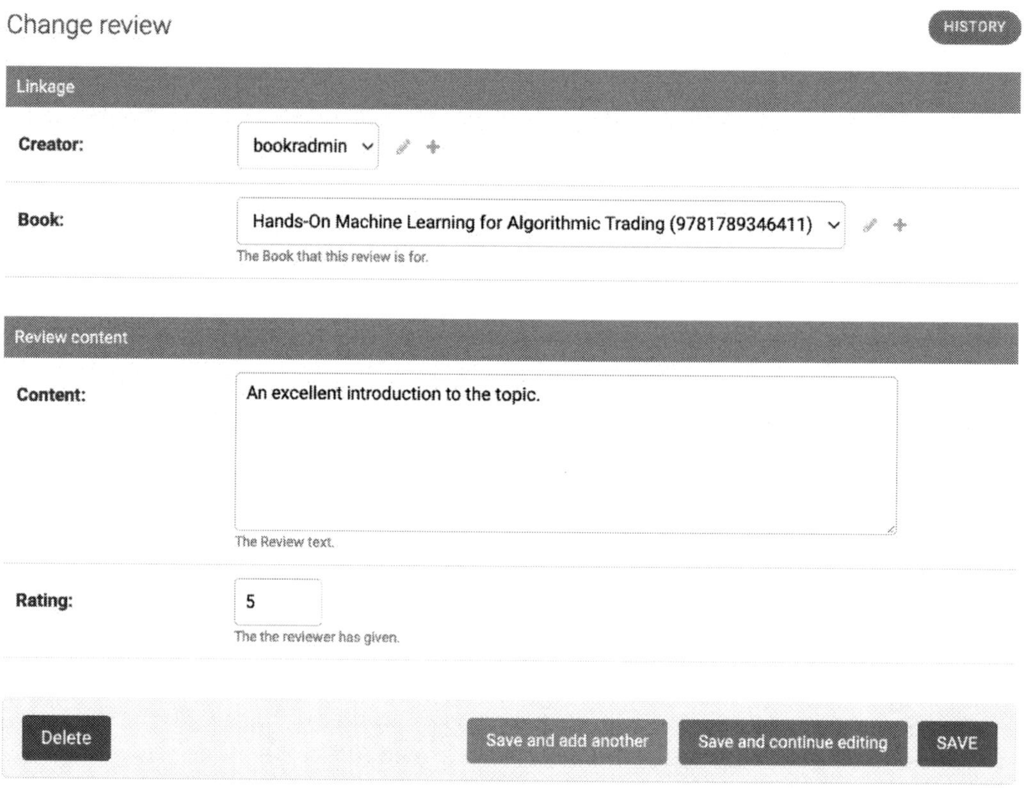

Figure 4.59: The review form with fieldsets

If we want to omit the title on a fieldset, we can do so by assigning the value **None** to it:

```
fieldsets = ((None, {'fields': ('creator', 'book')}),\
             ('Review content', \
                {'fields': ('content', 'rating')}))
```

Now, the review form should appear as shown in the following screenshot:

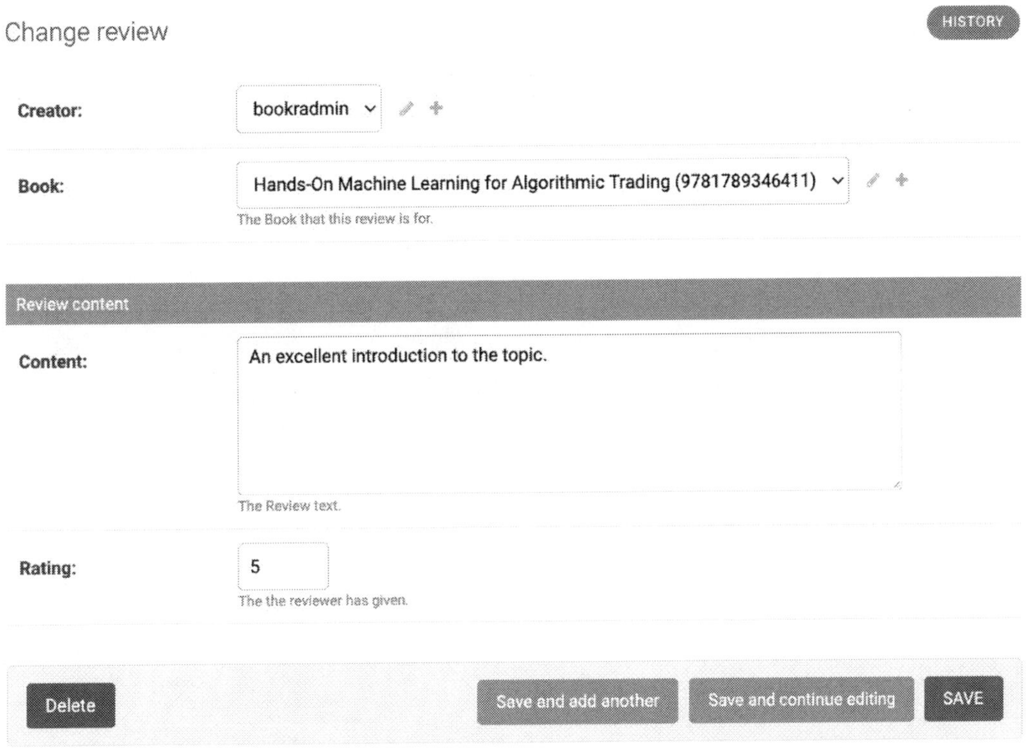

Change review

HISTORY

Creator: bookradmin

Book: Hands-On Machine Learning for Algorithmic Trading (9781789346411)
The Book that this review is for.

Review content

Content: An excellent introduction to the topic.

The Review text.

Rating: 5
The the reviewer has given.

Delete | Save and add another | Save and continue editing | SAVE

Figure 4.60: The review form with the first fieldset untitled

ACTIVITY 4.02: CUSTOMIZING THE MODEL ADMINS

In our data model, the **Contributor** class is used to store data for book contributors -- they can be authors, contributors, or editors. This activity focuses on modifying the **Contributor** class and adding a **ContributorAdmin** class to improve the user-friendliness of the admin app. At present, the **Contributor** change list defaults to a single column, **FirstNames**, based on the __str__ method created in *Chapter 2, Models and Migrations*. We will investigate some alternative ways of representing this. These steps will help you complete the activity:

1. Edit **reviews/models.py** to add additional functionality to the **Contributor** model.

2. Add an **initialled_name** method to **Contributor** that takes no arguments (like the **Book.isbn13** method).

3. The **initialled_name** method will return a string containing **Contributor.last_names** followed by a comma and the initials of the given names. For example, for a **Contributor** object with **first_names** of **Jerome David** and **last_names** of **Salinger**, **initialled_name** will return **Salinger, JD**.

4. Replace the **__str__** method for **Contributor** with one that calls **initialled_name()**.

   At this point, the **Contributors** display list will look like this:

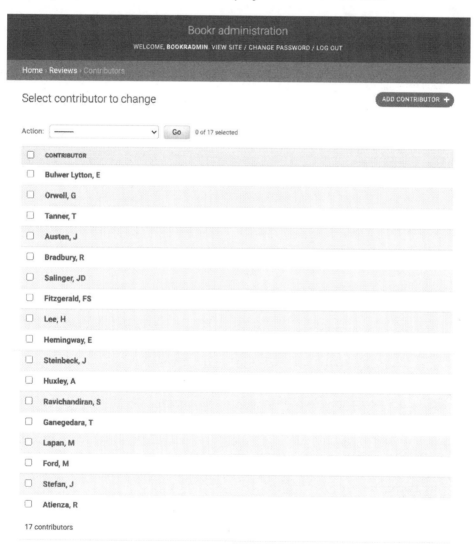

Figure 4.61: Contributors display list

5. Add a **ContributorAdmin** class in **reviews/admin.py**. It should inherit from **admin.ModelAdmin**.

6. Modify it so that on the **Contributors** change list, records are displayed with two sortable columns – **Last Names** and **First Names**.

7. Add a search bar that searches on **Last Names** and **First Names**. Modify it so that it only matches the start of **Last Names**.

8. Add a filter on **Last Names**.

By completing the activity, you should be able to see something like this:

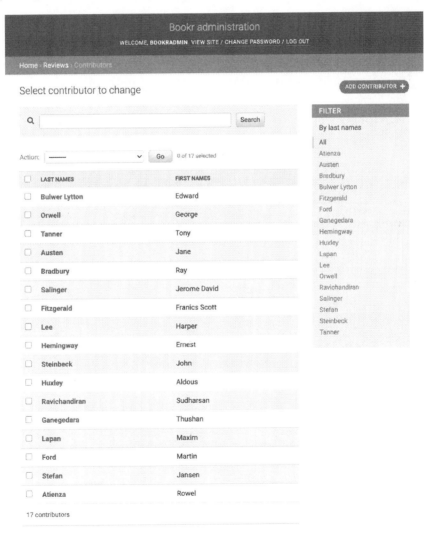

Figure 4.62: Expected output

Changes such as these can be made to improve the functionality of the admin user interface. By implementing **First Names** and **Last Names** columns as separate columns in the **Contributors** change list, we are giving the user an option to sort on either of the fields. By considering what columns are most useful in search retrieval and filter selections, we can improve the efficient retrieval of records.

> **NOTE**
>
> The solution to this activity can be found at http://packt.live/2Nh1NTJ.

SUMMARY

In this chapter, we saw how to create superusers through the Django command line and how to use them to access the admin app. After a brief tour of the admin app's basic functionality, we examined how to register our models with it to produce a CRUD interface for our data.

Then we learned how to refine this interface by modifying site-wide features. We altered how the admin app presents model data to the user by registering custom model admin classes with the admin site. This allowed us to make fine-grained changes to the representation of our models' interfaces. These modifications included customizing change list pages by adding additional columns, filters, date hierarchies, and search bars. We also modified the layout of the model admin pages by grouping and excluding fields.

This was only a very shallow dive into the functionality of the admin app. We will revisit the rich functionality of **AdminSite** and **ModelAdmin** in *Chapter 10, Advanced Django Admin and Customization*. But first, we need to learn some more intermediate features of Django. In the next chapter, we will learn how to organize and serve static content, such as CSS, JavaScript, and images, from a Django app.

5

SERVING STATIC FILES

OVERVIEW

In this chapter, you will start by learning the difference between static and dynamic responses. You will then see how the Django `staticfiles` app helps manage static files. Continuing work on the Bookr app, you will enhance it with images and CSS. You'll learn the different ways you can lay out your static files for your project and examine how Django consolidates them for production deployment. Django includes tools to reference static files in templates and you'll see how these tools help reduce the amount of work needed when deploying an application to production. After this, you'll explore the `findstatic` command, which can be used to debug issues with your static files. Later, you'll get an overview of how to write code for storing static files on a remote service. Finally, you'll look at caching web assets and how Django can help with cache invalidation.

INTRODUCTION

A web application with just plain **Hypertext Markup Language** (**HTML**) is quite limiting. We can enhance the look of web pages with **Cascading Style Sheets** (**CSS**) and images, and we can add interaction with JavaScript. We call all these kinds of files "static files." They are developed and then deployed as part of the application. We can compare these to dynamic responses, which are generated in real time when a request is made. All the views you have written generate a dynamic response by rendering a template. Note that we will not consider templates to be static files as they are not sent verbatim to a client; instead, they are rendered first and sent as part of a dynamic response.

During development, the static files are created on the developer's machine, and they must then be moved to the production web server. If you have to move to production in a short timeframe (say, a few hours), then it can be time-consuming to collect all the static assets, move them to the correct directory, and upload them to the server. When developing web applications using other frameworks or languages, you might need to manually put all of your static files into a specific directory that your web server hosts. Making changes to the URL from which static files are served might mean updating values throughout your code.

Django can manage static assets for us to make this process easier. It provides tools for serving them with its development server during development. When your application goes to production, it can also collect all your assets and copy them to a folder for a dedicated web server to host. This allows you to keep your static files segregated in a meaningful way during development and automatically bundle them for deployment.

This functionality is provided by Django's built-in `staticfiles` app. It adds several useful features for working with and serving static files:

- The `static` template tag to automatically build the static URL for an asset and include it in your HTML.

- A view (called `static`) that serves static files in development.

- Static file finders to customize where assets are found on your filesystem.

- The `collectstatic` management command, which finds all static files and moves them into a single directory for deployment.

- The `findstatic` management command, which shows which static file on disk is loaded for a particular request. This also helps to debug if a particular file is not being loaded.

In the exercises and activities in this chapter, we will be adding static files (images and CSS) to the Bookr application. Each file will be stored inside the Bookr project directory during development. We need to generate a URL for each so that the templates can reference them, and the browser can download them. Once the URL is generated, Django needs to serve these files. When we deploy the Bookr application to production, all the static files need to be found and moved to a directory where they can be served by the production web server. If there are static files that are not loading as expected, we need some method of determining what the cause is.

For the sake of simplicity, let's take a single static file as an example: `logo.png`. We will briefly introduce the role of each feature we mentioned in the previous paragraph and explain them in depth throughout the chapter:

- The **static** template tag is used to convert a filename to a URL or path that can be used in a template, for example, from **logo.png** to **/static/logo.png**.

- The **static** view receives a request to load the static file at the path **/static/logo.png**. It reads the file and sends it to the browser.

- A static file finder (or just **finder**) is used by the **static** view to locate the static file on the disk. There are different finders, but in this example, a finder is just converting from the URL path **/static/logo.png** to the path on disk **bookr/static/logo.png**.

- When deploying to production, the **collectstatic** management command is used. This will copy the **logo.png** file from the **bookr** project directory to a web server directory, such as **/var/www/bookr/static/logo.png**.

- If a static file is not working (for example, a request for it returns a **404 Not Found** response, or the wrong file is being served), then we can use the **findstatic** management command to try to determine the reason. This command takes the filename as a parameter and will output which directories were looked through and where it was able to locate that requested file.

These are the most common features that are used day to day, but there are others that we will also discuss.

STATIC FILE SERVING

In the introduction, we mentioned that Django includes a view function called **static** that serves static files. The first important point to make regarding the serving of static files is that Django is not intended to serve them in production. It is not Django's role, and in production, Django will refuse to serve static files. This is normal and intended behavior. If Django is just reading from the filesystem and sending out a file, then it has no advantage over a normal web server, which would probably be more performant at this task. Furthermore, if you serve static files with Django, you will keep the Python process busy for the duration of the request and it will be unable to serve the dynamic requests to which it is more suited.

For these reasons, the Django **static** view is designed only for use during development and will not work if your **DEBUG** setting is **False**. Since during development we only usually have one person accessing the site at a time (the developer), Django is fine to serve static files. Soon, we will discuss more how the **staticfiles** app supports production deployment. The entire production deployment process will be covered in *Chapter 17, Deployment of a Django Application (Part 1 – Server Setup)*. This chapter can be downloaded from the GitHub repository of this book, at http://packt.live/2Kx6FmR.

A URL mapping to the **static** view is automatically set up when running the Django development server, provided that your **settings.py** file meets the following conditions:

*   Has **DEBUG** set to **True**

*   Contains **'django.contrib.staticfiles'** in its **INSTALLED_APPS**

Both settings exist by default.

The URL mapping that is created is roughly equivalent to having the following map in your **urlpatterns**:

```
path(settings.STATIC_URL, django.conf.urls.static)
```

Any URL starting with **settings.STATIC_URL** (which is **/static/** by default) gets mapped to the **static** view.

> **NOTE**
>
> You can still use the **static** view without having **staticfiles** in **INSTALLED_APPS**, but you must set up an equivalent URL mapping manually.

INTRODUCTION TO STATIC FILE FINDERS

There are three times when Django needs to locate static files on disk, and for this, it uses a **static file finder**. A static file finder could be thought of like a plugin. It is a class that implements methods for converting URL paths to disks and iterates through the project directory to find static files.

The first time Django needs to locate static files on disk is when the Django **static** view receives a request to load a particular static file; it then needs to convert the path in the URL to a location on disk. For example, the URL's path is **/static/logo.png**, and it is converted to the path **bookr/static/logo.png** on the disk. As we noted in the previous section, this is only during development. On a production server, Django should not receive this request as it will be handled directly by the web server.

The second time is when using the **collectstatic** management command. This gathers up all the static files in the project directory and copies them to a single directory to be served by the production web server. **bookr/static/logo.png** will get copied to the web server root, for example, **/var/www/bookr/static/logo.png**. The static file finder contains code to locate all the static files inside your project directory.

The last time a static file finder is used is during the execution of the **findstatic** management command. This is similar to the first usage in that it accepts a static file's name (such as **logo.png**), but it outputs the full path (**bookr/static/logo.png**) to the terminal instead of loading the file content.

Django comes with some built-in finders, but you can also write your own if you want to store static files in a custom directory layout. The list of finders Django uses is defined by the **STATICFILES_FINDERS** setting in **settings. py**. In this chapter, we will cover the behavior of the default static file finders, **AppDirectoriesFinder** and **FileSystemFinder**, in the *AppDirectoriesFinder* and *FileSystemFinder* sections, respectively.

> **NOTE**
>
> If you look in **settings.py**, you won't see that **STATICFILES_
> FINDERS** setting defined by default. This is because Django will use its
> built-in default for the setting, which is defined as the list **['django.
> contrib.staticfiles.finders.FileSystemFinder',
> 'django.contrib.staticfiles.finders.
> AppDirectoriesFinder']**. If you add the **STATICFILES_
> FINDERS** setting to your **settings.py** file to include a custom finder,
> be sure to include these defaults if you're using them.

First, we will discuss static file finders and their use in the first case – responding to a request. Then we will introduce some more concepts and return to the behavior of **collectstatic** and how it uses static file finders. Later in the chapter, we will work with the **findstatic** command to see how to use it.

STATIC FILE FINDERS: USE DURING A REQUEST

When Django receives a request for a static file (remember, Django will only serve static files during development), each static file finder that has been defined will be queried until a file on disk has been found. If none of the finders can locate a file, the **static** view will return an **HTTP 404 Not Found** response.

For example, the URL of the request will be something like **/static/main.css** or **/static/reviews/ logo.png**. Each finder will be queried in turn with the path from the URL and will return a path such as **bookr/static/main.css** for the first file and **bookr/reviews/static/reviews/logo.png** for the second. Each finder will use its own logic to convert from a URL path to a filesystem path – we will discuss this logic in the upcoming *AppDirectoriesFinder* and *FileSystemFinder* sections.

APPDIRECTORIESFINDER

The **AppDirectoriesFinder** class is used to find static files inside each app directory, in a directory called **static**. The application must be listed in the **INSTALLED_APPS** setting in your **settings.py** file (we did this in *Chapter 1, Introduction to Django*). As we also mentioned in *Chapter 1, Introduction to Django*, it is good for apps to be self-contained. By letting each application have its own **static** directory, we can continue the self-contained design by also storing app-specific static files inside the app directory too.

Before we use **AppDirectoriesFinder**, we will explain a problem that can occur if multiple static files have the same name, and also how to solve this problem.

STATIC FILE NAMESPACING

In the *Static File Finders: Use during a Request* section, we discussed serving a file named **logo.png**. This would provide a logo for the **reviews** application. The filename (**logo.png**) could be quite common – you could imagine that if we added a **store** app (for purchasing books), it would also have a logo. Not to mention that third-party Django apps might also want to use a common name like **logo.png**. The problem we are about to describe could apply to any static file that has a common name, such as **styles.css** or **main.js**.

Let's consider the **reviews** and **store** examples. We can add a **static** directory in each of these apps. Then, each **static** directory would have a **logo.png** file (although it would be a different logo). The directory structure is as shown in *Figure 5.1*:

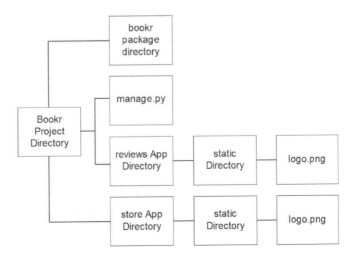

Figure 5.1: Directory layout with static directories inside app directories

The URL path that we use to download a static file is relative to the static directory. Therefore, it is unclear which **logo.png** is being referenced if we make an HTTP request for **/static/logo.png**. Django will check the **static** directory for each application in turn (in the order they are specified in the **INSTALLED_APPS** setting). The first **logo.png** it locates, it will serve. There is no way, in this directory layout, to specify which **logo.png** you want to load.

We can solve this problem by **namespacing** our static files. This is the process of using another directory inside the **static** directory, named the same as the app. The **reviews** app has a **reviews** directory inside its **static** directory, and the **store** app has a **store** directory inside its **static** directory. The respective **logo.png** files are then moved inside these subdirectories. The new directory layout is as shown in *Figure 5.2*:

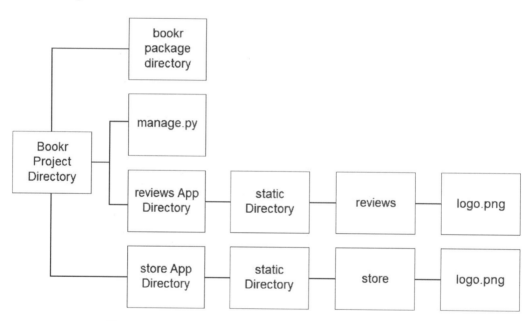

Figure 5.2: Directory layout with namespaced directories

To load a specific file, we include the namespaced directory too. For the **reviews** logo, the URL path is **/static/reviews/logo.png**, which maps to **bookr/reviews/static/review/logo.png** on disk. Similarly, for the store logo, its path is **/static/store/logo.png**, which maps to **bookr/store/static/store/logo.png**. You might have noticed that the examples path for the **logo.png** file is already namespaced in the *Static File Finders: Use during a Request* section.

> **NOTE**
>
> If you are considering writing a Django app that might be released as its own standalone plugin, you could use an even more explicit sub-directory name. For example, choose one that contains the entire dotted project path: *bookr/reviews/static/bookr.reviews*. In most cases, though, it is fine for the sub-directory name to be unique to just your project.

Now that we have introduced **AppDirectoriesFinder** and static file namespacing, we can use them to serve our first static file. In the first exercise of the chapter, we will create a new Django project for a basic business site. We will then serve a logo file from an app called **landing** that we will create in this project. The **AppDirectoriesFinder** class is used to find static files inside each app directory, in a directory called **static**. The application must be listed in the **INSTALLED_APPS** setting in your **settings.py** file. As we have mentioned in *Chapter 1, Introduction to Django*, it is good for apps to be self-contained. By letting each application have its own **static** directory, we can continue the self-contained design by also storing app-specific static files inside the app directory too.

The easiest way to serve a static file is from an app directory. This is because we do not need to make any settings changes. Instead, we just need to create the files in the correct directory, and they will be served using the default Django configuration.

> **THE BUSINESS SITE PROJECT**
>
> For the exercises in this chapter, we'll create a new Django project and use it to demonstrate the static file concepts. The project will be a basic business site with a simple landing page that has a logo. The project will have one app, calling **landing**.
>
> You can refer to *Exercise 1.01, Creating a Project and App, and Starting the dev server* from *Chapter 1, Introduction to Django*, to refresh your memory on creating a Django project.

EXERCISE 5.01: SERVING A FILE FROM AN APP DIRECTORY

In this exercise, you will add a logo file for the **landing** app. This will be done by putting a **logo.png** file in a **static** directory inside the **landing** app directory. After this is done, you can test that the static file is being served correctly and confirm the URL that will serve it:

1. Start by creating the new Django project. You can reuse the **bookr** virtual environment that already has Django installed. Open a new terminal and activate the virtual environment (refer to the *Preface* for instructions on how to create and activate a virtual environment). Then, run the **django-admin** command in the terminal (or command shell) to start a Django project named **business_ site**. To do this, run this command:

```
django-admin startproject business_site
```

    There will not be any output. This command will scaffold the Django project in a new directory named **business_site**.

2. Create a new Django app in this project by using the **startapp** management command. The app should be called *landing*. To do this, **cd** into the **business_ site** directory, then run this:

```
python3 manage.py startapp landing
```

    Note that there will not be any output again. The command will create the **landing** app directory inside the **business_site** directory.

> **NOTE**
>
> Remember that on Windows the command is **python manage.py startapp landing**.

3. Launch PyCharm, then open the **business_site** directory. If you already have a project open, you can do this by choosing **File** -> **Open**; otherwise, just click **Open** in the **Welcome to PyCharm** window. Navigate to the **business_ site** directory, select it, then click **Open**. The **business_site** project window should be shown like *Figure 5.3*:

> **NOTE**
>
> For detailed instructions on how to set up and configure PyCharm to work with your Django project, refer to *Exercise 1.02, Project Setup in PyCharm*, in *Chapter 1, Introduction to Django*.

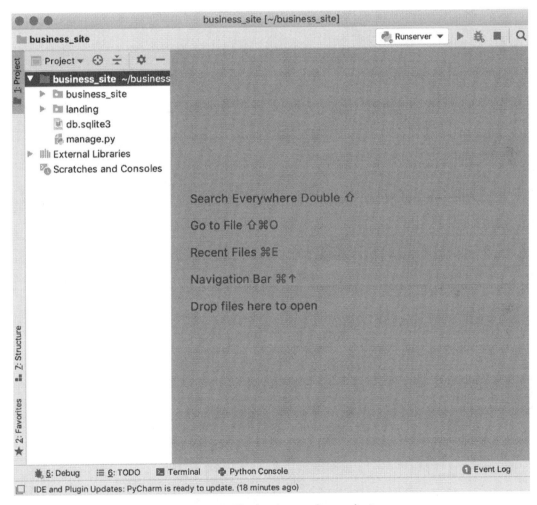

Figure 5.3: The business_site project

4. Create a new run configuration to execute **manage.py runserver** for the project. You can reuse the **bookr** virtual environment again. The **Run/Debug Configurations** window should look like *Figure 5.4*. when you are done:

> **NOTE**
>
> Note that if you are not sure how to configure these settings in PyCharm, refer to *Exercise 1.02*, *Project Setup in PyCharm*, from *Chapter 1*, *Introduction to Django*.

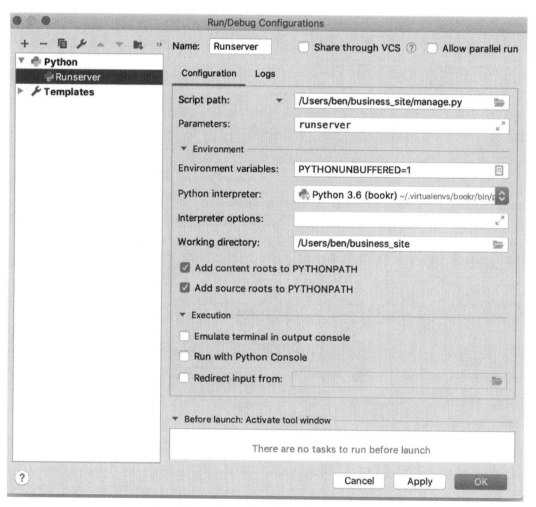

Figure 5.4: Run/Debug Configurations for Runserver

You can test that the configuration is set up correctly by clicking the **Run** button, then visiting **http://127.0.0.1:8000/** in your browser. You should see the Django welcome screen. If the debug server fails to start or you see the Bookr main page, then you probably still have the Bookr project running. Try stopping the Bookr **runserver** process (press *Ctrl + C* in the terminal that is running it) and then starting the new one you just set up.

5. Open **settings.py** in the **business_site** directory and add **'landing'** to the **INSTALLED_APPS** setting. Remember we learned how to do this in *step 1* of *Exercise 1.05, Creating a Templates Directory and Base Template*, in *Chapter 1, Introduction to Django.*

6. In PyCharm, right-click the **landing** directory in the **Project** pane and select **New** -> **Directory**.

7. Enter the name **static** and click **OK**:

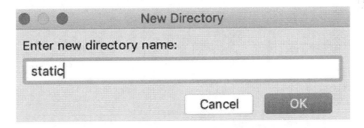

Figure 5.5: Naming the directory static

8. Right-click the **static** directory you just created and select **New** -> **Directory** again.

9. Enter the name **landing** and click **OK**. This is to implement namespacing of the static files directory as we discussed earlier:

Figure 5.6: Naming the new directory landing, to implement namespacing

10. Download **logo.png** from https://packt.live/2KM6kfT and move it into the **landing/static/landing** directory.

11. Start the Django dev server, if it is not already running, then navigate to `http://127.0.0.1:8000/static/landing/logo.png`. You should see the image being served in your browser:

Figure 5.7: Image served by Django

If you see the image as in *Figure 5.7*, you have set up static file serving correctly. Now let us look at how to automatically insert this URL into your HTML code.

GENERATING STATIC URLS WITH THE STATIC TEMPLATE TAG

In *Exercise 5.01*, *Serving a File from an App Directory*, you set up an image file to be served by Django. You saw that the URL of the image was `http://127.0.0.1:8000/static/landing/logo.png`, which you could use inside an HTML template. For example, to display the image with an **img** tag, you could use this code in your template:

```
<img src="http://127.0.0.1:8000/static/landing/logo.png">
```

Or, since Django is also serving the media and has the same host as the dynamic template response, you can simplify this by just including the path, as follows:

```
<img src="/static/landing/logo.png">
```

Both addresses (URLs and paths) have been hardcoded into the template; that is, we include the full path to the static file and make assumptions about where the file is being hosted. This works fine with the Django dev server or if you host your static files and Django website on the same domain. For more performance as your site becomes more popular, you might consider serving static files from their own domain or **Content Delivery Network (CDN)**.

> **NOTE**
>
> A **CDN** is a service that can host parts or all of your website for you. They provide several web servers and can seamlessly speed up the loading of your website. For example, they might serve files to a user from the server that is geographically closest to them. There are several CDN providers, and depending on how they are set up, they might require you to specify a certain domain from which to serve your static files.

Take, for instance, a common separation approach: using a different domain for static file serving. You host your main website at **https://www.example.com** but want to serve static files from **https://static.example.com**. During development, we could use just the path to the logo file as in the example we just saw. But when we deploy to the production server, our URLs would need to change to include the domain, like so:

```
<img src="https://static.example.com/landing/logo.png">
```

Since all the links are hardcoded, this would need to be done for every URL throughout our templates, every time we deploy to production. Once they were changed, though, the URL would no longer work in the Django dev server. Luckily, Django provides a solution to this problem.

The **staticfiles** app provides a template tag, **static**, to dynamically generate the URL to a static file inside a template. Since the URLs are all being dynamically generated, we can change the URL for all of them by changing just one setting (**STATIC_URL** in **settings.py** – more on this soon). Furthermore, later we will introduce a method of invalidating browser caches for static files that relies on the use of the **static** template tag.

The **static** tag is very simple: it takes a single argument, which is the project-relative path to a static asset. It will then output this path prepended with the **STATIC_URL** setting. It must first be loaded into the template with the **{% load static %}** template tag.

Django has a set of default template tags and filters (or tag sets) that it automatically makes available to every template. Django (and third-party libraries) also provides tag sets that are not automatically loaded. In these cases, we need to load these extra template tags and filters into a template before we can use them. This is done with the use of the **load** template tag, which should come near the start of a template (although it must be after the **extends** template tag, if one is used). The **load** template tag takes one or more packages/libraries to load, for example:

```
{% load package_one package_two package_three %}
```

This would load the template tag and filters set provided by the (made-up) **package_one**, **package_two**, and **package_three** packages.

The **load** template tag must be used in the actual template that requires the loaded package. In other words, if your template extends another template and that base template has loaded a certain package, your dependent template does not automatically have access to that package. Your template must still **load** the package to access the new tag set. The **static** template tag is not part of the default set, which is why we need to load it.

Then, it can be used to interpolate anywhere inside the template file. For example, by default, Django uses **/static/** as **STATIC_URL**. If we wanted to generate the static URL for our **logo.png** file, we would use the tag in a template like this:

```
{% static landing/logo.png' %}
```

The output inside the template would be this:

```
/static/landing/logo.png
```

This would be made clearer with an example, so let's look at how the **static** tag could be used to generate a URL for a number of different assets.

We can include the logo as an image on the page with an **img** tag, as follows:

```
<img src="{% static 'landing/logo.png' %}">
```

This is rendered in the template as follows:

```
<img src="/static/landing/logo.png">
```

Or we could use the **static** tag to generate the URL for a linked CSS file, as follows:

```
<link href="{% static 'path/to/file.css' %}"
            rel="stylesheet">
```

This will be rendered as this:

```
<link href="/static/path/to/file.css"
            rel="stylesheet">
```

It can be used in a **script** tag to include a JavaScript file, using the following line of code:

```
<script src="{% static 'path/to/file.js' %}">
    </script>
```

This is rendered as this:

```
<script src="/static/path/to/file.js"></script>
```

We can even use it to generate a link to a static file for download:

```
<a href="{% static 'path/to/document.pdf' %}">
    Download PDF</a>
```

> **NOTE**
>
> Note that this won't generate the actual PDF content; it will just create a link to an already-existing file.

This is rendered as follows:

```
<a href="/static/path/to/document.pdf">
    Download PDF</a>
```

Referring to these examples, we can now demonstrate the advantage of using the **static** tag instead of hardcoding. When we are ready to deploy to production, we can just change the **STATIC_URL** value in **settings.py**. None of the values in the templates need to be changed.

For example, we can change **STATIC_URL** to **https://static.example.com/**, and then when the page next gets rendered, the examples we've seen will automatically update as follows.

The following line shows this for the image:

```
<img src="https://static.example.com/landing/logo.png">
```

The following is for the CSS link:

```
<link href=
    "https://static.example.com/path/to/files.css"
    rel="stylesheet">
```

For the script, it's as follows:

```
<script src="
    https://static.example.com/path/to/file.js">
    </script>
```

And finally, the following is for the link:

```
<a href="
    https://static.example.com/path/to/document.pdf">
    Download PDF</a>
```

Note that in all these examples, a literal string is being passed as an argument (it is quoted). You can also use a variable as an argument. For example, say you were rendering a template with a context such as in this example code:

```
def view_function(request):
    context = {"image_file": "logofile.png"}
    return render(request, "example.html", context)
```

We are rendering the **example.html** template with an **image_file** variable. This variable has the value **logo.png**.

You would pass this variable to the **static** tag without quotes:

```
<img src="{% static image_file %}">
```

It would render like this (assuming we changed **STATIC_URL** back to **/static/**):

```
<img src="/static/logo.png">
```

The template tag can also be used with the **as [variable]** suffix to assign the result to a variable for use later in the template. This can be useful if the static file lookup takes a long time and you want to refer to the same static file multiple times (like when including an image in multiple places).

The first time you refer to the static URL, give it a variable name to assign to. In this case, we are creating the **logo_path** variable:

```
<img src="{% static 'logo.png' as logo_path %}">
```

This renders the same as the examples we've seen before:

```
<img src="/static/logo.png">
```

However, we can then use the assigned variable (**logo_path**) again later in the template:

```
<img src="{{ logo_path }}">
```

That renders the same again:

```
<img src="/static/logo.png">
```

This variable is now just a normal context variable in the template scope and can be used anywhere in the template. Be careful, though, as you might override a variable that has already been defined – although this a general warning when using any of the template tags that assign variables (for example, **{% with %}**).

In the next exercise, we will put the **static** template into practice to add the Bookr reviews logo to the Bookr site.

EXERCISE 5.02: USING THE STATIC TEMPLATE TAG

In *Exercise 5.01*, *Serving a File from an App Directory*, you tested serving the **logo.png** file from the static directory. In this exercise, you will continue with the business site project and create an **index.html** file as the template for our landing page. Then you'll include the logo inside this page, using the {% **static** %} template tag:

1. In PyCharm (make sure you're in the **business_site** project), right-click the **business_site** project directory and create a new folder called **templates**. Right-click this directory and select **New -> HTML File**. Select **HTML 5 file** and name it **index.html**:

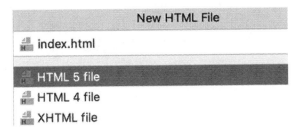

Figure 5.8: new index.html

2. **index.html** will open. First, load the **static** tag library to make the **static** tag available in the template. Do this with the **load** template tag. On the second line of the file (just after the **<!DOCTYPE html>**), add this line to load the static library:

```
{% load static %}
```

3. You can also make the template a bit nicer with some extra content. Enter the text **Business Site** inside the **<title>** tags:

```
<title>Business Site</title>
```

Then, inside the body, add an **<h1>** element with the text **Welcome to my Business Site**:

```
<h1>Welcome to my Business Site</h1>
```

4. Underneath the heading text, use the **{% static %}** template tag to set the source of **<img>**. You will use it to refer to the logo from *Exercise 5.01, Serving a File from an App Directory*:

```
<img src="{% static 'landing/logo.png' %}">
```

5. Finally, to flesh out the site a bit, add a **<p>** element under **<img>**. Give it some text about the business:

```
<p>Welcome to the site for my Business.
    For all your Business needs!</p>
```

Although the extra text and title are not too important, they give an idea of how to use the **{% static %}** template tag around the rest of the content. Save the file. It should look like this once complete: http://packt.live/37RUVnE.

6. Next, set up a URL to use to render the template. You will also use the built-in **TemplateView** to render the template without having to create a view. Open **urls.py** in the **business_site** package directory. At the start of the file, import **TemplateView** as follows:

```
from django.views.generic import TemplateView
```

You can also remove this Django admin import line since we're not using it in this project:

```
from django.contrib import admin
```

7. Add a URL map from **/** to a **TemplateView**. The **as_view** method of **TemplateView** takes **template_name** as an argument, which is used in the same way as a path that you might pass to the **render** function. Your **urlpatterns** should look like this:

```
urlpatterns = [path('', TemplateView.as_view\
                    (template_name='index.html')),]
```

Save the **urls.py** file. Once complete, it should look like this: http://packt.live/2KLTrlY.

8. Since we're not using the **landing** app template directory to store this template, you need to tell Django to use the **templates** directory you created in *step 1*. Do this by adding the directory to the **TEMPLATES['DIRS']** list in **settings.py**.

Open **settings.py** in the **business_site** directory. Scroll down until you find the **TEMPLATES** setting. It will look like this:

```
TEMPLATES = \
[{'BACKEND': 'django.template.backends.django.DjangoTemplates',\
  'DIRS': [],\
  'APP_DIRS': True,\
  'OPTIONS': {'context_processors': \
              ['django.template.context_processors.debug',\
               'django.template.context_processors.request',\
               'django.contrib.auth.context_processors.auth',\
               'django.contrib.messages.context_processors\
               .messages',\
    ],\
  },\
},]
```

Add **os.path.join(BASE_DIR, 'templates')** into the **DIRS** setting, so the **TEMPLATES** setting looks like this:

```
TEMPLATES = \
[{'BACKEND': 'django.template.backends.django.DjangoTemplates',\
  'DIRS': [os.path.join(BASE_DIR, 'templates')],\
  'APP_DIRS': True,\
  'OPTIONS': {'context_processors': \
              ['django.template.context_processors.debug',\
               'django.template.context_processors.request',\
```

```
                      'django.contrib.auth.context_processors.auth',\
                      'django.contrib.messages.context_processors\
                      .messages',\
            ],\
          },\
       },]
```

Depending on the version of Django you have, it might not be importing the **os** module in **settings.py**. To fix this, at the top of the **settings.py** file, just add this line:

```
import os
```

Save and close **settings.py**. It should look like this: http://packt.live/3pz4rlo.

9. Start the Django dev server, if it's not already running. Navigate to **http://127.0.0.1:8000/** in your browser. You should see your new landing page as in *Figure 5.9*:

Welcome to my Business Site

Welcome to the site for my Business. For all your Business needs!

Figure 5.9: The site with the logo

In this exercise, we added a base template for **landing** and loaded the static library into the template. Once the static library was loaded, we were able to use the **static** template tag to load an image. We then were able to see our business logo rendered in the browser.

All of the static file loading has so far used **AppDirectoriesFinder**, because it required no extra configuration to use it. In the next section, we will look at **FileSystemFinder**, which is more flexible but requires a small amount of configuration to use it.

FILESYSTEMFINDER

We've learned about **AppDirectoriesFinder**, which loads static files inside Django app directories. However, well-designed apps should be self-contained and therefore should only contain static files that they themselves rely on. If we have other static files that are used throughout the website or across different apps, we should store them outside the app directory.

> **NOTE**
>
> As a general rule, your CSS is probably consistent throughout your site and could be kept in a global directory. Some images and JavaScript code could be specific to apps, so these would be stored in the static directory for that application. This is just general advice, though: you can store static files anywhere that makes the most sense for your project.

In our business site application, we will be storing a CSS file in a site static directory, as it will be used not only in the **landing** app but throughout the site as we add more apps.

Django provides support for serving static files from arbitrary directories using its **FileSystemFinder** static file finder. The directories can be anywhere on the disk. Usually, you will have a **static** directory inside your project directory, but if your company has a global static directory that is used in many different projects (including non-Django web applications), then you could use this as well.

FileSystemFinder uses the **STATICFILES_DIRS** setting in the **settings. py** file to determine which directories to search for static files in. This is not present when the project is created and must be set by the developer. We will add it in the next exercise. There are two options for building this list:

- Setting a list of directories
- Setting a list of tuples in the form **(prefix, directory)**

The second use case will be easier to understand once we have covered some more of the fundamentals, so we will return to it after explaining and demonstrating the first case. It is covered after *Exercise 5.04, Collecting Static Files for Production*, in the *STATICFILES_DIRS Prefixed Mode* section. For now, we will just explain the first use case, which is just a list of one or more directories.

In **business_site**, we will add a **static** directory inside the project directory (that is, in the same directory that contains the **landing** app and the **manage. py** file). We can use the **BASE_DIR** setting when building the list to assign to **STATICFILES_DIRS**:

```
STATICFILES_DIRS = [os.path.join(BASE_DIR, 'static')]
```

We also mentioned earlier in this section that you might want to set multiple directory paths in this list, for example, if you had some company-wide static data shared by multiple web projects. Simply add extra directories to the **STATICFILES_DIRS** list:

```
STATICFILES_DIRS = [os.path.join(BASE_DIR, 'static'), \
                    '/Users/username/projects/company-static/']
```

Each of these directories would be checked in order to find a matching file. If a file existed in both directories, the first one found would be served. For example, if the **static/main.css** (inside the **business_site** project directory) and **/Users/ username/projects/company-static/bar/main.css** files both existed, a request for **/static/main.css** would serve the **business_site** project's **main.css** as it is first in the list. Keep this in mind when deciding the order in which you add directories to **STATICFILES_DIRS**; you may choose to prioritize your project static files over the global ones or vice versa.

In our business site (and later with Bookr), we will only use one **static** directory in this list, so we won't have to worry about this problem.

In the next exercise, we will add a **static** directory with a CSS file inside. Then we will configure the **STATICFILES_DIRS** setting to serve from the **static** directory.

EXERCISE 5.03: SERVING FROM A PROJECT STATIC DIRECTORY

We have already shown an example of serving an application-specific image file in *Exercise 5.01, Serving a File from an App Directory*. Now we want to serve a CSS file that is to be used throughout our project to set styles, so we will serve this from a static directory right inside the project folder.

In this exercise, you'll set up your project to serve static files from a specific directory, and then use the **{% static %}** template tag again to include it in the template. This will be done using the **business_site** example project:

1. Open the **business_site** project in In PyCharm, if it's not already open. Then, right-click the **business_site** project directory (the top-level **business_site** directory, not the **business_site** package directory) and select **New -> Directory**.

2. In the **New Directory** dialog, enter **static** and then click **OK**.

3. Right-click the **static** directory you just created and select **New -> File**.

4. In the **Name New File** dialog, enter **main.css** and click **OK**.

5. The blank **main.css** file should open automatically. Enter a couple of simple CSS rules, to center the text, and set a font and background color. Enter this text into the **main.css** file:

```
body {
    font-family: Arial, sans-serif;
    text-align: center;
    background-color: #f0f0f0;
}
```

You can now save and class **main.css**. You can take a look at the complete file for reference: http://packt.live/38H8a9N.

6. Open **business_site/settings.py**. Here, set a list of directories to the **STATICFILES_DIRS** settings. In this case, the list will have just one item. Define a new **STATICFILES_DIRS** variable at the bottom of **settings.py**, using this code:

```
STATICFILES_DIRS = [os.path.join(BASE_DIR, 'static')]
```

In the **settings.py** file, **BASE_DIR** is a variable that contains the path to the project directory. You can build the full path to the **static** directory you created in *step 2* by joining **static** to **BASE_DIR**. You then put this inside a list. The complete **settings.py** file should look like this: http://packt.live/3hnQQKW.

7. Start the Django dev server if it is not running. You can verify that the settings are correct by checking whether you can load the **main.css** file. Note that this is not namespaced so the URL is **http://127.0.0.1:8000/static/main.css**. Open this URL in your browser and check that the content matches what you just entered and saved:

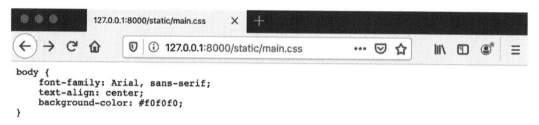

Figure 5.10: CSS served by Django

If the file does not load, check your **STATICFILES_DIRS** settings. You may need to restart the Django dev server if it was running while you made changes to **settings.py**.

8. You now need to include **main.css** in your index template. Open **index.html** in the **templates** folder. Before the closing **</head>** tag, add this **<link>** tag to load the CSS:

```
<link rel="stylesheet" href="{% static 'main.css' %}">
```

This links in the **main.css** file, using the **{% static %}** template tag. As mentioned earlier, since **main.css** is not namespaced, you can just include its name. Save the file. It should look like this: http://packt.live/392aedP.

9. Load **http://127.0.0.1:8000/** in your browser and you should see the background color, fonts, and alignment all change:

Figure 5.11: CSS applied with custom fonts visible

Your business landing page should look like *Figure 5.11*. Since you included the CSS in the **base.html** template, it will be available in all templates that extend this template (although none do at the moment, it's good planning for the future).

In this exercise, we put some CSS rules into their own file and served them using Django's **FileSystemFinder**. This was accomplished by creating a **static** directory inside the **business_site** project directory and specifying it in the Django settings (the **settings.py** file) using the **STATICFILES_DIRS** setting. We linked in the **main.css** file using the **static** template tag into the **base.html** template. We loaded the main page in our browser and saw that the font and color changes applied.

We've now covered how static file finders are used during a request (to load a specific static file when given a URL). We'll now look at their other use case: finding and copying static files for production deployment, when running the **collectstatic** management command.

STATIC FILE FINDERS: USE DURING COLLECTSTATIC

Once we have finished working on our static files, they need to be moved into a specific directory that can be served by our production web server. We can then deploy our website by copying our Django code and static files to our production web server. In the case of **business_site**, we will want to move **logo.png** and **main.css** (along with other static files that Django itself includes) into a single directory that can be copied to the production web server. This is the role of the **collectstatic** management command.

We have already discussed how Django uses static file finders during request handling. Now, we will cover the other use case: collecting static files for deployment. Upon running the **collectstatic** management command, Django uses each finder to list static files on the disk. Every static file that is found is then copied into the **STATIC_ROOT** directory (also defined in **settings.py**). This is a little bit like the reverse of handling a request. Instead of getting a URL path and mapping to a filesystem path, the filesystem path is being copied to a location that is predictable by the frontend web server. This allows the frontend web server to handle a request for a static file independently of Django.

> **NOTE**
>
> A frontend web server is designed to route requests to applications (like Django) or read static files from disk. It can handle requests faster but is not able to generate dynamic content in the same way as something like Django. Frontend web servers include software such as Apache HTTPD, Nginx, and lighttpd.

For some specific examples of how **collectstatic** works, we'll use the two files from *Exercise 5.01, Serving a File from an App Directory*, and *Exercise 5.03, Serving from a Project Status Directory*, respectively: **landing/static/landing/logo.png** and **static/main.css**.

Assume that **STATIC_ROOT** is set to a directory being served by a normal web server – this would be something like **/var/www/business_site/static**. The destination for these files would be **/var/www/business_site/static/reviews/logo.png** and **/var/www/business_site/static/main.css**, respectively.

Now when a request for a static file comes in, the web server will easily be able to serve it because the paths are mapped consistently:

- **/static/main.css** is served from the **/var/www/business_site/ static/main.css** file.

- **/static/reviews/logo.png** is served from the **/var/www/business_ site/static/reviews/logo.png** file.

This means the web server root is **/var/www/business_site/** and static paths are just loaded directory from disk in the usual manner that a web server would load files.

We have demonstrated how Django locates static files during development and can serve them itself. In production, we need the frontend web server to be able to serve static files without involving Django, for both safety and speed.

Without having run **collectstatic**, a web server would not be able to map a URL back to a path. For example, it would not know that **main.css** must be loaded from the project static directory while **logo.png** is to be loaded from the **landing** app directory – it has no concept of the Django directory layout.

You might be tempted to serve files directly from the Django project directory by setting your web server root to this directory – do not do this. There is a security risk in sharing your entire Django project directory as it would make it possible to download our **settings.py** or other sensitive files. Running **collectstatic** will copy the files to a directory that can be moved outside the Django project directory to the web server root for security.

So far, we have talked about using Django to copy static files directly to the web server root. You could also have Django copy them to an intermediary directory and have your deployment process move to a CDN or another server afterward. We will not go into detail on specific deployment processes; how you choose to copy static files to the web server will depend on yours or your company's existing setup (for example, a continuous delivery pipeline).

> **NOTE**
>
> The **collectstatic** command does not take into consideration the use of **static** template tags. It will collect all the static files inside **static** directories, even those that your project does not include inside a template.

In the next exercise, we will see the **collectstatic** command in action. We will use it to copy all the **business_site** static files that we have so far into a temporary directory.

EXERCISE 5.04: COLLECTING STATIC FILES FOR PRODUCTION

While we won't be covering deployment to a web server in this chapter, we can still use the **collectstatic** management command and see its result. In this exercise, we will create a temporary holding location for the static files to be copied into. This directory will be called **static_production_test** and will be located inside the **business_site** project directory. As part of the deployment process, you could copy this directory to your production web server. However, since we won't be setting up a web server until *Chapter 17, Deployment of a Django Application (Part 1 – Server Setup)*, we will just examine its contents to understand how files are copied and organized:

1. In PyCharm, create a temporary directory to put the collected files in. Right-click the **business_site** project directory (this is the top-level folder, not the **business_site** module) and select **New -> Directory**.

2. In the **New Directory** dialog, enter the name **static_production_test** and click **OK**.

3. Open **settings.py** and at the bottom of the file, define a new setting for **STATIC_ROOT**. Set it to the path of the directory you just created:

```
STATIC_ROOT = os.path.join(BASE_DIR, 'static_production_test')
```

This will join **static_dir** to **BASE_DIR** (the business site project path) to generate the full path. Save the **settings.py** file. It should look like this: http://packt.live/2Jq59Cc.

4. In a terminal, run the **collectstatic manage** command:

```
python3 manage.py collectstatic
```

You should see output similar to the following:

```
132 static files copied to \
   '/Users/ben/business_site/static_production_test'.
```

This might seem like a lot if you were expecting it to copy just two files but remember that it will copy all the files for all installed apps. In this case, as you have the Django admin app installed, most of the 132 files are to support that.

5. Let us look through the **static_production_test** directory to see what has been created. An expanded view of this directory (from the PyCharm project page) is shown in *Figure 5.12*, for reference. Yours should be similar.

Figure 5.12: Destination directory of the collectstatic command

You should notice three items inside:

The admin directory: This contains files from the Django admin app. If you look inside this, you'll see it has been organized into subfolders: **css**, **fonts**, **img**, and **js**.

The landing directory: This is the **static** directory from your landing app. Inside is the **logo.png** file. This directory has been created to match the namespacing of the directory that we created.

The main.css file: This is from your project **static** directory. Since you didn't place it inside a namespacing directory, this has been placed directly inside **STATIC_ROOT**.

If you want, you can open up any of these files and verify that their content matches the files you have just been working on – they should do, as they are simply copies of the original files.

In this exercise, we collected all the static files from **business_site** (including the **admin** static files that Django includes). They were copied into the directory defined by the **STATIC_ROOT** setting (**static_production_test** inside the **business_site** project directory). We saw that **main.css** was directly inside this folder but other static files were namespaced inside their app directories (**admin** and **reviews**). This folder could have been copied to a production web server to deploy our project.

STATICFILES_DIRS PREFIXED MODE

As mentioned earlier, the **STATICFILES_DIRS** setting also accepts items as tuples in the form **(prefix, directory)**. These modes of operation are not mutually exclusive, **STATICFILES_DIRS** may contain both non-prefixed (string) or prefixed (tuple) items. Essentially, this allows you to map a certain URL prefix to a directory. In Bookr, we do not have enough static assets to warrant setting this up, but it can be useful if you want to organize your static assets differently. For example, you can keep all your images in a certain directory, and all your CSS in another directory. You might need to do this if you use a third-party CSS generation tool such as Node.js with **LESS**.

> **NOTE**
>
> LESS is a CSS pre-processor that uses Node.js. It allows you to write CSS using variables and other programming-like concepts that don't exist natively. Node.js will then compile this to CSS. A more in-depth explanation is outside the scope of this book – suffice to say that if you use it (or a similar tool), then you might want to serve directly from the directory to which it saves its compiled output.

The easiest way to explain how prefixed mode works is with a short example. This will expand on the **STATICFILES_DIRS** setting created in *Exercise 5.03, Serving from a Project Static Directory*. In this example, two prefixed directories are added to this setting, one for serving images and one for serving CSS:

```
STATICFILES_DIRS = [os.path.join(BASE_DIR, 'static'),\
                    ('images', os.path.join\
                          (BASE_DIR, 'static_images')),\
                    ('css', os.path.join(BASE_DIR, 'static_css'))]
```

As well as the **static** directory that was already being served with no prefix, we have added the serving of the **static_images** directory inside the **business_site** project directory. This has the prefix **images**. We have also added the serving of the **static_css** directory inside the Bookr project directory, with the prefix **css**.

Then we can serve three files, **main.js**, **main.css**, and **main.jpg**, from the **static**, **static_css**, and **static_images** directories, respectively. The directory layout would be as shown in *Figure 5.13*:

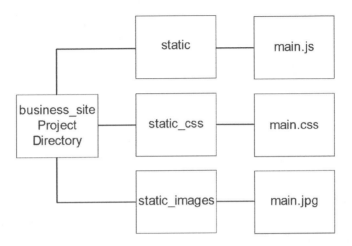

Figure 5.13: Directories layout for use with prefixed URLs

In terms of accessing these through URLs, the mapping is as shown in *Figure 5.14*:

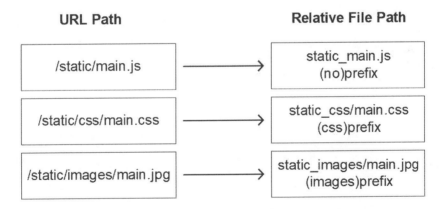

Figure 5.14: Mappings of URLs to files, based on the prefix

Django routes any static URL with a prefix to the directory that matches that prefix.

When using the **static** template tag, use the prefix and filename, not the directory name. For example:

```
{% static 'images/main.jpg' %}
```

When the static files are gathered using the **collectstatic** command, they are moved into a directory with the prefix name, inside **STATIC_ROOT**. The source paths and the target paths inside the **STATIC_ROOT** directory are shown in *Figure 5.15*:

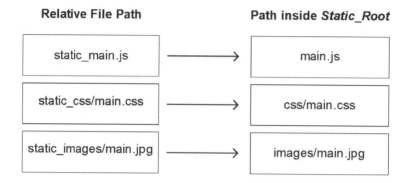

Figure 5.15: Mappings of paths in project directories to paths in STATIC_ROOT

Django creates the prefix directories inside **STATIC_ROOT**. Because of this, the paths can be kept consistent even when using a web server and not routing the URL lookup through Django.

THE FINDSTATIC COMMAND

The **staticfiles** application also provides one more management command: **findstatic**. This command allows you to enter the relative path to a static file (the same as what would be used inside a **static** template tag) and Django will tell you where that file was located. It can also be used in a verbose mode to output the directories it is searching through.

> **NOTE**
>
> You may not be familiar with the concept of verbosity or verbose mode. Having a higher verbosity (or simply turning on verbose mode) will cause a command to generate more output. Many command-line applications can be executed with more or less verbosity. This can be helpful when trying to debug the programs you are using. To see an example of the verbose mode in action, you can try running the Python shell in verbose mode. Enter **python -v** (instead of just **python**) and hit **Enter**. Python will start in verbose mode and print out the path of every file it imports.

This command is mostly useful for debugging/troubleshooting purposes. If the wrong file is loading, or a particular file cannot be found, you can use this command to try to find out why. The command will display which file on disk is being loaded for a specific path, or let you know that the file cannot be found and what directories were searched.

This can help solve issues where multiple files have the same name, and the precedence is not what you expect. See the *FileSystemFinder* section for a note about precedence in the **STATICFILES_DIRS** setting. You might also see that Django is not searching in a directory you expect for the file, in which case the static directory might need to be added to the **STATICFILES_DIRS** setting.

In the next exercise, you will execute the **findstatic** management command, so you are familiar with what some of the output is for good (file found correctly) and bad (file missing) scenarios.

EXERCISE 5.05: FINDING FILES USING FINDSTATIC

You will now run the **findstatic** command with a variety of options and understand what its output means. First, we will use it to find a file that exists and see that it displays the path to the file. Then, we will try to find a file that does not exist and check the error that is output. We will then repeat this process with multiple levels of verbosity and different ways of interacting with the command. While this exercise will not make changes to or progress the Bookr project, it is good to be familiar with the command in case you need to use it when working on your own Django applications:

1. Open a terminal and navigate to the **business_site** project directory.

2. Execute the **findstatic** command with no options. It will output some help explaining how it is used:

```
python3 manage.py findstatic
```

The help output is displayed:

```
usage: manage.py findstatic
       [-h] [--first] [--version] [-v {0,1,2,3}]
       [--settings SETTINGS] [--pythonpath PYTHONPATH]
       [--traceback] [--no-color] [--force-color]
       [--skip-checks]
       staticfile [staticfile ...]

manage.py findstatic: error: Enter at least one label.
```

3. You can find one or more files at a time; let's start with the one that we know exists, **main.css**:

```
python3 manage.py findstatic main.css
```

The command outputs the path at which **main.css** was found:

```
Found 'main.css' here:
   /Users/ben/business_site/static/main.css
```

Your full path will be different (unless you are also called Ben), but you can see that when Django locates **main.css** in a request it will load the **main.css** file from the project **static** directory.

This can be useful if a third-party application you have installed has not namespaced its static files correctly and is conflicting with one of your files.

4. Let's try finding a file that does not exist, **logo.png**:

```
python3 manage.py findstatic logo.png
```

Django displays an error saying that the file could not be found:

```
No matching file found for 'logo.png'.
```

Django is unable to locate this file because we have namespaced it – we must include the full relative path, the same as we have used in the **static** template tag.

5. Try finding **logo.png** again, but this time using the full path:

```
python3 manage.py findstatic landing/logo.png
```

Django can find the file now:

```
Found 'landing/logo.png' here:
   /Users/ben/business_site/landing/static/landing/logo.png
```

6. Finding multiple files at once is done by adding each file as an argument:

```
python3 manage.py findstatic landing/logo.png missing-file.js main.css
```

The location status for each file is shown:

```
No matching file found for 'missing-file.js'.
Found 'landing/logo.png' here:
   /Users/ben/business_site/landing/static/landing/logo.png
Found 'main.css' here:
   /Users/ben/business_site/static/main.css
```

7. The command can be executed with a verbosity of **0**, **1**, or **2**. By default, it executes at verbosity **1**. To set the verbosity, use the `--verbosity` or `-v` flag. Decrease the verbosity to **0** to only output the paths it locates without any extra information. No errors are displayed for missing paths:

```
python3 manage.py findstatic -v0 landing/logo.png missing-file.js main.
css
```

The output shows only found paths – notice no error is shown for the missing file, **missing-file.js**:

```
/Users/ben/business_site/landing/static/landing/logo.png
/Users/ben/business_site/static/main.css
```

This level of verbosity can be useful if you are piping the output to another file or command.

8. To get more information about which directories Django is searching in for the file you have requested, increase the verbosity to **2**:

```
python3 manage.py findstatic -v2 landing/logo.png missing-file.js main.
css
```

The output contains much more information, including the directories that have been searched for the requested file. You can see that as the **admin** application is installed, Django is also searching in the Django admin application directory for static files:

```
(bookr) → business_site python3 manage.py findstatic -v2 landing/logo.png missing-file.js main.css
No matching file found for 'missing-file.js'.

Looking in the following locations:
  /Users/ben/business_site/static
  /Users/ben/.virtualenvs/bookr/lib/python3.7/site-packages/django/contrib/admin/static
  /Users/ben/business_site/landing/static
Found 'landing/logo.png' here:
  /Users/ben/business_site/landing/static/landing/logo.png
Looking in the following locations:
  /Users/ben/business_site/static
  /Users/ben/.virtualenvs/bookr/lib/python3.7/site-packages/django/contrib/admin/static
  /Users/ben/business_site/landing/static
Found 'main.css' here:
  /Users/ben/business_site/static/main.css
Looking in the following locations:
  /Users/ben/business_site/static
  /Users/ben/.virtualenvs/bookr/lib/python3.7/site-packages/django/contrib/admin/static
  /Users/ben/business_site/landing/static
```

Figure 5.16: findstatic executed with verbosity 2, showing exactly which directories were searched

The **findstatic** command is not something that you will use day to day when working with Django, but it is useful to know about when trying to troubleshoot problems with static files. We saw the command output the full path to a file that existed, as well as the error messages when files did not exist. We also ran the command and supplied multiple files at once and saw that information about all the files was output. Finally, we ran the command with different levels of verbosity. The **-v0** flag suppressed errors about missing files. **-v1** was the default and displayed found paths and errors. Increasing the verbosity using the **-v2** flag also printed out the directories that were being searched through for a particular static file.

SERVING THE LATEST FILES (FOR CACHE INVALIDATION)

If you are not familiar with caching, the basic idea is that some operations can take a long time to perform. We can speed up a system by storing the results of an operation in a place that is faster to access so that the next time we need them, they can be retrieved quickly. The operation that takes a long time can be anything – from a function that takes a long time to run or an image that takes a long time to render, to a large asset that takes a long time to download over the internet. We are most interested in this last scenario.

You might have noticed that the first time you ever visit a particular website, it is slow to load, but then the next time it loads much faster. This is because your browser has cached some (or all) of the static files the site needs to load.

To use our business site as an example, we have a page that includes the **logo. png** file. The first time we visit the business site, we have to download the dynamic HTML, which is small and quick to transfer. Our browser parses the HTML and sees that **logo.png** should be included. It can then download this file too, which is much larger and can take longer to download. Note that this scenario assumes that the business site is now hosted on a remote server and not on our local machine – which is very fast for us to access.

If the web server is set up correctly, the browser will store **logo.png** on the computer. The next time we visit the *landing* page (or indeed any page that includes **logo.png**), your browser recognizes the URL can load the file from disk instead of having to download it again, thus speeding up the browsing experience.

> **NOTE**
>
> We said that the browser will cache "if the web server is set up correctly."
> What does this mean? The frontend web server should be configured to
> send special HTTP headers as part of a static file response. It can send a
> `Cache-Control` header, which can have values such as `no-cache`
> (the file should never be cached; in other words, the latest version should
> be requested every time) or `max-age=<seconds>` (the file should
> only be downloaded again if it was last retrieved more than `<seconds>`
> seconds ago). The response could also contain the `Expires` header, with
> the value being a date. The file is considered to be "stale" once this date is
> reached, and at that point, the new version should be requested.

One of the hardest problems in computer science is cache invalidation. For instance, if we change `logo.png`, how does our browser know it should download the new version? The only surefire way of knowing it had changed would be to download the file again and compare it with the version we had already saved every time. Of course, this defeats the purpose of caching since we would still be downloading every time the file changed (or not). We can cache for an arbitrary or server-specified amount of time, but if the static file changed before that time was up, we would not know. We would use the old version until we considered it expired, at which time we would download the new version. If we had a 1-week expiry and the static file changed the next day, we would still be using the old one for 6 days. Of course, the browser can be made to reload the page without using the cache (how this is done depends on the browser, for example, *Shift + F5* or *Cmd + Shift + R*) if you want to force downloading of all static assets again.

There is no need to try to cache our dynamic responses (rendered templates). Since they are designed to be dynamic, we would want to make sure that the user gets the latest version on every page load, and so they should not be cached. They are also quite small in size (compared to assets like images), so there is not much speed advantage when caching them.

Django provides a built-in solution. During the **collectstatic** phase, when the files are copied, Django can append a hash of their content to the filename. For example, the **logo.png** source file will be copied to **static_production_ test/landing/logo.f30ba08c60ba.png**. This is only done when using the **ManifestFilesStorage** storage engine. Since the filename is changing only when the content changes, the browser will always download the new content.

Using **ManifestFilesStorage** is just one way of invalidating caches. There may be other options that are more suitable for your application.

> **NOTE**
>
> A hash is a one-way function that generates a string of a fixed length regardless of the length of the input. There are several different hash functions available, and Django uses **MD5** for the content hashing. While no longer cryptographically secure, it is adequate for this purpose. To illustrate the fixed-length property, the MD5 hash of the string **a** is **0cc175b9c0f1b6a831c399e269772661**. The MD5 hash of the string (a much longer string) is **69fc4316c18cdd594a58ec2d59462b97**. They are both 32 characters long.

Choosing the storage engine is done by changing the **STATICFILES_STORAGE** value in **settings.py**. This is a string with a dotted path to the module and class to use. The class that implements the hash-addition functionality is **django. contrib.staticfiles.storage.ManifestStaticFilesStorage**.

Using this storage engine doesn't require any changes to your HTML templates, provided you are including static assets with the **static** template tag. Django generates a manifest file (**staticfiles.json**, in JSON format) that contains a mapping between the original filename and the hashed filename. It will automatically insert the hashed filename when using the **static** template tag. If you are including your static files without using the **static** tag and instead just manually insert the static URL, then your browser will attempt to load the non-hashed path and the URL will not automatically be updated when the cache should be invalidated.

For example, we include **logo.png** with the **static** tag here:

```
<img src="{% static 'reviews/logo.png' %}">
```

When the page is rendered, the latest hash will be retrieved from **staticfiles. json** and the output will be like this:

```
<img src="/static/landing/logo.f30ba08c60ba.png">
```

If we had not used the **static** tag and instead hardcoded the path, it would always appear as written:

```
<img src="/static/landing/logo.png">
```

Since this does not contain a hash, our browser will not see the path changing and thus never attempt to download the new file.

Django retains the previous version of files with the old hash when running **collectstatic**, so older versions of your application can still refer to it if they need to. The latest version of the file is also copied with no hash so non-Django applications can refer to it without needing to look up the hash.

In the next exercise, we will change our project settings to use the **ManifestFilesStorage** engine, then run the **collectstatic** management command. This will copy all the static assets as in *Exercise 5.04, Collecting Static Files for Production*; however, they will now have their hash included in the filename.

EXERCISE 5.06: EXPLORING THE MANIFESTFILESSTORAGE STORAGE ENGINE

In this exercise, you will temporarily update *settings.py* to use **ManifestFilesStorage**, then run **collectstatic** to see how the files are generated with a hash:

1. In PyCharm (still in the **business_site** project), open **settings.py**. Add a **STATICFILES_STORAGE** setting at the bottom of the file:

```
STATICFILES_STORAGE = \
'django.contrib.staticfiles.storage.ManifestStaticFilesStorage'
```

The completed file should look like this: http://packt.live/2Jq59Cc.

2. Open a terminal and navigate to the **business_site** project directory. Run the **collectstatic** command as you have before:

```
python3 manage.py collectstatic
```

If your **static_production_test** directory is not empty (which will probably be the case as files were moved there during *Exercise 5.04, Collecting Static Files for Production*) then you will be prompted to allow the overwrite of the existing files:

```
(bookr) → business_site python3 manage.py collectstatic

You have requested to collect static files at the destination
location as specified in your settings:

    /Users/ben/business_site/static_production_test

This will overwrite existing files!
Are you sure you want to do this?

Type 'yes' to continue, or 'no' to cancel:
```

Figure 5.17: Prompt to allow overwrite during collectstatic

Just type **yes** and then press *Enter* to allow the overwrite.

The output from this command will tell you the number of files copied as well as the number that were processed and had the hash added to the filename:

```
0 static files copied to '/Users/ben/business_site
/static_production_test', 132 unmodified,
28 post-processed.
```

Since you haven't changed any files since we last ran **collectstatic**, no files are copied. Instead, Django is just post-processing the files (28 of them), that is, generating their hash and appending the filename.

The static files were copied into the **static_production_test** directory as they were before; however, there are now two copies of each file: one named with the hash and one without.

static/main.css has been copied to **static_production_test/ main.856c74fb7029.css** (this filename might be different if your CSS file contents differ, for example, if it has extra spaces or newlines):

▼ 📁 static_production_test
   ▶ 📁 admin
   ▼ 📁 landing
       🖼 logo.ba8b3d8fe184.png
       🖼 logo.png
    📄 main.856c74fb7029.css
    📄 main.css
    📄 staticfiles.json

Figure 5.18: Expanded static_production_test directory with hashed filenames

Figure 5.18 shows the expanded **static_production_test** directory layout. You can see two copies of each static file and the **staticfiles.json** manifest file. To take **logo.png** as an example, you can see that **landing/ static/landing/logo.png** has been copied to the same directory as **static_production_test/landing/logo.ba8d3d8fe184.png**.

3. Let's make a change to the **main.css** file and see how the hash changes. Add some blank lines at the end of the file then save it. This won't change the effect of the CSS but the change in the file will affect its hash. Rerun the **collectstatic** command in a terminal:

```
python3 manage.py collectstatic
```

Once again, you may have to enter **yes** to confirm the overwrite:

```
You have requested to collect static files at the \
   destination location as specified in your settings:

    /Users/ben/business_site/static_production_test

This will overwrite existing files!
Are you sure you want to do this?
```

```
Type 'yes' to continue, or 'no' to cancel: yes

1 static file copied to '/Users/ben/business_site\
  /static_production_test', 131 unmodified, 28 post-processed.
```

Since only one file was changed, only one static file was copied (**main.css**).

4. Look inside the **static_production_test** directory again. You should see the old file with the old hash was retained, and a new file with a new hash has been added:

```
▼ 📁 static_production_test
   ▶ 📁 admin
   ▼ 📁 landing
        🖼 logo.ba8b3d8fe184.png
        🖼 logo.png
   📄 main.856c74fb7029.css
   📄 main.css
   📄 main.df1234ac4e63.css
   📄 staticfiles.json
```

Figure 5.19: Another main.css file with the latest hash was added

In this case, we have **main.856c74fb7029.css** (existing), **main.df1234ac4e63.css** (new), and **main.css**. Your hashes may differ.

The **main.css** file (no hash) always contains the newest content; that is to say, the contents of the **main.df1234ac4e63.css** and **main.css** files are identical. During the execution of **collectstatic**, Django will copy the file with a hash, as well as without a hash.

5. Now examine the **staticfiles.json** file that Django generates. This is the mapping that allows Django to look up the hashed path from the normal path. Open **static_production_test/staticfiles.json**. All the content may appear in one line; if it does, enable text soft wrapping from the **View** menu -> **Active Editor** -> **Soft Wrap**. Scroll to the end of the file and you should see an entry for the **main.css** file, for example:

```
"main.css": "main.df1234ac4e63.css"
```

This is how Django is able to populate the correct URL in a template when using the **static** template tag: by looking up the hashed path in this mapping file.

6. We're finished with **business_site**, which we were just using for testing. You can delete the project or keep it around for reference during the activities.

> **NOTE**
>
> Unfortunately, we can't examine how the hashed URL is interpolated in the template, because when running in debug mode, Django does not look up the hashed version of the file. As we know, the Django dev server only runs in debug mode, so if we turned debug mode off to try to view the hashed interpolation, then the Django dev server would not start. You will need to examine this interpolation yourself when going to production when using a frontend web server.

In this exercise, we configured Django to use **ManifestFilesStorage** for its static file storage, by adding the **STATICFILES_STORAGE** setting to **settings.py**. We then executed the **collectstatic** command to see how the hashes are generated and added to the filename of the copied files. We saw the manifest file called **staticfiles.json**, which stored a lookup from the original path to the hashed path. Finally, we cleaned up the settings and directories that we added in this exercise and *Exercise 5.04, Collecting Static Files for Production*. These were the **STATIC_ROOT** setting, the **STATICFILES_STORAGE** setting, and the **static_product_test** directory.

CUSTOM STORAGE ENGINES

In the previous section, we set the storage engine to **ManifestFilesStorage**. This class is provided by Django, but it is also possible to write a custom storage engine. For example, you could write a storage engine that uploads your static files to a CDN, Amazon S3, or a Google Cloud bucket when you run **collectstatic**.

Writing a custom storage engine is beyond the scope of this book. There already exist third-party libraries that support uploading to a variety of cloud services; one such library is **django-storages**, which can be found at https://django-storages.readthedocs.io/.

The following code is a short skeleton indicating which methods you should implement to create a custom file storage engine:

```
from django.conf import settings
from django.contrib.staticfiles import storage
class CustomFilesStorage(storage.StaticFilesStorage):
    def __init__(self):
    """

    The class must be able to be instantiated
    without any arguments.
    Create custom settings in settings.py and read them instead.
    """

    self.setting = settings.CUSTOM_STORAGE_SETTING
```

The class must be able to be instantiated without any arguments. The __init__ function must be able to load any settings from global identifiers (in this case, from our Django settings):

```
def delete(self, name):
    """

    Implement delete of the file from the remote service.
    """
```

This method should be able to delete the file, specified by the **name** argument, from the remote service:

```
def exists(self, name):
    """

    Return True if a file with name exists in the remote service.
    """
```

This method should query the remote service to check whether the file specified by name exists. It should return **True** if the file exists, or **False** if it doesn't:

```
def listdir(self, path):
    """

    List a directory in the remote service. Return should
    be a 2-tuple of lists, the first a list of directories,
    the second a list of files.
    """
```

This method should query the remote service to list the directory at **path**. It should then return a 2-tuple of lists. The first element should be a list of directories inside **path**, and the second element should be a list of files. For example:

```
return (['directory1', 'directory2'], \
        ['code.py', 'document.txt', 'image.jpg'])
```

If **path** contains no directories or no files, then an empty list should be returned for that element. You would return two empty lists if the directory was empty:

```
def size(self, name):
    """
    Return the size in bytes of the file with name.
    """
```

This method should query the remote service and get the size of the file specified by **name**:

```
def url(self, name):
    """
    Return the URL where the file of with name can be
    access on the remote service. For example, this
    might be URL of the file after it has been uploaded
    to a specific remote host with a specific domain.
    """
```

This method should determine the URL to access the file specified by **name**. This could be built by appending **name** to a specific static hosting URL:

```
def _open(self, name, mode='rb'):
    """
    Return a File-like object pointing to file with
    name. For example, this could be a URL handle for
    a remote file.
    """
```

This method will provide a handle remote file, specified by **name**. How you implement this will depend on the type of remote service. You might have to download the file and then use a memory buffer (such as an **io.BytesIO** object) to simulate the opening of the file:

```
def _save(self, name, content):
    """
    Write the content for a file with name. In this
```

```
method you might upload the content to a
remote service.
"""
```

This method should save **content** to the remote file at **name**. The method of implementing this will depend on your remote service. It might transfer the file over SFTP, or upload to a CDN.

While this example does not implement any transferring to or from a remote service, you can refer to it to get an idea of how to implement a custom storage engine.

After implementing your custom storage engine, you can make it active by setting its dotted module path in the **STATICFILES_STORAGE** setting in **settings.py**.

ACTIVITY 5.01: ADDING A REVIEWS LOGO

The Bookr app should have a logo that is specific for pages in the **reviews** app. This will involve adding a base template just for the **reviews** app and updating our current **reviews** templates to inherit from it. Then you will include the Bookr **reviews** logo on this base template.

These steps will help you complete this activity:

1. Add a CSS rule to position the logo. Put this rule into the existing **base.html**, after the **.navbar-brand** rule:

```
.navbar-brand > img {
   height: 60px;
}
```

2. Add a **brand block** template tag that inheriting templates can override. Put this inside the **<a>** element with the **navbar-brand** class. The default contents of **block** should be left as **Book Review**.

3. Add a static directory inside the **reviews** app, containing a namespaced directory. Download the reviews **logo.png** from https://packt.live/2WYIGjP and put it inside this directory.

4. Create the **templates** directory for the Bookr project (inside the Bookr project directory). Then move the **reviews** app's current **base.html** into this directory, so it becomes a base template for the whole project.

5. Add the new **templates** directory's path to the **TEMPLATES['DIRS']** setting in **settings.py** (the same as what you did in *Exercise 5.02, Using the static Template Tag.*

6. Create another **base.html** template specifically for the **reviews** app. Put it inside the **reviews** app's **templates** directory. The new template should extend the existing **base.html**.

7. The new **base.html** should override the content of the **brand** block. This block should contain just an **<img>** instance whose **src** attribute is set using the **{% static %}** template tag. The image source should be the logo added in *step 2*.

8. The index view in **views.py** should render the project **base.html** instead of the **reviews** one.

Refer to the following screenshots to see what your pages should be like after these changes. Note that although you are making changes to the base template, it will not change the layout of the main page:

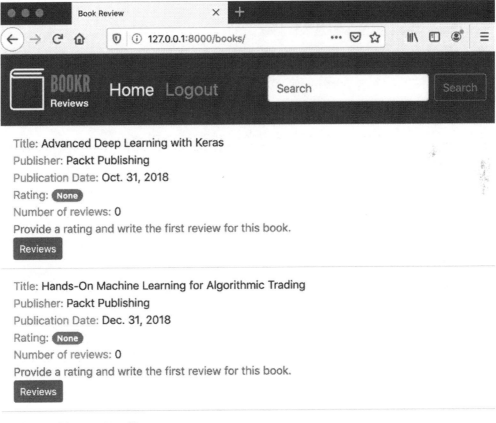

Figure 5.20: Book list page after adding reviews logos

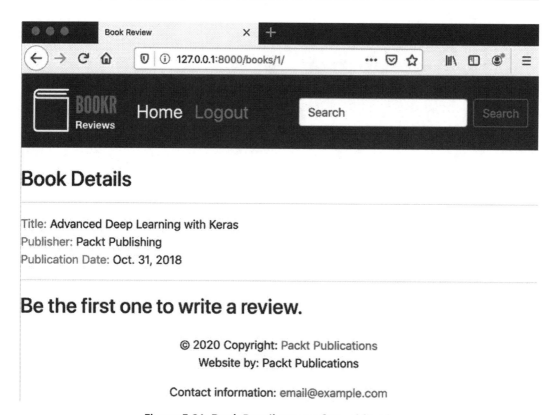

Figure 5.21: Book Details page after adding logo

> **NOTE**
>
> The solution to this activity can be found at http://packt.live/2Nh1NTJ.

ACTIVITY 5.02: CSS ENHANCEMENTS

Currently, the CSS is kept inline in the **base.html** template. For best practice, it should be moved into its own file so that it can be cached separately and decrease the size of the HTML downloads. As part of this, you'll also add some CSS enhancements, such as fonts and colors, and link in Google Fonts CSS to support these changes.

These steps will help you complete this activity:

1. Create a directory named **static** in the Bookr project directory. Then, create a new file inside it named **main.css**.

2. Copy the contents of the **<style>** element from the main **base.html** template into the new **main.css** file, then remove the **<style>** element from the template. Add these extra rules to the end of the CSS file:

```css
body {
    font-family: 'Source Sans Pro', sans-serif;
      background-color: #e6efe8
    color: #393939;
}


h1, h2, h3, h4, h5, h6 {
    font-family: 'Libre Baskerville', serif;
}
```

3. Link to the new **main.css** file with a **<link rel="stylesheet" href="...">** tag. Use the **{% static %}** template tag to generate the URL for the **href** attribute, and don't forget to **load** the **static** library.

4. Link in the Google fonts CSS, by adding this code to the base template:

```html
<link rel="stylesheet"
  href="https://fonts.googleapis.com/css?family
    =Libre+Baskerville|Source+Sans+Pro&display=swap">
```

> **NOTE**
>
> You will need to have an active internet connection so that your browser can include this remote CSS file.

5. Update your Django settings to add **STATICFILES_DIRS**, set to the **static** directory created in *step 1*. When you're finished, your Bookr application should look like *Figure 5.22*:

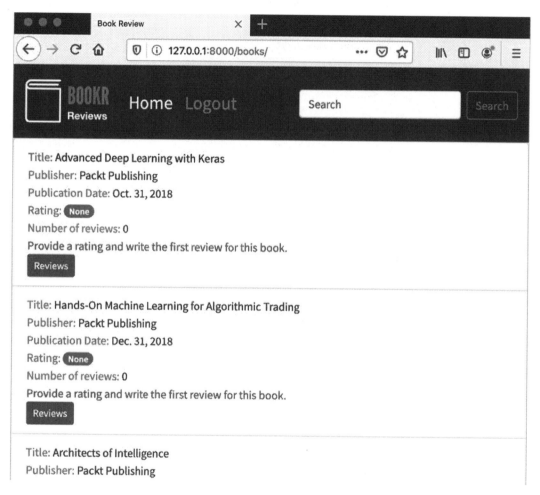

Figure 5.22: Book list with the new font and background color

Notice the new font and background color. These should be displayed on all the Bookr pages.

> **NOTE**
>
> The solution to this activity can be found at http://packt.live/2Nh1NTJ.

ACTIVITY 5.03: ADDING A GLOBAL LOGO

You have already added a logo that is served on pages for the **reviews** app. We have another logo to be used globally as a default, but other apps will be able to override it:

1. Download the Bookr logo (**logo.png**) from https://packt.live/2Jx7Ge4.

2. Save it in the main **static** directory for the project.

3. Edit the main **base.html** file. We already have a block for the logo (**brand**), so an **<img>** instance can be placed inside here. Use the **static** template tag to refer to the logo you just downloaded.

4. Check that your pages work. On the main URL, you should see the Bookr logo, but on the book list and details pages, you should see the Bookr Reviews logo.

   When you're finished, you should see the Bookr logo on the main page:

Figure 5.23: Bookr logo on the main page

When you visit a page that had the Bookr Reviews logo before, such as the book list page, it should still show the Bookr Reviews logo:

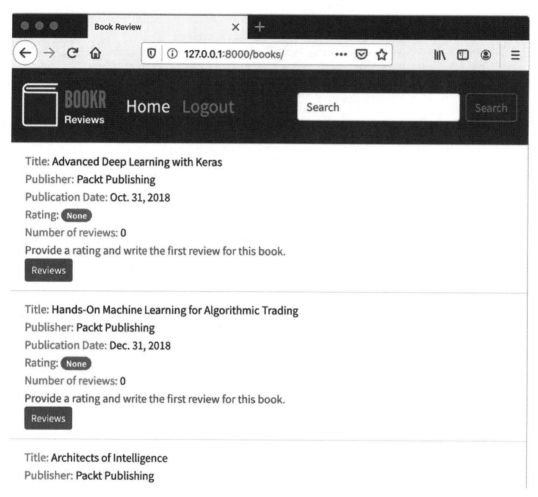

Figure 5.24: Bookr Reviews logo still shows on the Reviews pages

NOTE

The solution to this activity can be found at http://packt.live/2Nh1NTJ.

SUMMARY

In this chapter, we showed how to use Django's **staticfiles** app to find and serve static files. We used the built-in **static** view to serve these files with the Django dev server in **DEBUG** mode. We showed different places to store static files, using a directory that is global to the project or a specific directory for the application; global resources should be stored in the former while application-specific resources should be stored in the latter. We showed the importance of namespacing static file directories to prevent conflicts. After serving the assets, we used the **static** tag to include them in our template. We then demonstrated how the **collectstatic** command copies all the assets into the **STATIC_ROOT** directory, for production deployment. We showed how to use the **findstatic** command to debug the loading of static files. To invalidate caches automatically, we looked at using **ManifestFilesStorage** to add a hash of the file's content to the static file URL. Finally, we briefly talked about using a custom file storage engine.

So far, we have only fetched web pages using content that already existed. In the next chapter, we will start adding forms so we can interact with web pages by sending data to them over HTTP.

6

FORMS

OVERVIEW

This chapter introduces web forms, a method of sending information from the browser to the web server. It starts with an introduction to forms in general and discusses how data is encoded to be sent to the server. You will learn about the differences between sending form data in a **GET** HTTP request and sending it in a **POST** HTTP request, and how to choose which one to use. By the end of the chapter, you will know how Django's form library is used to build and validate forms automatically and how it cuts down the amount of manual HTML you need to write.

INTRODUCTION

So far, the views we have been building for Django have been one-way only. Our browser is retrieving data from the views we have written but it does not send any data back to them. In *Chapter 4, Introduction to Django Admin*, we created model instances using the Django admin and submitting forms, but those were using views built into Django, not created by us. In this chapter, we will use the Django Forms library to start accepting user-submitted data. The data will be provided through **GET** requests in the URL parameters, and/or **POST** requests in the body of the request. But before we get into the details, first let us understand what are forms in Django.

WHAT IS A FORM?

When working with an interactive web app, we not only want to provide data to users but also accept data from them to either customize the responses we are generating or let them submit data to the site. When browsing the web, you will most definitely have used forms. Whether you're logging in to your internet banking account, surfing the web with a browser, posting a message on social media, or writing an email in an online email client, in all these cases, you are entering data in a form. A form is made up of inputs that define key-value pairs of data to submit to the server. For example, when logging in to a website, the data being sent would have the keys *username* and *password*, with the values of your username and your password, respectively. We will go into the different types of inputs in more detail in the *Types of Inputs* section. Each input in the form has a *name*, and this is how its data is identified on the server-side (in a Django view). There can be multiple inputs with the same *name*, whose data is available in a list containing all the posted values with this name – for example, a list of checkboxes with permissions to apply to users. Each checkbox would have the same name but a different value. The form has attributes that specify which URL the browser should submit the data to and what method it should use to submit the data (browsers only support **GET** or **POST**).

The GitHub login form shown in the next figure is an example of a form:

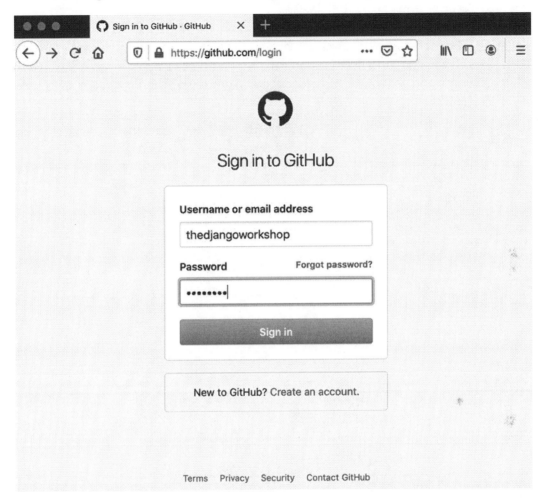

Figure 6.1: The GitHub login page is an example of a form

It has three visible inputs: a text field (**Username**), a **password** field (**Password**), and a **submit** button (**Sign in**). It also has a field that is not visible – its type is **hidden**, and it contains a special token for security called a **Cross-Site Request Forgery (CSRF)** token. We will discuss this later in the chapter. When you click the **Sign In** button, the form data is submitted with a **POST** request. If you entered a valid username and password, you are logged in; otherwise, the form will display an error as follows:

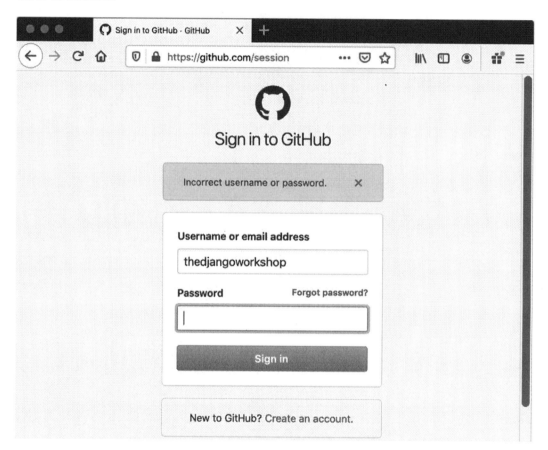

Figure 6.2: Form submitted with an incorrect username or password

There are two states a form can have: **pre-submit** and **post-submit**. The first is the initial state when the page is first loaded. All the fields will have a default value (usually empty) and no errors will be displayed. If all the information that has been entered into a form is valid, then usually when it is submitted you will be taken to a page showing the results of submitting the form. This might be a search results page, or a page showing you the new object that you created. In this case, you will not see the form in its post-submit state.

If you did not enter valid information into the form, then it will be rendered again in its post-submit state. In this state, you will be shown the information that you entered as well as any errors to help you resolve the problems with the form. The errors may be **field errors** or **non-field errors**. Field errors apply to a specific field. For example, leaving a required field blank or entering a value that is too large, too small, too long, or too short. If a form required you to enter your name and you left it blank, this would be displayed as a field error next to that field.

Non-field errors either do not apply to a field, or apply to multiple fields, and are displayed at the top of the form. In *Figure 6.2*, we see a message that either the username or password may be incorrect when logging in. For security, GitHub does not reveal whether a username is valid, and so this is displayed as a non-field error rather than a field error for the username or password (Django also follows this convention). Non-field errors also apply to fields that depend on each other. For example, on a credit card form, if the payment is rejected, we might not know if the credit card number or security code is incorrect; therefore, we cannot show that error on a specific field. It applies to the form as a whole.

THE <FORM> ELEMENT

All inputs used during form submission must be contained inside a **<form>** element. There are three HTML attributes that you will be using to modify the behavior of the form:

- **method**

  This is the HTTP method used to submit the form, either **GET** or **POST**. If omitted, this defaults to **GET** (because this is the default method when typing a URL into the browser and hitting *Enter*).

- **action**

  This refers to the URL (or path) to send the form data to. If omitted, the data gets sent back to the current page.

- **enctype**

  This sets the encoding type of the form. You only need to change this if you are using the form to upload files. The most common values are **application/x-www-form-urlencoded** (the default if this value is omitted) or **multipart/form-data** (set this if uploading files). Note that you don't have to worry about the encoding type in your view; Django handles the different types automatically.

Here is an example of a form without any of its attributes set:

```
<form>
    <!-- Input elements go here -->
</form>
```

It will submit its data using a **GET** request, to the current URL that the form is being displayed on, using the `application/x-www-form-urlencoded` encoding type.

In this next example, we will set all three attributes on a form:

```
<form method="post" action="/form-submit" enctype="multipart/form-data">
    <!-- Input elements go here -->
</form>
```

This form will submit its data with a **POST** request to the `/form-submit` path, encoding the data as `multipart/form-data`.

How do **GET** and **POST** requests differ in how the data is sent? Recall in *Chapter 1, Introduction to Django*, we discussed what the underlying HTTP request and response data that your browser sends looks like. In these next two examples, we will submit the same form twice, the first time using **GET** and the second time using **POST**. The form will have two inputs, a first name, and the last name.

A form submitted using **GET** sends its data in the URL, like this:

```
GET /form-submit?first_name=Joe&last_name=Bloggs HTTP/1.1
Host: www.example.com
```

A form submitted using **POST** sends its data in the body of the request, like this:

```
POST /form-submit HTTP/1.1
Host: www.example.com
Content-Length: 31
Content-Type: application/x-www-form-urlencoded

first_name=Joe&last_name=Bloggs
```

You will notice that the form data is encoded the same way in both cases; it is just placed differently for the **GET** and **POST** requests. In an upcoming section, we will discuss how to choose between these two types of requests.

TYPES OF INPUTS

We have seen four examples of inputs so far (*text*, *password*, *submit*, and *hidden*). Most inputs are created with an **<input>** tag, and their type is specified with its **type** attribute. Each input has a **name** attribute that defines the key for the key-value pairs that are sent to the server in the HTTP request.

In the next exercise, let's look at how we can build a form in HTML. This will allow you to get up to speed on many different form fields.

> **NOTE**
>
> The code for all the exercises and activities used in this chapter can be found on the book's GitHub repository at http://packt.live/2KGjlaM.

EXERCISE 6.01: BUILDING A FORM IN HTML

For the first few exercises of this chapter, we will need an HTML form to test with. We will manually code one in this exercise. This will also allow you to experiment with how different fields are validated and submitted. This will be done in a new Django project so that we don't interfere with Bookr. You can refer to *Chapter 1, Introduction to Django*, to refresh your memory on creating a Django project:

1. We will start by creating the new Django project. You can re-use the **bookr** virtual environment that already has Django installed. Open a new terminal and activate the virtual environment. Then, use **django-admin** to start a Django project named **form_project**. To do this, run the command:

```
django-admin startproject form_project
```

This will scaffold the Django project in a directory named **form_example**.

2. Create a new Django app in this project by using the **startapp** management command. The app should be called **form_example**. To do this, **cd** into the **form_project** directory, then run this:

```
python3 manage.py startapp form_example
```

This will create the **form_example** app directory inside the **form_project** directory.

3. Launch PyCharm, then open the **form_project** directory. If you already have a project open, you can do this by choosing **File** -> **Open**; otherwise, just click **Open** in the **Welcome to PyCharm** window. Navigate to the **form_project** directory, select it, then click **Open**. The **form_project** project window should be shown similar to this:

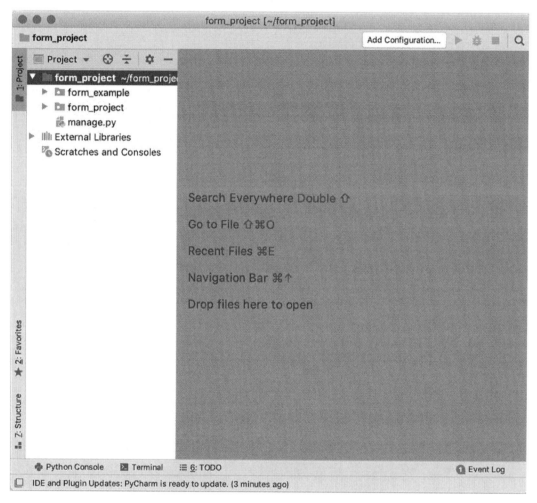

Figure 6.3: The form_project project open

4. Create a new run configuration to execute **manage.py runserver** for the project. You can re-use the **bookr** virtual environment again. The **Run/Debug Configurations** window should look similar to the following figure when you're done:

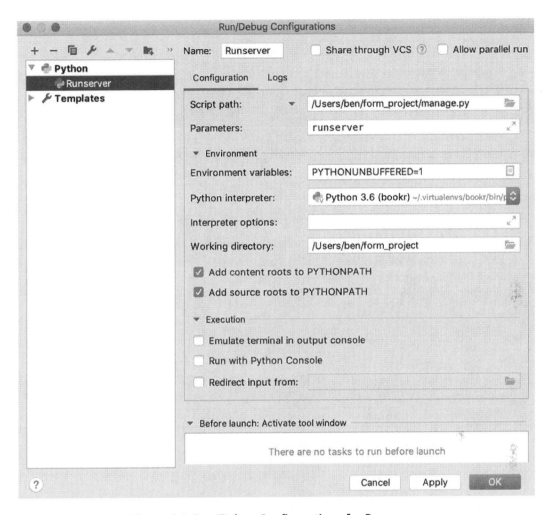

Figure 6.4: Run/Debug Configurations for Runserver

You can test that the configuration is set up correctly by clicking the **Run** button, then visiting **http://127.0.0.1:8000/** in your browser. You should see the Django welcome screen. If the debug server fails to start or you see the Bookr main page, then you probably still have the Bookr project running. Try stopping the Bookr **runserver** process and then starting the new one you just set up.

5. Open **settings.py** in the **form_project** directory and add **'form_example'** to the **INSTALLED_APPS** setting.

6. The last step in setting up this new project is to create a **templates** directory for the **form_example** app. Right-click on the **form_example** directory and then select **New** -> **Directory**. Name it **templates**.

7. We need an HTML template to display our form. Create one by right-clicking the **templates** directory you just created and choosing **New** -> **HTML File**. In the dialog box that appears, enter the name **form-example.html** and hit *Enter* to create it.

8. The **form-example.html** file should now be open in the editor pane of PyCharm. Start by creating the **form** element. We will set its **method** attribute to **post**. The **action** attribute will be omitted, which means the form will submit back to the same URL on which it was loaded.

   Insert this code between the **<body>** and **</body>** tags:

```
<form method="post">
</form>
```

9. Now let us add a few inputs. To add a little bit of spacing between each input, we will wrap them inside **<p>** tags. We will start with a text field and password field. This code should be inserted between the **<form>** tags you just created:

```
<p>
    <label for="id_text_input">Text Input</label><br>
    <input id="id_text_input" type="text" name=
      "text_input" value="" placeholder="Enter some text">
</p>
<p>
    <label for="id_password_input">Password Input</label><br>
    <input id="id_password_input" type="password" name="password_
input"
        value="" placeholder="Your password">
</p>
```

10. Next, we will add two checkboxes and three radio buttons. Insert this code after the HTML you added in the previous step; it should come before the **</form>** tag:

```
<p>
    <input id="id_checkbox_input" type="checkbox"
      name="checkbox_on" value="Checkbox Checked" checked>
    <label for="id_checkbox_input">Checkbox</label>
```

```
    </p>
    <p>
        <input id="id_radio_one_input" type="radio"
          name="radio_input" value="Value One">
        <label for="id_radio_one_input">Value One</label>

        <input id="id_radio_two_input" type="radio"
          name="radio_input" value="Value Two" checked>
        <label for="id_radio_two_input">Value Two</label>

        <input id="id_radio_three_input" type="radio"
          name="radio_input" value="Value Three">
        <label for="id_radio_three_input">Value Three</label>
    </p>
```

11. Next is a dropdown select menu to allow the user to choose a favorite book. Add this code after that of the previous step but before the **</form>** tag:

```
    <p>
        <label for="id_favorite_book">Favorite Book</label><br>
        <select id="id_favorite_book" name="favorite_book">
            <optgroup label="Non-Fiction">
                <option value="1">Deep Learning with Keras</option>
                <option value="2">Web Development with Django</option>
            </optgroup>
            <optgroup label="Fiction">
                <option value="3">Brave New World</option>
                <option value="4">The Great Gatsby</option>
            </optgroup>
        </select>
    </p>
```

It will display four options that are split into two groups. The user will only be able to select one option.

12. The next is a multiple select (achieved by using the **multiple** attribute). Add this code after that of the previous step but before the **</form>** tag:

```
    <p>
        <label for="id_books_you_own">Books You Own</label><br>
        <select id="id_books_you_own" name="books_you_own" multiple>
            <optgroup label="Non-Fiction">
                <option value="1">Deep Learning with Keras</option>
                <option value="2">Web Development with Django</option>
            </optgroup>
            <optgroup label="Fiction">
```

```
            <option value="3">Brave New World</option>
            <option value="4">The Great Gatsby</option>
        </optgroup>
    </select>
</p>
```

The user can select zero or more options from the four. They are displayed in two groups.

13. Next is **textarea**. It is like a text field but has multiple lines. This code should be added like in the previous steps, before the closing **</form>** tag:

```
<p>
    <label for="id_text_area">Text Area</label><br>
    <textarea name="text_area" id="id_text_area"
      placeholder="Enter multiple lines of text"></textarea>
</p>
```

14. Next, add some fields for specific data types: **number**, **email**, and **date** inputs. Add this all before the **</form>** tag:

```
<p>
    <label for="id_number_input">Number Input</label><br>
    <input id="id_number_input" type="number"
      name="number_input" value="" step="any" placeholder="A number">
</p>
<p>
    <label for="id_email_input">Email Input</label><br>
    <input id="id_email_input" type="email"
      name="email_input" value="" placeholder="Your email address">
</p>
<p>
    <label for="id_date_input">Date Input</label><br>
    <input id="id_date_input" type="date" name=
      "date_input" value="2019-11-23">
</p>
```

15. Now add some buttons to submit the form. Once again, insert this before the closing **</form>** tag:

```
<p>
    <input type="submit" name="submit_input" value="Submit Input">
</p>
<p>
    <button type="submit" name="button_element" value="Button
Element">
        Button With <strong>Styled</strong> Text
    </button>
</p>
```

This demonstrates two ways of creating submit buttons, either as **<input>** or **<button>**.

16. Finally, add a hidden field. Insert this before the closing **</form>** tag:

```
<input type="hidden" name="hidden_input" value="Hidden Value">
```

This field cannot be seen or edited so it has a fixed value. You can save and close **form-example.html**.

17. As with any template, we cannot see it unless we have a view to render it. Open the **form_example** app's **views.py** file and add a new view called **form_example**. It should render and return the template you just created, like so:

```
def form_example(request):
    return render(request, "form-example.html")
```

You can now save and close **views.py**.

18. You should be familiar with the next step now, which is to add a URL mapping to the view. Open the **urls.py** file in the **form_project** package directory. Add a mapping for the path **form-example** to your **form_example** view, to the **urlpatterns** variable. It should look like this:

```
path('form-example/', form_example.views.form_example)
```

Make sure you also add an import of **form_example.views**. Save and close **urls.py**.

19. Start the Django dev server (if it is not already running), then load your new view in your web browser; the address is `http://127.0.0.1:8000/form-example/`. Your page should look like this:

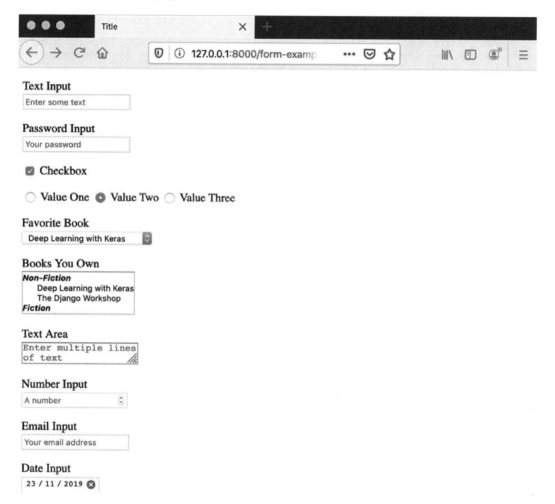

Figure 6.5: Example inputs page

You can now familiarize yourself with the behavior of the web forms and see how they are generated from the HTML you specified. One activity to try is to enter invalid data into the number, date, or email inputs and click the submit button – the built-in HTML validation should prevent the form from being submitted:

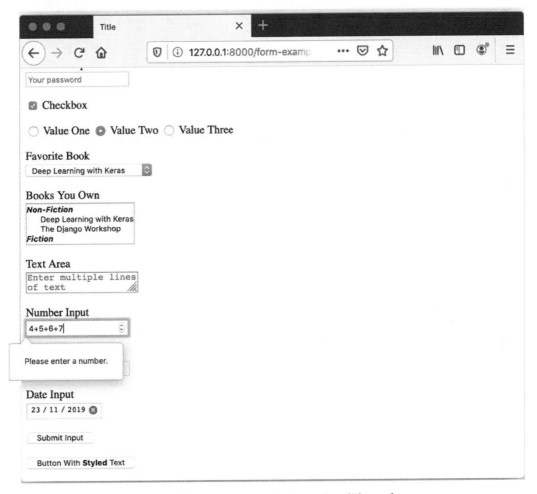

Figure 6.6: Browser error due to an invalid number

We have not yet set up everything for form submission, so if you correct all the errors in the form and try to submit it (by clicking either of the submit buttons), you will receive an error stating **CSRF verification failed. Request aborted.**, as we can see in the next figure. We will talk about what this means, and how to fix it, later in the chapter:

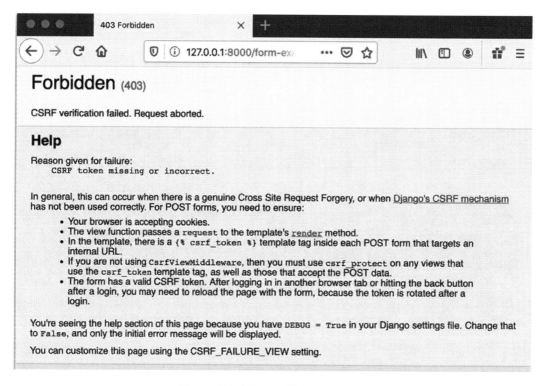

Figure 6.7: CSRF verification error

20. If you do receive the error, just go back in your browser to return to the input example page.

In this exercise, you created an example page showcasing many HTML inputs, then created a view to render it and a URL to map to it. You loaded the page in your browser and experimented with changing data and trying to submit the form when it contained errors.

FORM SECURITY WITH CROSS-SITE REQUEST FORGERY PROTECTION

Throughout the book, we have mentioned features that Django includes to prevent certain types of security exploits. One of these features is protection against CSRF.

A CSRF attack exploits the fact that a form on a website can be submitted to any other website. The **action** attribute of **form** just needs to be set appropriately. Let's take an example for Bookr. We don't have this set up yet, but we will be adding a view and URL that allows us to post a review for a book. To do this, we'll have a form for posting the review content and selecting the rating. Its HTML is like this:

```
<form method="post" action="http://127.0.0.1:8000/books/4/reviews/">
    <p>
        <label for="id_review_text">Your Review</label><br/>
        <textarea id="id_review_text" name="review_text"
          placeholder="Enter your review"></textarea>
    </p>
    <p>
        <label for="id_rating">Rating</label><br/>
        <input id="id_rating" type="number" name="rating"
          placeholder="Rating 1-5">
    </p>
    <p>
        <button type="submit">Create Review</button>
    </p>
</form>
```

And on a web page, it would look like this:

Figure 6.8: Example review creation form

Someone could take this form, make a few changes, and host it on their own website. For example, they could make the inputs hidden and hardcode a good review and rating for a book, and then make it look like some other kind of form, like this:

```
<form method="post" action="http://127.0.0.1:8000/books/4/reviews/">
    <input type="hidden" name="review_text" value="This book is great!">
    <input type="hidden" name="rating" value="5">
    <p>
```

```
            <button type="submit">Enter My Website</button>
      </p>
</form>
```

Of course, the hidden fields don't display, so the form looks like this on the malicious website.

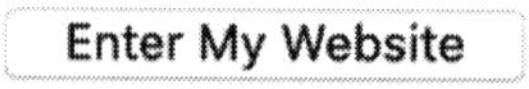

Enter My Website

Figure 6.9: Hidden inputs are not visible

The user would think they were clicking a button to enter a website, but while clicking it, they would submit the hidden values to the original view on Bookr. Of course, a user could check the source code of the page they were on to check what data is being sent and where, but most users are unlikely to inspect every form they come across. The attacker could even have the form with no submit button and just use JavaScript to submit it, which means the user would be submitting the form without even realizing it.

You may think that requiring the user to log in to Bookr will prevent this type of attack, and it does limit its effectiveness somewhat, as the attack would then only work for logged-in users. But because of the way authentication works, once a user is logged in, they have a cookie set in their browser that identifies them to the Django application. This cookie is sent on every request so that the user does not have to provide their login credentials on every page. Because of the way web browsers work, they will include the server's authentication cookie in *all* requests they send to that particular server. Even though our form is hosted on a malicious site, ultimately it is sending a request to our application, so it will send through our server's cookies.

How can we prevent CSRF attacks? Django uses something called a CSRF token, which is a small random string that is unique to each site visitor – in general, you can consider a visitor to be one browser session. Different browsers on the same computer would be different visitors, and the same Django user logged in on two different browsers would also be different visitors. When the form is read, Django puts the token into the form as a hidden input. The CSRF token must be included in all **POST** requests being sent to Django, and it must match the token Django has stored on the server-side for the visitor, otherwise, a 403 status HTTP response is returned. This protection can be disabled – either for the whole site or for an individual view – but it is not advisable to do so unless you really need to. The CSRF token must be added into the HTML for every form being sent and is done with the `{% csrf_token %}` template tag. We'll add it to our example review form now, and the code in the template will look like this:

```
<form method="post" action="http://127.0.0.1:8000/books/4/reviews/">
    {% csrf_token %}
    <p>
        <label for="id_review_text">Your Review</label><br/>
        <textarea id="id_review_text" name="review_text"
          placeholder="Enter your review"></textarea>
    </p>
    <p>
        <label for="id_rating">Rating</label><br/>
        <input id="id_rating" type="number" name="rating"
          placeholder="Rating 1-5">
    </p>
    <p>
        <button type="submit">Enter My Website</button>
    </p>
</form>
```

When the template gets rendered, the template tag is interpolated, so the output HTML ends up like this (note that the inputs are still in the output; they have just been removed here for brevity):

```
<form method="post" action="http://127.0.0.1:8000/books/4/reviews/">
    <input type="hidden" name="csrfmiddlewaretoken"
value="tETZjLDUXev1tiYqGCSbMQkhWiesHCnutxpt6mutHI6YH64F0nin5k2JW3B68IeJ">
    ...
</form>
```

Since this is a hidden field, the form on the page does not look any different from how it did before.

The CSRF token is unique to every visitor on the site and periodically changes. If an attacker were to copy the HTML from our site, they would get their own CSRF token that would not match that of any other user, so Django would reject the form when it was posted by someone else.

CSRF tokens also change periodically. This limits how long the attacker would have to take advantage of a particular user and token combination. Even if they were able to get the CSRF token of a user that they were trying to exploit, they would have a short window of time to be able to use it.

ACCESSING DATA IN THE VIEW

As we discussed in *Chapter 1, Introduction to Django*, Django provides two **QueryDict** objects on the **HTTPRequest** instances that are passed to the view function. These are **request.GET**, which contains parameters passed in the URL, and **request.POST**, which contains parameters in the HTTP request body. Even though **request.GET** has **GET** in its name, this variable is populated even for non-**GET** HTTP requests. This is because the data it contains is parsed from the URL. Since all HTTP requests have a URL, all HTTP requests may contain **GET** data, even if they are **POST** or **PUT**, and so on. In the next exercise, we will add code to our view to read and display the **POST** data.

EXERCISE 6.02: WORKING WITH POST DATA IN A VIEW

We will now add some code to our example view to print out the received **POST** data to the console. We will also insert the HTTP method that was used to generate the page into the HTML output. This will allow us to be sure of what method was used to generate the page (**GET** or **POST**) and see how the form differs for each type:

1. First, in PyCharm, open the **form_example** app's **views.py** file. Alter the **form_example** view to print each value in the **POST** request to the console by adding this code inside the function:

```
for name in request.POST:
    print("{}: {}".format(name, request.POST.getlist(name)))
```

This code iterates over each key in the request **POST** data **QueryDict** and prints the key and list of values to the console. We already know that each **QueryDict** can have multiple values for a key, so we use the **getlist** function to get them all.

2. Pass **request.method** to the template in a context variable named **method**. Do this by updating the call to **render** in the view, so that it's like this:

```
return render(request, "form-example.html", \
              {"method": request.method})
```

3. We will now display the **method** variable in the template. Open the **form-example.html** template and use an **<h4>** tag to show the **method** variable. Put this just after the opening **<body>** tag, like so:

```
<body>
    <h4>Method: {{ method }}</h4>
```

Note that we could access the method directly inside the template without passing it in a context dictionary, by using the **request** method variable and attribute properly. We know from *Chapter 3, URL Mapping, Views, and Templates*, that by using the render shortcut function, the request is always available in the template. We just demonstrated how to access the method in the view here because later on, we will change the behavior of the page based on the method.

4. We also need to add the CSRF token to the form HTML. We do this by putting the **{% csrf_token %}** template tag after the opening **<form>** tag. The start of the form should look like this:

```
<form method="post">
    {% csrf_token %}
```

Now, save the file.

5. Start the Django dev server if it's not already running. Load the example page (**http://127.0.0.1:8000/form-example/**) in your browser, and you should see it now displays the method at the top of the page (**GET**):

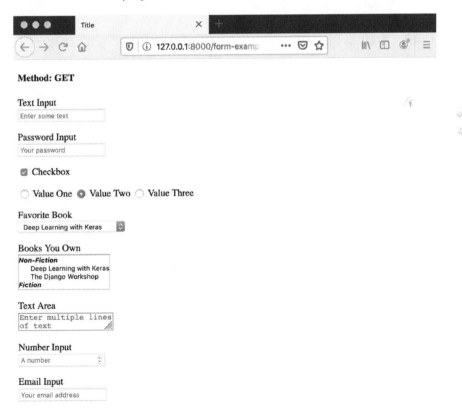

Figure 6.10: Method at the top of the page

6. Enter some text or data in each of the inputs and submit the form, by clicking the **Submit Input** button:

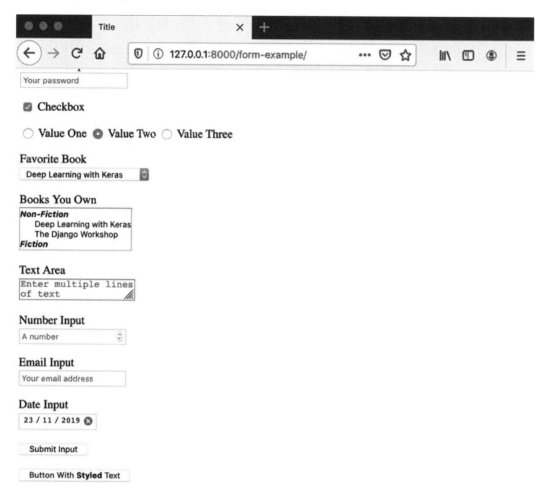

Figure 6.11: Clicking the Submit Input button to submit the form

You should see the page reload and the method displayed change to **POST**:

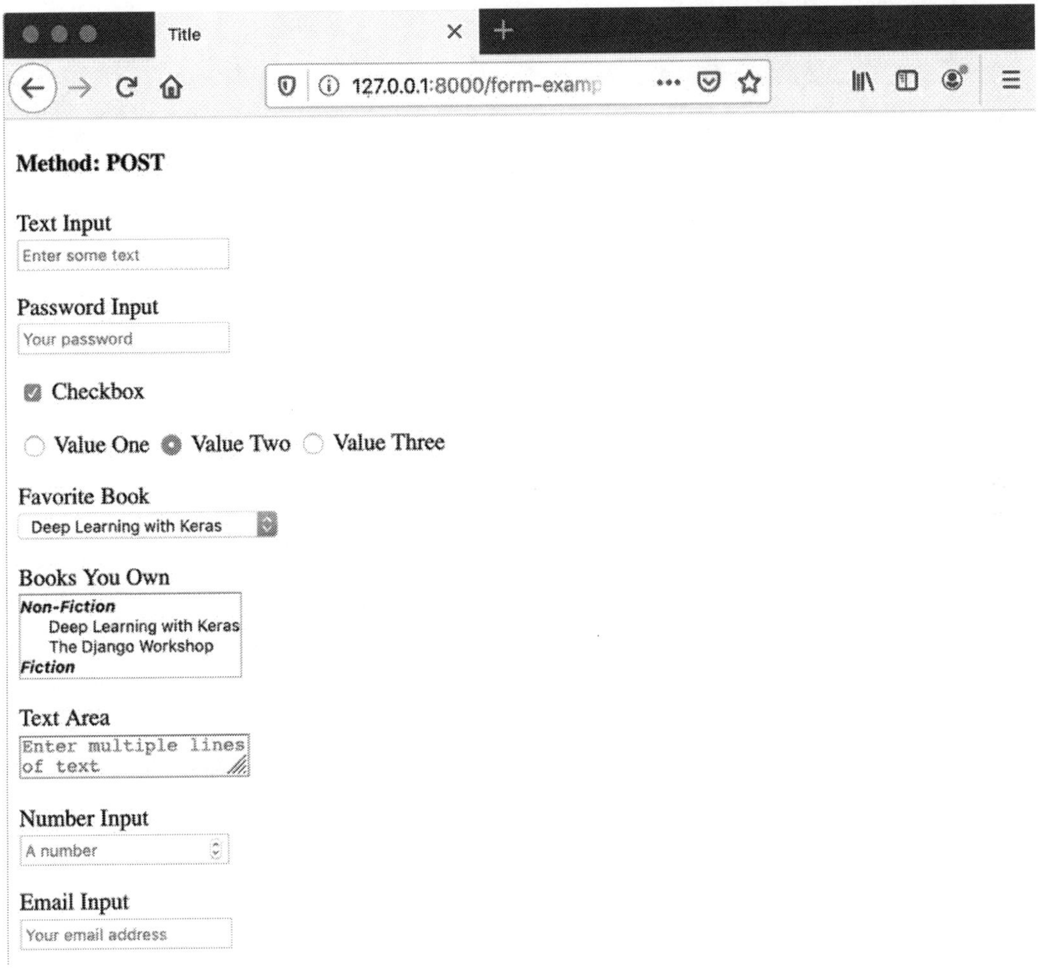

Method: POST

Text Input
`Enter some text`

Password Input
`Your password`

☑ Checkbox

○ Value One ◉ Value Two ○ Value Three

Favorite Book
`Deep Learning with Keras`

Books You Own
Non-Fiction
    Deep Learning with Keras
    The Django Workshop
Fiction

Text Area
`Enter multiple lines of text`

Number Input
`A number`

Email Input
`Your email address`

Figure 6.12: Method updated to POST after the form is submitted

7. Switch back to PyCharm and look in the **Run** console at the bottom of the window. If it is not visible, click the **Run** button at the bottom of the window to show it:

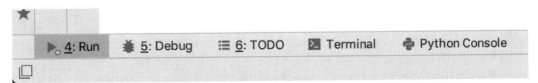

Figure 6.13: Click the Run button at the bottom of the window to display the console

Inside the **Run** console, a list of the values that were posted to the server should be displayed:

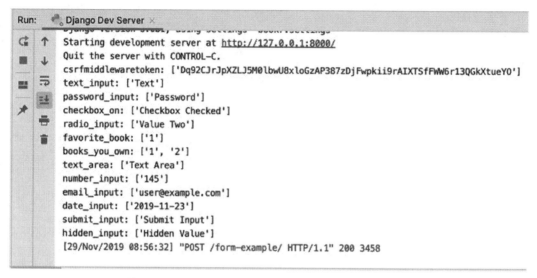

```
Run:      Django Dev Server ×
          Starting development server at http://127.0.0.1:8000/
          Quit the server with CONTROL-C.
          csrfmiddlewaretoken: ['Dq92CJrJpXZLJ5M0lbwU8xloGzAP387zDjFwpkii9rAIXTSfFWW6r13QGkXtueYO']
          text_input: ['Text']
          password_input: ['Password']
          checkbox_on: ['Checkbox Checked']
          radio_input: ['Value Two']
          favorite_book: ['1']
          books_you_own: ['1', '2']
          text_area: ['Text Area']
          number_input: ['145']
          email_input: ['user@example.com']
          date_input: ['2019-11-23']
          submit_input: ['Submit Input']
          hidden_input: ['Hidden Value']
          [29/Nov/2019 08:56:32] "POST /form-example/ HTTP/1.1" 200 3458
```

Figure 6.14: Input values shown in the Run console

Some things you should notice are as follows:

- All values are sent as text, even **number** and **date** inputs.

- For the **select** inputs, the selected **value** attributes of the selected options are sent, not the text content of the **option** tag.

- If you select multiple options for **books_you_own**, then you will see multiple values in the request. This is why we use the **getlist** method since multiple values are sent for the same input name.

- If the checkbox was checked, you will have a **checkbox_on** input in the debug output. If it was not checked, then the key will not exist at all (that is, there is no key, instead of having the key existing with an empty string or **None** value).

- We have a value for the name **submit_input**, which is the text **Submit Input**. You submitted the form by clicking the **Submit Input** button, so we receive its value. Notice that no value is set for the **button_element** input since that button was not clicked.

8. We will experiment with two other ways of submitting the form, first by hitting *Enter* when your cursor is in a text-like input (such as *text*, *password*, *date*, and *email*, but not *text area*, as hitting *Enter* there will add a new line).

If you submit a form in this way, the form will act as though you had clicked the first submit button on the form, so the **submit_input** input value will be included. The output you see should match that of the previous figure.

The other way to submit the form is by clicking the **Button Element** submit input, in which we will try clicking this button to submit the form. You should see that **submit_button** is no longer in the list of posted values, while **button_element** is now present:

```
csrfmiddlewaretoken: ['jfdrTNWqPwXvPwJWTL01]
text_input: ['Text']
password_input: ['Password']
checkbox_on: ['Checkbox Checked']
radio_input: ['Value Two']
favorite_book: ['2']
text_area: ['Some text']
number_input: ['4']
email_input: ['user@example.com']
date_input: ['2019-11-23']
button_element: ['Button Element']
hidden_input: ['Hidden Value']
```

Figure 6.15: submit_button is now gone from the inputs, and button_element is added

You can use this multiple-submit technique to alter how your view behaves depending on which button was clicked. You can even have multiple submit buttons with the same *name* attribute to make the logic easier to write.

In this exercise, you added a CSRF token to your **form** element by using the **{% csrf_token %}** template tag. This means that your form could then be submitted to Django successfully without generating an HTTP Permission Denied response. We then added some code to output the values that our form contained when it was submitted. We tried submitting the form with various values to see how they are parsed into Python variables on the **request.POST QueryDict**. We will now discuss some more theory around the difference between **GET** and **POST** requests, then move on to the Django Forms library, which makes designing and validating forms easier.

CHOOSING BETWEEN GET AND POST

Choosing when to use a **GET** or **POST** request requires the consideration of a number of factors. The most important is deciding whether or not the request should be idempotent. A request can be said to be idempotent if it can be repeated and produce the same result each time. Let us look at some examples.

If you type any web address into your browser (such as any of the Bookr pages we have built so far), it will perform a **GET** request to fetch the information. You can refresh the page, and no matter how many times you click refresh, you will get the same data back. The request you are making will not affect the content on the server. You would say these requests are idempotent.

Now, remember when you added data through the Django admin interface (in *Chapter 4, Introduction to Django Admin*)? You typed in the information for the new book in a form, then clicked **Save**. Your browser made a **POST** request to create a new book on the server. If you repeated that **POST** request, the server would create *another* book and would do so each time you repeated the request. Since the request is updating information, it is not idempotent. Your browser will warn you about this. If you have ever tried to refresh a page that you were sent to after submitting a form, you may have received a message asking if you want to *"Repost form data?"* (or something more verbose, as in the following figure). This is a warning that you are sending the form data again, which might cause the action you just undertook to be repeated:

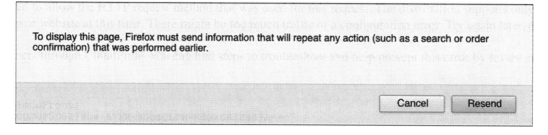

To display this page, Firefox must send information that will repeat any action (such as a search or order confirmation) that was performed earlier.

Cancel   Resend

Figure 6.16: Firefox confirming whether information should be resent

This is not to suggest that all **GET** requests are idempotent and all **POST** requests are not – your backend application can be designed in any way you want. Although it is not best practice, a developer might have decided to make data get updated during a **GET** request in their web application. When you are building your applications, you should try to make sure **GET** requests are idempotent and leave data-altering to **POST** requests only. Stick to these principles unless you have a good reason not to.

Another point to consider is that Django only applies CSRF projection to **POST** requests. Any **GET** request, including one that alters data, can be accessed without a CSRF token.

Sometimes, it can be hard to decide if a request is idempotent or not; for example, a login form. Before you submitted your username and password, you were not logged in, and afterward, the server considered you to be logged in, so could we consider that non-idempotent as it changed your authentication status with the server? On the other hand, once logged in, if you were able to send your credentials again, you would remain logged in. This implies that the request is idempotent and repeatable. So, should the request be **GET** or **POST**?

This brings us to the second point to consider when choosing what method to use. If sending form data with a **GET** request, the form parameters will be visible in the URL. For example, if we made a login form use a **GET** request, the login URL might be `https://www.example.com/login?username=user&password=password1`. The username, and worse, the password, is visible in the web browser's address bar. It would also be stored in the browser history, so anyone who used the browser after the real user could log in to the site. The URL is often stored in web server log files as well, meaning the credentials would be visible there too. In short, regardless of the idempotency of a request, don't pass sensitive data through URL parameters.

Sometimes, knowing that the parameter will be visible in the URL might be something you desire. For example, when searching with a search engine, usually the search parameter will be visible in the URL. To see this in action, try visiting https://www.google.com and searching for something. You'll notice that the page with the results has your search term as the **q** parameter. A search for **Django** will take you to the URL https://www.google.com/search?q=Django, for example. This allows you to share search results with someone else by sending them this URL. In *Activity 6.01, Book Searching*, you will add a search form that similarly passes a parameter.

Another consideration is that the maximum length of a URL allowed by a browser can be short compared to the size of a **POST** body – sometimes only around 2,000 characters (or about 2 KB) compared to many megabytes or gigabytes that a **POST** body can be (assuming your server is set up to allow these sizes of requests).

As we mentioned earlier, URL parameters are available in `request.GET` regardless of the type of request being made (**GET**, **POST**, **PUT**, and so on). You might find it useful to send some data in URL parameters and others in the request body (available in `request.POST`). For example, you could specify a `format` argument in the URL that sets what format some output data will be transformed to, but the input data is provided in the **POST** body.

WHY USE GET WHEN WE CAN PUT PARAMETERS IN THE URL?

Django allows us to easily define URL maps that contain variables. We could, for example, set up a URL mapping for a search view like this:

```
path('/search/<str:search>/', reviews.views.search)
```

This probably looks like a good approach at first, but when we start wanting to customize the results view with arguments, it can get complicated quickly. For example, we might want to be able to move from one results page to the next, so we add a page argument:

```
path('/search/<str:search>/<int:page>', reviews.views.search)
```

And then we might also want to order the search results by a specific category, such as the author name or the date of publishing, so we add another argument for that:

```
path('/search/<str:search>/<int:page>/<str:order >', \
      reviews.views.search)
```

You might be able to see the problem with this approach – we can't order the results without providing a page. If we wanted to also add a **results_per_page** argument too, we wouldn't be able to use that without setting **page** and **order** keys.

Contrast this to using query parameters: all of them are optional, so you could search like this:

```
?search=search+term:
```

Or you could set a page like this:

```
?search=search+term&page=2
```

Or you could just set the results ordering like this:

```
?search=search+term&order=author
```

Or you could combine them all:

```
?search=search+term&page=2&order=author
```

Another reason for using URL query parameters is that when submitting a form, the browser always sends the input values in this manner; it cannot be changed so that parameters are submitted as path components in the URL. Therefore, when submitting a form using **GET**, the URL query parameters must be used as the input data.

THE DJANGO FORMS LIBRARY

We've looked at how to manually write forms in HTML and how to access the data on the request object using **QueryDict**. We saw that the browser provides some validation for us for certain field types, such as email or numbers, but we have not tried validating the data in the Python view. We should validate the form in the Python view for two reasons:

- It is not safe to rely solely on browser-based validation of input data. A browser may not implement certain validation features, meaning the user could post any type of data. For example, older browsers don't validate number fields, so a user can type in a number outside the range we are expecting. Furthermore, a malicious user could try to send harmful data without using a browser at all. The browser validation should be considered as a nicety for the user and that's all.

- The browser does not allow us to do cross-field validation. For example, we can use the **required** attribute for inputs that are mandatory to be filled in. Often, though, we want to set the **required** attribute, based on the value of another input. For example, the email address input should only be set as **required** if the user has checked the **Register My Email** checkbox.

The Django Forms library allows you to quickly define a form using a Python class. This is done by creating a subclass of the base Django **Form** class. You can then use an instance of this class to render the form in your template and validate the input data. We refer to our classes as forms, similar to how we subclass Django models to create our own **Model** classes. Forms contain one or more fields of a certain type (such as text fields, number fields, or email fields). You'll notice this sounds like Django models, and forms *are* similar to models but use different field classes. You can even automatically create a form from a model – we will cover this in *Chapter 7, Advanced Form Validation and Model Forms*.

DEFINING A FORM

Creating a Django form is similar to creating a Django model. You define a class that inherits from the **django.forms.Form** class. The class has attributes, which are instances of different **django.forms.Field** subclasses. When rendered, the attribute name in the class corresponds to its input **name** in HTML. To give you a quick idea of what fields there are, some examples are **CharField**, **IntegerField**, **BooleanField**, **ChoiceField**, and **DateField**. Each field generally corresponds to one input when rendered in HTML, but there's not always a one-to-one mapping between a form field class and an input type. Form fields are more coupled to the type of data they collect rather than how they are displayed.

To illustrate this, consider a **text** input and a **password** input. They both accept some typed-in text data, but the main difference between them is that the text is visibly displayed in a **text** input, whereas with a **password** input the text is obscured. In a Django form, both of these fields are represented using **CharField**. The difference in how they are displayed is set by changing the *widget* the field is using.

> **NOTE**
>
> If you're not familiar with the word *widget*, it is a term to describe the actual input that is being interacted with and how it is displayed. Text inputs, password inputs, select menus, checkboxes, and buttons are all examples of different widgets. The inputs we have seen in HTML correspond one-to-one with widgets. In Django, this is not the case, and the same type of **Field** class can be rendered in multiple ways depending on the widget that is specified.

Django defines a number of **Widget** classes that define how a **Field** should be rendered as HTML. They inherit from **django.forms.widgets.Widget**. A widget can be passed to the **Field** constructor to change how it is rendered. For example, a **CharField** instance renders as **text <input>** by default. If we use the **PasswordInput** widget, it will instead render as **password <input>**. The other widgets we will use are as follows:

- **RadioSelect**, which renders a **ChoiceField** instance as radio buttons instead of a **<select>** menu

- **Textarea**, which renders a **CharField** instance as **<textarea>**

- **HiddenInput**, which renders a field as a hidden **<input>**

We will look at an example form and add fields and features one by one. First, let's just create a form with a text input and a password input:

```
from django import forms


class ExampleForm(forms.Form):
    text_input = forms.CharField()
    password_input = forms.CharField(widget=forms.PasswordInput)
```

The **widget** argument can be just a widget subclass, which can be fine a lot of the time. If you want to further customize the display of the input and its attributes, you can set the widget argument to an instance of the **widget** class instead. We will look at further customizing widget displays soon. In this case, we're using just the **PasswordInput** class, since we are not customizing it beyond changing the type of input being displayed.

When the form is rendered in a template, it looks like this:

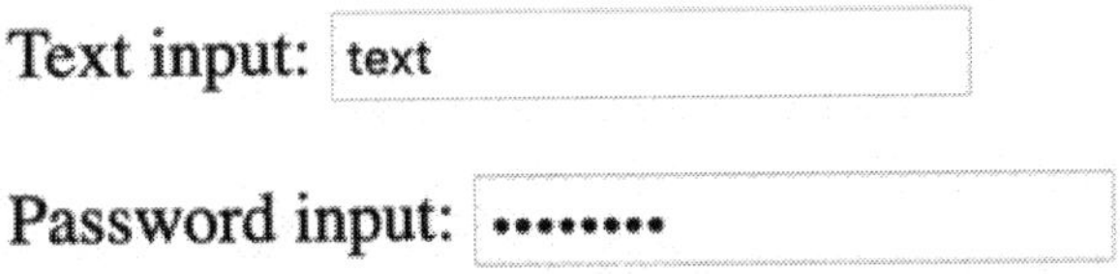

Text input: text

Password input: ••••••••

Figure 6.17: Django form rendered in a browser

Note that the inputs do not contain any content when the page loads; the text has been entered to illustrate the different input types.

If we examine the page source, we can see the HTML that Django generates. For the first two fields, it looks like this (some spacing added for readability):

```
<p>
    <label for="id_text_input">Text input:</label>
    <input type="text" name="text_input" required id="id_text_input">
</p>
<p>
    <label for="id_password_input">Password input:</label>
    <input type="password" name="password_input" required id="id_
password_input">
</p>
```

Notice that Django has automatically generated a **label** instance with its text derived from the field name. The **name** and **id** attributes have been set automatically. Django also automatically adds the **required** attribute to the input. Similar to model fields, form field constructors also accept a **required** argument – this defaults to **True**. Setting this to **False** removes the **required** attribute from the generated HTML.

Next, we'll look at how a checkbox is added to the form:

- A checkbox is represented with **BooleanField**, as it can have only two values, checked or unchecked. It's added to the form in the same way as the other field:

```
class ExampleForm(forms.Form):
    ...
    checkbox_on = forms.BooleanField()
```

The HTML that Django generates for this new field is similar to the previous two fields:

```
<label for="id_checkbox_on">Checkbox on:</label>
<input type="checkbox" name="checkbox_on" required id="id_checkbox_
on">
```

Next are the select inputs:

- We need to provide a list of choices to display in the **<select>** dropdown.

- The field class constructor takes a **choices** argument. The choices are provided as a tuple of two-element tuples. The first element in each sub-tuple is the value of the choice and the second element is the text or description of the choice. For example, choices could be defined like this:

```
BOOK_CHOICES = (('1', 'Deep Learning with Keras'),\
                ('2', 'Web Development with Django'),\
                ('3', 'Brave New World'),\
                ('4', 'The Great Gatsby'))
```

Note that you can use lists instead of tuples if you want (or a combination of the two). This can be useful if you want your choices to be mutable:

```
BOOK_CHOICES = (['1', 'Deep Learning with Keras'],\
                ['2', 'Web Development with Django'],\
                ['3', 'Brave New World'],\
                ['4', 'The Great Gatsby']]
```

- To implement **optgroup**, we can nest the choices. To implement the choices the same way as our previous examples, we use a structure like this:

```
BOOK_CHOICES = (('Non-Fiction', \
                (('1', 'Deep Learning with Keras'),\
                ('2', 'Web Development with Django'))),\
                ('Fiction', \
                (('3', 'Brave New World'),\
                ('4', 'The Great Gatsby')))))
```

The **select** functionality is added to the form by using a **ChoiceField** instance. The widget defaults to a **select** input so no configuration is necessary apart from setting **choices**:

```
class ExampleForm(forms.Form):
    ...
    favorite_book = forms.ChoiceField(choices=BOOK_CHOICES)
```

This is the HTML that is generated:

```
<label for="id_favorite_book">Favorite book:</label>
<select name="favorite_book" id="id_favorite_book">
    <optgroup label="Non-Fiction">
        <option value="1">Deep Learning with Keras</option>
        <option value="2">Web Development with Django</option>
    </optgroup>
    <optgroup label="Fiction">
        <option value="3">Brave New World</option>
        <option value="4">The Great Gatsby</option>
    </optgroup>
</select>
```

Making a multiple select requires the use of **MultipleChoiceField**. It takes a **choices** argument in the same format as the regular **ChoiceField** for single selects:

```
class ExampleForm(forms.Form):
    ...
    books_you_own = forms.MultipleChoiceField(choices=BOOK_CHOICES)
```

And its HTML is similar to that of the single select, except it has the **multiple** attribute added:

```
<label for="id_books_you_own">Books you own:</label>
<select name="books_you_own" required id="id_books_you_own" multiple>
    <optgroup label="Non-Fiction">
        <option value="1">Deep Learning with Keras</option>
        <option value="2">Web Development with Django</option>
    </optgroup>
    <optgroup label="Fiction">
        <option value="3">Brave New World</option>
        <option value="4">The Great Gatsby</option>
    </optgroup>
</select>
```

Choices can also be set after the form is instantiated. You may want to generate the choices **list/tuple** inside your view dynamically and then assign it to the field's **choices** attribute. See the following, for example:

```
form = ExampleForm()
form.fields["books_you_own"].choices = \
[("1", "Deep Learning with Keras"), …]
```

Next are the radio inputs, which are similar to selects:

- Like selects, radio inputs use **ChoiceField**, as they provide a single choice between multiple options.

- The options to choose between are passed into the field constructor with the **choices** argument.

- The choices are provided as a tuple of two-element tuples, also like selects:

```
choices = (('1', 'Option One'),\
           ('2', 'Option Two'),\
           ('3', 'Option Three'))
```

ChoiceField defaults to displaying as a **select** input, so the widget must be set to **RadioSelect** to have it rendered as radio buttons. Putting the choice setting together with this, we add radio buttons to the form like this:

```
RADIO_CHOICES = (('Value One', 'Value One'),\
                 ('Value Two', 'Value Two'),\
                 ('Value Three', 'Value Three'))



class ExampleForm(forms.Form):
    ...
    radio_input = forms.ChoiceField(choices=RADIO_CHOICES,\
                                    widget=forms.RadioSelect)
```

Here is the HTML that is generated:

```
<label for="id_radio_input_0">Radio input:</label>
<ul id="id_radio_input">
<li>
    <label for="id_radio_input_0">
        <input type="radio" name="radio_input"
          value="Value One" required id="id_radio_input_0">
        Value One
    </label>
</li>
<li>
    <label for="id_radio_input_1">
        <input type="radio" name="radio_input"
          value="Value Two" required id="id_radio_input_1">
        Value Two
    </label>
</li>
<li>
    <label for="id_radio_input_2">
        <input type="radio" name="radio_input"
          value="Value Three" required id="id_radio_input_2">
        Value Three
    </label>
</li>
</ul>
```

Django automatically generates a unique label and ID for each of the three radio buttons:

- To create a **textarea** instance, use **CharField** with a **Textarea** widget:

```
class ExampleForm(forms.Form):
    ...
    text_area = forms.CharField(widget=forms.Textarea)
```

You might notice that **textarea** is much larger than the previous ones we have seen (see the following figure):

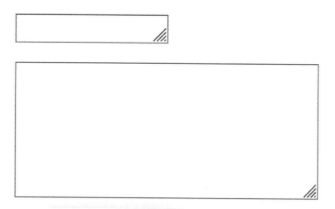

Figure 6.18: Normal textarea (top) versus Django's default textarea (bottom)

This is because Django automatically adds **cols** and **rows** attributes. These set the number of columns and rows, respectively, that the text field displays:

```
<label for="id_text_area">Text area:</label>
<textarea name="text_area" cols="40"
  rows="10" required id="id_text_area"></textarea>
```

- Note that the **cols** and **rows** settings do not affect the amount of text that can be entered into a field, only the amount that is displayed at a time. Also note that the size of **textarea** can be set using CSS (for example, the **height** and **width** properties). This will override the **cols** and **rows** settings.

To create **number** inputs, you might expect Django to have a **NumberField** type, but it does not.

Remember that the Django form fields are data-centric rather than display-centric, so instead, Django provides different **Field** classes depending on what type of numeric data you want to store:

- For integers, use **IntegerField**.

- For floating-point numbers, use **FloatField** or **DecimalField**. The latter two differ in how they convert their data to a Python value.

- **FloatField** will convert to a float while **DecimalField** is a decimal.

- Decimal values offer better accuracy in representing numbers than float values but may not integrate well into your existing Python code.

We'll add all three fields to the form at once:

```
class ExampleForm(forms.Form):
    ...
    integer_input = forms.IntegerField()
    float_input = forms.FloatField()
    decimal_input = forms.DecimalField()
```

Here's the HTML for all three:

```
<p>
    <label for="id_integer_input">Integer input:</label>
    <input type="number" name="integer_input"
      required id="id_integer_input">
</p>
<p>
    <label for="id_float_input">Float input:</label>
    <input type="number" name="float_input"
      step="any" required id="id_float_input">
</p>
<p>
    <label for="id_decimal_input">Decimal
      input:</label>
    <input type="number" name="decimal_input"
      step="any" required id="id_decimal_input">
</p>
```

The **IntegerField** generated HTML is missing the **step** attribute that the other two have, which means the widget will only accept integer values. The other two fields (**FloatField** and **DecimalField**) generate very similar HTML. Their behavior is the same in the browser; they differ only when their values are used in Django code.

As you might have guessed, an **email** input can be created with **EmailField**:

```
class ExampleForm(forms.Form):
    ...
    email_input = forms.EmailField()
```

Its HTML is similar to the **email** input we created manually:

```
<label for="id_email_input">Email input:</label>
<input type="email" name="email_input" required id="id_email_input">
```

Following our manually created form, the next field we will look at is **DateField**:

- By default, Django will render **DateField** as **text** input, and the browser will not show a calendar popup when the field is clicked.

We can add **DateField** to the form with no arguments, like this:

```
class ExampleForm(forms.Form):
    ...
    date_input = forms.DateField()
```

When rendered, it just looks like a normal **text** input:

Date input:

Figure 6.19: Default DateField display in a form

Here is the HTML generated by default:

```
<label for="id_date_input">Date input:</label>
<input type="text" name="date_input" required id="id_date_input">
```

The reason for using a **text** input is that it allows the user to enter the date in a number of different formats. For example, by default, the user can type in the date in *Year-Month-Day* (dash-separated) or *Month/Day/Year* (slash-separated) formats. The accepted formats can be specified by passing a list of formats to the **DateField** constructor using the **input_formats** argument. For example, we could accept dates in the formats of *Day/Month/Year* or *Day/Month/Year-with-century*, like this:

```
DateField(input_formats = ['%d/m/%y', '%d/%m/%Y'])
```

We can override any attributes on a field's widget by passing the **attrs** argument to the widget constructor. This accepts a dictionary of attribute key/values that will be rendered into the input's HTML.

We have not used this yet, but we will see it again in the next chapter when we customize the field rendering further. For now, we'll just set one attribute, **type**, that will overwrite the default input type:

```
class ExampleForm(forms.Form):
    ...
    date_input = forms.DateField\
                (widget=forms.DateInput(attrs={'type': 'date'}))
```

When rendered, it now looks like the date field we had before, and clicking on it brings up the calendar date picker:

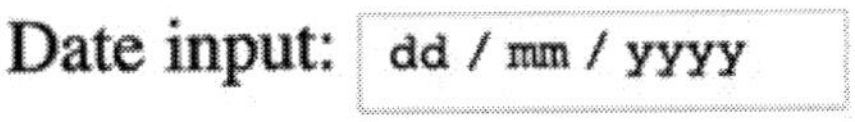

Date input: `dd / mm / yyyy`

Figure 6.20: DateField with date input

Examining the generated HTML now, we can see it uses the **date** type:

```
<label for="id_date_input">Date input:</label>
<input type="date" name="date_input" required id="id_date_input">
```

The final input that we are missing is the hidden input.

Once again, due to the data-centric nature of Django forms, there is no **HiddenField**. Instead, we choose the type of field that needs to be hidden and set its **widget** to **HiddenInput**. We can then set the value of the field using the field constructor's **initial** argument:

```
class ExampleForm(forms.Form):
    ...
    hidden_input = forms.CharField\
                (widget=forms.HiddenInput, \
                initial='Hidden Value')
```

Here is the generated HTML:

```
<input type="hidden" name="hidden_input"
    value="Hidden Value" id="id_hidden_input">
```

Note that as this is a **hidden** input, Django does not generate a **label** instance or any surrounding **p** elements. There are other form fields that Django provides that work in similar ways. These range from **DateTimeField** (for capturing a date and time) to **GenericIPAddressField** (for either IPv4 or IPv6 addresses) and **URLField** (for URLs). A full list of fields is available at https://docs.djangoproject.com/en/3.0/ref/forms/fields/.

RENDERING A FORM IN A TEMPLATE

We've now seen how to create a form and add fields, and we've seen what the form looks like and what HTML is generated. But how is the form actually rendered in the template? We simply instantiate the **Form** class and pass it to the **render** function in a view, using the context, just like any other variable.

For example, here's how to pass our **ExampleForm** to a template:

```
def view_function(request):
    form = ExampleForm()
    return render(request, "template.html", {"form": form})
```

Django does not add the **<form>** element or submit button(s) for you when rendering the template; you should add these around where your form is placed in the template. The form can be rendered like any other variable.

We mentioned briefly earlier that the form is rendered in the template using the **as_p** method. This layout method was chosen as it most closely matches the example form we built manually. Django offers three layout methods that can be used:

- **as_table**

  The form is rendered as table rows, with each input on its own row. Django does not generate the surrounding **table** element, so you should wrap the form yourself. See the following example:

```
<form method="post">
    <table>
        {{ form.as_table }}
    </table>
</form>
```

`as_table` is the default rendering method, so `{{ form.as_table }}` and `{{ form }}` are equivalent. When rendered, the form looks like this:

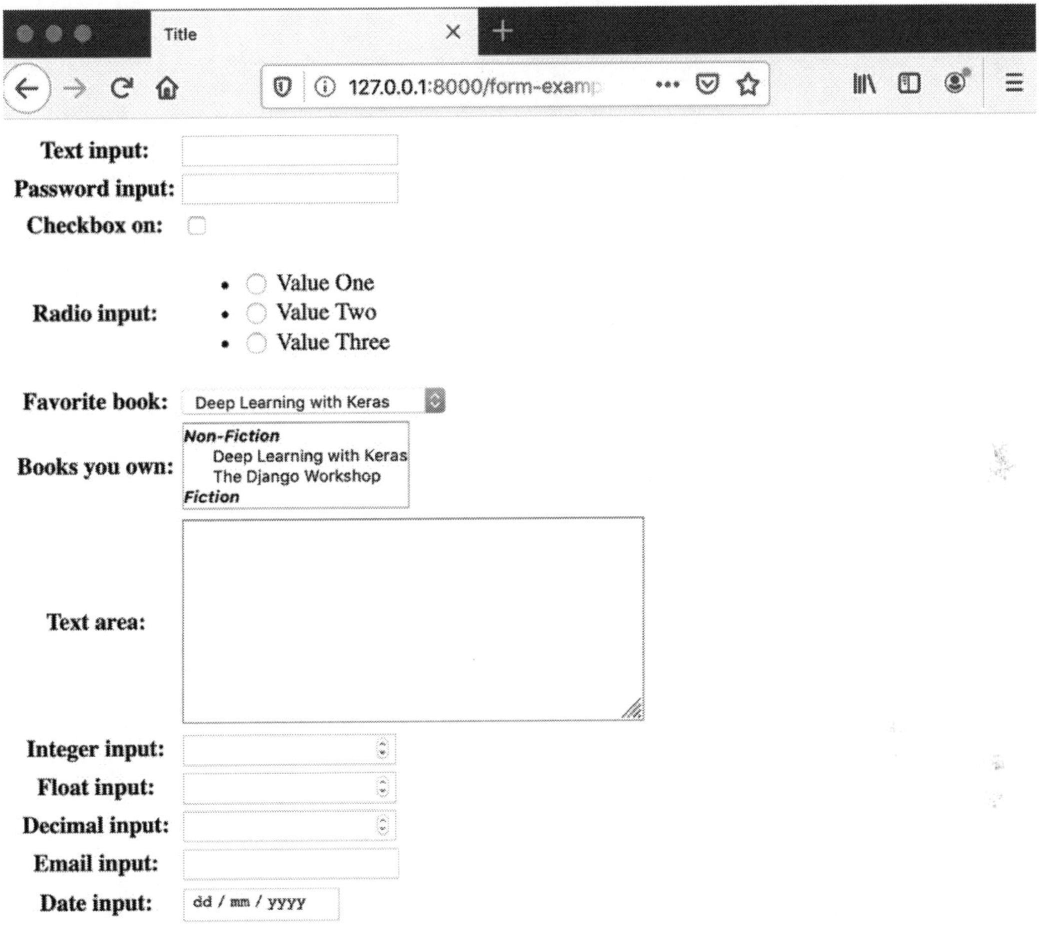

Figure 6.21: Form rendered as a table

Here is a small sample of HTML that is generated:

```
<tr>
    <th>
        <label for="id_text_input">Text input:</label>
    </th>
    <td>
        <input type="text" name="text_input" required id="id_text_
input">
    </td>
</tr>
<tr>
    <th>
        <label for="id_password_input">Password input:</label>
    </th>
    <td>
        <input type="password" name="password_input" required id="id_
password_input">
    </td>
</tr>
```

- **as_ul**

    This renders the form fields as list items (**li**) inside either a **ul** or **ol** element. Like with **as_table**, the containing element (**<ul>** or **<ol>**) is not created by Django and must be added by you:

```
<form method="post">
    <ul>
        {{ form.as_ul }}
    </ul>
</form>
```

Here's how the form renders using **as_ul**:

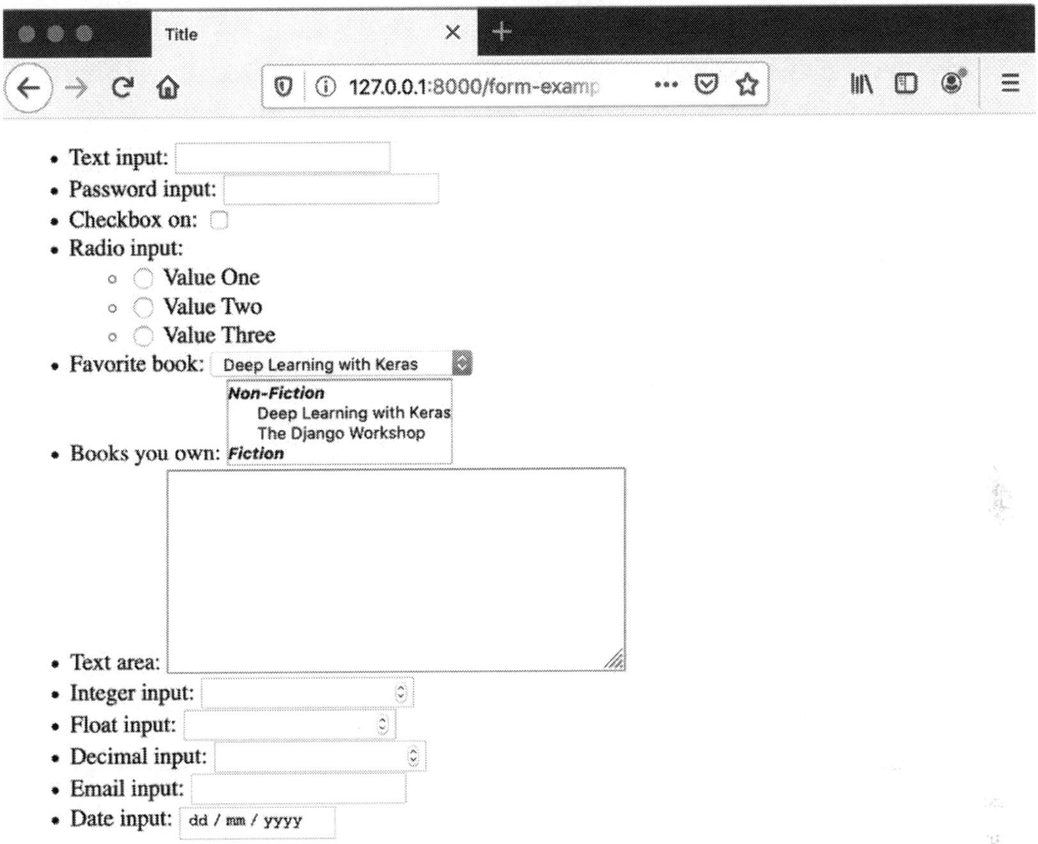

Figure 6.22: Form rendered using as_ul

And here's a sample of the generated HTML:

```
<li>
    <label for="id_text_input">Text input:</label>
    <input type="text" name="text_input" required id="id_text_input">
</li>
<li>
    <label for="id_password_input">Password input:</label>
    <input type="password" name="password_input" required id="id_
password_input">
</li>
```

- **as_p**

  Finally, there is the **as_p** method, which we were using in our previous examples. Each input is wrapped within **p** tags, which means that you don't have to wrap the form manually (in **<table>** or **<ul>**) like you did with the previous methods:

```
<form method="post">
    {{ form.as_p }}
</form>
```

Here's what the rendered form looks like: 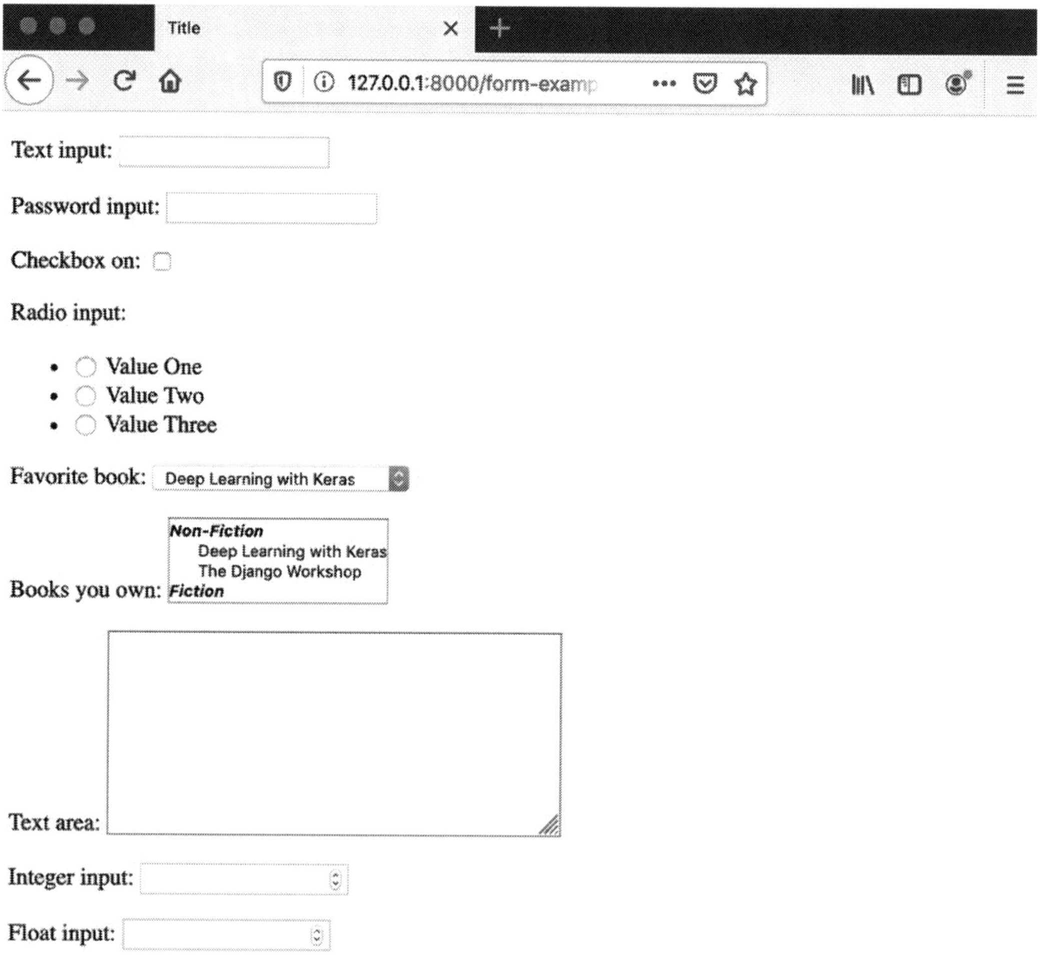

Figure 6.23: Form rendered using as_p

And you've seen this before, but once again, here's a sample of the HTML generated:

```
<p>
    <label for="id_text_input">Text input:</label>
    <input type="text" name="text_input" required id="id_text_input">
</p>
<p>
    <label for="id_password_input">Password input:</label>
    <input type="password" name="password_input" required
        id="id_password_input">
</p>
```

It is up to you to decide which method you want to use to render your form, depending on which suits your application best. In terms of their behavior and use with your view, all of the methods are all identical. In *Chapter 15, Django Third Party Libraries*, we will also introduce a method of rendering forms that will make use of the Bootstrap CSS classes.

Now that we have been introduced to Django Forms, we can now update our example form page to use a Django Form instead of manually writing all the HTML ourselves.

EXERCISE 6.03: BUILDING AND RENDERING A DJANGO FORM

In this exercise, you will build a Django form using all the fields we have seen. The form and view will behave similarly to the form that we built manually; however, you will be able to see how much less code is required when writing forms using Django. Your form will also automatically get field validation, and if we make changes to the form, we don't have to then make changes to the HTML, as it will update dynamically based on the form definition:

1. In PyCharm, create a new file called **forms.py** inside the **form_example** app directory.

2. Import the Django **forms** library at the top of your **forms.py** file:

    ```
    from django import forms
    ```

3. Define the choices for the radio buttons by creating a **RADIO_CHOICES** variable. Populate it as follows:

    ```
    RADIO_CHOICES = (("Value One", "Value One Display"),\
                     ("Value Two", "Text For Value Two"),\
                     ("Value Three", "Value Three's Display Text"))
    ```

You will use this soon when you create a **ChoiceField** instance called **radio_input**.

4. Define the nested choices for the book select inputs by creating a **BOOK_CHOICES** variable. Populate it as follows:

```
BOOK_CHOICES = (("Non-Fiction", \
                (("1", "Deep Learning with Keras"),\
                ("2", "Web Development with Django"))),\
                ("Fiction", \
                (("3", "Brave New World"),\
                ("4", "The Great Gatsby")))))
```

5. Create a class called **ExampleForm** that inherits from the **forms.Form** class:

```
class ExampleForm(forms.Form):
```

Add all of the following fields as attributes on the class:

```
text_input = forms.CharField()
password_input = forms.CharField\
                    (widget=forms.PasswordInput)
checkbox_on = forms.BooleanField()
radio_input = forms.ChoiceField\
                (choices=RADIO_CHOICES, \
                widget=forms.RadioSelect)
favorite_book = forms.ChoiceField(choices=BOOK_CHOICES)
books_you_own = forms.MultipleChoiceField\
                (choices=BOOK_CHOICES)
text_area = forms.CharField(widget=forms.Textarea)
integer_input = forms.IntegerField()
float_input = forms.FloatField()
decimal_input = forms.DecimalField()
email_input = forms.EmailField()
date_input = forms.DateField\
                (widget=forms.DateInput\
                    (attrs={"type": "date"}))
hidden_input = forms.CharField\
                (widget=forms.HiddenInput, initial="Hidden Value")
```

Save the file.

6. Open your **form_example** app's **views.py** file. At the top of the file, add a line to import **ExampleForm** from your **forms.py** file:

```
from .forms import ExampleForm
```

7. Inside the **form_example** view, instantiate the **ExampleForm** class and assign it to the **form** variable:

```
form = ExampleForm()
```

8. Add the **form** variable into the context dictionary, using the **form** key. The **return** line should look like this:

```
return render(request, "form-example.html",\
                  {"method": request.method, "form": form})
```

Save the file. Make sure you haven't removed the code that prints out the data the form has sent, as we will use it again later in this exercise.

9. Open the **form-example.html** file, inside the **form_example** app's **templates** directory. You can remove nearly all of the contents of the **form** element, except the **{% csrf_token %}** template tag and the submit buttons. When you're done, it should look like this:

```
<form method="post">
    {% csrf_token %}


    <p>
        <input type="submit" name="submit_input" value="Submit
Input">
    </p>
    <p>
        <button type="submit" name="button_element" value="Button
Element">
            Button With <strong>Styled</strong> Text
        </button>
    </p>
</form>
```

10. Add a rendering of the **form** variable using the **as_p** method. Put this on the line after the **{% csrf_token %}** template tag. The whole **form** element should now look like this:

```
<form method="post">
    {% csrf_token %}
    {{ form.as_p }}
```

```
      <p>
          <input type="submit" name="submit_input" value="Submit
    Input">
      </p>
      <p>
          <button type="submit" name="button_element"
            value="Button Element">
              Button With <strong>Styled</strong> Text
          </button>
      </p>
  </form>
```

11. Start the Django dev server if it is not already running, then visit the form example page in your browser, at **http://127.0.0.1:8000/form-example/**. It should look as follows:

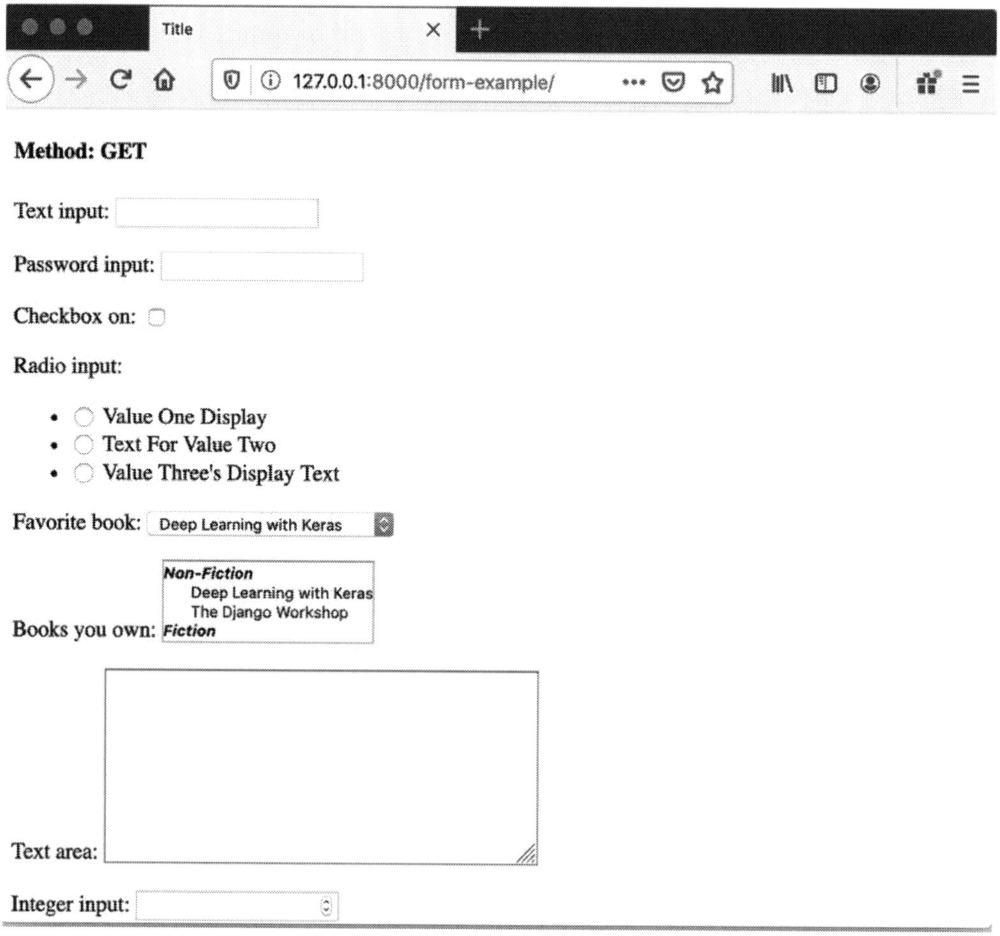

Figure 6.24: Django ExampleForm rendered in the browser

12. Enter some data in the form – since Django marks all fields as required, you will need to enter some text or select values for all fields, including ensuring that the checkbox is checked. Submit the form.

13. Switch back to PyCharm and look in the Debug Console at the bottom of the window. You should see all the values being submitted by the form are printed out to the console, similar to *Exercise 6.02, Working with POST Data in a View*:

```
csrfmiddlewaretoken: ['rZ5I3cs3xV0LS2oUU2rkXJyIktyDSX4yrSBcQNjChpBI6Qu9eNRwgdgakeVhj3VN']
text_input: ['Text']
password_input: ['password']
checkbox_on: ['on']
radio_input: ['Value Two']
favorite_book: ['1']
books_you_own: ['1', '2']
text_area: ['Some text in the text area.']
integer_input: ['10']
float_input: ['10.5']
decimal_input: ['11.5']
email_input: ['user@example.com']
date_input: ['2020-04-20']
hidden_input: ['Hidden Value']
submit_input: ['Submit Input']
```

Figure 6.25: Values as submitted by the Django form

You can see that the values are still strings, and the names match those of the attributes of **ExampleForm** class. Notice that the submit button that you clicked is included, as well as the CSRF token. The form you submit can be a mix of Django form fields and arbitrary fields you add; both will be contained in the **request.POST QueryDict** object.

In this exercise, you created a Django form, with many different types of form fields. You instantiated it into a variable in your view, then passed it to **form-example. html** where it was rendered as HTML. Finally, you submitted the form and looked at the values it posted. Notice that the amount of code we had to write to generate the same form was greatly reduced. We did not have to manually code any HTML and we now have one place that both defines how the form will display and how it will validate. In the next section, we will examine how Django forms can automatically validate the submitted data, as well as how the data is converted from strings to Python objects.

VALIDATING FORMS AND RETRIEVING PYTHON VALUES

So far, we have seen how Django Forms makes it much simpler to define a form using Python code and have it automatically rendered. We will now look at the other part of what makes Django forms useful: their ability to automatically validate the form and then retrieve native Python objects and values from them.

In Django, a form can either be *unbound* or *bound*. These terms describe whether or not the form has had the submitted **POST** data sent to it for validation. So far, we have only seen unbound forms – they are instantiated without arguments, like this:

```
form = ExampleForm()
```

A form is bound if it is called with some data to be used for validation, such as the **POST** data. A bound form can be created like this:

```
form = ExampleForm(request.POST)
```

A bound form allows us to start using built-in validation-related tools: first, the **is_valid** method to check the form's validity, then the **cleaned_data** attribute on the form, which contains the values converted from strings to Python objects. The **cleaned_data** attribute is only available after the form has been *cleaned*, which means the process of "cleaning up" the data and converting it from strings to Python objects. The cleaning process runs during the **is_valid** call. You will get **AttributeError** raised if you try to access **cleaned_data** before calling **is_valid**.

A short example of how to access the cleaned data of **ExampleForm** follows:

```
form = ExampleForm(request.POST)

if form.is_valid():
    # cleaned_data is only populated if the form is valid
    if form.cleaned_data["integer_input"] > 5:
        do_something()
```

In this example, **form.cleaned_data["integer_input"]** is the integer value **10**, so it can be compared to the number *5*. Compare this to the value that was posted, which is the string **"10"**. The cleaning process performs this conversion for us. Other fields such as dates or Booleans are converted accordingly.

The cleaning process also sets any errors on the form and fields that will be displayed when the form is rendered again. Let's see all this in action. Modern browsers provide a large amount of client-side validation, so they prevent forms from being submitted unless their basic validation rules are met. You might have already seen this if you tried to submit the form in the previous exercise with empty fields:

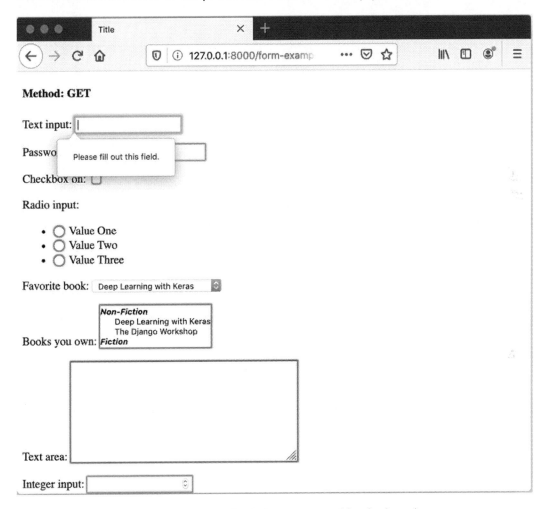

Figure 6.26: Form submission prevented by the browser

Figure 6.26 shows the browser preventing form submission. Since the browser is preventing the submission, Django never gets the opportunity to validate the form itself. To allow the form to be submitted, we need to add some more advanced validation that the browser is unable to validate itself.

We will discuss the different types of validations that can be applied to form fields in the next section, but for now, we will just add a **max_digits** setting of **3** to **decimal_input** for our **ExampleForm**. This means the user should not enter more than three digits into the form.

> **NOTE**
>
> Why should Django validate the form if the browser is already doing this and preventing submission? A server-side application should never trust input from the user: the user might be using an older browser or another HTTP client to send the request, thus not receiving any errors from their "browser." Also, as we have just mentioned, there are types of validation that the browser does not understand, and so Django must validate these on its end.

ExampleForm is updated like this:

```
class ExampleForm(forms.Form):
    ...
    decimal_input = forms.DecimalField(max_digits=3)
    ...
```

Now the view should be updated to pass **request.POST** to the **Form** class when the method is **POST**, for example, like this:

```
if request.method == "POST":
    form = ExampleForm(request.POST)
else:
    form = ExampleForm()
```

If you pass **request.POST** into the form constructor when the method is not **POST**, then the form will always contain errors when first rendered, as **request.POST** will be empty. Now the browser will let us submit the form, but we will get an error displayed if the **decimal_input** contains more than three digits:

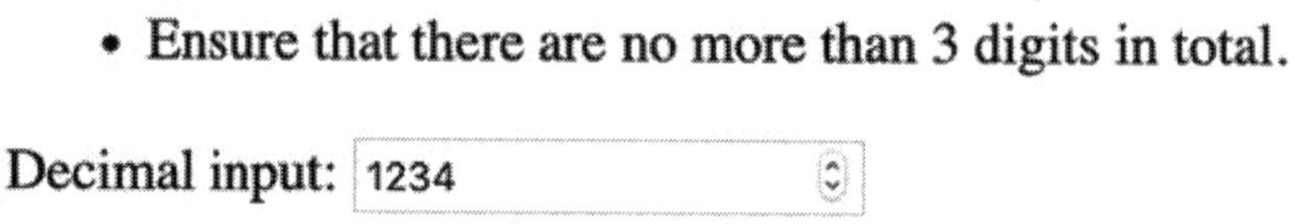

- Ensure that there are no more than 3 digits in total.

Decimal input: 1234

Figure 6.27: An error displayed when a field is not valid

Django is automatically rendering the form differently in the template when it has errors. But how can we make the view behave differently depending on the validity of the form? As we mentioned earlier, we should use the form's **is_valid** method. A view using this check might have code like this:

```
form = ExampleForm(request.POST)

if form.is_valid():
    # perform operations with data from form.cleaned_data
    return redirect("/success-page")   # redirect to a success page
```

In this example, we are redirecting to a success page if the form is valid. Otherwise, assume the execution flow continues as before and passes the invalid form back to the **render** function to be displayed to the user with errors.

> **NOTE**
>
> Why do we return a redirect on success? For two reasons: first, an early return prevents the execution of the rest of the view (that is, the failure branch); second, it prevents the message about resending the form data if the user then reloads the page.

In the next exercise, we will see the form validation in action and change the view execution flow based on the validity of the form.

EXERCISE 6.04: VALIDATING FORMS IN A VIEW

In this exercise, we will update the example view to instantiate the form differently depending on the HTTP method. We will also change the form to print out the cleaned data instead of the raw **POST** data, but only if the form is valid:

1. In PyCharm, open the **forms.py** file inside the **form_example** app directory. Add a **max_digits=3** argument to **decimal_input** of **ExampleForm**:

```
class ExampleForm(forms.Form):
    ...
    decimal_input = forms.DecimalField(max_digits=3)
```

Once this argument is added, we can submit the form, since the browser does not know how to validate this rule, but Django does.

2. Open the **reviews** app's **views.py** file. We need to update the **form_example** view so that if the request's method is **POST**, the **ExampleForm** is instantiated with the **POST** data; otherwise, it's instantiated without arguments. Replace the current form initialization with this code:

```
def form_example(request):
    if request.method == "POST":
        form = ExampleForm(request.POST)
    else:
        form = ExampleForm()
```

3. Next, also for the **POST** request method, we will check whether the form is valid using the **is_valid** method. If the form is valid, we will print out all of the cleaned data. Add a condition after the **ExampleForm** instantiation to check **form.is_valid()**, then move the debug print loop inside this condition. Your **POST** branch should look like this:

```
if request.method == "POST":
    form = ExampleForm(request.POST)
    if form.is_valid():
        for name in request.POST:
            print("{}: {}".format\
                        (name, request.POST.getlist(name)))
```

4. Instead of iterating over the raw **request.POST QueryDict** (in which all the data are **string** instances), we will iterate over **cleaned_data** of **form**. This is a normal dictionary and contains the values converted to Python objects. Replace the **for** line and **print** line with these two:

```
for name, value in form.cleaned_data.items():
    print("{}: ({}) {}".format\
                (name, type(value), value))
```

We don't need to use **getlist()** anymore, as **cleaned_data** has already converted the multi-value fields into **list** instances.

5. Start the Django dev server, if it is not already running. Switch to your browser and browse to the example form page at **http://127.0.0.1:8000/form-example/**. The form should look as it did before. Fill in all the fields, but be sure to enter four or more numbers into the **Decimal input** field to make the form invalid. Submit the form, and you should see the error message for **Decimal input** show up when the page refreshes:

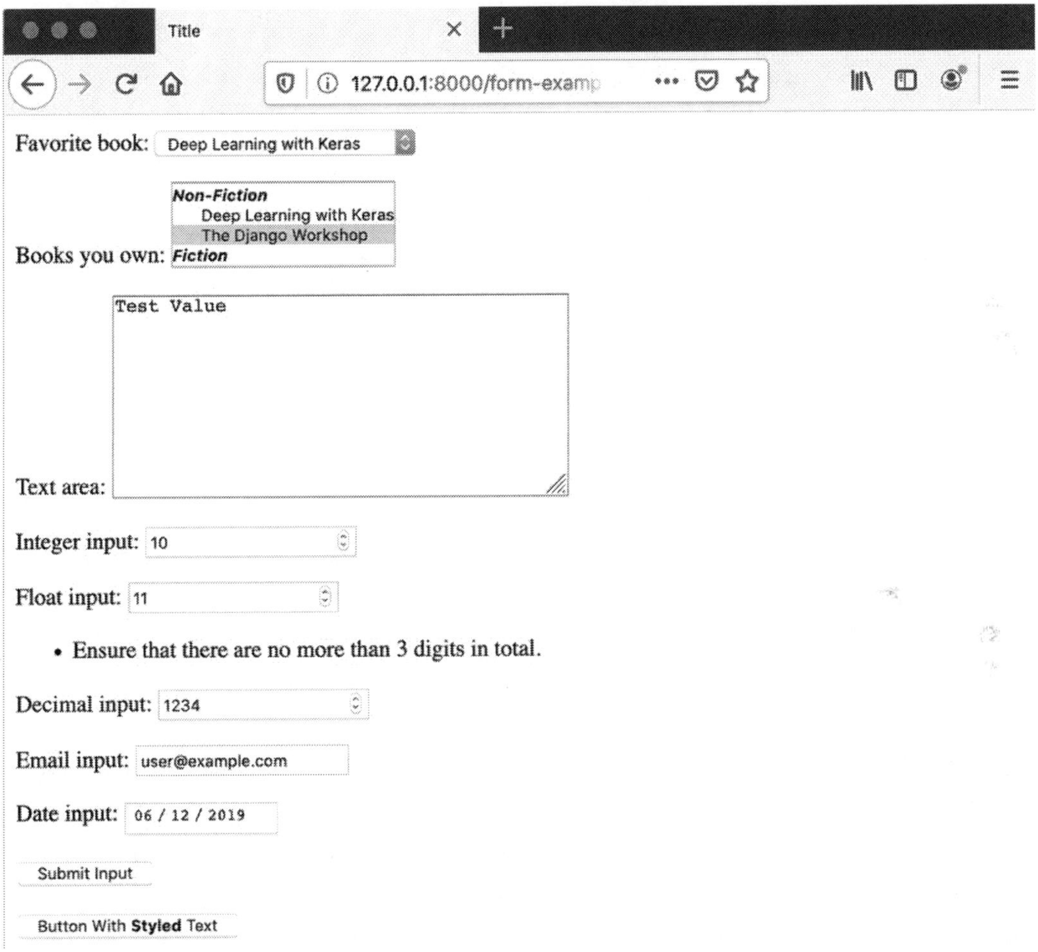

Figure 6.28: Decimal input error displayed after the form is submitted

6. Fix the form errors by making sure only three digits are in the **Decimal input** field, then submit the form again. Switch back to PyCharm and check the debug console. You should see that all the cleaned data has been printed out:

```
text_input: (<class 'str'>) Text
password_input: (<class 'str'>) password
checkbox_on: (<class 'bool'>) True
radio_input: (<class 'str'>) Value Two
favorite_book: (<class 'str'>) 1
books_you_own: (<class 'list'>) ['2', '3']
text_area: (<class 'str'>) Test Value
integer_input: (<class 'int'>) 10
float_input: (<class 'float'>) 11.0
decimal_input: (<class 'decimal.Decimal'>) 123
email_input: (<class 'str'>) user@example.com
date_input: (<class 'datetime.date'>) 2019-12-06
hidden_input: (<class 'str'>) Hidden Value
```

Figure 6.29: Cleaned data from the form printed out

Notice the conversions that have taken place. The **CharField** instances have been converted to **str**, **BooleanField** to **bool**, and **IntegerField**, **FloatField**, and **DecimalField** to **int**, **float**, and **Decimal**, respectively. **DateField** becomes **datetime.date** and the choice fields retain the string values of their initial choice values. Notice that **books_you_own** is automatically converted to a **list** of **str** instances.

Also, note that unlike when we iterated over all of the **POST** data, **cleaned_data** only contains form fields. The other data (such as the CSRF token and the submit button that was clicked) is present in the **POST QueryDict** but is not included as it does not include form fields.

In this exercise, you updated **ExampleForm** so the browser allowed it to be submitted even though Django would consider it to be invalid. This allowed Django to perform its validation on the form. You then updated the **form_example** view to instantiate the **ExampleForm** class differently depending on the HTTP method; passing in the request's **POST** data for a **POST** request. The view also had its debug output code updated to **print** out the **cleaned_data** dictionary. Finally, you tested submitting valid and invalid form data to see the different execution paths and the types of data that the form generated. We saw that Django automatically converted the **POST** data from strings to Python types based on the field class.

Next, we will look at how to add more validation options to fields, which will allow us to more tightly control the values that can be entered.

BUILT-IN FIELD VALIDATION

We have not yet discussed the standard validation arguments that can be used on fields. Although we already mentioned the **required** argument (which is **True** by default), many others can be used to more tightly control the data being entered into a field. Here are a few useful ones:

- **max_length**

  Sets the maximum number of characters that can be entered into the field; available on **CharField** (and **FileField**, which we will cover in *Chapter 8, Media Serving and File Uploads*).

- **min_length**

  Sets the minimum number of characters that must be entered into the field; available on **CharField** (and **FileField**; again, more about this in *Chapter 8, Media Serving and File Uploads*).

- **max_value**

  Sets the maximum value that can be entered into a numeric field; available on **IntegerField**, **FloatField**, and **DecimalField**.

- **min_value**

  Sets the minimum value that can be entered into a numeric field; available on **IntegerField**, **FloatField**, and **DecimalField**.

- **max_digits**

  This sets the maximum number of digits that can be entered; this includes digits before and after a decimal point (if one exists). For example, the number *12.34* has four digits, and the number *56.7* has three. Used in **DecimalField**.

- **decimal_places**

  This sets the maximum number of digits that can be after the decimal point. This is used in conjunction with **max_digits**, and the number of decimal places will always count toward the number of digits even if that number of decimals has not been entered after the decimal place. For example, imagine using **max_digits** of four and **decimal_places** of three: if the number *12.34* was entered, it would actually be interpreted as the value *12.340*; that is, zeros are appended until the number of digits after the decimal point is equal to the **decimal_places** setting. Since we set three as the value for **decimal_places**, the total number of digits ends up being five, which exceeds the **max_digits** setting of four. The number *1.2* would be valid since even after expanding to *1.200*, the total number of digits is only four.

You can mix and match the validation rules (provided that the fields support them). **CharField** can have **max_length** and **min_length**, numeric fields can have both **min_value** and **max_value**, and so on.

If you need more validation options, you can write custom validators, which we will cover in the next section. Right now, we will add some validators to our **ExampleForm** to see them in action.

EXERCISE 6.05: ADDING EXTRA FIELD VALIDATION

In this exercise, we will add and modify the validation rules for the fields of **ExampleForm**. We will then see how these changes affect how the form behaves, both in the browser and when Django validates the form:

1. In PyCharm, open the **forms.py** file inside the **form_example** app directory.

2. We will make **text_input** require at most three characters. Add a **max_length=3** argument to the **CharField** constructor:

```
text_input = forms.CharField(max_length=3)
```

3. Make **password_input** more secure by requiring a minimum of eight characters. Add a **min_length=8** argument to the **CharField** constructor:

```
password_input = forms.CharField(min_length=8, \
                                 widget=forms.PasswordInput)
```

4. The user may have no books, so the **books_you_own** field should not be required. Add a **required=False** argument to the **MultipleChoiceField** constructor:

```
books_you_own = forms.MultipleChoiceField\
                (required=False, choices=BOOK_CHOICES)
```

5. The user should only be able to enter a value between 1 and 10 in **integer_input**. Add **min_value=1** and **max_value=10** arguments to the **IntegerField** constructor:

```
integer_input = forms.IntegerField\
                (min_value=1, max_value=10)
```

6. Finally, add **max_digits=5** and **decimal_places=3** to the **DecimalField** constructor:

```
decimal_input = forms.DecimalField\
                (max_digits=5, decimal_places=3)
```

Save the file.

7. Start the Django dev server if it's not already running. We do not have to make any changes to any other files to get these new validation rules, since Django automatically updates the HTML generation and validation logic. This is a great benefit you get from using Django forms. Just visit or refresh **http://127.0.0.1:8000/form-example/** in your browser and the new validation will be automatically added. The form should not look any different until you try to submit it with incorrect values, in which case your browser can automatically show errors. Some things to try are as follows:

Enter more than three characters into the **Text input** field; you will not be able to.

Type fewer than eight characters into the **Password** field then click away from it. The browser should show an error indicating that this is not valid.

Do not select any values for the **Books you own** field. This will not prevent you from submitting the form anymore.

Use the stepper buttons on **Integer input**. You will only be able to enter a value between **1** and **10**. If you type in a value outside this range, your browser should show an error.

Decimal input is the only field that does not validate the Django rules in the browser. You will need to type in an invalid value (such as **123.456**) and submit the form before an error (generated by Django) is displayed.

The following figure shows some of the fields that the browser can validate itself:

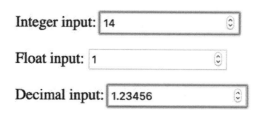

Figure 6.30: Browser performing validation with the new rules

Figure 6.31 shows an error that can only be generated by Django as the browser does not understand the **DecimalField** validation rules:

- Ensure that there are no more than 5 digits in total.

Decimal input: 123.456

Figure 6.31: The browser considers the form valid, but Django does not

In this exercise, we implemented some basic validation rules on our form fields. We then loaded the form example page in the browser, without having to make any changes to our template or view. We tried to submit the form with different values to see how the browser can validate the form compared to Django.

In the activity for this chapter, we will implement the Book Search view using a Django form.

ACTIVITY 6.01: BOOK SEARCHING

In this activity, you will finish the Book Search view that was started in *Chapter 1, Introduction to Django*. You will build a **SearchForm** instance that submits and accepts a search string from **request.GET**. It will have a **select** field to choose to search for **title** or **contributor**. It will then search for all **Book** instances containing the given text in **title** or in **first_names** or **last_names** of **Contributor**. You will then render this list of books in the **search-results. html** template. The search term should not be required, but if it exists, it should have a length of three or fewer characters. Since the view will search even when using the **GET** method, the form will always have its validation checked. If we made the field **required**, it would always show an error whenever the page loads.

There will be two ways of performing the search. The first is by submitting the search form that is in the **base.html** template and thus in the top-right corner of every page. This will only search through **Book** titles. The other method is by submitting a **SearchForm** instance that is rendered on the **search-results.html** page. This form will display the **ChoiceField** instance for choosing between **title** or **contributor** search.

These steps will help you complete this activity:

1. Create a **SearchForm** instance in your **forms.py** file.

2. **SearchForm** should have two fields. The first is a **CharField** instance with the name **search**. This field should not be required but should have a minimum length of **3**.

3. The second field on **SearchForm** is a **ChoiceField** instance named **search_in**. This will allow selecting between **title** and **contributor** (with **Title** and **Contributor** labels, respectively). It should not be **required**.

4. Update the **book_search** view to instantiate a **SearchForm** instance using data from **request.GET**.

5. Add code to search for **Book** models using **title__icontains** (for case-insensitive searching). This should be done if searching by **title**. The search should only be performed if the form is valid and contains some search text. The **search_in** value should be retrieved from **cleaned_data** using the **get** method since it might not exist, as it's not required. Set its default to **title**.

6. When searching for contributors, use **first_names__icontains** or **last_names__icontains**, then iterate the contributors and retrieve the books for each contributor. This should be done if searching by **contributor**. The search should only be performed if the form is valid and contains some search text. There are many ways to combine the search results for a first or last name. The easiest method, using the techniques that you have been introduced to so far, is to perform two queries, one for matching first names and then for last names, and iterating them separately.

7. Update the **render** call to include the **form** variable and the books that were retrieved in the context (as well as **search_text** that was already being passed). The location of the template was changed in *Chapter 3, URL Mapping, Views, and Templates*, so update the second argument to **render** accordingly.

8. The **search-results.html** template we created in *Chapter 1, Introduction to Django*, is essentially redundant now, so you can clear its content. Update the **search-results.html** file to extend from **base.html** instead of being a standalone template file.

9. Add a **title** block that will display **Search Results for <search_text>** if the form is valid and **search_text** was set and will otherwise just display **Book Search**. This block will also be added to **base.html** later in this activity.

10. Add a **content** block, which should show an **<h2>** heading with the text **Search for Books**. Under the **<h2>** heading, render the form. The **<form>** element can have no attributes and it will default to making a **GET** request to the same URL that it's on. Add a submit button as we have used in previous activities, with the **btn btn-primary** class.

11. Under the form, show a **Search results for <search_text>** message if the form is valid and search text was entered, otherwise show no message. This should be displayed in an **<h3>** heading, and the search text should be wrapped in **<em>**.

12. Iterate over the search results and render each one. Show the book title and contributor's first and last names. The book title should link to the **book_detail** page. If the books list is empty, show the text **No results found**. You should wrap the results in **<ul>** with **class list-group**, and each result should be an **<li>** instance with **class list-group-item**. This will be similar to the **book_list** page; however, we won't show as much information (just the title and contributors).

13. Update **base.html** to include an action attribute in the search **<form>** tag. Use the **url** template tag to generate the URL for this attribute.

14. Set the **name** attribute of the search field to **search** and the **value** attribute to the search text that was entered. Also, ensure that the minimum length of the field is **3**.

15. In **base.html**, add a **title** block to the **title** tag that was overridden by other templates (as in *step 9*). Add a **block** template tag inside the **<title>** HTML element. It should have the content **Bookr**.

After completing this activity, you should be able to open the Book Search page at **http://127.0.0.1:8000/book-search/** and it will look like *Figure 6.32*:

Figure 6.32: Book Search page without a search

When searching for something using just two characters, your browser should prevent you from submitting either of the search fields. If you search for something that returns no results, you will see a message that there were no results. Searching by title (this can be done with either field) will show matching results.

Similarly, when searching by the contributor (although this can only be done in the lower form), you should see something like the following:

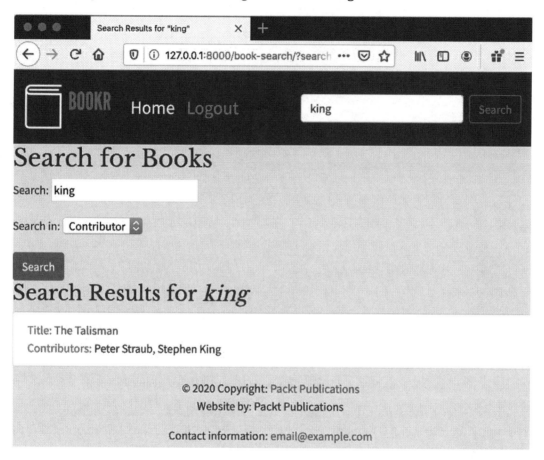

Figure 6.33: A contributor search

> **NOTE**
>
> The solution to this activity can be found at http://packt.live/2Nh1NTJ.

SUMMARY

This chapter was an introduction to forms in Django. We introduced some HTML inputs for entering data onto a web page. We talked about how data is submitted to a web application and when to use **GET** and **POST** requests. We then looked at how Django's form classes can make generating the form HTML simpler, as well as allowing the automatic building of forms using models. We enhanced Bookr some more by building the book search functionality.

In the next chapter, we will go deeper into forms and learn how to customize the display of form fields, how to add more advanced validation to your form, and how to automatically save model instances by using the `ModelForm` class.

7

ADVANCED FORM VALIDATION AND MODEL FORMS

OVERVIEW

Continuing your journey with the Bookr application, you will begin this chapter by adding a new form to your app with custom multi-field validation and form cleaning. You will learn how to set the initial values on your form and customize the widgets (the HTML input elements that are being generated). Then you will be introduced to the **ModelForm** class, which allows a form to be automatically created from a model. You will use it in a view to automatically save the new or changed **Model** instance.

By the end of this chapter, you will know how to add extra multi-field validation to Django forms, how to customize and set form widgets for fields, how to use **ModelForms** to automatically create a form from a Django model, and how to automatically create **Model** instances from **ModelForms**.

INTRODUCTION

This chapter builds upon the knowledge we gained in *Chapter 6, Forms*, where we learned how to submit data from an HTML form to a Django view, both with a manually built HTML form and with a Django form. We used Django's **form** library to build and automatically validate forms with basic validation. For example, now we can build forms that check whether a date is entered in its desired format, whether a number is input where a user must enter their age, and whether a dropdown is selected before the user clicks the **Submit** button. However, most large-scale websites require validation that is a bit more advanced.

For instance, a certain field might only be required if another field is set. Let's say we want to add a checkbox to allow users to sign up for our monthly newsletter. It has a textbox below it that lets them enter their email address. With some basic validation, we can check whether:

- The user has checked the checkbox.

- The user has entered their email address.

When the user clicks the **Submit** button, we will be able to validate whether both fields are actioned. But what if the user doesn't want to sign up for our newsletter? If they click the **Submit** button, ideally, both fields should be blank. That's where validating each individual field might not work.

Another example could be a case where we have two fields and each has a maximum value of, say, 50. But the total of values added to each one must be less than 75. We will start the chapter by looking at how to write custom validation rules to solve such problems.

Later, as we progress in the chapter, we will look at how to set initial values on a form. This can be useful when automatically filling out information that is already known to the user. For example, we can automatically put a user's contact information into a form if that user is logged in.

We will finish the chapter by looking at model forms, which will let us automatically create a form from a Django **Model** class. This cuts down the amount of code that needs to be written to create a new **Model** instance.

CUSTOM FIELD VALIDATION AND CLEANING

We have seen how a Django form converts values from an HTTP request, which are strings, into Python objects. In a non-custom Django form, the target type is dependent on the field class. For example, the Python type derived from **IntegerField** is **int**, and string values are given to us verbatim, as the user entered them. But we can also implement methods on our **Form** class to alter the output values from our fields in any way we choose. The allows us to clean or filter the user's input data to fit what we expect better. We could round an integer to the nearest multiple of ten to fit into a batch size for ordering specific items. Or we could transform an email address to lowercase so that the data is consistent for searching.

We can also implement some custom validators. We will look at a couple of different ways of validating fields: by writing a custom validator, and by writing a custom **clean** method for the field. Each method has its pros and cons: a custom validator can be applied to different fields and forms, so you do not have to write the validation logic for each field; a custom **clean** method must be implemented on each form you want to clean, but is more powerful and allows validation using other fields in the form or changing the cleaned value that the field returns.

CUSTOM VALIDATORS

A validator is simply a function that accepts a value and raises **django.core. exceptions.ValidationError** if the value is invalid – the validity is determined by the code you write. The value is a Python object (that is, **cleaned_data** that has already been converted from the **POST** request string).

Here is a simple example that validates whether a value is lowercase:

```
from django.core.exceptions import ValidationError


def validate_lowercase(value):
  if value.lower() != value:
    raise ValidationError("{} is not lowercase."\
                     .format(value))
```

Notice the function does not return anything, for either success or failure. It will just raise **ValidationError** if the value is not valid.

> **NOTE**
>
> Note that the behavior and handling of **ValidationError** differ from how other exceptions behave in Django. Normally, if you raise an exception in your view, you will end up with a **500** response from Django (if you do not handle the exception in your code).
>
> When raising **ValidationError** in your validation/cleaning code, the Django **form** class will catch the error for you and then the **is_valid** method of **form** will return **False**. You do not have to write **try/except** handlers around the code that might raise **ValidationError**.

The validator can be passed to the **validators** argument of a field constructor on a form, inside a list; for example, to our **text_input** field from our **ExampleForm**:

```
class ExampleForm(forms.Form):
    text_input = forms.CharField(validators=[validate_lowercase])
```

Now, if we submit the form and the fields contain uppercase values, we will get an error, as shown in the following figure:

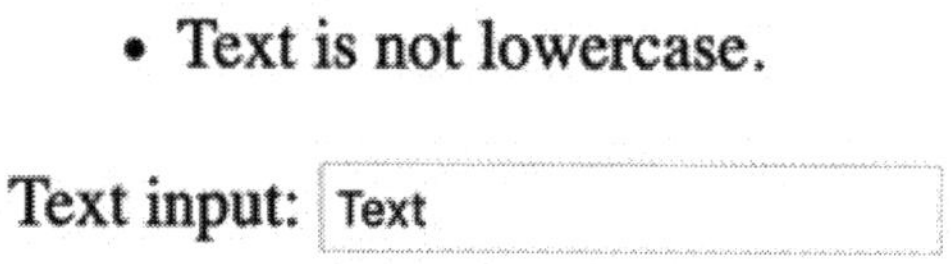

- Text is not lowercase.

Text input: `Text`

Figure 7.1: Lowercase text validator in action

The validator function can be used on any number of fields. In our example, if we wanted lots of fields to have lowercase enforced, **validate_lowercase** could be passed to all of them. Let's now look at how we could implement this another way, with a custom **clean** method.

CLEANING METHODS

A **clean** method is created on the **Form** class and is named in the format **clean_field-name**. For example, the **clean** method for **text_input** would be called **clean_text_input**, the **clean** method for **books_you_own** would be **clean_books_you_own**, and so on.

Cleaning methods take no arguments; instead, they should use the **cleaned_data** attribute on **self** to access the field data. This dictionary will contain the data after being cleaned in the standard Django way, as we saw in the previous example. The **clean** method must return the cleaned value, which will replace the original value in the **cleaned_data** dictionary. Even if the method does not change the value, a value must be returned. You can also use the **clean** method to raise **ValidationError**, and the error will be attached to the field (the same as with a validator).

Let's re-implement the lowercase validator as a **clean** method, like this:

```python
class ExampleForm(forms.Form):
    text_input = forms.CharField()

    ...

    def clean_text_input(self):
        value = self.cleaned_data['text_input']
        if value.lower() != value:
            raise ValidationError("{} is not lowercase."\
                                  .format(value))\
        return value
```

You can see the logic is essentially the same, except we must return the validated value at the end. If we submit the form, we get the same result as the previous time we tried (*Figure 7.1*).

Let's look at one more cleaning example. Instead of raising an exception when the value is invalid, we could just convert the value to lowercase. We would implement that with this code:

```python
class ExampleForm(forms.Form):
    text_input = forms.CharField()

    ...

    def clean_text_input(self):
        value = self.cleaned_data['text_input']
        return value.lower()
```

Now, consider that we enter text into the input as uppercase:

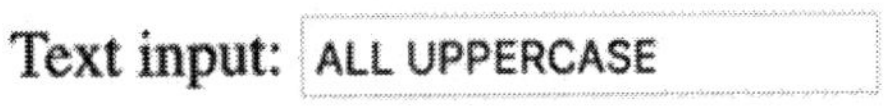

Text input: ALL UPPERCASE

Figure 7.2: ALL UPPERCASE text entered

If we were to examine the cleaned data using our debug output from the view, we would see that it is lowercase:

```
text_input: (<class 'str'>) all uppercase
```

Figure 7.3: The cleaned data has been transformed to lowercase

These were just a couple of simple examples of how to validate fields using both validators and **clean** methods. You can, of course, make each type of validation much more complex if you wish and transform the data in more complex ways using a **clean** method.

So far, you have only learned simple methods for form validation, where you have treated each field independently. A field is valid (or not) based only on the information it contains and nothing else. What if the validity of one field depends on what the user entered into another field? An example of this might be that you have an **email** field to collect someone's email address if they want to be signed up to a mailing list. The field is only required if they check a checkbox that indicates they wanted to be signed up. Neither of these fields is required on their own – we do not want the checkbox to be required to be checked, but if it is checked, then the **email** field should be required too.

In the next section, we will show how you can validate a form whose fields depend on each other by overriding the **clean** method in your form.

MULTI-FIELD VALIDATION

We have just looked at the **clean_<field-name>** methods that can be added to a Django form, to clean a specific field. Django also allows us to override the **clean** method, in which we can access all the **cleaned_data** from all fields, and we know that all custom field methods have been called. This allows the validation of fields based on another field's data.

Referring to our previous example with a form that has an email address that is only required if a checkbox is checked, we will see how we can implement this using the **clean** method.

First, create a **Form** class and add two fields – make them both optional with the **required=False** argument:

```
class NewsletterSignupForm(forms.Form):
    signup = forms.BooleanField\
            (label="Sign up to newsletter?", required=False)
    email = forms.EmailField\
```

```
(help_text="Enter your email address to subscribe", \
    required=False)
```

We have also introduced two new arguments that can be used for any field:

- **`label`**

  This allows setting the label text for a field. As we have seen, Django will automatically generate label text from the field name. If you set the **`label`** argument, you can override this default. Use this argument if you want to have a more descriptive label.

- **`help_text`**

  If you need to have more information displayed regarding what input a field requires, you can use this argument. By default, it is displayed after the field.

When rendered, the form looks like this:

Figure 7.4: Email signup form with custom label and help text

If we were to submit the form now, without entering any data, nothing would happen. Neither field is required, so the form validates fine.

Now we can add the multi-field validation to the **`clean`** method. We will check whether the **`signup`** checkbox is checked, and then check that the **`email`** field has a value. The built-in Django methods have already validated that the email address is valid at this point, so we then just need to check that a value exists for it. We will then use the **`add_error`** method to set an error for the **`email`** field. This is a method you haven't seen before but it's very simple; it takes two arguments – the name of the field to set the error on, and the text of the error.

Here is the code for the **clean** method:

```
class NewsletterSignupForm(forms.Form):

  ...
  def clean(self):
    cleaned_data = super().clean()

    if cleaned_data["signup"] and not cleaned_data.get("email"):
    self.add_error\
    ("email", \
     "Your email address is required if signing up for the newsletter.")
```

Your **clean** method must always call the **super().clean()** method to retrieve the cleaned data. When **add_error** is called to add errors to the form, the form will no longer validate (the **is_valid** method returns **False**).

Now if we submit the form without the checkbox checked, there is still no error generated, but if you check the checkbox without an email address, you will receive the error we just wrote the code for:

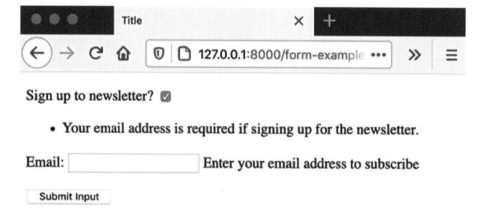

Figure 7.5: Error displayed when attempting to sign up with no email address

You might notice that we are retrieving the email from the **cleaned_data** dictionary using the **get** method. The reason for doing this is if the **email** value in the form is invalid, then the **email** key will not exist in the dictionary. The browser should prevent the user from submitting the form if an invalid email has been entered, but a user might be using an older browser that does not support this client-side validation, so for safety, we use the **get** method. Since the **signup** field is **BooleanField**, and not required, it will only be invalid if a custom validation function is used. We are not using one here, so it is safe to access its value using square bracket notation.

There is one more validation scenario to consider before moving on to our first exercise, and that is adding errors that are not specific to any field. Django calls these *non-field errors*. There are many scenarios where you might want to use these when multiple fields are dependent on each other.

Take, for example, a shopping website. Your order form could have two numeric fields whose totals could not exceed a certain value. If the total were exceeded, the value of either field could be decreased to bring the total below the maximum value, so the error is not specific to either one of the fields. To add a non-field error, call the **add_error** method with **None** as the first argument.

Let us look at how to implement this. In this example, we will have a form where the user can specify a certain number of items to order, for item A or item B. The user cannot order more than 100 items in total. The fields will have a **max_value** of **100**, and **min_value** of **0**, but custom validation in the **clean** method will need to be written to handle the validation of the total amount:

```
class OrderForm(forms.Form):
    item_a = forms.IntegerField(min_value=0, max_value=100)
    item_b = forms.IntegerField(min_value=0, max_value=100)\
    def clean(self):
        cleaned_data = super().clean()
        if cleaned_data.get("item_a", 0) + cleaned_data.get\
                                    ("item_b", 0) > 100:
            self.add_error\
            (None, \
             "The total number of items must be 100 or less.")
```

The fields (**item_a** and **item_b**) are added in the normal way, with standard validation rules. You can see that we have used the **clean** method the same way we used it before. Moreover, we have implemented the maximum item logic inside this method. The following line is what registers the non-field error if the maximum items are exceeded:

```
self.add_error(None, \
                "The total number of items must be 100 or less.")
```

Once again, we access the values of **item_a** and **item_b** using the **get** method, with a default value of **0**. This is in case the user has an older browser (from 2011 or earlier) and was able to submit the form with invalid values.

In a browser, the field-level validation ensures values between 0 and 100 have been entered in each field, and prevents the form from being submitted otherwise:

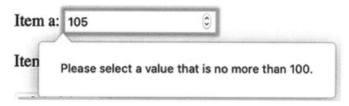

Figure 7.6: The form cannot be submitted if one field exceeds the maximum value

However, if we put in two values that sum to more than 100, we can see how Django displays the non-field error:

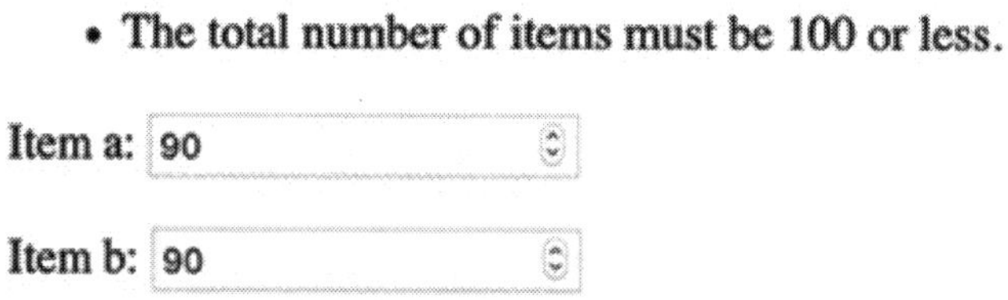

- **The total number of items must be 100 or less.**

Item a: 90

Item b: 90

Figure 7.7: Django non-field error displayed at the start of the form

Django non-field errors are always displayed at the start of a form, before other fields or errors. In the next exercise, we will build a form that implements a validation function, a field clean method, and a form clean method.

EXERCISE 7.01: CUSTOM CLEAN AND VALIDATION METHODS

In this exercise, you will build a new form that allows the user to create an order for books or magazines. It must have the following validation criteria:

- The user may order up to 80 magazines and/or 50 books, but the total number of items must not be more than 100.

- The user can choose to receive an order confirmation, and if they do, they must enter an email address.

- The user should not enter an email address if they have not chosen to receive an order confirmation.

- To ensure they are part of our company, the email address must be part of our company domain (in our case, we will just use `example.com`).

- For consistency with other email addresses in our fictional company, the address should be converted to lowercase.

This sounds like a lot of rules, but with Django, it is simple if we tackle them one by one. We will carry on with the **form_project** app we started in *Chapter 6, Forms*. If you haven't completed *Chapter 6, Forms*, you can download the code from http://packt.live/2LRCczP:

1. In PyCharm, open the **form_example** app's **forms.py** file.

> **NOTE**
>
> Make sure the Django dev server is not running, otherwise, it may crash as you make changes to this file, causing PyCharm to jump into the debugger.

2. Since our work with **ExampleForm** is done, you can remove it from this file.

3. Create a new class called **OrderForm** that inherits from **forms.Form**:

```
class OrderForm(forms.Form):
```

4. Add four fields to the class as follows:

- **magazine_count, IntegerField** with **min_value** of **0** and **max_value** of **80**

- **book_count, IntegerField** with **min_value** of **0** and **max_value** of **50**

- **send_confirmation, BooleanField**, which is not required

- **email, EmailField**, which is also not required

The class should look like this:

```
class OrderForm(forms.Form):
  magazine_count = forms.IntegerField\
                    (min_value=0, max_value=80)
  book_count = forms.IntegerField\
                (min_value=0, max_value=50)
  send_confirmation = forms.BooleanField\
                      (required=False)
  email = forms.EmailField(required=False)
```

5. Add a validation function to check that the user's email address is on the right domain. First, **ValidationError** needs to be imported; add this line at the top of the file:

```
from django.core.exceptions import ValidationError
```

Then write this function after the **import** line (before the **OrderForm** class implementation):

```
def validate_email_domain(value):
  if value.split("@")[-1].lower() != "example.com":\
     raise ValidationError\
        ("The email address must be on the domain example.com.")
```

The function splits the email address on the @ symbol, then checks whether the part after it is equal to **example.com**. This function alone would validate non-email addresses. For example, the string **not-valid@ someotherdomain@example.com** would not cause **ValidationError** to be raised in this function. This is acceptable in our case because as we are using **EmailField**, the other standard field validators will check the email address validity.

6. Add the **validate_email_domain** function as a validator to the **email** field on **OrderForm**. Update the **EmailField** constructor call to add a **validators** argument, passing in a list containing the validation function:

```
class OrderForm(forms.Form):
  ...
  email = forms.EmailField\
         (required=False, \
          validators=[validate_email_domain])
```

7. Add a **clean_email** method to the form to make sure the email address is lowercase:

```
class OrderForm(forms.Form):
  # truncated for brevity
  def clean_email(self):
  return self.cleaned_data['email'].lower()
```

8. Now, add the **clean** method to perform all the cross-field validation. First, we will just add the logic for making sure that an email address is only entered if an order confirmation is requested:

```
class OrderForm(forms.Form):
  # truncated for brevity
  def clean(self):
    cleaned_data = super().clean()
    if cleaned_data["send_confirmation"] and \
    not cleaned_data.get("email"):
```

```
        self.add_error\
        ("email", \
         "Please enter an email address to "\
         "receive the confirmation message.")\
    elif cleaned_data.get("email") and \
    not cleaned_data["send_confirmation"]:
        self.add_error("send_confirmation", \
                       "Please check this if you want to receive \
                       "a confirmation email.")
```

This will add an error to the **email** field if **Send confirmation** is checked but no email address is added:

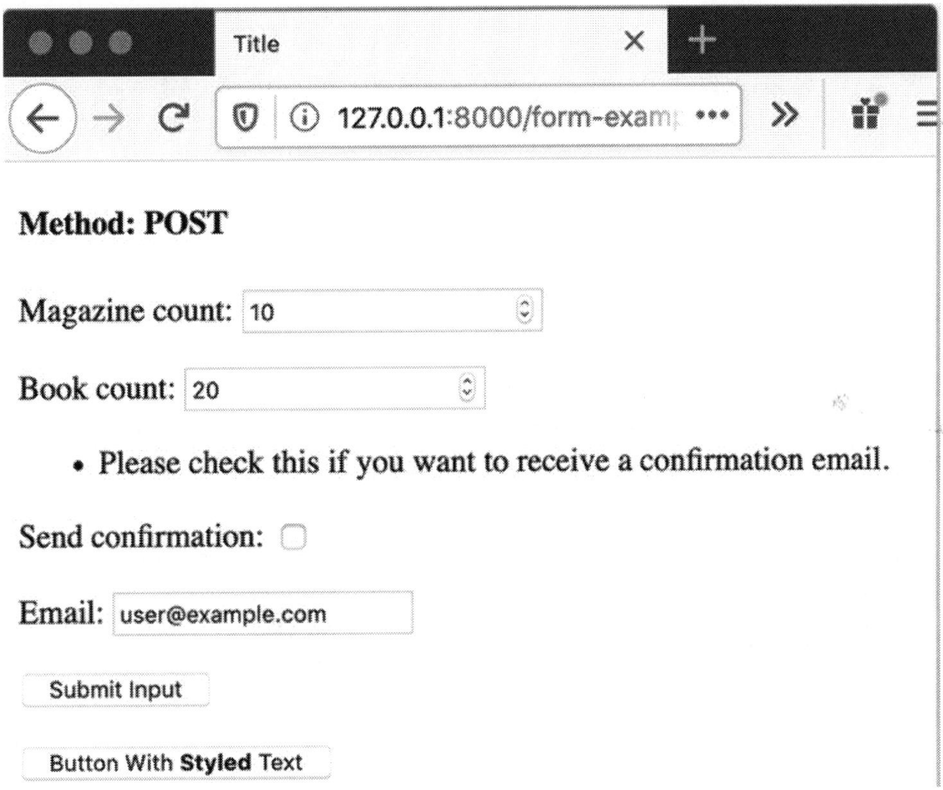

Figure 7.8: Error if Send confirmation is checked but no email address is added

Similarly, an error will be added to **email** if an email address is entered but **Send confirmation** is not checked:

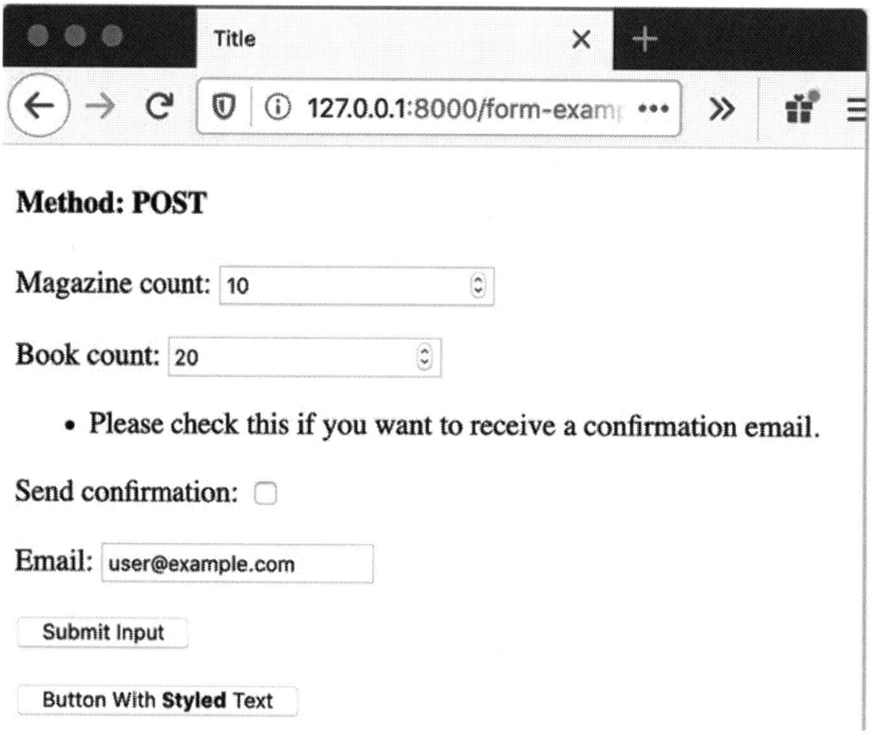

Figure 7.9: Error because an email has been entered but the user has not chosen to receive confirmation

9. Add the final check, also inside the **clean** method. The total number of items should not be more than 100. We will add a non-field error if the sum of **magazine_count** and **book_count** is greater than 100:

```
class OrderForm(forms.Form):
    ...
    def clean(self):
        ...
        item_total = cleaned_data.get("magazine_count", 0) \
                     + cleaned_data.get("book_count", 0)

        if item_total > 100:
            self.add_error(None, \
                    "The total number of items "\
                    "must be 100 or less.")
```

This will add a non-field error by passing **None** as the first argument to the **add_error** call.

> **NOTE**
>
> Refer to http://packt.live/3nMP3R7 for the complete code.

Save **forms.py**.

10. Open the **reviews** app's **views.py** file. We will change the form **import** so that **OrderForm** is being imported instead of **ExampleForm**. Consider the following import line:

```
from .forms import ExampleForm, SearchForm
```

Change it as follows:

```
from .forms import OrderForm, SearchForm
```

11. In the **form_example** view, change the two lines that use **ExampleForm** to use **OrderForm** instead. Consider the following line of code:

```
form = ExampleForm(request.POST)
```

Change this as follows:

```
form = OrderForm(request.POST)
```

Similarly, consider the following line of code:

```
form = ExampleForm()
```

Change this as follows:

```
form = OrderForm()
```

The rest of the function can stay as it is.

We don't have to make changes to the template. Start the Django dev server and navigate to **http://127.0.0.1:8000/form-example/** in your browser. You should see the form rendered as in *Figure 7.10*:

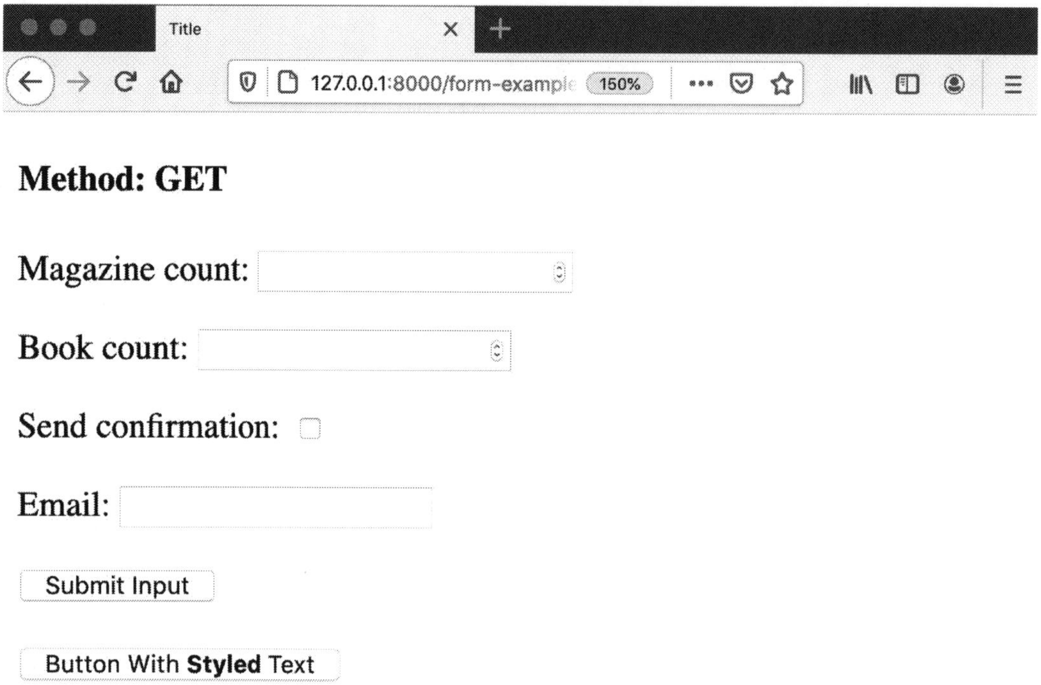

Figure 7.10: OrderForm in the browser

12. Try submitting the form with a **Magazine count** of **80** and **Book count** of **50**. The browser will allow this, but as they sum to more than 100, an error will be triggered by the **clean** method in the form and displayed on the page:

Method: POST

• The total number of items must be 100 or less.

Magazine count: 80

Book count: 50

Send confirmation: ☐

Email:

Submit Input

Button With **Styled** Text

Figure 7.11: A non-field error displayed on the form when the maximum number of allowed items is exceeded

13. Try submitting the form with **Send confirmation** checked but the **Email** field blank. Then fill the **Email** textbox but uncheck **Send confirmation**. Either combination will give an error that both must be present. The error will differ based on which field is missing:

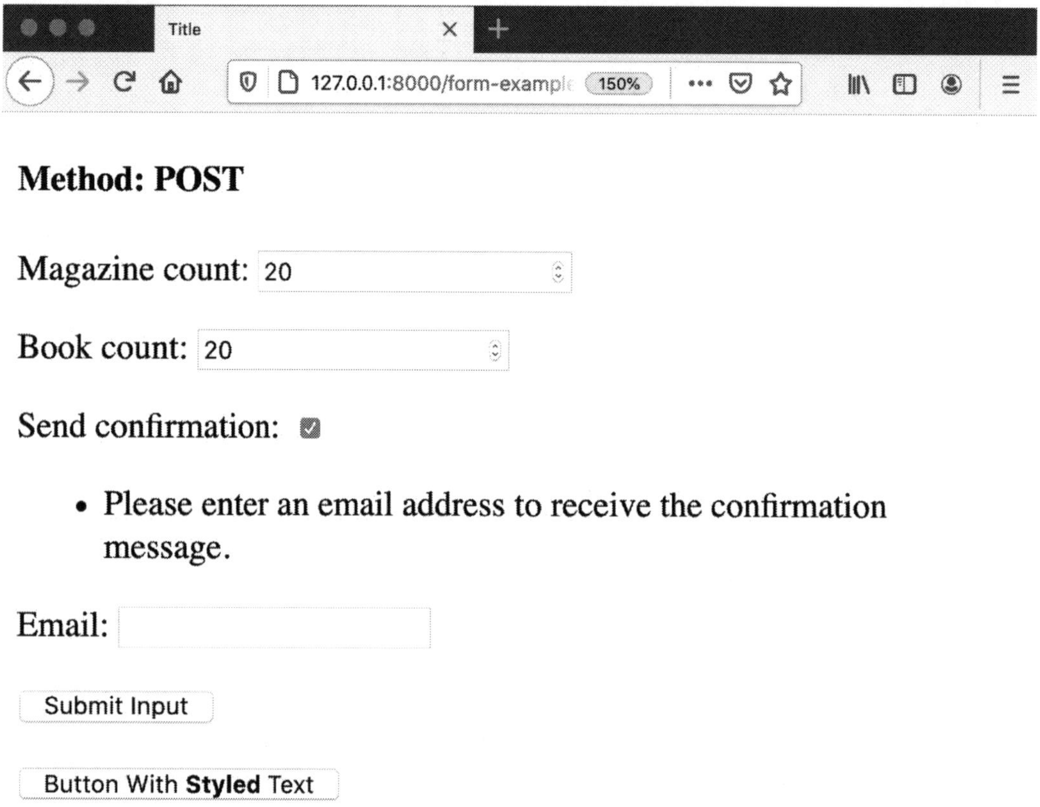

Figure 7.12: Error message if no email address is present

14. Now try submitting the form with **Send confirmation** checked and an email address that is on the **example.com** domain. You should receive a message that your email address must have the domain **example.com**. You should also receive a message that **email** must be set – since email does not end up in the **cleaned_data** dictionary, as it is not valid:

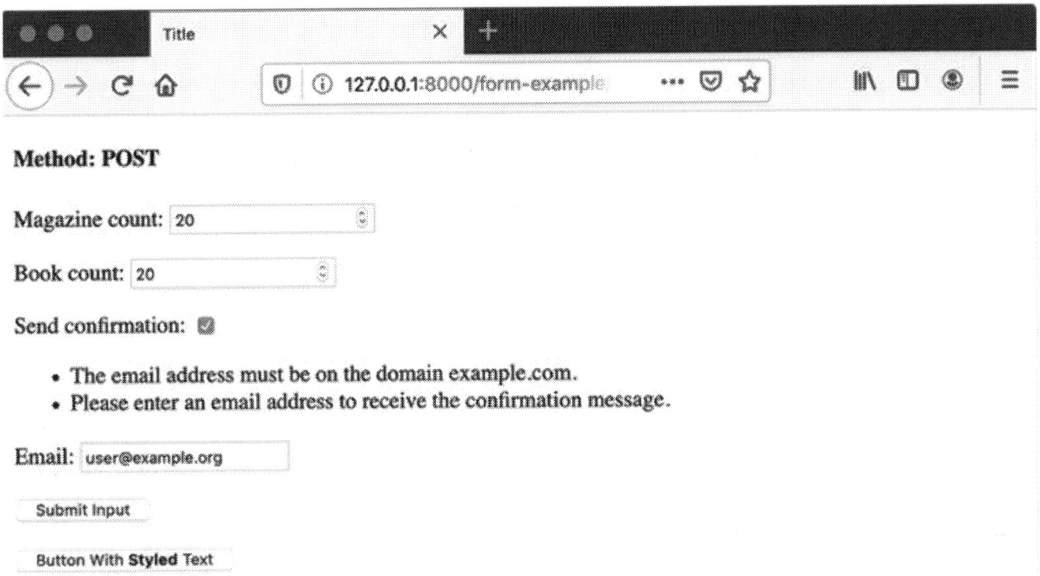

Figure 7.13: The error message is shown when the email domain is not example.com

15. Finally, enter valid values for **Magazine count** and **Book count** (such as **20** and **20**). Check **Send confirmation**, and enter **UserName@Example. Com** as the email (make sure you match the letter case, including the mixed uppercase and lowercase characters):

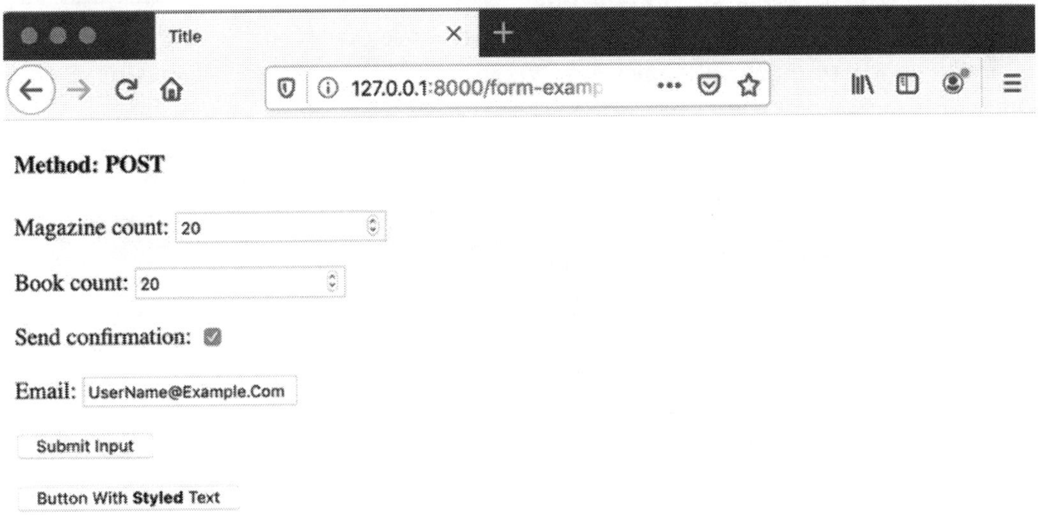

Figure 7.14: The form after being submitted with valid values

16. Switch to PyCharm and look in the debug console. You'll see that the email has been converted to lowercase when it is printed by our debug code:

```
magazine_count: (<class 'int'>) 20
book_count: (<class 'int'>) 20
send_confirmation: (<class 'bool'>) True
email: (<class 'str'>) username@example.com
```

Figure 7.15: Email in lowercase, as well as other fields

This is our `clean_email` method in action – even though we entered data in both uppercase and lowercase, it has been converted to all lowercase.

In this exercise, we created a new **OrderForm** that implemented form and field clean methods. We used a custom validator to ensure that the **Email** field met our specific validation rules – only a specific domain was allowed. We used a custom field cleaning method (`clean_email`) to convert the email address to lowercase. We then implemented a **clean** method to validate the forms that were dependent on each other. In this method, we added both field and non-field errors. In the next section, we will cover how to add placeholders and initial values to the form.

PLACEHOLDERS AND INITIAL VALUES

There are two things our first manually built form had that our current Django form still does not have –placeholders and initial values. Adding placeholders is simple; they are just added as an attribute to the widget constructor for the form field. This is similar to what we have already seen for setting the type of **DateField** in our previous examples.

Here is an example:

```
class ExampleForm(forms.Form):
  text_field = forms.CharField\
              (widget=forms.TextInput\
              (attrs={"placeholder": "Text Placeholder"}))
  password_field = forms.CharField(\
    widget=forms.PasswordInput\
          (attrs={"placeholder": "Password Placeholder"}))
  email_field = forms.EmailField\
              (widget=forms.EmailInput\
              (attrs={"placeholder": "Email Placeholder"}))
```

```
text_area = forms.CharField\
        (widget=forms.Textarea\
        (attrs={"placeholder": "Text Area Placeholder"}))
```

This is what the preceding form looks like when rendered in the browser:

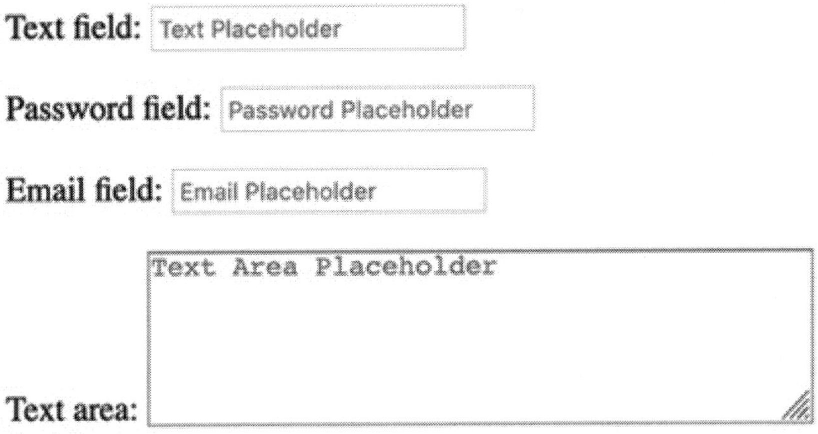

Text field: Text Placeholder

Password field: Password Placeholder

Email field: Email Placeholder

Text area: Text Area Placeholder

Figure 7.16: Django form with placeholders

Of course, if we are manually setting **Widget** for each field, we need to know which **Widget** class to use. The ones that support placeholders are **TextInput**, **NumberInput**, **EmailInput**, **URLInput**, **PasswordInput**, and **Textarea**.

While we are examining the **Form** class itself, we will look at the first of two ways of setting an initial value for a field. We can do it by using the **initial** argument on a **Field** constructor, like this:

```
text_field = forms.CharField(initial="Initial Value", …)
```

The other method is to pass in a dictionary of data when instantiating the form in our view. The keys are the field names. The dictionary should have zero or more items (that is, an empty dictionary is valid). Any extra keys are ignored. This dictionary should be supplied as the **initial** argument in our view as follows:

```
initial = {"text_field": "Text Value", \
          "email_field": "user@example.com"}
form = ExampleForm(initial=initial)
```

Or for a **POST** request, pass in **request.POST** as the first argument, as usual:

```
initial = {"text_field": "Text Value", \
          "email_field": "user@example.com"}
form = ExampleForm(request.POST, initial=initial)
```

Values in **request.POST** will override values in **initial**. This means that even if we have an initial value for a required field, if it is left blank when submitted, then it will not validate. The field will not fall back to the value in **initial**.

Whether you decide to set initial values in the **Form** class itself or the view is up to you and depends on your use case. If you had a form that was used in multiple views but usually had the same value, it would be better to set the **initial** value in the form. Otherwise, it can be more flexible to use **setting** in the view.

In the next exercise, we will add placeholders and initial values to the **OrderForm** class from the previous exercise.

EXERCISE 7.02: PLACEHOLDERS AND INITIAL VALUES

In this exercise, you will enhance the **OrderForm** class by adding placeholder text. You will simulate passing an initial email address to the form. It will be a hardcoded address, but once the user can log in, it could be an email address associated with their account – you will learn about sessions and authentication in *Chapter 9, Sessions and Authentication*:

1. In PyCharm, open the **reviews** app's **forms.py** file. You will add placeholders to the **magazine_count**, **book_count**, and **email** fields on the **OrderForm**, which means also setting the **widget**.

   To the **magazine_count** field, add a **NumberInput widget** with **placeholder** in the **attrs** dictionary. The **placeholder** should be set to *Number of Magazines*. Write the following code:

   ```
   magazine_count = forms.IntegerField\
                   (min_value=0, max_value=80,\
                    widget=forms.NumberInput\
                    (attrs={"placeholder": "Number of Magazines"}))
   ```

2. Add a placeholder to the **book_count** field in the same manner. The placeholder text should be **Number of Books**:

   ```
   book_count = forms.IntegerField\
               (min_value=0, max_value=50,\
                widget=forms.NumberInput\
                (attrs={"placeholder": "Number of Books"}))
   ```

3. The final change to **OrderForm** is to add a placeholder to the email field. This time the widget is **EmailInput**. The placeholder text should be **Your company email address**:

```
email = forms.EmailField\
        (required=False, validators=[validate_email_domain],\
        widget=forms.EmailInput\
        (attrs={"placeholder": "Your company email address"}))
```

Note that the **clean_email** and **clean** methods should remain as they were in *Exercise 7.01, Custom Clean and Validation Methods*. Save the file.

4. Open the **reviews** app's **views.py** file. In the **form_example** view function, create a new dictionary variable called **initial** with one key, **email**, like this:

```
initial = {"email": "user@example.com"}
```

5. In the two places that you are instantiating **OrderForm**, also pass in the **initial** variable using the **initial** kwarg. The first instance is as follows:

```
form = OrderForm(request.POST, initial=initial)
```

The second instance is as follows:

```
form = OrderForm(initial=initial)
```

The complete code for **views.py** can be found at http://packt.live/3szaPM6.

Save the **views.py** file.

6. Start the Django dev server if it is not already running. Browse to **http://127.0.0.1:8000/form-example/** in your browser. You should see that your form now has placeholders and an initial value set:

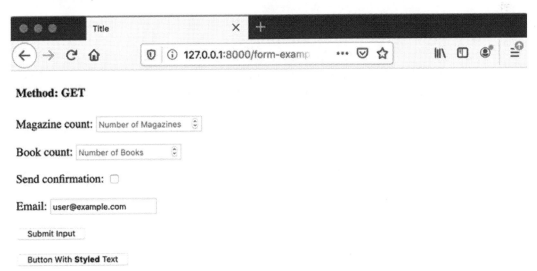

Figure 7.17: Order form with initial values and placeholders

In this exercise, we added placeholders to form fields. This was done by setting a **form** widget when defining the **form** field on the form class and setting a *placeholder* value in the **attrs** dictionary. We also set an initial value for the form using a dictionary and passing it to the **form** instance using the **initial** kwarg.

In the next section, we will talk about how to work with Django models using data from forms, and how **ModelForm** makes this easier.

CREATING OR EDITING DJANGO MODELS

You have seen how to define a form, and in *Chapter 2, Models and Migrations*, you learned how to create Django model instances. By using these things together, you could build a view that displayed a form and also saved a model instance to the database. This gives you an easy method to save data without having to write a lot of boilerplate code or create custom forms. In Bookr, we will use this method to allow users to add reviews without requiring access to the Django admin site. Without using **ModelForm**, we could do something like this:

- We can create a form based on an existing model, for example, **Publisher**. The form would be called **PublisherForm**.

- We can manually define the fields on **PublisherForm**, using the same rules defined on the **Publisher** model, as shown here:

```
class PublisherForm(forms.Form):
  name = forms.CharField(max_length=50)
  website = forms.URLField()
  …
```

- In the view, the **initial** values would be retrieved from the model queried from the database, then passed to the form using the **initial** argument. If we were creating a new instance, the **initial** value would be blank – something like this:

```
if create:
  initial = {}
else:
  publisher = Publisher.objects.get(pk=pk)
  initial = {"name": publisher.name, \
             "website": publisher.website, …}

form = PublisherForm(initial=initial)
```

- Then, in the **POST** flow of the view, we can either create or update the model based on **cleaned_data**:

```
form = PublisherForm(request.POST, initial=initial)
if create:
  publisher = Publisher()
else:
  publisher = Publisher.objects.get(pk=pk)

publisher.name = form.cleaned_data['name']
publisher.website = forms.cleaned_data['website']
...
publisher.save()
```

This is a lot of work, and we have to consider how much duplicated logic we have. For example, we are defining the length of the name in the **name** form field. If we made a mistake here, we could allow a longer name in the field than the model allows. We also have to remember to set all the fields in the **initial** dictionary, as well as setting the values on the new or updated model with **cleaned_data** from the form. There are many opportunities to make mistakes here, as well as remembering to add or remove field setting data for each of these steps if the model changes. All this code would have to be duplicated for each Django model you work with as well, expounding the duplication problem.

THE MODELFORM CLASS

Luckily, Django provides a method of building **Model** instances from forms much more simply, with the **ModelForm** class. **ModelForm** is a form that is built automatically from a particular model. It will inherit the validation rules from the model (such as whether fields are required or the maximum length of **CharField** instances, and so on). It provides an extra **__init__** argument (called **instance**) to automatically populate the initial values from an existing model. It also adds a **save** method to automatically persist the form data to the database. All that needs to be done to set up **ModelForm** is to specify its model and what fields should be used: this is done on the **class Meta** attribute of the **form** class. Let us see how to build a form from **Publisher**.

Inside the file that contains the form (for example, the **forms.py** file we have been working with), the only change is that the model must be imported:

```
from .models import Publisher
```

Then the **Form** class can then be defined. The class requires a **class Meta** attribute, which in turn must define a **model** attribute and either **fields** or **excludes** attributes:

```
class PublisherForm(forms.ModelForm):
  class Meta:
    model = Publisher
    fields = ("name", "website", "email")
```

fields is a list or tuple of the fields to include in the form. When manually setting the list of fields, if you add extra fields to the model, you must also add their name here to have them displayed on the form.

You can also use the special value __**all**__ instead of a list or tuple to automatically include all the fields, like this:

```
class PublisherForm(forms.ModelForm):
  class Meta:
    model = Publisher
    fields = "__all__"
```

If the **model** field has its **editable** attribute set to **False**, then it will not be automatically included.

On the contrary, the **exclude** attribute sets the fields to not display in the form. Any fields added to the model will automatically be added to the form. We could define the preceding form using **exclude** with any empty tuple since we want all the fields. The code is like this:

```
class PublisherForm(forms.ModelForm):
  class Meta:
    model = Publisher
    exclude = ()
```

This saves some work because you don't need to add a field to both the model and in the **fields** list, however, it is not as safe, as you might automatically expose fields to the end user that you don't want to. For example, if you had a **User** model with **UserForm**, you might add an **is_admin** field to the **User** model to give admin users extra privileges. If this field did not have the **exclude** attribute, it would be displayed to the user. A user would then be able to make themselves an administrator, which is something you probably wouldn't want.

Whichever of these three approaches to choosing the forms to display that we decide to use, in our case, they will display the same in the browser. This is because we are choosing to display *all* the fields. They all look like this when rendered in the browser:

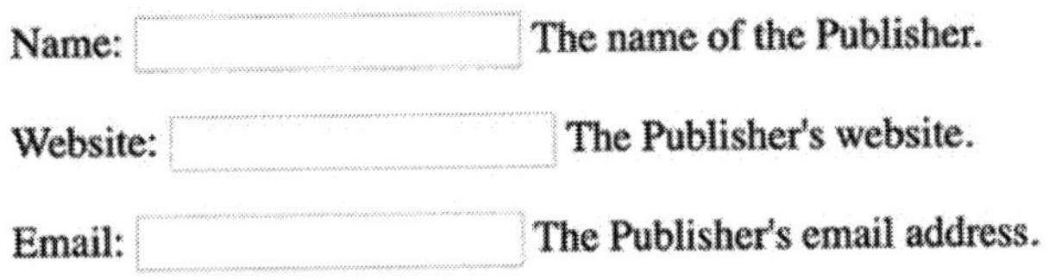

Name: [   ] The name of the Publisher.

Website: [   ] The Publisher's website.

Email: [   ] The Publisher's email address.

Figure 7.18: PublisherForm

Note that **help_text** from the **Publisher** model is automatically rendered as well.

Usage in a view is similar to the other forms we have seen. Also, as mentioned, there is an extra argument that can be provided, called **instance**. This can be set to **None**, which will render an empty form.

Assuming, in your view function, you have some method of determining whether you are creating or editing a model instance (we will discuss how to do this later), this will determine a variable called **is_create** (**True** if creating an instance, or **False** if editing an existing one). Your view function to create the form could then be written like this:

```
if is_create:
    instance = None
else:
    instance = get_object_or_404(Publisher, pk=pk)


if request.method == "POST":
    form = PublisherForm(request.POST, instance=instance)
    if form.is_valid():
        # we'll cover this branch soon
else:
    form = PublisherForm(instance=instance)
```

As you can see, in either branch, the instance is passed to the **PublisherForm** constructor, although it is **None** if we are in create mode.

If the form is valid, we can then save the **model** instance. This is done simply by calling the **save** method on the form. This will automatically create the instance, or simply save changes to the old one:

```
if form.is_valid():
  form.save()
  return redirect(success_url)
```

The **save** method returns the **model** instance that was saved. It takes one optional argument, **commit**, which determines whether the changes should be written to the database. You can pass **False** instead, which allows you to make additional changes to the instance before manually saving the changes. This would be required to set attributes that have not been included in the form. As we mentioned, maybe you would set the **is_admin** flag to **False** on a **User** instance:

```
if form.is_valid():
  new_user = form.save(False)
  new_user.is_admin = False
  new_user.save()
  return redirect(success_url)
```

In *Activity 7.02, Review Creation UI*, at the end of this chapter, we will be using this feature as well.

If your model uses **ManyToMany** fields, and you also call **form.save(False)**, you should also call **form.save_m2m()** to save any many-to-many relationships that have been set. It is not necessary to call this method if you call the form **save** method with **commit** set to **True** (that is, the default).

Model forms can be customized by making changes to their **Meta** attributes. The **widgets** attribute can be set. It can contain a dictionary keyed on the field names, with widget classes or instances as the values. For example, this is how to set up **PublisherForm** to have placeholders:

```
class PublisherForm(forms.ModelForm):
  class Meta:
    model = Publisher
    fields = "__all__"
    widgets = {"name": forms.TextInput\
              (attrs={"placeholder": "The publisher's name."})}
```

The values behave the same as setting the **kwarg** widget in the field definition; they can be a class or an instance. For example, to display **CharField** as a password input, the **PasswordInput** class can be used; it does not need to be instantiated:

```
widgets = {"password": forms.PasswordInput}
```

Model forms can also be augmented with extra fields added in the same way as they are added to a normal form. For example, suppose we wanted to give the option of sending a notification email after saving a **Publisher** object. We can add an **email_on_save** field to **PublisherForm** like this:

```
class PublisherForm(forms.ModelForm):
  email_on_save = forms.BooleanField\
               (required=False, \
                  help_text="Send notification email on save")


  class Meta:
    model = Publisher
    fields = "__all__"
```

When rendered, the form looks like this:

Name:	The name of the Publisher.
Website:	The Publisher's website.
Email:	The Publisher's email address.
Email on save: ☑	Send notification email on save

Figure 7.19: PublisherForm with an additional field

Additional fields are placed after the **Model** fields. The extra fields are not handled automatically – they do not exist on the model, so Django won't attempt to save them on the **model** instance. Instead, you should handle the saving of their values by examining the **cleaned_data** values of the form, as you would with a standard form, for example (inside your view function):

```
if form.is_valid():
  if form.cleaned_data.get("email_on_save"):
    send_email()
      # assume this function is defined elsewhere
```

```
# save the instance regardless of sending the email or not
form.save()
return redirect(success_url)
```

In the next exercise, you will write a new view function to create or edit a **Publisher**.

EXERCISE 7.03: CREATING AND EDITING A PUBLISHER

In this exercise, we will return to Bookr. We want to add the ability to create and edit a **Publisher** without using the Django admin. To do this, we will add a **ModelForm** for the **Publisher** model. It will be used in a new view function. The view function will take an optional argument, **pk**, which will either be the ID of the **Publisher** being edited or **None** to create a new **Publisher**. We will add two new URL maps to facilitate this. When this is complete, we will be able to see and update any publisher using their ID. For example, information for **Publisher 1** will be viewable/editable at URL path **/publishers/1**:

1. In PyCharm, open the **reviews** app's **forms.py** file. After the **forms** import, also import the **Publisher** model:

    ```
    from .models import Publisher
    ```

2. Create a **PublisherForm** class, inheriting from **forms.ModelForm**:

    ```
    class PublisherForm(forms.ModelForm):
    ```

3. Define the **class Meta** attribute on **PublisherForm**. The attributes that **Meta** requires are the model (**Publisher**) and fields (**"__all__"**):

    ```
    class PublisherForm(forms.ModelForm):
      class Meta:
        model = Publisher
        fields = "__all__"
    ```

    Save **forms.py**.

    > **NOTE**
    >
    > The complete file can be found at http://packt.live/3qh9bww.

4. Open the **reviews** app's **views.py** file. At the top of the file, import **PublisherForm**:

    ```
    from .forms import PublisherForm, SearchForm
    ```

5. Make sure you import the **get_object_or_404** and **redirect** functions from **django.shortcuts**, if you aren't already:

```
from django.shortcuts import render, get_object_or_404, redirect
```

6. Also make sure you're importing the **Publisher** model if you aren't already. You may already be importing this and other models:

```
from .models import Book, Contributor, Publisher
```

7. The final import you will need is the **messages** module. This will allow us to register a message letting the user know that a **Publisher** object was edited or created:

```
from django.contrib import messages
```

Once again, add this import if you do not already have it.

8. Create a new view function called **publisher_edit**. It takes two arguments, **request** and **pk** (the ID of the **Publisher** object to edit). This is optional, and if it is **None**, then a **Publisher** object will be created instead:

```
def publisher_edit(request, pk=None):
```

9. Inside the view function, we need to try to load the existing **Publisher** instance if **pk** is not **None**. Otherwise, the value of **publisher** should be **None**:

```
def publisher_edit(request, pk=None):
    if pk is not None:
        publisher = get_object_or_404(Publisher, pk=pk)
    else:
        publisher = None
```

10. After getting a **Publisher** instance or **None**, complete the branch for a **POST** request. Instantiate the form in the same way as seen earlier in the chapter, but now make sure that it takes **instance** as a kwarg. Then, if the form is valid, save it using the **form.save()** method. The method will return the updated **Publisher** instance, which is stored in the **updated_publisher** variable. Then, register a different success message depending on whether the **Publisher** instance was created or updated. Finally, redirect back to this **publisher_edit** view, since **updated_publisher** will always have an ID at this point:

```
def publisher_edit(request, pk=None):
    ...
    if request.method == "POST":
```

```
        form = PublisherForm(request.POST, instance=publisher)
        if form.is_valid():
        updated_publisher = form.save()
          if publisher is None:
            messages.success\
            (request, "Publisher \"{}\" was created."\
                    .format(updated_publisher))
          else:
            messages.success\
            (request, "Publisher \"{}\" was updated."\
                    .format(updated_publisher))\
        return redirect("publisher_edit", updated_publisher.pk)
```

If the form is not valid, the execution falls through to just return the **render** function call with the invalid form (this will be implemented in *step 12*). The redirect uses a named URL map, which will be added later in the exercise.

11. Next, fill in the non-**POST** branch of the code. In this case, just instantiate the form with the **instance**:

```
def publisher_edit(request, pk=None):
  ...
  if request.method == "POST":
    ...
  else:
     form = PublisherForm(instance=publisher)
```

12. Finally, you can reuse the **form-example.html** file that you've used in previous exercises. Render it with the **render** function, passing in the HTTP method and **form** as the context:

```
def publisher_edit(request, pk=None):
  ...
  return render(request, "form-example.html", \
              {"method": request.method, "form": form})
```

Save this file. You can refer to it at http://packt.live/3nl62En.

13. Open **urls.py** in the **reviews** directory. Add two new URL maps; they will both go to the **publisher_edit** view. One will capture the ID of **Publisher** we want to edit and pass it into the view as the **pk** argument. The other will use the word **new** instead, and will not pass the **pk**, which will indicate we want to create a new **Publisher**.

To your **urlpatterns** variable, add the path **'publishers/<int:pk>/'** mapping to the view **reviews.views.publisher_edit**, with the name of **'publisher_edit'**.

Also, add the path **'publishers/new/'** mapping to the **reviews.views. publisher_edit** view, with the name of **'publisher_create'**:

```
urlpatterns = [
   ...
  path('publishers/<int:pk>/',views.publisher_edit, \
       name='publisher_edit'),\
  path('publishers/new/',views.publisher_edit, \
       name='publisher_create')]
```

Since the second mapping does not capture anything, the **pk** that is passed to the **publisher_detail** view function is **None**.

Save the **urls.py** file. The completed version for reference is at http://packt. live/39CpUnw.

14. Create a **form-example.html** file inside the **reviews** app's **templates** directory. Since this is a standalone template (it does not extend any other templates), we need to render the messages inside it. Add this code just after the opening **<body>** tag to iterate through all the messages and display them:

```
{% for message in messages %}
<p><em>{{ message.level_tag|title }}:</em> {{ message }}</p>
{% endfor %}
```

This will loop over the messages we have added and display the tag (in our case, **Success**) and then the message.

15. Then, add the normal form rendering and submission code:

```
<form method="post">
  {% csrf_token %}
  {{ form.as_p }}
  <p>
    <input type="submit" value="Submit">
  </p>
</form>
```

Save and close this file.

You can refer to the full version of this file at http://packt.live/38I8XZx.

16. Start the Django dev server, then navigate to **http://127.0.0.1:8000/ publishers/new/**. You should see a blank **PublisherForm** being displayed:

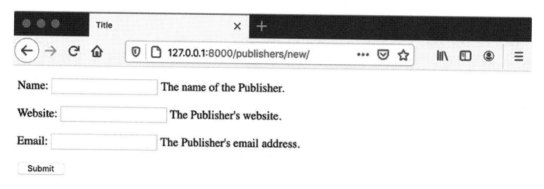

Figure 7.20: Blank publisher form

17. The form has inherited the model's validation rules, so you cannot submit the form with too many characters for **Name**, or with an invalid **Website** or **Email**. Put in some valid information, then submit the form. After submission, you should see the success message and the form will be populated with information that was saved to the database:

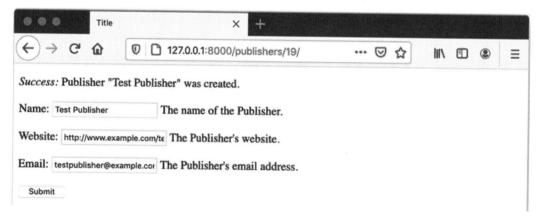

Figure 7.21: Form after submission

Notice that the URL has also been updated and now includes the ID of the publisher that was created. In this case, it is **http://127.0.0.1:8000/ publishers/19/** but the ID on your setup will depend on how many **Publisher** instances were already in your database.

Notice that if you refresh the page, you will not receive a message confirming whether you want to re-send the form data. This is because we redirected after saving, so it is safe to refresh this page as many times as you want, and no new **Publisher** instances will be created. If you had not redirected it, then every time the page was refreshed, a new **Publisher** instance would be created.

If you have other **Publisher** instances in your database, you can change the ID in the URL to edit other ones. Since the ID in this instance is **3**, we can assume that **Publisher 1** and **Publisher 2** already exist and can substitute in their IDs to see the existing data. Here is the view of the existing **Publisher 1** (at **http://127.0.0.1:8000/publishers/1/**) – your information may be different:

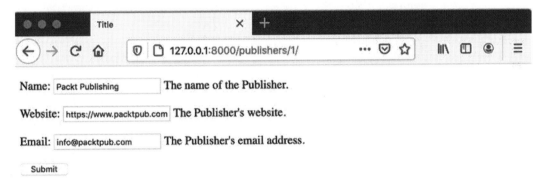

Figure 7.22: Existing Publisher 1 information

Try making changes to the existing **Publisher** instance. Notice that after you save, the message is different – it is telling the user that the **Publisher** instance was *updated* rather than *created*:

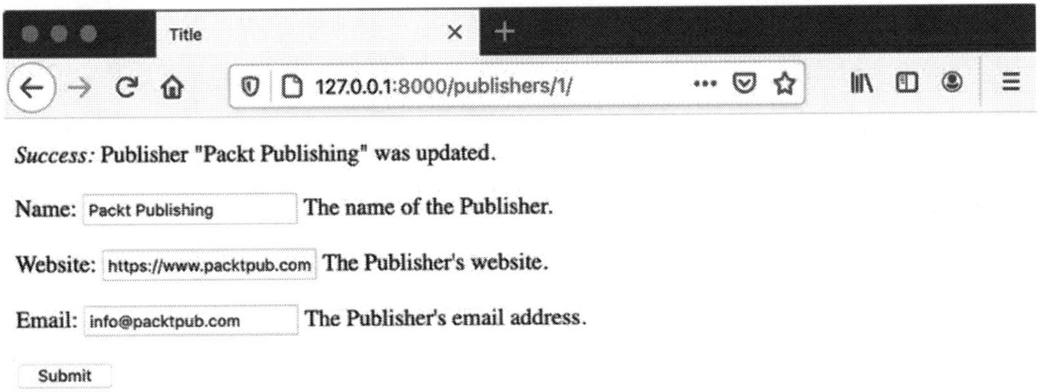

Figure 7.23: Publisher after updating instead of creating

In this exercise, we implemented a **ModelForm** from a model (**PublisherForm** was created from **Publisher**) and saw how Django automatically generated the form fields with the correct validation rules. We then used the form's built-in **save** method to save changes to the **Publisher** instance (or automatically create it) inside the **publisher_edit** view. We mapped two URLs to the view. The first URL, which was for editing an existing **Publisher**, passed **pk** to the view. The other did not pass **pk** to the view, indicating that the **Publisher** instance should be created. Finally, we used the browser to experiment with creating a new **Publisher** instance and then editing an existing one.

ACTIVITY 7.01: STYLING AND INTEGRATING THE PUBLISHER FORM

In *Exercise 7.03*, *Creating and Editing a Publisher*, you added **PublisherForm** to create and edit **Publisher** instances. You built this with a standalone template that did not extend any other templates, so it lacked the global styles. In this activity, you will build a generic form detail page that will display a Django form, similar to **form-example.html** but extending from a base template. The template will accept a variable to display the type of model being edited. You will also update the main **base.html** template to render the Django messages, using Bootstrap styling.

These steps will help you complete this activity:

1. Start by editing the **base.html** project. Wrap the **content** block in a container **div** for a nicer layout with some spacing. Surround the existing **content** block with a **<div>** element with **class="container-fluid"**.

2. Render each **message** in **messages** (similar to *step 14* of *Exercise 7.03*, *Creating and Editing a Publisher*). Add the **{% for %}** block after the **<div>** you just created but before the **content** block. You should use the Bootstrap framework classes – this snippet will help you:

```
<div class="alert alert-{% if message.level_tag
  == 'error' %}danger{% else %}{
    {message.level_tag }}{% endif %}"

    role="alert">
  {{ message }}
</div>
```

The Bootstrap class and Django **message** tags have corresponding names for the most part (for example, **success** and **alert-success**). The exception is Django's **error** tag. The corresponding Bootstrap class is **alert-danger**. See more information about Bootstrap alerts at https://getbootstrap.com/docs/4.0/components/alerts/. This is why you need to use the **if** template tag in this snippet.

3. Create a new template called **instance-form.html**, inside the **reviews** app's namespaced **templates** directory.

4. **instance-form.html** should extend from the **reviews** app's **base.html**.

5. The context being passed to this template will contain a variable called **instance**. This will be the **Publisher** instance being edited, or **None** if we are creating a new **Publisher** instance. The context will also contain a **model_type** variable, which is a string indicating the model type (in this case, **Publisher**). Use these two variables to populate the **title** block template tag:

    If the instance is **None**, the title should be **New Publisher**.

    Otherwise, the title should be **Editing Publisher <Publisher Name>**.

6. **instance-form.html** should contain a **content block** template tag to override the **base.html content** block.

7. Add an **<h2>** element inside the **content** block and populate it using the same logic as the title. For better styling, wrap the publisher name in an **<em>** element.

8. Add a **<form>** element to the template with a **method** of **post**. Since we are posting back to the same URL, an **action** does not need to be specified.

9. Include the CSRF token template tag in the **<form>** body.

10. Render the Django form (its context variable will be **form**) inside **<form>**, using the **as_p** method.

11. Add a **submit <button>** to the form. Its text should depend on whether you are editing or creating. Use the text **Save** for editing or **Create** for creating. You can use the Bootstrap classes for the button styling here. It should have the attribute **class="btn btn-primary"**.

12. In **reviews/views.py**, the **publisher_edit** view does not need many changes. Update the **render** call to render **instance-form.html** instead of **form-example.html**.

13. Update the context dictionary being passed to the **render** call. It should include the **Publisher** instance (the **publisher** variable that was already defined) and **model_type** string. The context dictionary already includes **form** (a **PublisherForm** instance). You can remove the **method** key.

14. Since we're finished with the **form-example.html** template, it can be deleted.

    When you've finished, the **Publisher** creation page (at **http://127.0.0.1:8000/publishers/new/**) should look like *Figure 7.24*:

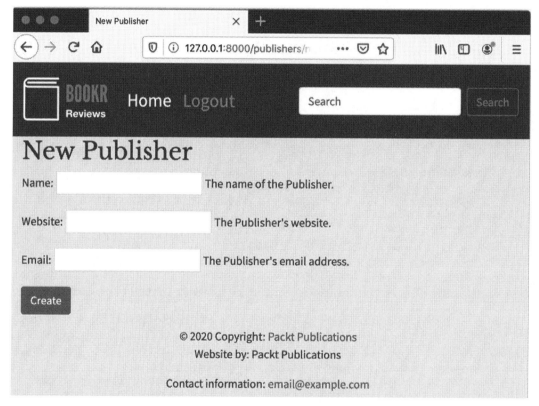

Figure 7.24: The Publisher creation page

When editing a **Publisher** (for example, at the URL
http://127.0.0.1:8000/publishers/1/), your page should look like
Figure 7.25:

Figure 7.25: The Editing Publisher page

After saving a **Publisher** instance, whether creating or editing, you should see the success message at the top of the page (*Figure 7.26*):

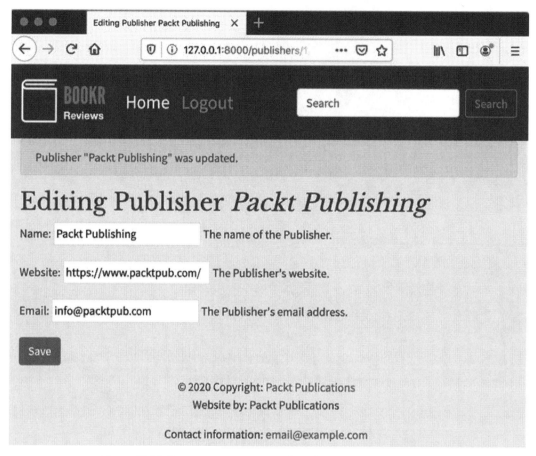

Figure 7.26: Success message rendered as a Bootstrap alert

> **NOTE**
>
> The solution to this activity can be found at http://packt.live/2Nh1NTJ.

ACTIVITY 7.02: REVIEW CREATION UI

Activity 7.01, Styling and Integrating the Publisher Form, was quite extensive; however, by completing it, you have created a foundation that makes it easier to add other *edit* and *create* views. You will experience this first-hand in this activity when you will build forms for creating and editing reviews. Because the **instance-form.html** template was made generically, you can reuse it in other views.

In this activity, you will create a review **ModelForm**, then add a **review_edit** view to create or edit a **Review** instance. You can reuse **instance-form.html** from *Activity 7.01, Styling and Integrating the Publisher Form*, and pass in different context variables to make it work with the **Review** model. When working with reviews, you will operate within the context of a book, that is, the **review_edit** view must accept a book's **pk** as an argument. You will fetch the **Book** instance separately and assign it to the **Review** instance that you create.

These steps will help you complete this activity:

1. In **forms.py**, add a **ReviewForm** subclass of **ModelForm**; its model should be **Review** (make sure you **import** the **Review** model).

    ReviewForm should exclude the **date_edited** and **book** fields since the user should not be setting these in the form. The database allows any rating, but we can override the **rating** field with an **IntegerField** that requires a minimum value of *0* and a maximum value of *5*.

2. Create a new view called **review_edit**. It should accept two arguments after **request**: **book_pk**, which is required, and **review_pk**, which is optional (defaults to **None**). Fetch the **Book** instance and **Review** instance using the **get_object_or_404** shortcut (call it once for each type). When fetching the review, make sure the review belongs to the book. If **review_pk** is **None**, then the **Review** instance should be **None** too.

3. If the **request** method is **POST**, then instantiate a **ReviewForm** using **request.POST** and the review instance. Make sure you **import** the **ReviewForm**.

    If the form is valid, save the form but set the **commit** argument to **save** to **False**. Then, set the **book** attribute on the returned **Review** instance to the book fetched in *step 2*.

4. If the **Review** instance was being updated instead of created, then you should also set the **date_edited** attribute to the current date and time. Use the **from django.utils.timezone.now()** function. Then, save the **Review** instance.

5. Finish the valid form branch by registering a success message and redirecting back to the **book_detail** view. Since the **Review** model doesn't really contain a meaningful text description, use the book title in the message. For example, **Review for "<book title>" created**.

6. If the **request** method is not **POST**, instantiate a **ReviewForm** and just pass in the **Review** instance.

7. Render the **instance-form.html** template. In the context dictionary, include the same items as were used in **publisher_view**: **form, instance**, and **model_type (Review)**. Include two extra items, **related_model_type**, which should be **Book**, and **related_instance**, which will be the **Book** instance.

8. Edit **instance-form.html** to add a place to display the related instance information added in *step 6*. Under the **<h2>** element, add a **<p>** element that is only displayed if both **related_model_type** and **related_instance** are set. It should show the text **For <related_model_type> <related_instance>**. For example: **For Book Advanced Deep Learning with Keras**. Put the **related_instance** output in an **<em>** element for better readability.

9. In the **reviews** app's **urls.py** file, add URL maps to the **review_edit** view. The URLs **/books/** and **/books/<pk>/** are already configured. Add the URLs **/books/<book_pk>/reviews/new/** to create a review, and **/books/<book_pk>/reviews/<review_pk>/** to edit a review. Make sure you give these names such as **review_create** and **review_edit**.

10. Inside the **book_detail.html** template, add links that a user can click to create or edit a review. Add a link inside the **content** block, just before the **endblock** closing template tag. It should use the **url** template tag to link to the **review_edit** view when in creation mode. Also, use the attribute **class="btn btn-primary"** to make the link display like a Bootstrap button. The link text should be **Add Review**.

11. Finally, add a link to edit a review, inside the **for** loop that iterates over **Reviews** for **Book**. After all the instances of **text-info <span>**, add a link to the **review_edit** view using the **url** template tag. You will need to provide **book.pk** and **review.pk** as arguments. The text of the link should be **Edit Review**. When you are finished, the **Review Comments** page should look like *Figure 7.27*:

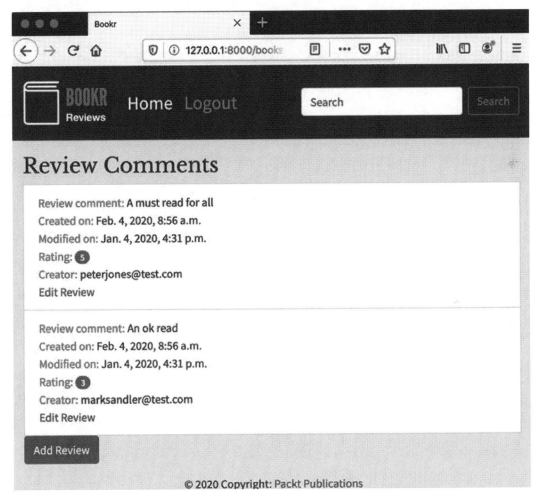

Figure 7.27: Book detail page with added Add Review button

You can see the **Add Review** button. Clicking it will take you to the **Create Book Review** page, which should look like *Figure 7.28*:

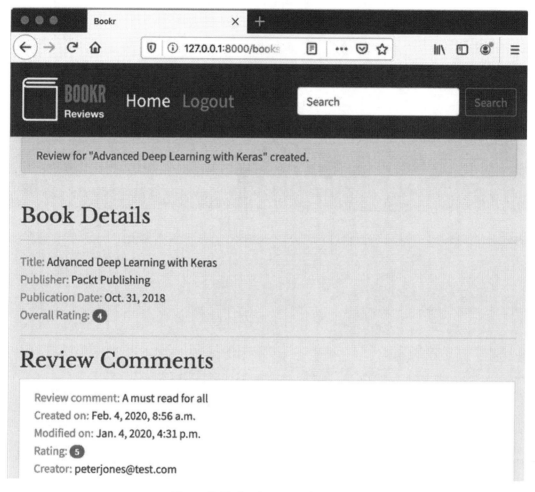

Figure 7.28: Review creation page

Enter some details in the form and click **Create**. You will be redirected to the **Book Details** page, and you should see the success message and your review, as in *Figure 7.29*:

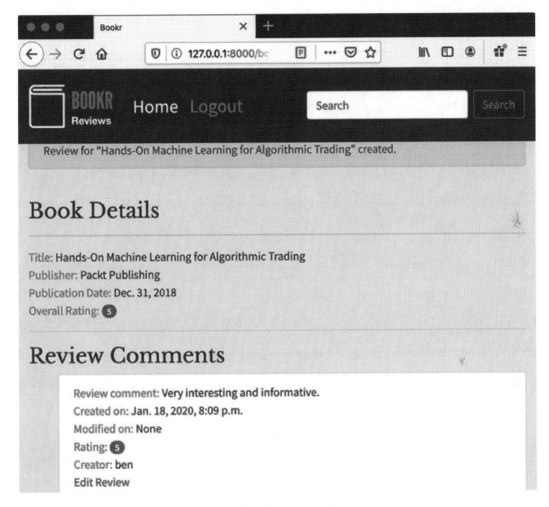

Figure 7.29: Book Details page with review added

You can also see the **Edit Review** link, and if you click it, you will be taken to a form that is pre-populated with your review data (see *Figure 7.30*):

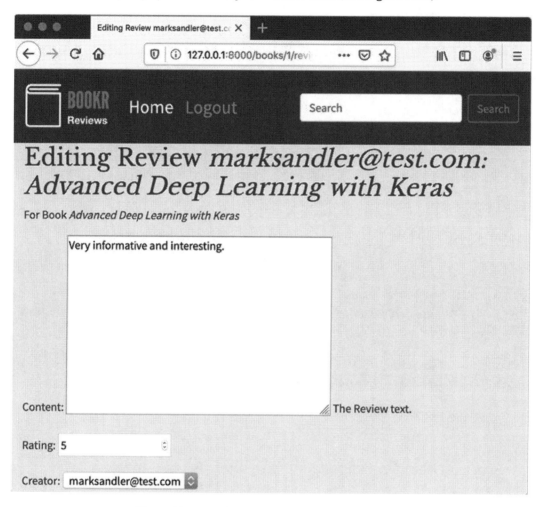

Figure 7.30: Review form when editing a review

After saving an existing review, you should see the **Modified on** date is updated on the **Book Details** page (*Figure 7.31*):

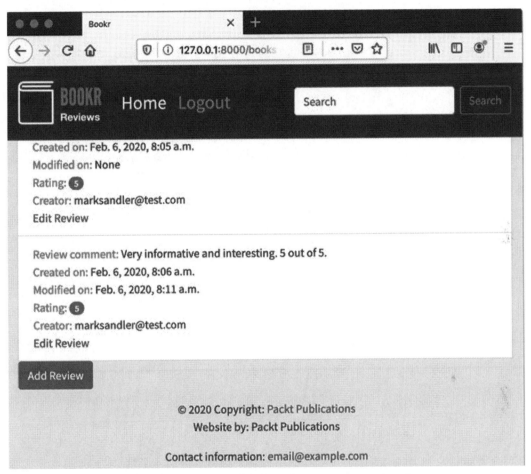

Figure 7.31: The Modified on date is now populated

NOTE

The solution to this activity can be found at http://packt.live/2Nh1NTJ.

SUMMARY

This chapter was a deep dive into forms. We saw how to enhance Django forms with custom validation advanced rules for cleaning data and validating fields. We saw how custom cleaning methods can transform the data that we get out of forms. A nice feature we saw that can be added to forms is the ability to set initial and placeholder values on fields, so the user does not have to fill them out.

We then looked at how to use the **ModelForm** class to automatically create a form from a Django model. We saw how to only show some fields to the user and how to apply custom form validation rules to the **ModelForm**. We also saw how Django can automatically save the new or updated model instance to the database inside the view. In the activities for this chapter, we enhanced Bookr some more by adding forms for creating and editing publishers and submitting reviews. The next chapter will carry on the theme of submitting user input, and along with that, we'll discuss how Django handles uploading and downloading files.

8

MEDIA SERVING AND FILE UPLOADS

OVERVIEW

This chapter starts by introducing you to media files and then teaching you how to set up Django to serve them. Once you have understood this, you will learn how to build a form in HTML that can upload files to a view for storage to disk. To enhance this process and reduce the amount of code, you will use Django forms to generate and validate a form and learn how to process file uploads through it. You will then look at some enhancements that Django provides specifically for working with image files and use the **Python Imaging Library** to resize an image. You will then create a model that uses `FileField` and `ImageField` to store a file and image respectively and upload to it using a Django form. After this, you will build a `ModelForm` instance automatically from the model and save the model and the files using just one line of code. At the end of this chapter, you will enhance the Bookr app by adding a cover image and book excerpt to the `Book` model.

INTRODUCTION

Media files refer to extra files that can be added after deployment to enrich your Django application. Usually, they are extra images that you would use in your site, but any type of file (including video, audio, PDF, text, documents, or even HTML) can be served as media.

You can think of them as somewhere between dynamic data and static assets. They are not dynamic data that Django generates on the fly, like when rendering a template. They also are not the static files that are included by the site developer when the site is deployed. Instead, they are extra files that can be uploaded by users or generated by your application for later retrieval.

Some common examples of media files (that you will see in *Activity 8.01, Image and PDF Uploads of Books*, later in this chapter) are book covers and preview PDFs that can be attached to a **Book** object. You can also use media files to allow users to upload images for a blog post or avatars for a social media site. If you wanted to use Django to build your own video sharing platform, you would store the uploaded videos as media. Your website will not function well if all these files are static files, as users won't be able to upload their own book covers, videos, and so on, and will be stuck with the ones you deployed.

SETTINGS FOR MEDIA UPLOADS AND SERVING

In *Chapter 5, Serving Static Files*, we looked at how Django can be used to serve static files. Serving media files is quite similar. Two settings must be configured in **settings.py**: **MEDIA_ROOT** and **MEDIA_URL**. These are analogous to **STATIC_ROOT** and **STATIC_URL** for serving static files.

- **MEDIA_ROOT**

  This is the path on the disk where the media (such as uploaded files) will be stored. As with static files, your web server should be configured to serve directly from this directory, to take the load off Django.

- **MEDIA_URL**

  This is similar to **STATIC_URL**, but as you might guess, it's the URL that should be used to serve media. It must end in a **/**. Generally, you will use something like **/media/**.

> **NOTE**
>
> For security reasons, the path for **MEDIA_ROOT** must not be the same as the path for **STATIC_ROOT**, and **MEDIA_URL** must not be the same as **STATIC_URL**. If they were the same, a user might replace your static files (such as JavaScript or CSS files) with malicious code and exploit your users.

MEDIA_URL is designed to be used in templates so that you are not hardcoding the URL and it can be changed easily. For example, you might want to set it to a specific host or **Content Delivery Network** (**CDN**) when you deploy to production. We will discuss the use of **MEDIA_URL** in templates in an upcoming section.

SERVING MEDIA FILES IN DEVELOPMENT

As with static files, when serving media in production, your web server should be configured to serve directly from the **MEDIA_ROOT** directory to prevent Django from being tied up servicing the request. The Django dev server can serve media files in development. However, unlike static files, the URL mapping and view is not set up automatically for media files.

Django provides the **static** URL mapping that can be added to your existing URL maps to serve media files. It is added to your **urls.py** file like this:

```
from django.conf import settings
from django.conf.urls.static import static



urlpatterns = [
    # your existing URL maps
]
if settings.DEBUG:
    urlpatterns += static(settings.MEDIA_URL,\
                        document_root=settings.MEDIA_ROOT)
```

This will serve the **MEDIA_ROOT** setting defined in **settings.py** to the **MEDIA_URL** setting that is also defined there. The reason we check for **settings.DEBUG** before appending the map is so we don't add this map in production.

For example, if your **MEDIA_ROOT** was set to **/var/www/bookr/media**, and your **MEDIA_URL** was set to **/media/**, then the **/var/www/bookr/media/image. jpg** file would be available at **http://127.0.0.1:8000/media/image.jpg**.

The **static** URL map does not work when the Django **DEBUG** setting is **False**, and so it can't be used in production. However, as mentioned earlier, in production your web server should be serving these requests, so Django will not need to handle them.

In the first exercise, you will create and add a new **MEDIA_ROOT** and **MEDIA_URL** to your **settings.py** file. You will then add the **static** media serving URL map and add a test file to ensure media serving is configured correctly.

EXERCISE 8.01: CONFIGURING MEDIA STORAGE AND SERVING MEDIA FILES

In this exercise, you will set up a new Django project as an example project to use throughout this chapter. Then you'll configure it to be able to serve media files. You'll do this by creating a **media** directory and adding the **MEDIA_ROOT** and **MEDIA_URL** settings. Then you'll set up the URL mapping for **MEDIA_URL**.

To check that everything is configured and being served correctly, you will put a test file inside the **media** directory:

1. As with the previous example Django projects you've set up, you can reuse the existing **bookr** virtual environment. In a terminal, activate the **bookr** virtual environment. Then, start a new project named **media_project**, using **django-admin.py**:

   > **NOTE**
   >
   > To learn how to create and activate a virtual environment, refer to the *Preface*.

   ```
   django-admin.py startproject media_project
   ```

   Change (or **cd**) into the **media_project** directory that was created, then use the **startapp** management command to start an app called **media_example**:

   ```
   python3 manage.py startapp media_example
   ```

2. Open the **media_project** directory in PyCharm. Set up a run configuration for the **runserver** command in the same manner as for the other Django projects you've opened:

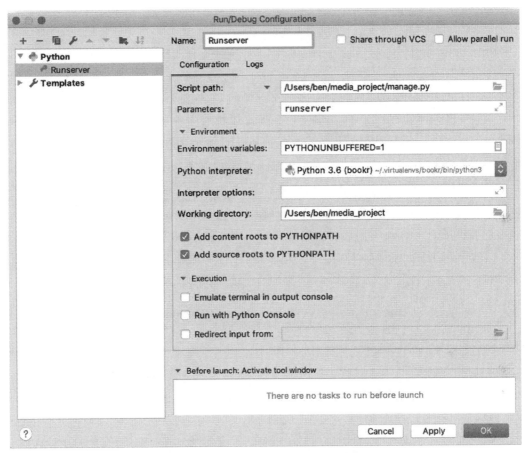

Figure 8.1: Runserver configuration

Figure 8.1 shows the **runserver** configuration of the project in PyCharm.

3. Create a new directory named **media** inside the **media_project** project directory. Then, create a new file in this directory named **test.txt**. The directory structure of this will look like *Figure 8.2*:

        media
           test.txt

Figure 8.2: media directory and test.txt layout

4. **test.txt** will also open automatically. Enter the text **Hello, world!** into it, then you can save and close the file.

5. Open **settings.py** inside the **media_project** package directory. At the end of the file, add a setting for **MEDIA_ROOT**, using the path to the media directory you just created. Make sure to import the **os** module at the top of the file:

```
import os
```

Then use it to join it to **BASE_DIR** using the **os.path.join** function:

```
MEDIA_ROOT = os.path.join(BASE_DIR, 'media')
```

6. Directly below the line added in *step 5*, add another setting for **MEDIA_URL**. This should just be **'/media/'**:

```
MEDIA_URL = '/media/'
```

After this, save **settings.py**. Here's what it should look like:

```
STATIC_URL = '/static/'


MEDIA_ROOT = os.path.join(BASE_DIR, 'media')
MEDIA_URL = '/media/'
```

With these changes made, your **settings.py** should look like this: http://packt.live/34RdhU1.

7. Open the **media_project** package's **urls.py** file. After the **urlpatterns** definition, add the following code to add the media serving URL if running in **DEBUG** mode. First, you will need to import the Django settings and static serving view by adding the highlighted import lines above the **urlpatterns** definition:

```
from django.contrib import admin
from django.urls import path
from django.conf import settings
```

```
from django.conf.urls.static import static

urlpatterns = [path('admin/', admin.site.urls),]
```

8. Then, add the following code right after your **urlpatterns** definition (refer to the code block in the previous step) to conditionally add a mapping from **MEDIA_URL** to the **static** view, which will serve from **MEDIA_ROOT**:

```
if settings.DEBUG:
    urlpatterns += static(settings.MEDIA_URL,\
                    document_root=settings.MEDIA_ROOT)
```

You can now save this file. It should look like this: http://packt.live/3nVUiPn.

9. Start the Django dev server if it is not already running, then visit **http://127.0.0.1:8000/media/test.txt**. If you did everything correctly, then you should see the text **Hello, world!** in your browser:

Figure 8.3: Serving a media file

If your browser looks like *Figure 8.3*, it means that the media files are being served from the **MEDIA_ROOT** directory. The **test.txt** file we created was just for testing, but we will use it in *Exercise 8.02, Template Settings and Using MEDIA_ URL in Templates*, so don't delete it yet.

In this exercise, we configured Django to serve media files. We served a test file just to make sure everything works as expected, and it did. We'll now look at how we can automatically generate media URLs in templates.

CONTEXT PROCESSORS AND USING MEDIA_URL IN TEMPLATES

To use **MEDIA_URL** in a template, we could pass it in through the rendering context dictionary, in our view. For example:

```
from django.conf import settings

def my_view(request):
    return render(request, "template.html",\
                {"MEDIA_URL": settings.MEDIA_URL,\
                "username": "admin"})
```

This will work, but the problem is that **MEDIA_URL** is a common variable that we might want to use in many places, and so we'd have to pass it through in practically every view.

Instead, we can use a **context processor**, which is a way of adding one or more variables automatically to the context dictionary on every **render** call.

A context processor is a function that accepts one argument, the current request. It returns a dictionary of context information that will be merged with the dictionary that was passed to the **render** call.

We can look at the source code of the **media** context processor, which illustrates how they work:

```
def media(request):
    """
    Add media-related context variables to the context.
    """
    return {'MEDIA_URL': settings.MEDIA_URL}
```

With the media context processor activated, **MEDIA_URL** will be added to our context dictionaries. We could change our **render** call, seen previously, to this:

```
return render(request, "template.html", {"username": "admin"})
```

The same data would be sent to the template, as the context processor would add **MEDIA_URL**.

The full module path to the **media** context processor is **django.template. context_processors.media**. Some examples of other context processors that Django provides are:

- **django.template.context_processors.debug**

  This returns the dictionary **{"DEBUG": settings.DEBUG}**.

- **django.template.context_processors.request**

  This returns the dictionary **{"request": request}**, that is, it just adds the current HTTP request to the context.

To enable a context processor, its module path must be added to the **context_ processors** option of your **TEMPLATES** setting. For example, to enable the media context processor, add **django.template.context_processors.media**. We will cover how to do this in detail in *Exercise 8.02, Template Settings and Using MEDIA_ URL in Templates*.

Once the **media** context processor is enabled, the **MEDIA_URL** variable can be accessed inside a template just like a normal variable:

```
{{ MEDIA_URL }}
```

You could use it, for example, to source an image:

```
<img src="{{ MEDIA_URL }}uploads/image.jpg">
```

Note that, unlike with static files, there is no template tag for loading media files (that is, there is no equivalent to the **{% static %}** template tag).

Custom context processors can also be written. For example, referring back to the Bookr application that we have been building, we might want to show a list of the five latest reviews in a sidebar that's on every page. A context processor like this would perform this:

```
from reviews.models import Review



def latest_reviews(request):
    return {"latest_reviews": \
            Review.objects.order_by('-date_created')[:5]}.
```

This would be saved in a file named **context_processors.py** in the Bookr project directory, then referred to in the **context_processors** setting by its module path, **context_processors.latest_reviews**. Or we could save it inside the **reviews** app and refer to it as **reviews.context_processors.latest_reviews**. It is up to you to decide whether a context processor should be considered project-wide or app-specific. However, bear in mind that regardless of where it is stored, once activated, it applies to all **render** calls for all apps.

A context processor can return a dictionary with multiple items, or even zero items. It would do this if it had conditions to only add items if certain criteria were met, for example, showing the latest reviews only if the user is logged in. Let's explore this in detail in the next exercise.

EXERCISE 8.02: TEMPLATE SETTINGS AND USING MEDIA_URL IN TEMPLATES

In this exercise, you will continue with **media_project** and configure Django to automatically add the **MEDIA_URL** setting to every template. You do this by adding **django.template.context_processors.media** to the **TEMPLATES context_processors** setting. You'll then add a template that uses this new variable, and an example view to render it. You will make changes to the view and template throughout the exercises in this chapter:

1. In PyCharm, open **settings.py**. First, you will need to add **media_example** to the **INSTALLED_APPS** setting, since it wasn't done when the project was set up:

```
INSTALLED_APPS = [# other apps truncated for brevity\
    'media_example']
```

2. About halfway down the file, you will find the **TEMPLATES** setting, which is a dictionary. Inside it is the item **OPTIONS** (another dictionary). Inside **OPTIONS** is the **context_processors** setting.

    To the end of this list, add this:

```
'django.template.context_processors.media'
```

    The full list should look like this:

```
TEMPLATES = \
[{'BACKEND': 'django.template.backends.django.DjangoTemplates',
  'DIRS': [],
  'APP_DIRS': True,
  'OPTIONS': {'context_processors': \
              ['django.template.context_processors.debug',\
               'django.template.context_processors.request',\
               'django.contrib.auth.context_processors.auth',\
               'django.contrib.messages.context_processors.messages',\
               'django.template.context_processors.media'\
           ],\
       },\
    },\
 ]
```

    The complete file should look like this: http://packt.live/3nVOpSx.

3. Open the **media_example** app's **views.py** and create a new view called **media_example**. For now, it can just render a template named **media-example.html** (you will create this in *step 5*). The entire code of the view function is like this:

```
def media_example(request):
    return render(request, "media-example.html")
```

Save **views.py**. It should look like this: http://packt.live/3pvEGCB.

4. You need a URL mapping to the **media_example** view. Open the **media_project** package's **urls.py** file.

First, **import media_example.views** with the other imports in the file:

```
import media_example.views
```

Then add a **path** into **urlpatterns** to map **media-example/** to the **media_example** view:

```
path('media-example/', media_example.views.media_example)
```

Your full **urlpatterns** should look like this code block:

```
from django.conf.urls.static import static

import media_example.views

urlpatterns = [path('admin/', admin.site.urls),\
               path('media-example/', \
                    media_example.views.media_example)]

if settings.DEBUG:
    urlpatterns += static(settings.MEDIA_URL,\
                          document_root=settings.MEDIA_ROOT)
```

You can save and close the file.

5. Create a **templates** directory inside the **media_example** app directory. Then, create a new HTML file inside the **media_project** project's **templates** directory. Select **HTML 5 file** and name the file **media-example.html**:

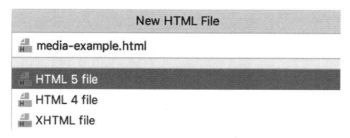

Figure 8.4: Create media-example.html

6. The **media-example.html** file should open automatically. You are just going to add a link inside the file to the **test.txt** file you created in *Exercise 8.01, Configuring Media Storage and Serving*. Inside the **<body>** element, add the highlighted code:

```
<body>
    <a href="{{ MEDIA_URL }}test.txt">Test Text File</a>
</body>
```

Note that there is no **/** between **MEDIA_URL** and the filename – this is because we already added a trailing slash when we defined it in **settings.py**. You can save the file. The complete file will look like this: http://packt.live/3nYTvgF.

7. Start the Django dev server if it is not already running, then visit **http://127.0.0.1:8000/media-example/**. You should see a simple page, like in *Figure 8.5*:

Figure 8.5: Basic media link page

If you click the link, you will be taken to the **test.txt** display and see the **Hello, world!** text you created in *Exercise 8.01, Configuring Media Storage and Serving Media Files* (*Figure 8.3*). This means you have configured the Django **context_processors** settings correctly.

We have finished with **test.txt**, so you can delete the file now. We will use the **media_example** view and template in the other exercises, so leave them around. In the next section, we will talk about how to upload files using a web browser, and how Django accesses them in a view.

FILE UPLOADS USING HTML FORMS

In *Chapter 6*, *Forms*, we learned about HTML forms. We discussed how to use the **method** attribute of **<form>** for **GET** or **POST** requests. Though we have only submitted text data using a form so far, it is also possible to submit one or more files using a form.

When submitting files, we must ensure that there are at least two attributes on the form: **method** and **enctype**. You may still also need other attributes, such as **action**. A form that supports file uploads might look like this:

```
<form method="post" enctype="multipart/form-data">
```

File uploads are only available for **POST** requests. They are not possible with **GET** requests as it would be impossible to send all the data for a file through a URL. The **enctype** attribute must be set to let the browser know it should send the form data as multiple parts, one part for the text data of the form, and separate parts for each of the files that have been attached to the form. This encoding is seamless to the user; they do not know how the browser is encoding the form, nor do they need to do anything different.

To attach files to a form, you need to create an input of type **file**. You can manually write the HTML code, like this:

```
<input type="file" name="file-upload-name">
```

When the input is rendered in the browser it looks like this when empty:

Browse...   No file selected.

Figure 8.6: Empty file input

The title of the button might be different depending on your browser.

Clicking the **Browse**... button will display a *file open* dialog box:

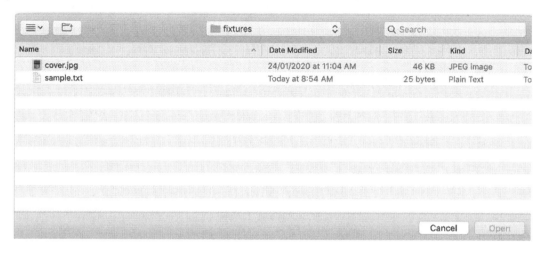

Figure 8.7: File browser on macOS

And after selecting a file, the name of the file is shown in the field:

Browse...   cover.jpg

Figure 8.8: File input with cover.jpg selected

Figure 8.8 shows a file input with a file named **cover.jpg** having been selected.

WORKING WITH UPLOADED FILES IN A VIEW

In addition to text data, if a form also contains file uploads, Django will populate the **request.FILES** attribute with these files. **request.FILES** is a dictionary-like object that is keyed on the **name** attribute given to the **file** input.

In the form example in the previous section, the file input had the name **file-upload-name**. So, the file would be accessible in the view using **request.FILES["file-upload-name"]**.

The objects that **request.FILES** contains are file-like objects (specifically, a **django.core.files.uploadedfile.UploadedFile** instance), so to use them, you must read their data. For example, to get the content of an uploaded file in your view, you can write:

```
content = request.FILES["file-upload-name"].read()
```

A more common action is to write the file contents to disk. When files are uploaded, they are stored in a temporary location (in memory if they are under 2.5 MB, otherwise in a temporary file on disk). To store the file data in a known location, the contents must be read and then written to disk at the desired location. An **UploadedFile** instance has a **chunks** method that will read the file data one chunk at a time to prevent too much memory from being used by reading the entirety of the file at once.

So, instead of simply using the **read** and **write** functions, use the **chunks** method to only read small chunks of the file into memory at a time:

```python
with open("/path/to/output.jpg", "wb+") as output_file:
    uploaded_file = request.FILES["file-upload-name"]
    for chunk in uploaded_file.chunks():
        output_file.write(chunk)
```

Note that in some of the upcoming examples, we will refer to this code as the **save_file_upload** function. Assume the function is defined like this:

```python
def save_file_upload(upload, save_path):
    with open(save_path, "wb+") as output_file:
        for chunk in upload.chunks():
            output_file.write(chunk)
```

The previous example code could then be refactored to call the function:

```python
uploaded_file = request.FILES["file-upload-name"]
save_file_upload(uploaded_file, "/path/to/output.jpg")
```

Each **UploadedFile** object (the **uploaded_file** variable in the previous example code snippets) also contains extra metadata about the uploaded file, such as the file's name, size, and content type. The attributes you will find most useful are:

- **size**: As the name suggests, this is the size of the uploaded file in bytes.

- **name**: This refers to the name of the uploaded file, for example, **image.jpg**, **file.txt**, **document.pdf**, and so on. This value is sent by the browser.

- **content_type**: The content type (MIME type) of the uploaded file. For example, **image/jpeg**, **text/plain**, **application/pdf**, and so on. Like **name**, this value is sent by the browser.

- **charset**: This refers to the charset or text encoding of the uploaded file, for text files. This will be something like **utf8** or **ascii**. Once again, this value is also determined and sent by the browser.

Here is a quick example of accessing these attributes (such as inside a view):

```
upload = request.FILES["file-upload-name"]
size = upload.size
name = upload.name
content_type = upload.content_type
charset = upload.charset
```

SECURITY AND TRUST OF BROWSERS' SENT VALUES

As we just described, the values of an **UploadedFile** for **name**, **content_type**, and **charset** are determined by the browser. This is important to consider because a malicious user could send fake values in place of real ones to disguise the actual files being uploaded. Django does not automatically try to determine the content type or charset of the uploaded file, and so it relies on the client to be accurate when it sends this information.

If we manually handle the saving of tile uploads without suitable checks, then a scenario like this could happen:

1. A user of the site uploads a malicious executable **malware.exe** but sends the content type **image/jpeg**.

2. Our code checks the content type and considers it to be safe, and so saves **malware.exe** to the **MEDIA_ROOT** file.

3. Another user of the site downloads what they think is a book cover image but is the **malware.exe** executable. They open the file, and their computer is infected with malware.

This scenario has been simplified – the malicious file would probably have a name that was not so obvious (maybe something like **cover.jpg.exe**), but the general process has been illustrated.

How you choose to handle the security of your uploads will depend on the specific use case, but for most cases, these tips will help:

- When you save the file to disk, generate a name instead of using the one provided by the uploader. You should replace the file extension with what you expect. For example, if a file is named **cover.exe** but the content type is **image/jpeg**, save the file as **cover.jpg**. You could also generate a completely random filename for extra security.

- Check that the file name extension matches the content type. This method is not foolproof as there are so many mime types that if you are handling uncommon files you might not get a match. The built-in **mimetypes** Python module can help you here. Its **guess_type** function takes a filename and returns a tuple of **mimetype** (content type) and **encoding**. Here is a short snippet showing its use, in a Python console:

```
>>> import mimetypes
>>> mimetypes.guess_type('file.jpg')
('image/jpeg', None)
>>> mimetypes.guess_type('text.html')
('text/html', None)
>>> mimetypes.guess_type('unknownfile.abc')
(None, None)
>>> mimetypes.guess_type('archive.tar.gz')
('application/x-tar', 'gzip')
```

Either element of the tuple might be **None** if the type or encoding cannot be guessed. Once it is imported into your file by doing **import mimetypes**, you would use it like this in your view function:

```
upload = request.FILES["file-upload-name"]
mimetype, encoding = mimetypes.guess_type(upload.name)
if mimetype != upload.content_type:
    raise TypeError("Mimetype doesn't match file extension.")
```

This method will work for common file types such as images, but as mentioned, many uncommon types may return **None** for **mimetype**.

- If you are expecting image uploads, use the **Pillow** library to try to open the uploaded file as an image. If it is not a valid image, then **Pillow** will be unable to open it. This is what Django does when using its **ImageField** to upload images. We will show how to use this technique to open and manipulate an image in *Exercise 8.05, Image Uploads using Django Forms*.

- You can also consider the **python-magic** Python package, which examines the actual content of files to try to determine their type. It is installable using **pip**, and its GitHub project is https://github.com/ahupp/python-magic. Once installed, and imported into your file with **import magic**, you can use it like this in your view function:

```
upload = request.FILES["field_name"]
mimetype = magic.from_buffer(upload.read(2048), mime=True)
```

You could then verify that **mimetype** was in a list of allowed types.

This is not a definitive list of all the ways of protecting against malicious file uploads. The best approach will depend on what type of application you are building. You might build a site for hosting arbitrary files, in which case you would not need any kind of content checking at all.

Let us now see how we can build an HTML form and view that will allow files to be uploaded. We will then store them inside the **media** directory and retrieve the downloaded files in our browser.

EXERCISE 8.03: FILE UPLOAD AND DOWNLOAD

In this exercise, you will add a form with a file field to the **media-example.html** template. This will allow you to upload a file to the **media_example** view using your browser. You will also update the **media_example** view to save the file to the **MEDIA_ROOT** directory so that it's available for download. You will then test that this all works by downloading the file again:

1. In PyCharm, open the **media-example.html** template located inside the **templates** folder. Inside the **<body>** element, remove the **<a>** link that was added in *step 6* of *Exercise 8.02, Template Settings and Using MEDIA_URL in Templates*. Replace it with a **<form>** element (highlighted here). Make sure the opening tag has **method="post"** and **enctype="multipart/form-data"**:

```
</head>
<body>
    <form method="post" enctype="multipart/form-data">

    </form>
</body>
```

2. Insert the **{% csrf_token %}** template tag inside the **<form>** body.

3. After **{% csrf_token %}**, add an **<input>** element, with **type="file"** and **name="file_upload"**:

```
<input type="file" name="file_upload">
```

4. Finally, before the closing **</form>** tag, add a **<button>** element with **type="submit"** and the text content **Submit**:

```
<button type="submit">Submit</button>
```

Your HTML body should now look like this:

```
<body>
    <form method="post" enctype="multipart/form-data">
        {% csrf_token %}
        <input type="file" name="file_upload">
        <button type="submit">Submit</button>
    </form>
</body>
```

Now, save and close the file. It should look like this: http://packt.live/37XJPh3.

5. Open the **media_example** app's **views.py**. Inside the **media_example** view, add code to save the uploaded file to the **MEDIA_ROOT** directory. For this, you need access to **MEDIA_ROOT** from settings, so import the Django settings at the top of the file:

```
from django.conf import settings
```

You will also need to use the **os** module to build the save path, so import that as well (also at the top of the file):

```
import os
```

6. The uploaded file should only be saved if the request method is **POST**. Inside the **media_example** view, add an **if** statement to validate that **request. method** is **POST**:

```
def media_example(request):
    if request.method == 'POST':
        ...
```

7. Inside the **if** statement added in the previous step, generate the output path by joining the uploaded filename to **MEDIA_ROOT**. Then, open this path in **wb** mode and iterate over the uploaded file using the **chunks** method. Finally, write each chunk to the saved file:

```
def media_example(request):
    if request.method == 'POST':
        save_path = os.path.join\
                    (settings.MEDIA_ROOT, \
                    request.FILES["file_upload"].name)
```

```
        with open(save_path, "wb") as output_file:
            for chunk in request.FILES["file_upload"].chunks():
                output_file.write(chunk)


    return render(request, "media-example.html")
```

Note that the uploaded file and its metadata are being accessed from the **request.FILES** dictionary, using the key that matches the name given to the file input (in our case, this is **file_upload**). You can save and close **views.py**. It should now look like this:

http://packt.live/37TwxSr.

8. Start the Django dev server if it is not already running, then navigate to **http://127.0.0.1:8000/media-example/**. You should see the file upload field and **Submit** button, as can be seen here:

Figure 8.9: File upload form

Click **Browse**... (or the equivalent in your browser) and select a file to upload. The name of the file will appear in the file input. Then, click **Submit**. The page will reload, and the form will be empty again. This is normal – in the background, the file should have been saved.

9. Try to download the file you uploaded using **MEDIA_URL**. In this example, a file named **cover.jpg** was uploaded. It will be downloadable at **http://127.0.0.1:8000/media/cover.jpg**. Your URL will depend on the name of the file you uploaded.

Figure 8.10: Uploaded file visible inside MEDIA_URL

If you uploaded an image file, HTML file, or another type of file your browser can display, you will be able to view it inside the browser. Otherwise, your browser will just download it to disk again. In both cases, it means the upload was successful.

You can also confirm the upload was successful by looking inside the **media** directory in the **media_project** project directory:

Figure 8.11: cover.jpg inside the media directory

Figure 8.11 shows **cover.jpg** inside the **media** directory in PyCharm.

In this exercise, you added an HTML form with **enctype** set to **multipart/form-data** so that it would allow file uploads. It contained a **file** input to select a file to upload. You then added saving functionality to the **media_example** view to save the uploaded file to disk.

In the next section, we will look at how to simplify form generation and add validation using Django forms.

FILE UPLOADS WITH DJANGO FORMS

In *Chapter 6, Forms*, we saw how Django makes it easy to define forms and automatically render them to HTML. In the previous example, we defined our form manually and wrote the HTML. We can replace this with a Django form, and implement the file input with a **FileField** constructor.

Here is how a **FileField** is defined on a form:

```
from django import forms


class ExampleForm(forms.Form):
    file_upload = forms.FileField()
```

The **FileField** constructor can take the following keyword arguments:

- **required**: This should be **True** for required fields and **False** if the field is optional.

- **max_length**: This refers to the maximum length of the filename of the file being uploaded.

- **allow_empty_file**: A field with this argument is valid even if the uploaded file is empty (has a size of **0**).

Apart from these three keyword arguments, the constructor can also accept the standard **Field** arguments, such as **widget**. The default widget class for a **FileField** is **ClearableFileInput**. This is a file input that can display a checkbox that can be checked to send a null value and clear the saved file on a model field.

Using a form with a **FileField** in a view is similar to other forms, but when the form has been submitted (that is, **request.METHOD** is **POST**), then **request.FILES** should be passed into the form constructor as well. This is because Django needs to access **request.FILES** to find information about uploaded files when validating the form.

The basic flow in a **view** function is therefore like this:

```
def view(request):
    if request.method == "POST":
        # instantiate the form with POST data and files
        form = ExampleForm(request.POST, request.FILES)
        if form.is_valid():
            # process the form and save files
            return redirect("success-url")
    else:
        # instantiate an empty form as we've seen before
        form = ExampleForm()

    # render a template, the same as for other forms
    return render(request, "template.html", {"form": form})
```

When working with uploaded files and forms, you can interact with the uploaded files by accessing them through **request.FILES**, or through **form.cleaned_data**: the values will return to the same object. In our above example, we could process the uploaded file like this:

```
if form.is_valid():
    save_file_upload("/path/to/save.jpg", \
                        request.FILES["file_upload"])
    return redirect("/success-url/")
```

Or, since they contain the same object, you can use **form.cleaned_data**:

```
if form.is_valid():
    save_file_upload("/path/to/save.jpg", \
                        form.cleaned_data["file_upload"])
    return redirect("/success-url/")
```

The data that is saved will be the same.

> **NOTE**
>
> In *Chapter 6, Forms*, you experimented with forms and submitting them with invalid values. When the page refreshed to show the form errors, the data that you had previously entered was populated when the page reloaded. This does not occur with file fields; instead, the user will have to navigate and select the file again if the form is invalid.

In the next exercise, we will put what we have seen with **FileFields** into practice by building an example form, then modifying our view to save the file only if the form is valid.

EXERCISE 8.04: FILE UPLOADS WITH A DJANGO FORM

In the previous exercise, you created a form in HTML and used it to upload a file to a Django view. If you tried submitting the form without selecting a file, you would get a Django exception screen. You did not do any validation on the form, so this method is quite fragile.

In this exercise, you will create a Django form with a **FileFIeld**, which will allow you to use form validation functions to make the view more robust as well to reduce the amount of code:

1. In PyCharm, inside the **media_example** app, create a new file named **forms.py**. It will open automatically. At the start of the file, import the Django **forms** library:

```
from django import forms
```

Then, create a **forms.Form** subclass, and name it **UploadForm**. Add one field to it, a **FileField** named **file_upload**. Your class should have this code:

```
class UploadForm(forms.Form):
    file_upload = forms.FileField()
```

You can save and close this file. The complete file should look like this: http://packt.live/34S5hBV.

2. Open the **form_example** app's **views.py** file. At the start of the file, right below the existing **import** statements, you will need to import your new class, like this:

```
from .forms import UploadForm
```

3. If you are in the **POST** branch of the view, **UploadForm** needs to be instantiated with both **request.POST** and **request.FILES**. If you do not pass in **request.FILES**, then the **form** instance will not be able to access the uploaded files. Under the **if request.method == "POST"** check, instantiate the **UploadForm** with these two arguments:

```
form = UploadForm(request.POST, request.FILES)
```

4. The existing lines that define the **save_path** and store the file contents can be retained, but they should be indented by one block and put inside a form validity check, so they are only executed if the form is valid. Add the **if form.is_valid():** line and then indent the other lines so the code looks like this:

```
if form.is_valid():
    save_path = os.path.join\
                (settings.MEDIA_ROOT, \
                request.FILES["file_upload"].name)

    with open(save_path, "wb") as output_file:
        for chunk in request.FILES["file_upload"].chunks():
            output_file.write(chunk)
```

5. Since you are using a form now, you can access the file upload through the form. Replace usages of **request.FILES["file_upload"]** with **form.cleaned_data["file_upload"]**:

```
if form.is_valid():
    save_path = os.path.join\
                (settings.MEDIA_ROOT,\
                form.cleaned_data["file_upload"].name)

    with open(save_path, "wb") as output_file:
        for chunk in form.cleaned_data["file_upload"].chunks():
            output_file.write(chunk)
```

6. Finally, add an **else** branch to handle non-**POST** requests, which simply instantiates a form without any arguments:

```
if request.method == 'POST':
    ...
else:
    form = UploadForm()
```

7. Add a context dictionary argument to the **render** call and set the **form** variable in the **form** key:

```
return render(request, "media-example.html", \
              {"form": form})
```

You can now save and close this file. It should look like this: http://packt.live/3psXxyc.

8. Finally, open the **media-example.html** template and remove your manually defined file **<input>**. Replace it with **form**, rendered using the **as_p** method (highlighted):

```
<body>
    <form method="post" enctype="multipart/form-data">
        {% csrf_token %}
        {{ form.as_p }}
        <button type="submit">Submit</button>
    </form>
</body>
```

You should not change any other parts of the file. You can save and close this file. It should look like this: http://packt.live/3qHHSMi.

9. Start the Django dev server if it is not already running, then navigate to **http://127.0.0.1:8000/media-example/**. You should see the **File upload** field and the **Submit** button, as follows:

Figure 8.12: File upload Django form rendered in the browser

10. Since we are using a Django form, we get its built-in validation automatically. If you try to submit the form without selecting a file, your browser should prevent you and show an error, as can be seen here:

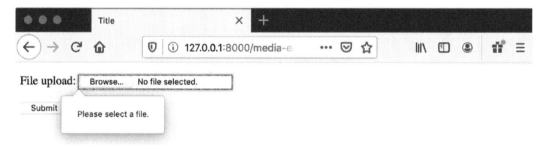

Figure 8.13: Form submission prevented by the browser

11. Finally, repeat the upload test that you performed in *Exercise 8.03, File Upload and Download*, by selecting a file and submitting the form. You should then be able to retrieve the file using **MEDIA_URL**. In this case, a file named **cover.jpg** is being uploaded again (see the following figure):

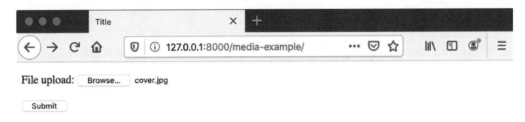

Figure 8.14: Uploading a file named cover.jpg

You can then retrieve the file at **http://127.0.0.1:8000/media/cover. jpg**, and you can see it in the browser as follows:

Figure 8.15: The file uploaded using a Django form is also visible in the browser

In this exercise, we replaced a manually built form with a Django form containing a **FileField**. We instantiated the form in the view by passing in both **request. POST** and **request.FILES**. We then used the standard **is_valid** method to check the validity of the form, and only saved the file upload if the form was valid. We tested the file uploading and saw we were able to retrieve uploaded files using **MEDIA_URL**.

In the next section, we will look at **ImageField**, which is like a **FileField** but specifically for images.

IMAGE UPLOADS WITH DJANGO FORMS

If you want to work with images in Python, the most common library that you will use is called **Pillow**. This is the library that Django uses to validate images. Originally, there was a library called **Python Imaging Library**, or **PIL**. It was not kept up to date and, eventually, a fork of the library was created and is still maintained – this is Pillow. To maintain backward compatibility, the package is still called PIL when installed. For example, the **Image** object is imported from PIL:

```
from PIL import Image
```

> **NOTE**
>
> The terms Python Imaging Library, PIL, and Pillow are often used interchangeably. You can assume that if someone refers to PIL, they mean the latest Pillow library.

Pillow provides various methods of retrieving data about or manipulating images. You can find out the width and height of images, or scale, crop, and apply transformations to them. There are too many operations available to cover in this chapter, so we will just introduce a simple example (scaling an image), which you will use in the next exercise.

Since images are one of the most common types of files that a user may want to upload, Django also includes an **ImageField** instance. This behaves similarly to **FileField** instance but also automatically validates that the data is an image file. This helps mitigate security issues where we expect an image, but the user uploads a malicious file.

An **UploadedFile** from an **ImageField** has all the same attributes and methods as that of a **FileField** (**size**, **content_type**, **name**, **chunks()**, and so on) but adds an extra attribute: **image**. This is an instance of the PIL **Image** object that is used to verify that the file being uploaded is a valid image.

After checking that the form is valid, the underlying PIL **Image** object is closed. This is to free up memory and prevent the Python process from holding too many files open, which could cause performance issues. What this means for the developer is that you can access some of the metadata about the image (such as its **width**, **height**, and **format**) but you can't access the actual image data without re-opening the image.

To illustrate, we will have a form with an **ImageField**, named **picture**:

```
class ExampleForm(forms.Form):
    picture = ImageField()
```

Inside the view function, the **picture** field can be accessed in the form's **cleaned_data**:

```
if form.is_valid():
    picture_field = form.cleaned_data["picture"]
```

Then, the **picture** field's **Image** object can be retrieved:

```
image = picture_field.image
```

Now that we have a reference to the image in the view, we can get some metadata:

```
w = image.width   # an integer, e.g. 600
h = image.height  # also an integer, e.g. 420
# the format of the image as a string, e.g. "PNG"
f = image.format
```

Django will also automatically update the **content_type** attribute of **UploadedFile** to the correct type for the **picture** field. This overwrites the value that the browser sent when uploading the file.

Attempting to use a method that accesses the actual image data (rather than just the metadata) will cause an exception to be raised. This is because Django has already closed the underlying image file.

For example, the following code snippet will raise an **AttributeError**:

```
image.getdata()
```

Instead, we need to re-open the image. The image data can be opened with the **ImageField** reference, after importing the **Image** class:

```
from PIL import Image

image = Image.open(picture_field)
```

Now that the image has been opened, you can perform operations on it. In the next section, we will look at a simple example – resizing the uploaded image.

RESIZING AN IMAGE WITH PILLOW

Pillow supports many operations that you might want to perform on an image before saving it. We cannot explain them all in this book, so we will just use a common operation: resizing an image to a specific size before saving it. This will help us save storage space and improve the download speed. For example, a user may upload large cover images in Bookr that are bigger than are needed for our purposes. When saving the file (writing it back to disk) we must specify the format to use. We could determine the type of image that was uploading with a number of methods (such as checking the **content_type** of the uploaded file or the **format** from the **Image** object), but in our example, we will always just save the image as a **JPEG** file.

The PIL **Image** class has a **thumbnail** method that will resize an image to a maximum size while retaining the aspect ratio. For example, we could set a maximum size of 50px by 50px. A 200px by 100px image would be resized to 50px by 25px: the aspect ratio is retained by setting the maximum dimension to 50px. Each dimension is scaled by a factor of 0.25:

```
from PIL import Image

size = 50, 50  # a tuple of width, height to resize to
image = Image.open(image_field)  # open the image as before
image.thumbnail(size)  # perform the resize
```

At this point, the resize has been done in memory only. The change is not saved to disk until the **save** method is called, like so:

```
image.save("path/to/file.jpg")
```

The output format is automatically determined from the file extension used, in this case, JPEG. The **save** method can also take a format argument to override it. For example:

```
image.save("path/to/file.png", "JPEG")
```

Despite having the extension **png**, the format is specified as **JPEG** and so the output will be in JPEG format. As you might imagine, this can be very confusing, so you might decide to stick with specifying the extension only.

In the next exercise, we will change the **UploadForm** we have been working with to use an **ImageField** instead of a **FileField**, then implement the resizing of an uploaded image before saving it to the media directory.

EXERCISE 8.05: IMAGE UPLOADS USING DJANGO FORMS

In this exercise, you will update the **UploadForm** class you created in *Exercise 8.04, File Uploads with a Django Form*, to use an **ImageField** instead of a **FileField** (this will involve simply changing the field's class). You will then see that the form renders it in the browser. Next, you will try uploading some non-image files and see how Django validates the form to disallow them. Finally, you will update your view to use PIL to resize the image before saving it, and then test it in action:

1. Open the **media_example** app's **forms.py** file. In the **UploadForm** class, change **file_upload** so it's an instance of **ImageField** instead of **FileField**. After updating, your **UploadForm** should look like this:

```
class UploadForm(forms.Form):
    file_upload = forms.ImageField()
```

Save and close the file. Your **forms.py** file should look like this: http://packt.live/2KAootD.

2. Start the Django dev server if it is not already running, then navigate to
    http://127.0.0.1:8000/media-example/. You should see the form
    rendered, and it will look identical as to when we used a **FileField** (see the
    following figure):

Figure 8.16: The ImageField looks the same as a FileField

3. You will notice the difference when you try to upload a non-image file. Click the
    Browse... button and try to select a non-image file. Depending on your browser
    or operating system, you might not be able to select anything other than an
    image file, as in *Figure 8.17*:

Figure 8.17: Only image files are selectable

Your browser may allow selecting an image but show an error in the form after
selection. Or your browser may allow you to select a file and submit the form,
and Django will raise a **ValidationError**. Regardless, you can be sure that
in your view, the form's **is_valid** view will only return **True** if an image has
been uploaded.

> **NOTE**
>
> You do not need to test uploading a file at this point, as the result would be
> the same as in *Exercise 8.04, File Uploads with a Django Form*.

4. The first thing you will need to do is to make sure the Pillow library is installed. In a terminal (making sure your virtual environment has been activated), run:

```
pip3 install pillow
```

(In Windows, this is **pip install pillow**.) You will get output like *Figure 8.18*:

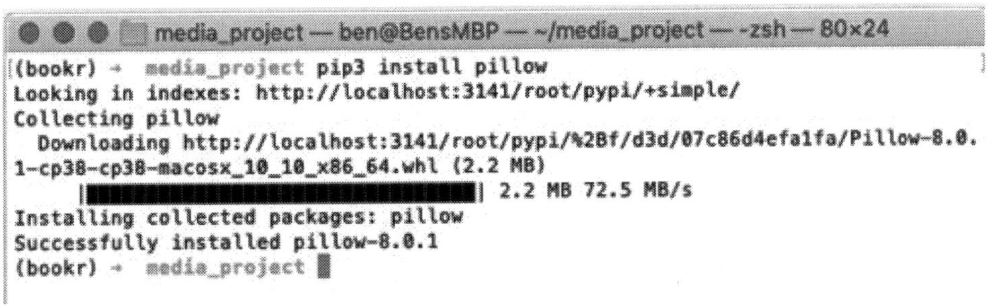

```
● ● ●  media_project — ben@BensMBP — ~/media_project — -zsh — 80×24
(bookr) →  media_project pip3 install pillow
Looking in indexes: http://localhost:3141/root/pypi/+simple/
Collecting pillow
  Downloading http://localhost:3141/root/pypi/%2Bf/d3d/07c86d4efa1fa/Pillow-8.0.
1-cp38-cp38-macosx_10_10_x86_64.whl (2.2 MB)
     |████████████████████████████████| 2.2 MB 72.5 MB/s
Installing collected packages: pillow
Successfully installed pillow-8.0.1
(bookr) →  media_project █
```

Figure 8.18: pip3 installing Pillow

Or if Pillow was already installed, you will see the output message **Requirement already satisfied**.

5. Now we can update the **media_example** view to resize the image before saving it. Switch back to PyCharm and open the **media_example** app's **views.py** file, then import PIL's **Image** class. So, add this import line below the **import os** statement near the top of the file:

```
from PIL import Image
```

6. Go to the **media_example** view. Under the line that generates the **save_path**, take out the three lines that open the output file, iterate over the uploaded file, and write out its chunks. Replace this with the code that opens the uploaded file with PIL, resizes it, then saves it:

```
image = Image.open(form.cleaned_data["file_upload"])
image.thumbnail((50, 50))
image.save(save_path)
```

The first line creates an **Image** instance by opening the uploaded file, the next performs the thumbnail conversion (to a maximum size of 50px by 50px), and the third line saves the file to the same save path that we have been generating in previous exercises. You can save the file. It should look like this: http://packt.live/34PWvof.

7. The Django dev server should still be running from *step 2*, but you should start it if it is not. Then, navigate to **http://127.0.0.1:8000/media-example/**. You will see the familiar **UploadForm**. Select an image and submit the form. If the upload and resize was successful, the form will refresh and be empty again.

8. View the uploaded image using **MEDIA_URL**. For example, a file named **cover. jpg** will be downloadable from **http://127.0.0.1:8000/media/cover. jpg**. You should see the image has been resized to have a maximum dimension of just 50px:

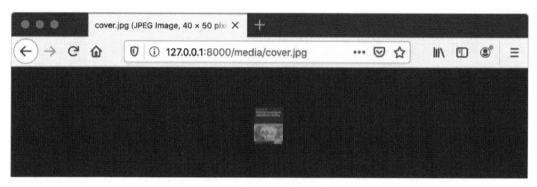

Figure 8.19: Resized logo

While a thumbnail this size might not be that useful, it at least lets us be sure that the image resize has worked correctly.

In this exercise, we changed the **FileField** on **UploadForm** to an **ImageField**. We saw that the browser wouldn't let us upload anything other than images. We then added code to the **media_example** view to resize the uploaded image using PIL.

We have encouraged the use of a separate web server to serve static and media files, for performance reasons. However, in some cases, you might want to use Django to serve files, for example, to provide authentication before allowing access. In the next section, we will discuss how to use Django to serve media files.

SERVING UPLOADED (AND OTHER) FILES USING DJANGO

Throughout this chapter and *Chapter 5, Serving Static Files*, we have discouraged serving files using Django. This is because it would needlessly tie up a Python process just serving a file – something that the web server is capable of handling. Unfortunately, web servers do not usually provide dynamic access control, that is, allowing only authenticated users to download a file. Depending on your web server used in production, you might be able to have it authenticate against Django and then serve the file itself; however, the specific configuration of specific web servers is outside the scope of this book.

One approach you can take is to specify a subdirectory of your **MEDIA_ROOT** directory and have your web server prevent access to just this specific folder. Any protected media should be stored inside it. If you do this, only Django will be able to read the files inside. For example, your web server could serve everything in the **MEDIA_ROOT** directory, except for a **MEDIA_ROOT/protected** directory.

Another approach would be to configure a Django view to serve a specific file from disk. The view will determine the path of the file on disk to send, then send it using the **FileResponse** class. The **FileResponse** class takes an open filehandle as an argument and tries to determine the correct content type from the file's content. Django will close the filehandle after the request completes.

The view function will accept the request and a relative path to the file to be downloaded, as parameters. This relative path is the path inside the **MEDIA_ROOT/protected** folder.

In our case, we will just check whether the user is anonymous (not logged in). We will do this by checking the **request.user.is_anonymous** property. If they are not logged in then we will raise a **django.core.exceptions.PermissionDenied** exception, which returns an HTTP **403 Forbidden** response to the browser. This will stop the execution of the view and not return any file:

```
import os.path
from django.conf import settings
from django.http import FileResponse
from django.core.exceptions import PermissionDenied


def download_view(request, relative_path):
    if request.user.is_anonymous:
        raise PermissionDenied
    full_path = os.path.join(settings.MEDIA_ROOT, \
```

```
                          "protected", relative_path)
    file_handle = open(full_path, "rb")
    return FileResponse(file_handle)
# Django sends the file then closes the handle
```

The URL mapping to this view could be like this, using the **<path>** path converter. Inside your **urls.py** file:

```
urlpatterns = [
    ...
    path("downloads/<path:relative_path>", views.download_view)]
```

There are many ways that you could choose to implement a view that sends files. The important thing is that you use the **FileResponse** class, which is designed to stream the file to the client in chunks instead of loading it all into memory. This will reduce the load on the server and lessen the impact on resource usage if you have to resort to sending files with Django.

STORING FILES ON MODEL INSTANCES

So far, we have manually managed the uploading and saving of files. You can also associate a file with a model instance by assigning the path to which it was saved to a **CharField**. However, as with much of Django, this capability (and more) is already provided with the **models.FileField** class. **FileField** instances do not actually store the file data; instead, they store the path where the file is stored (like a **CharField** would), but they also provide helper methods. These methods assist with loading files (so you do not have to manually open them) and generating disk paths for you based on the ID of the instance (or other attributes).

FileField can accept two specific optional arguments in its constructor (as well as the base **Field** arguments, such as **required**, **unique**, **help_text**, and so on):

- **max_length**: Like **max_length** in the form's **ImageField**, this is the maximum length of the filename that is allowed.

- **upload_to**: The **upload_to** argument has three different behaviors depending on what type of variable is passed to it. Its simplest use is with a string or **pathlib.Path** object. The path is simply appended to **MEDIA_ROOT**.

In this example, **upload_to** is just defined as a string:

```
class ExampleModel(models.Model):
    file_field = models.FileField(upload_to="files/")
```

Files saved to this **FileField** would be stored in the **MEDIA_ROOT/files** directory.

You could achieve the same result using a **pathlib.Path** instance too:

```
import pathlib

class ExampleModel(models.Model):
    file_field = models.FileField(upload_to=pathlib.Path("files/"))
```

The next way of using **upload_to** is with a string that contains **strftime** formatting directives (for example, **%Y** to substitute the current year, **%m** for the current month, and **%d** for the current day of the month). The full list of these directives is extensive and can be found at https://docs.python.org/3/library/time.html#time.strftime. Django will automatically interpolate these values when saving the file.

For example, say you defined the model and **FileField** like this:

```
class ExampleModel(models.Model):
    file_field = models.FileField(upload_to="files/%Y/%m/%d/")
```

For the first file uploaded on a specific day, Django would create the directory structure for that day. For example, for the first file uploaded on January 1, 2020, Django would create the directory **MEDIA_ROOT/2020/01/01** and then store the uploaded file in there. The next file (and all subsequent ones) uploaded on the same day would also be stored in that directory. Similarly, on January 2, 2020, Django would create the **MEDIA_ROOT/2020/01/02** directory, and files would be stored there.

If you have many thousands of files being uploaded every day, you could even have the files split up further by including the hour and minute in the **upload_to** argument (**upload_to="files/%Y/%m/%d/%H/%M/"**). This may not be necessary if you only have a small volume of uploads though.

By utilizing this method of the **upload_to** argument, you can have Django automatically segregate uploads and prevent too many files from being stored within a single directory (which can be hard to manage).

The final method of using **upload_to** is by passing a function that will be called to generate the storage path. Note that this is different than the other uses of **upload_to** as it should generate the full path, including filename, rather than just the directory. The function takes two arguments: **instance** and **filename**. **instance** is the model instance that the **FileField** is attached to, and **filename** is the name of the uploaded file.

Here is an example function that takes the first two characters of a filename to generate the saved directory. This will mean that each uploaded file will be grouped into parent directories, which can help organize files and prevent there from being too many in one directory:

```
def user_grouped_file_path(instance, filename):
    return "{}/{}/{}/{}".format(instance.username, \
                                filename[0].lower(), \
                                filename[1].lower(), filename)
```

If this function is called with the filename **Test.jpg**, it will return **<username>/t/e/Test.jpg**. If called with **example.txt**, it will return **<username>e/x/example.txt**, and so on. **username** is retrieved from the instance that is being saved. To illustrate, here is a model with a **FileField** that uses this function. It also has a username, which is a **CharField**:

```
class ExampleModel(models.Model):
    file_field = models.FileField\
                    (upload_to=user_grouped_file_path)
    username = models.CharField(unique=True)
```

You can use any attribute of the instance in the **upload_to** function, but be aware that if this instance is in the process of being created, then the file save function will be called before it is saved to the database. Therefore, some of the automatically generated attributes on the instance (such as **id/pk**) will not yet be populated and should not be used to generate a path.

Whatever path is returned from the **upload_to** function, it is appended to **MEDIA_ROOT** so the uploaded files would be saved at **MEDIA_ROOT/<username>/t/e/Test.jpg** and **MEDIA_ROOT/<username>/e/x/example.txt** respectively.

Note that **user_grouped_file_path** is just an illustrative function that has intentionally been kept short, so it will not work correctly with single-character filenames or if the username has invalid characters. For example, if the username has a **/** in it, then this would act as a directory separator in the generated path.

Now we have done a deep dive into setting up a **FileField** on a model, but how do we actually save an uploaded file to it? It is as easy as assigning the uploaded file to the attribute of the model, as you would with any type of value. Here is a quick example with a view, and the simple **ExampleModel** class we were using as an example earlier in this section:

```
class ExampleModel(models.Model):
    file_field = models.FileField(upload_to="files/")


def view(request):
    if request.method == "POST":
        m = ExampleModel()  # Create a new ExampleModel instance
        m.file_field = request.FILES["uploaded_file"]
        m.save()
    return render(request, "template.html")
```

In this example, we create a new **ExampleModel** class and assign the uploaded file (which had the name **uploaded_file** in the form) to its **file_field** attribute. When we save the model instance, Django automatically writes the file with its name to the **upload_to** directory path. If the uploaded file had the name **image.jpg**, the save path would be **MEDIA_ROOT/upload_to/image.jpg**.

We could just have easily updated the file field on an existing model or used a form (validating it before saving). Here is another simple example demonstrating this:

```
class ExampleForm(forms.Form):
    uploaded_file = forms.FileField()


def view(request, model_pk):
    form = ExampleForm(request.POST, request.FILES)
    if form.is_valid():
        # Get an existing model instance
        m = ExampleModel.object.get(pk=model_pk)

        # store the uploaded file on the instance
        m.file_field = form.cleaned_data["uploaded_file"]
        m.save()
    return render(request, "template.html")
```

You can see that updating a **FileField** on an existing model instance is the same process as setting it on a new instance; and if you choose to use a Django form, or just access **request.FILES** directly, the process is just as simple.

STORING IMAGES ON MODEL INSTANCES

While a **FileField** can store any type of file, including images, there is also an **ImageField**. As you would expect, this is only for storing images. The relationship between models' **forms.FileField** and **forms.ImageField** is similar to that between **models.FileField** and **models.ImageField**, that is, **ImageField** extends **FileField** and adds extra methods for working with images.

The **ImageField** constructor takes the same arguments as **FileField**, and adds two extra optional arguments:

- **height_field**: This is the name of the field of the model that will be updated with the height of the image every time the model instance is saved.

- **width_field**: The width counterpart to **height_field**, the field that stores the width of the image that is updated every time the model instance is saved.

Both of these arguments are optional, but the fields they name must exist if used. That is, it is valid to have **height_field** or **width_field** unset, but if they are set to the name of a field that does not exist, then an error will occur. The purpose of this is to assist with searching the database for files of a particular dimension.

Here is an example model using an **ImageField**, which updates the image dimension fields:

```
class ExampleModel(models.Model):
    image = models.ImageField(upload_to="images/%Y/%m/%d/", \
                              height_field="image_height",\
                              width_field="image_width")
    image_height = models.IntegerField()
    image_width = models.IntegerField()
```

Notice that the **ImageField** is using the **upload_to** parameter with date formatting directives that are updated on save. The behavior of **upload_to** is identical to that of **FileField**.

Upon saving an **ExampleModel** instance, its **image_height** field would be updated with the height of the image, and **image_width** with the width of the image.

We will not show examples for setting **ImageField** values in a view, as the process is the same as for a plain **FileField**.

WORKING WITH FIELDFILE

When you access a **FileField** or **ImageField** attribute of a model instance, you will not get a native Python **file** object. Instead, you will be working with a **FieldFile** object. The **FieldFile** class is a wrapper around a **file** that adds extra methods. Yes, it can be confusing to have classes called **FileField** and **FieldFile**.

The reason that Django uses **FieldFile** instead of just a **file** object is twofold. First, it adds extra methods to open, read, delete, and generate the URL of the file. Second, it provides an abstraction to allow alternative storage engines to be used.

CUSTOM STORAGE ENGINES

We looked at custom storage engines in *Chapter 5, Serving Static Files*, regarding storing static files. We will not examine custom storage engines in detail about media files, since the code outlined in *Chapter 5, Serving Static Files*, for static files also applies to media files. The important thing to note is that the storage engine you are using can be changed without updating your other code. This means that you can have your media files stored on your local drive during development and then saved to a CDN when your application is deployed to production.

The default storage engine class can be set with **DEFAULT_FILE_STORAGE** in **settings.py**. The storage engine can also be specified on a per-field basis (for **FileField** or **ImageField**) with the **storage** argument. For example:

```
storage_engine = CustomStorageEngine()


class ExampleModel(models.Model):
    image_field = ImageField(storage=storage_engine)
```

This demonstrates what actually happens when you upload or retrieve a file. Django delegates to the storage engine to write or read it, respectively. This happens even while saving to disk; however, it is fundamental and is invisible to the user.

READING A STORED FIELDFILE

Now that we have learned about custom storage engines, let us look at reading from a **FieldFile**. In the previous sections, we saw how to set the file on the model instance. Reading the data back again is just as easy – we have a couple of different methods that can help us, depending on our use case.

In the following few code snippets, assume we are inside a view and have retrieved our model instance in some manner, and it is stored in a variable, **m**. For example:

```
m = ExampleModel.object.get(pk=model_pk)
```

We can read all the data from the file with the **read** method:

```
data = m.file_field.read()
```

Or we can manually open the file with the **open** method. This might be useful if we want to write our own generated data to the file:

```
with m.file_field.open("wb") as f:
    chunk = f.write(b"test")   # write bytes to the file
```

If we wanted to read the file in chunks, we can use the **chunks** method. This works the same as reading chunks from the uploaded file, as we saw earlier:

```
for chunk in m.file_field.chunks():
    # assume this method is defined somewhere
    write_chunk(open_file, chunk)
```

We can also manually open the file ourselves by using its **path** attribute:

```
open(m.file_field.path)
```

If we want to stream a **FileField** for download, the best way is by using the **FileResponse** class as we saw earlier. Combine this with the **open** method on the **FileField**. Note that if we are just trying to serve a media file, we should only implement a view to do this if we are trying to restrict access to the file. Otherwise, we should just serve the file using **MEDIA_URL** and allow the web server to handle the request. Here is how we'd write our **download_view** to use a **FileField** instead of the manually specified path:

```
def download_view(request, model_pk):
    if request.user.is_anonymous:
        raise PermissionDenied
```

```
    m = ExampleModel.objects.get(pk=model_pk)
    # Django sends the file then closes the handle
    return FileResponse(m.file_field.open())
```

Django opens the correct path and closes it after the response. Django will also attempt to determine the correct mime type for the file. We assume that this **FileField** has its **upload_to** attribute set to a protected directory that the web server is preventing direct access to.

STORING EXISTING FILES OR CONTENT IN FILEFIELD

We've seen how to store an uploaded file in an image field – simply assign it to the field like so:

```
m.file_field = request.FILES["file_upload"]
```

But how can we set the **field** value to that of an existing file that we might already have on disk? You might think you can use a standard Python **file** object, but this won't work:

```
# Don't do this
m.file_field = open("/path/to/file.txt", "rb")
```

You might also try setting the file using some content:

```
m.file_field = "new file content"  # Don't do this
```

This won't work either.

You instead need to use the **save** method of **FileField**, which accepts an instance of a Django **File** or **ContentFile** object (these classes' full paths are **django.core.files.File** and **django.core.files.base.ContentFile**, respectively). We will briefly discuss the **save** method and its arguments then return to these classes.

The **save** method of **FileField** takes three arguments:

- **name**: The name of the file you are saving. This is the name the file will have when saved to the storage engine (in our case, to disk, inside **MEDIA_ROOT**).

- **Content**: This is an instance of **File** or **ContentFile**, which we just saw; again, we will discuss these soon.

- **Save**: This argument is optional and defaults to **True**. This indicates whether or not to save the model instance to the database after saving the file. If set to **False** (that is, the model is not saved), then the file will still be written to the storage engine (to disk), but the association is not stored on the model. The previous file path (or no file if one was not set) will still be stored in the database until the model instance's **save** method is called manually. You should only set this argument to **False** if you intend to make other changes to the model instance and then save it manually.

Back to **File** and **ContentFile**: the one to use depends on what you want to store in a **FileField**.

File is used as a wrapper around a Python **file** object, and you should use it if you have an existing **file** or file-like object that you want to save. File-like objects include **io.BytesIO** or **io.StringIO** instances. To instantiate a **File** instance, just pass the native **file** object to the constructor, for example:

```
f = open("/path/to/file.txt", "rb")
file_wrapper = File(f)
```

Use **ContentFile** when you already have some data loaded, either a **str** or **bytes** object. Pass the data to the **ContentFile** constructor:

```
string_content = ContentFile("A string value")
bytes_content = ContentField(b"A bytes value")
```

Now that you have either a **File** or **ContentFile** instance, saving the data to the **FileField** is easy, using the **save** method:

```
m = ExampleModel.objects.first()
with open("/path/to/file.txt") as f:
    file_wrapper = File(f)
    m.file_field.save("file.txt", f)
```

Since we did not pass a value for **save** to the **save** method, it will default to **True**, so the model instance is automatically persisted to the database.

Next, we will look at how to store an image that has been manipulated with a PIL back to an image field.

WRITING PIL IMAGES TO IMAGEFIELD

In *Exercise 8.05, Image Uploads Using Django Forms*, you used PIL to resize an image and save it to disk. When working with a model, you might want to perform a similar operation, but have Django handle the file storage using the **ImageField** so that you do not have to do it manually. As in the exercise, you could save the image to disk and then use the **File** class to wrap the stored path – something like this:

```
image = Image.open(request.FILES["image_field"])
image.thumbnail((150, 150))
# save thumbnail to temp location
image.save("/tmp/thumbnail.jpg")

with open("/tmp/thumbnail.jpg", "rb") as f:
    image_wrapper = File(f)
    m.image_field.save("thumbnail.jpg", image_wrapper)

os.unlink("/tmp/thumbnail.jpg")   # clean up temp file
```

In this example, we're having PIL stored to a temporary location with the **Image. save()** method, and then re-opening the file.

This method works but is not ideal as it involves writing the file to disk and then reading it out again, which can sometimes be slow. Instead, we can perform this whole process in memory.

> ### NOTE
>
> **io.BytesIO** and **io.StringIO** are useful objects. They behave like files but exist in memory only. **BytesIO** is used for storing raw bytes, and **StringIO** accepts Python 3's native Unicode strings. You can **read**, **write**, and **seek** them, just like a normal file. Unlike a normal file though, they do not get written to disk and instead will disappear when your program terminates, or they go out of scope and are garbage-collected. They are very useful if a function wants to write to something like a file, but you want to access the data immediately.

First, we will save the image data to an **io.BytesIO** object. Then, we will wrap the **BytesIO** object in a **django.core.files.images.ImageFile** instance (a subclass of **File** that is specifically for images and provides **width** and **height** attributes). Once we have this **ImageFile** instance, we can use it in the **save** method of **ImageField**.

> **NOTE**
>
> An **ImageFile** is a file or file-like wrapper just like **File**. It provides two extra attributes: **width**, and **height**. **ImageFile** does not generate any errors if you use it to wrap a non-image. For example, you could **open()** a text file and pass the filehandle to the **ImageFile** constructor without any issue. You can check whether the image file you passed in was valid by trying to access the **width** or **height** attributes: if these are **None**, then PIL was unable to decode the image data. You could check for the validity of these values yourself and throw an exception if they were **None**.

Let us have a look at this in practice, in a view:

```
from io import BytesIO
from PIL import Image
from django.core.files.images import ImageFile


def index(request, pk):
    # trim out logic for checking if method is POST

    # get a model instance, or create a new one
    m = ExampleModel.objects.get(pk=pk)

    # store the uploaded image in a variable for shorter code
    uploaded_image = request.FILES["image_field"]

    # load a PIL image instance from the uploaded file
    image = Image.open(uploaded)

    # perform the image resize
    image.thumbnail((150, 150))
```

```
    # Create a BytesIO file-like object to store
    image_data = BytesIO()

    # Write the Image data back out to the BytesIO object
    # Retain the existing format from the uploaded image
    image.save(fp=image_data, uploaded_image.format)

    # Wrap the BytesIO containing the image data
    image_file = ImageFile(image_data)

    # Save the wrapped image file data with the original name
    m.image_field.save(uploaded_image.name, image_file)
    # this also saves the model instance
    return redirect("/success-url/")
```

You can see this is a little bit more code, but it saves on writing the data to disk. You can choose to use either method (or another one that you come up with) depending on your needs.

REFERRING TO MEDIA IN TEMPLATES

Once we have uploaded a file, we want to be able to refer to it in a template. For an uploaded image, such as a book cover, we will want to be able to display the image on the page. We saw in *Exercise 8.02, Template Settings and Using MEDIA_URL in Templates*, how to build a URL using **MEDIA_URL** in a template. When working with **FileField** or **ImageField** on a model instance, it is not necessary to do this as Django provides this functionality for you.

The **url** attribute of a **FileField** will automatically generate the full URL to the media file, based on the **MEDIA_URL** in your settings.

> **NOTE**
>
> Note that references we make to a **FileField** in this section also apply to **ImageField**, as it is a subclass of **FileField**.

This can be used anywhere that you have access to the instance and field, such as in a view or a template. For example, in a view:

```
instance = ExampleModel.objects.first()
url = instance.file_field.url  # Get the URL
```

Or in a template (assuming the **instance** has been passed to the template context):

```
<img src="{{ instance.file_field.url }}">
```

In the next exercise, we will create a new model with a **FileField** and **ImageField**, then show how Django can automatically save these. We'll also demonstrate how to retrieve the URL for an uploaded file.

EXERCISE 8.06: FILEFIELD AND IMAGEFIELD ON MODELS

In this exercise, we will create a model with a **FileField** and **ImageField**. After doing this, we will have to generate a migration and apply it. We will then change the **UploadForm** we have been using so it has both a **FileField** and an **ImageField**. The **media_example** view will be updated to store the uploaded files in the model instance. Finally, we will add an **<img>** into the example template to show the previously uploaded image:

1. In PyCharm, open the **media_example** app's **models.py** file. Create a new model called **ExampleModel**, with two fields: an **ImageField** named **image_field**, and a **FileField** called **file_field**. The **ImageField** should have its **upload_to** set to **images/**, and the **FileField** should have its **upload_to** set to **files/**. The finished model should look like this:

```
class ExampleModel(models.Model):
    image_field = models.ImageField(upload_to="images/")
    file_field = models.FileField(upload_to="files/")
```

Your **models.py** should now look like this: http://packt.live/3p4bfrr.

2. Open a terminal and navigate to the **media_project** project directory. Make sure your **bookr** virtual environment is active. Run the **makemigrations** management command to generate the migrations for this new model (for Windows, you can use **python** instead of **python3** in the following code):

```
python3 manage.py makemigrations
```

> **NOTE**
>
> To learn how to create and activate a virtual environment, refer to the *Preface*.

You should get output like the following:

```
(bookr)$ python3 manage.py makemigrations
Migrations for 'media_example':
  media_example/migrations/0001_initial.py
    - Create model ExampleModel
```

3. Apply the migration by running the **migrate** management command:

```
python3 manage.py migrate
```

The output is like the following:

```
(bookr)$ python3 manage.py migrate
Operations to perform:
  Apply all migrations: admin, auth, contenttypes, reviews, sessions
Running migrations:
  # output trimmed for brevity
  Applying media_example.0001_initial... OK
```

Note that all the initial Django migrations will also be applied since we did not apply those after creating the project.

4. Switch back to PyCharm and open the **reviews** app's **forms.py** file. Rename the existing **ImageField** from **file_upload** to **image_upload**. Then, add a new **FileField** named **file_upload**. After making these changes, your **UploadForm** code should look like this:

```
class UploadForm(forms.Form):
    image_upload = forms.ImageField()
    file_upload = forms.FileField()
```

You can save and close the file. It should look like this: http://packt.live/37RZcaG.

5. Open the **media_example** app's **views.py** file. First, import **ExampleModel** into the file. To do this, add this line at the top of the file after the existing **import** statements:

```
from .models import ExampleModel
```

Some imports will no longer be required, so you can remove these lines:

```
import os
from PIL import Image
from django.conf import settings
```

6. In the **media_example** view, set a default for the instance that you will render, in case one is not created. After the function definition, define a variable called **instance**, and set it to **None**:

```
def media_example(request):
    instance = None
```

7. You can completely remove the contents of the **form.is_valid()** branch as you no longer need to manually save the file. Instead, it will automatically be saved when the **ExampleModel** instance is saved. You will instantiate an **ExampleModel** instance and set the **file** and **image** fields from the uploaded form.

    Add this code under the **if form.is_valid():** line:

```
instance = ExampleModel()
instance.image_field = form.cleaned_data["image_upload"]
instance.file_field = form.cleaned_data["file_upload"]
instance.save()
```

8. Pass the instance through to the template in the context dictionary that is passed to **render**. Use the key **instance**:

```
return render(request, "media-example.html", \
              {"form": form, "instance": instance})
```

    Now, your completed **media_example** view should look like this:
    http://packt.live/3hqyYz7.

    You can now save and close this file.

9. Open the **media-example.html** template. Add an **<img>** element that displays the last uploaded image. Under the closing **</form>** tag, add an **if** template tag that checks if an **instance** has been provided. If so, display an **<img>** with a **src** attribute of **instance.image_field.url**:

```
{% if instance %}
    <img src="{{ instance.image_field.url }}">
{% endif %}
```

    You can save and close this file. It should now look like this:
    http://packt.live/2X5d5w9.

10. Start the Django dev server if it is not already running, then navigate to **http://127.0.0.1:8000/media-example/**. You should see the form rendered with two fields:

Figure 8.20: UploadForm with two fields

11. Select a file for each field – for the **ImageField** you must select an image, but any type of file is allowed for the **FileField**. See *Figure 8.21*, which shows the fields with files selected:

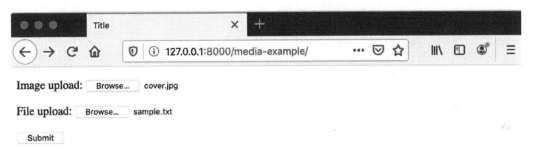

Figure 8.21: ImageField and FileField with files selected

Then, submit the form. If the submission was successful, the page will reload and the last image you uploaded will be displayed (*Figure 8.22*):

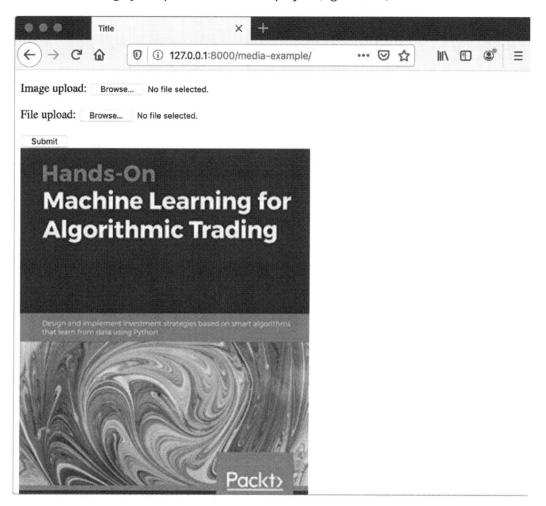

Figure 8.22: The last image that was uploaded is displayed

12. You can see how Django stores the files by looking in the **MEDIA_ROOT** directory. *Figure 8.23* shows the directory layout in PyCharm:

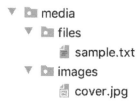

Figure 8.23: Uploaded files that Django has created

You can see that Django has created the **files** and **images** directories. These were what you set in the **upload_to** arguments on the **ImageField** and **FileField** of the model. You could also verify these uploads by attempting to download them, for example, at **http://127.0.0.1:8000/media/files/ sample.txt** or **http://127.0.0.1:8000/media/images/cover.jpg**.

In this exercise, we created **ExampleModel** with **FileField** and **ImageField** and saw how to store uploaded files in it. We saw how to generate a URL to an uploaded file for use in a template. We tried uploading some files and saw that Django automatically created the **upload_to** directories (**media/files** and **media/images**), then stored the files inside.

In the next section, we will look at how we can simplify the process even further by using a **ModelForm** to generate the form and save the model without having to manually set the files in the view.

MODELFORMS AND FILE UPLOADS

We have seen how using a **form.ImageField** on a form can prevent non-images being uploaded. We have also seen how **models.ImageField** makes it easy to store an image for a model. But we need to be aware that Django does not stop you from setting a non-image file to an **ImageField**. For example, consider a form that has both a **FileField** and **ImageField**:

```
class ExampleForm(forms.Form):
    uploaded_file = forms.FileField()
    uploaded_image = forms.ImageField()
```

In the following view, the form would not validate if the **uploaded_image** field on the form was not an image, so some data validity is ensured for uploaded data. For example:

```
def view(request):
    form = ExampleForm(request.POST, request.FILES)
    if form.is_valid():
        m = ExampleModel()
        m.file_field = form.cleaned_data["uploaded_file"]
        m.image_field = forms.cleaned_data["uploaded_image"]
        m.save()
    return render(request, "template.html")
```

Since we are sure the form is valid, we know that **forms.cleaned_ data["uploaded_image"]** must contain an image. Therefore, we would never assign a non-image to the model instance's **image_field**.

However, say we made a mistake in our code and wrote something like this:

```
m.image_field = forms.cleaned_data["uploaded_file"]
```

That is, if we accidentally reference the **FileField** by mistake, Django does not validate that a (potential) non-image is being assigned to an **ImageField**, and so it does not throw an exception or generate any kind of error. We can mitigate the potential for issues like this by using a **ModelForm**.

We introduced **ModelForm** in *Chapter 7, Advanced Form Validation and Model Forms* – these are forms whose fields are automatically defined from a model. We saw that a **ModelForm** has a **save** method that automatically creates or updates the model data in the database. When used with a model that has a **FileFIeld** or **ImageField**, then the **ModelForm save** method will also save uploaded files.

Here is an example of using a **ModelForm** to save a new model instance in a view. Here, we are just making sure to pass **request.FILES** to the **ModelForm** constructor:

```
class ExampleModelForm(forms.Model):
    class Meta:
        model = ExampleModel
        # The same ExampleModel class we've seen previously
        fields = "__all__"


def view(request):
    if request.method == "POST":
        form = ExampleModelForm(request.POST, request.FILES)
        form.save()
        return redirect("/success-page")
    else:
        form = ExampleModelForm()
    return (request, "template.html", {"form": form})
```

As with any **ModelForm**, the **save** method can be called with the **commit** argument set to **False**. Then the model instance will not be saved to the database, and the **FileField/ImageField** files will not be saved to disk. The **save** method should be called on the model instance itself – this will commit changes to the database and save the files. In this next short example, we set a value on the model instance before saving it:

```
def view(request):
    if request.method == "POST":
        form = ExampleModelForm(request.POST, request.FILES)
        m = form.save(False)
        # Set arbitrary value on the model instance before save
        m.attribute = "value"
        # save the model instance, also write the files to disk
        m.save()
        return redirect("/success-page/")
    else:
        form = ExampleModelForm()
    return (request, "template.html", {"form": form})
```

Calling the **save** method on the model instance both saves the model data to the database and the uploaded files to disk. In the next exercise, we will build a **ModelForm** from **ExampleModel**, which we created in *Exercise 8.06, FileField and ImageField on Models*, then test uploading files with it.

EXERCISE 8.07: FILE AND IMAGE UPLOADS USING A MODELFORM

In this exercise, you will update **UploadForm** to be a subclass of **ModelForm** and have it built automatically from **ExampleModel**. You will then change the **media_ example** view to save the instance automatically from the form, so you can see how the amount of code can be reduced:

1. In PyCharm, open the **media_example** apps' **forms.py** file. You need to use **ExampleModel** in this chapter, so **import** it at the top of the file after the **from django import forms** statement. Insert this line:

```
from .models import ExampleModel
```

2. Change **UploadForm** to be a subclass of **forms.ModelForm**. Remove the **class** body and replace it with a **class** **Meta** definition; its **model** should be **ExampleModel**. Set the **fields** attribute to **__all__**. After completing this step, your **UploadForm** should look like this:

```
class UploadForm(forms.ModelForm):
    class Meta:
        model = ExampleModel
        fields = "__all__"
```

Save and close the file. It should now look like this: http://packt.live/37X49ig.

3. Open the **media_example** app's **views.py** file. Since you no longer need to reference the **ExampleModel** directly, you can remove its **import** at the top of the file. Remove the following line:

```
from .models import ExampleModel
```

4. In the **media_example** view, remove the entirety of the **form.is_valid()** branch and replace it with a single line:

```
instance = form.save()
```

The form's **save** method will handle persisting the instance to the database and saving the files. It will return an instance of **ExampleModel**, the same as the other instances of **ModelForm** we have worked with in *Chapter 7, Advanced Form Validation and Model Forms*.

After completing this step, your **media_example** function should look like this: http://packt.live/37V0ly2. Save and close **views.py**.

5. Start the Django dev server if it is not already running, then navigate to **http://127.0.0.1:8000/media-example/**. You should see the form rendered with two fields, **Image field** and **File field** (*Figure 8.24*):

Figure 8.24: UploadForm as a ModelForm rendered in the browser

Note that the names of these fields now match those of the model rather than the form, as the form just uses the model's fields.

6. Browse and select an image and file (*Figure 8.25*), then submit the form:

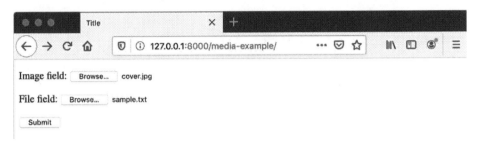

Figure 8.25: Image and file selected

7. The page will reload, and as in *Exercise 8.06, FileField and ImageField on Models*, you will see the previously uploaded image (*Figure 8.26*):

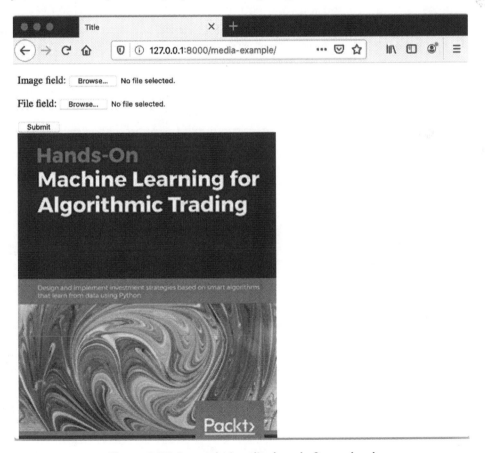

Figure 8.26: Image being displayed after upload

8. Finally, examine the contents of the **media** directory. You should see the directory layout matches that of *Exercise 8.06, FileField and ImageField on Models*, with images inside the **images** directory, and files inside the **files** directory:

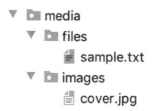

Figure 8.27: The uploaded files directory matches Exercise 8.06

In this exercise, we changed **UploadForm** to be a **ModelForm** subclass, which allowed us to automatically generate the upload fields. We could replace the code that stored the uploaded files on the models with a call to the form's **save** method.

We have now covered everything you need to start enhancing Bookr with file uploads. In the activity for this chapter, we will add support for uploading a cover image and sample document (PDF, text file, and more) for a book. The book cover will be resized using PIL before it is saved.

ACTIVITY 8.01: IMAGE AND PDF UPLOADS OF BOOKS

In this activity, you will start by cleaning up (deleting) the example views, templates, forms, models, and URL maps that we have used throughout the exercises in this chapter. You will then need to generate and apply a migration to delete **ExampleModel** from the database.

You can then start adding the Bookr enhancements, first by adding an **ImageField** and **FileField** to the **Book** model to store the book **cover** and **sample**. Then you will create a migration and apply it to add these fields to the database. You can then build a form that will display just these new fields. You will add a view that uses this form to save the model instance with the uploaded files, after first resizing the image to thumbnail size. You will be able to reuse the **instance-form.html** template from *Chapter 7, Advanced Form Validation and Model Forms*, with a minor change to allow file uploads.

These steps will help you complete the activity:

1. Update the Django settings to add the settings **MEDIA_ROOT** and **MEDIA_URL**.

2. The **/media/** URL mapping should be added to **urls.py**. Use the **static** view and utilize **MEDIA_ROOT** and **MEDIA_URL** from Django settings. Remember, this mapping should only be added if **DEBUG** is true.

3. Add an **ImageField** (named **cover**) and **FileField** (named **sample**) to the **Book** model. The fields should upload to **book_covers/** and **book_samples/**, respectively. They should both allow **null** and **blank** values.

4. Run **makemigrations** and **migrate** again to apply the **Book** model changes to the database.

5. Create a **BookMediaForm** as a subclass of **ModelForm**. Its model should be **Book**, and the fields should only be the fields you added in *step 3*.

6. Add a **book_media** view. This will not allow you to create a **Book**, instead, it will only allow you to add media to an existing **Book** (so it must take **pk** as a required argument).

7. The **book_media** view should validate the form, and **save** it, but not **commit** the instance. The uploaded cover should first be resized using the **thumbnail** method as demonstrated in the *Writing PIL Images to ImageField* section. The maximum size should be 300 by 300 pixels. It should then be stored on the instance and the instance saved. Remember that the **cover** field is not required so you should check this before trying to manipulate the image. On a successful **POST**, register a success message that the **Book** was updated, then redirect to the **book_detail** view.

8. Render the **instance-form.html**, passing a context dictionary containing **form**, **model_type**, and **instance**, as you did in *Chapter 6, Forms*. Also pass another item, **is_file_upload**, set to **True**. This variable will be used in the next step.

9. In the **instance-form.html** template, use the **is_file_upload** variable to add the correct **enctype** attribute to the form. This will allow you to switch the modes for the form to enable file uploads when required.

10. Finally, add a URL map that maps **/books/<pk>/media/** to the **book_media** view.

When you are finished, you should be able to start the Django dev server and load the **book_media** view at **http://127.0.0.1:8000/books/\<pk\>/media/**, for example, **http://127.0.0.1:8000/books/2/media/**. You should see the **BookMediaForm** rendered in the browser, like in *Figure 8.28*:

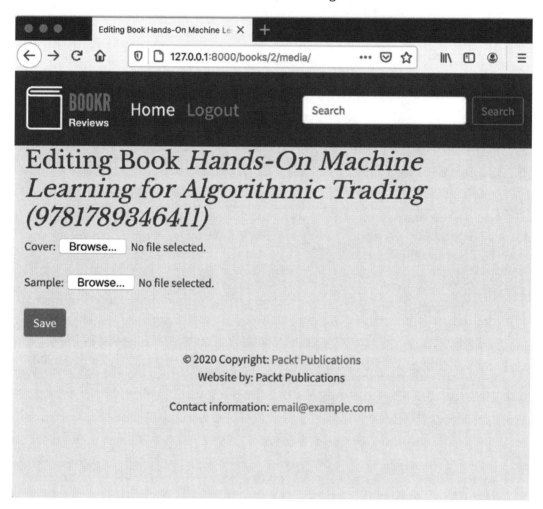

Figure 8.28: BookMediaForm in the browser

Select a cover image and sample file for the book. You can use the image at
http://packt.live/2KyIapl and PDF at http://packt.live/37VycHn (or you can use any
other image/PDF of your choosing).

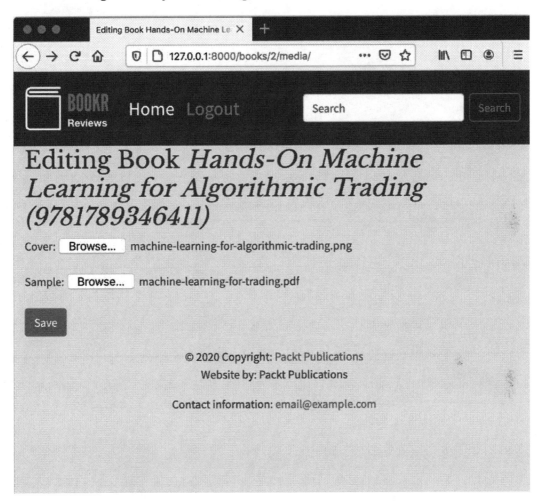

Figure 8.29: Book Cover image and Sample selected

After submitting the form, you will be redirected to the **Book Details** view and see the success message (*Figure 8.30*):

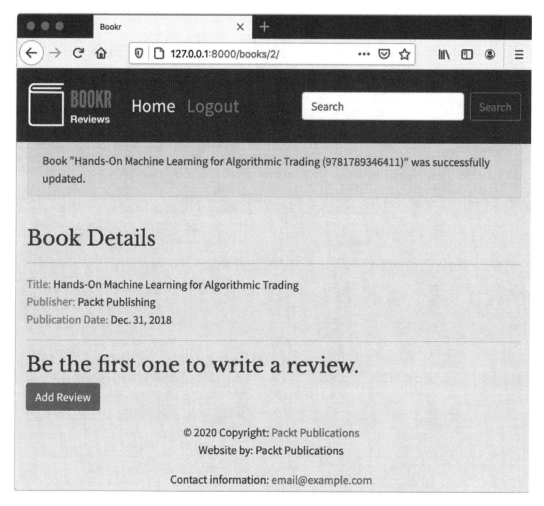

Figure 8.30: Success message on the Book Details page

If you go back to the same book's media page, you should see the fields are now filled in, with an option to clear the data from them:

Figure 8.31: BookMediaForm with existing values

In *Activity 8.02, Displaying Cover and Sample Links*, you will add these uploaded files to the **Book Details** view, but for now, if you want to check that uploads have worked, you can look inside the **media** directory in the Bookr project:

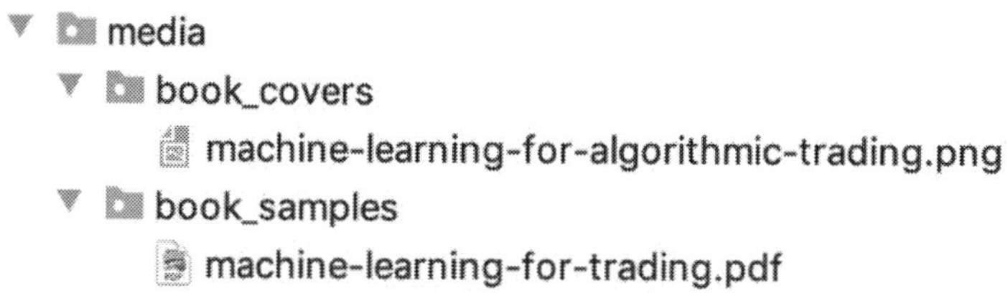

▼ 🗀 media
    ▼ 🗀 book_covers
        🖾 machine-learning-for-algorithmic-trading.png
    ▼ 🗀 book_samples
        🖾 machine-learning-for-trading.pdf

Figure 8.32: Book media

You should see the directories that were created and the uploaded files, as per *Figure 8.32*. Open an uploaded image, and you should see its maximum dimension is 300 pixels.

> **NOTE**
>
> The solution to this activity can be found at http://packt.live/2Nh1NTJ.

ACTIVITY 8.02: DISPLAYING COVER AND SAMPLE LINKS

In this activity, you will update the **book_detail.html** template to show the cover for the **Book** (if one is set). You will also add a link to download the sample, again, only if one is set. You will use the **FileField** and **ImageField url** attributes to generate the URLs to the media files.

These steps will help you complete this activity:

1. Inside the **Book Details** display in the **book_detail.html** view, add an **<img>** element if the book has a **cover** image. Then, display the cover of the book inside it. Use **
** after the **<img>** tag so the image is on its own line.

2. After the **Publication Date** display, add a link to the sample file. It should only be displayed if a **sample** file has been uploaded. Make sure you add another **
** tag so it displays correctly.

3. In the section that has a link to add a review, add another link that goes to the media page for the book. Follow the same styling as the **Add Review** link.

When you have completed these steps, you should be able to load a book detail page. If the book has no **cover** or **sample**, then the page should look very similar to what it did before, except you should see the new link to the **Media** page at the bottom (*Figure 8.33*):

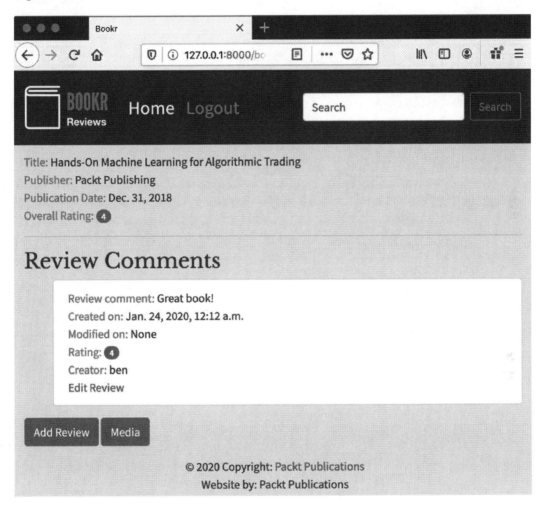

Figure 8.33: New Media button visible on the book detail page

Once you have uploaded a **cover** and/or a **sample** for a **Book**, the cover image and sample link should be displayed (*Figure 8.34*):

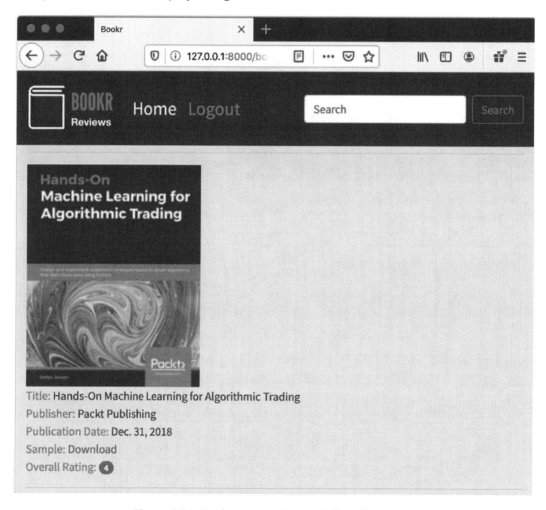

Figure 8.34: Book cover and sample link displayed

NOTE

The solution to this activity can be found at http://packt.live/2Nh1NTJ.

SUMMARY

In this chapter, we added the **MEDIA_ROOT** and **MEDIA_URL** settings and a special URL map to serve media files. We then created a form and a view to upload files and save them to the **media** directory. We saw how to add the media context processor to automatically have access to the **MEDIA_URL** setting in all our templates. We then enhanced and simplified our form code by using a Django form with a **FileField** or **ImageField**, instead of manually defining one in HTML.

We looked at some of the enhancements Django provides for images with the **ImageField**, and how to interact with an image using Pillow. We showed an example view that would be able to serve files that required authentication, using the **FileResponse** class. Then, we saw how to store files on models using the **FileField** and **ImageField** and refer to them in a template using the **FileField.url** attribute. We were able to reduce the amount of code we had to write by automatically building a **ModelForm** from a **model** instance. Finally, in the two activities at the end, we enhanced Bookr by adding a cover image and sample file to the **Book** model. In *Chapter 9, Sessions and Authentication*, we will learn how to add authentication to a Django application to protect it from unauthorized users.

9

SESSIONS AND AUTHENTICATION

OVERVIEW

This chapter begins with a brief introduction to **middleware** before delving into the concepts of **authentication models** and **session engines**. You will implement Django's authentication model to restrict permissions to only a specific set of users. Then, you will see how you can leverage Django authentication to provide a flexible approach to application security. After that, you will learn how Django supports multiple session engines to retain user data. By the end of the chapter, you will be proficient at using sessions to retain information on past user interactions and to maintain user preferences for when pages are revisited.

INTRODUCTION

Up until now, we have used Django to develop dynamic applications that allow users to interact with application models, but we have not attempted to secure these applications from unwanted use. For example, our Bookr app allows unauthenticated users to add reviews and upload media. This is a critical security issue for any online web app as it leaves the site open to the posting of spam or other inappropriate material and the vandalism of existing content. We want the creation and modification of content to be strictly limited to authenticated users who have registered with the site.

The **authentication app** supplies Django with the models for representing users, groups, and permissions. It also provides middleware, utility functions, decorators, and mixins that help integrate user authentication into our apps. Furthermore, the authentication app allows grouping and naming certain sets of users.

In *Chapter 4, Introduction to Django Admin*, we used the Admin app to create a help desk user group with the permissions "Can view log entry," "Can view permission," "Can change user," and "Can view user." Those permissions could be referenced in our code using their corresponding codenames: `view_logentry`, `view_permissions`, `change_user`, and `view_user`. In this chapter, we will learn how to customize Django behavior based on specific user permissions.

Permissions are directives that delineate what is permissible by classes of users. Permissions can be assigned either to groups or directly to individual users. From an administrative point of view, it is cleaner to assign permissions to groups. Groups make it easier to model roles and organizational structures. If a new permission is created, it is less time-consuming to modify a few groups than to remember to assign it to a subset of users.

We are already familiar with creating users and groups and assigning permissions using several methods, such as the option of instantiating users and groups through the model using scripts and the convenience of creating them through the Django Admin app. The authentication app also offers us programmatic ways of creating and deleting users, groups, and permissions and assigning relations between them.

As we go through this chapter, we'll learn how to use authentication and permissions to implement application security and how to store user-specific data to customize the user's experience. This will help us secure the `bookr` project from unauthorized content changes and make it contextually relevant for different types of users. Adding this basic security to our `bookr` project is crucial before we consider deploying it on the internet.

Authentication, as well as session management (which we'll learn about in the *Sessions* section), is handled by something known as a **middleware stack**. Before we implement authentication in our **bookr** project, let's learn a bit about this middleware stack and its modules.

MIDDLEWARE

In *Chapter 3, URL Mapping, Views, and Templates*, we discussed Django's implementation of the request/response process along with its view and rendering functionality. In addition to these, another feature that plays an extremely important role when it comes to Django's core web processing is **middleware**. Django's middleware refers to a variety of software components that intervene in this request/response process to integrate important functionalities such as security, session management, and authentication.

So, when we write a view in Django, we don't have to explicitly set a series of important security features in the response header. These additions to the response object are automatically made by the **SecurityMiddleware** instance after the view returns its response. As middleware components wrap the view and perform a series of pre-processes on the request and post-processes on the response, the view is not cluttered with a lot of repetitive code and we can concentrate on coding application logic rather than worrying about low-level server behavior. Rather than building these functionalities into the Django core, Django's implementation of a middleware stack allows these components to be both optional and replaceable.

MIDDLEWARE MODULES

When we run the **startproject** subcommand, a default list of middleware modules is added to the **MIDDLEWARE** variable in the **<project>/settings.py** file, as follows:

```
MIDDLEWARE = ['django.middleware.security.SecurityMiddleware',\
              'django.contrib.sessions.middleware.SessionMiddleware',\
              'django.middleware.common.CommonMiddleware',\
              'django.middleware.csrf.CsrfViewMiddleware',\
              'django.contrib.auth.middleware.AuthenticationMiddleware',\
              'django.contrib.messages.middleware.MessageMiddleware',\
              'django.middleware.clickjacking.XFrameOptionsMiddleware',\]
```

This is a minimal middleware stack that is suitable for most Django applications. The following list elaborates on the general purpose of each module:

- **SecurityMiddleware** provides common security enhancements such as handling SSL redirects and adding response headers to prevent common hacks.

- **SessionMiddleware** enables session support and seamlessly associates a stored session with the current request.

- **CommonMiddleware** implements a lot of miscellaneous features, such as rejecting requests from the **DISALLOWED_USER_AGENTS** list, implementing URL rewrite rules, and setting the **Content-Length** header.

- **CsrfViewMiddleware** adds protection against **Cross-Site Request Forgery (CSRF)**.

- **AuthenticationMiddleware** adds the **user** attribute to the **request** object.

- **MessageMiddleware** adds "flash" message support.

- **XFrameOptionsMiddleware** protects against **X-Frame-Options** header clickjacking attacks.

The middleware modules are loaded in the order that they appear in the **MIDDLEWARE** list. This makes sense because we want to call the middleware that deals with initial security issues first so that dangerous requests are rejected before further processing occurs. Django also comes with several other middleware modules that perform important functions, such as using **gzip** file compression, redirect configuration, and web cache configuration.

This chapter is devoted to discussing two important aspects of stateful application development that are implemented as middleware components – **SessionMiddleware** and **AuthenticationMiddleware**.

The **process_request** method of **SessionMiddleware** adds a **session** object as an attribute of the **request** object. The **process_request** method of **AuthenticationMiddleware** adds a **user** object as an attribute of the **request** object.

It is possible to write a Django project without these layers of the middleware stack if a project does not require user authentication or a means of preserving the state of individual interactions. However, most of the default middleware plays an important role in application security. If you don't have a good reason for changing the middleware components, it is best to maintain these initial settings. In fact, the Admin app requires **SessionMiddleware**, **AuthenticationMiddleware**, and **MessageMiddleware** to run, and the Django server will throw errors such as these if the Admin app is installed without them:

```
django.core.management.base.SystemCheckError: SystemCheckError: System
check identified some issues:

ERRORS:
?: (admin.E408) 'django.contrib.auth.middleware.AuthenticationMiddleware'
must be in MIDDLEWARE in order to use the admin application.
?: (admin.E409) 'django.contrib.messages.middleware.MessageMiddleware'
must be in MIDDLEWARE in order to use the admin application.
?: (admin.E410) 'django.contrib.sessions.middleware.SessionMiddleware'
must be in MIDDLEWARE in order to use the admin application.
```

Now that we know about the middleware modules, let's look at one approach to enable authentication in our project using the authentication app's views and templates.

IMPLEMENTING AUTHENTICATION VIEWS AND TEMPLATES

We have already encountered the login form on the Admin app in *Chapter 4, Introduction to Django Admin*. This is the authentication entry point for staff users who have access to the Admin app. We also need to create a login capability for ordinary users who want to give book reviews. Fortunately, the authentication app comes with the tools to make this possible.

As we work through the forms and views of the authentication app, we encounter a lot of flexibility in its implementation. We are free to implement our own login pages, define either very simple or fine-grained security policies at the view level, and authenticate against external authorities.

The authentication app exists to accommodate a lot of different approaches to authentication so that Django doesn't rigidly enforce a single mechanism. For a first-time user encountering the documentation, this can be quite bewildering. For the most part in this chapter, we will follow Django's defaults, but some of the important configuration options will be noted.

A Django project's **settings** object contains attributes for login behavior. **LOGIN_ URL** specifies the URL of the login page. **'/accounts/login/'** is the default value. **LOGIN_REDIRECT_URL** specifies the path where a successful login is redirected to. The default path is **'/accounts/profile/'**.

The authentication app supplies standard forms and views for carrying out typical authentication tasks. The forms are located in **django.contrib.auth.forms** and the views are in **django.contrib.auth.views**.

The views are referenced by these URL patterns present in **django.contrib. auth.urls**:

```
urlpatterns = [path('login/', views.LoginView.as_view(), \
                name='login'),
            path('logout/', views.LogoutView.as_view(), \
                name='logout'),
            path('password_change/', \
                views.PasswordChangeView.as_view()),\
                (name='password_change'),\
            path('password_change/done/', \
                views.PasswordChangeDoneView.as_view()),\
                (name='password_change_done'),\
            path('password_reset/', \
                views.PasswordResetView.as_view()),\
                (name='password_reset'),\
            path('password_reset/done/', \
                views.PasswordResetDoneView.as_view()),\
                (name='password_reset_done'),\
            path('reset/<uidb64>/<token>/', \
                views.PasswordResetConfirmView.as_view()),\
                (name='password_reset_confirm'),\
            path('reset/done/', \
                views.PasswordResetCompleteView.as_view()),\
                (name='password_reset_complete'),]
```

If this style of views looks unfamiliar, it is because they are class-based views rather than the function-based views that we have previously encountered. We will learn more about class-based views in *Chapter 11, Advanced Templates and Class-Based Views*. For now, note that the authentication app makes use of class inheritance to group the functionality of views and prevent a lot of repetitive coding.

If we want to maintain the default URLs and views that are presupposed by the authentication app and Django settings, we can include the authentication app's URLs in our project's **urlpatterns**.

By taking this approach, we have saved a lot of work. We need only include the authentication app's URLs to our **<project>/urls.py** file and assign it the **'accounts'** namespace. Designating this namespace ensures that our reverse URLs correspond to the default template values of the views:

```
urlpatterns = [path('accounts/', \
                include(('django.contrib.auth.urls', 'auth')),\
                (namespace='accounts')),\
            path('admin/', admin.site.urls),\
            path('', include('reviews.urls'))]
```

Though the authentication app comes with its own forms and views, it lacks the templates needed to render these components as HTML. *Figure 9.1* lists the templates that we require to implement the authentication functionality in our project. Fortunately, the Admin app does implement a set of templates that we can utilize for our purposes.

We could just copy the template files from the Django source code in the **django/ contrib/admin/templates/registration** directory and **django/ contrib/admin/templates/admin/login.html** to our project's **templates/registration** directory.

> **NOTE**
>
> When we say Django source code, it's the directory where your Django installation resides. If you installed Django in a virtual environment (as detailed in the *Preface*), you can find these template files at the following path: **<name of your virtual environment>/ lib/python3.X/site-packages/django/contrib/admin/ templates/registration/**. Provided your virtual environment is activated and Django is installed in it, you can also retrieve the complete path to the **site-packages** directory by running the following command in a terminal: **python -c "import sys; print(sys.path)"**.

Template Path
`templates/registration/login.html`
`templates/registration/password_reset_email.html`
`templates/registration/password_change_form.html`
`templates/registration/password_change_done.html`
`templates/registration/password_reset_form.html`
`templates/registration/password_reset_done.html`
`templates/registration/password_reset_confirm.html`
`templates/registration/password_reset_complete.html`
`templates/registration/logged_out.html`

Figure 9.1: Default paths for authentication templates

> **NOTE**
>
> We need only copy the templates that are dependencies for the views and should avoid copying the **base.html** or **base_site.html** files.

This gives a promising result at first, but as they stand, the admin templates do not meet our precise needs as we can see from the login page (*Figure 9.2*):

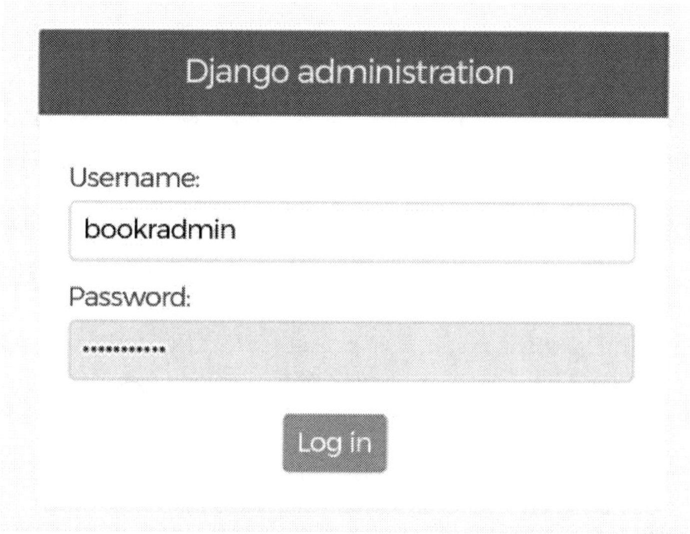

Figure 9.2: A first attempt at a user login screen

As these authentication pages inherit from the Admin app's **admin/base_site.html** template, they follow the style of the Admin app. We would prefer for these pages to follow the style of the **bookr** project that we have developed. We can do this by following these three steps on each Django template that we have copied from the Admin app to our project:

1. The first change that needs to be made is to replace the **{% extends "admin/base_site.html" %}** tag with **{% extends "base.html" %}**.

2. Given that **template/base.html** only contains the following block definitions – **title**, **brand**, and **content** – we should remove all other block substitutions from our templates in the **bookr** folder. We are not using the content from the **userlinks** and **breadcrumbs** blocks in our app, so these blocks can be removed entirely.

   Some of these blocks, such as **content_title** and **reset_link**, contain HTML content that is relevant to our application. We should strip the block from around this HTML and put it inside the content block.

   For example, the **password_change_done.html** template contains an extensive number of blocks:

```
{% extends "admin/base_site.html" %}
{% load i18n %}
{% block userlinks %}{% url 'django-admindocs-docroot' as docsroot %}
  {% if docsroot %}<a href="{{ docsroot }}">{% trans 'Documentation'
%}
    </a> / {% endif %}{% trans 'Change password' %} / <a href="{% url
      'admin:logout' %}">{% trans 'Log out' %}</a>{% endblock %}


{% block breadcrumbs %}
<div class="breadcrumbs">
<a href="{% url 'admin:index' %}">{% trans 'Home' %}</a>
&rsaquo; {% trans 'Password change' %}
</div>
{% endblock %}


{% block title %}{{ title }}{% endblock %}
{% block content_title %}<h1>{{ title }}</h1>{% endblock %}


{% block content %}
<p>{% trans 'Your password was changed.' %}</p>
{% endblock %}
```

It will be simplified to this template in the **bookr** project:

```
{% extends "base.html" %}
{% load i18n %}



{% block title %}{{ title }}{% endblock %}
{% block content %}
<h1>{{ title }}</h1>
<p>{% trans 'Your password was changed.' %}</p>
{% endblock %}
```

3. Likewise, there are reverse URL patterns that need to change to reflect the current path, so **{% url 'login' %}** gets replaced by **{% url 'accounts:login' %}**.

Given these considerations, the next exercise will focus on transforming the Admin app's login template into a login template for the **bookr** project.

> **NOTE**
>
> The **i18n** module is used for creating multilingual content. If you intend to develop multilingual content for your website, leave the **i18n** import, **trans** tags, and **transblock** statements in the templates. For brevity, we will not be covering those in detail in this chapter.

EXERCISE 9.01: REPURPOSING THE ADMIN APP LOGIN TEMPLATE

We started this chapter without a login page for our project. By adding the URL patterns for authentication and copying the templates from the Admin app to our own project, we can implement the functionality of a login page. But this login page is not satisfactory as it is directly copied from the Admin app and is disconnected from the Bookr design. In this exercise, we will follow the steps needed to repurpose the Admin app's login template for our project. The new login template will need to inherit its style and format directly from the **bookr** project's **templates/base.html**:

1. Create a directory inside your project for **templates/registration**.

2. The Admin login template is located in the Django source directory at the **django/contrib/admin/templates/admin/login.html** path. It begins with an **extends** tag, a **load** tag, the importing of the **i18n** and **static** modules, and a series of block extensions that over-ride the blocks defined in the child template, **django/contrib/admin/templates/admin/base.html**. A truncated snippet of the **login.html** file is shown in the following code block:

```
{% extends "admin/base_site.html" %}
{% load i18n static %}

{% block extrastyle %}{{ block.super }}...
{% endblock %}

{% block bodyclass %}{{ block.super }} login{% endblock %}
{% block usertools %}{% endblock %}
{% block nav-global %}{% endblock %}
{% block content_title %}{% endblock %}
{% block breadcrumbs %}{% endblock %}
```

3. Copy this Admin login template, **django/contrib/admin/templates/admin/login.html**, into **templates/registration** and begin editing the file using PyCharm.

4. As the login template you are editing is located at **templates/registration/login.html** and extends the base template (**templates/base.html**), replace the argument of the **extends** tag at the top of **templates/registration/login.html**:

```
{% extends "base.html" %}
```

5. We don't need most of the contents of this file. Just retain the **content** block, which contains the login form. The remainder of the template will consist of loading the **i18n** and **static** tag libraries:

```
{% load i18n static %}

{% block content %}
...
{% endblock %}
```

6. Now you must replace the paths and reverse URL patterns in **templates/ registration/login.html** with ones that are appropriate to your project. As you don't have an **app_path** variable defined in your template, it needs to be replaced with the reverse URL for the login, **'accounts:login'**. So, consider the following line:

```
<form action="{{ app_path }}" method="post" id="login-form">
```

This line changes as follows:

```
<form action="{% url 'accounts:login' %}" method="post" id="login-form">
```

There is no **'admin_password_reset'** defined in your project paths, so it will be replaced with **'accounts:password_reset'**.

Consider the following line:

```
{% url 'admin_password_reset' as password_reset_url %}
```

This line changes as follows:

```
{% url 'accounts:password_reset' as password_reset_url %}
```

Your login template will look as follows:

templates/registration/login.html

```
1   {% extends "base.html" %}
2   {% load i18n static %}
3
4   {% block content %}
5   {% if form.errors and not form.non_field_errors %}
6   <p class="errornote">
7   {% if form.errors.items|length == 1 %}{% trans "Please correct the error
    below." %}{% else %}{% trans "Please correct the errors below." %}{% endif %}
8   </p>
9   {% endif %}
```

You can find the complete code for this file at http://packt.live/2MILJtF.

7. To use the standard Django authentication views, we must add the URLs mapping to them. Open the **urls.py** file in the **bookr** project directory, then add this URL pattern:

```
urlpatterns = [path('accounts/', \
                    include(('django.contrib.auth.urls', 'auth')),\
                    (namespace='accounts')),\
                path('admin/', admin.site.urls),\
                path('', include('reviews.urls'))]
```

8. Now when you visit the login link at **http://127.0.0.1:8000/accounts/login/**, you will see this page:

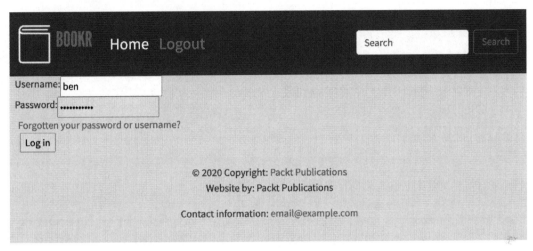

Figure 9.3: The Bookr login page

By completing this exercise, you have created the template required for non-admin authentication in your project.

> **NOTE**
>
> Before you proceed, you'll need to make sure the rest of the templates in the **registration** directory follow the **bookr** project's style; that is, they inherit from the Admin app's **admin/base_site.html** template. You've already seen this done with **password_change_done.html** and the **login.html** templates. Go ahead and apply what you've learned in this exercise (and the section before it) to the rest of the files in the **registration** directory. Alternatively, you may download the modified files from the GitHub repo: http://packt.live/3s4R5iU.

PASSWORD STORAGE IN DJANGO

Django does not store passwords in plain text form in the database. Instead, passwords are digested with a hashing algorithm, such as **PBKDF2/SHA256**, **BCrypt/SHA256**, or **Argon2**. As hashing algorithms are a one-way transformation, this prevents a user's password from being decrypted from the hash stored in the database. This often comes as a surprise to users who expect a system administrator to retrieve their forgotten password, but it is best practice in security design. So, if we query the database for the password, we will see something like this:

```
sqlite> select password from auth_user;pbkdf2_
sha256$180000$qgDCHSUv1E4w$jnh69TEIO6kypHMQPOknkNWMlE1e2ux8Q1Ow4AHjJDU=
```

The components of this string are `<algorithm>$<iterations>$<salt>$<hash>`. As several hashing algorithms have been compromised over time and we sometimes need to work with mandated security requirements, Django is flexible enough to accommodate new algorithms and can maintain data encrypted in multiple algorithms.

THE PROFILE PAGE AND THE REQUEST.USER OBJECT

When a login is successful, the login view redirects to **/accounts/profile**. However, this path is not included in the existing **auth.url** nor does the authentication app provide a template for it. To avoid a **Page not Found** error, a view and an appropriate URL pattern are required.

Each Django request has a **request.user** object. If the request is made by an unauthenticated user, **request.user** will be an **AnonymousUser** object. If the request is made by an authenticated user, then **request.user** will be a **User** object. This makes it easy to retrieve personalized user information in a Django view and render it in a template.

In the next exercise, we will add a profile page to our **bookr** project.

EXERCISE 9.02: ADDING A PROFILE PAGE

In this exercise, we will add a profile page to our project. To do so, we need to include the path to it in our URL patterns and also include it in our views and templates. The profile page will simply display the following attributes from the **request.user** object:

- **username**
- **first_name** and **last_name**
- **date_joined**
- **email**
- **last_login**

Perform the following steps to complete this exercise:

1. Add **bookr/views.py** to the project. It needs a trivial profile function to define our view:

```python
from django.shortcuts import render


def profile(request):
    return render(request, 'profile.html')
```

2. In the templates folder of your main **bookr** project, create a new file called **profile.html**. In this template, the attributes of the **request.user** object can easily be referenced by using a notation such as **{{ request.user. username }}**:

```html
{% extends "base.html" %}


{% block title %}Bookr{% endblock %}


{% block content %}
<h2>Profile</h2>
<div>
  <p>
      Username: {{ request.user.username }} <br>
      Name: {{ request.user.first_name }} {{ request.user.last_name
}}<br>
      Date Joined: {{ request.user.date_joined }} <br>
      Email: {{ request.user.email }}<br>
      Last Login: {{ request.user.last_login }}<br>
```

```
    </p>
  </div>
  {% endblock %}
```

Also, we added a block containing profile details of the user. More importantly, we made sure that **profile.html** extends **base.html**.

3. Finally, this path needs to be added to the top of the **urlpatterns** list in **bookr/urls.py**. First, import the new views and then add a path linking the URL **accounts/profile/** to **bookr.views.profile**:

```
from bookr.views import profile

urlpatterns = [path('accounts/', \
                include(('django.contrib.auth.urls', 'auth')),\
                (namespace='accounts')),\
              path('accounts/profile/', profile, name='profile'),\
              path('admin/', admin.site.urls),\
              path('', include('reviews.urls'))]
```

This is a good start on a user profile page. When Alice is logged in and visits **http://localhost:8000/accounts/profile/**, it is rendered as shown in the screenshot in *Figure 9.4*. Remember, if the server needs to be started, use the **python manage.py runserver** command:

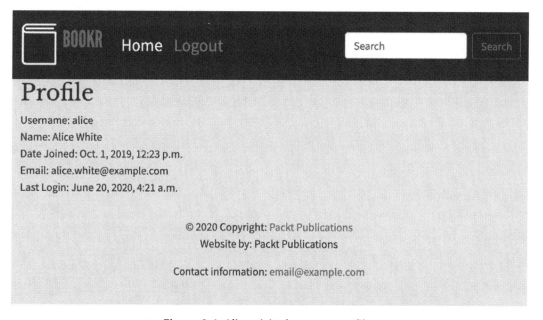

Figure 9.4: Alice visits her user profile

We've seen how we can redirect a user to their profile page, once they've successfully logged in. Let's now discuss how we can give content access to specific users only.

AUTHENTICATION DECORATORS AND REDIRECTION

Now that we have learned how to allow ordinary users to log in to our project, we can discover how to restrict content to authenticated users. The authentication module comes with some useful decorators that can be used to secure views according to the current user's authentication or access.

Unfortunately, if, say, a user named Alice was to log out of Bookr, the profile page would still render and display empty details. Instead of this happening, it would be preferable for any unauthenticated visitor to be directed to the login screen:

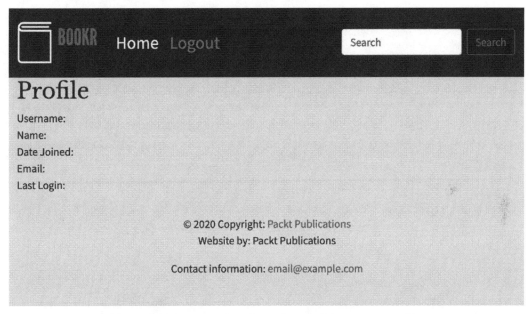

Figure 9.5: An unauthenticated user visits a user profile

The authentication app comes with useful decorators for adding authentication behavior to Django views. In this situation of securing our profile view, we can use the **login_required** decorator:

```
from django.contrib.auth.decorators import login_required


@login_required
def profile(request):
    ...
```

Now if an unauthenticated user visits the **/accounts/profile** URL, they will be redirected to **http://localhost:8000/accounts/login/?next=/ accounts/profile/**.

This URL takes the user to the login URL. The **next** parameter in the **GET** variables tells the login view where to redirect to after a successful login. The default behavior is to redirect back to the current view, but this can be overridden by specifying the **login_url** argument to the **login_required** decorator. For example, if we had some need to redirect to a different page after login, we could have explicitly stated it in the decorator call like this:

```
@login_required(login_url='/accounts/profile2')
```

If we had rewritten our login view to expect the redirection URL to be specified in a different URL argument to **'next'**, we could explicate this in the decorator call with the **redirect_field_name** argument:

```
@login_required(redirect_field_argument='redirect_to')
```

There are often situations where a URL should be restricted to users or groups holding a specific condition. Consider the case where we have a page for staff users to view any user profile. We don't want this URL to be accessible to all users, so we want to limit this URL to users or groups with the **'view_user'** permission and to forward the unauthorized requests to the login URL:

```
from django.contrib.auth.decorators \
import login_required, permission_required

...

@permission_required('view_group')
def user_profile(request, uid):
    user = get_object_or_404(User, id=uid)
    permissions = user.get_all_permissions()
    return render(request, 'user_profile.html',\
                  {'user': user, 'permissions': permissions}
```

So with this decorator applied on our **user_profile** view, an unauthorized user visiting **http://localhost:8000/accounts/users/123/profile/** would be redirected to **http://localhost:8000/accounts/login/?next=/ accounts/users/123/profile/**.

Sometimes, though, we need to structure more subtle conditional permissions that don't fall into the scope of these two directors. For this purpose, Django provides a custom decorator that takes an arbitrary function as an argument. The **user_passes_test** decorator requires a **test_func** argument:

```
user_passes_test(test_func, login_url=None, redirect_field_name='next')
```

Here's an example where we have a view, **veteran_features**, that is only available to users who have been registered on the site for more than a year:

```
from django.contrib.auth.decorators import (login_required),\
                                            (permission_required),\
                                            (user_passes_test)


...


def veteran_user(user):
    now = datetime.datetime.now()
    if user.date_joined is None:
        return False
    return now - user.date_joined > datetime.timedelta(days=365)


@user_passes_test(veteran_user)
def veteran_features(request):
    user = request.user
    permissions = user.get_all_permissions()
    return render(request, 'veteran_profile.html',\
            {'user': user, 'permissions': permissions}
```

Sometimes the logic in our views cannot be handled with one of these decorators and we need to apply the redirect within the control flow of the view. We can do this using the **redirect_to_login** helper function. It takes the same arguments as the decorators, as shown in the following snippet:

```
redirect_to_login(next, login_url=None, redirect_field_name='next')
```

EXERCISE 9.03: ADDING AUTHENTICATION DECORATORS TO THE VIEWS

Having learned about the flexibility of the authentication app's permission and authentication decorators, we will now set about putting them to use in the Reviews app. We need to ensure that only authenticated users can edit reviews and that only staff users can edit publishers. There are several ways of doing this, so we will attempt a few approaches. All the code in these steps is in the **reviews/views.py** file:

1. Your first instinct to solve this problem would be to think that the **publisher_edit** method needs an appropriate decorator to enforce that the user has **edit_publisher** permission. For this, you could easily do something like this:

```
from django.contrib.auth.decorators import permission_required
...


@permission_required('edit_publisher')
def publisher_edit(request, pk=None):
    ...
```

2. Using this method is fine and it's one way to add permissions checking to a view. You can also use a slightly more complicated but more flexible method. Instead of using a permission decorator to enforce permission rights on the **publisher_edit** method, you will create a test function that requires a staff user and apply this test function to **publisher_edit** with the **user_passes_test** decorator. Writing a test function allows more customization on how you validate users' access rights or permissions. If you made changes to your **views.py** file in *step 1*, feel free to comment the decorator out (or delete it) and write the following test function instead:

```
from django.contrib.auth.decorators import user_passes_test
...




def is_staff_user(user):
    return user.is_staff


@user_passes_test(is_staff_user)
    ...
```

3. Ensure that login is required for the **review_edit** and **book_media** functions by adding the appropriate decorator:

```
...

from django.contrib.auth.decorators import login_required, \
                                            user_passes_test

...
@login_required
def review_edit(request, book_pk, review_pk=None):


@login_required
def book_media(request, pk):
...
```

4. In the **review_edit** method, add logic to the view that requires that the user be either a staff user or the owner of the review. The **review_edit** view controls the behavior of both review creation and review updates. The constraint that we are developing only applies to the case where an existing review is being updated. So, the place to add code is after a **Review** object has been successfully retrieved. If the user is not a staff account or the review's creator doesn't match the current user, we need to raise a **PermissionDenied** error:

```
...

from django.core.exceptions import PermissionDenied
from PIL import Image
from django.contrib import messages

...

@login_required
def review_edit(request, book_pk, review_pk=None):
    book = get_object_or_404(Book, pk=book_pk)

    if review_pk is not None:
        review = get_object_or_404(Review), \
                            (book_id=book_pk), \
                            (pk=review_pk)

        user = request.user
        if not user.is_staff and review.creator.id != user.id:
            raise PermissionDenied
```

```
        else:
            review = None
    ...
```

Now, when a non-staff user attempts to edit another user's review, a **Forbidden** error will be thrown, as in *Figure 9.6*. In the next section, we will look at applying conditional logic in templates so that users aren't taken to pages that they don't have sufficient permission to access:

403 Forbidden

Figure 9.6: Access is forbidden to non-staff users

In this exercise, we have used authentication decorators to secure views in a Django app. The authentication decorators that were applied provided a simple mechanism to restrict views from users lacking necessary permissions, non-staff users, and unauthenticated users. Django's authentication decorators provide a robust mechanism that follows Django's role and permission framework, while the **user_passes_test** decorator provides an option to develop custom authentication.

ENHANCING TEMPLATES WITH AUTHENTICATION DATA

In *Exercise 9.02, Adding a Profile Page*, we saw that we can pass the **request.user** object to the template to render the current user's attributes in the HTML. We can also take the approach of giving different template renderings according to the user type or permissions held by a user. Consider that we want to add an edit link that only appears to staff users. We might apply an **if** condition to achieve this:

```
{% if user.is_staff %}
  <p><a href="{% url 'review:edit' %}">Edit this Review</a></p>
{% endif %}
```

If we didn't take the time to conditionally render links based on permissions, users would have a frustrating experience navigating the application as many of the links that they click on would lead to **403 Forbidden** pages. The following exercise will show how we can use templates and authentication to present contextually appropriate links in our project.

EXERCISE 9.04: TOGGLING LOGIN AND LOGOUT LINKS IN THE BASE TEMPLATE

In the **bookr** project's base template, located in **templates/base.html**, we have a placeholder logout link in the header. It is coded in HTML as follows:

```
<li class="nav-item">
  <a class="nav-link" href="#">Logout</a>
</li>
```

We don't want the logout link to appear after a user has logged out. So, this exercise aims to apply conditional logic in the template so that **Login** and **Logout** links are toggled depending on whether the user is authenticated:

1. Edit the **templates/base.html** file. Copy the structure of the **Logout** list element and create a **Login** list element. Then, replace the placeholder links with the correct URLs for the **Logout** and **Login** pages – **/accounts/logout** and **/accounts/login**, respectively – as follows:

```
<li class="nav-item">
  <a class="nav-link" href="/accounts/logout">Logout</a>
</li>
<li class="nav-item">
  <a class="nav-link" href="/accounts/login">Login</a>
</li>
```

2. Now put our two **li** elements inside an **if** … **else** … **endif** conditional block. The logic condition that we are applying is **if user.is_authenticated**:

```
{% if user.is_authenticated %}
  <li class="nav-item">
    <a class="nav-link" href="/accounts/logout">Logout</a>
  </li>
    {% else %}
```

```
    <li class="nav-item">
      <a class="nav-link" href="/accounts/login">Login</a>
    </li>
  {% endif %}
```

3. Now visit the user profile page at **http://localhost:8000/accounts/profile/**. When authenticated, you will see the **Logout** link:

Figure 9.7: An authenticated user sees the Logout link

4. Now click the **Logout** link; you will be taken to the **/accounts/logout** page. The **Login** link appears in the menu, confirming that the link is contextually dependent on the authentication state of the user:

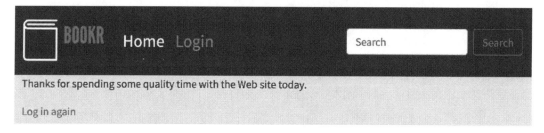

Figure 9.8: An unauthenticated user sees the Login link

This exercise was a simple example of how Django templates can be used with authentication information to create a stateful and contextual user experience. We also do not want to provide links that a user does not have access to or actions that are not permissible for the user's permission level. The following activity will use this templating technique to fix some of these problems in Bookr.

ACTIVITY 9.01: AUTHENTICATION-BASED CONTENT USING CONDITIONAL BLOCKS IN TEMPLATES

In this activity, you will apply conditional blocks in templates that modify content based on user authentication and user status. Users should not be presented with links that they are not permitted to visit or actions that they are not authorized to carry out. The following steps will help you complete this activity:

1. In the **book_detail** template, in the file at **reviews/templates/ reviews/book_detail.html**, hide the **Add Review** and **Media** buttons from non-authenticated users.

2. Also, hide the heading that says "*Be the first one to write a review*," as that is not an option for non-authenticated users.

3. In the same template, make the **Edit Review** link only appear for the staff or the user that wrote the review. The conditional logic for the template block is very similar to the conditional logic that we used in the **review_edit** view in the previous section:

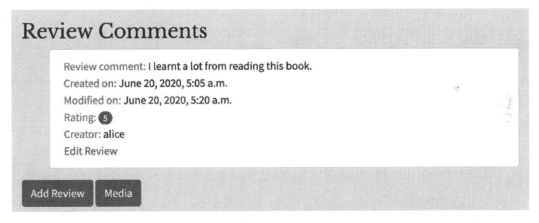

Figure 9.9: The Edit Review link appears on Alice's review when Alice is logged in

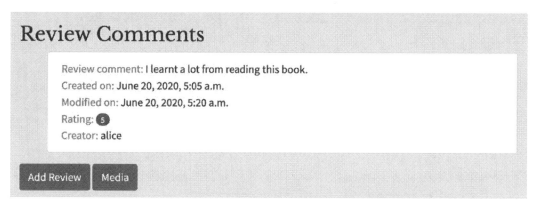

Figure 9.10: There is no Edit Review link on Alice's review when Bob is logged in

4. Modify **template/base.html** so that it displays the currently authenticated user's username to the right of the search form in the header, linking to the user profile page.

   By completing this activity, you will have added dynamic content to the template that reflects the authentication state and identity of the current user, as can be seen from the following screenshot:

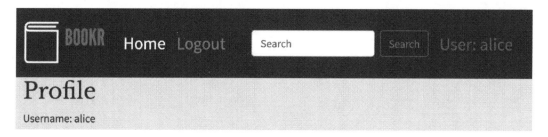

Figure 9.11: An authenticated user's name appears after the search form

> **NOTE**
>
> The solution to this activity can be found at http://packt.live/2Nh1NTJ.

SESSIONS

It is worth looking at some theory to understand why sessions are a common solution in web applications for managing user content. The HTTP protocol defines the interactions between a client and a server. It is said to be a "stateless" protocol as no stateful information is retained by the server between requests. This protocol design worked well for delivering hypertextual information in the early days of the World Wide Web, but it did not suit the needs of secured web applications delivering customized information to specific users.

We are now acquainted with seeing websites adapt to our personal viewing habits. Shopping sites recommend similar products to the ones that we have recently viewed and tell us about products that are popular in our region. These features all required a stateful approach to website development. One of the most common ways to implement a stateful web experience is through **sessions**. A session refers to a user's current interaction with a web server or application and requires that data is persisted for the duration of the interaction. This may include information about the links that the user has visited, the actions that they have performed, and the preferences that they have made in their interactions.

If a user sets a blogging site to a dark theme on one page, there is an expectation that the next page will use the same theme as well. We describe this behavior as "maintaining state." A session key is stored client-side as a browser cookie, which can be identified with server-side information that persists while the user is logged in.

In Django, sessions are implemented as a form of middleware. When we initially created the app in *Chapter 4, Introduction to Django Admin*, session support was activated by default.

THE SESSION ENGINE

Information about current and expired sessions needs to be stored somewhere. In the early days of the World Wide Web, this was done through saving session information in files on the server, but as web server architectures have become more elaborate and their performance demands have increased, other more efficient strategies such as a database or in-memory storage have become the norm. By default, in Django, session information is stored in a project's database.

This is a reasonable default for most small projects. However, Django's middleware implementation of sessions gives us the flexibility to store our project's session information in a variety of ways to suit our system architecture and performance requirements. Each of these different implementations is called a session engine. If we want to change the session configuration, we need to specify the **SESSION_ENGINE** setting in the project's **settings.py** file:

- **Cached sessions**: In some environments, caching session information in memory or in a database is an approach that is suited to high performance. Django provides the **django.contrib.sessions.backends.cache** and **django.contrib.sessions.backends.cached_db** session engines for this purpose.

- **File-based sessions**: As stated earlier, this is a somewhat antiquated way of maintaining session information but may suit some sites where performance is not an issue and there are reasons not to store dynamic information in a database.

- **Cookie-based sessions**: Rather than keeping session information server-side, you can keep them entirely in the web browser client by serializing the contents of the session as JSON and storing it in a browser-based cookie.

DO YOU NEED TO FLAG COOKIE CONTENT?

All of Django's implementations of sessions require storing a session ID in a cookie on the user's web browser.

Regardless of the session engine employed, all these middleware implementations involve storing a site-specific cookie in the web browser. In the early days of web development, it was not uncommon to pass session IDs as URL arguments, but this approach has been eschewed in Django for reasons of security.

In many jurisdictions, including the European Union, websites are legally required to warn users if the site sets cookies in their browsers. If there are such legislative requirements in the region where you intend to operate your site, it is your responsibility to ensure that the code meets these obligations. Be sure to use up-to-date implementations and avoid using abandoned projects that have not kept pace with legislative changes.

> **NOTE**
>
> To cater to these changes and legislative requirements, there are many useful apps, such as **Django Simple Cookie Consent** and **Django Cookie Law**, that are designed to work with several legislative frameworks. You can find more by going to the following links:
>
> https://pypi.org/project/django-simple-cookie-consent/
>
> https://github.com/TyMaszWeb/django-cookie-law
>
> Many JavaScript modules exist that implement similar cookie consent mechanisms.

PICKLE OR JSON STORAGE

Python provides the **pickle** module in its standard library for serializing Python objects into a byte stream representation. A pickle is a binary structure that has the benefit of being interoperable between different architectures and different versions of Python, so that a Python object can be serialized to a pickle on a Windows PC and deserialized to a Python object on a Linux Raspberry Pi.

This flexibility comes with security vulnerabilities and it is not recommended that it is used to represent untrusted data. Consider the following Python object, which contains several types of data. It can be serialized using `pickle`:

```
import datetime
data = dict(viewed_books=[17, 18, 3, 2, 1],\
        search_history=['1981', 'Machine Learning', 'Bronte'],\
        background_rgb=(96, 91, 92),\
        foreground_rgb=(17, 17, 17),\
        last_login_login=datetime.datetime(2019, 12, 3, 15, 30, 30),\
        password_change=datetime.datetime(2019, 9, 2, 8, 41, 25),\
        user_class='Veteran',\
        average_rating=4.75,\
        reviewed_books={18, 3, 7})
```

Using the **dumps** (dump string) method of the **pickle** module, we can serialize the data object to produce a byte representation:

```
import pickle
data_pickle = pickle.dumps(data)
```

JSON stands for **JavaScript Object Notation**. The syntax of JSON is a small subset of the JavaScript language. It is a widespread standard for messaging and data exchange, commonly used for transferring data between web browsers and servers. We can serialize JSON with a similar approach to the one that we outlined with the **pickle** format:

```
import json
data_json = json.dumps(data)
```

Because data contains Python **datetime** and **set** objects, which aren't serializable with JSON, when we attempt to serialize the structure a type error will be thrown:

```
TypeError: Object of type datetime is not JSON serializable
```

For serializing to JSON, we could convert the **datetime** objects to **string** and **set** to a list:

```
data['last_login_login'] = data['last_login_login'].
strftime("%Y%d%m%H%M%S")
data['password_change'] = data['password_change'].
strftime("%Y%d%m%H%M%S")
data['reviewed_books'] = list(data['reviewed_books'])
```

As JSON data is human readable, it is easy to examine:

```
{"viewed_books": [17, 18, 3, 2, 1], "search_history": ["1981", "Machine
Learning", "Bronte"], "background_rgb": [96, 91, 92], "foreground_rgb":
[17, 17, 17], "last_login_login": "20190312153030", "password_change":
"20190209084125", "user_class": "Veteran", "average_rating": 4.75,
"reviewed_books": [18, 3, 7]}
```

Note that we had to explicitly convert the **datetime** and **set** objects, but the tuple is automatically converted to a list by the JSON. Django ships with **PickleSerializer** and **JSONSerializer**. If the situation arises where the serializer needs to be altered, it can be changed by setting the **SESSION_SERIALIZER** variable in the project's **settings.py** file:

```
SESSION_SERIALIZER = 'django.contrib.sessions.serializers.JSONSerializer'
```

EXERCISE 9.05: EXAMINING THE SESSION KEY

The purpose of this exercise is to query the project's SQLite database and perform queries on the session table, so as to become familiar with how session data is stored. You will then create a Python script for examining session data that is stored using **JSONSerializer**:

1. At a command prompt, open the project database using this command:

```
sqlite3 db.sqlite3
```

2. Use the **.schema** directive to observe the structure of the **django_session** table as follows:

```
sqlite> .schema django_session
CREATE TABLE IF NOT EXISTS "django_session" ("session_key"
varchar(40) NOT NULL PRIMARY KEY, "session_data" text NOT NULL,
"expire_date" datetime NOT NULL);
CREATE INDEX "django_session_expire_date_a5c62663" ON "django_
session" ("expire_date");
```

This reveals that the **django_session** table in the database stores session information in the following fields:

session_key

session_data

expire_date

3. Query the data in the **django_session** table by using the SQL command **select * from django_session;**:

```
sqlite> select * from django_session;
gh4iesm01784g0uq4v3jq9iaoofymxca|MjM0YTkyZDZmYWZmMmQxMzM2OTI3YjdhOGM2NWMxNTg5ODc
4NWUwMjp7Il9hdXRoX3VzZXJfaWQiOiIxIiwiX2F1dGhfdXNlcl9iYWNrZW5kIjoiZGphbmdvLmNvbnR
yaWIuYXV0aC5iYWNrZW5kcy5Nb2RlbEJhY2tlbmQiLCJfYXV0aF9hc2VyX2hhc2giOiIyMGFlMDI3Nzd
hZWQ0OTNmOTk1YWFmMmY2JiMmRkYTcyOTg2ZjY5OTM4In0=|2019-10-18 06:46:44.504781
0oygh7wfg3hrnofazx61hjnkpd9kg00i|MjM0YTkyZDZmYWZmMmQxMzM2OTI3YjdhOGM2NWMxNTg5ODc
4NWUwMjp7Il9hdXRoX3VzZXJfaWQiOiIxIiwiX2F1dGhfdXNlcl9iYWNrZW5kIjoiZGphbmdvLmNvbnR
yaWIuYXV0aC5iYWNrZW5kcy5Nb2RlbEJhY2tlbmQiLCJfYXV0aF9hc2VyX2hhc2giOiIyMGFlMDI3Nzd
hZWQ0OTNmOTk1YWFmMmY2JiMmRkYTcyOTg2ZjY5OTM4In0=|2019-11-03 01:16:50.981512
```

Figure 9.12: Querying data in the django_session table

> **NOTE**
>
> To exit **sqlite3**, hit *Ctrl + D* on Linux and macOS or *Ctrl + Z* and *Enter* on Windows.

4. We have observed that the session data is encoded in **base64** format. We can decrypt this data at the Python command line using the **base64** module. Once decoded from **base64**, the **session_key** data contains a **binary_key** and a JSON payload separated by a colon:

```
b'\x82\x1e"z\xc9\xb4\xd7\xbf8\x83K…5e02:{"_auth_user_id":"1"…}'
```

This Python code shows how to obtain the payload:

```
>>> import base64
>>> import json
>>>
>>> session_key = 'gh4iesm01784g0uq4v3jq9iaoofymxca|MjM0YTkyZDZmYWZmMmQxMzM2OTI3
YjdhOGM2NWMxNTg5ODc4NWUwMjp7Il9hdXRRoX3VzZXJfaWQiOiIxIiwiX2F1dGhfdXNlcl9iYWNrZW5k
IjoiZGphbmdvLmNvbnRyaWIuYXV0aC5iYWNrZW5kcy5Nb2RlbEJhY2tlbmQiLCJfYXV0aF91c2VyX2hh
c2giOiIyMGFlMDI3NzdhZWQ0OTNmOTk1YWFmY2JiMmRkYTcyOTg2ZjY5OTM4In0='
>>>
>>> binary_key, payload = base64.b64decode(session_key).split(b':', 1)
>>> json.loads(payload.decode())
{'_auth_user_id': '1', '_auth_user_backend': 'django.contrib.auth.backends.Model
Backend', '_auth_user_hash': '20ae02777aed493f995aafcbb2dda72986f69938'}
>>> █
```

Figure 9.13: Decoding the session key with the Python shell

We can see the structure that is encoded in the payload. The payload represents the minimal data stored in a session. It contains keys for **_auth_user_id**, **_auth_user_backend**, and **_auth_user_hash** with values obtained from **User.id**, the **ModelBackend** class name, and the hash that is derived from the user's for password information. We will learn how to add additional data in the next section.

5. We will develop a simple Python utility for decrypting this session information. It requires modules that we have used as well as **pprint** for formatting output and the **sys** module for checking command-line arguments:

```
import base64
import json
import pprint
import sys
```

6. After the **import** statements, write a function that decodes the session key and loads the JSON payload as a Python dictionary:

```
def get_session_dictionary(session_key):
    binary_key, payload = base64.b64decode\
                          (session_key).split(b':', 1)
    session_dictionary = json.loads(payload.decode())
    return session_dictionary
```

7. Add a code block so that when this utility is run, it takes a **session_key** argument specified at the command line and converts it to a dictionary using the **get_session_dictionary** function. Then, use the **pprint** module to print an indented version of the dictionary structure:

```
if __name__ == '__main__':
    if len(sys.argv)>1:
        session_key = sys.argv[1]
        session_dictionary = get_session_dictionary(session_key)
        pp = pprint.PrettyPrinter(indent=4)
        pp.pprint(session_dictionary)
```

8. Now you can use this Python script to examine session data that is stored in the database. You can call it on the command line by passing the session data as an argument as follows:

```
python session_info.py <session_data>
```

It will be useful for debugging session behavior when you attempt the final activity:

```
> python session_info.py 'gh4iesm01784g0uq4v3jq9iaoofymxca|MjM0YTkyZDZmYWZmMmQxM
zM2OTI3YjdhOGM2NWMxNTg5ODc4NWUwMjp7I19hdXRoX3VzZXJfaWQiOiIxIiwiX2F1dGhfdXNlcl9iY
WNrZW5kIjoiZGphbmdvLmNvbnRyaWIuYXV0aC5iYWNrZW5kcy5Nb2RlbEJhY2tlbmQiLCJfYXV0aF91c
2VyX2hhc2giOiIyMGFlMDI3NzdhZWQ0OTNmOTk1YWFmY2JiMmRkYTcyOTg2ZjY5OTM4In0='
{    '_auth_user_backend': 'django.contrib.auth.backends.ModelBackend',
     '_auth_user_hash': '20ae02777aed493f995aafcbb2dda72986f69938',
     '_auth_user_id': '1'}
>
```

Figure 9.14: Python script

This script outputs the decoded session information. At present, the session only contains three keys:

_auth_user_backend is a string representation of the class of the user backend. As our project stores user credentials in the model, **ModelBackend** is used.

_auth_user_hash is a hash of the user's password.

_auth_user_id is the user ID obtained from the model's **User.id** attribute.

This exercise helped you become familiar with how session data is stored in Django. We will now turn our attention to adding additional information to Django sessions.

STORING DATA IN SESSIONS

We've covered the way sessions are implemented in Django. Now we are going to briefly examine some of the ways that we can make use of sessions to enrich our user experience. In Django, the session is an attribute of the **request** object. It is implemented as a dictionary-like object. In our views, we can assign keys to the **session** object like a typical dictionary, as here:

```
request.session['books_reviewed_count'] = 39
```

But there are some restrictions. First, the keys in the session must be strings, so integers and timestamps are not allowed. Secondly, keys starting with an underscore are reserved for internal system use. Data is limited to values that can be encoded as JSON, so some byte sequences that can't be decoded as UTF-8, such as the **binary_ key** listed previously, can't be stored as JSON data. The other warning is to avoid reassigning **request.session** to a different value. We should only assign or delete keys. So, don't do this:

```
request.session = {'books_read_count':30, 'books_reviewed_count': 39}
```

Instead, do this:

```
request.session['books_read_count'] = 30
request.session['books_reviewed_count'] = 39
```

With those restrictions in mind, we will investigate the use that we can make of session data in our Reviews application.

EXERCISE 9.06: STORING RECENTLY VIEWED BOOKS IN SESSIONS

The purpose of this exercise is to use the session to keep information about the **10** books that have been most recently browsed by the authenticated user. This information will be displayed on the profile page of the **bookr** project. When a book is browsed, the **book_detail** view is called. In this exercise, we will edit **reviews/views.py** and add some additional logic to the **book_detail** method. We will add a key to the session called **viewed_books**. Using basic knowledge of HTML and CSS, the page can be created to show the profile details and viewed books stored in separate divisions of the page, as follows:

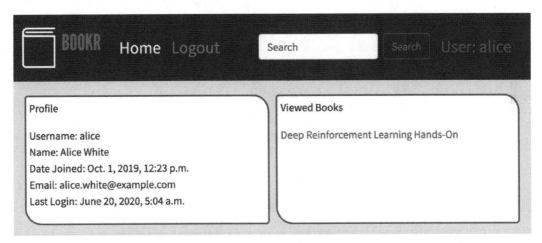

Figure 9.15: The Profile page incorporating Viewed Books

1. Edit **reviews/views.py** and the **book_detail** method. We are only interested in adding session information for authenticated users, so add a conditional statement to check whether the user is authenticated and set **max_viewed_books_length**, the maximum length of the viewed books list, to **10**:

```
def book_detail(request, pk):
    ...
    if request.user.is_authenticated:
        max_viewed_books_length = 10
```

2. Within the same conditional block, add code to retrieve the current value of **request.session['viewed_books']**. If this key isn't present in the session, start with an empty list:

```
viewed_books = request.session.get('viewed_books', [])
```

3. If the current book's primary key is already present in **viewed_books**, the following code will remove it:

```
viewed_book = [book.id, book.title]
if viewed_book in viewed_books:
    viewed_books.pop(viewed_books.index(viewed_book))
```

4. The following code inserts the current book's primary key to the start of the **viewed_books** list:

```
viewed_books.insert(0, viewed_book)
```

5. Add the following key to only keep the first 10 elements of the list:

```
viewed_books = viewed_books[:max_viewed_books_length]
```

6. The following code will add our **viewed_books** back to **session['viewed_books']**, so that it is available in subsequent requests:

```
request.session['viewed_books'] = viewed_books
```

7. As before, at the end of the **book_detail** function, render the **reviews/book_detail.html** template given the request and context data:

```
return render(request, "reviews/book_detail.html", context)
```

Once complete, the **book_detail** view will have this conditional block:

```
def book_detail(request, pk):
    ...
    if request.user.is_authenticated:
        max_viewed_books_length = 10
        viewed_books = request.session.get('viewed_books', [])
        viewed_book = [book.id, book.title]
        if viewed_book in viewed_books:
            viewed_books.pop(viewed_books.index(viewed_book))
        viewed_books.insert(0, viewed_book)
        viewed_books = viewed_books[:max_viewed_books_length]
        request.session['viewed_books'] = viewed_books
    return render(request, "reviews/book_detail.html", context)
```

8. Modify the page layout and CSS of **templates/profile.html** to accommodate the viewed book division. As we may add more divisions to this page in the future, one convenient layout concept is the **flexbox**. We will add this CSS and separate the content into nested **div** instances that will be arranged horizontally on the page. We will refer to the internal **div** instances as **infocell** instances and style them with green borders and rounded edges:

```
<style>
.flexrow { display: flex;
           border: 2px black;
}
.flexrow > div { flex: 1; }

.infocell {
  border: 2px solid green;
  border-radius: 5px 25px;
  background-color: white;
  padding: 5px;
  margin: 20px 5px 5px 5px;
}

</style>

  <div class="flexrow" >
    <div class="infocell" >
      <p>Profile</p>

      ...

    </div>

    <div class="infocell" >
      <p>Viewed Books</p>

      ...

    </div>
  </div>
```

9. Modify the **Viewed Books div** in **templates/profile.html** so that if there are books present, their titles are displayed, linked to the individual book detail pages. This will be rendered as follows:

```
<a href="/books/1">Advanced Deep Learning with Keras</a><br>
```

There should be a message displayed if the list is empty. The entire **div**, including the iteration through **request.session.viewed_books**, will look like this:

```
<div class="infocell" >
  <p>Viewed Books</p>
  <p>
  {% for book_id, book_title in request.session.viewed_books %}
  <a href="/books/{{ book_id }}">{{ book_title }}</a><br>
  {% empty %}
        No recently viewed books found.
  {% endfor %}
  </p>
</div>
```

This will be the complete profile template once all these changes have been incorporated:

templates/profile.html

```
1  {% extends "base.html" %}
2
3  {% block title %}Bookr{% endblock %}
4
5  {% block heading %}Profile{% endblock %}
6
7  {% block content %}
8
9  <style>
```

You can find the complete code for this file at http://packt.live/3btvSJZ.

This exercise has enhanced the profile page by adding a list of recently viewed books. Now when you visit the login link at **http://127.0.0.1:8000/accounts/profile/**, you will see this page:

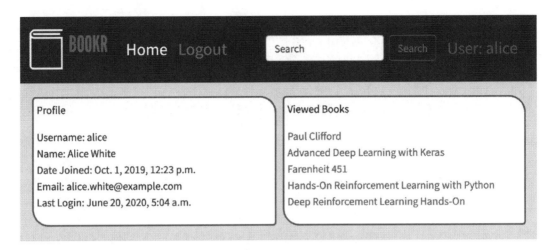

Figure 9.16: Recently viewed books

We can use the **session_info.py** script that we developed in *Exercise 9.04,
Toggling Login and Logout Links in the Base Template,* to examine the user's session
once this feature is implemented. It can be called on the command line by passing the
session data as an argument:

```
python session_info.py <session_data>
```

We can see that the book IDs and titles are listed in the **viewed_books** key.
Remember that the encoded data is obtained by querying the **django_session**
table in the SQLite database:

```
> python session_info.py 'clbdr0hg5gzszlnif987ir31cpvw327r|MTg2OTUzMGM3YjY3
YzhkOWFiODMyYjJkY2JjZDczNWZiMTY0MjIwZDp7Il9hdXRoX3VzZXJfaWQiOiI2IiwiX2F1dGh
fdXNlc19iYWNrZW5kIjoiMphipmdvLmNvbnRyaWIuYXV0aC5iYWNrZW5kcy5Nb2RlbEJhY2t1bm
QiLCJfYXV0aF91c2VyX2hhc2giOiI1MDkzMzQwNjY2YmQxNmZlZDQ1YmI5ODU0Y2QzM2U0NmZlY
jI1Zjk4Iiwidmlld2VkX2Jvb2tzIjpbWzE3LCJQYXVsIENsaWZmb3JkIl0sWzEsIkFkdmFuY2Vk
IERlZXAgTGVhcm5pbmcgd2l0aCBLZXJhcyJdLFsxMywiRmFyZW5oZWl0IDQ1MSJdLFs2LCJIYW5
kcy1PbiBSZWluZm9yY2VtZW50IExlYXJuaW5nIHdpdGggUH10aG9uIl0sWzQsIkR1ZXAgUmVpbm
ZvcmNlbWVudCBMZWFybmluZyBIYW5kcy1PbiJdXSwic2VhcmNoX2hpc3RvcnkiOltbImNvbnRya
WJ1dG9yIiwiMTk4NCJdXX0='
{   '_auth_user_backend': 'django.contrib.auth.backends.ModelBackend',
    '_auth_user_hash': '5093340666bd16fed45bb9854cd33e46feb25f98',
    '_auth_user_id': '6',
    'viewed_books': [   [17, 'Paul Clifford'],
                        [1, 'Advanced Deep Learning with Keras'],
                        [13, 'Farenheit 451'],
                        [6, 'Hands-On Reinforcement Learning with Python'],
                        [4, 'Deep Reinforcement Learning Hands-On']]}
>
```

Figure 9.17: The viewed books are stored in the session data

In this exercise, we have used Django's session mechanism to store ephemeral information about user interactions with the Django project. We have learned how this information can be retrieved from the user session and be displayed in a view that informs users about their recent activity.

ACTIVITY 9.02: USING SESSION STORAGE FOR THE BOOK SEARCH PAGE

Sessions are a useful way to store short-lived information that assists in maintaining a stateful experience on a site. Users frequently revisit pages such as search forms, and it would be convenient to store their most recently used form settings when they return to those pages. In *Chapter 3, URL Mapping, Views, and Templates*, we developed a book search feature for the **bookr** project. The book search page has two options for **Search in** – **Title** and **Contributor**. Currently, each time the page is visited, it defaults to **Title**:

Figure 9.18: The Search and Search in fields of the book search form

In this activity, you will use session storage so that when the book search page, **/book-search**, is visited, it will default to the most recently used search option. You will also add a third **infocell** to the profile page that contains a list of links to the most recently used search terms. These are the steps that you need to complete this activity:

1. Edit the **book_search** view and retrieve **search_history** from the session.

2. When the form has received valid input and a user is logged in, append the search option and search text to the session's search history list.

   In the case that the form hasn't been filled (for example, when the page is first visited), render the form with the previously used **Search in** option selected, that is, either **Title** or **Contributor** (*Figure 9.19*):

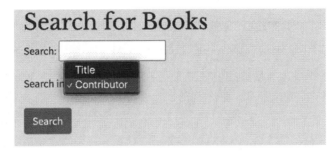

Figure 9.19: Selecting Contributor in the search page

3. In the profile template, include an additional **infocell** division for **Search History**.

4. List the search history as a series of links to the book search page. The links will take this form: **/book-search?search=Python&search_in=title**.

This activity will challenge you to apply session data to solve a usability issue in a web form. This approach will have applicability in many real-world situations and will give you some idea of the use of sessions in creating a stateful web experience. After completing this activity, the profile page will contain the third **infocell** as in *Figure 9.20*:

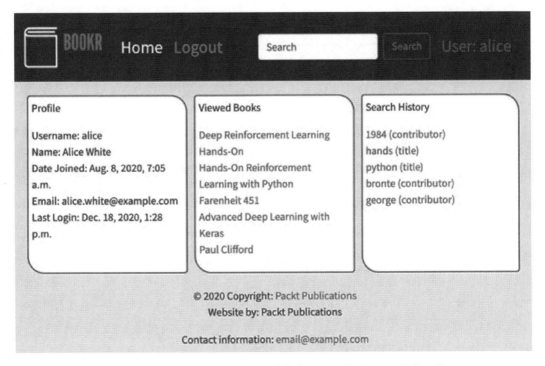

Figure 9.20: The profile page with the Search History infocell

> **NOTE**
>
> The solution to this activity can be found at http://packt.live/2Nh1NTJ.

SUMMARY

In this chapter, we have examined Django's middleware implementation of authentication and sessions. We have learned how to incorporate authentication and permission logic into views and templates. We can set permissions on specific pages and limit their access to authenticated users. We have also examined how to store data in a user's session and render it in subsequent pages.

Now you have the skills to customize a Django project to deliver a personalized web experience. You can limit the content to authenticated or privileged users and you can personalize a user's experience based on their prior interactions. In the next chapter, we will revisit the Admin app and learn some advanced techniques to customize our user model and apply fine-grained changes to the admin interface for our models.

10

ADVANCED DJANGO ADMIN AND CUSTOMIZATIONS

OVERVIEW

This chapter introduces you to advanced customizations to the **Django Admin** site so that you can tailor the appearance of the Django Admin dashboard to make it blend with the rest of your web project. You will see how new features and capabilities can be added to your web project's Django admin interface to make it substantially more powerful and useful for your project's goals. These customizations are driven by the addition of custom templates that help modify the look and feel of existing pages. These custom templates also add new views that can help extend the default functionalities of the Admin dashboard. Completing this chapter will equip you with skills that not only let you customize the interface, but also the functionality of your project's Django-based admin page.

INTRODUCTION

Let's say we want to customize the front page of a large organization's admin site. We want to show the health of the different systems in the organization and see any high-priority alerts that are active. If this were an internal website built on top of Django, we would need to customize it. Adding these kinds of functionalities will require the developers in the IT team to customize the default admin panel and create their own custom **AdminSite** module, which will render a different index page in comparison to what is provided by the default admin site. Fortunately, Django makes these kinds of customizations easy.

In this chapter, we will look at how we can leverage Django's framework and its extensibility to customize Django's default admin interface (as shown in *Figure 10.1*). We'll not just learn how to make the interface more personal; we will also learn how we can control the different aspects of the admin site to make Django load a custom admin site instead of the one that ships with the default framework. Such customization can come in handy when we want to introduce features into the admin site that are not present by default.

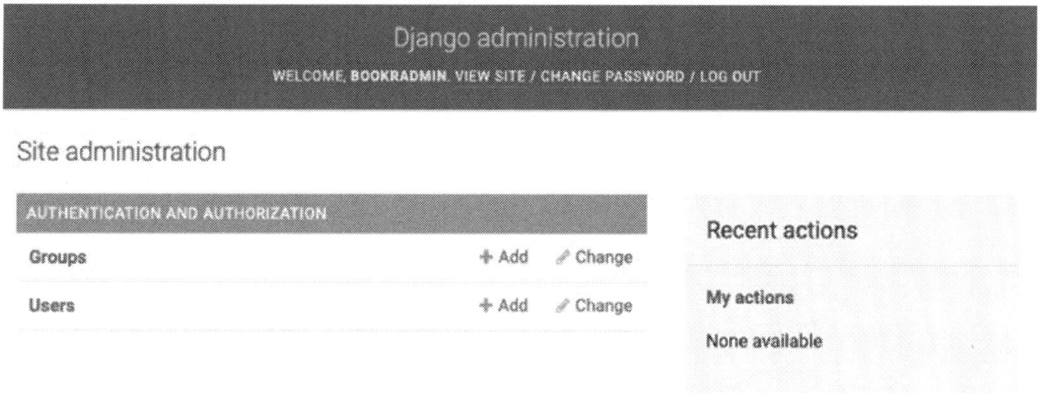

Figure 10.1: Default Django administration panel interface

This chapter builds upon the skills we practiced in *Chapter 4, Introduction to Django Admin*. Just to recap, we learned how to use the Django admin site to take control of the administration and authorization for our Bookr app. We also learned how to register models to read and edit their contents and also to customize Django's admin interface using the **admin.site** properties. Now, let's expand our knowledge further by taking a look at how we can start customizing the admin site by utilizing Django's **AdminSite** module to add powerful new functionalities to the admin portal of our web application.

CUSTOMIZING THE ADMIN SITE

Django as a web framework provides a lot of customization options for building web applications. We will be using this same freedom provided by Django when we are working on building the admin application for our project.

In *Chapter 4, Introduction to Django Admin*, we looked at how we can use the **admin. site** properties to customize the elements of our Django's admin interface. But what if we require more control over how our admin site behaves? For example, let's say we wanted to use a custom template for the login page (or the logout page) to show to users whenever they visited the Bookr admin panel. In this case, the **admin.site** properties provided might not be enough, and we will need to build customizations that can extend the default admin site's behavior. Luckily, this can be easily achieved by extending the **AdminSite** class from Django's admin model. But before we jump into building our admin site, let's first understand how Django discovers admin files and how we can use this admin file discovery mechanism to build a new app inside Django that will act as our admin site app.

DISCOVERING ADMIN FILES IN DJANGO

When we build applications in our Django project, we use the **admin.py** file frequently to register our models or create **ModelAdmin** classes that customize our interactions with the models inside the admin interface. These **admin.py** files store and provide this information to our project's admin interface. The discovery of these files is affected automatically by Django once we add **django.contrib.admin** to our **INSTALLED_APPS** section inside our **settings.py** file:

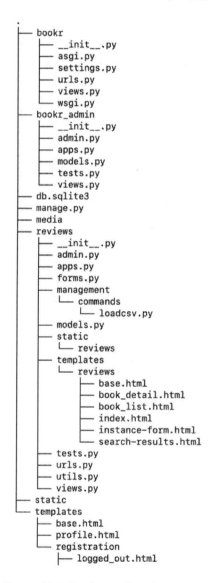

```
.
├── bookr
│   ├── __init__.py
│   ├── asgi.py
│   ├── settings.py
│   ├── urls.py
│   ├── views.py
│   └── wsgi.py
├── bookr_admin
│   ├── __init__.py
│   ├── admin.py
│   ├── apps.py
│   ├── models.py
│   ├── tests.py
│   └── views.py
├── db.sqlite3
├── manage.py
├── media
├── reviews
│   ├── __init__.py
│   ├── admin.py
│   ├── apps.py
│   ├── forms.py
│   ├── management
│   │   └── commands
│   │       └── loadcsv.py
│   ├── models.py
│   ├── static
│   │   └── reviews
│   ├── templates
│   │   └── reviews
│   │       ├── base.html
│   │       ├── book_detail.html
│   │       ├── book_list.html
│   │       ├── index.html
│   │       ├── instance-form.html
│   │       └── search-results.html
│   ├── tests.py
│   ├── urls.py
│   ├── utils.py
│   └── views.py
├── static
└── templates
    ├── base.html
    ├── profile.html
    └── registration
        ├── logged_out.html
```

Figure 10.2: Bookr application structure

As we can see in the preceding figure, we have an **admin.py** file under the **reviews** application directory that is used by Django to customize the admin site for Bookr.

When the admin application gets added, it tries to find the **admin** module inside every app of the Django project we are working on and, if a module is found, it loads the contents from that module.

DJANGO'S ADMINSITE CLASS

Before we start customizing Django's admin site, we must understand how the default admin site is generated and handled by Django.

To provide us with the default admin site, Django packages a module known as the **admin** module, which holds a class known as **AdminSite**. This class implements a lot of useful functionalities and intelligent defaults that the Django community thinks will be important for implementing a useful administration panel for most Django websites. The default **AdminSite** class provides a lot of inbuilt properties that not only control the look and feel of how the default admin site is rendered in the web browser, but also control the way we can interact with it and how a particular interaction will result in an action. Some of these defaults include the site template properties, such as text to be shown in the site header, text to show in the title bar of the web browser, integration with Django's **auth** module for authenticating to the admin site, and a host of other properties.

As we progress on our path to building a custom admin site for our Django web project, it is more than desirable to retain a lot of the useful functionalities that are already built into Django's **AdminSite** class. This is where the concepts of Python object-oriented programming come to our rescue.

As we start to create our custom admin site, we will try to leverage the existing useful set of functionalities that are provided by Django's default **AdminSite** class. For this, instead of building everything from scratch, we will work on creating a new child class that inherits from Django's **AdminSite** class to leverage the existing set of functionalities and useful integration that Django already provides us with. This kind of approach allows us to focus on adding a new and useful set of functionalities to our custom admin site, rather than spending time on implementing the basic set of functionalities from scratch. For example, the following code snippet shows how we can create a child class of Django's **AdminSite** class:

```
class MyAdminSite(admin.AdminSite):
    ...
```

To start working on our custom admin site for our web application, let's start by overriding some of the basic properties of Django's admin panel through the use of the custom **AdminSite** class we are going to work on.

Some of the properties that can be overridden include **site_header**, **site_title**, and others.

> **NOTE**
>
> When creating a custom admin site, we will have to register once again any **Model** and **ModelAdmin** classes that we might have registered using the default **admin.site** variable earlier. This happens because a custom admin site doesn't inherit the instance details from the default admin site provided by Django and so unless we re-register our **Model** and **ModelAdmin** interfaces, our custom admin site will not show them.

Now, with the knowledge of how Django discovers what to load into the admin interface and how we can start building our custom admin site, let's go ahead and try to create our custom admin app for Bookr, which extends the existing **admin** module provided by Django. In the exercise that follows, we are going to create a custom admin site interface for our Bookr application using Django's **AdminSite** class.

EXERCISE 10.01: CREATING A CUSTOM ADMIN SITE FOR BOOKR

In this exercise, you will create a new application that extends the default Django admin site and allows you to customize the components of the interface. Consequently, you will customize the default title of Django's admin panel. Once that is done, you will override the default value of Django's **admin.site** property to point to your custom admin site:

1. Before you can start working on your custom admin site, you first need to make sure that you are in the correct directory in your project from where you can run your Django application's management commands. For this, use the Terminal or Windows Command Prompt to navigate to the **bookr** directory and then create a new application named **bookr_admin**, which is going to act as the admin site for Bookr, by running the following commands:

```
python3 manage.py startapp bookr_admin
```

Once this command is executed successfully, you should have a new directory named **bookr_admin** inside your project.

2. Now, with the default structure configured, the next step is to create a new class named **BookrAdmin**, which will extend the **AdminSite** class provided by Django to inherit the properties of the default admin site. To do this, open the **admin.py** file under the **bookr_admin** directory inside PyCharm. Once the file is open, you will see that the file already has the following code snippet present inside it:

```
from django.contrib import admin
```

Now, keeping this **import** statement as is, starting from the next line, create a new class named **BookrAdmin**, which inherits from the **AdminSite** class provided by the **admin** module you imported earlier:

```
class BookrAdmin(admin.AdminSite):
```

Inside this new **BookrAdmin** class, override the default value for the **site_header** variable, which is responsible for rendering the site header in Django's admin panel by setting the **site_header** property, as shown next:

```
site_header = "Bookr Administration"
```

With this, the custom admin site class is now defined. To use this class, you will first create an instance of this class. This can be done as follows:

```
admin_site = BookrAdmin(name='bookr_admin')
```

3. Save the file but don't close it yet; we'll revisit it in *step 6*. Next, let's edit the **urls.py** file in the **bookr** app.

4. With the custom class now defined, the next step is to modify the **urlpatterns** list to map the **/admin** endpoint in our project to the new **AdminSite** class you created. To do this, open the **urls.py** file under the **Bookr** project directory inside PyCharm and change the mapping of the **/admin** endpoint to point to our custom site:

```
from bookr_admin.admin import admin_site

urlpatterns = [....,\
               path('admin/', admin_site.urls)]
```

We first imported the **admin_site** object from the admin module of the **bookr_admin** app. Then, we used the **urls** property of the object to map to the **admin** endpoint in our application as follows:

```
path('admin/', admin_site.urls)
```

In this case, the **urls** property of our **admin_site** object is being automatically populated by the **admin.AdminSite** base class provided by Django's **admin** module. Once complete, your **urls.py** file should look like this: http://packt.live/3qjx46J.

5. Now, with the configuration done, let's run our admin app in the browser. For this, run the following command from the root of your project directory where the **manage.py** file is located:

```
python manage.py runserver localhost:8000
```

Then, navigate to **http://localhost:8000/admin** (or **http://127.0.0.1:8000/admin**), which opens a page that resembles the following screenshot:

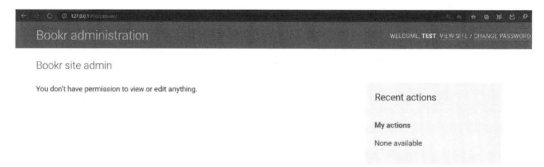

Figure 10.3: Home page view for the custom Bookr admin site

In the preceding screenshot (*Figure 10.3*), you will see that Django displays the message, **You don't have permission to view or edit anything**. The issue of not having adequate permissions happens because, up till now, we have not registered any models with our custom **AdminSite** instance. The issue also applies to the **User and Groups** models that are shipped along with the Django **auth** module. So, let's make our custom admin site a bit more useful by registering the **User** model from Django's **auth** module.

6. To register the **User** model from Django's **auth** module, open the **admin.py** file under the **bookr_admin** directory inside PyCharm, and add the following line at the top of the file:

```
from django.contrib.auth.admin import User
```

At the end of the file, use your **BookrAdmin** instance to register this model as follows:

```
admin_site.register(User)
```

By now, your **admin.py** file should look like this:

```
from django.contrib import admin
from django.contrib.auth.admin import User

class BookrAdmin(admin.AdminSite):
    site_header = "Bookr Administration"

admin_site = BookrAdmin(name='bookr_admin')
admin_site.register(User)
```

Once this is done, reload the web server and visit **http://localhost:8000/admin**. Now, you should be able to see the **User** model being displayed for editing inside the admin interface, as shown here:

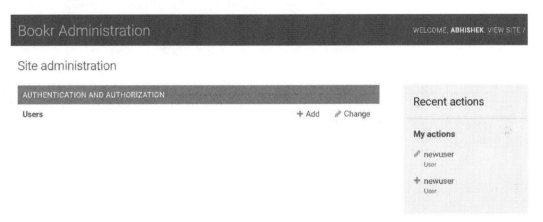

Figure 10.4: Home page view showing our registered models on the Bookr Administration site

With this, we just created our admin site application, and we can also now validate the fact that the custom site has a different header—**Bookr Administration**.

OVERRIDING THE DEFAULT ADMIN.SITE

In the previous section, after we created our own **AdminSite** application, we saw that we had to register models manually. This happens because most of the apps that we have built prior to our custom admin site still use the **admin.site** property to register their models and, if we want to use our **AdminSite** instance, we will have to update all those applications to use our instance, which can become cumbersome if there are a lot of applications inside a project.

Luckily, we can avoid this additional burden by overriding the default **admin.site** property. To do this, we first have to create a new **AdminConfig** class, which will override the default **admin.site** property for us, so that our application is marked as the default admin site and hence overrides the **admin.site** property inside our project. In the next exercise, we'll look at how we can map our custom admin site as a default admin site for an application.

EXERCISE 10.02: OVERRIDING THE DEFAULT ADMIN SITE

In this exercise, you will use the **AdminConfig** class to override the default admin site for your project such that you can keep on using the default **admin.site** variable to register models, override site properties, and more:

1. Open the **admin.py** file under the **bookr_admin** directory and remove the import for the **User** model and the **BookrAdmin** instance creation, which you wrote in *step 6* of *Exercise 10.01, Creating a Custom Admin Site for Bookr*. Once this is done, the file contents should resemble the following:

```
from django.contrib import admin


class BookrAdmin(admin.AdminSite):
    site_header = "Bookr Administration"
```

2. You will then need to create an **AdminConfig** class for the custom admin site, such that Django recognizes the **BookrAdmin** class as an **AdminSite** and overrides the **admin.site** property. To do this, open up the **apps.py** file inside the **bookr_admin** directory and overwrite the contents of the file with the contents shown here:

```
from django.contrib.admin.apps import AdminConfig


class BookrAdminConfig(AdminConfig):
    default_site = 'bookr_admin.admin.BookrAdmin'
```

In this, we first imported the **AdminConfig** class from Django's **admin** module. This class is used to define the application that should be used as a default admin site, and also to override the default behavior of the Django admin site.

For our use case, we created a class with the name **BookrAdminConfig**, which acts as a child class of Django's **AdminConfig** class and overrides the **default_site** property to point to our **BookrAdmin** class, which is our custom admin site:

```
default_site = 'bookr_admin.admin.BookrAdmin'
```

Once this is done, we need to set our application as an admin application inside our **Bookr** project. To achieve this, open the **settings.py** file of the **Bookr** project and, under the **INSTALLED_APPS** section, replace **'reviews.apps.ReviewsAdminConfig'** with **'bookr_admin.apps. BookrAdminConfig'**. The **settings.py** file should look like this: http:// packt.live/3siv1lf.

3. With the application mapped as the admin application, the final step involves modifying the URL mapping such that the **'admin/'** endpoint uses the **admin. site** property to find the correct URL. For this, open the **urls.py** file under the bookr project. Consider the following entry in the **urlpatterns** list:

```
path('admin/', admin_site.urls)
```

Replace it with the following entry:

```
from django.contrib import admin

urlpatterns = [....\
                path('admin/', admin.site.urls)]
```

Remember that **admin_site.urls** is a module, while **admin.site** is a Django internal property.

Once the preceding steps are complete, let's reload our web server and check whether our admin site loads by visiting `http://localhost:8000/admin`. If the website that loads looks like the one shown here, we have our own custom admin app now being used for the admin interface:

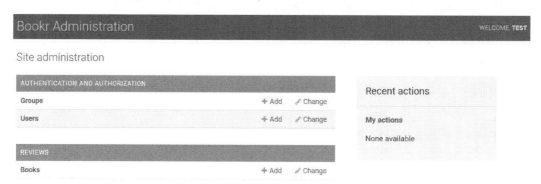

Figure 10.5: Home page view of the custom Bookr Administration site

As you can see, once we override **admin.site** with our admin app, the models that were registered earlier using the **admin.site.register** property start to show up automatically.

With this, we now have a custom base template, which we can now utilize to build the remainder of our Django admin customizations on. As we work through the chapter, we will discover some interesting customizations that allow us to make the admin dashboard an integrated part of our application.

CUSTOMIZING ADMIN SITE TEXT USING ADMINSITE ATTRIBUTES

Just as we can use the **admin.site** properties to customize the text for our Django application, we can also use the attributes exposed by the **AdminSite** class to customize these texts. In *Exercise 10.02, Overriding the Default Admin Site*, we took a look at updating the **site_header** property of the admin site. Similarly, there are many other properties we can modify. Some of the properties that can be overridden are described as follows:

- **site_header**: Text to display at the top of every admin page (defaults to **Django Administration**).

- **site_title**: Text to display in the title bar of the browser (defaults to **Django Admin Site**).

- **`site_url`**: The link to use for the **View Site** option (defaults to **/**). This is overridden when the site is running on a custom path and the redirection should take the user to the subpath directly.

- **`index_title`**: This is the text that should be shown on the index page of the admin application (defaults to **Site administration**).

> **NOTE**
>
> For more information on all the **adminsite** attributes, refer to the official Django documentation at https://docs.djangoproject.com/en/3.1/ref/contrib/admin/#adminsite-attributes.

If we want to override these attributes in our custom admin site, the process is very simple:

```
class MyAdminSite(admin.AdminSite):
    site_header = "My web application"
    site_title = "My Django Web application"
    index_title = "Administration Panel"
```

As we have seen in the examples so far, we have created a custom admin application for Bookr and then made it the default admin site for our project. An interesting question arises here. Since the properties that we have customized so far can also be customized by using the **admin.site** object directly, why should we create a custom admin application? Can't we just modify the **admin.site** properties?

As it turns out, there could be multiple reasons why someone would opt for a custom admin site; for example, they might want to change the layout of the default admin site to make it align with the overall layout of their application. This is quite common when creating a web application for a business where the homogeneity of the content is very important. Here is a short list of requirements that may compel a developer to go ahead and build a custom admin site as opposed to simply modifying the properties of the **admin.site** variable:

- A need to override the index template for the admin interface

- A need to override the login or logout template

- A need to add a custom view to the admin interface

CUSTOMIZING ADMIN SITE TEMPLATES

Just like some of the customizable common texts, such as **site_header** and **site_title**, that appear across the admin site, Django also allows us to customize the templates, which are used to render different pages inside the admin site by setting certain properties in the **AdminSite** class.

These customizations can include the modification of templates that are used to render the index page, login page, model data page, and more. These customizations can be easily done by leveraging the templating system provided by Django. For example, the following code snippet shows how we can add a new template to the Django admin dashboard:

```
{% extends "admin/base_site.html" %}


{% block content %}
  <!-- Template Content -->
{% endblock %}
```

In this custom template, there are a couple of important aspects that we need to understand.

When customizing the existing Django admin dashboard by modifying how certain pages inside the dashboard appear or by adding a new set of pages to the dashboard, we might not want to write every single piece of HTML again from scratch to maintain the basic look and feel of the Django admin dashboard.

Usually, while customizing the admin dashboard, we want to retain the layout in which Django organizes the different elements displayed on the dashboard such that we can focus on modifying parts of the page that matter to us. This basic layout of the page, along with the common page elements, such as the page header and page footer, are defined inside the Django admin's base template, which also acts as a master template for all the pages inside the default Django admin website.

To retain the way the common elements inside the Django admin pages are organized and rendered, we need to extend from this base template such that our custom template pages provide a user experience consistent with the other pages inside the Django admin dashboard. This can be done by using the template extension tags and extending the **base_site.html** template from the **admin** module provided by Django:

```
{% extends "admin/base_site.html" %}
```

Once this is done, the next part is to define our own content for the custom template. The **base_site.html** template provided by Django provides a block-based placeholder for developers to add their own content to the template. To add this content, a developer has to put the logic for their own custom elements for the page inside the **{% block content %}** tags. This essentially overrides any content defined by the **{% block content %}** tag inside the **base_site.html** template, following the concepts of template inheritance in Django.

Now, let's look at how we can customize the template, which is used to render the logout page, once the user clicks the Logout button in the admin panel.

EXERCISE 10.03: CUSTOMIZING THE LOGOUT TEMPLATE FOR THE BOOKR ADMIN SITE

In this exercise, you are going to customize the template that is used to render the logout page once the user clicks the **Logout** button on the admin site. Such overrides can come in handy in banking websites. Once a user clicks **Logout**, the bank might want to show the user a page with detailed instructions on how to make sure that their banking session is securely closed.

1. Under the **templates** directory which you must have created in the earlier chapters, create another directory named **admin** which will be used for storing templates for your custom admin site.

    > **NOTE**
    >
    > Before proceeding, make sure that the templates directory is added to the **DIRS** list in your **settings.py** file (under the **bookr/ project**).

2. Now, with the directory structure setup complete, and Django configured to load the templates, the next step involves writing your custom logout template that you want to render. For this, let's create a new file named **logout.html** under the **templates/admin** directory we created in *step 1* and add the following content to it:

```
{% extends "admin/base_site.html" %}

{% block content %}
<p>You have been logged out from the Admin panel. </p>
<p><a href="{% url 'admin:index' %}">Login Again</a> or
  <a href="{{ site_url }}">Go to Home Page</a></p>
{% endblock %}
```

In the preceding code snippet, we are doing a couple of things. First, for our custom logout template, we are going to use the same master layout as provided by the **django.contrib.admin** module. So, consider the following:

```
{% extends "admin/base_site.html" %}
```

When we write this, Django tries to find and load the **admin/base_site. html** template inside the **templates** directory provided by the **django. contrib.admin** module.

Now, with our base template all set to be extended, the next thing we do is try to override the HTML of the content block by executing the following command:

```
{% block content %}
...
{% endblock %}
```

The values of **admin:index** and **site_url** are provided by the **AdminSite** class automatically, based on the settings we define.

Using the value for **admin:index** and **site_url**, we create our **Login Again** hyperlink, which, when clicked, will take the user back to the login form, and the **Go to Home Page** link, which will take the user back to the home page of the website. The file should look like this now: http://packt.live/3oIGQPo.

3. Now, with the custom template defined, the next step is to make use of this custom template in our custom admin site. To do this, let's open the **admin.py** file under the **bookr_admin** directory and add the following field as the final value in the **BookrAdmin** class:

```
logout_template = 'admin/logout.html'
```

Save the file. It should look like this: http://packt.live/3oHHsVz.

4. Once all the preceding steps are complete, let's start our development server by running the following command:

```
python manage.py runserver localhost:8000
```

Then, we navigate to **http://localhost:8000/admin**.

Once you are there, try to do a login and then click **Logout**. Once you are logged out, you will see the following page rendered:

Figure 10.6: Logout view rendered to users after clicking the Logout button

With this, we have successfully overridden our first template. Similarly, we can also override other templates inside Django's admin panel, such as the templates for the index view and the login form.

ADDING VIEWS TO THE ADMIN SITE

Just like general applications inside Django, which can have multiple views associated with them, Django allows developers to add custom views to the admin site as well. This allows the developer to increase the scope of what the admin site interface can do.

The ability to add your own views to the admin site provides a lot of extensibility to the admin panel of the website, which can be leveraged for several additional use cases. For example, as we discussed at the start of the chapter, an IT team of a big organization can add a custom view to the admin site, which can then be used to both monitor the health of the different IT systems in the organization and to provide the IT team with the ability to quickly look at any urgent alerts that need to be addressed.

Now, the next question we need to answer is: *How can we add a custom view to the admin site?*

As it turns out, adding a new view inside the admin template is quite easy and follows the same approach we used while creating views for our applications, though with some minor modifications. In the next section, we will look at how we can add a new view to our Django admin dashboard.

CREATING THE VIEW FUNCTION

The first step to adding a new view to the Django application is to create a view function that implements the logic to handle the view. In the previous chapters, we created the view functions inside a separate file known as **views.py**, which was used to hold all our method- and class-based views.

When it comes to adding a new view to the Django admin dashboard, to create a new view, we need to define a new view function inside our custom **AdminSite** class. For example, to add a new view that renders a page showing the health of the different IT systems inside the organization, we can create a new view function named **system_ health_dashboard()** inside our custom **AdminSite** class implementation, as shown in the following code snippet:

```
class SysAdminSite(admin.AdminSite):
    def system_health_dashboard(self, request):
        # View function logic
```

Inside the view function, we can perform any operations we want in order to generate a view and finally use that response to render a template. Inside this view function, there are some important pieces of logic we need to make sure are implemented correctly.

The first one is to set the **current_app** property for the **request** field inside the view function. This is required in order to allow Django's URL resolver inside the templates to correctly resolve the view functions for an application. To set this value inside the custom view function we just created, we need to set the **current_app** property as shown in the following code snippet:

```
request.current_app = self.name
```

The **self.name** field is automatically populated by Django's **AdminSite** class and we don't need to initialize it explicitly. With this, our minimal custom view implementation will appear as shown in the following code snippet:

```
class SysAdminSite(admin.AdminSite):
    def system_health_dashboard(self, request):
        request.current_app = self.name
        # View function logic
```

ACCESSING COMMON TEMPLATE VARIABLES

When creating a custom view function, we might want access to the common template variables, such as **site_header** and **site_title**, in order to render them correctly in the template associated with our view function. As it turns out, this is quite easy to achieve with the use of the **each_context()** method provided by the **AdminSite** class.

The **each_context()** method of the **AdminSite** class takes a single parameter, **request**, which is the current request context, and returns the template variables that are to be inserted in all the admin site templates.

For example, if we wanted to access the template variables inside our custom view function, we could implement code similar to the following code snippet:

```
def system_health_dashboard(self, request):
    request.current_app = self.name
    context = self.each_context(request)
    # view function logic
```

The value returned by the **each_context()** method is a dictionary containing the name of the variable and the associated value.

MAPPING URLS FOR THE CUSTOM VIEW

Once the view function is defined, the next step involves mapping this view function to a URL such that a user can access it or allow the other views to link to it. For the views defined inside **AdminSite**, this URL mapping to views is controlled by the **get_urls()** method implemented by the **AdminSite** class. The **get_urls()** method returns the **urlpatterns** list that maps to the **AdminSite** views.

If we would like to add a URL mapping for our custom view, the preferred approach includes overriding the implementation of **get_urls()** in our custom **AdminSite** class and adding the URL mapping there. This approach is demonstrated in the following code snippet:

```
class SysAdminSite(admin.AdminSite):
    def get_urls(self):
        base_urls = super().get_urls(). # Get the existing set of URLs
        # Define our URL patterns for custom views
        urlpatterns = [path("health_dashboard/"),\
                        (self.system_health_dashboard)]
        # Return the updated mapping
        return base_urls + urlpatterns.
```

The **get_urls()** method is generally called automatically by Django and there is no need to perform any manual processing on it.

Once this is done, the last step involves making sure that our custom admin view is only accessible through the admin site and non-admin users should not be able to access it. Let's take a look at how that can be achieved.

RESTRICTING CUSTOM VIEWS TO THE ADMIN SITE

If you followed all the previous sections thoroughly, you would now have a custom **AdminSite** view ready for use. However, there is a small glitch. This view is also directly accessible to any user who is not on the admin site.

To ensure that such a situation does not arise, we need to restrict this view to the admin site. This can be achieved quite simply by wrapping our URL path inside the **admin_view()** call, as shown in the following code snippet:

```
urlpatterns = [self.admin_view\
               (path("health_dashboard/"),\
               (self.system_health_dashboard))]
```

The **admin_view** function makes sure the path provided to it is restricted just to the admin dashboard and that no non-admin-privilege user can access it.

Now, let's add a new custom view to our admin site.

EXERCISE 10.04: ADDING CUSTOM VIEWS TO THE ADMIN SITE

In this exercise, you will add a custom view to the admin site, which will render a user profile and will show the user the options to modify their email or add a new profile picture. To build this custom view, follow the steps described:

1. Open the **admin.py** file under the **bookr_admin** directory and add the following imports. These will be required to build our custom view inside the admin site application:

```
from django.template.response import TemplateResponse
from django.urls import path
```

2. Open the **admin.py** file under the **bookr_admin** directory and create a new method named **profile_view**, which takes in a **request** variable as its parameter, inside the **BookrAdmin** class:

```
def profile_view(self, request):
```

Next, inside the method, get the name of the current application and set that in the **request** context. For this, you can use the **name** property of the class, which is auto-populated by Django. To get this property and set it in your **request** context, you need to add the following line:

```
request.current_app = self.name
```

Once you have the application name populated to the request context, the next step is to fetch the template variables, which are required to render the contents, such as **site_title**, **site_header**, and more, in the admin templates. For this, leverage the **each_context()** method of the **AdminSite** class, which provides the dictionary of the admin site template variables from the class:

```
context = self.each_context(request)
```

Once you have the data in place, the last step is to return a **TemplateResponse** object, which will render the custom profile template when someone visits the URL endpoint mapped to your custom view:

```
return TemplateResponse(request, "admin/admin_profile.html", \
                        context)
```

3. With the view function now created, the next step is to make **AdminSite** return the URLs mapping the view to a path inside **AdminSite**. To do this, you need to create a new method with the name **get_urls()**, which overrides the **AdminSite.get_urls()** method and returns the mapping of your new view. This can be done by first creating a new method named **get_urls()** inside the **BookrAdmin** class you have created for your custom admin site:

```
def get_urls(self):
```

Inside this method, the first thing you need to do is to get the list of the URLs that are already mapped to the admin endpoint. This is a required step, otherwise, your custom admin site will not be able to load any results associated with the model editing pages, logout page, and so on, in case this mapping is lost. To get this mapping, call the **get_urls()** method of the base class from which the **BookrAdmin** class is derived:

```
urls = super().get_urls()
```

Once the URLs from the base class are captured, the next step is to create a list of URLs that map our custom view to a URL endpoint in the admin site. For this, we create a new list named **url_patterns** and map our **profile_view** method to the **admin_profile** endpoint. To do this, we use the **path** utility function from Django, which allows us to map the view function with a string-based API endpoint path:

```
url_patterns = [path("admin_profile", self.profile_view)]
return urls + url_patterns
```

Save the **admin.py** file. It should look like this: http://packt.live/38Jlyvz.

4. Now, with the **BookrAdmin** class configured for the new view, the next step is to create your template for the admin profile page. For this, create a new file named **admin_profile.html** under the **templates/admin** directory of your project root. Inside this file, first, add an **extend** tag to make sure that you are extending from the default **admin** template:

```
{% extends "admin/index.html" %}
```

This step ensures that all of your admin template style sheets and HTML are available for use inside your custom view template. For example, without having this **extend** tag, your custom view will not show any specific content already mapped to your admin site, such as **site_header**, **site_title**, or any links to log out or go to another page.

Once the extend tag is added, add a **block** tag and provide it with the value of content. This makes sure that the code you add between the pair of **{% block content %}**...**{% endblock %}** segments overrides whatever value is present in the **index.html** template that comes pre-packaged with the Django admin module:

```
{% block content %}
```

Inside the **block** tag, add the HTML required to render the profile view that was created in *step 2* of this exercise:

```
<p>Welcome to your profile, {{ username }}</p>
<p>You can do the following operations</p>
<ul>
    <li><a href="#">Change E-Mail Address</a></li>
    <li><a href="#">Add Profile Picture</a></li>
</ul>
{% endblock %}
```

The file should look like this: http://packt.live/2MZhU8d.

5. Now, with the preceding steps complete, reload your application server by running **python manage.py runserver localhost:8000** and then visiting **http://localhost:8000/admin/admin_profile**.

When the page opens, you can expect to see something like the following screenshot:

Figure 10.7: Profile page view in the administration site

> **NOTE**
>
> The view created so far will render just fine irrespective of whether the user is logged into the admin application.

To make sure that this view is only accessible to the logged-in admins, you need to make a small modification inside your **get_urls()** method, which you defined in *step 3* of this exercise.

Inside the **get_urls()** method, modify the **url_patterns** list to look something like the one shown here:

```
url_patterns = [path("admin_profile", \
                self.admin_view(self.profile_view)),]
```

In the preceding code, you wrapped your **profile_view** method inside the **admin_view()** method.

The **AdminSite.admin_view()** method causes the view to be restricted to those users who are logged in. If a user who is currently not logged into the admin site tries to visit the URL directly, they will get redirected to the login page, and only in the event of a successful login will they be allowed to see the contents of our custom page.

During this exercise, we leveraged our existing understanding of writing views for Django applications and merged it with the context of the **AdminSite** class to build a custom view for our admin dashboard. With this knowledge, we can now move on and add useful functionalities to our Django admin to supercharge its usefulness.

PASSING ADDITIONAL KEYS TO THE TEMPLATES USING TEMPLATE VARIABLES

Inside the admin site, the variable values passed to the templates are passed through the use of template variables. These template variables are prepared and returned by the **AdminSite.each_context()** method.

Now, if there is a value that you would like to pass to all the templates of your admin site, you can override the **AdminSite.each_context()** method and add the required fields to the **request** context. Let's look at an example to see how we can achieve this outcome.

Consider the **username** field, which we passed to our **admin_profile** template earlier. If we want to pass it to every template inside our custom admin site, we first need to override the **each_context()** method inside our **BookrAdmin** class, as shown here:

```
def each_context(self, request):
    context = super().each_context(request)
    context['username'] = request.user.username
    return context
```

The **each_context()** method takes a single argument (we're not considering self here) of the **HTTPRequest** type, which it uses to evaluate certain other values.

Now, inside our overridden **each_context()** method, we first make a call to the base class **each_context()** method so as to retrieve the **context** dictionary for the admin site:

```
context = super().each_context(request)
```

Once that is done, the next thing we do is to add our **username** field to the **context** and set its value to the value of the **request.user.username** field:

```
context['username'] = request.user.username
```

Once this is done, the last thing that remains is to return this modified context.

Now, whenever a template is rendered by our custom admin site, the template will be passed with this additional username variable.

ACTIVITY 10.01: BUILDING A CUSTOM ADMIN DASHBOARD WITH BUILT-IN SEARCH

In this activity, you will use the knowledge you gained about the different aspects of creating a custom admin site to build a custom admin dashboard for Bookr. Inside this dashboard, you will introduce the capability of allowing a user to search the books by using either the name of the book or by using the name of the book publisher and allowing the user to modify or delete these book records.

The following steps will help you build a custom admin dashboard and add the ability to search a book record by using the name of the publisher:

1. Create a new application inside the Bookr project named **bookr_admin**, if not created already. This is going to store the logic for our custom admin site.

2. Inside the **admin.py** file under the **bookr_admin** directory, create a new class, **BookrAdmin**, which inherits from the **AdminSite** class of Django's admin module.

3. Inside the newly created **BookrAdmin** class in *step 2*, add any customizations for the site title or any other branding component of the admin dashboard.

4. Inside the **apps.py** file under the **bookr_admin** directory, create a new **BookrAdminConfig** class, and inside this new **BookrAdminConfig** class, set the default site attribute to the fully qualified module name for our custom admin site class, **BookrAdmin**.

5. Inside the **settings.py** file of your Django project, add the fully qualified path of the **BookrAdminConfig** class created in *step 4* as the first installed application.

6. To register the **Books** model from the **reviews** application inside Bookr, open the **admin.py** file inside the reviews directory and make sure that the Books model is registered to the admin site by using **admin.site.register(ModelClass)**.

7. To allow a search of the book according to the name of the publisher, inside the **admin.py** file of the **reviews** application, modify the **BookAdmin** class and add to it a property named **search_fields**, which contains **publisher_name** as a field.

8. To get the publisher's name correctly for the **search_fields** property, introduce a new method named **get_publisher** inside the **BookAdmin** class, which will return the name field of the publisher from the **Book** model.

9. Make sure that the **BookAdmin** class is registered as a Model admin class for the Book model inside our Django admin dashboard by using **admin.site. register(Book, BookModel)**.

After completing this activity, once you start the application server and visit **http://localhost:8000/admin** and navigate to the Book model, you should be able to search for books by using the publisher's name and, in the event of a successful search, see a page that resembles the one shown in the following screenshot:

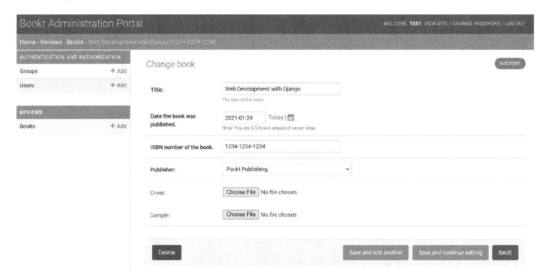

Figure 10.8: Book editing page inside the Bookr administration dashboard

NOTE

The solution to this activity can be found at http://packt.live/2Nh1NTJ.

SUMMARY

In this chapter, we looked at how Django allows the customization of its admin site. It does so by providing easy-to-use properties for some of the more general parts of the site, such as title fields, headings, and home links. Beyond this, we learned how to build a custom admin site by leveraging the concepts of object-oriented programming in Python and creating a child class of `AdminSite`.

This functionality was further enhanced by implementing a custom template for the logout page. We also learned how we can supercharge our admin dashboard by adding a new set of views to allow enhanced usage of the dashboard.

As we move on to the next chapter, we will build upon what we have learned so far by learning how to create our own custom tags and filters for templates. Furthermore, using class-based views, we will gain the ability to build our views in an object-oriented style.

11

ADVANCED TEMPLATING AND CLASS-BASED VIEWS

OVERVIEW

In this chapter, you will learn how to use Django's templating API to create custom template tags and filters. You will also write **class-based views** that will help you perform CRUD operations. By the end of this chapter, you will have a clear understanding of how Django handles advanced templating and how you can build custom views that support CRUD-based operations. You will be able to use classes to define views inside Django and be able to build custom tags and filters to complement the powerful templating engine provided by Django.

INTRODUCTION

In *Chapter 3, URL Mapping, Views, and Templates*, we learned how to build views and create templates in Django. Then, we learned how to use those views to render the templates we built. In this chapter, we will build upon our knowledge of developing views by using **class-based views**, which allow us to write views that can group logical methods into a single entity. This skill comes in handy when developing a view that maps to multiple HTTP request methods for the same **Application Programming Interface (API)** endpoint. With method-based views, we may end up using a lot of `if-else` conditions to successfully handle the different types of HTTP request methods. In contrast, class-based views allow us to define separate methods for every HTTP request method we want to handle. Then, based on the type of request received, Django takes care of calling the correct method in the class-based view.

Beyond the ability to build views based on different development techniques, Django also comes packed with a powerful templating engine. This engine allows developers to build reusable templates for their web applications. This reusability of the templating engine is further enhanced by using **template tags** and **filters**, which help easily implement commonly used features inside templates, features such as iterating over lists of data, formatting the data in a given style, extracting a piece of text from a variable to display, and overriding the content in a specific block of a template. All these features also expand the reusability of a Django template.

As we go through this chapter, we will look at how we can expand the default set of template filters and template tags provided by Django by leveraging Django's ability to define our own custom template tags and filters. These custom template tags and filters can then be used to implement some common features in a reusable fashion across our web application. For example, while building a user profile badge that can be shown in several places inside a web application, it is better to leverage the ability to write a custom template inclusion tag that just inserts the template of the badge in any of the views we desire, rather than rewriting the entire code for the badge template or by introducing additional complexity to the templates.

TEMPLATE FILTERS

While developing templates, developers often just want to change the value of a template variable before rendering it to the user. For example, consider that we are building a profile page for a Bookr user. There, we want to show the number of books the user has read. Below that, we also want to show a table listing the books they have read.

To achieve this, we can pass two separate variables from our view to the HTML template. One can be named **books_read**, which denotes the number of books read by the user. The other can be **book_list**, containing the list of names of the books read by the user, for example:

```
<span class="books_read">You have read {{ books_read }} books</span>
<ul>
{% for book in book_list %}
<li>{{ book }} </li>
{% endfor %}
</ul>
```

Or we can use **Template filters**. Template filters in Django are simple Python-based functions that accept a variable as an argument (and any additional data in the context of the variable), change its value as per our requirements, and then render the changed value.

Now, the same outcome from writing the previous snippet can also be obtained without the use of two separate variables by using template filters in Django, as follows:

```
<span class="books_read">You have read {{ book_list|length }}</span>
<ul>
{% for book in book_list %}
<li>{{ book }}</li>
{% endfor %}
</ul>
```

Here, we used the built-in **length** filter provided by Django. The use of this filter causes the length of the **book_list** variable to be evaluated and returned, which is then inserted into our HTML template during rendering.

Like **length**, there are a lot of other template filters that come pre-packaged with Django and that are ready to be used. For example, the **lowercase** filter converts the text to all lowercase format, the **last** filter can be used to return the last item in the list, and the **json_script** filter can be used to output a Python object passed to the template as a JSON value wrapped in a **<script>** tag in your template.

> **NOTE**
>
> You can refer to Django's official documentation for the complete list of template filters offered by Django: https://docs.djangoproject.com/en/3.1/ref/templates/builtins/.

CUSTOM TEMPLATE FILTERS

Django supplies a lot of useful filters that we can use in our templates while we are working on our projects. But what if someone wants to format a specific piece of text and render it with different fonts? Or say if someone wants to translate an error code to a user-friendly error message based on the mapping of the error code in the backend. In these cases, predefined filters do not suffice, and we would like to write our own filter that we can reuse across the project.

Luckily, Django supplies an easy-to-use API that we can use to write custom filters. This API provides developers with some useful decorator functions that can be used to quickly register a Python function as a custom template filter. Once a Python function is registered as a custom filter, a developer can start using the function in templates.

An instance of this **template** library method is required to access these filters. This instance can be created by instantiating the **Library()** class in Django from Django's **template** module, as shown here:

```
from django import template
register = template.Library()
```

Once the instance is created, we can now use the filter decorator from the template library instance to register our filters.

TEMPLATE FILTERS

To create custom template filters, there are a couple of steps we need to take. Let's try to understand what these steps are and how they help us with the creation of a custom template filter.

SETTING UP THE DIRECTORY FOR STORING TEMPLATE FILTERS

It is important to note that when creating a custom template filter or template tag, we need to put them in a directory named **templatetags** under the application directory. This requirement arises because Django is internally configured to look for custom template tags and filters when loading a web application. A failure to name the directory as **templatetags** will result in Django not loading the custom template filters and tags created by us.

To create this directory, first, navigate to the application folder inside which you want to create custom template filters, and then run the following command in the terminal:

```
mkdir templatetags
```

Once the directory is created, the next step is to create a new file inside the **templatetags** directory to store the code for our custom filters. This can be done by executing the following command inside the **templatetags** directory:

```
touch custom_filter.py
```

> **NOTE**
>
> The aforementioned command won't work on Windows. You can, however, navigate to the desired directory and create a new file using Windows Explorer.

Alternatively, this can be done by using the GUI interface provided by PyCharm.

SETTING UP THE TEMPLATE LIBRARY

Once the file for storing the code for the custom filter is created, we can now start working on implementing our custom filter code. For custom filters to work in Django, they need to be registered to Django's template library before they can be used inside templates. To that end, the first step is to set up an instance of the template library, which will be used to register our custom filters. For this, inside the **custom_filters.py** file we created in the previous section, we first need to import the template module from the Django project:

```
from django import template
```

Once the import is resolved, the next step is to create an instance of the template library by adding the following line of code:

```
register = template.Library()
```

The **Library** class from Django's template module is implemented as a **Singleton** class that returns the same object that is only initialized once at the start of the application.

Once the template library instance is set up, we are now good to proceed with implementing our custom filter.

IMPLEMENTING THE CUSTOM FILTER FUNCTION

Custom filters inside Django are nothing more than simple Python functions that essentially take the following parameters:

1. The value on which the filter is being applied (mandatory)

2. Any additional parameters (zero or more) that need to be passed to the filter (optional)

To behave as template filters, these functions need to be decorated with the **filter** attribute from Django's template library instance. For example, the generic implementation of a custom filter will look like the following:

```
@register.filter
def my_filter(value, arg):
    # Implementation logic of the filter
```

With this, we have learned the basics of how to implement custom filters. Before we head to our first exercise, let's quickly learn how to use them.

USING CUSTOM FILTERS INSIDE TEMPLATES

Once the filter is created, it's simple to start using it inside our templates. To do that, the filter first needs to be imported into the template. This can be easily done by adding the following line to the top of the template file:

```
{% load custom_filter %}
```

When Django's templating engine is parsing the template files, the preceding line is automatically resolved by Django to find the correct module specified under the **templatetags** directory. Consequently, all the filters mentioned inside the **custom_filter** module are automatically made available inside the template.

Using our custom filter inside the template is as simple as adding the following line:

```
{{ some_value|generic_filter:"arg" }}
```

Equipped with this knowledge, let's now create our first custom filter.

EXERCISE 11.01: CREATING A CUSTOM TEMPLATE FILTER

In this exercise, you will write a custom filter named **explode**, which, when provided with a string and a user-supplied separator, returns a list of strings. For example, consider the following string:

```
names = "john,doe,mark,swain"
```

You will apply the following filter to this string:

```
{{ names|explode:"," }}
```

The output after applying this filter should be as follows:

```
["john", "doe", "mark", "swain"]
```

1. Create a new application inside the **bookr** project that you can use for demo purposes:

```
python manage.py startapp filter_demo
```

The preceding command will set up a new application inside your Django project.

2. Now, create a new directory named **templatetags** inside your **filter_demo** application directory to store the code for your custom template filters. To create the directory, run the following command from inside the **filter_demo** directory from the terminal app or command prompt:

```
mkdir templatetags
```

3. Once the directory is created, create a new file named **explode_filter.py** inside the **templatetags** directory.

4. Open the file and add the following lines to it:

```
from django import template

register = template.Library()
```

The preceding code creates an instance of the Django library that can be used to register our custom filter with Django.

5. Add the following code to implement the **explode** filter:

```
@register.filter
def explode(value, separator):
    return value.split(separator)
```

The **explode** filter takes two arguments; one is **value** on which the filter was used, and the second is **separator** passed from the template to the filter. The filter will use this separator to convert the string into a list.

6. With the custom filter ready, create a template where this filter can be applied. For this, first, create a new folder named **templates** under the **filter_demo** directory and then create a new file named **index.html** inside it with the following contents:

```
<html>
<head>
  <title>Custom Filter Example</title>
<body>
{% load explode_filter %}

{{ names|explode:"," }}
</body>
</html>
```

In the first line, Django's template engine loads the custom filter from the **explode_filter** module so that it can be used inside the templates. To achieve this, Django will look for the **explode_filter** module under the **templatetags** directory and if, found, will load it for use.

In the next line, you pass the **names** variable passed to the template and apply the **explode** filter to it, while also passing in the comma "**,**" as a separator value to the filter.

7. Now, with the template created, the next thing is to create a Django view that can render this template and pass the **name** variable to the template. For this, open the **views.py** file and add the following highlighted code:

```
from django.shortcuts import render


def index(request):
    names = "john,doe,mark,swain"
    return render(request, "index.html", {'names': names})
```

The preceding code snippet performs some basic operations. It first imports the **render** helper from the **django.shortcuts** module, which helps render the templates. Once the import is complete, it defines a new view function named **index()**, which renders **index.html**.

8. Now map the view to a URL that can then be used to render the results in the browser. To do this, create a new file named **urls.py** inside the **filter_demo** directory and add the following code to it:

```
from django.urls import path
from . import views


urlpatterns = [path('', views.index, name='index')]
```

9. Add the **filter_demo** application to the project URL mapping. To do this, open **urls.py** in the **bookr** project directory and add the following highlighted line inside **urlpatterns**:

```
urlpatterns = [path('filter_demo/', include('filter_demo.urls')),\
    ....]
```

10. Finally, add the application under the **INSTALLED_APPS** section under **settings.py** of the **bookr** project:

```
INSTALLED_APPS = [....,\
                    'filter_demo']
```

This requirement arises due to the security guidelines implemented by Django, which require that the application implementing custom filters/tags needs to be added to the **INSTALLED_APPS** section.

11. To view whether the custom filter works, run the following command:

```
python manage.py runserver localhost:8000
```

Now, navigate to the following page in your browser: **http://localhost:8000/filter_demo** (or **127.0.0.1** instead of **localhost**).

This page should appear as shown in *Figure 11.1*:

['john', 'doe', 'mark', 'swain']

Figure 11.1: Index page displayed by using the explode filter

With this, we saw how we can quickly create a custom filter inside Django and then use it in our templates. Now, let's take a look at another type of filter, namely, string filters, which work solely on string type values.

STRING FILTERS

In *Exercise 11.01, Creating a Custom Template Filter*, we built a custom filter, which allowed us to split a provided string with a separator and generate a list from it. This filter can take any kind of variable and split it as a list of values based on a delimiter provided. But what if we wanted to restrict our filter to work only with strings and not with any other type of values, such as integers?

To develop filters that work only on *strings*, we can use the **stringfilter** decorator provided by Django's template library. When the **stringfilter** decorator is used to register a Python method as a filter in Django, the framework ensures that the value being passed to the filter is converted to a string before the filter executes. This reduces any potential issues that may arise when non-string values are passed to our filter.

The steps to implement a **String Filter** are similar to the ones we followed for building a custom filter, with some minor changes. Remember the `custom_filter.py` file we created in the *Setting Up the Directory for Storing Template Filters* section? We can add a new Python function inside it that will act as our string filter.

Before we can implement a string filter though, we first need to import the `stringfilter` decorator, which demarcates a custom filter function as a string filter. We can add this decorator by adding the following **import** statement inside the `custom_filters.py` file:

```
from django.template.defaultfilters import stringfilter
```

Now, to implement our custom string filter, the following syntax can be used:

```
@register.filter
@stringfilter
def generic_string_filter(value, arg):
    # Logic for string filter implementation
```

With this approach, we can build as many string filters as we want and use them just like any other filter.

TEMPLATE TAGS

Template tags are a powerful feature of Django's templating engine. They allow developers to build powerful templates by generating HTML through the evaluation of certain conditions and help avoid the repetitive writing of common code.

One example where we may use template tags is the sign up/login options in the navigation bar of a website. In this case, we can use template tags to evaluate whether the visitor on the current page is logged in. Based on that, we can render either a profile banner or a sign up/login banner.

Tags are also a common occurrence while developing templates. For example, consider the following line of code, which we used to import the custom filters inside our templates in *Exercise 11.01, Creating a Custom Template Filter*:

```
{% load explode_filter %}
```

This uses a template tag known as **load,** which is responsible for loading the **explode** filter into the template. Template tags are much more powerful compared to filters. While filters have access only to the values they are operating on, template tags have access to the context of the whole template and hence they can be used to build a lot of complex functionalities inside a template.

Let's look at the different types of template tags that are supported by Django and how we can build our own custom template tags.

TYPES OF TEMPLATE TAGS

Django majorly supports two types of template tags:

- **Simple tags**: These are the tags that operate on the variable data provided (and any additional variables to them) and render in the same template they have been called in. For example, one such use case can include the rendering of a custom welcome message to the user based on their username or displaying the last login time of the user based on their username.

- **Inclusion tags**: These tags take in the provided data variables and generate an output by rendering another template. For example, the tag can take in a list of objects and iterate over them to generate an HTML list.

In the next sections, we will take a look at how we can create these different types of tags and use them in our application.

SIMPLE TAGS

Simple tags provide a way for developers to build template tags that take in one or more variables from the template, process them, and return a response. The response returned from the template tag is used to replace the template tag definition provided inside the HTML template. These kinds of tags can be used to build several useful functionalities, for example, the parsing of dates, or displaying any active alerts, if there are any, that we want to show to the user.

The simple tags can be created easily using the **simple_tag** decorator provided by the template library, by decorating the Python method that should act as a template tag. Now, let us look at how we can implement a custom simple tag using Django's template library.

HOW TO CREATE A SIMPLE TEMPLATE TAG

Creating simple template tags follows the same conventions we discussed in the *Custom Template Filters* section, with some subtle differences. Let us go over the process of understanding how template tags can be created for use in our Django templates.

SETTING UP THE DIRECTORY

Just like custom filters, custom template tags also need to be created inside the same **templatetags** directory to make them discoverable by Django's templating engine. The directory can be created either directly using the PyCharm GUI or by running the following command inside the application directory where we want to create our custom tags:

```
mkdir templatetags
```

Once this is done, we can now create a new file that will store the code for our custom template tags by using the following command:

```
touch custom_tags.py
```

> **NOTE**
>
> The aforementioned command won't work on Windows. You can, however, create a new file using Windows Explorer.

SETTING UP THE TEMPLATE LIBRARY

Once the directory structure is set up and we have a file in place for keeping the code for our custom template tags, we can now proceed and start creating our template tags. But before that, we need to set up an instance of Django's template library as we did earlier. This can be done by adding the following lines of code to our **custom_tag.py** file:

```
from django import template
register = template.Library()
```

Like custom filters, the template library instance is used here to register the custom template tags for use inside Django templates.

IMPLEMENTING A SIMPLE TEMPLATE TAG

Simple template tags inside Django are Python functions that can take any number of arguments as desired by us. These Python functions need to be decorated with the **simple_tag** decorator from the template library such that those functions are registered as simple template tags. The following snippet of code shows how a simple template tag is implemented:

```
@register.simple_tag
def generic_simple_tag(arg1, arg2):
    # Logic to implement a generic simple tag
```

USING SIMPLE TAGS INSIDE TEMPLATES

Using simple tags inside Django templates is quite easy. Inside the template file, we need to first make sure that we have the tag imported inside the template by adding the following to the top of the template file:

```
{% load custom_tag %}
```

The preceding statement will load all the tags from the **custom_tag.py** file we defined earlier and make them available inside our template. Then we can use our custom simple tag by adding the following command:

```
{% custom_simple_tag "argument1" "argument2" %}
```

Now, let's put this knowledge into practice and create our first custom simple tag.

EXERCISE 11.02: CREATING A CUSTOM SIMPLE TAG

In this exercise, you will create a simple tag that will take in two arguments: the first one will be a greeting message, and the second will be the name of the user. This tag will print a formatted greeting message:

1. Following up on the example shown in *Exercise 11.01, Creating a Custom Template Filter*, let us re-use the same directory structure to store the code for the simple tag inside. So, first, create a new file named **simple_tag.py** under the **filter_demo/template_tags** directory. Inside this file, add the following code:

```
from django import template


register = template.Library()
```

```
@register.simple_tag
def greet_user(message, username):
    return\
    "{greeting_message},\
    {user}!!!".format(greeting_message=message, user=username)
```

In this case, you create a new Python method, **greet_user()**, which takes in two arguments, **message**, the message to use for the greeting, and **username**, the name of the user who should be greeted. This method is then decorated with **@register.simple_tag**, which indicates that this method is a simple tag and can be used as a template tag in the templates.

2. Now, create a new template that will use your simple tag. For this, create a new file named **simple_tag_template.html** under the **filter_demo/ templates** directory and add the following code to it:

```
<html>
<head>
<title>Simple Tag Template Example</title>
</head>
<body>
{% load simple_tag %}
{% greet_user "Hey there" username %}
</body>
</html>
```

In the preceding code snippet, you just created a bare-bones HTML page that will use your custom simple tag. The semantics of loading a custom template tag is similar to that of loading a custom template filter and requires the use of a **{% load %}** tag in the template. The process will look for the **simple_tag.py** module under the **templatetags** directory and, if found, will load the tags that have been defined under the module.

The following line shows how you can use the custom template tag:

```
{% greet_user "Hey there" username %}
```

In this, you first used Django's tag specifier, **{% %}**, and inside it, the first argument you passed is the name of the tag that needs to be used, followed by the first argument, **Hey there**, which is the greeting message, and the second argument, **username**, which will be passed to the template from the view function.

3. With the template created, the next step involves creating a view that will render your template. For this, add the following code under the **views.py** file under the **filter_demo** directory:

```
def greeting_view(request):
    return render(request),\
                ('simple_tag_template.html', {'username': 'jdoe'})
```

In the preceding code snippet, you created a simple function-based view, which will render your **simple_tag_template** defined in *step 2* and pass the value **'jdoe'** to the variable called **username**.

4. With the view created, the next step is to map it to a URL endpoint in your application. To do this, open the **urls.py** file under the **filter_demo** directory and add the following inside the **urlpatterns** list:

```
path('greet', views.greeting_view, name='greeting')
```

With this, **greeting_view** is now mapped to the URL endpoint **/greet** for your **filter_demo** application.

5. To see the custom tag in action, start your web server by running the following command:

```
python manage.py runserver localhost:8000
```

After visiting **http://localhost:8000/filter_demo/greet** in the browser (or **127.0.0.1** instead of **localhost**), you should see the following page:

Hey there, jdoe!!!

Figure 11.2: Greeting message generated with the help of the custom simple tag

With this, we have created our first custom template tag and used it successfully to render our template, as shown in *Figure 11.2*. Now, let's look at another important aspect of simple tags, which is associated with passing the context variables available in the template to the template tag.

PASSING THE TEMPLATE CONTEXT IN A CUSTOM TEMPLATE TAG

In the previous exercise, we created a simple tag to which we passed two arguments, namely, the greeting message and the username. But what if we wanted to pass a large number of variables to the tag? Or simply, what if we did not want to pass the username of the user explicitly to the tag?

There are times when developers would like to have access to all the variables and data that is present in the template to be available inside the custom tag. Fortunately for us, this is easy to implement.

Using our previous example of the **greet_user** tag, let's create a new tag named **contextual_greet_user** and see how we can pass the data available in the template directly to the tag instead of passing it manually as an argument.

The first modification we need to make is to modify our decorator to look like the following:

```
@register.simple_tag(takes_context=True)
```

With this, we tell Django that when our **contextual_greet_user** tag is used, Django should also pass it the template context, which has all the data that is passed from the view to the template. With this addition done, the next thing we need to do is to change our **contextual_greet_user** implementation to accept the added context as an argument. The following code shows the modified form of the **contextual_greet_user** tag, which uses our template context to render a greeting message:

```
@register.simple_tag(takes_context=True)
def contextual_greet_user(context, message):
    username = context['username']
    return "{greeting_message},\
            {user}".format(greeting_message=message, user=username)
```

In the preceding code example, we can see how the **contextual_greet_user()** method was modified to accept the passed context as the first argument, followed by the greeting message passed by the user.

To leverage this modified template tag, all we need to do is to change our call to the **contextual_greet_user** tag inside **simple_tag_template.html** under **filter_demo** to look like this:

```
{% contextual_greet_user "Hey there" %}
```

Then, when we reload our Django web application, the output at **http://localhost:8000/filter_demo/greet** should look similar to what was shown in *step 5* of *Exercise 11.02, Creating a Custom Simple Tag*.

With this, we got to know how we can build a simple tag and handle passing the template context to the tag. Now, let us look at how we can build an inclusion tag that can be used to render data in a certain format as described by another template.

INCLUSION TAGS

Simple tags allow us to build tags that accept one or more input variables, do some processing on them, and return an output. This output is then inserted at the place where the simple tag was used.

But what if we wanted to build tags that, instead of returning text output, return an HTML template, which can then be used to render the parts of the page. For example, a lot of web applications allow users to add custom widgets to their profiles. These individual widgets can be built as an inclusion tag and rendered over independently. This kind of approach keeps the code for the base page template and the individual templates separate and hence allows for easy reuse as well as refactoring.

Developing custom inclusion tags is a similar process to how we develop our simple tags. This involves the use of the **inclusion_tag** decorator provided by the template library. So, let's take a look at how we can do it.

IMPLEMENTING INCLUSION TAGS

Inclusion tags are those tags that are used for rendering a template as a response to their usage inside a template. These tags can be implemented in a similar manner to how other custom template tags are implemented, with some minor modifications.

Inclusion tags are also simple Python functions that can take multiple parameters, where each parameter maps to an argument passed from the template where the tag was called. These tags are decorated using the **inclusion_tag** decorator from Django's template library. The **inclusion_tag** decorator takes a single parameter, the name of the template, which should be rendered as a response to the processing of the inclusion tag.

A generic implementation of an inclusion tag will look like the one shown in the following code snippet:

```
@register.inclusion_tag('template_file.html')
def my_inclusion_tag(arg):
    # logic for processing
    return {'key1': 'value1'}
```

Notice the return value in this case. An inclusion tag is supposed to return a dictionary of values that will be used to render the **template_file.html** file specified as an argument in the **inclusion_tag** decorator.

USING AN INCLUSION TAG INSIDE A TEMPLATE

An inclusion tag can easily be used inside a template file. This can be done by first importing the tag as follows:

```
{% load custom_tags %}
```

And then by using the tag like any other tag:

```
{% my_inclusion_tag "argument1" %}
```

The response of the rendering of this tag will be a sub-template that will be rendered inside our primary template where the inclusion tag was used.

EXERCISE 11.03: BUILDING A CUSTOM INCLUSION TAG

In this exercise, we are going to build a custom **inclusion** tag, which will render the list of books read by a user:

1. For this exercise, you will continue to use the same demo folders as in earlier exercises. First, create a new file named **inclusion_tag.py** under the **filter_demo/templatetags** directory and write the following code inside it:

```
from django import template

register = template.Library()

@register.inclusion_tag('book_list.html')
def book_list(books):
    book_list = [book_name for book_name, \
                 book_author in books.items()]
    return {'book_list': book_list}
```

The @**register.inclusion_tag** decorator is used to mark the method as a custom inclusion tag. This decorator takes the name of the template as an argument that should be used to render the data returned by the tag function.

After the decorator, you define a function that implements the logic of your custom inclusion tag. This function takes a single argument called **books**. This argument will be passed from the template file and will contain a list of books that the reader has read (in the form of a **Python** dictionary). Inside the definition, you convert the dictionary into a Pythonic list of book names. The key in the dictionary is mapped to the name of the book and the value is mapped to the author:

```
books_list = [book_name for book_name, \
              book_author in books.items()]
```

Once the list is formed, the following code returns the list as a context for the template passed to the inclusion tag (in this example, **book_list.html**):

```
return {'book_list': books_list}
```

The value returned by this method will be passed by Django to the **book_list. html** template and the contents will then be rendered.

2. Next, create the actual template, which will contain the rendering structure for the template tag. For this, create a new template file, **book_list.html**, under the **filter_demo/templates** directory, and add the following content to it:

```
<ul>
   {% for book in book_list %}
<li>{{ book }}</li>
   {% endfor %}
</ul>
```

Here, in the new template file, you created an unordered list that will hold the list of books a user has read. Next, using the **for** template tag, you iterate over the values within **book_list** that will be provided by the custom template function:

```
{% for book in book_list %}
```

This iteration results in the creation of several list items, as defined by the following:

```
<li>{{ book }}</li>
```

The list item is generated with the contents from **book_list**, which was passed to the template. The **for** tag executes as many times as the number of items present in **book_list**.

3. With the template defined for the **book_list** tag, modify the existing greeting template to make this tag available inside it and use it to show a list of books that the user has read. For this, modify the **simple_tag_template.html** file under the **filter_demo/templates** directory and change the code to look as follows:

```
<html>
<head>
  <title>Simple Tag Template Example</title>
</head>
<body>
{% load simple_tag inclusion_tag %}
{% greet_user "Hey" username %}
  <br />
  <span class="message">You have read the following books
    till date</span>
{% book_list books %}
</body>
</html>
```

In this snippet, the first thing you did was load the **inclusion_tag** module by writing the following:

```
{% load simple_tag inclusion_tag %}
```

Once the tag is loaded, you can now use it anywhere in the template. To use it, you added the **book_list** tag in the following format:

```
{% book_list books %}
```

This tag takes a single argument, which is a dictionary of the books, inside which the key is the book title and the value of the key is the author of the book. At this point, you can even customize the greeting message; in this step, we have gone with a simple "**Hey**" instead of "**Hey there**".

4. With the template now modified, the final step involves passing the required data to the template. To achieve this, modify **views.py** in the **filter_demo** directory and change the greeting view function to look like this:

```
def greeting_view(request):
    books = {"The night rider": "Ben Author",\
             "The Justice": "Don Abeman"}
    return render(request),\
                  ('simple_tag_template.html'),\
                  ({'username': 'jdoe', 'books': books})
```

Here, you modified the **greeting_view** function to add a dictionary of books and their authors and then you passed it to the **simple_tag_template** context.

5. With the preceding changes implemented, it's time to render the modified template. To do this, restart your Django application server by running the following command:

```
python manage.py runserver localhost:8080
```

Navigate to **http://localhost:8080/filter_demo/greet**, which should now render a page similar to the following screenshot:

Hey, jdoe!!!
You have read the following books till date

- The night rider
- The Justice

Figure 11.3: List of books read by a user when they visit the greeting endpoint

The page shows the list of books read by a user when they visit the greeting endpoint. The list you see on the page is rendered using inclusion tags. The template for listing these books is created separately first and then, using the inclusion tag, it is added to the page.

> **NOTE**
>
> Our work with the `filter_demo` app is complete. You can continue to customize this app further if you wish to practice the concepts you learned. Since the app was created solely to explain the concepts of custom template filters and template tags, and is unrelated to the `bookr` app we're building, you won't find it included in the `final/bookr` application folder on the GitHub repository.

With this, we now have the foundations on which we can build highly complex template filters or custom tags that can be helpful in the development of the projects we want to work on.

Now, let's revisit Django views and dive into a new territory of views called **Class-Based Views**. Provided by Django, these help us leverage the power of object-oriented programming and allow the re-use of code for the rendering of a view.

DJANGO VIEWS

To recall, a view in Django is a piece of Python code that allows a request to be taken in, performs an action based on the request, and then returns a response to the user, and hence forms an important part of our Django applications.

Inside Django, we have the option of building our views by following two different methodologies, one of which we have already seen in the preceding examples and is known as function-based views, while the other one, which we will be covering soon, is known as class-based views:

- **Function-Based Views** (**FBVs**): FBVs inside Django are nothing more than generic Python functions that are supposed to take an **HTTPRequest** type object as their first positional parameter and return an **HTTPResponse** type object, which corresponds to the action the view wants to perform once the request is processed by it. In the preceding exercise, `index()` and `greeting_view()` were examples of FBVs.

- **Class-Based Views (CBVs)**: CBVs are views that closely adhere to the Python object-oriented principles and allow mapping of the view calls in a class-based representation. These views are specialized in nature and a given type of CBV performs a specific operation. The benefits that CBVs provide include easy extensibility of the view and the re-use of code, which may turn out to be a complex task with FBVs.

Now, with the basic definitions clear, and with knowledge of FBVs already in our arsenal, let's look at CBVs and see what they have in store for us.

CLASS-BASED VIEWS

Django provides different ways in which developers can write views for their applications. One way is to map a Python function to act as a view function to create FBVs. Another way of creating views is to use Python object instances (which are based on top of Python classes). These are known as CBVs. An important question that arises is, what is the need for a CBV when we can already create views using the FBV approach?

The idea here, when creating FBVs, is that at times, we may be replicating the same logic again and again, for example, the processing of certain fields, or logic for handling certain request types. Although it is completely possible to create logically separate functions that handle a particular piece of logic, the task becomes difficult to manage as the complexity of the application increases.

This is where CBVs come in handy, where they abstract away implementation of the common repetitive code that we need to write to handle certain tasks, such as the rendering of templates. At the same time, they also make it easy to re-use pieces of code through the use of inheritance and mix-ins. For example, the following code snippet shows the implementation of a CBV:

```
from django.http import HttpResponse
from django.views import View


class IndexView(View):

    def get(self, request):
        return HttpResponse("Hey there!")
```

In the preceding example, we built a simple CBV by inheriting from the built-in view class, which is provided by Django.

Using these CBVs is also quite easy. For example, let's say we wanted to map **IndexView** to a URL endpoint in our application. In this case, all we need to do is to add the following line to our **urlpatterns** list inside the **urls.py** file of the application:

```
urlpatterns = [path('my_path', IndexView.as_view(), \
                     name='index_view')]
```

In this, as we can observe, we used the **as_view()** method of the CBV we created. Every CBV implements the **as_view()** method, which allows the view class to be mapped to a URL endpoint by returning the instance of the view controller from the view class.

Django provides a couple of built-in CBVs that provide the implementation of a lot of common tasks, such as how to render a template, or how to process a particular request. The built-in CBVs help to avoid the rewriting of code from scratch when handling basic functionality, thereby enabling the reusability of code. Some of these in-built views include the following:

- **View**: The base class for all CBVs available in Django that allows a custom CBV to be written with all the features provided and overridable. A user can implement their own definitions for different HTTP **Request** methods, such as **GET**, **POST**, **PUT**, and **DELETE**, and the view will automatically delegate the call to the method that is responsible for handling the request based on the type of request received.

- **TemplateView**: A view that can be used to render a template based on the parameters for the template data provided in the URL of the call. This allows developers to easily render a template without writing any logic related to how the rendering should be handled.

- **RedirectView**: A view that can be used to automatically redirect a user to the correct resource based on the request they have made.

- **DetailView**: A view that is mapped to a Django model and can be used to render the data obtained from the model using a template of choice.

The preceding views are just some of the built-in views that Django provides by default and we will cover more of them as we move through the chapter.

Now, to better understand how CBVs work inside Django, let's try to build our first CBV.

EXERCISE 11.04: CREATING A BOOK CATALOG USING A CBV

In this exercise, you will create a class-based form view that will help build a book catalog. This catalog will consist of the name of the book and the name of the author of the book.

> **NOTE**
>
> To understand the concept of class-based views, we will create a separate application inside Bookr with its own set of models and forms such that our existing code from previous exercises is not affected. Just like `filter_demo`, we won't be including this app in the `final/bookr` folder on our GitHub repo.

1. To get started, create a new application inside our **bookr** project and name it **book_management**. This can be done by simply running the following command:

```
python manage.py startapp book_management
```

2. Now, before building the book catalog, you first need to define a Django model that will help you store the records inside the database. To do this, open the **models.py** file under the **book_management** app you just created and define a new model named **Book**, as shown here:

```
from django.db import models


class Book(models.Model):
    name = models.CharField(max_length=255)
    author = models.CharField(max_length=50)
```

The model contains two fields, the name of the book and the name of the author. With the model in place, you'll need to migrate the model to your database such that you can start storing your data inside the database.

3. Once all the preceding steps are complete, add your book_management application to the **INSTALLED_APPS** list such that it can be discovered by Django and you can use your model properly. For this, open the **settings.py** file under the bookr directory and add the following code at the final position in the **INSTALLED_APPS** section:

```
INSTALLED_APPS = [...., \
                        'book_management']
```

4. Migrate your model to the database by running the following two commands. These will first create a Django migrations file and then create a table in your database:

```
python manage.py makemigrations
python manage.py migrate
```

5. Now, with the database model in place, let's create a new form that we will use to capture information about the books, such as the book title, author, and ISBN. For this, create a new file named **forms.py** under the **book_management** directory and add the following code inside it:

```
from django import forms


from .models import Book



class BookForm(forms.ModelForm):
    class Meta:
        model = Book
        fields = ['name', 'author']
```

In the preceding code snippet, you first imported Django's forms module, which will allow you to easily create forms and will also provide the rendering capability for the form. The next line imports the model that will store the data for the form:

```
from django import forms
from .models import Book
```

In the next line, you created a new class named **BookForm**, which inherits from the **ModelForm**. This is nothing but a class that maps the fields of the model to the form. To successfully achieve this mapping between the model and the form, you defined a new subclass named **Meta** under the **BookForm** class and set the attribute model to point to the **Book** model and the attribute fields to the list of fields that you want to display in the form:

```
class Meta:
    model = Book
    fields = ['name', 'author']
```

This allows for **ModelForm** to render the correct form HTML when expected to do so. The **ModelForm** class provides a built-in **Form.save()** method, which, when used, writes the data in the form to the database, and so helps avoid having to write redundant code.

6. Now that you have both your model and the form ready, go ahead and implement a view that will render the form and accept input from the user. For this, open **views.py** under the book_management directory and add the following lines of code to the file:

```
from django.http import HttpResponse
from django.views.generic.edit import FormView
from django.views import View

from .forms import BookForm

class BookRecordFormView(FormView):
    template_name = 'book_form.html'
    form_class = BookForm
    success_url = '/book_management/entry_success'

    def form_valid(self, form):
        form.save()
        return super().form_valid(form)


class FormSuccessView(View):
    def get(self, request, *args, **kwargs):
        return HttpResponse("Book record saved successfully")
```

In the preceding code snippet, you created two major views, one being **BookRecordFormView**, which is also responsible for rendering the book catalog entry form, and the other being **FormSuccessView**, which you will use to render the success message if the form data is saved successfully. Let's now look at both the views individually and understand what we are doing.

First, you created a new view named the **BookRecordFormView** CBV, which inherits from **FormView**:

```
class BookRecordFormView(FormView)
```

The **FormView** class allows you to easily create views that deal with forms. To this class, you need to provide certain parameters, such as the name of the template it will render to show the form, the form class that it should use to render the form, and the success URL to redirect to when the form is processed successfully:

```
template_name = 'book_form.html'
form_class = BookForm
success_url = '/book_management/entry_success'
```

The **FormView** class also provides a **form_valid()** method, which is called when the form successfully finishes the validation. Inside the **form_valid()** method, we can decide what we want to do. For our use case, when the form validation completes successfully, we first call the **form.save()** method, which persists the data for our form into the database, and then call the base class **form_valid()** method, which will cause the form view to redirect to the successful URL if form validation was a success:

```
def form_valid(self, form):
    form.save()
    return super().form_valid(form)
```

> **NOTE**
>
> The **form_valid()** method should always return an
> **HttpResponse** object.

This completes the implementation of **BookRecordFormView**. The next thing we have to do is to build a view named **FormSuccessView**, which we will use to render the success message once the data is saved successfully for the book record form we just created. This is done by creating a new view class named **FormSuccessView**, which inherits from the view base class of Django CBVs:

```
class FormSuccessView(View)
```

Inside this class, we override the **get()** method, which will be rendered when the form is saved successfully. Inside the **get()** method, we render a simple success message by returning a new **HttpResponse**:

```
def get(self, request, *args, **kwargs):
    return HttpResponse("Book record saved successfully")
```

7. Now, create a template that will be used to render the form. For this, create a new **templates** folder under the **book_management** directory and create a new file named **book_form.html**. Add the following lines of code inside the file:

```html
<html>
  <head>
    <title>Book Record Insertion</title>
  </head>
  <body>
    <form method="POST">
      {% csrf_token %}
      {{ form.as_p }}
      <input type="submit" value="Save record" />
    </form>
  </body>
</html>
```

Inside this code snippet, two important things need to be discussed.

The first is the use of the **{% csrf_token %}** tag. This tag is inserted to prevent the form from running into **Cross-Site Request Forgery** (**CSRF**) attacks. The **csrf_token** tag is one of the built-in template tags provided by Django to avoid such attacks. It does so by generating a unique token for every form instance that is rendered.

The second is the use of the **{{ form.as_p }}** template variable. The data for this variable is provided by our **FormView**-based view automatically. The **as_p** call causes the form fields to be rendered inside the **<p></p>** tags.

8. With the CBVs now built, go ahead and map them to URLs, such that you can start using them to add new book records. To do this, create a new file named **urls.py** under the book_management directory and add the following code to it:

```
from django.urls import path

from .views import BookRecordFormView, FormSuccessView

urlpatterns = [path('new_book_record',\
        BookRecordFormView.as_view(),\
        name='book_record_form'),\
        path('entry_success', FormSuccessView.as_view()),\
        (name='form_success')]
```

Most parts of the preceding snippet are similar to the ones that you have written earlier, but there is one thing different in the way we map our CBVs under the URL patterns. When using CBVs, instead of directly adding the function name, we use the class name and use its **as_view** method, which maps the class object to the view. For example, to map **BookRecordFormView** as a view, we will use **BookRecordFormView.as_view()**.

9. With the URLs added to our **urls.py** file, the next thing is to add our application URL mapping to our **bookr** project. To do this, open the **urls.py** file under the **bookr** application and add the following line to **urlpatterns**:

```
urlpatterns = [path('book_management/',\
        include('book_management.urls')),\
        ....]
```

10. Now, start your development server by running the following command:

```
python manage.py runserver localhost:8080
```

Then, visit **http://localhost:8080/book_management/new_book_record** (or **127.0.0.1** instead of **localhost**.)

If everything works fine, you will see a page as shown here:

Figure 11.4: View for adding a new book to the database

Upon clicking **Save record**, your record will be written to the database and the following page will show up:

Figure 11.5: Template rendered when the record is successfully inserted

With this, we have created our own CBV, which allows us to save records for new books. With our knowledge of CBVs in tow, let's now take a look at how we can perform Create, Read, Update, Delete (CRUD) operations with the help of CBVs.

CRUD OPERATIONS WITH CBVS

While working with Django models, one of the most common patterns we run into involves the creation, reading, updating, and deletion of objects that are stored inside our database. The Django admin interface allows us to achieve these CRUD operations easily, but what if we wanted to build custom views to give us the same capability?

As it turns out, Django's CBVs allow us to achieve this quite easily. All we need to do is to write our custom CBVs and inherit from the built-in base classes provided by Django. Building on our existing example of book record management, let's see how we can build CRUD-based views in Django.

CREATE VIEW

To build a view that helps in object creation, we'll need to open the **view.py** file under the **book_management** directory and add the following lines of code to it:

```
from django.views.generic.edit import CreateView
from .models import Book


class BookCreateView(CreateView):
model = Book
    fields = ['name', 'author']
    template_name = 'book_form.html'
    success_url = '/book_management/entry_success'
```

With this, we have created our **CreateView** for the book resource. Before we can use it, we will need to map it to a URL. To do this, we can open the **urls.py** file under the book_management directory and add the following entry under the **urlpatterns** list:

```
urlpatterns = [....,\
                path('book_record_create'),\
                    (BookCreateView.as_view(), name='book_create')]
```

Now, when we visit **http://127.0.0.1:8000/book_management/book_record_create**, we will be greeted with the following page:

Figure 11.6: A view to insert a new book record based on Create view

This looks similar to the one that we got when using the Form view. On filling in the data and clicking **Save record**, Django will save the data to the database.

UPDATE VIEW

In this view, we want to update the data for a given record. To do this, we would need to open the **view.py** file under the **book_management** directory and add the following lines of code to it:

```
from django.views.generic.edit import UpdateView
from .models import Book


class BookUpdateView(UpdateView):
    model = Book
    fields = ['name', 'author']
    template_name = 'book_form.html'
    success_url = '/book_management/entry_success'
```

In the preceding code snippet, we have used the built-in **UpdateView** template, which allows us to update the stored records. The fields attribute here should take in the name of the fields that we would like to allow the user to update.

Once the view is created, the next step is to add the URL mapping. To do this, we can open the **urls.py** file under the **book_management** directory and add the following lines of code:

```
urlpatterns = [path('book_record_update/<int:pk>'),\
                    (BookUpdateView.as_view(), name='book_update')]
```

In this example, we have appended **<int:pk>** to the URL field. This signifies the field input we are going to have to retrieve the record for. Inside Django models, Django inserts a primary key of the integer type, which is used to uniquely identify the records. Inside the URL mapping, this is the field that we have been asking to insert.

Now, when we try to open **http://127.0.0.1:8000/book_management/book_record_update/1**, it should show us a record of the first record that we inserted into our database and allow us to edit it:

Figure 11.7: View displaying the book record update template based on the Update view

DELETE VIEW

Delete view, as the name suggests, is a view that deletes the record from our database. To implement such a view for our **Book** model, you will need to open the **views.py** file under the **book_management** directory and add the following code snippet to it:

```python
from django.views.generic.edit import DeleteView
from .models import Book


class BookDeleteView(DeleteView):
    model = Book
    template_name = 'book_delete_form.html'
    success_url = '/book_management/delete_success
```

With this, we have just created a Delete view for our book records. As we can see, this view uses a different template where all we would like to confirm from the user is, do they really want to delete the record or not? To achieve this, you can create a new template file, **book_delete_form.html**, and add the following code to it:

```html
<html>
  <head>
    <title>Delete Book Record</title>
  </head>
  <body>
    <p>Delete Book Record</p>
    <form method="POST">
      {% csrf_token %}
      Do you want to delete the book record?
      <input type="submit" value="Delete record" />
    </form>
  </body>
</html>
```

Then we can add a mapping for our Delete view by modifying the **urlpatterns** list inside the **urls.py** file under the **book_management** directory as follows:

```
urlpatterns = [....,\
            path('book_record_delete/<int:pk>'),\
            (BookDeleteView.as_view(), name='book_delete')]
```

Now, when visiting **http://127.0.0.1:8000/book_management/book_record_delete/1**, we should be greeted with the following page:

Figure 11.8: Delete Book Record view based on the Delete view class

Upon clicking the **Delete record** button, the record will be deleted from the database and the Deletion success page will be rendered.

READ VIEW

In this view, we would like to see a list of records that our database stores for the books. To achieve this, we are going to build a view named **DetailView**, which will render details about the book we are requesting. To build this view, we can add the following lines of code to our **views.py** file under the **book_management** directory:

```
from django.views.generic import DetailView


class BookRecordDetailView(DetailView):
    model = Book
    template_name = 'book_detail.html'
```

In the preceding code snippet, we are creating **DetailView**, which will help us to render the details about the book ID we are asking for. The Detail view internally queries our database model with the book ID we provide to it and, if a record is found, renders the template with the data stored inside the record by passing it as an object variable inside the template context.

Once this is done, the next step is to create the template for our book details. For this we'll need to create a new template file named **book_detail.html** under our **templates** directory inside the **book_management** application with the following contents:

```
<html>
  <head>
    <title>Book List</title>
  </head>
  <body>
    <span>Book Name: {{ object.name }}</span><br />
    <span>Author: {{ object.author }}</span>
  </body>
</html>
```

Now, with the template created, the last thing we need to do is to add a URL mapping for the Detail view. This can be done by appending the following to the **urlpatterns** list under the **urls.py** file of the **book_management** application:

```
path('book_record_detail/<int:pk>'),\
    (BookRecordDetail.as_view(), name='book_detail')
```

Now, with all of this configured, if we now go and open **http://127.0.0.1:8000/book_management/book_record_detail/1**, we will get to see the details pertaining to our book, as shown here:

Figure 11.9: View rendered when we try to access a previously stored book record

With the preceding examples, we just enabled CRUD operations for our **Book** model, and all of that while using CBVs.

ACTIVITY 11.01: RENDERING DETAILS ON THE USER PROFILE PAGE USING INCLUSION TAGS

In this activity, you will create a custom inclusion tag that helps to develop a user profile page that renders not only the users' details but also lists the books they have read.

The following steps should help you to complete this activity successfully:

1. Create a new **templatetags** directory under the **reviews** application inside the **bookr** project to provide a place where you can create your custom template tags.

2. Create a new file named **profile_tags.py**, which will store the code for your inclusion tag.

3. Inside the **profile_tags.py** file, import Django's template library and use it to initialize an instance of the template library class.

4. Import the **Review** model from the reviews application to fetch the reviews written by a user. This will be used to filter the reviews for the current user to render on the user profile page.

5. Next, create a new Python function named **book_list**, which will contain the logic for your inclusion tag. This function should only take a single parameter, the username of the currently logged-in user.

6. Inside the body of the **book_list** function, add the logic for fetching the reviews for this user and extract the name of the books this user has read. Assume that a user has read all those books for which they have provided a review.

7. Decorate this **book_list** function with the **inclusion_tag** decorator and provide it with a template name **book_list.html**.

8. Create a new template file named **book_list.html**, which was specified to the inclusion tag decorator in *step* 7. Inside this file, add code to render a list of books. This can be done by using a **for** loop construct and rendering HTML list tags for every item inside the list provided.

9. Modify the existing **profile.html** file under the **templates** directory, which will be used to render the user profile. Inside this template file, include the custom template tag and use it to render the list of books read by the user.

Once you implement all the aforementioned steps, starting the application server and visiting the user profile page should render a page that is similar to the one shown in *Figure 11.10*:

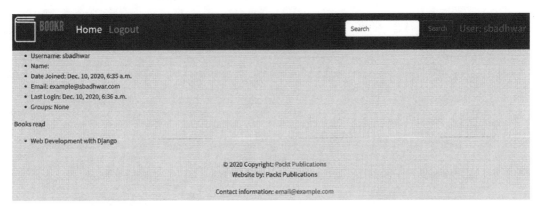

Figure 11.10: User profile page with the list of books read by the user

> **NOTE**
>
> The solution to this activity can be found at http://packt.live/2Nh1NTJ.

SUMMARY

In this chapter, we learned about the advanced templating concepts in Django and understood how we can create custom template tags and filters to fit a myriad of use cases and support the reusability of components across the application. We then looked at how Django provides us with the flexibility to implement FBVs and CBVs to render our responses.

While exploring CBVs, we learned how they can help us avoid code duplication and how we can leverage the built-in CBVs to render forms that save data, help us update existing records, and implement CRUD operations on our database resources.

As we move to the next chapter, we will now utilize our knowledge of building CBVs to work on implementing REST APIs in Django. This will allow us to perform well-defined HTTP operations on our data inside our Bookr application without maintaining any state inside the application.

12

BUILDING A REST API

OVERVIEW

This chapter introduces **REST APIs** and **Django REST Framework (DRF)**. You will start by implementing a simple API for the Bookr project. Next, you will learn about the serialization of model instances, which is a key step in delivering data to the frontend side of Django applications. You will explore different types of API views, including both functional and class-based types. By the end of this chapter, you will be able to implement custom API endpoints, including simple authentication.

INTRODUCTION

In the previous chapter, we learned about templates and class-based views. These concepts greatly help expand the range of functionalities we can provide to the user on the frontend (that is, in their web browser). However, that is not sufficient to build a modern web application. Web apps typically have the frontend built with an entirely separate library, such as **ReactJS** or **AngularJS**. These libraries provide powerful tools for building dynamic user interfaces; however, they do not communicate directly with our backend Django code or database. The frontend code simply runs in the web browser and does not have direct access to any data on our backend server. Therefore, we need to create a way for these applications to "talk" to our backend code. One of the best ways to do this in Django is by using REST APIs.

API stands for **Application Programming Interface**. APIs are used to facilitate interaction between different pieces of software, and they communicate using **HTTP** (**Hypertext Transfer Protocol**). This is the standard protocol for communication between servers and clients and is fundamental to information transfer on the web. APIs receive requests and send responses in HTTP format.

In our use case in this chapter, an API will help facilitate interaction between our Django backend, and our frontend JS code. For example, imagine that we want to create a frontend application that allows users to add new books to the Bookr database. The user's web browser would send a message (an HTTP request) to our API to say that they want to create an entry for a new book, and perhaps include some details about the book in that message. Our server would send back a response to report on whether the book was successfully added or not. The web browser would then be able to display to the user the outcome of their action.

REST APIS

REST stands for **Representational State Transfer**. Most modern web APIs can be classified as REST APIs. REST APIs are simply a type of API that focuses on communicating and synchronizing the *state* of objects between the database server and frontend client.

For example, imagine that you are updating your details on a website for which you are signed into your account. When you go to the account details page, the web server tells your browser about the various details attached to your account. When you change the values on that page, the browser sends back the updated details to the web server and tells it to update these details on the database. If the action is successful, the website will show you a confirmation message.

This is a very simple example of what is known as **decoupled** architecture between frontend and backend systems. Decoupling allows greater flexibility and makes it easier to update or change components in your architecture. So, let's say you want to create a new frontend website. In such a case, you don't have to change the backend code at all, as long as your new frontend is built to make the same API requests as the old one.

REST APIs are *stateless*, which means that neither the client nor the server stores any states in-between to do the communication. Every time a request is made, the data is processed, and a response is sent back without having to store any intermediate data by the protocol itself. What this means is that the API is processing each request in isolation. It doesn't need to store information regarding the session itself. This is in contrast to a stateful protocol (such as **TCP**), which maintains information regarding the session during its life.

So, a **RESTful web service**, as the name suggests, is a collection of REST APIs used to carry out a set of tasks. For example, if we develop a set of REST APIs for the Bookr application to carry out a certain set of tasks, then we can call it a RESTful web service.

DJANGO REST FRAMEWORK

Django REST Framework, also called **DRF** for short, is an open-source Python library that can be used to develop REST APIs for a Django project. DRF has most of the necessary functionality built in to help develop APIs for any Django project. Throughout this chapter, we will be using it to develop APIs for our Bookr project.

INSTALLATION AND CONFIGURATION

Install **djangorestframework** in the **virtual env** setup along with PyCharm. Enter the following code in your Terminal app or Command Prompt to do this:

```
pip install djangorestframework
```

Next, open the **settings.py** file and add **rest_framework** to **INSTALLED_APPS** as shown in the following snippet:

```
INSTALLED_APPS = ['django.contrib.admin',\
                  'django.contrib.auth',\
                  <django.contrib.contenttypes>,\
                  'django.contrib.sessions',\
                  'django.contrib.messages',\
                  'django.contrib.staticfiles',\
```

```
<rest_framework>,\
<reviews>]
```

You are now ready to start using DRF to create your first simple API.

FUNCTIONAL API VIEWS

In *Chapter 3, URL Mapping, Views, and Templates*, we learned about simple functional views that take a request and return a response. We can write similar functional views using DRF. However, note that class-based views are more commonly used, and will be covered next. A functional view is created by simply adding the following decorator onto a normal view, as follows:

```
from rest_framework.decorators import api_view


@api_view
def my_view(request):
    ...
```

This decorator takes the functional view and turns it into a subclass of the DRF **APIView**. It's a quick way to include an existing view as part of your API.

EXERCISE 12.01: CREATING A SIMPLE REST API

In this exercise, you will create your first REST API using DRF and implement an endpoint using a functional view. You will create this endpoint to view the total number of books in the database:

> **NOTE**
>
> You'll need to have DRF installed on your system to proceed with this exercise. If you haven't already installed it, make sure you refer to the section titled *Installation and Configuration* earlier in this chapter.

1. Create **api_views.py** in the **bookr/reviews** folder.

    REST API views work like Django's conventional views. We could have added the API views, along with the other views, in the **views.py** folder. However, having our REST API views in a separate file will help us maintain a cleaner code base.

2. Add the following code in **api_views.py**:

```
from rest_framework.decorators import api_view
from rest_framework.response import Response
```

```
from .models import Book


@api_view()
def first_api_view(request):
    num_books = Book.objects.count()
    return Response({"num_books": num_books})
```

The first line imports the **api_view** decorator, which will be used to convert our functional view into one that can be used with DRF, and the second line imports **Response**, which will be used to return a response.

The **view** function returns a **Response** object containing a dictionary with the number of books in our database (see the highlighted part).

Open **bookr/reviews/urls.py** and import the **api_views** module. Then, add a new path to the **api_views** module in the URL patterns that we have developed throughout this course, as follows:

```
from . import views, api_views


urlpatterns = [path('api/first_api_view/)',\
               path(api_views.first_api_view)

    ...
]
```

Start the Django service with the **python manage.py runserver** command and go to **http://0.0.0.0:8000/api/first_api_view/** to make your first API request. Your screen should appear as in *Figure 12.1*:

Figure 12.1: API view with the number of books

Calling this URL endpoint made a default **GET** request to the API endpoint, which returned a JSON key-value pair (**"num_books": 0**). Also, notice how DRF provides a nice interface to view and interact with the APIs.

3. We could also use the Linux **curl** (client URL) command to send an HTTP request as follows:

```
curl http://0.0.0.0:8000/api/first_api_view/
{"num_books":0}
```

Alternatively, if you are using Windows 10, you can make an equivalent HTTP request with **curl.exe** from Command Prompt as follows:

```
curl.exe http://0.0.0.0:8000/api/first_api_view/
```

In this exercise, we learned how to create an API view using DRF and a simple functional view. We will now look at a more elegant way to convert between information stored in the database and what gets returned by our API using serializers.

SERIALIZERS

By now, we are well versed in the way Django works with data in our application. Broadly, the columns of a database table are defined in a class in **models.py**, and when we access a row of the table, we are working with an instance of that class. Ideally, we often just want to pass this object to our frontend application. For example, if we wanted to build a website that displayed a list of books in our Bookr app, we would want to call the **title** property of each book instance to know what string to display to the user. However, our frontend application knows nothing about Python and needs to retrieve this data through an HTTP request, which just returns a string in a specific format.

This means that any information translated between Django and the frontend (via our API) must be done by representing the information in **JavaScript Object Notation (JSON)** format. JSON objects look similar to a Python dictionary, except there are some extra rules that constrict the exact syntax. In our previous example in *Exercise 12.01, Creating a Simple REST API*, the API returned the following JSON object containing the number of books in our database:

```
{"num_books": 0}
```

But what if we wanted to return the full details about an actual book in our database with our API? DRF's **serializer** class helps to convert complex Python objects into formats such as JSON or XML so that they can be transmitted across the web using the HTTP protocol. The part of DRF that does this conversion is named **serializer**. Serializers also perform deserialization, which refers to converting serialized data back into Python objects, so that the data can be processed in the application.

EXERCISE 12.02: CREATING AN API VIEW TO DISPLAY A LIST OF BOOKS

In this exercise, you will use serializers to create an API that returns a list of all books present in the **bookr** application:

1. Create a file named **serializers.py** in the **bookr/reviews** folder. This is the file where we will place all the serializer code for the APIs.

2. Add the following code to **serializers.py**:

```python
from rest_framework import serializers


class PublisherSerializer(serializers.Serializer):
    name = serializers.CharField()
    website = serializers.URLField()
    email = serializers.EmailField()


class BookSerializer(serializers.Serializer):
    title = serializers.CharField()
    publication_date = serializers.DateField()
    isbn = serializers.CharField()
    publisher = PublisherSerializer()
```

Here, the first line imports the serializers from the **rest_framework** module.

Following the imports, we have defined two classes, **PublisherSerializer** and **BookSerializer**. As the names suggest, they are serializers for the **Publisher** and **Book** models respectively. Both these serializers are subclasses of **serializers.Serializer** and we have defined field types for each serializer such as **CharField**, **URLField**, and **EmailField**, and so on.

Look at the **Publisher** model in the **bookr/reviews/models.py** file.
The **Publisher** model has **name**, **website**, and **email** attributes. So,
to serialize a **Publisher** object, we need **name**, **website**, and **email**
attributes in the **serializer** class, which we have defined accordingly in
PublisherSerializer. Similarly, for the **Book** model, we have defined
title, **publication_date**, **isbn**, and **publisher** as the desired
attributes in **BookSerializer**. Since **publisher** is a foreign key for the
Book model, we have used **PublisherSerializer** as the serializer for the
publisher attribute.

3. Open **bookr/reviews/api_views.py**, remove any pre-existing code, and
add the following code:

```
from rest_framework.decorators import api_view
from rest_framework.response import Response

from .models import Book
from .serializers import BookSerializer


@api_view()
def all_books(request):
    books = Book.objects.all()
    book_serializer = BookSerializer(books, many=True)
    return Response(book_serializer.data)
```

In the second line, we have imported the newly created **BookSerializer**
from the **serializers** module.

We then add a functional view, **all_books** (as in the previous exercise). This
view takes a query set containing all books and then serializes them using
BookSerializer. The **serializer** class is also taking an argument,
many=True, which indicates that the **books** object is a **queryset** or a list of
many objects. Remember that serialization takes Python objects and returns
them in a JSON serializable format, as follows:

```
[OrderedDict([('title', 'Advanced Deep Learning with Keras'),
('publication_date', '2018-10-31'), ('isbn', '9781788629416'),
('publisher', OrderedDict([('name', 'Packt Publishing'),
('website', 'https://www.packtpub.com/'), ('email', 'info@packtpub.
com')]))]), OrderedDict([('title', 'Hands-On Machine Learning for
Algorithmic Trading'), ('publication_date', '2018-12-31'), ('isbn',
'9781789346411'), ('publisher', OrderedDict([('name', 'Packt
Publishing'), ('website', 'https://www.packtpub.com/'), ('email',
'info@packtpub.com')]))])] …
```

4. Open **bookr/reviews/urls.py**, remove the previous example path for **first_api_view**, and add the **all_books** path as shown in the following code:

```
from django.urls import path
from . import views, api_views

urlpatterns = [path('api/all_books/'),\
               path(api_views.all_books),\
               path(name='all_books')
    ...
]
```

This newly added path calls the view function **all_books** when it comes across the **api/all_books/** path in the URL.

5. Once all the code is added, run the Django server with the **python manage. py runserver** command and navigate to **http://0.0.0.0:8000/api/ all_books/**. You should see something similar to *Figure 12.2*:

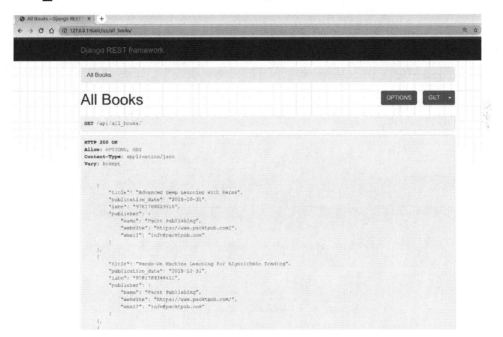

Figure 12.2: List of books shown in the all_books endpoint

The preceding screenshot shows that the list of all books is returned upon calling the **/api/all_books** endpoint. And with that, you have successfully used a serializer to return data efficiently in your database, with the help of a REST API.

Till now, we have been focusing on functional views. However, you will now learn that class-based views are more commonly used in DRF and will make your life much easier.

CLASS-BASED API VIEWS AND GENERIC VIEWS

Similar to what we learned in *Chapter 11, Advanced Templating and Class-Based Views*, we can write class-based views for REST APIs as well. Class-based views are the most preferred way for writing views among developers as a lot can be achieved by writing very little code.

Just as with conventional views, DRF offers a set of generic views that makes writing class-based views even simpler. Generic views are designed keeping in mind some of the most common operations needed while creating APIs. Some of the generic views offered by DRF are **ListAPIView**, **RetrieveAPIView**, and so on. In *Exercise 12.02, Creating an API View to Display a List of Books*, our functional view was responsible for creating a **queryset** of the objects and then calling the serializer. Equivalently, we could use **ListAPIView** to do the same thing:

```
class AllBooks(ListAPIView):
    queryset = Book.objects.all()
    serializer_class = BookSerializer
```

Here, the **queryset** of objects is defined as a class attribute. Passing the **queryset** through to the **serializer** is handled by methods on **ListAPIView**.

MODEL SERIALIZERS

In *Exercise 12.02, Creating an API View to Display a List of Books*, our serializer was defined as follows:

```
class BookSerializer(serializers.Serializer):
    title = serializers.CharField()
    publication_date = serializers.DateField()
    isbn = serializers.CharField()
    publisher = PublisherSerializer()
```

However, our model for **Book** looks like this (note how similar the definitions of the model and serializer appear to be):

```
class Book(models.Model):
    """A published book."""
    title = models.CharField(max_length=70),\
                        (help_text="The title of the book.")
```

```
    publication_date = models.DateField\
                    (verbose_name="Date the book was published.")
    isbn = models.CharField(max_length=20),\
                    (verbose_name="ISBN number of the book.")
    publisher = models.ForeignKey(Publisher),\
                    (on_delete=models.CASCADE)
    contributors = models.ManyToManyField('Contributor'),\
                    (through="BookContributor")


    def __str__(self):
        return self.title
```

We would prefer not to specify that the title must be **serializers.CharField()**. It would be easier if the serializer just looked at how **title** was defined in the model and could figure out what serializer field to use.

This is where model serializers come in. They provide shortcuts to create serializers by utilizing the definition of the fields on the model. Instead of specifying that **title** should be serialized using a **CharField**, we just tell the model serializer we want to include the **title**, and it uses the **CharField** serializer because the **title** field on the model is also a **CharField**.

For example, suppose we wanted to create a serializer for the **Contributor** model in **models.py**. Instead of specifying the types of serializers that should be used for each field, we can give it a list of the field names, and let it figure out the rest:

```
from rest_framework import serializers

from .models import Contributor


class ContributorSerializer(serializers.ModelSerializer):

    class Meta:
        model = Contributor
        fields = ['first_names', 'last_names', 'email']
```

In the following exercise, we will see how we can use a model serializer to avoid the duplication of code in the preceding classes.

EXERCISE 12.03: CREATING CLASS-BASED API VIEWS AND MODEL SERIALIZERS

In this exercise, you will create class-based views to display a list of all books while using model serializers:

1. Open the file **bookr/reviews/serializers.py**, remove any pre-existing code, and replace it with the following code:

```python
from rest_framework import serializers

from .models import Book, Publisher


class PublisherSerializer(serializers.ModelSerializer):

    class Meta:
        model = Publisher
        fields = ['name', 'website', 'email']


class BookSerializer(serializers.ModelSerializer):
    publisher = PublisherSerializer()

    class Meta:
        model = Book
        fields = ['title', 'publication_date', 'isbn', 'publisher']
```

Here, we have included two model serializer classes, **PublisherSerializer** and **BookSerializer**. Both these classes inherit the parent class **serializers.ModelSerializer**. We do not need to specify how each field gets serialized, instead, we can simply pass a list of field names, and the field types are inferred from the definition in **models.py**.

Although mentioning the field inside **fields** is sufficient for the model serializer, under certain special cases, such as this one, we may have to customize the field since the **publisher** field is a foreign key. Hence, we must use **PublisherSerializer** to serialize the **publisher** field.

2. Next, open **bookr/reviews/api_views.py**, remove any pre-existing code, and add the following code:

```
from rest_framework import generics

from .models import Book
from .serializers import BookSerializer


class AllBooks(generics.ListAPIView):
    queryset = Book.objects.all()
    serializer_class = BookSerializer
```

Here, we use the DRF class-based **ListAPIView** instead of a functional view. This means that the list of books is defined as a class attribute, and we do not have to write a function that directly handles the request and calls the serializer. The book serializer from the previous step is also imported and assigned as an attribute of this class.

Open the **bookr/reviews/urls.py** file and modify the **/api/all_books** API path to include the new class-based view as follows:

```
urlpatterns = [path('api/all_books/'),\
               path(api_views.AllBooks.as_view()),\
               path(name='all_books')]
```

Since we are using a class-based view, we have to use the class name along with the **as_view()** method.

3. Once all the preceding modifications are completed, wait till the Django service restarts or start the server with the **python manage.py runserver** command, and then open the API at **http://0.0.0.0:8000/api/all_books/** in the web browser. You should see something like *Figure 12.3*:

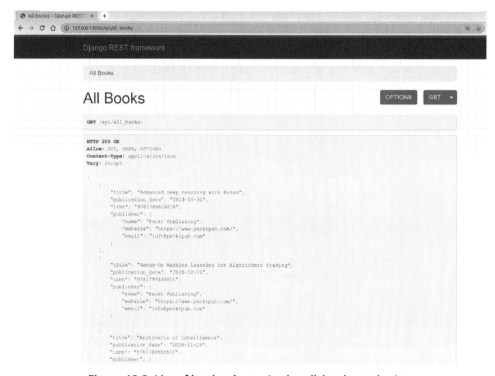

Figure 12.3: List of books shown in the all_books endpoint

Like what we saw in *Exercise 12.02, Creating an API View to Display a List of Books*, this is a list of all books present in the book review application. In this exercise, we used model serializers to simplify our code, and the generic class-based **ListAPIView** to return a list of the books in our database.

ACTIVITY 12.01: CREATING AN API ENDPOINT FOR A TOP CONTRIBUTORS PAGE

Imagine that your team decides to create a web page that displays the top contributors (that is, authors, coauthors, and editors) in your database. They decide to enlist the services of an external developer to create an app in React JavaScript. To integrate with the Django backend, the developer will need an endpoint that provides the following:

- A list of all contributors in the database

- For each contributor, a list of all books they contributed to

- For each contributor, the number of books they contributed to

- For each book they contributed to, their role in the book

The final API view should look like this:

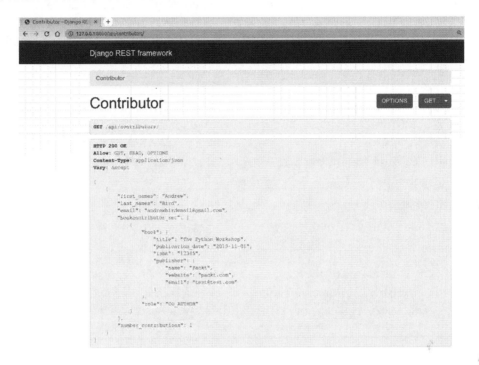

Figure 12.4: Top contributors endpoint

To perform this task, execute the following steps:

1. Add a method to the **Contributor** class that returns the number of contributions made.

2. Add **ContributionSerializer**, which serializes the **BookContribution** model.

3. Add **ContributorSerializer**, which serializes the **Contributor** model.

4. Add **ContributorView**, which uses **ContributorSerializer**.

5. Add a pattern to **urls.py** to enable access to **ContributorView**.

> **NOTE**
>
> The solution to this activity can be found at http://packt.live/2Nh1NTJ.

VIEWSETS

We have seen how we can optimize our code and make it more concise using class-based generic views. **Viewsets** and **Routers** help us further simplify our code. As the name indicates, viewsets are a set of views represented in a single class. For example, we used the **AllBooks** view to return a list of all books in the application and the **BookDetail** view to return the details of a single book. Using viewsets, we could combine both these classes into a single class.

DRF also provides a class named **ModelViewSet**. This class not only combines the two views mentioned in the preceding discussion (that is, list and detail) but also allows you to create, update, and delete model instances. The code needed to implement all this functionality could be as simple as specifying the serializer and **queryset**. For example, a view that allows you to manage all these actions for your user model could be defined as tersely as the following:

```
class UserViewSet(viewsets.ModelViewSet):
    serializer_class = UserSerializer
    queryset = User
```

Lastly, DRF provides a **ReadOnlyModelViewSet** class. This is a simpler version of the preceding **ModelViewSet**. It is identical, except that it only allows you to list and retrieve specific users. You cannot create, update, or delete records.

ROUTERS

Routers, when used along with a viewset, take care of automatically creating the required URL endpoints for the viewset. This is because a single viewset is accessed at different URLs. For example, in the preceding **UserViewSet**, you would access a list of users at the URL **/api/users/**, and a specific user record at the URL **/api/users/123**, where **123** is the primary key of that user record. Here is a simple example of how you might use a router in the context of the previously defined **UserViewSet**:

```
from rest_framework import routers
router = routers.SimpleRouter()
router.register(r'users', UserViewSet)
urlpatterns = router.urls
```

Now, let's try to combine the concepts of routers and viewsets in a simple exercise.

EXERCISE 12.04: USING VIEWSETS AND ROUTERS

In this exercise, we will combine the existing views to create a viewset and create the required routing for the viewset:

1. Open the file **bookr/reviews/serializers.py**, remove the pre-existing code, and add the following code snippet:

reviews/serializers.py

```
01   from django.contrib.auth.models import User
02   from django.utils import timezone
03   from rest_framework import serializers
04   from rest_framework.exceptions import NotAuthenticated, PermissionDenied
05
06   from .models import Book, Publisher, Review
07   from .utils import average_rating
08
09   class PublisherSerializer(serializers.ModelSerializer):
```

You can find the complete code snippet at http://packt.live/3osYJli.

Here, we added two new fields to **BookSerializer**, namely **reviews** and **rating**. The interesting thing about these fields is that the logic behind them is defined as a method on the serializer itself. This is why we use the **serializers.SerializerMethodField** type to set the **serializer** class attributes.

2. Open the file **bookr/reviews/api_views.py**, remove the pre-existing code, and add the following:

```
from rest_framework import viewsets
from rest_framework.pagination import LimitOffsetPagination


from .models import Book, Review
from .serializers import BookSerializer, ReviewSerializer



class BookViewSet(viewsets.ReadOnlyModelViewSet):
    queryset = Book.objects.all()
    serializer_class = BookSerializer



class ReviewViewSet(viewsets.ModelViewSet):
    queryset = Review.objects.order_by('-date_created')
    serializer_class = ReviewSerializer
```

```
pagination_class = LimitOffsetPagination
authentication_classes = []
```

Here, we have removed the **AllBook** and the **BookDetail** views and replaced them with **BookViewSet** and **ReviewViewSet**. In the first line, we import the **ViewSets** module from **rest_framework**. The **BookViewSet** class is a subclass of **ReadOnlyModelViewSet**, which ensures that the views are used for the **GET** operation only.

Next, open the **bookr/reviews/urls.py** file, remove the first two URL patterns starting with **api/**, and then add the following (highlighted) code:

```
from django.urls import path, include
from rest_framework.routers import DefaultRouter

from . import views, api_views

router = DefaultRouter()
router.register(r'books', api_views.BookViewSet)
router.register(r'reviews', api_views.ReviewViewSet)

urlpatterns = [path('api/', include((router.urls, 'api'))),\
            path('books/', views.book_list, \
                name='book_list'),
            path('books/<int:pk>/', views.book_detail, \
                name='book_detail'),
            path('books/<int:book_pk>/reviews/new/', \
                views.review_edit, name='review_create'),
            path('books/<int:book_pk>/reviews/<int:review_pk>/', \
                views.review_edit, name='review_edit'),
            path('books/<int:pk>/media/', views.book_media, \
                name='book_media'),
            path('publishers/<int:pk>/', views.publisher_edit, \
                name='publisher_detail'),
            path('publishers/new/', views.publisher_edit, \
                name='publisher_create')]
```

Here, we have combined the **all_books** and **book_detail** paths into a single path called **books**. We have also added a new endpoint under the path **reviews** which we will need in a later chapter.

We start by importing the **DefaultRouter** class from **rest_framework.routers**. Then, we create a **router** object using the **DefaultRouter** class and then register the newly created **BookViewSet** and **ReviewViewSet**, as can be seen from the highlighted code. This ensures that the **BookViewSet** is invoked whenever the API has the **/api/books** path.

3. Save all the files, and once the Django service restarts (or you start it manually with the **python manage.py runserver** command), go to the URL **http://0.0.0.0:8000/api/books/** to get a list of all the books. You should see the following view in the API explorer:

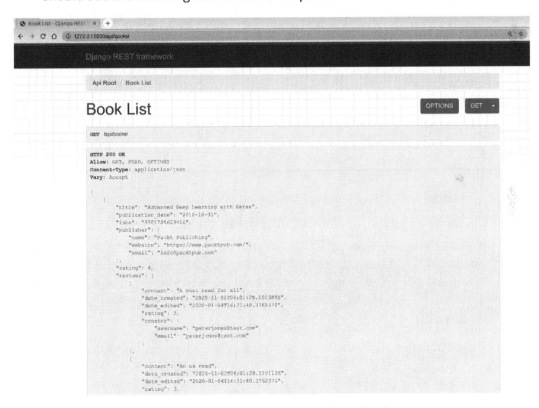

Figure 12.5: Book list at the path /api/books

4. You can also access the details for a specific book using the URL
    http://0.0.0.0:8000/api/books/1/. In this case, it will return details
    for the book with a primary key of **1** (if it exists in your database):

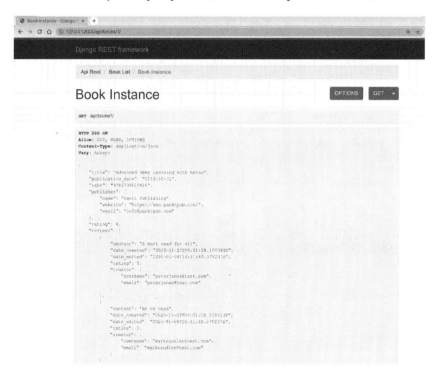

Figure 12.6: Book details for "Advanced Deep Learning with Keras"

In this exercise, we saw how we can use viewsets and routers to combine the list and
detail views into a single viewset. Using viewsets will make our code more consistent
and idiomatic, making it easier to collaborate with other developers. This becomes
particularly important when integrating with a separate frontend application.

AUTHENTICATION

As we learned in *Chapter 9, Sessions and Authentication*, it is important to authenticate
the users of our application. It is good practice to only allow those users who have
registered in the application to log in and access information from the application.
Similarly, for REST APIs too, we need to design a way to authenticate and authorize
users before any information is passed on. For example, suppose Facebook's website
makes an API request to get a list of all comments for a post. If they did not have
authentication on this endpoint, you could use it to programmatically get comments
for any post you want. They obviously don't want to allow this, so some sort of
authentication needs to be implemented.

There are different authentication schemes, such as **Basic Authentication**, **Session Authentication**, **Token Authentication**, **Remote User Authentication**, and various third-party authentication solutions. For the scope of this chapter, and for our Bookr application, we will use **Token Authentication**.

> **NOTE**
>
> For further reading on all the authentication schemes, please refer to the official documentation at https://www.django-rest-framework.org/api-guide/authentication.

TOKEN-BASED AUTHENTICATION

Token-based authentication works by generating a unique token for a user in exchange for the user's username and password. Once the token is generated, it will be stored in the database for further reference and will be returned to the user upon every login.

This token is unique for a user and the user can then use this token to authorize every API request they make. Token-based authentication eliminates the need to pass the username and password on every request. It is much safer and is best suited to client-server communication, such as a JavaScript-based web client interacting with the backend application via REST APIs.

An example of this would be a ReactJS or AngularJS application interacting with a Django backend via REST APIs.

The same architecture can be used if you are developing a mobile application to interact with the backend server via REST APIs, for instance, an Android or iOS application interacting with a Django backend via REST APIs.

EXERCISE 12.05: IMPLEMENTING TOKEN-BASED AUTHENTICATION FOR BOOKR APIS

In this exercise, you will implement token-based authentication for the **bookr** application's APIs:

1. Open the **bookr/settings.py** file and add **rest_framework.authtoken** to **INSTALLED_APPS**:

```
INSTALLED_APPS = ['django.contrib.admin',\
                  'django.contrib.auth',\
                  <django.contrib.contenttypes>,\
```

```
'django.contrib.sessions',\
'django.contrib.messages',\
'django.contrib.staticfiles',\
<rest_framework>,\
<rest_framework.authtoken>,\
<reviews>]
```

2. Since the **authtoken** app has associated database changes, run the **migrate** command in the command line/terminal as follows:

```
python manage.py migrate
```

3. Open the **bookr/reviews/api_views.py** file, remove any pre-existing code, and replace it with the following:

/reviews/api_views.py

```
from django.contrib.auth import authenticate
from rest_framework import viewsets
from rest_framework.authentication import TokenAuthentication
from rest_framework.authtoken.models import Token
from rest_framework.pagination import LimitOffsetPagination
from rest_framework.permissions import IsAuthenticated
from rest_framework.response import Response
from rest_framework.status import HTTP_404_NOT_FOUND, HTTP_200_OK
from rest_framework.views import APIView
```

You can find the complete code for this file at http://packt.live/2JQebbS.

Here, we have defined a view called **Login**. The purpose of this view is to allow a user to get (or create if it does not already exist) a token that they can use to authenticate with the API.

We override the **post** method of this view because we want to customize the behavior when a user sends us data (that is, their login details). First, we use the **authenticate** method from Django's **auth** library to check whether the username and password are correct. If they are correct, then we will have a **user** object. If not, we return an **HTTP 404** error. If we do have a valid **user** object, then we simply get or create a token, and return it to the user.

4. Next, let's add the authentication class to our **BookViewSet**. This means that when a user tries to access this viewset, it will require them to authenticate using token-based authentication. Note that it's possible to include a list of different accepted authentication methods, not just one. We also add the **permissions_classes** attribute, which just uses DRF's built-in class that checks to see if the given user has permission to view the data in this model:

```
class BookViewSet(viewsets.ReadOnlyModelViewSet):
    queryset = Book.objects.all()
```

```
        serializer_class = BookSerializer
        authentication_classes = [TokenAuthentication]
        permission_classes = [IsAuthenticated]
```

> **NOTE**
>
> The preceding code (highlighted) won't match the code you see on GitHub as we'll be modifying it later in *step 9*

5. Open **bookr/reviews/urls.py** file and add the following path into url patterns.

```
path('api/login', api_views.Login.as_view(), name='login')
```

6. Save the file and wait for the application to restart, or start the server manually with the **python manage.py runserver** command. Then access the application using the URL **http://0.0.0.0:8000/api/login**. Your screen should appear as follows:

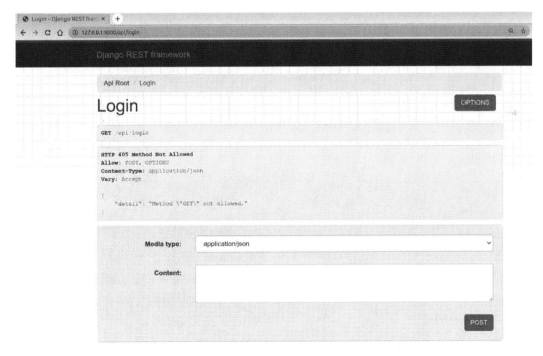

Figure 12.7: Login page

The API at **/api/login** is a **POST** only message, hence **Method GET not allowed** is displayed.

7. Next, enter the following snippet in the content and click on **POST**:

```
{
"username": "Peter",
"password": "testuserpassword"
}
```

You will need to replace this with an actual username and password for your account in the database. Now you can see the token generated for the user. This is the token we need to use to access **BookSerializer**:

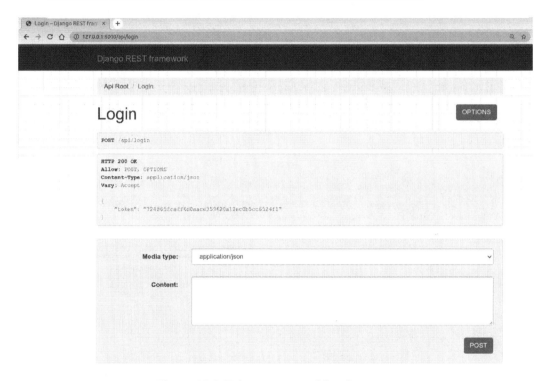

Figure 12.8: Token generated for the user

8. Try to access the list of books using the API that we previously created at **http://0.0.0.0:8000/api/books/**. Note that you are now not allowed to access it. This is because this viewset now requires you to use your token to authenticate.

The same API can be accessed using **curl** on the command line:

```
curl -X GET http://0.0.0.0:8000/api/books/

{"detail":"Authentication credentials were not provided."}
```

Since the token was not provided, the message **Authentication credentials were not provided** is displayed:

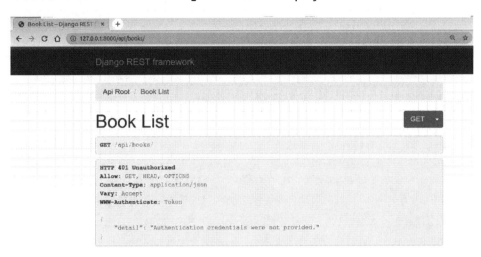

Figure 12.9: Message saying that the authentication details weren't provided

Note that if you're using Windows 10, replace **curl** in the preceding command with **curl.exe** and execute it from Command Prompt.

To pass the **Authorization** token (obtained in *step 7*) as a header, you can use the following command (Windows users can replace **curl** with **curl.exe**):

```
curl -X GET http://0.0.0.0:8000/api/books/ -H "Authorization: Token
724865fcaff6d0aace359620a12ec0b5cc6524f1"
```

> **NOTE**
>
> Before pasting this command, make sure you've replaced the token (highlighted) with the one you got when you ran *step 7* of this exercise. It will be different from the one we have shown here.

The preceding command should now return the list of books:

```
[{"title":"Advanced Deep Learning with Keras","publication_
date":"2018-10-31","isbn":"9781788629416","publisher":{"name":"Pa
ckt Publishing","website":"https://www.packtpub.com/","email":"info@
packtpub.com"},"rating":4,"reviews":[{"content":"A must read for
all","date_created":… (truncated)
```

This operation ensured that only an existing user of the application can access and fetch the collection of all books.

9. Before moving on, set the authentication and permission classes on
   BookViewSet to an empty string. Future chapters will not utilize these
   authentication methods, and we will assume for sake of simplicity that our API
   can be accessed by an unauthenticated user.

```
class BookViewSet(viewsets.ReadOnlyModelViewSet):
    queryset = Book.objects.all()
    serializer_class = BookSerializer
    authentication_classes = []
    permission_classes = []
```

In this exercise, we implemented token-based authentication in our Bookr app. We
created a login view that allows us to retrieve the token for a given authenticated
user. This then enabled us to make API requests from the command line by passing
through the token as a header in the request.

SUMMARY

This chapter introduced REST APIs, a fundamental building block in most real-world
web applications. These APIs facilitate communication between the backend server
and the web browser, so they are central to your growth as a Django web developer.
We learned how to serialize data in our database so that it can be transmitted via an
HTTP request. We also learned the various options DRF gives us to simplify the code
we write, taking advantage of the existing definitions of the models themselves. We
also covered viewsets and routers, and saw how they can be used to condense code
even further by combining the functionality of multiple views. We also learned about
authentication and authorization and implemented token-based authentication for
the book review app. In the next chapter, we will extend Bookr's functionality for its
users by learning how to generate CSVs, PDFs, and other binary filetypes.

13

GENERATING CSV, PDF, AND OTHER BINARY FILES

OVERVIEW

This chapter teaches you how to generate files in different data formats, such as **CSV**, **PDF**, and other binary file formats (for example, Excel-compatible files) using some of the common libraries that are available inside Python. This knowledge will help you build web projects that let your users export and download records from your site into familiar CSV or Excel-based formats. You will also learn how to generate graph plots inside Python and render them as HTML and display them inside your web applications. Moreover, you will be able to build features that let users export your data in PDF format.

INTRODUCTION

So far, we have learned the various aspects of the Django framework and explored how we can build web applications using Django with all the features and customizations we want.

Let's say that while building a web application, we need to do some analysis and prepare some reports. We may need to analyze user demographics about how the platform is being used or generate data that can be fed into machine learning systems to find patterns. We want our website to display some of the results of our analysis in a tabular format and other results as detailed graphs and charts. Furthermore, we also want to allow our users to export the reports and peruse them further in applications such as Jupyter Notebook and Excel.

As we work our way through this chapter, we will learn how to bring these ideas to fruition and implement functionality in our web application that allows us to export records into structured formats such as tables through the use of **Comma-Separated Value (CSV)** files or Excel files. We will also learn how to allow our users to generate visual representations of the data we have stored inside our web application and export it as PDF so it can be distributed easily for quick reference.

Let's start our journey by learning how to work with CSV files in Python. Learning this skill will help us create functionality that allows our readers to export our data for further analysis.

WORKING WITH CSV FILES INSIDE PYTHON

There are several reasons we may need to export the data in our application. One of the reasons may involve performing analysis of that data – for example, we may need to understand the demographics of users registered on the application or extract patterns of application usage. We may also need to find out how our application is working for users to design future improvements. Such use cases require data to be in a format that can be easily consumed and analyzed. Here, the CSV file format comes to the rescue.

CSV is a handy file format that can be used to quickly export data from an application in a row-and-column format. CSV files usually have data separated by simple delimiters, which are used to differentiate one column from another, and newlines, which are used to indicate the start of a new record (or row) inside the table.

Python has great support for working with CSV files in its standard library thanks to the **csv** module. This support enables the reading, parsing, and writing of CSV files. Let's take a look at how we can leverage the CSV module provided by Python to work on CSV files and read and write data from them.

WORKING WITH PYTHON'S CSV MODULE

The **csv** module from Python provides us with the ability to interact with files that are in CSV format, which is nothing but a text file format. That is, the data stored inside the CSV files is human-readable.

The **csv** module requires that the file is opened before the methods supplied by the **csv** module can be applied. Let's take a look at how we can start with the very basic operation of reading data from CSV files.

READING DATA FROM A CSV FILE

Reading data from CSV files is quite easy and consists of the following steps:

1. First, we open the file:

```
csv_file = open('path to csv file')
```

    Here, we are reading the file using the Python **open()** method and then passing it the name of the file from which the data is to be read.

2. Then, we read the data from the **file** object using the **csv** module's **reader** method:

```
import csv
csv_data = csv.reader(csv_file)
```

    In the first line, we imported the **csv** module, which contains the set of methods required to work on CSV files:

```
import csv
```

    With the file opened, the next step is to create a CSV **reader** object by using the **csv** module's **reader** method. This method takes in the **file** object as returned by the **open()** call and uses the **file** object to read the data from the CSV file:

```
csv_reader = csv.reader(csv_file)
```

The data read by the **reader()** method is returned as a list of a list, where every sub-list is a new record and every value inside the list is a value for the specified column. Generally, the first record in the list is referred to as a header, which denotes the different columns that are present inside the CSV file, but it is not necessary to have a **header** field inside a CSV file.

3. Once the data is read by the **csv** module, we can iterate over this data to perform any kind of operation we may desire. This can be done as follows:

```
for csv_record in csv_data:
    # do something
```

4. Once the processing is done, we close the CSV file simply by using the **close()** method in Python's file handler object:

```
csv_file.close()
```

Now let's look at our first exercise, where we will implement a simple module that helps us read a CSV file and output its contents on our screen.

EXERCISE 13.01: READING A CSV FILE WITH PYTHON

In this exercise, you will read and process a CSV file inside Python using Python's built-in **csv** module. The CSV file contains fictitious market data of several NASDAQ-listed companies:

1. First, download the **market_cap.csv** file from the GitHub repository for this book by clicking the following link: http://packt.live/2MNWzOV.

> **NOTE**
>
> The CSV file consists of randomly generated data and does not correspond to any historical market trends.

2. Once the file is downloaded, open it and take a look at its contents. You will realize that the file contains a set of comma-separated values with each different record on its own line:

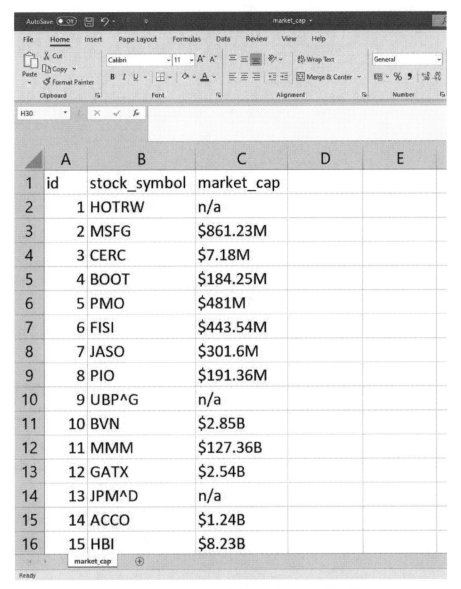

Figure 13.1: Contents of the market cap CSV file

3. Once the file is downloaded, you can proceed to write the first piece of code. For this, create a new file named **csv_reader.py** in the same directory where the CSV file was downloaded and add the following code inside it:

```python
import csv


def read_csv(filename):
    """Read and output the details of CSV file."""
```

```
    try:
        with open(filename, newline='') as csv_file:
            csv_reader = csv.reader(csv_file)
            for record in csv_reader:
                print(record)
    except (IOError, OSError) as file_read_error:
        print("Unable to open the csv file. Exception: {}".format(file_
read_error))

if __name__ == '__main__':
    read_csv('market_cap.csv')
```

Let's try to understand what you just implemented in the preceding snippet of code.

After importing the **csv** module, to keep the code modular, you created a new method named **read_csv()** that takes in a single parameter, the filename to read the data from:

```
try:
        with open(filename, newline='') as csv_file:
```

Now, if you are not familiar with the approach of opening the file shown in the preceding snippet, this is also known as the **try-with-resources** approach. In this case, any block of code that is encapsulated in the scope of the **with** block will have access to the **file** object, and once the code exits the scope of the **with** block, the file will be closed automatically.

> **NOTE**
>
> It is a good habit to encapsulate file I/O operations within a **try-except** block, since file I/O can fail for several reasons and showing stack traces to the users is not a good option.

The **reader()** method returns a **reader** object over which we can iterate to access the values just like we saw in the *Reading Data from a CSV File* section:

```
for record in csv_reader:
    print(record)
```

Once this is done, you write the entry point method, from which your code will begin executing, by calling the **read_csv()** method and passing the name of the CSV file to read:

```
if __name__ == '__main__':
    read_csv(market_cap.csv')
```

4. With this, you are done and ready to parse your CSV file now. You can do this by running your Python file in the Terminal or Command Prompt as shown here:

```
python3 csv_reader.py
```

NOTE

Or, on Windows, use **python csv_reader.py** as shown in *Figure 13.2*.

Once the code executes, you should expect to see the following output:

```
C:\Users\CV552\Documents\Chapter13\Exercise13.01>python csv_reader.py
['id', 'stock_symbol', 'market_cap']
['1', 'HOTRW', 'n/a']
['2', 'MSFG', '$861.23M']
['3', 'CERC', '$7.18M']
['4', 'BOOT', '$184.25M']
['5', 'PMO', '$481M']
['6', 'FISI', '$443.54M']
['7', 'JASO', '$301.6M']
['8', 'PIO', '$191.36M']
['9', 'UBP^G', 'n/a']
['10', 'BVN', '$2.85B']
['11', 'MMM', '$127.36B']
['12', 'GATX', '$2.54B']
['13', 'JPM^D', 'n/a']
['14', 'ACCO', '$1.24B']
['15', 'HBI', '$8.23B']
['16', 'Y', '$9.37B']
['17', 'DHX', '$128.99M']
['18', 'AGNCB', '$9.12B']
['19', 'BT', '$37.72B']
['20', 'GGP^A', 'n/a']
['21', 'XRAY', '$14.6B']
['22', 'ANCB', '$62.74M']
['23', 'MLP', '$386.9M']
['24', 'AEG', '$10.51B']
['25', 'CELGZ', 'n/a']
['26', 'ACXM', '$2.06B']
['27', 'JBSS', '$696.39M']
['28', 'MOBL', '$571.52M']
['29', 'FFHL', '$10.06M']
['30', 'ONEQ', '$798.86M']
['31', 'FBNC', '$768.07M']
['32', 'WSBF', '$568.57M']
['33', 'AGU', '$12.97B']
```

Figure 13.2: Output from the CSV reader program

With this, now you know how to read CSV file contents. Also, as you can see from the output of *Exercise 13.01*, *Reading a CSV File with Python*, the output for individual rows is represented in the form of a list.

Now, let's look at how we can use the Python **csv** module to create new CSV files.

WRITING TO CSV FILES USING PYTHON

In the previous section, we explored how we can use the **csv** module in Python to read the contents of the CSV-formatted files. Now, let us learn how we can write CSV data to files.

Writing CSV data follows a similar approach as reading from a CSV file, with some minor differences. The following steps outline the process of writing data to CSV files:

1. Open the file in writing mode:

```
csv_file = open('path to csv file', 'w')
```

2. Obtain a CSV writer object, which can help us write data that is correctly formatted in the CSV format. This is done by calling the **writer()** method of the **csv** module, which returns a **writer** object, which can be used to write CSV format-compatible data to a CSV file:

```
csv_writer = csv.writer(csv_file)
```

3. Once the **writer** object is available, we can start writing the data. This is facilitated by the **write_row()** method of the **writer** object. The **write_row()** method takes in a list of values that it writes to the CSV file. The list itself indicates a single row and the values inside the list indicate the values of columns:

```
record = ['value1', 'value2', 'value3']
csv_writer.writerow(record)
```

If you want to write multiple records in a single call, you can also use the **writerows()** method of the CSV writer. The **writerows()** method behaves similarly to the **writerow()** method but takes a list of lists and can write multiple rows in one go:

```
records = [['value11', 'value12', 'value13'],\
           ['value21', 'value22', 'value23']]
csv_writer.writerows(records)
```

4. Once the records are written, we can then close the CSV file:

```
csv_file.close()
```

Now, let's apply what we've learned in the next exercise and implement a program that will help us in writing values to CSV files.

EXERCISE 13.02: GENERATING A CSV FILE USING PYTHON'S CSV MODULE

In this exercise, you will use the Python **csv** module to create new CSV files:

1. Create a new file named **csv_writer.py**, inside which you will write the code for the CSV writer. Inside this file, add the following code:

```
import csv

def write_csv(filename, header, data):
    """Write the provided data to the CSV file.

    :param str filename: The name of the file \
        to which the data should be written
    :param list header: The header for the \
        columns in csv file
    :param list data: The list of list mapping \
        the values to the columns
    """
    try:
        with open(filename, 'w') as csv_file:
            csv_writer = csv.writer(csv_file)
            csv_writer.writerow(header)
            csv_writer.writerows(data)
    except (IOError, OSError) as csv_file_error:
        print\
        ("Unable to write the contents to csv file. Exception: {}"\
        .format(csv_file_error))
```

With this code, you should now be able to create new CSV files easily. Now, going step by step, let's understand what you are trying to do in this code:

You define a new method called **write_csv()**, which takes three parameters: the name of the file to which the data should be written (**filename**), the list of column names that should be used as headers (**header**), and lastly a list of a list that contains the data that needs to be mapped to individual columns (**data**):

```
def write_csv(filename, header, data):
```

Now, with the parameters in place, the next step is to open the file to which the data needs to be written and map it to an object:

```
with open(filename, 'w') as csv_file:
```

Once the file is opened, you perform three main steps: first, obtain a new CSV writer object by using the **writer()** method from the **csv** module and passing it to the file handler that holds a reference to your opened file:

```
csv_writer = csv.writer(csv_file)
```

The next step involves using the CSV writer's **writerow()** method to write your dataset's header fields into the file:

```
csv_writer.writerow(header)
```

Once you have written the header, the last step is to write the data to the CSV file for the individual columns that are present. For this, use the **csv** module's **writerows()** method to write multiple rows at once:

```
csv_writer.writerows(data)
```

> **NOTE**
>
> We could also have merged the step of writing the header and data into a single line of code by having the header list as the first element of the data list and calling the **writerows()** method with the data list as a parameter.

2. When you have created the methods that can write the provided data to a CSV file, you write the code for the entry point call, and inside it, set up the values for the header, data, and filename fields, and finally call the **write_csv()** method that you defined earlier:

```
if __name__ == '__main__':
    header = ['name', 'age', 'gender']
    data = [['Richard', 32, 'M'], \
```

```
            ['Mumzil', 21, 'F'], \
            ['Melinda', 25, 'F']]
    filename = 'sample_output.csv'
    write_csv(filename, header, data)
```

3. Now with the code in place, execute the file you just created and see whether it creates the CSV file. To execute, run the following command:

```
python3 csv_writer.py
```

Once the execution finishes, you will see that a new file has been created in the same directory as the one in which you executed the command. When you open the file, the contents should resemble what you see in the following figure:

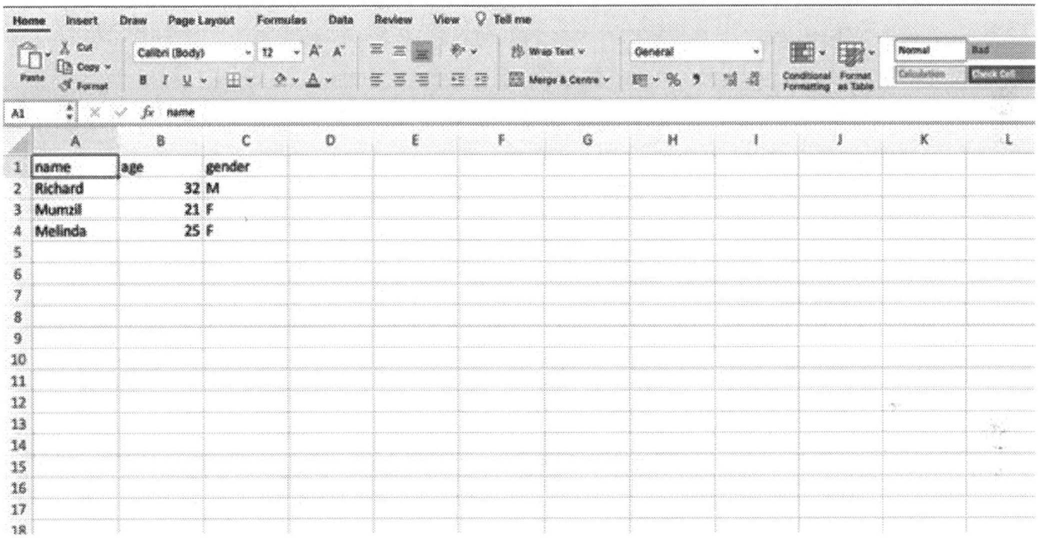

Figure 13.3: Output from the CSV writer sample_output.csv

With this, now you are well equipped to read and write the contents of CSV files.

With this exercise, we have learned how to write data to a CSV file. Now, it is time to look at some enhancements that can make reading and writing data to CSV files as a developer more convenient.

A BETTER WAY TO READ AND WRITE CSV FILES

Now, there is one important thing that needs to be taken care of. If you remember, the data read by the CSV reader usually maps values to a list. Now, if you want to access the values of individual columns, you need to use list indexes to access them. This way is not natural and causes a higher degree of coupling between the program responsible for writing the file and the one responsible for reading the file. For example, what if the writer program shuffled the order of the rows? In this case, you now have to update the reader program to make sure it identifies correct rows. So, the question arises, do we have a better way to read and write values that, instead of using list indexes, uses column names while preserving the context?

The answer to this is yes, and the solution is provided by another set of CSV modules known as **DictReader** and **DictWriter**, which provide the functionality of mapping objects in a CSV file to **dict**, rather than to a list.

This interface is easy to implement. Let's revisit the code you wrote in *Exercise 13.01, Reading a CSV File with Python*. If you wanted to parse the code as dict, the implementation of the **read_csv()** method would need to be changed as shown here:

```
def read_csv(filename):
    """Read and output the details of CSV file."""
    try:
        with open(filename, newline='') as csv_file:
            csv_reader = csv.DictReader(csv_file)
            for record in csv_reader:
                print(record)
    except (IOError, OSError) as file_read_error:
        print\
            ("Unable to open the csv file. Exception: {}"\
            .format(file_read_error))
```

As you will notice, the only change we did was to change **csv.reader()** to **csv.DictReader()**, which should represent individual rows in the CSV file as **OrderedDict**. You can also verify this by making this change and executing the following command:

```
python3 csv_reader.py
```

This should result in the following output:

```
(venv) sbadhwar@sbadhwar-mn1 Exercise13.01 % python3 csv_reader.py
{'id': '1', 'stock_symbol': 'HOTRW', 'market_cap': 'n/a'}
{'id': '2', 'stock_symbol': 'MSFG', 'market_cap': '$861.23M'}
{'id': '3', 'stock_symbol': 'CERC', 'market_cap': '$7.18M'}
{'id': '4', 'stock_symbol': 'BOOT', 'market_cap': '$184.25M'}
{'id': '5', 'stock_symbol': 'PMO', 'market_cap': '$481M'}
{'id': '6', 'stock_symbol': 'FISI', 'market_cap': '$443.54M'}
{'id': '7', 'stock_symbol': 'JASO', 'market_cap': '$301.6M'}
{'id': '8', 'stock_symbol': 'PIO', 'market_cap': '$191.36M'}
{'id': '9', 'stock_symbol': 'UBP^G', 'market_cap': 'n/a'}
{'id': '10', 'stock_symbol': 'BVN', 'market_cap': '$2.85B'}
{'id': '11', 'stock_symbol': 'MMM', 'market_cap': '$127.36B'}
{'id': '12', 'stock_symbol': 'GATX', 'market_cap': '$2.54B'}
{'id': '13', 'stock_symbol': 'JPM^D', 'market_cap': 'n/a'}
{'id': '14', 'stock_symbol': 'ACCO', 'market_cap': '$1.24B'}
{'id': '15', 'stock_symbol': 'HBI', 'market_cap': '$8.23B'}
{'id': '16', 'stock_symbol': 'Y', 'market_cap': '$9.37B'}
{'id': '17', 'stock_symbol': 'DHX', 'market_cap': '$128.99M'}
{'id': '18', 'stock_symbol': 'AGNCB', 'market_cap': '$9.12B'}
{'id': '19', 'stock_symbol': 'BT', 'market_cap': '$37.72B'}
{'id': '20', 'stock_symbol': 'GGP^A', 'market_cap': 'n/a'}
{'id': '21', 'stock_symbol': 'XRAY', 'market_cap': '$14.6B'}
{'id': '22', 'stock_symbol': 'ANCB', 'market_cap': '$62.74M'}
{'id': '23', 'stock_symbol': 'MLP', 'market_cap': '$386.9M'}
{'id': '24', 'stock_symbol': 'AEG', 'market_cap': '$10.51B'}
{'id': '25', 'stock_symbol': 'CELGZ', 'market_cap': 'n/a'}
```

Figure 13.4: Output with DictReader

As you can see in the preceding figure, the individual rows are mapped as key-value pairs in the dictionary. To access these individual fields in rows, we can use this:

```
print(record.get('stock_symbol'))
```

That should give us the value of the **stock_symbol** field from our individual records.

Similarly, you can also use the **DictWriter()** interface to operate on CSV files as dictionaries. To see this, let's take a look at the **write_csv()** method in *Exercise 13.02, Generating a CSV File Using Python's csv Module*, and modify it as follows:

```
def write_csv(filename, header, data):
    """Write the provided data to the CSV file.

    :param str filename: The name of the file \
        to which the data should be written
    :param list header: The header for the \
        columns in csv file
    :param list data: The list of dicts mapping \
        the values to the columns
```

```
"""
try:
    with open(filename, 'w') as csv_file:
        csv_writer = csv.DictWriter(csv_file, fieldnames=header)
        csv_writer.writeheader()
        csv_writer.writerows(data)
except (IOError, OSError) as csv_file_error:
    print\
    ("Unable to write the contents to csv file. Exception: {}"\
    .format(csv_file_error))
```

In the preceding code, we replaced **csv.writer()** with **csv.DictWriter()**, which provides a dictionary-like interface to interact with CSV files. **DictWriter()** also takes in a **fieldnames** parameter, which is used to map the individual columns in a CSV file before writing.

Next, to write this header, call the **writeheader()** method, which writes the **fieldname** header to the CSV file.

The final call involves the **writerows()** method, which takes in a list of dictionaries and writes them to the CSV file. For the code to work correctly, you also need to modify the data list to resemble the one shown here:

```
data = [{'name': Richard, 'age': 32, 'gender': 'M'}, \
        {'name': Mumzil', 'age': 21, 'gender':'F'}, \
        {'name': 'Melinda', 'age': 25, 'gender': 'F'}]
```

With this, you will have enough knowledge to work with CSV files inside Python.

Since we are talking about how to deal with tabular data, specifically reading and writing it to files, let's take a look at one of the more well-known file formats used by one of the most popular tabular data editors – Microsoft Excel.

WORKING WITH EXCEL FILES IN PYTHON

Microsoft Excel is a world-renowned software in the field of book-keeping and tabular record management. Similarly, the XLSX file format that was introduced with Excel has seen rapid and widespread adoption and is now supported by all the major product vendors.

You will find that Microsoft Excel and its XLSX format are used quite a lot in the marketing and sales departments of many companies. Let's say, for one such company's marketing department, you are building a web portal in Django that keeps track of the products purchased by users. It also displays data about the purchases, such as the time of purchase and the location where the purchase was made. The marketing and sales teams are planning to use this data to generate leads or to create relevant advertisements.

Since the marketing and sales teams use Excel quite a lot, we might want to export the data available inside our web application in XLSX format, which is native to Excel. Soon, we will look at how we can make our website work with this XLSX format. But before that, let's quickly take a look at the usage of binary file formats.

BINARY FILE FORMATS FOR DATA EXPORTS

Until now, we have worked mainly with textual data and how we can read and write it from text files. But often, text-based formats are not enough. For example, imagine you want to export an image or a graph. How will you represent an image or a graph as text, and how will you read and write to these images?

In these situations, binary file formats can come to our rescue. They can help us read and write to and from a rich and diverse set of data. All commercial operating systems provide native support for working with both text and binary file formats, and it comes as no surprise that Python provides one of the most versatile implementations to work on binary data files. A simple example of this is the **open** command, which you use to state the format you would like to open a file in:

```
file_handler = open('path to file', 'rb')
```

Here, **b** indicates binary.

Starting from this section, we will now be dealing with how we can work on binary files and use them to represent and export data from our Django web application. The first of the formats we are going to look at is the XLSX file format made popular by Microsoft Excel.

So, let's dive into the handling of XLSX files with Python.

WORKING WITH XLSX FILES USING THE XLSXWRITER PACKAGE

In this section, we will learn more about the XLSX file format and understand how we can work with it using the **XlsxWriter** package.

XLSX FILES

XLSX files are binary files that are used to store tabular data. These files can be read by any software that implements support for this format. The XLSX format arranges data into two logical partitions:

- **Workbooks**: Each XLSX file is called a workbook and is supposed to contain datasets related to a particular domain. In *Figure 13.5*, `Example_file.xlsx` is a workbook **(1)**:

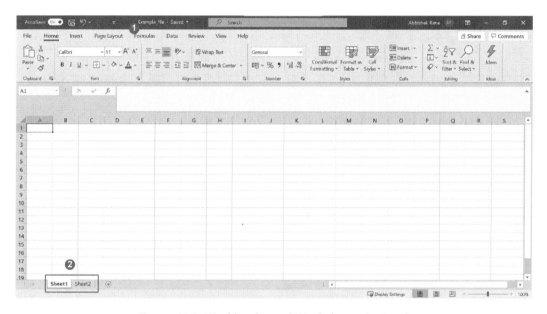

Figure 13.5: Workbooks and Worksheets in Excel

- **Worksheets**: Inside each workbook, there can be one or more worksheets, which are used to store data about different but logically related datasets in a tabular format. In *Figure 13.5*, `Sheet1` and `Sheet2` are two worksheets **(2)**.

When working with XLSX format, these are the two units that we generally work on. If you know about relational databases, you can think of workbooks as databases and worksheets as tables.

With that, let's try to understand how we can start working on XLSX files inside Python.

THE XLSXWRITER PYTHON PACKAGE

Python does not provide native support for working with XLSX files through its standard library. But thanks to the vast community of developers within the Python ecosystem, it is easy to find a number of packages that can help us manage our interaction with XLSX files. One popular package in this category is **XlsxWriter**.

XlsxWriter is an actively maintained package by the developer community, providing support for interacting with XLSX files. The package provides a lot of useful functionalities and supports the creation and management of workbooks as well as worksheets in individual workbooks. You can install it by running the following command in Terminal or Command Prompt:

```
pip install XlsxWriter
```

Once installed, you can import the **xlsxwriter** module as follows:

```
import xlsxwriter
```

So, let's look at how we can start creating XLSX files with the support of the **XlsxWriter** package.

CREATING A WORKBOOK

To start working on XLSX files, we first need to create them. An XLSX file is also known as a workbook and can be created by calling the **Workbook** class from the **xlsxwriter** module as follows:

```
workbook = xlsxwriter.Workbook(filename)
```

The call to the **Workbook** class opens a binary file, specified with the **filename** argument, and returns an instance of **workbook** that can be used to further create worksheets and write data.

CREATING A WORKSHEET

Before we can start writing data to an XLSX file, we first need to create a worksheet. This can be done easily by calling the **add_worksheet()** method of the **workbook** object we obtained in the previous step:

```
worksheet = workbook.add_worksheet()
```

The **add_worksheet()** method creates a new worksheet, adds it to the workbook, and returns an object mapping the worksheet to a Python object, through which we can write data to the worksheet.

WRITING DATA TO THE WORKSHEET

Once a reference to the worksheet is available, we can start writing data to it by calling the **write** method of the **worksheet** object as shown:

```
worksheet.write(row_num, col_num, col_value)
```

As you can see, the **write()** method takes three parameters: a row number (**row_num**), a column number (**col_num**), and the data that belongs to the [**row_num, col_num**] pair as represented by **col_value**. This call can be repeated to insert multiple data items into the worksheet.

WRITING THE DATA TO THE WORKBOOK

Once all the data is written, to finalize the written datasets and cleanly close the XLSX file, you call the **close()** method on the workbook:

```
workbook.close()
```

This method writes any data that may be in the file buffer and finally closes the workbook. Now, let's use this knowledge to implement our own code, which will help us write data to an XLSX file.

> **FURTHER READING**
>
> It's not possible to cover all the methods and features the **XlsxWriter** package provides in this chapter. For more information, you can read the official documentation: https://xlsxwriter.readthedocs.io/contents.html.

EXERCISE 13.03: CREATING XLSX FILES IN PYTHON

In this exercise, you will use the **XlsxWriter** package to create a new Excel (XLSX) file and add data to it from Python:

1. For this exercise, you will need the **XlsxWriter** package installed on your system. You can install it by running the following command in your Terminal app or Command Prompt:

```
pip install XlsxWriter
```

Once the command finishes, you will have the package installed on your system.

2. With the package installed, you can start writing the code that will create the Excel file. Create a new file named **xlsx_demo.py** and add the following code inside it:

```
import xlsxwriter


def create_workbook(filename):
    """Create a new workbook on which we can work."""
    workbook = xlsxwriter.Workbook(filename)
    return workbook
```

In the preceding code snippet, you have created a new function that will assist you in creating a new workbook in which you can store your data. Once you have created a new workbook, the next step is to create a worksheet that provides you with the tabular format needed for you to organize the data to be stored inside the XLSX workbook.

3. With the workbook created, create a new worksheet by adding the following code snippet to your **xlsx_demo.py** file:

```
def create_worksheet(workbook):
    """Add a new worksheet in the workbook."""
    worksheet = workbook.add_worksheet()
    return worksheet
```

In the preceding code snippet, you have created a new worksheet using the **add_worksheet()** method of the **workbook** object provided by the **XlsxWriter** package. This worksheet will then be used to write the data for the objects.

4. The next step is to create a helper function that can assist in writing the data to the worksheet in a tabular format defined by the row and column numbering. For this, add the following snippet of code to your **xlsx_writer.py** file:

```
def write_data(worksheet, data):
    """Write data to the worksheet."""
    for row in range(len(data)):
        for col in range(len(data[row])):
            worksheet.write(row, col, data[row][col])
```

In the preceding code snippet, you have created a new function named **write_data()** that takes two parameters: the **worksheet** object to which the data needs to be written and the **data** object represented by a list of lists that needs to be written to the worksheet. The function iterates over the data passed to it and then writes the data to the row and column it belongs to.

5. With all the core methods now implemented, you can now add the method that can help close the **workbook** object cleanly, such that the data is written to the file without any file corruption happening. For this, implement the following code snippet in the **xlsx_demo.py** file:

```
def close_workbook(workbook):
    """Close an opened workbook."""
    workbook.close()
```

6. The last step in the exercise is to integrate all the methods you have implemented in the previous steps. For this, create a new entry point method as shown in the following code snippet in your **xlsx_demo.py** file:

```
if __name__ == '__main__':
    data = [['John Doe', 38], \
            ['Adam Cuvver', 22], \
            ['Stacy Martin', 28], \
            ['Tom Harris', 42]]
    workbook = create_workbook('sample_workbook.xlsx')
    worksheet = create_worksheet(workbook)
    write_data(worksheet, data)
    close_workbook(workbook)
```

In the preceding code snippet, you first created a dataset that you want to write to the XLSX file in the form of a list of lists. Once that was done, you obtained a new **workbook** object, which will be used to create an XLSX file. Inside this **workbook** object, you then created a worksheet to organize your data in a row-and-column format and then wrote the data to the worksheet and closed the workbook to persist the data to the disk.

7. Now, let's see whether the code you wrote works the way it is expected to work. For this, run the following command:

```
python3 xlsx_demo.py
```

Once the command is finished executing, you will see a new file with the name **sample_workbook.xlsx** being created in the directory where the command was executed. To verify whether it contains the correct results, open this file with either Microsoft Excel or Google Sheets and view the contents. It should resemble what you see here:

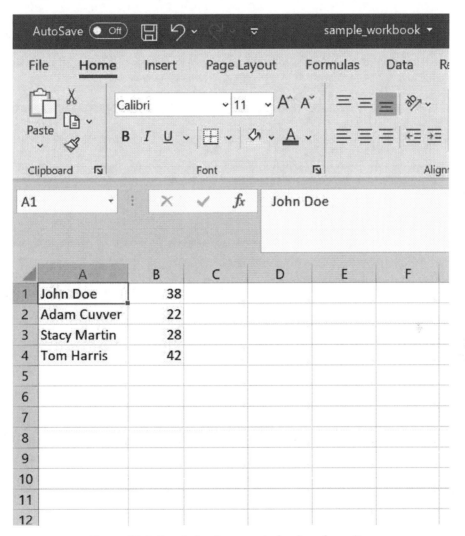

Figure 13.6: Excel sheet generated using xlsxwriter

With the help of the **xlsxwriter** module, you can also apply formulas to your columns. For example, if you wanted to add another row that shows the average age of the people in the spreadsheet, you can do that simply by modifying the **write_data()** method as shown here:

```
def write_data(worksheet, data):
    """Write data to the worksheet."""
    for row in range(len(data)):
        for col in range(len(data[row])):
            worksheet.write(row, col, data[row][col])
    worksheet.write(len(data), 0, "Avg. Age")
    # len(data) will give the next index to write to
    avg_formula = "=AVERAGE(B{}:B{})".format(1, len(data))
    worksheet.write(len(data), 1, avg_formula)
```

In the preceding code snippet, you added an additional **write** call to the worksheet and used the **AVERAGE** function provided by Excel to calculate the average age of the people in the worksheet.

With this, you now know how we can generate Microsoft Excel-compatible XLSX files using Python and how to export tabular content that's easily consumable by the different teams in your organization.

Now, let's cover another interesting file format that is widely used across the world.

WORKING WITH PDF FILES IN PYTHON

Portable Document Format or **PDF** is one of the most common file formats in the world. You must have encountered PDF documents at some point. These documents can include business reports, digital books, and more.

Also, do you remember ever having encountered websites that have a button that reads **Print page as PDF**? A lot of websites for government agencies readily provide this option, which allows you to print the web page directly as a PDF. So, the question arises, how can we do this for our web app? How should we add the option to export certain content as a PDF?

Over the years, a huge community of developers has contributed a lot of useful packages to the Python ecosystem. One of those packages can help us achieve PDF file generation.

CONVERTING WEB PAGES TO PDFS

Sometimes, we may run into situations where we want to convert a web page into a PDF. For example, we may want to print a web page to store it as a local copy. This also comes in handy when trying to print a certificate that is natively displayed as a web page.

To help us in such efforts, we can leverage a simple library known as **weasyprint**, which is maintained by a community of Python developers and allows the quick and easy conversion of web pages to PDFs. So, let's take a look at how we can generate a PDF version of a web page.

EXERCISE 13.04: GENERATING A PDF VERSION OF A WEB PAGE IN PYTHON

In this exercise, you will generate a PDF version of a website using Python. You will use a community-contributed Python module known as **weasyprint** that will help you generate the PDF:

1. To make the code in the upcoming steps work correctly, install the **weasyprint** module on your system. To do this, run the following command:

```
pip install weasyprint
```

> **NOTE**
>
> **weasyprint** depends on the **cairo** library. In case you haven't installed **cairo** libraries, usage of **weasyprint** might raise an error with the message: **libcairo-2.dll file not found**. If you're facing this issue or any other issue installing the module, use the **requirements.txt** file we've provided on our GitHub repository at http://packt.live/3btLoVV. Download the file to your disk and open your Terminal, shell or Command Prompt and type the following command (you will need to **cd** to the path where you saved this file locally): **pip install -r requirements.txt**. If that doesn't work, follow the steps as mentioned in the **weasyprint** documentation: https://weasyprint.readthedocs.io/en/stable/install.html.

2. With the package now installed, create a new file named **pdf_demo.py** that will contain the PDF generation logic. Inside this file, write the following code:

```
from weasyprint import HTML


def generate_pdf(url, pdf_file):
    """Generate PDF version of the provided URL."""
    print("Generating PDF...")
    HTML(url).write_pdf(pdf_file)
```

Now, let's try to understand what this code does. In the first line, you imported the **HTML** class from the **weasyprint** package, which you installed in *step 1*:

```
from weasyprint import HTML
```

This HTML class provides us with a mechanism through which we can read the HTML content of a website if we have its URL.

In the next step, you created a new method named **generate_pdf()** that takes in two parameters, namely, the URL that should be used as the source URL for the generation of the PDF and the **pdf_file** parameter, which takes in the name of the file to which the document should be written:

```
def generate_pdf(url, pdf_file):
```

Next, you passed the URL to the **HTML** class object you imported earlier. This caused the URL to be parsed by the **weasyprint** library and caused its HTML content to be read. Once this was done, you called the **write_pdf()** method of the **HTML** class object and provided to it the name of the file to which the content should be written:

```
HTML(url).write_pdf(pdf_file)
```

3. After this, write the entry point code that sets up the URL (for this exercise, we will use the text version of the **National Public Radio** (**NPR**) website) that should be used for your demo and the filename that should be used to write the PDF content to. Once that is set, the code calls the **generate_pdf()** method to generate the content:

```
if __name__ == '__main__':
    url = 'http://text.npr.org'
    pdf_file = 'demo_page.pdf'
    generate_pdf(url, pdf_file)
```

4. Now, to see the code in action, run the following command:

```
python3 pdf_demo.py
```

Once the command finishes executing, you will have a new PDF file named **demo_page.pdf** that is saved in the same directory where the command was executed. When you open the file, it should resemble what you see here:

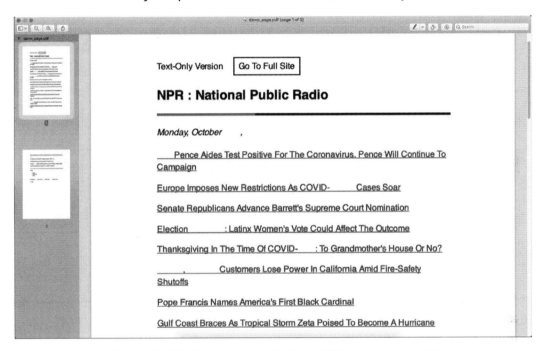

Figure 13.7: Web page converted to a PDF using weasyprint

In the PDF file generated, we can see that the content seems to lack the formatting that the actual website has. This happens because the **weasyprint** package reads the HTML content but does not parse the attached CSS stylesheets for the page, so the page formatting is lost.

weasyprint also makes it quite easy to change the formatting of a page. This can be done simply by introducing the stylesheet parameter to the **write_pdf()** method. A simple modification to our **generate_pdf()** method is described next:

```
from weasyprint import CSS, HTML


def generate_pdf(url, pdf_file):
    """Generate PDF version of the provided URL."""
    print("Generating PDF...")
```

```
css = CSS(string='body{ font-size: 8px; }')
HTML(url).write_pdf(pdf_file, stylesheets=[css])
```

Now, when the preceding code is executed, we will see that the font size for all the text inside the HTML body content of the page has a size of **8px** in the printed PDF version.

> **NOTE**
>
> The **HTML** class in **weasyprint** is also capable of taking any local files as well as raw HTML string content and can use those files to generate PDFs. For further information, please visit the **weasyprint** documentation at https://weasyprint.readthedocs.io.

So far, we have learned about how we can generate different types of binary files with Python, which can help us export our data in a structured manner or help us print PDF versions of our pages. Next, we will see how we can generate graph representations of our data using Python.

PLAYING WITH GRAPHS IN PYTHON

Graphs are a great way to visually represent data that changes within a specific dimension. We come across graphs quite frequently in our day-to-day lives, be it weather charts for a week, stock market movements, or student performance report cards.

Similarly, graphs can come in quite handy when we are working with our web applications. For Bookr, we can use graphs as a visual medium to show the user information about the number of books they read each week. Alternatively, we can show them the popularity of a book over time based on how many readers were reading the given book at a specific time. Now, let's look at how we can generate plots with Python and have them show up on our web pages.

GENERATING GRAPHS WITH PLOTLY

Graphs can come in quite handy when trying to visualize patterns in the data maintained by our applications. There are a lot of Python libraries that help developers in generating static or interactive graphs.

For this book, we will use **plotly**, a community-supported Python library that generates graphs and renders them on web pages. **plotly** is particularly interesting to us due to its ease of integration with Django.

To install it on your system, you can type in the following command in the command line:

```
pip install plotly
```

Now that's done, let's take a look at how we can generate a graph visualization using **plotly**.

SETTING UP A FIGURE

Before we can get started with generating a graph, we first need to initialize a **plotly Figure** object, which essentially acts as a container for our graph. A **plotly Figure** object is quite easy to initialize; it can be done by using the following code snippet:

```
from plotly.graph_objs import graphs
figure = graphs.Figure()
```

The **Figure()** constructor from the **graph_objs** module of **plotly** library returns an instance of the **Figure** graph container, inside which a graph can be generated. Once the **Figure** object is in place, the next thing that needs to be done is to generate a plot.

GENERATING A PLOT

A plot is a visual representation of a dataset. This plot could be a scatter plot, a line graph, a chart, and so on. For example, to generate a scatter plot, the following code snippet is used:

```
scatter_plot = graphs.Scatter(x_axis_values, y_axis_values)
```

The **Scatter** constructor takes in the values for the *X*-axis and *Y*-axis and returns an object that can be used to build a scatter plot. Once the **scatter_plot** object is generated, the next step is to add this plot to our **Figure**. This can be done as follows:

```
figure.add_trace(scatter_plot)
```

The **add_trace()** method is responsible for adding a plotting object to the figure and generating its visualization inside the figure.

RENDERING A PLOT ON A WEB PAGE

Once the plot is added to the figure, it can be rendered on a web page by calling the **plot** method from the **offline** plotting module of **plotly** library. This is shown in the following code snippet:

```
from plotly.offline import plot
visualization_html = plot(figure, output_type='div')
```

The **plot** method takes two primary parameters: the first is the figure that needs to be rendered and the second one is the HTML tag of the container inside which the figure HTML will be generated. The **plot** method returns fully integrated HTML that can be embedded in any web page or made a part of the template to render a graph.

Now, with this understanding of how graph plotting works, let's try a hands-on exercise to generate a graph for our sample dataset.

EXERCISE 13.05: GENERATING GRAPHS IN PYTHON

In this exercise, you will generate a Graph plot using Python. It will be a scatter plot that will represent two-dimensional data:

1. For this exercise, you will be using the **plotly** library. To use this library, you first need to install it on the system. To do this, run the following command:

```
pip install plotly
```

> **NOTE**
>
> You can install **plotly** and other dependencies for this exercise using the **requirements.txt** file we've provided on our GitHub repository: http://packt.live/38y5OLR.

2. With the library now installed, create a new file named **scatter_plot_demo.py** and add the following **import** statements inside it:

```
from plotly.offline import plot
import plotly.graph_objs as graphs
```

3. Once the imports are sorted, create a method named **generate_scatter_ plot()** that takes in two parameters, the values for the *X*-axis and the values for the *Y*-axis:

```
def generate_scatter_plot(x_axis, y_axis):
```

4. Inside this method, first, create an object to act as a container for the graph:

```
figure = graphs.Figure()
```

5. Once the container for the graph is set up, create a new **Scatter** object with the values for the *X*-axis and *Y*-axis and add it to the graph **Figure** container:

```
scatter = graphs.Scatter(x=x_axis, y=y_axis)
figure.add_trace(scatter)
```

6. Once the scatter plot is ready and added to the figure, the last step is to generate the HTML, which can be used to render this plot inside a web page. To do this, call the **plot** method and pass the graph container object to it, and render the HTML inside an HTML **div** tag:

```
return plot(figure, output_type='div')
```

The complete **generate_scatter_plot()** method should look like this now:

```
def generate_scatter_plot(x_axis, y_axis):
    figure = graphs.Figure()
    scatter = graphs.Scatter(x=x_axis, y=y_axis)
    figure.add_trace(scatter)
    return plot(figure, output_type='div')
```

7. Once the HTML for the plot is generated, it needs to be rendered somewhere. For this, create a new method named **generate_html()**, which will take in the plot HTML as its parameter and render an HTML file consisting of the plot:

```
def generate_html(plot_html):
    """Generate an HTML page for the provided plot."""
    html_content = "<html><head><title>Plot
      Demo</title></head><body>{}</body></html>".format(plot_html)
    try:
        with open('plot_demo.html', 'w') as plot_file:
            plot_file.write(html_content)
```

```
except (IOError, OSError) as file_io_error:
    print\
    ("Unable to generate plot file. Exception: {}"\
    .format(file_io_error))
```

8. Once the method is set up, the last step is to call it. For this, create a script entry point that will set up the values for the *X*-axis list and the *Y*-axis list and then call the **generate_scatter_plot()** method. With the value returned by the method, make a call to the **generate_html()** method, which will create an HTML page consisting of the scatter plot:

```
if __name__ == '__main__':
    x = [1,2,3,4,5]
    y = [3,8,7,9,2]
    plot_html = generate_scatter_plot(x, y)
    generate_html(plot_html)
```

9. With the code in place, run the file and see what output is generated. To run the code, execute the following command:

```
python3 scatter_plot_demo.py
```

Once the execution completes, there will be a new **plot_demo.html** file created in the same directory in which the script was executed. Upon opening the file, you should see the following:

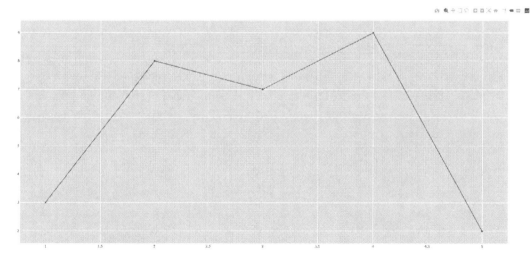

Figure 13.8: Graph generated in the browser using plotly

With this, we have generated our first scatter plot, where different points are connected by a line.

In this exercise, you used the **plotly** library to generate a graph that can be rendered inside a browser for your readers to visualize data.

Now, you know how you can work with graphs in Python and how to generate HTML pages from them.

But as a web developer, how you can use these graphs in Django? Let's find out.

INTEGRATING PLOTLY WITH DJANGO

The graphs generated by **plotly** are quite easy to embed in Django templates. Since the **plot** method returns a fully contained HTML that can be used to render a graph, we can use the HTML returned as a template variable in Django and pass it as it is. The Django templating engine will then take care of adding this generated HTML to the final template before it is shown in the browser.

Some sample code for doing this is shown next:

```
def user_profile(request):
    username = request.user.get_username()
    scatter_plot_html = scatter_plot_books_read(username)
    return render(request, 'user_profile.html'),\
               (context={'plt_div': scatter_plot_html})
```

The preceding code will cause the **{{ plt_div }}** content used inside the template to be replaced by the HTML stored inside the **scatter_plot_demo** variable, and the final template to render the scatter plot of the number of books read per week.

INTEGRATING VISUALIZATIONS WITH DJANGO

In the preceding sections, you have learned how data can be read and written in different formats that cater to the different needs of users. But how can we use what we've learned to integrate with Django?

For example, in Bookr, we might want to allow the user to export a list of books that they have read or visualize their book reading activity over a year. How can that be done? The next exercise in this chapter focuses on that aspect, where you will learn how the components we have seen so far can be integrated into Django web applications.

EXERCISE 13.06: VISUALIZING A USER'S READING HISTORY ON THE USER PROFILE PAGE

In this exercise, you will aim to modify the user's profile page such that the user can visualize their book reading history when they visit their profile page on Bookr.

Let's look at how this can be done:

1. To get started with integrating the ability to visualize the reading history of the user, you first need to install the **plotly** library. To do this, run the following command in your terminal:

```
pip install plotly
```

> **NOTE**
>
> You can install **plotly** and other dependencies for this exercise using the **requirements.txt** file we've provided on our GitHub repository: http://packt.live/3sclvPp.

2. Once the library is installed, the next step is to write the code that will fetch the total books read by the user as well as the books read by the user on a per-month basis. For this, create a new file named **utils.py** under the **bookr** application directory and add the required imports, which will be used to fetch the book reading history of the user from the **Review** model of the **reviews** application:

```
import datetime

from django.db.models import Count
from reviews.models import Review
```

3. Next, create a new utility method named **get_books_read_by_month()**, which takes in the username of the user for whom the reading history needs to be fetched.

4. Inside the method, we query the **Review** model and return a dictionary of books read by the user on a per-month basis:

```
def get_books_read_by_month(username):
    """Get the books read by the user on per month basis.

    :param: str The username for which the books needs to be returned
```

```
        :return: dict of month wise books read
        """

        current_year = datetime.datetime.now().year
        books = Review.objects.filter\
                (creator__username__contains=username),\
                (date_created__year=current_year)\
                .values('date_created__month')\
                .annotate(book_count=Count('book__title'))
        return books
```

Now, let's examine the following query, which is responsible for fetching the results of books read this year on a monthly basis:

```
Review.objects.filter(creator__username__contains=username,date_
created__year=current_year).values('date_created__month').
annotate(book_count=Count('book__title'))
```

This query can be broken down into the following components:

Filtration

```
Review.objects.filter(creator__username__contains=username,date_
created__year=current_year)
```

Here you filter the review records to choose all the records that belong to the current user as well as the current year. The **year** field can be easily accessed from our **date_created** field by appending **__year**.

Projection

Once the review records are filtered, you are not interested in all the fields that might be there. What you are mainly interested in is the month and the number of books read each month. For this, use the **values()** call to select only the **month** field from the **date_created** attribute of the **Review** model on which you are going to run the group by operation.

Group By

Here, you select the total number of books read in a given month. This is done by applying the **annotate** method to the **QuerySet** instance returned by the **values()** call.

5. Once you have the utilities file in place, the next thing is to write the view function, which is going to help in showing the books-read-per-month plot on the user's profile page. For this, open the **views.py** file under the **bookr** directory and start by adding the following imports to it:

```
from plotly.offline import plot
import plotly.graph_objects as graphs


from .utils import get_books_read_by_month
```

6. Once these imports are done, the next thing to do is to modify the view function that renders the profile page. Currently, the profile page is being handled by the **profile()** method inside the **views.py** file. Modify the method to resemble the one shown here:

```
@login_required
def profile(request):
    user = request.user
    permissions = user.get_all_permissions()
    # Get the books read in different months this year
    books_read_by_month = get_books_read_by_month(user.username)

    """
    Initialize the Axis for graphs, X-Axis is months,
    Y-axis is books read
    """
    months = [i+1 for i in range(12)]
    books_read = [0 for _ in range(12)]

    # Set the value for books read per month on Y-Axis
    for num_books_read in books_read_by_month:
        list_index = num_books_read['date_created__month'] - 1
        books_read[list_index] = num_books_read['book_count']

    # Generate a scatter plot HTML
    figure = graphs.Figure()
    scatter = graphs.Scatter(x=months, y=books_read)
    figure.add_trace(scatter)
    figure.update_layout(xaxis_title="Month"),\
                        (yaxis_title="No. of books read")
    plot_html = plot(figure, output_type='div')
```

```
# Add to template
return render(request, 'profile.html'),\
              ({'user': user, 'permissions': permissions,\
              'books_read_plot': plot_html})
```

In this method, you did a couple of things. The first thing was that you called the **get_books_read_by_month()** method and provided it with the username of the currently logged-in user. This method returns the list of books read by a given user on a per-month basis in the current year:

```
books_read_by_month = get_books_read_by_month(user.username)
```

The next thing you did was pre-initialize the X-axis and Y-axis for the graph with some default values. For this visualization, use the X-axis to display months and the Y-axis to display the number of books read.

Now, since you already know that a year is going to have only 12 months, pre-initialize the X-axis with a value between **1** and **12**:

```
months = [i+1 for i in range(12)]
```

For the books read, initialize the Y-axis with all the **12** indexes set to **0** as follows:

```
books_read = [0 for _ in range(12)]
```

Now, with the pre-initialization done, fill in some actual values for the books read per month. For this, iterate upon the list you got as a result of the call made to **get_books_read_by_month(user.username)** and extract the month and the book count for the month from it.

Once the book count and month are extracted, the next step is to assign the **book_count** value to the **books_read** list at the month index:

```
for num_books_read in books_read_by_month:
    list_index = num_books_read['date_created__month'] - 1
    books_read[list_index] = num_books_read['book_count']
```

Now, with the values for the axes set, generate a scatter plot using the **plotly** library:

```
figure = graphs.Figure()
scatter = graphs.Scatter(x=months, y=books_read)
figure.add_trace(scatter)
figure.update_layout(xaxis_title="Month", \
                     yaxis_title="No. of books read")
plot_html = plot(figure, output_type='div')
```

Once the HTML for the plot is generated, pass it to the template using the **render()** method such that it can be visualized on the profile page:

```
return render(request, 'profile.html',
        {'user': user, 'permissions': permissions,\
         'books_read_plot': plot_html}
```

7. With the view function done, the next step is to modify the template to render this graph. For this, open the **profile.html** file under the **templates** directory and add the following highlighted code to the file, just before the last **{% endblock %}** statement:

```
{% extends "base.html" %}

{% block title %}Bookr{% endblock %}

{% block heading %}Profile{% endblock %}

{% block content %}
  <ul>
      <li>Username: {{ user.username }} </li>
      <li>Name: {{ user.first_name }} {{ user.last_name }}</li>
      <li>Date Joined: {{ user.date_joined }} </li>
      <li>Email: {{ user.email }}</li>
      <li>Last Login: {{ user.last_login }}</li>
      <li>Groups: {{ groups }}{% if not groups %}None{% endif %} </li>
  </ul>
  {% autoescape off %}
      {{ books_read_plot }}
  {% endautoescape %}

{% endblock %}
```

This code snippet adds the **books_read_plot** variable passed in the view function to be used inside our HTML template. Also note that **autoescape** is set to off for this variable. This is required because this variable contains HTML generated by the **plotly** library and if you allow Django to escape the HTML, you will only see raw HTML in the profile page and not a graph visualization.

With this, you have successfully integrated the plot into the application.

8. To try the visualization, run the following command and then navigate to your user profile by visiting **http://localhost:8080**:

```
python manage.py runserver localhost:8080
```

You should see a page that resembles the one shown next:

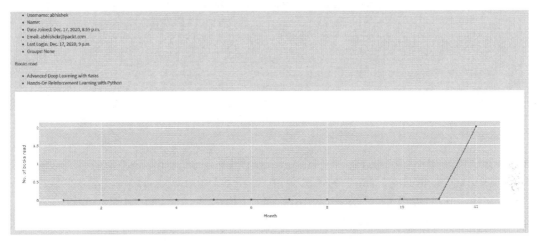

Figure 13.9: User book reading history scatter plot

In the preceding exercise, you saw how you can integrate a plotting library with Django to visualize the reading history of a user. Similarly, Django allows you to integrate any generic Python code into a web application, with the only constraint being that the data generated as a result of the integration should be transformed into a valid HTTP response that can be handled by any standard HTTP-compatible tool, such as a web browser or command-line tools such as CURL.

ACTIVITY 13.01: EXPORTING THE BOOKS READ BY A USER AS AN XLSLX FILE

In this activity, you will implement a new API endpoint inside Bookr that will allow your users to export and download a list of books they have read as an XLSX file:

1. Install the **XlsxWriter** library.

2. Inside the **utils.py** file created under the **bookr** application, create a new function that will help in fetching the list of books that have been read by the user.

3. Inside the **views.py** file under the **bookr** directory, create a new view function that will allow the user to download their reading history in the XLSX file format.

4. To create an XLSX file inside the view function, first create a **BytesIO**-based in-memory file that can be used to store the data from the **XlsxWriter** library.

5. Read the data stored inside the in-memory file using the **getvalue()** method of the temporary file object.

6. Finally, create a new **HttpResponse** instance with the **'application/vnd. ms-excel'** content type header, and then write the data obtained in step 5 to the response object.

7. With the response object prepared, return the response object from the view function.

8. With the view function ready, map it to a URL endpoint that can be visited by a user to download their book reading history.

Once you have the URL endpoint mapped, start the application and log in to it with your user account. Once done, visit the URL endpoint you just created, and if upon visiting the URL endpoint your browser starts to download an Excel file, you have successfully completed the activity.

> **NOTE**
>
> The solution to this activity can be found at http://packt.live/2Nh1NTJ.

SUMMARY

In this chapter, we looked at how we can deal with binary files and how Python's standard library, which comes pre-loaded with the necessary tools, can allow us to handle commonly used file formats such as CSV. We then moved on to learning how to read and write CSV files in Python using Python's CSV module. Later, we worked with the **XlsxWriter** package, which provides us with the ability to generate Microsoft Excel-compatible files right from our Python environment without worrying about the internal formatting of the file.

The second half of the chapter was dedicated to learning how to use the **weasyprint** library to generate PDF versions of HTML pages. This skill can come in handy when we want to provide our users with an easy option to print the HTML version of our page with any added CSS styling of our choosing. The last section of the chapter discussed how we can generate interactive graphs in Python and render them as HTML pages that can be viewed inside the browser using the **plotly** library.

In the next chapter, we will look at how we can test the different components we have been implementing in the previous chapters to make sure that code changes do not break our website's functionality.

14

TESTING

OVERVIEW

This chapter introduces you to the concept of testing Django web applications. You will learn about the importance of testing in software development and, more importantly, in building web applications. You will write unit tests for your Django application's components, such as **views**, **models**, and **endpoints**. Completing this chapter will equip you with the skills to write test cases for Django web applications. That way, you can ensure that your application code works the way you expect.

INTRODUCTION

In the preceding chapters, we have focused upon building our web application in Django by writing different components such as database models, views, and templates. We did all that to provide our users with an interactive application where they can create a profile and write reviews for the books they have read.

Apart from building and running the application, there is another important aspect of making sure that the application code works the way we expect it to work. This is ensured by a technique called **testing**. In testing, we run the different parts of the web application and check whether the output of the executed component matches the output we expected. If the output matches, we can say that the component was tested successfully, and if the output does not match, we say that the component failed to work as intended.

In this chapter, as we go through the different sections, we will learn why testing is important, what the different ways to test a web application are, and how we can build a strong testing strategy that will help us ensure that the web application we build is robust. Let us start our journey by learning about the importance of testing.

THE IMPORTANCE OF TESTING

Making sure that an application works the way it was designed to work is an important aspect of development efforts because, otherwise, our users might keep on encountering weird behaviors that will usually drive them away from engaging with the application.

The efforts we put into testing help us ensure that the different kinds of problems that we intend to solve are indeed being solved correctly. Imagine a case where a developer is building an online event scheduling platform. On this platform, users can schedule events on their calendars as per their local time zone. Now, what if, on this platform, users can schedule events as expected, but due to a bug, the events are scheduled in an incorrect time zone? It is such issues that tend to drive many users away.

That is why a lot of companies spend a huge amount of money making sure that the applications they are building have undergone thorough testing. That way, they ensure that they do not release a buggy product or a product that is far away from satisfying user requirements.

In brief, testing helps us achieve the following goals:

- Ensuring that the components of the application work according to specifications

- Ensuring interoperability with different infrastructure platforms: if an application can be deployed on a different operating system, such as Linux, Windows, and so on

- Reducing the probability of introducing a bug while refactoring the application code

Now, a common assumption many people make about testing is that they have to test all the components manually as they are developed to make sure each component works according to its specifications, and repeat this exercise every time a change is made, or a new component is added to the application. While this is true, this does not provide a complete picture of testing. Testing as a technique has grown to be very powerful with time, and as a developer, you can reduce a huge amount of testing effort by implementing **automated test cases**. So, what are these automated test cases? Or, in other words, what is **automation testing**? Let us find out.

AUTOMATION TESTING

Testing a whole application repeatedly when a single component is modified can turn out to be a challenging task, and even more so if that application consists of a large codebase. The size of the codebase could be due to the sheer number of features or the complexity of the problem it solves.

As we develop applications, it is important to make sure that the changes being made to these applications can be tested easily, so that we can verify whether there is something that is breaking. That is where the concept of automation testing comes in handy. The focus of automation testing is to write tests as code, such that the individual components of an application can be tested in isolation as well as in terms of their interaction with each other.

With this aspect, it now becomes important for us to define the different kinds of automation tests that can be done for applications.

Automation testing can be broadly categorized into five different types:

- **Unit Testing**: In this type of testing, the individual isolated units of code are tested. For example, a unit test can target a single method or a single isolated API. This kind of testing is performed to make sure the basic units of the application work according to their specification.

- **Integration Testing**: In this type of testing, the individual isolated units of code are merged to form a logical grouping. Once this grouping is formed, testing is performed on this logical group to make sure that the group works in the way it is expected to.

- **Functional Testing**: In this kind of testing, the overall functionality of the different components of the application is tested. This may include different APIs, user interfaces, and so on.

- **Smoke Testing**: In this kind of testing, the stability of the deployed application is tested to make sure that the application continues to remain functional as users interact with it, without causing a crash.

- **Regression Testing**: This kind of testing is done to make sure that the changes being made to the application do not degrade the previously built functionality of the application.

As we can see, testing is a big domain that takes time to master, and entire books have been written on this topic. To make sure we highlight the important aspects of testing, we are going to focus on the aspect of unit testing in this chapter.

TESTING IN DJANGO

Django is a feature-packed framework that aims to make web application development rapid. It provides a full-featured way of testing an application. It also provides a well-integrated module that allows application developers to write unit tests for their applications. This module is based on the Python `unittest` library that ships with most Python distributions.

Let us get started with understanding how we can write basic test cases in Django and how to leverage the framework-provided modules to test our application code.

IMPLEMENTING TEST CASES

When working on implementing mechanisms for testing your code, the first thing that needs to be understood is how this implementation can be logically grouped, such that modules that are closely related to each other are tested in one logical unit.

This is simplified by implementing a **test case**. A test case is nothing more than a logical unit that groups together tests that are related to logically similar units, such that all the common logic to initialize the environment for the test cases can be combined in the same place, hence avoiding duplication of work while implementing application testing code.

UNIT TESTING IN DJANGO

Now, with our basic understanding of the tests clear, let us look at how we can do unit testing inside Django. In the context of Django, a unit test consists of two major parts:

- A **TestCase** class, which wraps the different test cases that are grouped for a given module

- An actual test case, which needs to be executed to test the flow of a particular component

The class implementing a unit test should inherit from the **TestCase** class provided by Django's **test** module. By default, Django provides a **tests.py** file in every application directory, which can be used to store the test cases for the application module.

Once these unit tests are written, they can also be executed easily by running them directly using the provided **test** command in **manage.py** as follows:

```
python manage.py test
```

UTILIZING ASSERTIONS

An important part of writing tests is validating whether the test passed or failed. Generally, to implement such decisions inside a testing environment, we utilize something known as **assertions**.

Assertions are a common concept in software testing. They take in two operands and validate whether the value of the operand on the **left-hand side (LHS)** matches the value of the operand on the **right-hand side (RHS)**. If the value on the LHS matches the value on the RHS, an assertion is considered to be successful, whereas if the values differ, the assertion is considered to have failed.

An assertion evaluating to **False** essentially causes a test case to be evaluated as a failure, which is then reported to the user.

Assertions in Python are quite easy to implement and they use a simple keyword called **assert**. For example, the following code snippet shows a very simple assertion:

```
assert 1 == 1
```

The preceding assertion takes in a single expression, which evaluates to **True**. If this assertion were a part of a test case, the test would have succeeded.

Now, let us see how we can implement test cases using the Python **unittest** library. Doing so is quite easy and can be accomplished in a few easy-to-follow steps:

1. Import the **unittest** module, which allows us to build the test cases:

```
import unittest
```

2. Once the module is imported, you can create a class whose name starts with **Test**, which inherits from the **TestCase** class provided by the **unittest** module:

```
class TestMyModule(unittest.TestCase):
    def test_method_a(self):
        assert <expression>
```

Only if the **TestMyModule** class inherits the **TestCase** class will Django be able to run it automatically with full integration with the framework. Once the class is defined, we can implement a new method inside the class named **test_method_a()**, which validates an assertion.

> **NOTE**
>
> An important part to note here is the naming scheme for the test cases and test functions. The test cases being implemented should be prefixed with the name **test**, such that the test execution modules can detect them as valid test cases and execute them. The same rule applies to the naming of testing methods.

3. Once the test case is written, it can be simply executed by running the following command:

```
python manage.py test
```

Now, with our basic understanding of implementing test cases clarified, let us write a very simple unit test to see how the unit testing framework behaves inside Django.

EXERCISE 14.01: WRITING A SIMPLE UNIT TEST

In this exercise, you will write a simple unit test to understand how the Django unit testing framework works and use this knowledge to implement your first test case that validates a couple of simple expressions.

1. To get started, open the **tests.py** file under the **reviews** application of the **Bookr** project. By default, this file will contain only a single line that imports Django's **TestCase** class from the **test** module. In case the file already has a couple of test cases, you can remove all the lines in the file except the one which imports the **TestCase** class as shown next:

```
from django.test import TestCase
```

2. Add the following lines of code in the **tests.py** file you just opened:

```
class TestSimpleComponent(TestCase):
    def test_basic_sum(self):
        assert 1+1 == 2
```

Here, you created a new class named **TestSimpleComponent**, which inherits from the **TestCase** class provided by Django's **test** module. The **assert** statement will compare the expression on the left-hand side (**1 + 1**) with the one on the right (**2**).

3. Once you have written the test case, navigate back to the project folder, and run the following command:

```
python manage.py test
```

The following output should be generated:

```
% ./manage.py test
Creating test database for alias 'default'...
System check identified no issues (0 silenced).
.
----------------------------------------------------------------------
--
Ran 1 test in 0.001s

OK
Destroying test database for alias 'default'...
```

The preceding output signifies that Django's test runner executed one test case, which successfully passed the evaluation.

4. With the test case confirmed to be working and passing, now try to add another assertion at the end of the **test_basic_sum()** method, as shown in the following code snippet:

```
assert 1+1 == 3
```

5. With the **assert** statement added to **tests.py**, now execute the test cases by running the following command from the project folder:

```
python manage.py test
```

At this point, you will notice Django reporting that the execution of the test cases has failed.

With this, you now have an understanding of how test cases can be written in Django and how assertions can be used to validate whether the output generated from your method calls under test is correct or not.

TYPES OF ASSERTIONS

In *Exercise 14.01, Writing a Simple Unit Test,* we had a brief encounter with assertions when we came across the following **assert** statement:

```
assert 1+1 == 2
```

These assertion statements are simple and use the Python **assert** keyword. There are a few different types of assertions possible that can be tested inside a unit test while using the **unittest** library. Let us look at those:

- **assertIsNone**: This assertion is used to check whether an expression evaluates to **None** or not. For example, this type of assertion can be used in cases where a query to a database returns **None** because no records were found for the specified filtering criteria.

- **assertIsInstance**: This assertion is used to validate whether a provided object evaluates to an instance of the provided type. For example, we can validate whether the value returned by a method is indeed of a specific type, such as list, dict, tuple, and so on.

- **assertEquals**: This is a very basic function that takes in two arguments and checks whether the provided arguments to it are equal in value or not. This can be useful when you plan to compare the values of data structures that do not guarantee ordering.

- **assertRaises**: This method is used to validate whether the name of the method provided to it when called raises a specified exception or not. This is helpful when we are writing test cases where a code path that raises an exception needs to be tested. As an example, this kind of assertion can be useful when we want to want to make sure an exception is raised by a method performing a database query (say, to let us know if the database connection is not yet established).

These were just a small set of useful assertions that we can make in our test cases. The **unittest** module on top of which Django's testing library is built provides a lot more assertions that can be tested for.

PERFORMING PRE-TEST SETUP AND CLEANUP AFTER EVERY TEST CASE RUN

Sometimes while writing test cases, we may need to perform some repetitive tasks; for example, setting up some variables that will be required for the test. Once the test is over, we would want to clean up all the changes made to the test variables, such that any new test starts with a fresh instance.

Luckily, the **unittest** library provides a useful way through which we can automate our repetitive efforts of setting up the environment before every test case runs and cleaning it up after the test case is finished. This is achieved using the following two methods, which we can implement in **TestCase**.

setUp(): This method is called before the execution of every **test** method inside the **TestCase** class. It implements the code required to set up the test case's environment before the test executes. This method can be a good place to set up any local database instance or test variables that may be required for the test cases.

> **NOTE**
>
> The **setUp()** method is valid only for test cases written inside the **TestCase** class.

For example, the following example illustrates a simple definition of how the **setUp()** method is used inside a **TestCase** class:

```
class MyTestCase(unittest.TestCase):
    def setUp(self):
        # Do some initialization work
    def test_method_a(self):
```

```
        # code for testing method A
    def test_method_b(self):
        # code for testing method B
```

In the preceding example, when we try to execute the test cases, the **setUp()** method we defined here will be called every time before a **test** method executes. In other words, the **setUp()** method will be called before the execution of the **test_method_a()** call and then it will be called again before **test_method_b()** is called.

tearDown(): This method is called once the **test** function finishes execution and cleans up the variables and their values once the test case execution is finished. This method is executed no matter whether the test case evaluates to **True** or **False**. An example of using the **tearDown()** method is shown next:

```
class MyTestCase(unittest.TestCase):
    def setUp(self):
        # Do some initialization work
    def test_method_a(self):
        # code for testing method A
    def test_method_b(self):
        # code for testing method B
    def tearDown(self):
        # perform cleanup
```

In the preceding example, the **tearDown()** method will be called every time a **test** method finishes execution, that is, once **test_method_a()** finishes execution and again once after **test_method_b()** finishes execution.

Now, we are aware of the different components of writing test cases. Let us now look at how we can test the different aspects of a Django application using the provided test framework.

TESTING DJANGO MODELS

Models in Django are object-based representations of how the data will be stored inside the database of an application. They provide methods that can help us validate the data input provided for a given record, as well as performing any processing on the data before it is inserted into the database.

As easy as it is to create models in Django, it is equally easy to test them. Now, let us look at how Django models can be tested using the Django test framework.

EXERCISE 14.02: TESTING DJANGO MODELS

In this exercise, you will create a new Django model and write test cases for it. The test case will validate whether your model can correctly insert and retrieve the data from the database. These kinds of test cases that work on database models can turn out to be useful in cases where a team of developers is collaborating on a large project and the same database model may get modified by multiple developers over time. Implementing test cases for database models allows developers to pre-emptively identify potentially breaking changes that they may inadvertently introduce as a part of their work:

> **NOTE**
>
> To ensure we get a good hang of running tests from scratch on newly created apps, we'll be creating a new application called **bookr_test**. This application's code is independent of the main **bookr** application and consequently, we won't be including this app's files in the **final/bookr** folder. Upon completion of this chapter, we recommend you practice what you learned by writing similar tests for various components of the main **bookr** application.

1. Create a new application, which you will use for the exercises in this chapter. To do this, run the following command, which will set up a new application for your use case:

```
python manage.py startapp bookr_test
```

2. To make sure the **bookr_test** application behaves the same way as any other application in the Django project, add this application to our **INSTALLED_APPS** section of the **bookr** project. To do this, open the **settings.py** file in your **bookr** project and append the following code to the **INSTALLED_APPS** list:

```
INSTALLED_APPS = [...., \
                  ...., \
                  'bookr_test']
```

3. Now, with the application setup complete, create a new database model, which you will use for testing purposes. For this exercise, you are going to create a new model named **Publisher**, which will store the details about the book publisher in our database. To create the model, open the **models.py** file under the **bookr_test** directory and add the following code to it:

```
from django.db import models


class Publisher(models.Model):
    """A company that publishes books."""
    name = models.CharField\
            (max_length=50,\
             help_text="The name of the Publisher.")
    website = models.URLField\
                (help_text="The Publisher's website.")
    email = models.EmailField\
                (help_text="The Publisher's email address.")


    def __str__(self):
        return self.name
```

In the preceding code snippet, you have created a new class named **Publisher**, which inherits from the **Model** class of Django's **models** module, defining the class as a Django model, which will be used to store data about the publisher:

```
class Publisher(models.Model)
```

Inside this model, you have added three fields, which will act as the properties of the model:

name: The name of the publisher

website: The website belonging to the publisher

email: The email address of the publisher

Once this is done, you create a class method, **__str__()**, which defines how the string representation of the model will look.

4. Now, with the model created, you first need to migrate this model before you can run a test on it. To do this, run the following commands:

```
python manage.py makemigrations
python manage.py migrate
```

5. With the model now set up, write the test case with which you are going to test the model created in *step 3*. For this, open the **tests.py** file under the **bookr_ test** directory and add the following code to it:

```
from django.test import TestCase
from .models import Publisher


class TestPublisherModel(TestCase):
    """Test the publisher model."""
    def setUp(self):
        self.p = Publisher(name='Packt', \
                            website='www.packt.com', \
                            email='contact@packt.com')

    def test_create_publisher(self):
        self.assertIsInstance(self.p, Publisher)

    def test_str_representation(self):
        self.assertEquals(str(self.p), "Packt")
```

In the preceding code snippet, there are a couple of things worth exploring.

At the start, after importing the **TestCase** class from the Django **test** module, you imported the **Publisher** model from the **bookr_test** directory, which is going to be used for testing.

Once the required libraries were imported, you created a new class named **TestPublisherModel**, which inherits the **TestCase** class and is used for grouping the unit tests related to the **Publisher** model:

```
class TestPublisherModel(TestCase):
```

Inside this class, you defined a couple of methods. First, you defined a new method named **setUp()** and added the **Model** object creation code inside it such that the **Model** object is created every time a new **test** method is executed inside this test case. This **Model** object is stored as a class member, such that it can be accessed inside other methods without a problem:

```
def setUp(self):
    self.p = Publisher(name='Packt', \
                        website='www.packt.com', \
                        email='contact@packt.com')
```

The first test case validates whether the **Model** object for the **Publisher** model was created successfully or not. To do this, you created a new method named **test_create_publisher()**, inside which you check whether the created Model object points to an object of the **Publisher** type. If this **Model** object was not created successfully, your test will fail:

```
def test_create_publisher(self):
    self.assertIsInstance(self.p, Publisher)
```

If you check carefully, you are using the **assertIsInstance()** method of the **unittest** library here to assert whether the **Model** object belongs to the **Publisher** type or not.

The next test validates whether the string representation of the model is the same as what you expected it to be. From the code definition, the string representation of the **Publisher** model should output the name of the publisher. To test this, you create a new method named **test_str_representation()** and check whether the generated string representation of the model matches the one you are expecting:

```
def test_str_representation(self):
    self.assertEquals(str(self.p), "Packt")
```

To perform this validation, you use the **assertEquals** method of the **unittest** library, which validates whether the two values provided to it are equal or not.

6. With the test cases now in place, you can run them to check what happens. To run these test cases, run the following command:

```
python manage.py test
```

Once the command finishes execution, you will see an output that resembles the one shown here (your output may differ slightly, though):

```
% python manage.py test
Creating test database for alias 'default'...
System check identified no issues (0 silenced).
..
----------------------------------------------------------------------
--
Ran 2 tests in 0.002s

OK
Destroying test database for alias 'default'...
```

As you can see from the preceding output, the test cases are executed successfully, hence validating that the operations such as the creation of a new **Publisher** object and its string representation when fetched are being done correctly.

With this exercise, we got to see how we can write test cases for our Django models easily and validate their functioning, involving the creation of objects, their retrieval, and representation.

Also, there is an important line to notice in the output from this exercise:

```
"Destroying test database for alias 'default'..."
```

This happens because when there are test cases that require the data to be persisted inside a database, instead of using the production database, Django creates a new empty database for the test cases, which it uses to persist the value for the test case.

TESTING DJANGO VIEWS

Views in Django control the rendering of the HTTP response for users based on the URL they visit in a web application. In this section, we will get on to understand how we can test views inside Django. Imagine you are working on a website where a lot of **Application Programming Interface (API)** endpoints are required. An interesting question to ask would be, how will you be able to validate every new endpoint? If done manually, you will have to first deploy the application every time a new endpoint is added, then manually visit the endpoint in the browser to validate whether it is working fine or not. Such an approach may work out when the number of endpoints is low but may become extremely cumbersome if there are hundreds of endpoints.

Django provides a very comprehensive way of testing application views. This happens with the use of a testing client class provided by Django's **test** module. This class can be used to visit URLs mapped to the views and capture the output generated by visiting the URL endpoint. Then we can use the captured output to test whether the URLs are generating a correct response or not. This client can be used by importing the **Client** class from the Django **test** module and then initializing it as shown in the following snippet:

```
from django.test import Client

c = Client()
```

The client object supports several methods that can be used to simulate the different HTTP calls a user can make, namely, **GET**, **POST**, **PUT**, **DELETE**, and so on. An example of making such a request will look like this:

```
response = c.get('/welcome')
```

The response generated by the view is then captured by the client and gets exposed as a **response** object, which can then be queried to validate the output of the view.

With this knowledge, now let us look at how we can write test cases for our Django views.

EXERCISE 14.03: WRITING UNIT TESTS FOR DJANGO VIEWS

In this exercise, you will use the Django test client to write a test case for your Django view, which will be mapped to a specific URL. These test cases will help you validate whether your view function generates the correct response when visited using its mapped URL:

1. For this exercise, you are going to use the **bookr_test** application that was created in *step 1* of *Exercise 14.02, Testing Django Models*. To get started, open the **views.py** file under the bookr_test directory and add the following code to it:

```
from django.http import HttpResponse


def greeting_view(request):
    """Greet the user."""
    return HttpResponse("Hey there, welcome to Bookr!")\
                        ("Your one stop place")\
                        ("to review books.")
```

Here, you have created a simple Django view, which will be used to greet the user with a welcome message whenever they visit an endpoint mapped to the provided view.

2. Once this view is created, you need to map it to a URL endpoint, which can then be visited in a browser or a test client. To do this, open the **urls.py** file under the **bookr_test** directory and add the highlighted code to the **urlpatterns** list:

```
from django.urls import path
from . import views
```

```
urlpatterns = [path('test/greeting',views.greeting_view,\
                     name='greeting_view')]
```

In the preceding code snippet, you have mapped **greeting_view** to the **'test/greeting'** endpoint for the application by setting the path in the **urlpatterns** list.

3. Once this path is set up, you need to make sure that it is also identified by your project. To do this, you need to add this entry to the **bookr** project's URL mapping. To achieve that, open the **urls.py** file in the **bookr** directory and append the following highlighted line to the end of the **urlpatterns** list, as shown next:

```
urlpatterns = [....,\
               ....,\
               path('', include('bookr_test.urls'))]
```

Your **urls.py** file should look like this now: http://packt.live/3nF8Sdb.

4. Once the view is set up, validate whether it works correctly. Do this by running the following command:

```
python manage.py runserver localhost:8080
```

Then visit **http://localhost:8080/test/greeting** in your web browser. Once the page opens, you should see the following text, which you added to the greeting view in *step 1*, being displayed in the browser:

```
Hey there, welcome to Bookr! Your one stop place to review books.
```

5. Now, you are ready to write the test cases for **greeting_view**. In this exercise, you are going to write a test case that checks whether, on visiting the **/test/greeting** endpoint, you get a successful result or not. To implement this test case, open the **tests.py** file under the **bookr_test** directory and add the following code at the end of the file:

```
from django.test import TestCase, Client


class TestGreetingView(TestCase):
    """Test the greeting view."""
    def setUp(self):
        self.client = Client()
```

```
    def test_greeting_view(self):
        response = self.client.get('/test/greeting')
        self.assertEquals(response.status_code, 200)
```

In the preceding code snippet, you have defined a test case that helps in validating whether the greeting view is working fine or not.

This is done by first importing Django's test client, which allows testing views mapped to the URLs by making calls to them and analyzing the generated response:

```
from django.test import TestCase, Client
```

Once the import is done, you now create a new class named **TestGreetingView**, which will group the test cases related to the greeting view that you created in *step 2*:

```
class TestGreetingView(TestCase):
```

Inside this test case, you defined two methods, **setUp()** and **test_greeting_view()**. The **test_greeting_view()** method implements your test case. Inside this, you first make an HTTP **GET** call to the URL that is mapped to the greeting view and then store the response generated by the view inside the **response** object created:

```
response = self.client.get('/test/greeting')
```

Once this call finishes, you will have its HTTP response code, contents, and headers available inside the **response** variable. Next, with the following code, you make an assertion validating whether the status code generated by the call matches the status code for successful HTTP calls (**HTTP 200**):

```
self.assertEquals(response.status_code, 200)
```

With this, you are now ready to run the tests.

6. With the test case written, let's look at what happens when you run the test case:

```
python manage.py test
```

Once the command executes, you can expect to see an output like the one shown in the following snippet:

```
% python manage.py test
Creating test database for alias 'default'...
System check identified no issues (0 silenced).
...
```

```
------------------------------------------------------------------
--
Ran 3 tests in 0.006s

OK
Destroying test database for alias 'default'...
```

As you can see from the output, your test cases executed successfully, hence validating that the response generated by the **greeting_view()** method is as per your expectations.

In this exercise, you learned how you can implement a test case for a Django view function and use **TestClient** provided by Django to assert that the output generated by the view function matches the one that the developer should see.

TESTING VIEWS WITH AUTHENTICATION

In the previous example, we looked at how we can test views inside Django. An important part to be highlighted about this view is that the view we created could be accessed by anyone and is not protected by any authentication or login checks. Now imagine a case where a view should only be accessible if the user is logged in. For example, imagine implementing a view function that renders the profile page of a registered user of our web application. To make sure that only logged-in users can view the profile page for their account, you might want to restrict the view to logged-in users only.

With this, we now have an important question: *How can we test views that require authentication?*

Luckily, Django's test client provides this functionality through which we can log in to our views and then run tests on them. This result can be achieved by using Django's test client **login()** method. When this method is called, Django's test client performs an authentication operation against the service and if the authentication succeeds, it stores the login cookie internally, which it can then use for further test runs. The following code snippet shows how you can set up Django's test client to simulate a logged-in user:

```
login = self.client.login(username='testuser', password='testpassword')
```

The **login** method requires a username and password for the test user that we are going to test with, as will be shown in the next exercise. So, let us look at how we can test a flow that requires user authentication.

EXERCISE 14.04: WRITING TEST CASES TO VALIDATE AUTHENTICATED USERS

In this exercise, you will write test cases for views that require the user to be authenticated. As part of this, you will validate the output generated by the view method when a user who is not logged in tries to visit the page and when a user who is logged in tries to visit the page mapped to the view function:

1. For this exercise, you are going to use the **bookr_test** application that you created in *step 1* of *Exercise 14.02*, *Testing Django Models*. To get started, open the **views.py** file under the bookr_test application and add the following code to it:

```
from django.http import HttpResponse
from django.contrib.auth.decorators import login_required
```

Once the preceding code snippet is added, create a new function, **greeting_view_user()**, at the end of the file, as shown in the following code snippet:

```
@login_required
def greeting_view_user(request):
    """Greeting view for the user."""
    user = request.user
    return HttpResponse("Welcome to Bookr! {username}"\
                        .format(username=user))
```

With this, you have created a simple Django view that will be used to greet the logged-in user with a welcome message whenever they visit an endpoint mapped to the provided view.

2. Once this view is created, you need to map this view to a URL endpoint that can then be visited in a browser or a test client. To do this, open the **urls.py** file under the **bookr_test** directory and add the following highlighted code to it:

```
from django.urls import path
from . import views


urlpatterns = [path('test/greet_user',\
                     views.greeting_view_user,\
                     name='greeting_view_user')]
```

In the preceding code snippet (see the highlighted part), you have mapped **greeting_view_user** to the **'test/greet_user'** endpoint for the application by setting the path in the **urlpatterns** list. If you have followed the previous exercises, this URL should already be set up for detection in the project and no further steps are required to configure the URL mapping.

3. Once the view is set up, the next thing you need to do is to validate whether it works correctly. To do this, run the following command:

```
python manage.py runserver localhost:8080
```

Then visit **http://localhost:8080/test/greet_user** in your web browser.

If you are not logged in already, by visiting the preceding URL, you will be redirected to the login page for the project.

4. Now, write the test cases for **greeting_view_user**, which checks whether, on visiting the **/test/greet_user** endpoint, you get a successful result. To implement this test case, open the **tests.py** file under the **bookr_test** directory and add the following code to it:

```
from django.contrib.auth.models import User

class TestLoggedInGreetingView(TestCase):
    """Test the greeting view for the authenticated users."""
    def setUp(self):
        test_user = User.objects.create_user\
                    (username='testuser', \
                     password='test@#628password')
        test_user.save()
        self.client = Client()

    def test_user_greeting_not_authenticated(self):
        response = self.client.get('/test/greet_user')
        self.assertEquals(response.status_code, 302)

    def test_user_authenticated(self):
        login = self.client.login\
                (username='testuser', \
                 password='test@#628password')
        response = self.client.get('/test/greet_user')
        self.assertEquals(response.status_code, 200)
```

In the preceding code snippet, you have implemented a test case that checks the views that have authentication enabled before their content can be seen.

With this, you first imported the required classes and methods that will be used to define the test case and initialize a testing client:

```
from django.test import TestCase, Client
```

The next thing you require is the **User** model from Django's **auth** module:

```
from django.contrib.auth.models import User
```

This model is required because for the test cases requiring authentication, you will need to initialize a new test user. Next up, you created a new class named **TestLoggedInGreetingView**, which wraps your tests related to the **greeting_user** view (which requires authentication). Inside this class, you defined three methods, namely: **setUp()**, **test_user_greeting_not_authenticated()**, and **test_user_authenticated()**. The **setUp()** method is used to first initialize a test user, which you will use for authentication. This is a required step because a test environment inside Django is a completely isolated environment that doesn't use data from your production application, hence all the required models and objects are to be instantiated separately inside the test environment.

You then created the test user and initiated the test client using the following code:

```
test_user = User.objects.create_user\
            (username='testuser', \
             password='test@#628password')
test_user.save()
self.client = Client()
```

Next up, you wrote the test case for the **greet_user** endpoint when the user is not authenticated. Inside this, you should expect Django to redirect the user to the login endpoint. This redirect can be detected by checking the HTTP status code of the response, which should be set to **HTTP 302**, indicating a redirect operation:

```
def test_user_greeting_not_authenticated(self):
    response = self.client.get('/test/greet_user')
    self.assertEquals(response.status_code, 302)
```

Next, you wrote another test case to check whether the **greet_user** endpoint renders successfully when the user is authenticated. To authenticate the user, you first call the **login()** method of the test client and perform authentication by providing the username and password of the test user you created in the **setUp()** method as follows:

```
login = self.client.login\
        (username='testuser', \
         password='test@#628password')
```

Once the login is completed, you make an **HTTP GET** request to the **greet_user** endpoint and validate whether the endpoint generates a correct result or not by checking the HTTP status code of the returned response:

```
response = self.client.get('/test/greet_user')
self.assertEquals(response.status_code, 200)
```

5. With the test cases written, it is time to check how they run. For this, run the following command:

```
python manage.py test
```

Once the execution finishes, you can expect to see a response that resembles the one that follows:

```
% python manage.py test
Creating test database for alias 'default'...
System check identified no issues (0 silenced).
.....
----------------------------------------------------------------
--
Ran 5 tests in 0.366s

OK
Destroying test database for alias 'default'...
```

As we can see from the preceding output, our test cases have passed successfully, validating that the view we created generates the desired response of redirecting the user if the user is unauthenticated to the website, and allows the user to see the page if the user is authenticated.

In this exercise, we just implemented a test case where we can test the output generated by a view function regarding the authentication status of the user.

DJANGO REQUEST FACTORY

Till now, we have been using Django's test client to test the views we have created for our application. The test client class simulates a browser and uses this simulation to make calls to the required APIs. But what if we did not want to use the test client and its associated simulation of being a browser, but rather wanted to test the view functions directly by passing the request parameter? How can we do that?

To help us in such cases, we can leverage the **RequestFactory** class provided by Django. The **RequestFactory** class helps us provide the **request** object, which we can pass to our view functions to evaluate their working. The following object for **RequestFactory** can be created by instantiating the class as follows:

```
factory = RequestFactory()
```

The **factory** object thus created supports only HTTP methods such as **get()**, **post()**, **put()**, and others, to simulate a call to any URL endpoint. Let us look at how we can modify the test case that we wrote in *Exercise 14.04, Writing Test Cases to Validate Authenticated Users*, to use **RequestFactory**.

EXERCISE 14.05: USING A REQUEST FACTORY TO TEST VIEWS

In this exercise, you will use a request factory to test view functions in Django:

1. For this exercise, you are going to use the existing **greeting_view_user** view function, which you created earlier, in *step 1* of *Exercise 14.04, Writing Test Cases to Validate Authenticated Users*, which is shown as follows:

```
@login_required
def greeting_view_user(request):
    """Greeting view for the user."""
    user = request.user
    return HttpResponse("Welcome to Bookr! {username}"\
                        .format(username=user))
```

2. Next, modify the existing test case, **TestLoggedInGreetingView**, defined inside the **tests.py** file under the **bookr_test** directory. Open the **tests. py** file and make the following changes.

    First, you need to add the following import to use **RequestFactory** inside the test cases:

```
from django.test import RequestFactory
```

The next thing you need is an import for the **AnonymousUser** class from Django's **auth** module and the **greeting_view_user** view method from the **views** module. This is required to test the view functions with a simulated user who is not logged in. This can be done by adding the following code:

```
from django.contrib.auth.models import AnonymousUser
from .views import greeting_view_user
```

3. Once the **import** statements are added, modify the **setUp()** method of the **TestLoggedInGreetingView** class and change its contents to resemble the one shown next:

```
def setUp(self):
    self.test_user = User.objects.create_user\
                        (username='testuser', \
                        password='test@#628password')
    self.test_user.save()
    self.factory = RequestFactory()
```

In this method, you first created a **user** object and stored it as a class member such that you can use it later in the tests. Once the **user** object is created, then instantiate a new instance of the **RequestFactory** class to use it for testing our view function.

4. With the **setUp()** method now defined, modify the existing tests to use the **RequestFactory** instance. For the test for a non-authenticated call to the view function, modify the **test_user_greeting_not_authenticated** method to have the following contents:

```
def test_user_greeting_not_authenticated(self):
    request = self.factory.get('/test/greet_user')
    request.user = AnonymousUser()
    response = greeting_view_user(request)
    self.assertEquals(response.status_code, 302)
```

In this method, you first created a **request** object using the **RequestFactory** instance you defined in the **setUp()** method. Once that was done, you assigned an **AnonymousUser()** instance to the **request.user** property. Assigning the **AnonymousUser()** instance to the property makes the view function think that the user making the request is not logged in:

```
request.user = AnonymousUser()
```

Once this is done, you made a call to the **greeting_view_user()** view method and passed to it the **request** object you created. Once the call is successful, you capture the output of the method in the **response** variable using the following code:

```
response = greeting_view_user(request)
```

For the unauthenticated user, you expect to get a redirect response, which can be tested by checking the HTTP status code of the response as follows:

```
self.assertEquals(response.status_code, 302)
```

5. Once this is done, go ahead and modify the other method, **test_user_authenticated()**, similarly by using the **RequestFactory** instance as follows:

```
def test_user_authenticated(self):
    request = self.factory.get('/test/greet_user')
    request.user = self.test_user
    response = greeting_view_user(request)
    self.assertEquals(response.status_code, 200)
```

As you can see, most of the code resembles the code you wrote in the **test_user_greeting_not_authenticated** method, with the small change that, in this method, instead of using **AnonymousUser** for our **request.user** property, you are using **test_user**, which you created in our **setUp()** method:

```
request.user = self.test_user
```

With the changes done, it is time to run the tests.

6. To run the tests and validate whether the request factory works as expected, run the following command:

```
python manage.py test
```

Once the command executes, you can expect to see an output that resembles the one shown next:

```
% python manage.py test
Creating test database for alias 'default'...
System check identified no issues (0 silenced).
......
----------------------------------------------------------------------
--
```

```
Ran 6 tests in 0.248s

OK
Destroying test database for alias 'default'...
```

As we can see from the output, the test cases written by us have passed successfully, hence validating the behavior of the **RequestFactory** class.

With this exercise, we learned how we can write test cases for view functions leveraging **RequestFactory** and passing the **request** object directly to the view function, rather than simulating a URL visit using the test client approach, and hence allowing more direct testing.

TESTING CLASS-BASED VIEWS

In the previous exercise, we saw how we can test views defined as methods. But what about class-based views? How can we test those?

As it turns out, it is quite easy to test class-based views. For example, if we have a class-based view defined with the name **ExampleClassView(View)**, to test the view, all we need to do is to use the following syntax:

```
response = ExampleClassView.as_view()(request)
```

It is as simple as that.

A Django application generally consists of several different components that can work in isolation, such as models, and some other components that need to interact with the URL mapping and other parts of the framework to work. Testing these different components may require some steps that are common only to those components. For example, when testing a model, we might first want to create certain objects of the **Model** class before we start testing, or for views, we might first want to initialize a test client with user credentials.

As it turns out, Django also provides some other classes based on top of the **TestCase** class, which can be used to write test cases of specific types about the type of the component being used. Let us look at these different classes provided by Django.

TEST CASE CLASSES IN DJANGO

Beyond the base **TestCase** class provided by Django, which can be used to define a multitude of test cases for different components, Django also provides some specialized classes derived from the **TestCase** class. These classes are used for specific types of test cases based on the capabilities they provide to the developer.

Let us take a quick look at them.

SIMPLETESTCASE

This class is derived from the **TestCase** class provided by Django's **test** module and should be used for writing simple test cases that test the view functions. Usually, the class is not preferred when your test case involves making database queries. The class also provides a lot of useful features, such as the following:

- The ability to check for exceptions raised by a view function

- The ability to test form fields

- A built-in test client

- The ability to verify a redirect by a view function

- Matching the equality of two HTML, JSON, or XML outputs generated by the view functions

Now, with a basic idea of what **SimpleTestCase** is, let us try to understand another type of test case class that helps in writing test cases involving interaction with databases.

TRANSACTIONTESTCASE

This class is derived from the **SimpleTestCase** class and should be used when writing test cases that involve interaction with the database, such as database queries, model object creations, and so on.

The class provides the following added features:

- The ability to reset the database to a default state before a test case runs

- Skipping tests based on database features – this feature can come in handy if the database being used for testing does not support all the features of a production database

LIVESERVERTESTCASE

This class is like the **TransactionTestCase** class, but with the small difference that the test cases written in the class use a live server created by Django (instead of using the default test client).

This ability to run the live server for testing comes in handy when writing test cases that test for the rendered web pages and any interaction with them, which is not possible while using the default test client.

Such test cases can leverage tools such as **Selenium**, which can be used to build interactive test cases that modify the state of the rendered page by interacting with it.

MODULARIZING TEST CODE

In the previous exercises, we have seen how we can write test cases for different components of our project. But an important aspect to note is that, till now, we have written the test cases for all the components in a single file. This approach is okay when the application does not have a lot of views and models. But this can become problematic as our application grows because now our single **tests.py** file will be hard to maintain.

To avoid running into such scenarios, we should try to modularize our test cases such that the test cases for models are kept separately from test cases related to the views, and so on. To achieve this modularization, all we need to do is two simple steps:

1. Create a new directory named **tests** inside your application directory by running the following command:

    ```
    mkdir tests
    ```

2. Create a new empty file named **__init__.py** inside your tests directory by running the following command:

    ```
    touch __init__.py
    ```

    This **__init__.py** file is required by Django to correctly detect the **tests** directory we created as a module and not a regular directory.

Once the preceding steps are done, you can go ahead and create new testing files for the different components in your application. For example, to write test cases for your models, you can create a new file named **test_models.py** inside the tests directory and add any associated code for your model testing inside this file.

Also, you do not need to take any other additional steps to run your tests. The same command will work perfectly fine for your modular testing code base as well:

```
python manage.py test
```

With this, we have now understood how we can write test cases for our projects. So, how about we assess this knowledge by writing test cases for the Bookr project that we are working on?

ACTIVITY 14.01: TESTING MODELS AND VIEWS IN BOOKR

In this activity, you will implement test cases for the Bookr project. You will implement test cases to validate the functioning of the models created inside the **reviews** application of the Bookr project, and then you will implement a simple test case for validating the **index view** inside the **reviews** application.

The following steps will help you work through this activity:

1. Create a directory named **tests** inside the **reviews** application directory, such that all our test cases for the **reviews** application can be modularized.

2. Create an empty **__init__.py** file, such that the directory is considered not as a general directory, but rather a Python module directory.

3. Create a new file, **test_models.py**, for implementing the code that tests the models. Inside this file, import the models you want to test.

4. Inside **test_models.py**, create a new class that inherits from the **TestCase** class of the **django.tests** module and implements methods to validate the creation and reading of the **Model** objects.

5. To test the view function, create a new file named **test_views.py** inside the **tests** directory, which was created in *step 1*.

6. Inside the **test_views.py** file, import the test **Client** class from the **django.tests** module and the **index** view function from the **reviews** application's **views.py** file.

7. Inside the **test_views.py** file created in *step 5*, create a new **TestCase** class, and implement methods to validate the index view.

8. Inside the **TestCase** class created in *step 7*, create a new function, **setUp()**, inside which you should initialize an instance of **RequestFactory**, which will be used to create a **request** object that can be directly passed to the view function for testing.

9. Once the previous steps are done and the test cases are written, run the test cases by executing the **python manage.py** test to validate that the test cases pass.

Upon completing this activity, all test cases should pass successfully.

> **NOTE**
>
> The solution to this activity can be found at http://packt.live/2Nh1NTJ.

SUMMARY

Throughout this chapter, we looked at how we can write test cases for different components of our web application project with Django. We learned about why testing plays a crucial role in the development of any web application and the different types of testing techniques that are employed in the industry to make sure the application code they ship is stable and bug-free.

We then looked at how we can use the **TestCase** class provided by Django's **test** module to implement our unit tests, which can be used to test the models as well as views. We also looked at how we can use Django's **test** client to test our view functions that require or do not require the user to be authenticated. We also glanced over another approach of using **RequestFactory** to test method views and class-based views.

We concluded the chapter by understanding the predefined classes provided by Django and where they should be used and looked at how we can modularize our testing codebase to make it appear clean.

As we move on to the next chapter, we will try to understand how we can make our Django application more powerful by integrating third-party libraries into our project. This functionality will then be used to implement third-party authentication into our Django application and thus allow users to log in to the application using popular services such as Google Sign-In, Facebook Login, and more.

15

DJANGO THIRD-PARTY LIBRARIES

OVERVIEW

This chapter introduces you to Django third-party libraries. You will configure your database connection using URLs with `dj-database-urls` and inspect and debug your application with the **Django Debug Toolbar**. Using `django-crispy-forms`, you will enhance the look of your forms, as well as reduce the amount of code you have to write by using the `crispy` template tag. We will also cover the `django-allauth` library, which lets you authenticate users against third-party providers. In the final activity, we will enhance Bookr's forms with the use of `django-crispy-forms`.

INTRODUCTION

Because Django has been around since 2007, there is a rich ecosystem of third-party libraries that can be plugged into an application to give it extra features. So far, we have learned a lot about Django and used many of its features, including database models, URL routing, templating, forms, and more. We used these Django tools directly to build a web app, but now we will look at how to leverage the work of others to quickly add even more advanced features to our own apps. We have alluded to apps for storing files, (in *Chapter 5*, *Serving Static Files*, we mentioned an app, **django-storages**, that can store our static files in a CDN), but in addition to file storage, we can also use them to plug into third-party authentication systems, integrate with payment gateways, customize how our settings are built, modify images, build forms more easily, debug our site, use different types of databases, and much more. Chances are, if you want to add a certain feature, an app exists for it.

We don't have space to cover every app in this chapter, so we'll just focus on four that provide useful features across many different types of apps. **django-configurations** allows you to configure your Django settings using classes and take advantage of inheritance to simplify settings for different environments. This works in tandem with **dj-database-urls** to specify your database connection setting using just a URL. The *Django Debug Toolbar* lets you get extra information to help with debugging, right in your browser. The last app we'll look at is **django-crispy-forms**, which provides extra CSS classes to make forms look nicer, as well as making them easier to configure using just Python code.

For each of these libraries, we will cover installation and basic setup and use, mostly as they apply to Bookr. They also have more configuration options to further customize to fit your application. Each of these apps can be installed with **pip**.

We will also briefly introduce **django-allauth**, which allows a Django application to authenticate users against third-party providers (such as Google, GitHub, Facebook, and Twitter). We won't cover its installation and setup in detail but will provide some examples to help you configure it.

ENVIRONMENT VARIABLES

When we create a program, we often want the user to be able to configure some of its behavior. For example, say you have a program that connects to a database and saves all the records it finds into a file. Normally it would probably print out just a *success* message to the terminal, but you might also want to run it in *debug mode*, which makes it also print out all the SQL statements it is executing.

There are many ways of configuring a program like this. For example, you could have it read from a configuration file. But in some cases, the user may quickly want to run the Django server with a particular setting on (say, debug mode), and then run the server again with the same setting off. Having to change the configuration file each time can be inconvenient. In this case, we can read from an *environment variable*. Environment variables are key/value pairs that can be set in your operating system and then read by a program. There are several ways they can be set:

- Your shell (terminal) can read variables from a profile script when it starts, then each program will have access to these variables.

- You can set a variable inside a terminal and it will be made available to any programs that start subsequently. In Linux and macOS, this is done with the **export** command; Windows uses the **set** command. Any variables you set in this way override those in the profile script, but only for the current session. When you close the terminal, the variables are lost.

- You can set environment variables at the same time as running a command in a terminal. These will only persist for the program being run, and they override exported environment variables and those read from a profile script.

- You can set environment variables inside a running program, and they will be available only inside the program (or to programs your program starts). Environment variables set in this way will override all the other methods we have just set.

These might sound complicated, but we will explain them with a short Python script and show how variables can be set in the last three ways (the first method depends on what shell you use). The script will also show how environment variables are read.

Environment variables are available in Python using the **os.environ** variable. This is a dictionary-like object that can be used to access environment variables by name. It is safest to access values using the **get** method just in case they are not set. It also provides a **setdefault** method, which allows setting a value only if it is not set (that is, it doesn't overwrite an existing key).

Here is the example Python script that reads environment variables:

```
import os


# This will set the value since it's not already set
os.environ.setdefault('UNSET_VAR', 'UNSET_VAR_VALUE')


# This value will not be set since it's already passed
```

```
# in from the command line
os.environ.setdefault('SET_VAR', 'SET_VAR_VALUE')


print('UNSET_VAR:' + os.environ.get('UNSET_VAR', ''))
print('SET_VAR:' + os.environ.get('SET_VAR', ''))

# All these values were provided from the shell in some way
print('HOME:' + os.environ.get('HOME', ''))
print('VAR1:' + os.environ.get('VAR1', ''))
print('VAR2:' + os.environ.get('VAR2', ''))
print('VAR3:' + os.environ.get('VAR3', ''))
print('VAR4:' + os.environ.get('VAR4', ''))
```

We then set up our shell by setting some variables. In Linux or macOS, we use **export** (note there is no output from these commands):

```
$ export SET_VAR="Set Using Export"
$ export VAR1="Set Using Export"
$ export VAR2="Set Using Export"
```

In Windows, we would use the **set** command in the command line as follows:

```
set SET_VAR="Set Using Export"
set VAR1="Set Using Export"
set VAR2="Set Using Export"
```

In Linux and macOS, we can also provide environment variables by setting them before the command (the actual command is just **python3 env_example.py**):

```
$ VAR2="Set From Command Line" VAR3="Also Set From Command Line" python3
env_example.py
```

> **NOTE**
>
> Note that the above command will not work on Windows. For Windows, the environment variables must be set before execution and cannot be passed in at the same time.

The output from this command is:

```
UNSET_VAR:UNSET_VAR_VALUE
SET_VAR:Set Using Export
HOME:/Users/ben
VAR1:Set Using Export
VAR2:Set From Command Line
VAR3:Also Set From Command Line
VAR4:
```

- When the script runs **os.environ.setdefault('UNSET_VAR', 'UNSET_ VAR_VALUE')**, the value is set inside the script, since no value for **UNSET_VAR** was set by the shell. The value that is output is the one set by the script itself.

- When **os.environ.setdefault('SET_VAR', 'SET_VAR_VALUE')** is executed, the value is not set since one was provided by the shell. This was set with the **export SET_VAR="Set Using Export"** command.

- The value for **HOME** was not set by any of the commands that were run – this is one provided by the shell. It is the user's home directory. This is just an example of an environment variable that a shell normally provides.

- **VAR1** was set by **export** and was not overridden when executing the script.

- **VAR2** was set by **export** but was subsequently overridden when executing the script.

- **VAR3** was only set when executing the script.

- **VAR4** was never set – we use the **get** method to access it to avoid a **KeyError**.

Now that environment variables have been covered, we can return to discussing the changes that need to be made to **manage.py** to support **django-configurations**.

DJANGO-CONFIGURATIONS

One of the main considerations when deploying a Django application to production is how to configure it. As you have seen throughout this book, the **settings.py** file is where all your Django configuration is defined. Even third-party apps have their configuration in this file. You have already seen this in *Chapter 12, Building a REST API*, when working with the Django REST framework.

There are many ways to provide different configurations and switch between them in Django. If you have begun working on an existing application that already has a specific method of switching between configurations in development and production environments, then you should probably keep using that method.

When we release Bookr onto a product web server, in *Chapter 17, Deployment of a Django Application (Part 1 – Server Setup)*, we will need to switch to a production configuration, and that's when we will use **django-configurations**.

To install **django-configurations**, use **pip3** as follows:

```
pip3 install django-configurations
```

> **NOTE**
>
> For Windows, you can use **pip** instead of **pip3** in the preceding command.

The output will be as follows:

```
Collecting django-configurations
  Using cached https://files.pythonhosted.org/packages/96/ef/
bddcce16f3cd36f03c9874d8ce1e5d35f3cedea27b7d8455265e79a77c3d/django_
configurations-2.2-py2.py3-none-any.whl
Requirement already satisfied: six in /Users/ben/.virtualenvs/bookr/lib/
python3.6/site-packages (from django-configurations) (1.14.0)
Installing collected packages: django-configurations
Successfully installed django-configurations-2.2
```

django-configurations changes your **settings.py** file so that all the settings are read from a class you define, which will be a subclass of **configurations.Configuration**. Instead of the settings being global variables inside **settings.py**, they will be attributes on the class you define. By using this class-based method, we can take advantage of object-oriented paradigms, most notably inheritance. Settings, defined in a class, can inherit settings in another class. For example, the production settings class can inherit the development settings class and just override some specific settings – such as forcing **DEBUG** to **False** in production.

We can illustrate what needs to be done to the settings file by just showing the first few settings in the file. A standard Django **settings.py** file normally starts like this (comment lines have been removed):

```
import os


BASE_DIR =os.path.dirname\
          (os.path.dirname(os.path.abspath(__file__)))
SECRET_KEY =\
'y%ux@_^+#eahu3!^i2w71qtgidwpvs^o=w2*$=xy+2-y4r_!fw'
DEBUG = True
...
# The rest of the settings are not shown
```

To convert the settings to **django-configurations**, first import **Configuration** from **configurations**. Then define a **Configuration** subclass. Finally, indent all the settings to be under the class. In PyCharm, this is as simple as selecting all the settings and pressing *Tab* to indent them all.

After doing this, your **settings.py** file will look like this:

```
import os

from configurations import Configuration


class Dev(Configuration):
    BASE_DIR = os.path.dirname\
              (os.path.dirname(os.path.abspath(__file__)))
    SECRET_KEY = \
    'y%ux@_^+#eahu3!^i2w71qtgidwpvs^o=w2*$=xy+2-y4r_!fw'
    DEBUG = True
    ...
    # All other settings indented in the same manner
```

To have different configurations (different sets of settings), you can just extend your configuration classes and override the settings that should differ.

For example, one variable that needs overriding in production is **DEBUG**: it should be **False** (for security and performance reasons). A **Prod** class can be defined that extends **Dev** and sets **DEBUG**, like this:

```
class Dev(Configuration):
    DEBUG = True

    ...

    # Other settings truncated

class Prod(Dev):
    DEBUG = False
    # no other settings defined since we're only overriding DEBUG
```

Of course, you can override other production settings too, not just **DEBUG**. Usually, for security, you would also redefine **SECRET_KEY** and **ALLOWED_HOSTS**; and to configure Django to use your production database, you'd set the **DATABASES** value too. Any Django setting can be configured as you choose.

If you try to execute runserver (or other management commands) now, you will get an error because Django doesn't know how to find the **settings.py** file when the settings files are laid out like this:

```
django.core.exceptions.ImproperlyConfigured: django-configurations settings
importer wasn't correctly installed. Please use one of the starter
functions to install it as mentioned in the docs: https://django-
configurations.readthedocs.io/
```

We need to make some changes to the **manage.py** file before it starts to work again. But before we make them, we'll briefly discuss environment variables, in case you haven't used them before.

MANAGE.PY CHANGES

There are two lines that need to be added/changed in **manage.py** to enable **django-configurations**. First, we need to define a default environment variable that tells Django Configuration which **Configuration** class it should load.

This line should be added in the **main()** function to set the default value for the **DJANGO_CONFIGURATION** environment variable:

```
os.environ.setdefault('DJANGO_CONFIGURATION', 'Dev')
```

This sets the default to **Dev** – the name of the class we defined. As we saw in our example script, if this value is already defined, it won't be overwritten. This will allow us to switch between configurations using an environment variable.

The second change is to swap the **execute_from_command_line** function with one that **django-configurations** provides. Consider the following line:

```
from django.core.management import execute_from_command_line
```

This line is changed as follows:

```
from configurations.management import execute_from_command_line
```

From now on, **manage.py** will work as it did before, except it now prints out which **Configuration** class it's using when it starts (*Figure 15.1*):

```
(bookr) → bookr python3 manage.py runserver
django-configurations version , using configuration Dev
Watching for file changes with StatReloader
Performing system checks...

System check identified no issues (0 silenced).
January 25, 2020 - 09:26:33
Django version 3.0, using settings 'bookr.settings'
Starting development server at http://127.0.0.1:8000/
Quit the server with CONTROL-C.
```

Figure 15.1: django-configurations is using the configuration Dev

In the second line, you can see **django-configurations** output that is using the **Dev** class for settings.

CONFIGURATION FROM ENVIRONMENT VARIABLES

As well as switching between **Configuration** classes using environment variables, **django-configurations** allows us to give values for individual settings using environment variables. It provides **Value** classes that will automatically read values from the environment. We can define defaults if no values are provided. Since environment variables are always strings, the different **Value** classes are used to convert from a string to the specified type.

Let's look at this in practice with a few examples. We will allow **DEBUG**, **ALLOWED_HOSTS**, **TIME_ZONE**, and **SECRET_KEY** to be set with environment variables as follows:

```
from configurations import Configuration, values


class Dev(Configuration):
    DEBUG = values.BooleanValue(True)
    ALLOWED_HOSTS = values.ListValue([])
    TIME_ZONE = values.Value('UTC')
    SECRET_KEY =\
    'y%ux@_^+#eahu3!^i2w71qtgidwpvs^o=w2*$=xy+2-y4r_!fw'
    ...
    # Other settings truncated

class Prod(Dev):
    DEBUG = False
    SECRET_KEY = values.SecretValue()
    # no other settings are present
```

We'll explain the settings one at a time:

- In **Dev**, **DEBUG** is read from an environment variable and cast to a Boolean value. The values **yes**, **y**, **true**, and **1** become **True**; the values **no**, **n**, **false**, and **0** become **False**. This allows us to run with **DEBUG** off even on a development machine, which can be useful in some cases (for example, testing a custom exception page rather than Django's default one). In the **Prod** configuration, we don't want **DEBUG** to accidentally become **True**, so we set it statically.

- **ALLOWED_HOSTS** is required in production. It is a list of hosts for which Django should accept requests.

- The **ListValue** class will convert a comma-separated string into a Python list.

- For example, the string **www.example.com,example.com** is converted to **["www.example.com", "example.com"]**

- **TIME_ZONE** accepts just a string value, so it is set using the **Value** class. This class just reads the environment variable and does not transform it at all.

- **SECRET_KEY** is statically defined in the **Dev** configuration; it can't be changed with an environment variable. In the **Prod** configuration, it is set with **SecretValue**. This is like **Value** in that it is just a string setting; however, it does not allow a default. If a default is set, then an exception is raised. This is to ensure you don't ever put a secret value into **settings.py**, since it might be accidentally shared (for example, uploaded to GitHub). Note that since we do not use **SECRET_KEY** for **Dev** in production, we don't care if it's leaked.

By default, **django-configurations** expects the **DJANGO_** prefix for each environment variable. For example, to set **DEBUG**, use the **DJANGO_DEBUG** environment variable; to set **ALLOWED_HOSTS**, use **DJANGO_ALLOWED_HOSTS**, and so on.

Now that we've introduced **django-configurations** and the changes that need to be made to the project to support it, let's add it to Bookr and make those changes. In the next exercise, you will install and set up **django-configurations** in Bookr.

EXERCISE 15.01: DJANGO CONFIGURATIONS SETUP

In this exercise, you will install **django-configurations** using **pip**, then update **settings.py** to add a **Dev** and **Prod** configuration. You'll then make the necessary changes to **manage.py** to support the new configuration style, and test that everything is still working:

1. In a terminal, make sure you have activated the **bookr** virtual environment, then run this command to install **django-configurations** using **pip3**:

```
pip3 install django-configurations
```

> **NOTE**
>
> For Windows, you can use **pip** instead of **pip3** in the preceding command.

The install process will run, and you should have output like *Figure 15.2*:

```
(bookr) → bookr pip install django-configurations
Collecting django-configurations
  Using cached https://files.pythonhosted.org/packages/96/ef/bddcce16f3cd36f03c9074d8ce1e5d35f3cedea27b7d8455265e79a77c3d/django_configurations-2.2-py2.py3-none-any.whl
Requirement already satisfied: six in /Users/ben/.virtualenvs/bookr/lib/python3.6/site-packages (from django-configurations) (1.14.0)
Installing collected packages: django-configurations
Successfully installed django-configurations-2.2
```

Figure 15.2: django-configurations installation with pip

2. In PyCharm, open **settings.py** inside the **bookr** package. Underneath the existing **os** import, import **Configuration** and **values** from **configurations**, like this:

```
from configurations import Configuration, values
```

3. After the imports but before your first setting definition (the line that sets the **BASE_DIR** value), add a new **Configuration** subclass, called **Dev**:

```
class Dev(Configuration):
```

4. Now we need to move all the existing settings, so they are attributes of the **Dev** class rather than global variables. In PyCharm, this is as simple as selecting all the settings, and then pressing the *Tab* key to indent them. After doing this, your settings should look as follows:

```
from configurations import Configuration, values


class Dev(Configuration):
    # Build paths inside the project like this: os.path.join(BASE_DIR, ...)
    BASE_DIR = os.path.dirname(os.path.dirname(os.path.abspath(__file__)))

    # Quick-start development settings - unsuitable for production
    # See https://docs.djangoproject.com/en/dev/howto/deployment/checklist/

    # SECURITY WARNING: keep the secret key used in production secret!
    SECRET_KEY = 'y%ux@_^+#eahu3!^i2w71qtgidwpvs^o=w2*$=xy+2-y4r_!fw'

    # SECURITY WARNING: don't run with debug turned on in production!
    DEBUG = True
```

Figure 15.3: New Dev configuration

5. After indenting the settings, we will change some of the settings to be read from environment variables. First, change **DEBUG** to be read as **BooleanValue**. It should default to **True**. Consider this line:

```
DEBUG = True
```

And then change it to this:

```
DEBUG = values.BooleanValue(True)
```

This will automatically read **DEBUG** from the **DJANGO_DEBUG** environment variable and convert it to a Boolean. If the environment variable is not set, then it will default to **True**.

6. Also convert **ALLOWED_HOSTS** to be read from an environment variable, using the **values.ListValue** class. It should default to **[]** (empty list). Consider the following line:

```
ALLOWED_HOSTS = []
```

And change it to this:

```
ALLOWED_HOSTS = values.ListValue([])
```

ALLOWED_HOSTS will be read from the **DJANGO_ALLOWED_HOSTS** environment variable, and default to an empty list.

7. Everything you have done so far has been adding/changing attributes on the **Dev** class. Now, at the end of the same file, add a **Prod** class that inherits from **Dev**. It should define two attributes, **DEBUG = True** and **SECRET_KEY = values.SecretValue()**. The completed class should look like this:

```
class Prod(Dev):
    DEBUG = False
    SECRET_KEY = values.SecretValue()
```

Save **settings.py**.

8. If we try to run any management command now, we will receive an error that **django-configurations** is not set up properly. We need to make some changes to **manage.py** to make it work again. Open **manage.py** in the **bookr** project directory.

Consider the line that reads as follows:

```
os.environ.setdefault('DJANGO_SETTINGS_MODULE', 'bookr.settings')
```

Under it, add this line:

```
os.environ.setdefault('DJANGO_CONFIGURATION', 'Dev')
```

This will set the default configuration to the **Dev** class. It can be overridden by setting the **DJANGO_CONFIGURATION** environment variable (for example, to **Prod**).

9. Two lines below the line from the previous step, you must already have the following **import** statement:

```
from django.core.management import execute_from_command_line
```

Change this to:

```
from configurations.management import execute_from_command_line
```

This will make the **manage.py** script use Django Configuration's **execute_from_command_line** function, instead of the Django built-in one.

Save **manage.py**.

10. Start the Django dev server. If it begins without error, you can be confident that the changes you made have worked. To be sure, check that the pages load in your browser. Open **http://127.0.0.1:8000/** and try browsing around the site. Everything should look and feel as it did before:

Figure 15.4: The Bookr site should look and feel as it did before

In this exercise, we installed **django-configurations** and refactored our **settings.py** file to use its **Configuration** class to define our settings. We added **Dev** and **Prod** configurations and made **DEBUG, ALLOWED_HOSTS**, and **SECRET_KEY** settable with environment variables. Finally, we updated **manage.py** to use Django Configuration's **execute_from_command_line** function, which enabled the use of this new settings.py format.

In the next section, we will cover **dj-database-url**, a package that makes it possible to configure your Django database settings using URLs.

DJ-DATABASE-URL

dj-database-url is another app that helps with the configuration of your Django application. Specifically, it allows you to set the database (your Django app connects to) using a URL instead of a dictionary of configuration values. As you can see in your existing **settings.py** file, the **DATABASES** setting contains a couple of items and gets more verbose when using a different database that has more configuration options (for username, password, and so on). We can instead set these from a URL, which can contain all these values.

The URL's format will differ slightly depending on whether you are using a local SQLite database or a remote database server. To use SQLite on disk (as Bookr is currently), the URL is like this:

```
sqlite:///<path>
```

Note there are three slashes present. This is because SQLite doesn't have a hostname, so this is like a URL being like this:

```
<protocol>://<hostname>/<path>
```

That is, the URL has a blank hostname. All three slashes are therefore together.

To build a URL for a remote database server, the format is usually like this:

```
<protocol>://<username>:<password>@<hostname>:<port>/<database_name>
```

For example, to connect to a PostgreSQL database called **bookr_django** on the host, **db.example.com**, on port **5432**, with username **bookr** and password **b00ks**, the URL would be like this:

```
postgres://bookr:b00ks@db.example.com:5432/bookr_django
```

Now that we've seen the format for URLs, let's look at how we can actually use them in our **settings.py** file. First, **dj-database-url** must be installed using **pip3**:

```
pip3 install dj-database-url
```

> **NOTE**
>
> For Windows, you can use **pip** instead of **pip3** in the preceding command.

The output is as follows:

```
Collecting dj-database-url
  Downloading https://files.pythonhosted.org/packages/d4/
a6/4b8578c1848690d0c307c7c0596af2077536c9ef2a04d42b00fabaa7e49d/dj_
database_url-0.5.0-py2.py3-none-any.whl
Installing collected packages: dj-database-url
Successfully installed dj-database-url-0.5.0
```

Now **dj_database_url** can be imported into **settings.py**, and the **dj_
database_url.parse** method can be used to transform the URL into a dictionary
that Django can use. We can use its return value to set the **default** (or other) item
in the **DATABASES** dictionary:

```
import dj_database_url


DATABASES = {'default':dj_database_url.parse\
            ('postgres://bookr:b00ks@db.example.com:5432/\
            bookr_django')}
```

Or, for our SQLite database, we can utilize the **BASE_DIR** setting as we are already,
and include it in the URL:

```
import dj_database_url


DATABASES = {'default': dj_database_url.parse\
            ('sqlite:///{}/db.sqlite3'.format(BASE_DIR))}
```

After parsing, the **DATABASES** dictionary is similar to what we had defined before.
It includes some redundant items that do not apply to an SQLite database (**USER**,
PASSWORD, **HOST**, and so on), but Django will ignore them:

```
DATABASES = {'default': \
            {'NAME': '/Users/ben/bookr/bookr/db.sqlite3',\
            'USER': '',\
            'PASSWORD': '',\
            'HOST': '',\
            'PORT': '',\
            'CONN_MAX_AGE': 0,\
            'ENGINE': 'django.db.backends.sqlite3'}}
```

This method of setting the database connection information is not that useful since we are still statically defining the data in **settings.py**. The only difference is we are using a URL instead of a dictionary. **dj-database-url** can also automatically read the URL from an environment variable. This will allow us to override these values by setting them in the environment.

To read the data from the environment, use the dj_database_url.config function, like this:

```
import dj_database_url



DATABASES = {'default': dj_database_url.config()}
```

The URL is automatically read from the **DATABASE_URL** environment variable.

We can improve on this by also providing a **default** argument to the **config** function. This is the URL that will be used by default if one is not specified in an environment variable:

```
import dj_database_url



DATABASES = {'default':dj_database_url.config\
             (default='sqlite:///{}/db.sqlite3'\
              .format(BASE_DIR))}
```

In this way, we can specify a default URL that can be overridden by an environment variable in production.

We can also specify the environment variable that the URL is read from by passing in the **env** argument – this is the first positional argument. In this way, you could read multiple URLs for different database settings:

```
import dj_database_url

DATABASES = {'default':dj_database_url.config\
             (default='sqlite:///{}/db.sqlite3'\
                 .format(BASE_DIR)),\
             'secondary':dj_database_url.config\
                    ('DATABASE_URL_SECONDARY'\
                 default=\
                 'sqlite:///{}/db-secondary.sqlite3'\
                 .format(BASE_DIR)),}
```

In this example, the **default** item's URL is read from the **DATABASE_URL** environment variable, and **secondary** is read from **DATABASE_URL_SECONDARY**.

django-configurations also provides a config class that works in tandem with **dj_database_url: DatabaseURLValue**. This differs slightly from **dj_database_url.config** in that it generates the entire **DATABASES** dictionary including the **default** item. For example, consider the following code:

```
import dj_database_url


DATABASES = {'default': dj_database_url.config()}
```

This code is the equivalent to the following:

```
from configurations import values


DATABASES = values.DatabaseURLValue()
```

Do not write **DATABASES['default'] = values.DatabaseURLValue()** as your dictionary will be doubly nested.

If you need to specify multiple databases, you will need to fall back to **dj_database_url.config** directly rather than using **DatabaseURLValue**.

Like other **values** classes, **DatabaseURLValue** takes a default value as its first argument. You might also want to use the **environment_prefix** argument and set it to **DJANGO** so that its environment variable being read is consistent in naming to the others. A full example of using **DatabaseURLValue** would therefore be like this:

```
DATABASES = values.DatabaseURLValue\
            ('sqlite:///{}/db.sqlite3'.format(BASE_DIR),\
            environment_prefix='DJANGO')
```

By setting the **environment_prefix** like this, we can set the database URL using the **DJANGO_DATABASE_URL** environment variable (rather than just **DATABASE_URL**). This means it is consistent with other environment variable settings that also start with **DJANGO_**, such as **DJANGO_DEBUG** or **DJANGO_ALLOWED_HOSTS**.

Note that even though we are not importing **dj-database-url** in **settings.py**, **django-configurations** uses it internally, so it still must be installed.

In the next exercise, we will configure Bookr to use DatabaseURLValue to set its database configuration. It will be able to read from an environment variable and fall back to a default we specify.

EXERCISE 15.02: DJ-DATABASE-URL AND SETUP

In this exercise, we will install **dj-database-url** using **pip3**. Then we will update Bookr's **settings.py** to configure the **DATABASE** setting using a URL, which is read from an environment variable:

1. In a terminal, make sure you have activated the **bookr** virtual environment, then run this command to install **dj-database-url** using **pip3**:

```
pip3 install dj-database-url
```

The install process will run, and you should have output similar to this:

```
(bookr) → bookr pip3 install dj-database-url
Collecting dj-database-url
  Downloading https://files.pythonhosted.org/packages/d4/a6/4b8578c1848690d0c307c7c0596af2077536c9ef2a04d42b00fabaa7e49d/dj_database_url-0.5.0-py2.py3-none-any.whl
Installing collected packages: dj-database-url
Successfully installed dj-database-url-0.5.0
```

Figure 15.5: dj-database-url installation with pip

2. In PyCharm, open **settings.py** in the **bookr** package directory. Scroll down to find where the **DATABASES** attribute is being defined. Replace it with the **values.DatabaseURLValue** class. The first argument (default value) should be the URL to the SQLite database: **'sqlite:///{}/db.sqlite3'.format(BASE_DIR)**. Also pass in **environ_prefix**, set to **DJANGO**. After completing this step, you should be setting the attribute like this:

```
DATABASES = values.DatabaseURLValue\
            ('sqlite:///{}/db.sqlite3'.format(BASE_DIR),\
             environ_prefix='DJANGO')
```

Save **settings.py**.

3. Start the Django dev server. As with *Exercise 15.01, Django Configurations Setup*, if it starts fine, you can be confident that your change was successful. To be sure, open `http://127.0.0.1:8000/` in a browser and check that everything looks and behaves as it did before. You should visit a page that queries from the database (such as the **Books List** page) and check that a list of books is displayed:

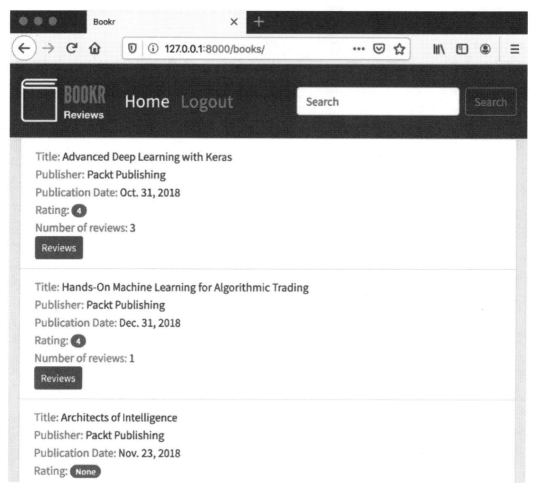

Figure 15.6: Bookr pages with database queries still work

In this exercise, we updated our **`settings.py`** to determine its **DATABASES** setting from a URL specified in an environment variable. We used the **`values.DatabaseURLValue`** class to automatically read the value, and provided a default URL. We also set the **`environ_prefix`** argument to **DJANGO** so that the environment variable name is **DJANGO_DATABASE_URL**, which is consistent with other settings.

In the next section, we will take a tour of the Django Debug Toolbar, an app that helps you debug your Django applications through the browser.

THE DJANGO DEBUG TOOLBAR

The Django Debug Toolbar is an app that displays debug information about a web page right in your browser. It includes information about what SQL commands were run to generate the page, the request and response headers, how long the page took to render, and more. These can be useful if:

- *A page is taking a long time to load – maybe it is running too many database queries.* You can see if the same queries are being run multiple times, in which case you could consider caching. Otherwise, some queries may be sped up by adding an index to the database.

- *You want to determine why a page is returning the wrong information.* Your browser may have sent headers you did not expect, or maybe some headers from Django are incorrect.

- *Your page is slow because it is spending time in non-database code* – you can profile the page to see what functions are taking the longest.

- *The page looks incorrect.* You can see what templates Django rendered. There might be a third-party template that is being rendered unexpectedly. You can also check all the settings that are being used (including the built-in Django ones that we are not setting). This can help to pinpoint a setting that is incorrect and causing the page to not behave correctly.

We'll explain how to use the Django Debug Toolbar to see this information. Before diving into how to set up the Django Debug Toolbar and how to use it, let's take a quick look at it. The toolbar is shown on the right of the browser window and can be toggled open and closed to display information:

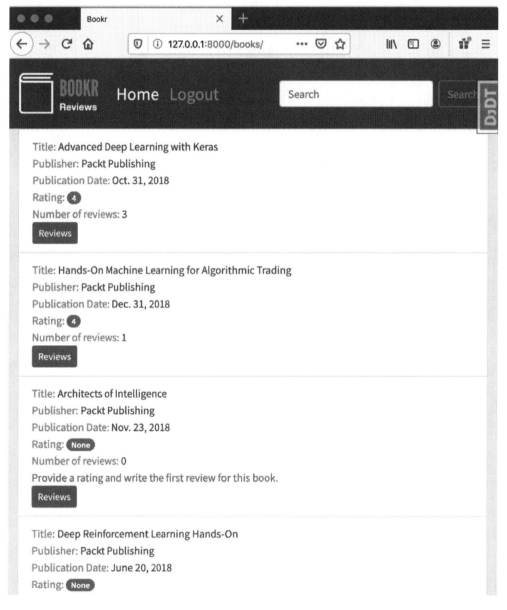

Figure 15.7: The Django Debug Toolbar closed

The preceding figure shows the Django Debug Toolbar in its closed state. Notice the toggle bar in the top-right corner of the window. Clicking the toolbar opens it:

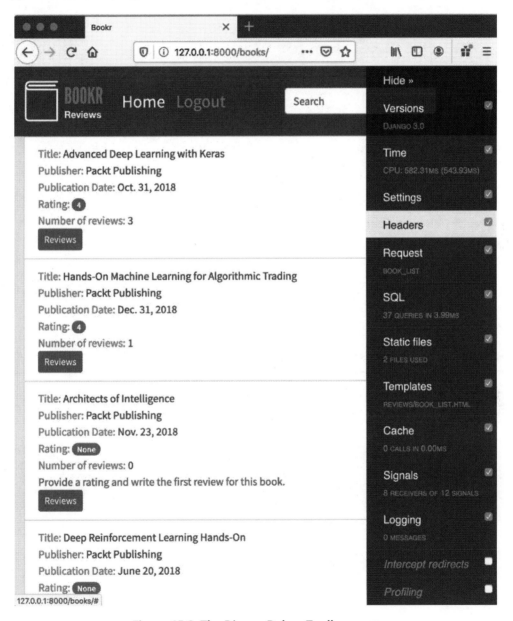

Figure 15.8: The Django Debug Toolbar open

Figure 15.8 shows the Django Debug Toolbar open.

Installing the Django Debug Toolbar is done using **pip**:

```
pip3 install django-debug-toolbar
```

> **NOTE**
>
> For Windows, you can use **pip** instead of **pip3** in the
> preceding command.

Then there are a few steps to set it up, mostly by making changes to **settings.py**:

1. Add **debug_toolbar** to the **INSTALLED_APPS** settings list.

2. Add **debug_toolbar.middleware.DebugToolbarMiddleware** to the
    MIDDLEWARE settings list. It should be done as early as possible; for Bookr,
    it can be the first item in this list. This is the middleware that all requests and
    responses pass through.

3. Add **'127.0.0.1'** to the **INTERNAL_IPS** settings list (this setting may have
    to be created). The Django Debug Toolbar will only show for IP addresses
    listed here.

4. Add the Django Debug Toolbar URLs to the base **urls.py** file. We want to add
    this mapping only if we are in **DEBUG** mode:

```
path('__debug__/', include(debug_toolbar.urls))
```

In the next exercise, we will go through these steps in detail.

Once the Django Debug Toolbar is installed and set up, any page you visit will
show the DjDT sidebar (you can open or close it using the DjDT menu). When
it's open, you'll be able to see another set of sections that you can click on to get
more information.

Each panel has a checkbox next to it, this allows you to enable or disable the collection of that metric. Each metric that is collected will slightly slow down the page load (although, usually, this is not noticeable). If you find that one metric collection is slow, you can turn it off here:

1. We'll go through each panel. The first is **Versions**, which shows the version of Django running. You can click it to open a large **Versions** display, which will also show the version of Python and the Django Debug Toolbar (*Figure 15.9*):

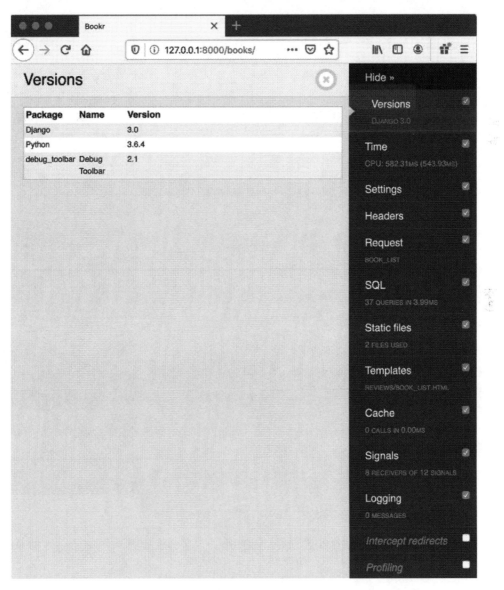

Figure 15.9: DjDT Versions panel (screenshot cropped for brevity)

2. The second panel is **Time**, which shows how long it took to process the request. It is broken down into system time and user time as well (*Figure 15.10*):

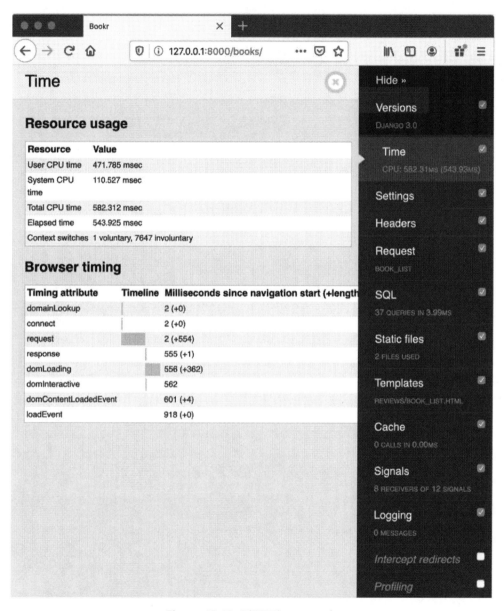

Figure 15.10: DjDT Time panel

The differences between these are beyond the scope of this book but, basically, system time is time spent in the kernel (for example, doing network or file reading/writing) and user time is code that is outside the operating system kernel (this includes the code you've written in Django, Python, and so on).

Also shown is time spent in the browser, such as the time taken to get the request and how long it took to render the page.

3. The third panel, `Settings`, shows all the settings your application is using (*Figure 15.11*):

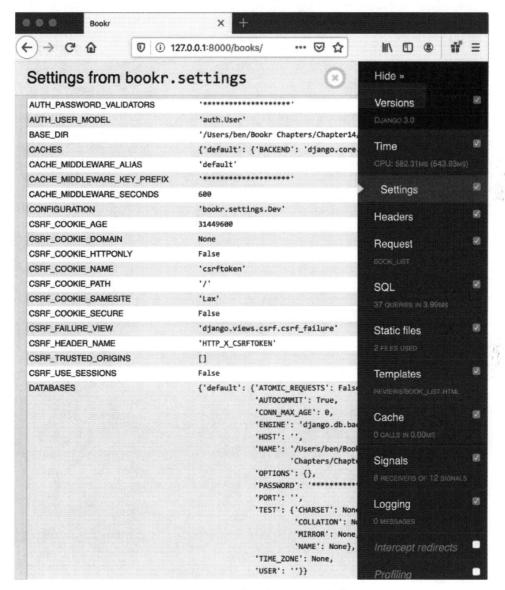

Figure 15.11: DjDT Settings panel

This is useful because it shows both your settings from `settings.py` and the default Django settings.

4. The fourth panel is **Headers** (*Figure 15.12*). It shows the headers of the request the browser made, and the response headers that Django has sent:

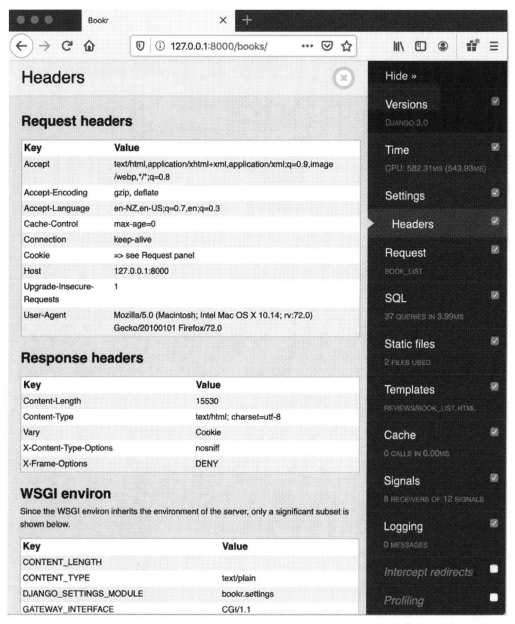

Figure 15.12: DjDT Headers panel

5. The fifth panel, **Request**, shows the view that generated the response, and the args and kwargs it was called with (*Figure 15.13*). You can also see the name of the URL used in its URL map:

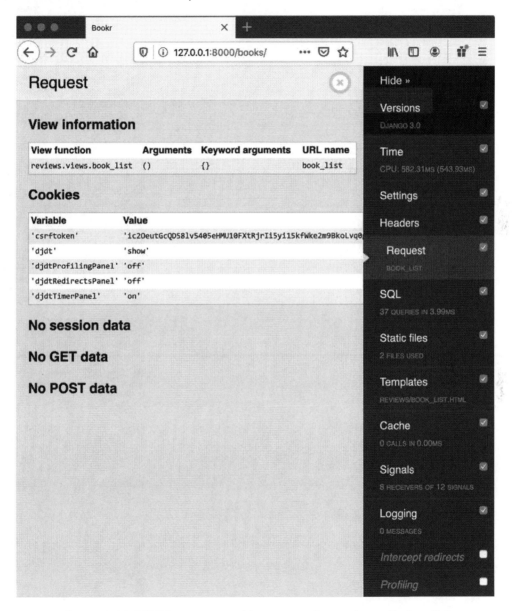

Figure 15.13: DjDT Request panel (some panels not shown for brevity)

It also shows the request's cookies, information stored in the session (sessions were introduced in *Chapter 8, Media Serving and File Upload*) as well as the `request.GET` and `request.POST` data.

6. The sixth panel, **SQL**, shows all the SQL database queries that were executing when building the response (Figure 15.14):

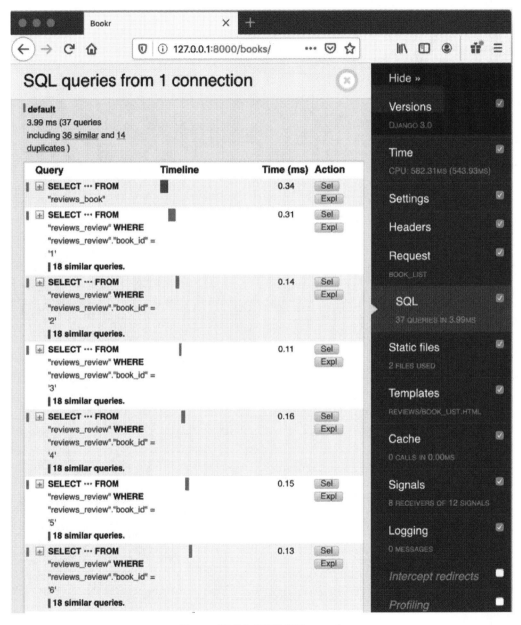

Figure 15.14: DjDT SQL panel

You can see how long each query took to execute and in what order they were executed. It also flags similar and duplicate queries so you can potentially refactor your code to remove them.

Each **SELECT** query displays two action buttons, **Sel**, short for select, and **Expl**, short for explain. These do not show up for **INSERT**, **UDPATE**, or **DELETE** queries.

The **Sel** button shows the **SELECT** statement that was executed and all the data that was retrieved for the query (*Figure 15.15*):

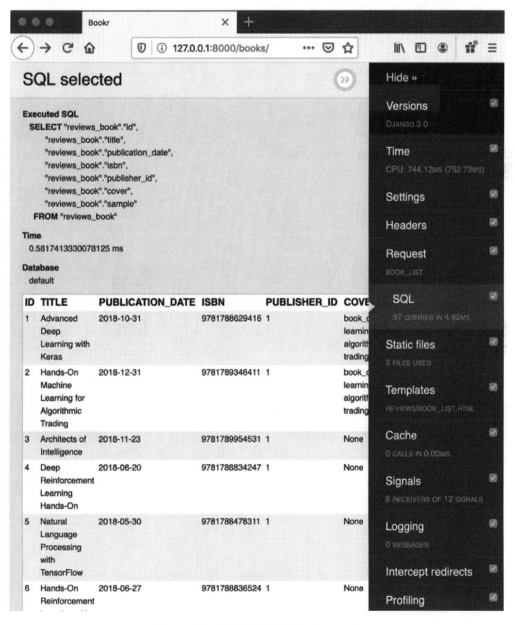

Figure 15.15: DjDT SQL Select panel

The **Expl** button shows the **EXPLAIN** query for the **SELECT** query (*Figure 15.16*):

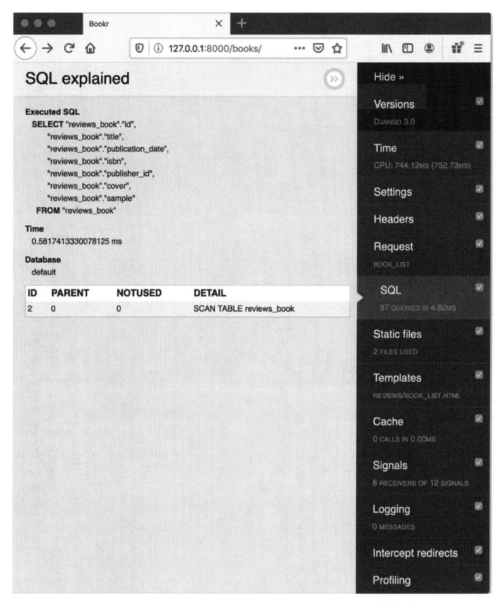

Figure 15.16: DjDT SQL Explain panel (some panels not shown for brevity)

EXPLAIN queries are beyond the scope of the book, but they basically show how the database tried to execute the **SELECT** query, for example, what database indexes were used. You might find that a query does not use an index and you can therefore get faster performance by adding one.

7. The seventh panel is **Static files**, and it shows you which static files were loaded in this request (*Figure 15.17*). It also shows you all the static files that are available and how they would be loaded (that is, which static file finder found them). The **Static files** panel's information is like the information you can get from the **findstatic** management command:

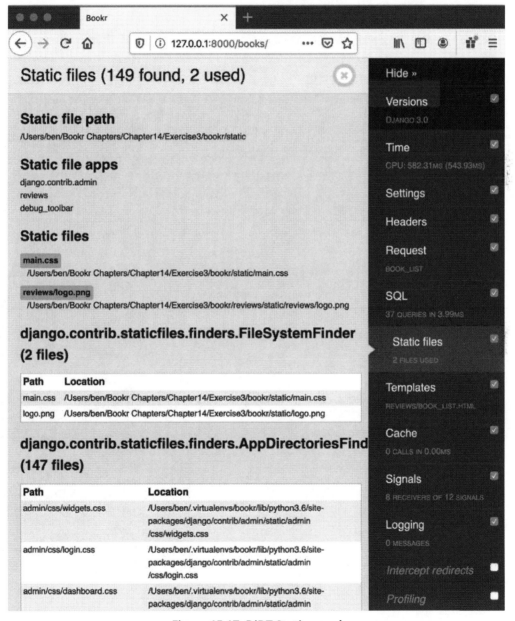

Figure 15.17: DjDT Static panel

8. The eighth panel, **Templates**, shows information about the templates that were rendered (*Figure 15.18*):

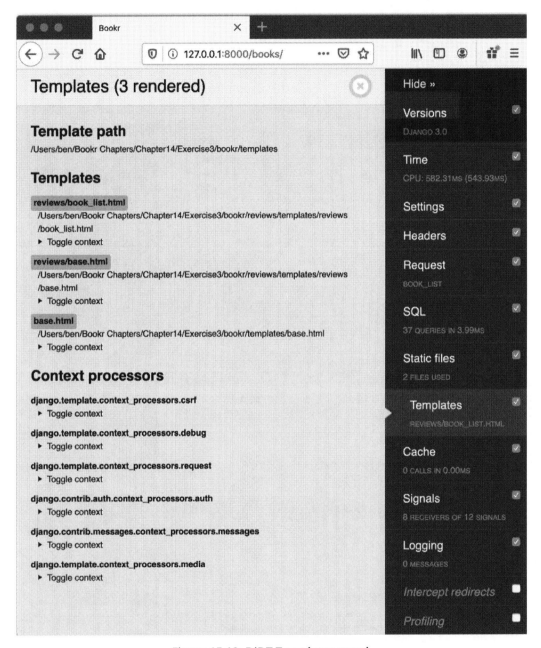

Figure 15.18: DjDT Templates panel

It shows the paths the templates were loaded from and the inheritance chain.

9. The ninth panel, `Cache`, shows information about data fetched from Django's cache:

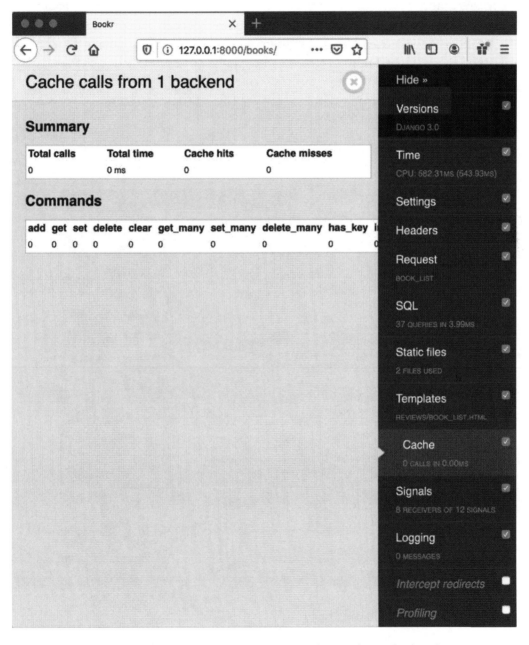

Figure 15.19: DjDT Cache panel (some panels not shown for brevity)

Since we aren't using caching in Bookr, this section is blank. If we were, we would be able to see how many requests to the cache had been made, and how many of those requests were successful in retrieving items. We would also see how many items had been added to the cache. This can give you an idea about whether you are using the cache effectively or not. If you are adding a lot of items to the cache but not retrieving any, then you should reconsider what data you are caching. On the contrary, if you have a lot of **Cache misses** (a miss is when you request data that is not in the cache), then you should be caching more data than you are already.

10. The tenth panel is **Signals**, which shows information about Django signals (*Figure 15.20*):

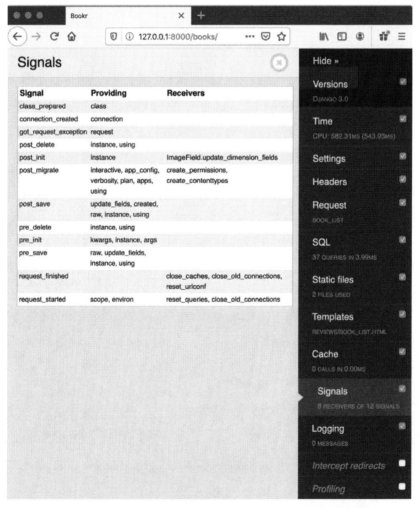

Figure 15.20: DjDT Signals panel (some panels not shown for brevity)

While we don't cover signals in this book, they are like events that you can hook into to execute functions when Django does something; for example, if a user is created, send them a welcome email. This section shows which signals were sent and which functions received them.

11. The eleventh panel, **Logging**, shows log messages that were generated by your Django app (*Figure 15.21*):

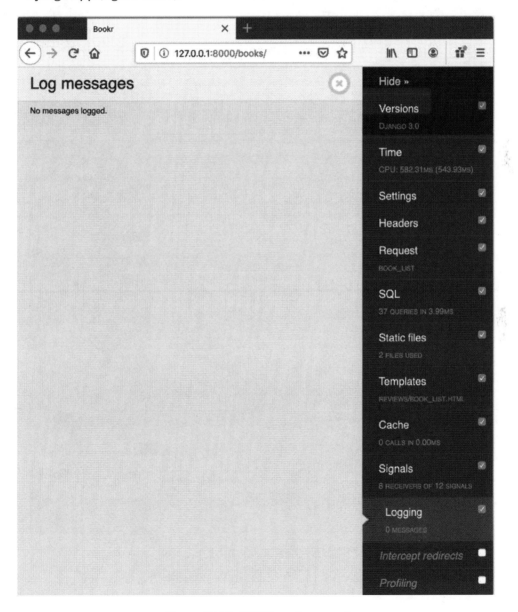

Figure 15.21: DjDT Logging panel

Since no log messages were generated in this request, this panel is empty.

The next option, **`Intercept redirects`**, is not a section with data. Instead, it lets you toggle redirect interception. If your view returns a redirect, it will not be followed. Instead, a page like *Figure 15.22* is displayed:

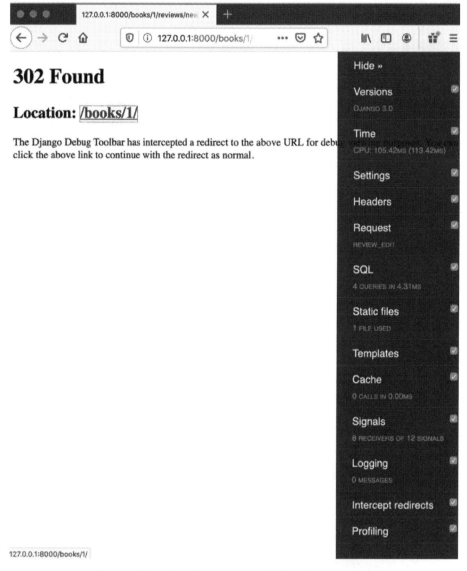

Figure 15.22: A redirect that DjDT has intercepted

This allows you to open the Django Debug Toolbar for the view that generated the redirect – otherwise, you'd only be able to see the information for the view that you were redirected to.

12. The final panel is **Profiling**. This is off by default as profiling can slow down your response quite a lot. Once it is turned on, you must refresh the page to generate the profiling information (shown in *Figure 15.23*):

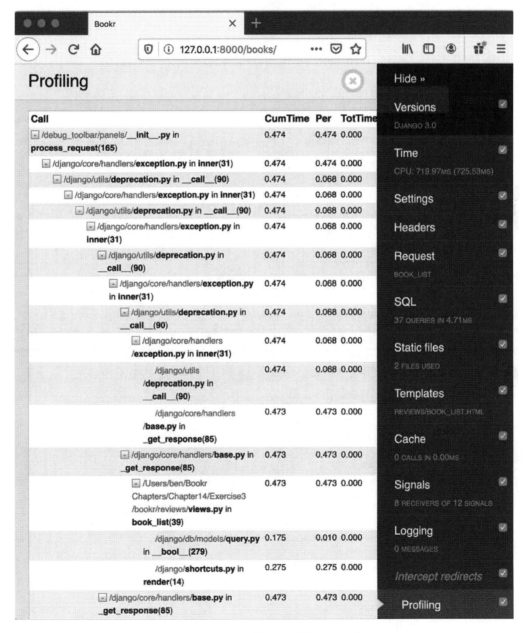

Figure 15.23: DjDT Profiling panel

The information shown here is a breakdown of how long each function call in your response took. The left of the page shows a stack trace of all the calls performed. On the right are columns with timing data. The columns are:

- **CumTime**: The cumulative amount of time spent in the function and any sub-functions it calls

- **Per**: The cumulative time divided by the number of calls (**Count**)

- **TotTime**: The amount of time spent in this function but not in any sub-function it calls

- **Per** (**second per**): The total time divided by the number of calls (**Count**)

- **Calls**: The number of calls of this function

This information can help you determine where to speed up your app. For example, it can be easier to speed up a function that is called 1,000 times by a small fraction, than to optimize a large function that is only called once. Any more in-depth tips on how to speed up your code are beyond the scope of this book.

EXERCISE 15.03: SETTING UP THE DJANGO DEBUG TOOLBAR

In this exercise, you will add the Django Debug Toolbar settings by modifying the **INSTALLED_APPS**, **MIDDLEWARE**, and **INTERNAL_IPS** settings. Then you'll add the **debug_toolbar.urls** map to the **bookr** package's **urls.py**. Then you will load a page with the Django Debug Toolbar in a browser and use it:

1. In a terminal, make sure you have activated the **bookr** virtual environment, then run this command to install the Django Debug Toolbar using **pip3**:

```
pip3 install django-debug-toolbar
```

> **NOTE**
>
> For Windows, you can use **pip** instead of **pip3** in the preceding command.

The install process will run, and you should have output similar to *Figure 15.24*:

```
(bookr) → bookr pip3 install django-debug-toolbar
Collecting django-debug-toolbar
  Downloading https://files.pythonhosted.org/packages/14/92/d923c1df1f927d539543Beb2dc0cab41884009fcaae13b4974eca1d821b2/django_debug_toolbar-2.1-py3-none-any.whl (198kB)
     |████████████████████████████████| 204kB 1.6MB/s
Requirement already satisfied: sqlparse>=0.2.0 in /Users/ben/.virtualenvs/bookr/lib/python3.6/site-packages (from django-debug-toolbar) (0.3.0)
Requirement already satisfied: Django>=1.11 in /Users/ben/.virtualenvs/bookr/lib/python3.6/site-packages (from django-debug-toolbar) (3.0)
Requirement already satisfied: asgiref~=3.2 in /Users/ben/.virtualenvs/bookr/lib/python3.6/site-packages (from Django>=1.11->django-debug-toolbar) (3.2.2)
Requirement already satisfied: pytz in /Users/ben/.virtualenvs/bookr/lib/python3.6/site-packages (from Django>=1.11->django-debug-toolbar) (2019.2)
Installing collected packages: django-debug-toolbar
Successfully installed django-debug-toolbar-2.1
```

Figure 15.24: django-debug-toolbar installation with pip

Open **settings.py** in the **bookr** package directory. Add **debug_toolbar** to the **INSTALLED_APPS** setting:

```
INSTALLED_APPS = [...\
                    'debug_toolbar']
```

This will allow Django to find the Django Debug Toolbar's static files.

2. Add **debug_toolbar.middleware.DebugToolbarMiddleware** to the **MIDDLEWARE** setting – it should be the first item in the list:

```
MIDDLEWARE = ['debug_toolbar.middleware.DebugToolbarMiddleware',\
               ...]
```

This will route requests and responses through **DebugToolbarMiddleware**, allowing the Django Debug Toolbar to inspect the request and insert its HTML into the response.

3. The final setting to add is to add the address **127.0.0.1** to **INTERNAL_IPS**. You will not yet have an **INTERNAL_IPS** setting defined, so add this as a setting:

```
INTERNAL_IPS = ['127.0.0.1']
```

This will make the Django Debug Toolbar only show up on the developer's computer. You can now save **settings.py**.

4. We now need to add the Django Debug Toolbar URLs. Open **urls.py** in the **bookr** package directory. We already have an **if** condition that checks for **DEBUG** mode then adds the media URL like so:

```
if settings.DEBUG:
    urlpatterns += static(settings.MEDIA_URL,\
                          document_root=settings.MEDIA_ROOT)
```

We will also add an **include** of **debug_toolbar.urls** inside this **if** statement, however, we will add it to the start of **urlpatterns** rather than appending it to the end. Add this code inside the **if** statement:

```
import debug_toolbar

urlpatterns = [path\
          ('__debug__/',\
          include(debug_toolbar.urls)),] + urlpatterns
```

Save **urls.py**.

5. Start the Django dev server if it is not already running and navigate to **http://127.0.0.1:8000**. You should see the Django Debug Toolbar open. If it is not open, click the **DjDT** toggle button at the top-right to open it:

Figure 15.25: DjDT toggle shown in the corner

6. Try going through some of the panels and visiting different pages to see what information you can find out. Try also turning on **Intercept redirects** and then create a new book review. After submitting the form, you should see the intercepted page rather than being redirected to the new review (*Figure 15.26*):

The Django Debug Toolbar has intercepted a redirect to the above URL for debug viewing purposes. You can click the above link to continue with the redirect as normal.

Figure 15.26: The redirect intercept page after submitting a new review

You can then click the **Location** link to go to the page that it was being redirected to.

7. You can also try turning on **Profiling** and see which functions are being called a lot and which are taking up most of the rendering time.

8. Once you are finished experimenting with the Django Debug Toolbar, turn off **Intercept redirects** and **Profiling**.

In this exercise, we installed and set up the Django Debug Toolbar by adding settings and URL maps. We then saw it in action and examined the useful information it can give us, including how to work with redirects and see profiling information.

In the next section, we will look at the **django-crispy-forms** app, which will let us reduce the amount of code needed to write forms.

DJANGO-CRISPY-FORMS

In Bookr, we are using the Bootstrap CSS framework. It provides styles that can be applied to forms using CSS classes. Since Django is independent of Bootstrap, when we use Django forms, it does not even know that we are using Bootstrap and so has no idea of what classes to apply to form widgets.

`django-crispy-forms` acts as an intermediary between Django Forms and Bootstrap forms. It can take a Django form and render it with the correct Bootstrap elements and classes. It not only supports Bootstrap but also other frameworks such as **Uni-Form** and **Foundation** (although Foundation support must be added through a separate package, `crispy-forms-foundation`).

Its installation and setup are quite simple. Once again, it is installed with **pip3**:

```
pip3 install django-crispy-forms
```

> **NOTE**
>
> For Windows, you can use **pip** instead of **pip3** in the preceding command.

Then there are just a couple of settings changes. First, add **crispy_forms** to your **INSTALLED_APPS**. Then, you need to tell **django-crispy-forms** what framework you are using, so it loads the correct templates. This is done with the **CRISPY_TEMPLATE_PACK** setting. In our case, it should be set to **bootstrap4**:

```
CRISPY_TEMPLATE_PACK = 'bootstrap4'
```

`django-crispy-forms` has two main modes of operation, either as a filter or a template tag. The former is easier to drop into an existing template. The latter allows more configuration options and moves more of the HTML generation into the **Form** class. We'll look at both of these in order.

THE CRISPY FILTER

The first method of rendering a form with **django-crispy-forms** is by using the **crispy** template. First, the filter must be loaded in the template. The library name is `crispy_forms_tags`:

```
{% load crispy_forms_tags %}
```

Then, instead of rendering a form with the **as_p** method (or another method), use the **crispy** filter. Consider the following line:

```
{{ form.as_p }}
```

And replace it with this:

```
{{ form|crispy }}
```

Here's a quick *before and after* showing the **Review Create** form. None of the rest of the HTML has been changed apart from the form rendering. *Figure 15.27* shows the standard Django form:

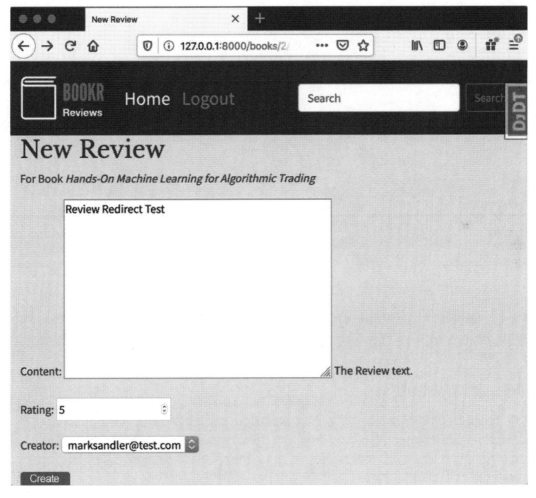

Figure 15.27: The Review Create form with default styling

Figure 15.28 shows the form after **django-crispy-forms** has added the Bootstrap classes:

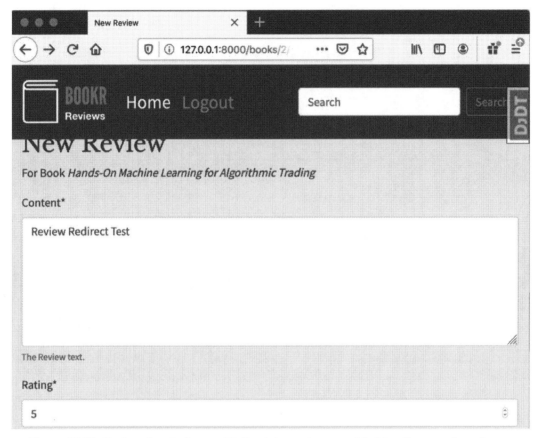

Figure 15.28: Review Create form with Bootstrap classes added by django-crispy-forms

When we integrate **django-crispy-forms** into Bookr, we will not use this method, however, it is worth knowing about because of how easy it is to drop it into your existing templates.

THE CRISPY TEMPLATE TAG

The other method of rendering a form with **django-crispy-forms** is with the use of the **crispy** template tag. To use it, the **crispy_forms_tags** library must first be loaded into the template (as we did in the previous section). Then, the form is rendered like this:

```
{% crispy form %}
```

How does this differ from the **crispy** filter? The **crispy** template tag will also render the **<form>** element and **{% csrf_token %}** template tag for you. So, consider for example that you used it like this:

```
<form method="post">
  {% csrf_token %}
  {% crispy form %}
</form>
```

The output for this would be as follows:

```
<form method="post" >
<input type="hidden" name="csrfmiddlewaretoken" value="...">
<form method="post">
<input type="hidden" name="csrfmiddlewaretoken" value="...">
    ... form fields ...
</form>
</form>
```

That is, the form and CSRF token fields are duplicated. In order to customize the **<form>** element that is generated, **django-crispy-forms** provides a **FormHelper** class that can be set as a **Form** instance's **helper** attribute. It is the **FormHelper** instance that the **crispy** template tag uses to determine what attributes the **<form>** should have.

Let us look at an **ExampleForm** with a helper added. First, import the required modules:

```
from django import forms
from crispy_forms.helper import FormHelper
```

Next, define a form:

```
class ExampleForm(forms.Form):
example_field = forms.CharField()
```

We could instantiate a **FormHelper** instance and then set it to the **form.helper** attribute (for example, in a view), but it's usually more useful to just create and assign it inside the form's **__init__** method. We haven't created a form with an __ **init__** method yet, but it's no different from any other Python class:

```
    def __init__(self, *args, **kwargs):
        super().__init__(*args, **kwargs)
```

Next, we set the helper and the form_method for the helper (which is then rendered in the form HTML):

```
self.helper = FormHelper()
self.helper.form_method = 'post'
```

Other attributes can be set on the helper, such as **form_action**, **form_id**, and **form_class**. We don't need to use these in Bookr though. We also do not need to manually set the **enctype** on the form or its helper, as the **crispy** form tag will automatically set this to **multipart/form-data** if the form contains file upload fields.

If we tried to render the form now, we wouldn't be able to submit it as there's no submit button (remember we added submit buttons to our forms manually, they are not part of the Django form). **django-crispy-forms** also includes layout helpers that can be added to the form. They will be rendered after the other fields. We can add a submit button like this – first, import the **Submit** class:

```
from crispy_forms.layout import Submit
```

> **NOTE**
>
> **django-crispy-forms** does not properly support using a **<button>** input to submit a form, but for our purposes, an **<input type="submit">** is functionally identical.

We then instantiate it and add it to the helper's inputs in a single line:

```
self.helper.add_input(Submit("submit", "Submit"))
```

The first argument to the **Submit** constructor is its *name*, and the second is its *label*.

django-crispy-forms is aware that we are using Bootstrap and will automatically render the button with the **btn btn-primary** classes.

The advantage of using a crispy template tag and **FormHelper** is that it means there is only one place where attributes and the behavior of the form are defined. We are already defining all the form fields in a **Form** class; this allows us to define the other attributes of the form in the same place. We could change a form from a **GET** submission to a **POST** submission easily here. The **FormHelper** instance will then automatically know that it needs to add a CSRF token to its HTML output when rendered.

We'll put all this into practice in the next exercise, where you will install **django-crispy-forms** and then update **SearchForm** to utilize a form helper, then render it using the **crispy** template tag.

EXERCISE 15.04: USING DJANGO CRISPY FORMS WITH THE SEARCHFORM

In this exercise, you will install **django-crispy-forms**, then convert the **SearchForm** to be usable with the **crispy** template tag. This will be done by adding an **__init__** method and building a **FormHelper** instance inside it:

1. In a terminal, make sure you have activated the **bookr** virtual environment, then run this command to install **django-crispy-forms** using **pip3**:

```
pip3 install django-crispy-forms
```

> **NOTE**
>
> For Windows, you can use **pip** instead of **pip3** in the preceding command.

The installation process will run, and you should have output similar to *Figure 15.29*:

```
(bookr) → bookr pip3 install django-crispy-forms
Collecting django-crispy-forms
  Using cached https://files.pythonhosted.org/packages/6e/27/9d6eef25ee96060b20a8df3cc6f6e5f98492900fada0b736767daf6f8f1c/django_crispy_forms-1.8.1-py2.py3-none-any.whl
Installing collected packages: django-crispy-forms
Successfully installed django-crispy-forms-1.8.1
```

Figure 15.29: django-crispy-forms installation with pip

Open **settings.py** in the **bookr** package directory, then add **crispy_forms** to your **INSTALLED_APPS** setting:

```
INSTALLED_APPS = [...\
                    'reviews',\
                    'debug_toolbar',\
                    'crispy_forms'\]
```

This will allow Django to find the required templates.

2. While in **settings.py**, add a new setting for **CRISPY_TEMPLATE_PACK** – its value should be **bootstrap4**. This should be added as an attribute on the **Dev** class:

```
CRISPY_TEMPLATE_PACK = 'bootstrap4'
```

This lets **django-crispy-forms** know that it should be using the templates designed for Bootstrap version 4 when rendering forms. You can now save and close **settings.py**.

3. Open the **reviews** app's **forms.py** file. First, we need to add two imports to the top of the file: **FormHelper** from **crispy_forms.helper**, and **Submit** from **crispy_forms.layout**:

```
from crispy_forms.helper import FormHelper
from crispy_forms.layout import Submit
```

4. Next, add an **__init__** method to **SearchForm**. It should accept ***args** and ****kwargs** as arguments, then call the super **__init__** method with them:

```
class SearchForm(forms.Form):
    ...

    def __init__(self, *args, **kwargs):
        super().__init__(*args, **kwargs)
```

This will simply pass through whatever arguments are provided to the superclass constructor.

5. Still inside the **__init__** method, set **self.helper** to an instance of **FormHelper**. Then set the helper's **form_method** to **get**. Finally, create an instance of **Submit**, passing in an empty string as the name (first argument), and **Search** as the button label (second argument). Add this to the helper with the **add_input** method:

```
self.helper = FormHelper()
self.helper.form_method = "get"
self.helper.add_input(Submit("", "Search"))
```

You can save and close **forms.py**.

6. In the **reviews** app's **templates** directory, open **search-results.html**. At the start of the file, after the **extends** template tag, use a **load** template tag to load **crispy_forms_tags**:

```
{% load crispy_forms_tags %}
```

7. Locate the existing **<form>** in the template. It should look like this:

```
<form>
    {{ form.as_p }}
<button type="submit" class="btn btn-primary">Search</button>
</form>
```

You can delete the entered **<form>** element and replace it with a **crispy** template tag:

```
{% crispy form %}
```

This will use the **django-crispy-forms** library to render the form, including the **<form>** element and submit button. After making this change, this portion of the template should look like *Figure 15.30*:

```
{% block content %}
<h2>Search for Books</h2>
{% crispy form %}
{% if form.is_valid and search_text %}
<h3>Search Results for <em>{{ search_text }}</em></h3>
```

Figure 15.30: search-results.html after replacing <form> with crispy form renderer

You can now save **search-results.html**.

8. Start the Django dev server if it is not already running and go to **http://127.0.0.1:8000/book-search/**. You should see the book search form like in *Figure 15.31*:

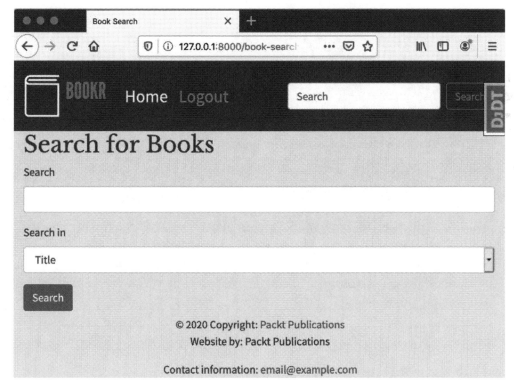

Figure 15.31: Book search form rendered with django-crispy-forms

You should be able to use the form in the same manner as you did before (*Figure 15.32*):

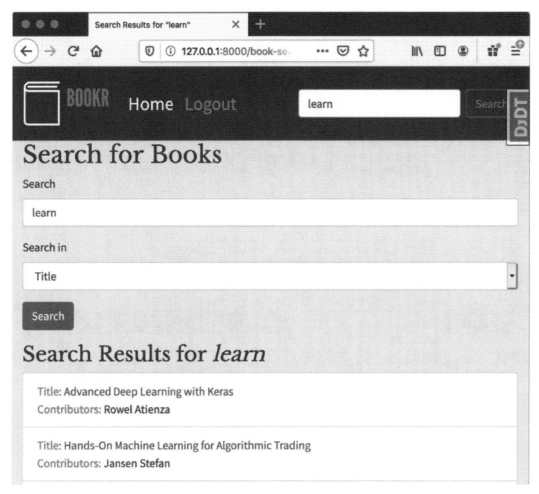

Figure 15.32: Performing a search with the updated search form

Try viewing the source of the page in your web browser to see the rendered output. You will see that the **<form>** element has been rendered with the **method="get"** attribute, as we specified to the **FormHelper** in *step 5*. Notice also that **django-crispy-forms** has not inserted a CSRF token field – it knows that one is not required for a form submitted using **GET**.

In this exercise, we installed **django-crispy-forms** using **pip3** (**pip** for Windows) and then configured it in **settings.py** by adding it to **INSTALLED_APPS** and defining the **CRISPY_TEMPLATE_PACK** we wanted to use (in our case, **bootstrap4**). We then updated the **SearchForm** class to use a **FormHelper** instance to control the attributes on the form and added a submit button using the **Submit** class. Finally, we changed the **search-results.html** template to use the **crispy** template tag to render the form, which allowed us to remove the **<form>** element we were using before and simplify form generation by moving all the form-related code into Python code (instead of being partially in HTML and partially in Python).

DJANGO-ALLAUTH

When browsing websites, you have probably seen buttons that allow you to log in using another website's credentials. For example, using your GitHub login:

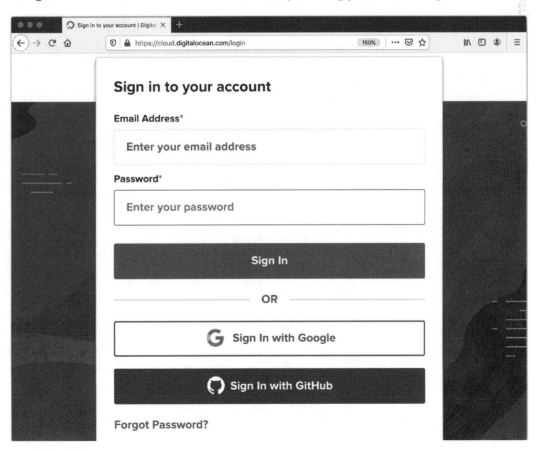

Figure 15.33: Sign In form with options to log in with Google or GitHub

Before we explain the process, let us introduce the terminology we will be using:

- **Requesting site**: The site the user is trying to log in to.

- **Authentication provider**: The third-party provider that the user is authenticating to (for example, Google, GitHub, and so on).

- **Authentication application**: This is something the creators of the requesting site set up at the authentication provider. It determines what permissions the requesting site will have with the authentication provider. For example, the requesting application can get access to your GitHub username, but won't have permission to write to your repositories. The user can stop the requesting site from accessing your information at the authentication provider by disabling access to the authentication application.

The process is generally the same regardless of which third-party sign-in option you choose. First, you will be redirected to the authentication provider site and be asked to allow the authentication application to access your account (*Figure 15.34*):

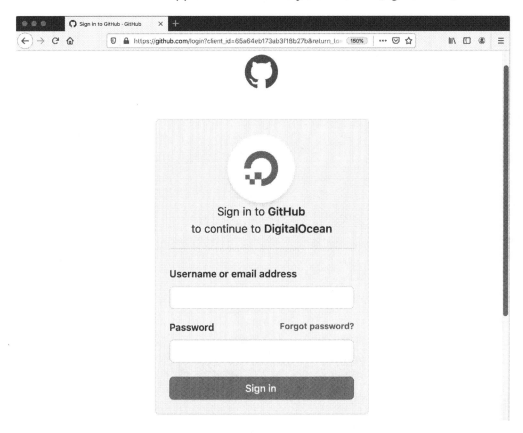

Figure 15.34: Authentication provider authorization screen

After you authorize the authentication application, the authentication provider will redirect back to the requesting site. The URL that you are redirected to will contain a secret token that the requesting site can use to request your user information in the backend. This allows the requesting site to verify who you are by communicating directly with the authentication provider. After validating your identity using a token, the requesting site can redirect you to your content. This flow is illustrated in a sequence diagram in *Figure 15.35*:

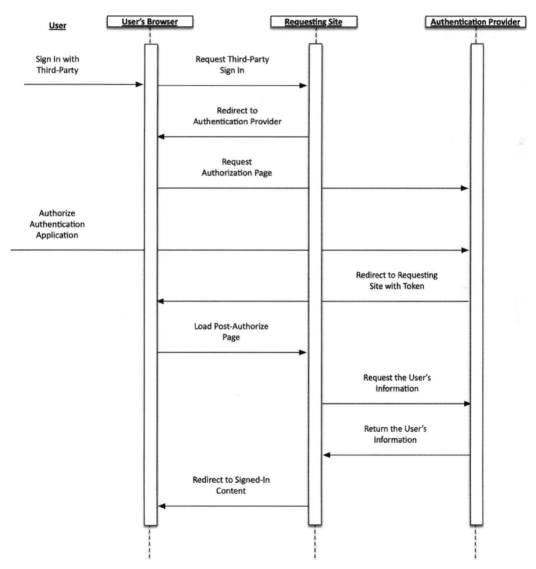

Figure 15.35: Third-party authentication flow

Now that we have introduced authenticating using a third-party service, we can discuss **django-allauth**. **django-allauth** is an app that easily plugs your Django application into a third-party authentication service, including Google, GitHub, Facebook, Twitter, and others. In fact, at the time of writing, **django-allauth** supports over 75 authentication providers.

The first time a user authenticates to your site, **django-allauth** will create a standard Django **User** instance for you. It also knows how to parse the callback/redirect URL that the authentication provider loads after the end user authorizes the authentication application.

django-allauth adds three models to your application:

- **SocialApplication**: This stores the information used to identify your authentication application. The information you enter will depend on the provider, who will give you a *client* ID, *secret* key, and (optionally) a *key*. Note that these are the names that **django-allauth** uses for these values and they will differ based on the provider. We will give some examples of these values later in this section. **SocialApplication** is the only one of the **django-allauth** models that you will create yourself, the others **django-allauth** creates automatically when a user authenticates.

- **SocialApplicationToken**: This contains the values needed to identify a Django user to the authentication provider. It contains a *token* and (optionally) a *token secret*. It also contains a reference to the **SocialApplication** that created it and the **SocialAccount** to which it applies.

- **SocialAccount**: This links a Django user to the provider (for example, Google or GitHub) and stores extra information that the provider may have given.

Since there are so many authentication providers, we will not cover how to set them all up, but we will give a short instruction on setup and how to map the auth tokens from the providers to the right fields in a **SocialApplication**. We will do this for the two auth providers we have been mentioning throughout the chapter: Google and GitHub.

DJANGO-ALLAUTH INSTALLATION AND SETUP

Like the other apps in this chapter, **django-allauth** is installed with **pip3**:

```
pip3 install django-allauth
```

We then need a few settings changes. **django-allauth** requires the **django. contrib.sites** app to run, so it needs to be added to **INSTALLED_APPS**. Then a new setting needs to be added to define a **SITE_ID** for our site. We can just set this to **1** in our **settings.py** file:

```
INSTALLED_APPS = [# this entry added
                 'django.contrib.sites',\
                 'django.contrib.admin',\
                 'django.contrib.auth',\
                 # the rest of the values are truncated]

SITE_ID = 1
```

We also need to add **allauth** and **allauth.socialaccount** to **INSTALLED_APPS**:

```
INSTALLED_APPS = [# the rest of the values are truncated
                 'allauth',\
                 'allauth.socialaccount',]
```

Then, each provider we want to support must also be added in the list of **INSTALLED_APPS**; for example, consider the following snippet:

```
INSTALLED_APPS = [# the rest of the values are truncated
                 'allauth.socialaccount.providers.github',\
                 'allauth.socialaccount.providers.google',]
```

After all this is done, we need to run the **migrate** management command, to create the **django-allauth** models:

```
python3 manage.py migrate
```

Once this is done, new social applications can be added through the Django Admin interface (*Figure 15.36*):

Figure 15.36: Adding a social application

To add a social application, select a **Provider** (this list will only show those in the **INSTALLED_APPS** list), enter a name (it can just be the same as the **Provider**), and enter the **Client ID** from the provider's website (we will go into detail on this soon). You may also need a **Secret key** and **Key**. Select the site it should apply to. (If you only have one **Site** instance, then its name does not matter, just select it. The site name can be updated in the **Sites** section of Django admin. You can also add more sites there.)

We will now look at the tokens used by our three example providers.

GITHUB AUTH SETUP

A new GitHub application can be set up under your GitHub profile. During development, your callback URL for the application should be set to `http://127.0.0.1:8000/accounts/github/login/callback/` and updated with the real hostname when you deploy to production. After creating the app, it will provide a `Client ID` and `Client Secret`. These are your `Client id` and `Secret key`, respectively, in `django-allauth`.

GOOGLE AUTH SETUP

The creation of a Google application is done through your Google Developers console. The authorized redirect URI should be set to `http://127.0.0.1:8000/accounts/google/login/callback/` during development and updated after production deployment. The app's `Client ID` is also Client id in `django-allauth`, and the app's `Client secret` is the `Secret key`.

INITIATING AUTHENTICATION WITH DJANGO-ALLAUTH

To initiate authentication through a third-party provider, you first need to add the `django-allauth` URLs in your URL maps. Somewhere inside your `urlpatterns` is one of your `urls.py` files, include `allauth.urls`:

```
urlpatterns = [path('allauth', include('allauth.urls')),]
```

You will then be able to initiate a login using URLs like `http://127.0.0.1:8000/allauth/github/login/?process=login` or `http://127.0.0.1:8000/allauth/google/login/?process=login`, and so on. django-allauth will handle all the redirects for you, then create/authenticate the Django user when they return to the site. You can have buttons on your login page with text such as Login with GitHub or Login with Google that link to these URLs.

OTHER DJANGO-ALLAUTH FEATURES

Other than authentication with third-party providers, `django-allauth` can also add some useful features that Django does not have built in. For example, you can configure it to require an email address for a user, and have the user verify their email address by clicking a confirmation link they receive before they log in, `django-allauth` can also handle generating a URL for a password reset that is emailed to the user. You can find the documentation for `django-allauth` that explains these features, and more, at https://django-allauth.readthedocs.io/en/stable/overview.html.

Now that we have covered the first four third-party apps in depth and given a brief overview of **django-allauth**, you can undertake the activity for this chapter. In this activity, you will refactor the **ModelForm** instances we are using to use the **CrispyFormHelper** class.

ACTIVITY 15.01: USING FORMHELPER TO UPDATE FORMS

In this activity, we will update the **ModelForm** instances (**PublisherForm**, **ReviewForm**, and **BookMediaForm**) to use the **CrispyFormHelper** class. Using **FormHelper**, we can define the text of the **Submit** button inside the **Form** class itself. We can then move the **<form>** rendering logic out of the **instance-form. html** template and replace it with a **crispy** template tag.

These steps will help you complete the activity:

1. Create an **InstanceForm** class that subclasses **forms.ModelForm**. This will be the base of the existing **ModelForm** classes.

2. In the **__init__** method of **InstanceForm**, set a **FormHelper** instance on **self**.

3. Add a **Submit** button to **FormHelper**. If the form is instantiated with an **instance**, then the button text should be **Save**, otherwise, it should be **Create**.

4. Update PublisherForm, ReviewForm, and BookMediaForm to extend from **InstanceForm**.

5. Update the **instance-form.html** template so that **form** is rendered using the **crispy** template tag. The rest of the **<form>** can be removed.

6. In the **book_media** view, the **is_file_upload** context item is no longer required.

When you are finished, you should see the forms rendered with Bootstrap themes. *Figure 15.37* shows the **New Publisher** page:

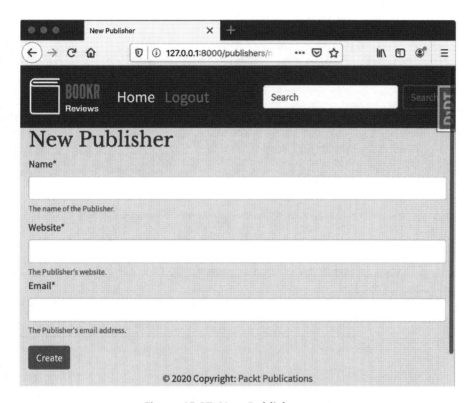

Figure 15.37: New Publisher page

Figure 15.38 shows the **New Review** page:

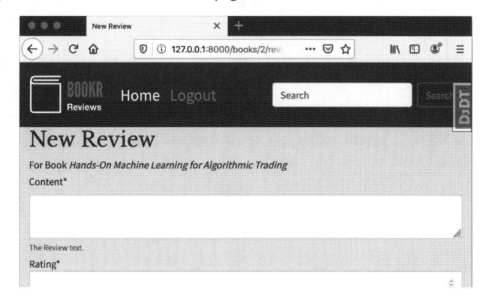

Figure 15.38: New Review form

Finally, the book media page is displayed in *Figure 15.39*:

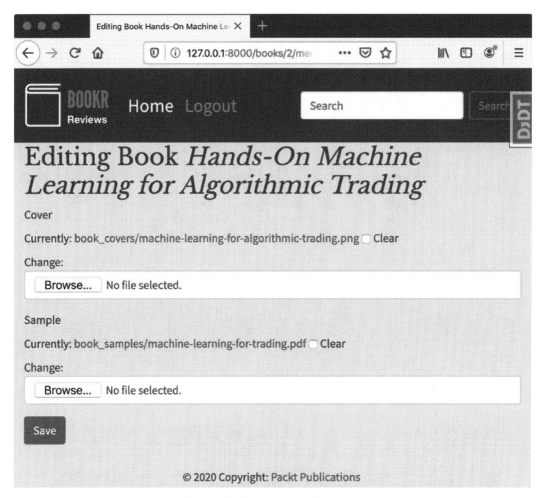

Figure 15.39: Book media page

You should notice the form still behaves fine and allows file uploads. **django-crispy-forms** has automatically added the **enctype="multipart/form-data"** attribute to **<form>**. You can verify this by viewing the page source.

> **NOTE**
>
> The solution to this activity can be found at http://packt.live/2Nh1NTJ.

SUMMARY

In this chapter, we introduced five third-party Django apps that can enhance your website. We installed and set up **django-configurations**, which allowed us to easily switch between different settings and change them using environment variables. **dj-database-url** also helped with settings, allowing us to make database settings changes using URLs. We saw how the Django Debug Toolbar could help us see what our app was doing and help us debug problems we were having with it. **django-crispy-forms** can not only render our forms using the Bootstrap CSS but also lets us save code by defining their behavior as part of the form class itself. We briefly looked at **django-allauth** and saw how it can be integrated into third-party authentication providers. In the activity for this chapter, we updated our **ModelForm** instances to use the **django-crispy-forms FormHelper** and remove some logic from the template by using the **crispy** template tag.

In the next chapter, we will look at how to integrate the React JavaScript framework into a Django application.

16

USING A FRONTEND JAVASCRIPT LIBRARY WITH DJANGO

OVERVIEW

This chapter introduces the basics of JavaScript and ends with building an interactive web frontend for Bookr using the React JavaScript framework. You will learn how to include the React JavaScript framework in a Django template, and how to build React components. This chapter also includes an introduction to **JSX**, a special format that combines JavaScript code and HTML – you will also learn how **Babel** transpiles JSX into plain JavaScript. Later, you will learn about the `fetch` JavaScript function which is used to retrieve information from a REST API. Toward the end of the chapter, you will be introduced to the Django `{% verbatim %}` template tag, which is used to include unparsed data in a Django template.

INTRODUCTION

Django is a great tool for building the backend of an application. You have seen how easy it is to set up the database, route URLs, and render templates. Without using JavaScript, though, when those pages are rendered to the browser, they are static and do not provide any form of interaction. By using JavaScript, your pages can be transformed into applications that are fully interactive in the browser.

This chapter will be a brief introduction to JavaScript frameworks and how to use them with Django. While it won't be a deep dive into how to build an entire JavaScript application from scratch (that would be a book in itself), we will give enough of an introduction so that you can add interactive components to your own Django application. In this chapter, we will primarily be working with the React framework. Even if you do not have any JavaScript experience, we will introduce enough about it so that, by the end of this chapter, you will be comfortable writing your own React components. In *Chapter 12*, *Building a REST API*, you built a REST API for Bookr. We will interact with that API using JavaScript to retrieve data. We will enhance Bookr by showing some review previews on the main page that are dynamically loaded and can be paged through.

> **NOTE**
>
> The code for the exercises and activities in this chapter can be found in this book's GitHub repository at http://packt.live/3iasIMl.

JAVASCRIPT FRAMEWORKS

These days, real-time interactivity is a fundamental part of web applications. While simple interactions can be added without a framework (developing without a framework is often called *Vanilla JS*), as your web application grows, it can be much easier to manage with the use of a framework. Without a framework, you would need to do all these things yourself:

- Manually define the database schema.

- Convert data from HTTP requests into native objects.

- Write form validation.

- Write SQL queries to save data.

- Construct HTML to show a response.

Compare this to what Django provides. Its **ORM (Object Relational Mapping)**, automatic form parsing and validation, and templating drastically cut down on the amount of code you need to write. JavaScript frameworks bring similar time-saving enhancements to JavaScript development. Without them, you would have to manually update the HTML elements in the browser as your data changes. Let's take a simple example: showing the count of the number of times a button has been clicked. Without a framework, you would have to do the following:

1. Assign a handler to the button click event.

2. Increment the variable that stored the count.

3. Locate the element containing the click count display.

4. Replace the element's text with the new click count.

When using a framework, the button count variable is bound to the display (HTML), so the process you have to code is as follows:

1. Handle the button click.

2. Increment the variable.

The framework takes care of automatically re-rendering the number display. This is just a simple example, though; as your application grows, the disparity in complexity between the two approaches expands. There are several JavaScript frameworks available, each with different features and some supported and used by large companies. Some of the most popular are React (https://reactjs.org), Vue (http://vuejs.org), Angular (https://angularjs.org), Ember (https://emberjs.com), and Backbone.js (https://backbonejs.org).

In this chapter, we will be using React, as it is easy to drop into an existing web application and allows *progressive enhancement*. This means that rather than having to build your application from scratch, targeting React, you can simply apply it to certain parts of the HTML that Django generates; for example, a single text field that automatically interprets Markdown and shows the result without reloading the page. We will also cover some of the features that Django offers that can help integrate several JavaScript frameworks.

There are several different levels that JavaScript can be incorporated into a web application at. *Figure 16.1* shows our current stack, with no JavaScript (note that the following diagrams do not show requests to the server):

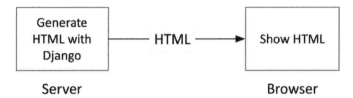

Figure 16.1: Current stack

You can base your entire application on JavaScript using **Node.js** (a server-side JavaScript interpreter), which would take the place of Python and Django in the stack. *Figure 16.2* shows how this might look:

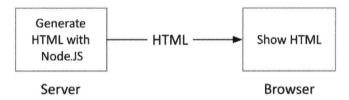

Figure 16.2: Using Node.js to generate HTML

Or, you can have your frontend and templates entirely in JavaScript, and just use Django to act as a REST API to provide data to render. *Figure 16.3* shows this stack:

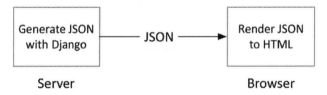

Figure 16.3: Sending JSON from Django and rendering it in the browser

The final approach is progressive enhancement, which is (as mentioned) what we will be using. In this way, Django is still generating the HTML templates and React sits on top of this to add interactivity:

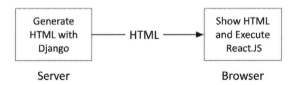

Figure 16.4: HTML generated with Django with React providing progressive enhancement

Note that it is common to use multiple techniques together. For example, Django may generate the initial HTML to which React is applied in the browser. The browser can then query Django for JSON data to be rendered, using React.

JAVASCRIPT INTRODUCTION

In this section, we will briefly introduce some basic JavaScript concepts, such as variables and functions. Different operators will be covered as we introduce them.

Loading JavaScript

JavaScript can either be inline in an HTML page or included from a separate JavaScript file. Both methods use the **<script>** tag. With inline JavaScript, the JavaScript code is written directly inside the **<script>** tags in an HTML file; for example, like this:

```
<script>
    // comments in JavaScript can start with //
    /* Block comments are also supported. This comment is multiple
       lines and doesn't end until we use a star then slash:
    */
    let a = 5; // declare the variable a, and set its value to 5
    console.log(a); // print a (5) to the browser console
</script>
```

Note that the **console.log** function prints out data to the browser console that is visible in the developer tools of your browser:

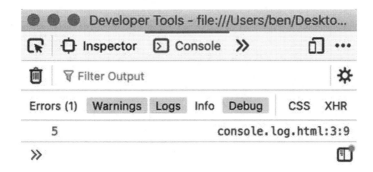

Figure 16.5: The result of the console.log(a) call – 5 is printed to the browser console

We could also put the code into its own file (we would not include the **<script>** tags in the standalone file). We then load it into the page using the **<script>** tag's **src** attribute, as we saw in *Chapter 5, Serving Static Files*:

```
<script src="{% static 'file.js' %}"></script>
```

The source code, whether inline or included, will be executed as soon as the browser loads the **<script>** tag.

Variables and Constants

Unlike in Python, variables in JavaScript must be declared, using either the **var**, **let**, or **const** keyword:

```
var a = 1; // variable a has the numeric value 1
let b = 'a'; // variable b has the string value 'a'
const pi = 3.14; // assigned as a constant and can't be redefined
```

Just like in Python, though, a type for a variable does not need to be declared. You will notice that the lines end with semicolons. JavaScript does not require lines to be terminated with semicolons – they are optional. However, some style guides enforce their use. You should try to stick with a single convention for any project.

You should use the **let** keyword to declare a variable. Variable declarations are scoped. For example, a variable declared with **let** inside a **for** loop will not be defined outside the loop. In this example, we'll loop through and sum the multiples of 10 till 90, and then print the result to **console.log**. You'll notice we can access variables declared at the function level inside the **for** loop, but not the other way around:

```
let total = 0;
for (let i = 0; i< 10; i++){  // variable i is scoped to the loop
    let toAdd = i * 10;   // variable toAdd is also scoped
    total += toAdd;   // we can access total since it's in the outer scope
}
console.log(total);   // prints 450
console.log(toAdd);   /* throws an exception as the variable is not
    declared in the outer scope */
console.log(i);   /* this code is not executed since an exception was
    thrown the line before, but it would also generate the same
        exception */
```

const is for constant data and cannot be redefined. That does not mean that the object it points to cannot be changed, though. For example, you couldn't do this:

```
const pi = 3.1416;
pi = 3.1;   /* raises exception since const values can't be
    reassigned */
```

The **var** keyword is required by older browsers that don't support **let** or **const**. Only 1% of browsers these days don't support those keywords, so throughout the rest of the chapter, we will only use **let** or **const**. Like **let**, variables declared with **var** can be reassigned; however, they are scoped at the function level only.

JavaScript supports several different types of variables, including strings, arrays, objects (which are like dictionaries), and numbers. We will cover arrays and objects in their own sections now.

Arrays

Arrays are defined similarly to how they are in Python, with square brackets. They can contain different types of data, just like with Python:

```
const myThings = [1, 'foo', 4.5];
```

Another thing to remember with the use of **const** is that it prevents reassigning the constant but does not prevent changing the variable or object being pointed to. For example, we would not be allowed to do this:

```
myThings = [1, 'foo', 4.5, 'another value'];
```

However, you could update the contents of the **myThings** array by using the **push** method (like Python's **list.append**) to append a new item:

```
myThings.push('another value');
```

Objects

JavaScript objects are like Python dictionaries, providing a key-value store. The syntax to declare them is similar as well:

```
const o = {foo: 'bar', baz: 4};
```

Note that, unlike Python, JavaScript object/dictionary keys do not need to be quoted when creating them – unless they contain special characters (spaces, dashes, dots, and more).

The values from **o** can be accessed either with item access or attribute access:

```
o.foo; // 'bar'
o['baz']; // 4
```

Also note that since **o** was declared as a constant, we cannot reassign it, but we can alter the object's attributes:

```
o.anotherKey = 'another value'  // this is allowed
```

Functions

There are a few different ways to define functions in JavaScript. We will look at three. You can define them using the **function** keyword:

```
function myFunc(a, b, c) {
   if (a == b)
      return c;
   else if (a > b)
      return 0;
   return 1;
}
```

All arguments to a function are optional in JavaScript; that is, you could call the preceding function like this: **myFunc()**, and no error would be raised (at least during call time). The **a**, **b**, and **c** variables would all be the special type **undefined**. This would cause issues in the logic of the function. **undefined** is kind of like **None** in Python – although JavaScript also has **null**, which is more similar to **None**. Functions can also be defined by assigning them to a variable (or constant):

```
const myFunc = function(a, b, c) {
    // function body is implemented the same as above
}
```

We can also define functions using an arrow syntax. For example, we can also define **myFunc** like this:

```
const myFunc = (a, b, c) => {
    // function body as above
}
```

This is more common when defining functions as part of an object, for example:

```
const o = {
myFunc: (a, b, c) => {
    // function body
    }
}
```

In this case, it would be called like this:

```
o.myFunc(3, 4, 5);
```

We will return to the reasons for using arrow functions after introducing classes.

Classes and Methods

Classes are defined with the **class** keyword. Inside a **class** definition, methods are defined without the **function** keyword. The JavaScript interpreter can recognize the syntax and tell that it is a method. Here is an example class, which takes a number to add (through **toAdd**) when instantiated. That number will be added to whatever is passed to the **add** method, and the result returned:

```
class Adder {
    // A class to add a certain value to any number

    // this is like Python's __init__ method
    constructor (toAdd) {
        //"this" is like "self" in Python
        //it's implicit and not manually passed into every method
        this.toAdd = toAdd;
    }

    add (n) {
        // add our instance's value to the passed in number
        return this.toAdd + n;
    }
}
```

Classes are instantiated with the **new** keyword. Other than that, their usage is very similar to classes in Python:

```
const a = new Adder(5);
console.log(a.add(3)); // prints "8"
```

Arrow Functions

Now that we've introduced the **this** keyword, we can return to the purpose of arrow functions. Not only are they shorter to write, but they also preserve the context of **this**. Unlike **self** in Python, which always refers to a specific object because it is passed into methods, the object that **this** refers to can change based on context. Usually, it is due to the nesting of functions, which is common in JavaScript.

Let's look at two examples. First, an object with a function called **outer**. This **outer** function contains an **inner** function. We refer to **this** in both the **inner** and **outer** functions:

> **NOTE**
>
> The next code example refers to the **window** object. In JavaScript, **window** is a special global variable that exists in each browser tab and represents information about that tab. It is an instance of the **window** class. Some examples of the attributes **window** has are **document** (which stores the current HTML document), **location** (which is the current location shown in the tab's address bar), and **outerWidth** and **outerHeight** (which represent the width and height of the browser window respectively). For example, to print the current tab's location to the browser console, you would write **console.log(window. location)**.

```
const o1 = {
    outer: function() {
        console.log(this);  // "this" refers to o1
        const inner = function() {
            console.log(this);  // "this" refers to the "window"
            object
        }
        inner();
    }
}
```

Inside the **outer** function, **this** refers to **o1** itself, whereas inside the **inner** function, **this** refers to the window (an object that contains information about the browser window).

Compare this to defining the inner function using arrow syntax:

```
const o2 = {
    outer: function() {
        console.log(this);  // refers to o2
        const inner = () => {
            console.log(this);  // also refers to o2
        }
```

```
        inner();
    }
}
```

When we use arrow syntax, **this** is consistent and refers to **o2** in both cases. Now that we have had a very brief introduction to JavaScript, let's introduce React.

> **FURTHER READING**
>
> Covering all the concepts of JavaScript is beyond the scope of this book. For a complete, hands-on course on JavaScript, you can always refer to *The JavaScript Workshop*: https://courses.packtpub.com/courses/javascript.

REACT

React allows you to build applications using components. Each component can *render* itself, by generating HTML to be inserted on the page.

A component may also keep track of its own *state*. If it does track its own state, when the state changes, the component will automatically re-render itself. This means if you have an action method that updates a state variable on a component, you don't need to then figure out whether the component needs to be redrawn; React will do this for you. A web app should track its own state so that it doesn't need to query the server to find out how it needs to update to display data.

Data is passed between components using properties, or *props* for short. The method of passing properties looks kind of like HTML attributes, but there are some differences, which we will cover later in the chapter. Properties are received by a component in a single **props** object.

To illustrate with an example, you might build a shopping list app with React. You would have a component for the list container (**ListContainer**), and a component for a list item (**ListItem**). **ListItem** would be instantiated multiple times, once for each item on the shopping list. The container would hold a state, containing a list of the items' names. Each item name would be passed to the **ListItem** instances as a *prop*. Each **ListItem** would then store the item's name and an **isBought** flag in its own state. As you click an item to mark it off the list, **isBought** would be set to **true**. Then React would automatically call **render** on that **ListItem** to update the display.

There are a few different methods of using React with your application. If you want to build a deep and complex React application, you should use **npm** (**Node Package Manager**, a tool for managing Node.js applications) to set up a React project. Since we are just going to be using React to enhance some of our pages, we can just include the React framework code using a **<script>** tag:

```
<script crossorigin src="https://unpkg.com/react@16/umd/react.
development.js"></script>
<script crossorigin src="https://unpkg.com/react-dom@16/umd/react-dom.
development.js"></script>
```

> **NOTE**
>
> The **crossorigin** attribute is for security and means cookies or other data cannot be sent to the remote server. This is necessary when using a public CDN such as https://unpkg.com/, in case a malicious script has been hosted there by someone.

These should be placed on a page that you want to add React to, just before the closing **</body>** tag. The reason for putting the tags here instead of in the **<head>** of the page is that the script might want to refer to HTML elements on the page. If we put the script tag in the head, it will be executed before the page elements are available (as they come after).

> **NOTE**
>
> The links to the latest React versions can be found at https://reactjs.org/docs/cdn-links.html.

COMPONENTS

There are two ways to build a component in React: with functions or with classes. Regardless of the approach, to get displayed on a page, the component must return some HTML elements to display. A functional component is a single function that returns elements, whereas a class-based component will return elements from its **render** method. Functional components cannot keep track of their own state.

React is like Django in that it automatically escapes HTML in strings that are returned from **render**. To generate HTML elements, you must construct them using their tag, the attributes/properties they should have, and their content. This is done with the **React.createElement** function. A component will return a React element, which may contain sub-elements.

Let us look at two implementations of the same component, first as a function then as a class. The functional component takes **props** as an argument. This is an object containing the properties that are passed to it. The following function returns an **h1** element:

```
function HelloWorld(props) {
return React.createElement('h1', null, 'Hello, ' +
  props.name + '!');
}
```

Note that it is conventional for the function to have an uppercase first character.

While a functional component is a single function that generates HTML, a class-based component must implement a **render** method to do this. The code in the **render** method is the same as in the functional component, with one difference: the class-based component accepts the **props** object in its constructor, and then **render** (or other) methods can refer to **props** using **this.props**. Here is the same **HelloWorld** component, implemented as a class:

```
class HelloWorld extends React.Component {
render() {
return React.createElement('h1', null, 'Hello, ' +
  this.props.name + '!');
  }
}
```

When using classes, all components extend from the **React.Component** class. Class-based components have an advantage over functional components, which is that they encapsulate the handling actions/event, and their own state. For simple components, using the functional style means less code. For more information on components and properties, see https://reactjs.org/docs/components-and-props.html.

Whichever method you choose to define a component, it is used in the same way. In this chapter, we will only be using class-based components.

To put this component onto an HTML page, we first need to add a place for React to render it. Normally, this is done using **<div>** with an **id** attribute. For example:

```
<div id="react_container"></div>
```

Note that **id** does not have to be **react_container**, it just needs to be unique for the page. Then, in the JavaScript code, after defining all your components, they are rendered on the page using the **ReactDOM.render** function. This takes two arguments: the root React element (not the component) and the HTML element in which it should be rendered.

We would use it like this:

```
const container = document.getElementById('react_container');
const componentElement = React.createElement(HelloWorld, {name:
  'Ben'});
ReactDOM.render(componentElement, container);
```

Note that the **HelloWorld** component (class/function) itself is not being passed to the **render** function, it is wrapped in a **React.createElement** call to instantiate it and transform it into an element.

As you might have guessed from its name, the **document.getElementById** function locates an HTML element in the document and returns a reference to it.

The final output in the browser when the component is rendered is like this:

```
<h1>Hello, Ben!</h1>
```

Let's look at a more advanced example component. Note that since **React.createElement** is such a commonly used function, it's common to alias to a shorter name, such as **e**: that's what the first line of this example does.

This component displays a button and has an internal state that keeps track of how many times the button was clicked. First, let's look at the component class in its entirety:

```
const e = React.createElement;

class ClickCounter extends React.Component {
  constructor(props) {
    super(props);
    this.state = { clickCount: 0 };
  }

  render() {
    return e(
      'button',  // the element name
      {onClick: () => this.setState({
        clickCount: this.state.clickCount + 1 }) },//element props
```

```
            this.state.clickCount    // element content
    );
  }
}
```

Some things to note about the **ClickCounter** class:

- The **props** argument is an object (dictionary) of attribute values that have been passed to the component when it is used in HTML. For example:

```
<ClickCounter foo="bar" rex="baz"/>
```

  The **props** dictionary would contain the key **foo** with a value of bar, and the key **rex** with the value **baz**.

- **super(props)** calls the super class's **constructor** method and passes the **props** variable. This is analogous to the **super()** method in Python.

- Each React class has a **state** variable, which is an object. **constructor** can initialize it. The state should be changed using the **setState** method, rather than being manipulated directly. When it is changed, the **render** method will be automatically called to redraw the component.

The **render** method returns a new HTML element, using the **React.createElement** function (remember, the **e** variable was aliased to this function). In this case, the arguments to **React.createElement** will return a **<button>** element with a click handler, and with the text content **this.state.clickCount**. Essentially, it will return an element like this (when **clickCount** is **0**):

```
<button onClick="this.setState(…)">
  0
</button>
```

The **onClick** function is set as an anonymous function with arrow syntax. This is similar to having a function as follows (although not quite the same since it's in a different context):

```
const onClick = () => {
this.setState({clickCount: this.state.clickCount + 1})
}
```

Since the function is only one line, we can also remove one set of wrapping braces, and we end up with this:

```
{ onClick: () => this.setState({clickCount:
  this.state.clickCount + 1}) }
```

We covered how to place **ClickCounter** onto a page earlier in this section, something like this:

```
ReactDOM.render(e(ClickCounter), document.getElementById
  ('react_container'));
```

The screenshot in the following figure shows the counter in the button when the page loads:

> **NOTE**
>
> In the following figure, **DjDt** refers to the debug toolbar that we learned about in the *Django Debug Toolbar* section in *Chapter 15, Django Third-Party Libraries*.

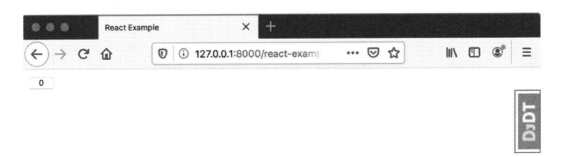

Figure 16.6: Button with 0 for the count

After clicking the button a few times, the button looks as shown in *Figure 16.7*:

Figure 16.7: Button after clicking seven times

Now, just to demonstrate how *not* to write the **render** function, we'll look at what happens if we just return HTML as a string, like this:

```
render() {
    return '<button>' + this.state.clickCount + '</button>'
}
```

Now the rendered page looks as shown in *Figure 16.8*:

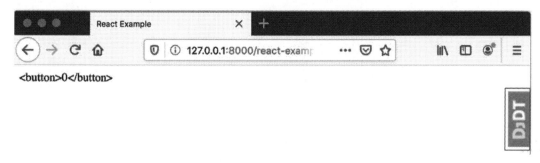

Figure 16.8: Returned HTML rendered as a string

This shows React's automatic escaping of HTML in action. Now that we have had a brief intro to JavaScript and React, let's add an example page to Bookr so you can see it in action.

EXERCISE 16.01: SETTING UP A REACT EXAMPLE

In this exercise, we will create an example view and template to use with React. Then we will implement the **ClickCounter** component. At the end of the exercise, you will be able to interact with it with the **ClickCounter** button:

1. In PyCharm, go to **New** -> **File** inside the project's **static** directory. Name the new file **react-example.js**.

2. Inside it, put this code, which will define the React component, then render it into the **react_container <div>** that we will be creating:

```
const e = React.createElement;

class ClickCounter extends React.Component {
  constructor(props) {
    super(props);
    this.state = { clickCount: 0 };
  }
```

```
    render() {
      return e(
        'button',
        { onClick: () => this.setState({
            clickCount: this.state.clickCount + 1
          })
      },
        this.state.clickCount
      );
    }
  }


ReactDOM.render(e(ClickCounter), document.getElementById
  ('react_container'))
```

You can now save **react-example.js**.

3. Go to **New** -> **HTML File** inside the project's **templates** directory:

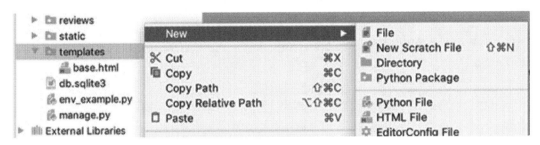

Figure 16.9: Create a new HTML file

Name the new file **react-example.html**:

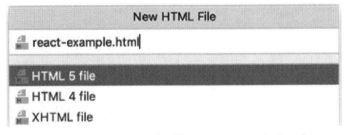

Figure 16.10: Name the file react-example.html

You can change the title inside the **<title>** element to *React Example*, but that is not necessary for this exercise.

4. **react-example.html** is created with some HTML boilerplate as we have seen before. Add the following **<script>** tags to include React just before the closing **</body>** tag:

```
<script crossorigin src="https://unpkg.com/react@16/umd/react.
development.js"></script>
<script crossorigin src="https://unpkg.com/react-dom@16/umd/react-
dom.development.js"></script>
```

5. The **react-example.js** file will be included using a **<script>** tag, and we need to generate the script path using the **static** template tag. First, **load** the static template library at the start of the file by adding this on the second line:

```
{% load static %}
```

The first few lines of your file will look like *Figure 16.11*:

```
<!DOCTYPE html>
{% load static %}
<html lang="en">
<head>
```

Figure 16.11: The load static template tag included

Then, just before the closing **</body>** tag, but after the **<script>** tags that were added in *step 4*, add this script tag to include your **react-example.js**:

```
<script src="{% static 'react-example.js' %}"></script>
```

6. We now need to add the containing **<div>** that React will render into. Add this element after the opening **<body>** tag:

```
<div id="react_container"></div>
```

You can save **react-example.html**.

7. Now we'll add a view to render the template. Open the **reviews** app's **views. py** and add a **react_example** view at the end of the file:

```
def react_example(request):
    return render(request, "react-example.html")
```

In this simple view, we are just rendering the **react-example.html** template with no context data.

8. Finally, we need to map a URL to the new view. Open the **bookr** package's **urls.py** file. Add this map to the **urlpatterns** variable:

```
path('react-example/', reviews.views.react_example)
```

You can save and close **urls.py**.

9. Start the Django dev server if it's not already running, then go to **http://127.0.0.1:8000/react-example/**. You should see the **ClickCount** button rendered as in *Figure 16.12*:

Figure 16.12: ClickCount button

Try clicking the button a few times and watch the counter increment.

In this example, we created our first React component, then added a template and view to render it. We included the React framework source from a CDN. In the next section, we will introduce **JSX**, which is a method of combining templates and code into a single file that can simplify our code.

JSX

It can be quite verbose to define each element using the **React.createElement** function – even when we alias to a shorter variable name. The verbosity is exacerbated when we start building larger components.

When using React, we can use JSX instead to build the HTML elements. JSX stands for JavaScript XML – since both JavaScript and XML are written in the same file. For example, consider the following code in which we are creating a button using the **render** method:

```
return React.createElement('button', { onClick: … },
    'Button Text')
```

Instead of this, we can return its HTML directly, as follows:

```
return <button onClick={…}>Button Text</button>;
```

Note that the HTML is not quoted and returned as a string. That is, we are not doing this:

```
return '<button onClick={…}>Button Text</button>';
```

Since JSX is an unusual syntax (a combination of HTML and JavaScript in a single file), we need to include another JavaScript library before it can be used: Babel (https://babeljs.io). This is a library that can *transpile* code between different versions of JavaScript. You can write code using the latest syntax and have it *transpiled* (a combination of translate and compile) into a version of code that older browsers can understand.

Babel can be included with a **<script>** tag like this:

```
<script crossorigin src="https://unpkg.com/babel-standalone@6/
   babel.min.js"></script>
```

This should be included on the page after your other React-related script tags, but before you include any files containing JSX.

Any JavaScript source code that includes JSX must have the **type="text/babel"** attribute added:

```
<script src="path/to/file.js" type="text/babel"></script>
```

This is so Babel knows to parse the file rather than just treating it as plain JavaScript.

> **NOTE**
>
> Note that using Babel in this way can be slow for large projects. It is designed to be used as part of the build process in an **npm** project and to have your JSX files transpiled ahead of time (rather than in real time as we are doing here). **npm** project setup is beyond the scope of this book. For our purposes and with the small amount of JSX we are using, using Babel will be fine.

JSX uses braces to include JavaScript data inside HTML, similar to Django's double braces in templates. JavaScript inside braces will be executed. We'll now look at how to convert our button creation example to JSX. Our **render** method can be changed to this:

```
render() {
    return <button onClick={() =>this.setState({
            clickCount: this.state.clickCount + 1
        })
    }>
    {this.state.clickCount}
</button>;
    }
```

Note that the **onClick** attribute has no quotes around its value; instead, it is wrapped in braces. This is passing the JavaScript function that is defined inline to the component. It will be available in that component's **props** dictionary that is passed to the **constructor** method. For example, imagine that we had passed it like this:

```
onClick="() =>this.setState..."
```

In such a case, it would be passed to the component as a string value and thus would not work.

We are also rendering the current value of **clickCount** as the content of the **button**. JavaScript could be executed inside these braces too. To show the click count plus one, we could do this:

```
{this.state.clickCount + 1}
```

In the next exercise, we will include Babel in our template and then convert our component to use JSX.

EXERCISE 16.02: JSX AND BABEL

In this exercise, we want to implement JSX in our component to simplify our code. To do this, we need to make a couple of changes to the **react-example.js** file and **react-example.html** file to switch to JSX to render **ClickCounter**:

1. In PyCharm, open **react-example.js** and change the **render** method to use JSX instead, by replacing it with the following code. You can refer to *step 2* from *Exercise 16.01*, *Setting Up a React Example*, where we defined this method:

```
render() {
return <button onClick={() => this.setState({
```

```
        clickCount: this.state.clickCount + 1
      })
    }>
    {this.state.clickCount}
</button>;
  }
```

2. We can now treat **ClickCounter** as an element itself. In the **ReactDOM. render** call at the end of the file, you can replace the first argument, **e(ClickCounter)**, with a **<ClickCounter/>** element, like this:

```
ReactDOM.render(<ClickCounter/>, document.getElementById
  ('react_container'));
```

3. Since we're no longer using the **React.create** function that we created in *step 2* of *Exercise 16.01, Setting Up a React Example*, we can remove the alias we created; delete the first line:

```
const e = React.createElement;
```

You can save and close the file.

4. Open the **react-example.html** template. You need to include the Babel library JavaScript. Add this code between the React **script** elements and the **react-example.js** element:

```
<script crossorigin src="https://unpkg.com/babel-standalone@6/babel.
min.js"></script>
```

5. Add a **type="text/babel"** attribute to the **react-example.html** **<script>** tag:

```
<script src="{% static 'react-example.js' %}" type="text/babel"></
script>
```

Save **react-example.html**.

6. Start the Django dev server if it is not already running and go to **http://127.0.0.1:8000/react-example/**. You should see the same button as we had before (*Figure 16.12*). When clicking the button, you should see the count increment as well.

In this exercise, we did not change the behavior of the **ClickCounter** React component. Instead, we refactored it to use JSX. This makes it easier to write the component's output directly as HTML and cut down on the amount of code we need to write. In the next section, we will look at passing properties to a JSX React component.

JSX PROPERTIES

Properties on JSX-based React components are set in the same way as attributes on a standard HTML element. The important thing to remember is whether you are setting them as a string or a JavaScript value.

Let's look at some examples using the **ClickCounter** component. Say that we want to extend **ClickCounter** so that a **target** number can be specified. When the target is reached, the button should be replaced with the text **Well done, <name>!**. These values should be passed into **ClickCounter** as properties.

When using variables, we have to pass them as JSX values:

```
let name = 'Ben'
let target = 5;


ReactDOM.render(<ClickCounter name={name} target={target}/>,
    document.getElementById('react_container'));
```

We can mix and match the method of passing the values too. This is also valid:

```
ReactDOM.render(<ClickCounter name="Ben" target={5}/>,
    document.getElementById('react_container'));
```

In the next exercise, we will update **ClickCounter** to read these values from properties and change its behavior when the target is reached. We will pass these values in from the Django template.

EXERCISE 16.03: REACT COMPONENT PROPERTIES

In this exercise, you will modify **ClickCounter** to read the values of **target** and **name** from its **props**. You will pass these in from the Django view and use the **escapejs** filter to make the **name** value safe for use in a JavaScript string. When you are finished, you will be able to click on the button until it reaches a target, and then see a **Well done** message:

1. In PyCharm, open the **reviews** app's **views.py**. We will modify the **react_example** view's **render** call to pass through a context containing **name** and **target**, like this:

    ```
    return render(request, "react-example.html", {"name": "Ben", \
                                                    "target": 5})
    ```

    You can use your own name and pick a different target value if you like. Save **views.py**.

2. Open the **react-example.js** file. We will update the **state** setting in the **constructor** method to set the name and target from **props**, like this:

```
constructor(props) {
    super(props);
    this.state = { clickCount: 0, name: props.name, target:
      props.target
    };
}
```

3. Change the behavior of the **render** method to return **Well done, <name>!** once **target** has been reached. Add this **if** statement inside the **render** method:

```
if (this.state.clickCount === this.state.target) {
    return <span>Well done, {this.state.name}!</span>;
}
```

4. To pass the values in, move the **ReactDOM.render** call into the template so that Django can render that piece of code. Cut this **ReactDOM.render** line from the end of **react-example.js**:

```
ReactDOM.render(<ClickCounter/>, document.getElementById
  ('react_container'));
```

We will paste it into the template file in *step 6*. **react-example.js** should now only contain the **ClickCounter** class. Save and close the file.

5. Open **react-example.html**. After all the existing **<script>** tags (but before the closing **</body>** tag), add opening and closing **<script>** tags with the **type="text/babel"** attribute. Inside them, we need to assign the Django context values that were passed to the template to JavaScript variables. Altogether, you should be adding this code:

```
<script type="text/babel">
let name = "{{ name|escapejs }}";
let target = {{ target }};
</script>
```

The first assigns the **name** variable with the **name** context variable. We use the **escapejs** template filter; otherwise, we could generate invalid JavaScript code if our name had a double quote in it. The second value, **target**, is assigned from **target**. This is a number, so it does not need to be escaped.

> **NOTE**
>
> Due to the way Django escapes the values for JavaScript, **name** cannot be passed directly to the component property like this:
>
> `<ClickCounter name="{{ name|escapejs }}"/>`
>
> The JSX will not un-escape the values correctly and you will end up with escape sequences.
>
> However, you could pass the numerical value target in like this:
>
> `<ClickCounter target="{ {{ target }} }"/>`
>
> Also, be aware of the spacing between the Django braces and JSX braces. In this book, we will stick with assigning all properties to variables first, then passing them to the component, for consistency.

6. Underneath these variable declarations, paste in the **ReactDOM.render** call that you copied from **react-example.js**. Then, add the **target={ target }** and **name={ name }** properties to **ClickCounter**. Remember, these are the JavaScript variables being passed in, not the Django context variables – they just happen to have the same name. The **<script>** block should now look like this:

```
<script type="text/babel">
    let name = "{{ name|escapejs }}";
    let target = {{ target }};
    ReactDOM.render(<ClickCounter name={ name }
       target={ target }/>, document.getElementById
         ('react_container'));
</script>
```

You can save **react-example.html**.

7. Start the Django dev server if it is not already running, then go to
    `http://127.0.0.1:8000/react-example/`. Try clicking the button a few
    times – it should increment until you click it **target** number of times. Then, it
    will be replaced with the **Well done, <name>!** text. See *Figure 16.13* for how
    it should look after you've clicked it enough times:

Figure 16.13: Well done message

In this exercise, we passed data to a React component using **props**. We escaped the
data when assigning it to a JavaScript variable using the **escapejs** template filter. In
the next section, we will cover how to fetch data over HTTP using JavaScript.

> **FURTHER READING**
>
> For a more detailed, hands-on course on React, you can always refer to *The
> React Workshop*: https://courses.packtpub.com/courses/react.

JAVASCRIPT PROMISES

To prevent blocking on long-running operations, many JavaScript functions are
implemented asynchronously. The way they work is by returning immediately, but
then invoking a callback function when a result is available. The object these types
of functions return is a **Promise**. Callback functions are provided to the **Promise**
object by calling its **then** method. When the function finishes running, it will
either **resolve** the **Promise** (call the **success** function) or **reject** it (call the
failure function).

We will illustrate the wrong and right way of using promises. Consider a hypothetical long-running function that performs a big calculation, called **getResult**. Instead of returning the result, it returns a **Promise**. You would not use it like this:

```
const result = getResult();
console.log(result);  // incorrect, this is a Promise
```

Instead, it should be invoked like this, with a callback function passed to **then** on the returned **Promise**. We will assume that **getResult** can never fail, so we only provide it with a **success** function for the resolve case:

```
const promise = getResult();
promise.then((result) => {
    console.log(result);  /* this is called when the Promise
        resolves*/
});
```

Normally, you wouldn't assign the returned **Promise** to a variable. Instead, you'd chain the **then** call to the function call. We'll show this in the next example, along with a failure callback (assume **getResult** can now fail). We'll also add some comments illustrating the order in which the code executes:

```
getResult().then(
(result) => {
        // success function
        console.log(result);
// this is called 2nd, but only on success
},
    () => {
        // failure function
        console.log("getResult failed");
        // this is called 2nd, but only on failure
})

// this will be called 1st, before either of the callbacks
console.log("Waiting for callback");
```

Now that we've introduced promises, we can look at the **fetch** function, which makes HTTP requests. It is asynchronous and works by returning promises.

FETCH

Most browsers (95%) support a function called **fetch**, which allows you to make HTTP requests. It uses an asynchronous callback interface with promises.

The **fetch** function takes two arguments. The first is the URL to make the request to and the second is an object (dictionary) with settings for the request. For example, consider this:

```
const promise = fetch("http://www.google.com", {…settings});
```

The settings are things such as the following:

- **method**: The request HTTP method (**GET**, **POST**, and more).

- **headers**: Another object (dictionary) of HTTP headers to send.

- **body**: The HTTP body to send (for **POST/PUT** requests).

- **credentials**: By default, **fetch** does not send any cookies. This means your requests will act like you are not authenticated. To have it set cookies in its requests, this should be set to the value **same-origin** or **include**.

Let's look at it in action with a simple request:

```
fetch('/api/books/', {
    method: 'GET',
    headers: {
        Accept: 'application/json'
    }
}).then((resp) => {
    console.log(resp)
})
```

This code will fetch from **/api/book-list/** and then call a function that logs the request to the browser's console using **console.log**.

Figure 16.14 shows the console output in Firefox for the preceding response:

```
▼ Response
  ▶ body: ReadableStream { locked: false }
    bodyUsed: false
  ▶ headers: Headers {  }
    ok: true
    redirected: false
    status: 200
    statusText: "OK"
    type: "basic"
    url: "http://127.0.0.1:8000/api/books/"
  ▶ <prototype>: ResponsePrototype { clone: clone(), arrayBuffer: arrayBuffer(), blob:
  blob(), … }
```

Figure 16.14: Response output in the console

As you can see, there isn't much information that is output. We need to decode the response before we can work with it. We can use the **json** method on the response object to decode the response body to a JSON object. This also returns a **Promise**, so we will ask to get the JSON, then work with the data in our callback. The full code block to do that looks like this:

```
fetch('/api/books/', {
    method: 'GET',
    headers: {
        Accept: 'application/json'
    }
}).then((resp) => {
    return resp.json(); // doesn't return JSON, returns a Promise
}).then((data) => {
    console.log(data);
});
```

This will log the decoded object that was in JSON format to the browser console. In Firefox, the output looks like *Figure 16.15*:

```
▼ (18) […]
  ▶ 0: Object { title: "Advanced Deep Learning with Keras", publication_date: "2018-10-31",
    isbn: "9781788629416", … }
  ▶ 1: Object { title: "Hands-On Machine Learning for Algorithmic Trading",
    publication_date: "2018-12-31", isbn: "9781789346411", … }
  ▶ 2: Object { title: "Architects of Intelligence", publication_date: "2018-11-23", isbn:
    "9781789954531", … }
  ▶ 3: Object { title: "Deep Reinforcement Learning Hands-On", publication_date:
    "2018-06-20", isbn: "9781788834247", … }
  ▶ 4: Object { title: "Natural Language Processing with TensorFlow", publication_date:
    "2018-05-30", isbn: "9781788478311", … }
  ▶ 5: Object { title: "Hands-On Reinforcement Learning with Python", publication_date:
    "2018-06-27", isbn: "9781788836524", … }
  ▶ 6: Object { title: "Brave New World", publication_date: "2006-10-18", isbn:
    "9780060850524", … }
  ▶ 7: Object { title: "The Grapes of Wrath", publication_date: "2006-03-28", isbn:
    "9780143039433", … }
  ▶ 8: Object { title: "For Whom The Bell Tolls", publication_date: "2019-07-16", isbn:
    "9781476787770", … }
  ▶ 9: Object { title: "To Kill A Mocking Bird", publication_date: "2002-01-01", isbn:
    "9780060935467", … }
  ▶ 10: Object { title: "The Great Gatsby", publication_date: "2004-09-30", isbn:
    "9780743273565", … }
  ▶ 11: Object { title: "The Catcher in the Rye", publication_date: "2001-01-30", isbn:
    "9780316769174", … }
  ▶ 12: Object { title: "Farenheit 451", publication_date: "2012-01-10", isbn:
    "9781451673319", … }
```

Figure 16.15: Decoded book list output to console

In *Exercise 16.04, Fetching and Rendering Books*, we will write a new React component that will fetch a list of books and then render each one as a list item (**<li>**). Before that, we need to learn about the JavaScript **map** method and how to use it to build HTML in React.

THE JAVASCRIPT MAP METHOD

Sometimes we want to execute the same piece of code (JavaScript or JSX) multiple times for different input data. In this chapter, it will be most useful to generate JSX elements with the same HTML tags but different content. In JavaScript, the **map** method iterates over the target array and then executes a callback function for each element in the array. Each of these elements is then added to a new array, which is then returned. For example, this short snippet uses **map** to double each number in the **numbers** array:

```
const numbers = [1, 2, 3];
const doubled = numbers.map((n) => {
    return n * 2;
});
```

The **doubled** array now contains the values **[2, 4, 6]**.

We can also create a list of JSX values using this method. The only thing to note is that each item in the list must have a unique **key** property set. In this next short example, we are transforming an array of numbers into **<li>** elements. We can then use them inside **<ul>**. Here is an example **render** function to do this:

```
render() {
    const numbers = [1, 2, 3];
    const listItems = numbers.map((n) => {
      return <li key={n}>{n}</li>;
      });
    return <ul>{listItems}</ul>
}
```

When rendered, this will generate the following HTML:

```
<ul>
<li>1</li>
<li>2</li>
<li>3</li>
</ul>
```

In the next exercise, we will build a React component with a button that will fetch the list of books from the API when it is clicked. The list of books will then be displayed.

EXERCISE 16.04: FETCHING AND RENDERING BOOKS

In this exercise, you will create a new component named **BookDisplay** that renders an array of books inside **<ul>**. The books will be retrieved using **fetch**. To do this, we add the React component into the **react-example.js** file. Then we pass the URL of the book list to the component inside the Django template:

1. In PyCharm, open **react-example.js**, which you previously used in *step 9* of *Exercise 16.03, React Component Properties*. You can delete the entire **ClickCounter** class.

2. Create a new class called **BookDisplay** that **extends** from **React.Component**.

3. Then, add a **constructor** method that takes **props** as an argument. It should call **super(props)** and then set its state like this:

```
this.state = { books: [], url: props.url, fetchInProgress:
   false };
```

This will initialize **books** as an empty array, read the API URL from the passed-in property **url**, and set a **fetchInProgress** flag to **false**. The code of your **constructor** method should be like this:

```
constructor(props) {
  super(props);
  this.state = { books: [], url: props.url, fetchInProgress:
  false };
}
```

4. Next, add a **doFetch** method. You can copy and paste this code to create it:

```
doFetch() {
  if (this.state.fetchInProgress)
      return;

  this.setState({ fetchInProgress: true })

    fetch(this.state.url, {
        method: 'GET',
        headers: {
            Accept: 'application/json'
```

```
        }
    }
  ).then((response) => {
      return response.json();
  }).then((data) => {
this.setState({ fetchInProgress: false, books: data })
  })
}
```

First, with the **if** statement, we check if a fetch has already been started. If so, we **return** from the function. Then, we use **setState** to update the state, setting **fetchInProgress** to **true**. This will both update our button display text and stop multiple requests from being run at once. We then **fetch** the **this.state.url** (which we will pass in through the template later in the exercise). The response is retrieved with the **GET** method and we only want to **Accept** a JSON response. After we get a response, we then return its JSON using the **json** method. This returns a **Promise**, so we use another **then** to handle the callback when the JSON is parsed. In that final callback, we set the state of the component, with **fetchInProgress** going back to **false**, and the **books** array being set to the decoded JSON data.

5. Next, create the **render** method. You can copy and paste this code too:

```
render() {
  const bookListItems = this.state.books.map((book) => {
      return <li key={ book.pk }>{ book.title }</li>;
  })

  const buttonText = this.state.fetchInProgress  ?
  'Fetch in Progress' : 'Fetch';

  return <div>
<ul>{ bookListItems }</ul>
<button onClick={ () =>this.doFetch() }
        disabled={ this.state.fetchInProgress }>
          {buttonText}
</button>
</div>;
}
```

This uses the **map** method to iterate over the array of books in **state**. We generate **<li>** for each book, using the book's **pk** as the **key** instance for the list item. The content of **<li>** is the book's title. We define a **buttonText** variable to store (and update) the text that the button will display. If we currently have a **fetch** operation running, then this will be *Fetch in Progress*. Otherwise, it will be *Fetch*. Finally, we return a **<div>** that contains all the data we want. The content of **<ul>** is the **bookListItems** variable (the array of **<li>** instances). It also contains a **<button>** instance added in a similar way to in the previous exercises. The **onClick** method calls the **doFetch** method of the class. We can make the button **disabled** (that is, the user can't click the button) if there is a fetch in progress. We set the button text to the **buttonText** variable we created earlier. You can now save and close **react-example.js**.

6. Open **react-example.html**. We need to replace the **ClickCounter** render (from *Exercise 16.03, React Component Properties*) with a **BookDisplay** render. Delete the **name** and **target** variable definitions. We will instead render the **<BookDisplay>**. Set the **url** property as a string and pass in the URL to the book list API, using the **{% url %}** template tag to generate it. The **ReactDOM.render** call should then look like this:

```
ReactDOM.render(<BookDisplay url="{% url 'api:book-list' %}" />,
    document.getElementById('react_container'));
```

You can now save and close **react-example.html**.

7. Start the Django dev server if it's not already running, then visit **http://127.0.0.1:8000/react-example/**. You should see a single **Fetch** button on the page (*Figure 16.16*):

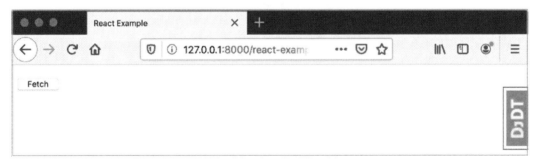

Figure 16.16: Book Fetch button

After clicking the **Fetch** button, it should become disabled and have its text changed to **Fetch in Progress**, as we can see here:

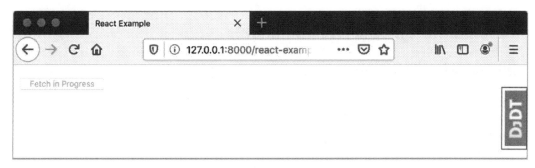

Figure 16.17: Fetch in Progress

Once the fetch is complete, you should see the list of books rendered as follows:

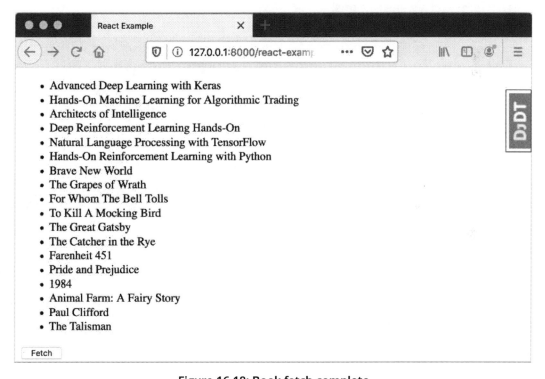

Figure 16.18: Book fetch complete

This exercise was a chance to integrate React with the Django REST API you built in *Chapter 12, Building a REST API*. We built a new component (**BookDisplay**) with a call to **fetch** to get a list of books. We used the JavaScript **map** method to transform the book array to some **<li>** elements. As we had seen before, we used **button** to trigger **fetch** when it was clicked. We then provided the book list API URL to the React component in the Django template. Later, we saw a list of books in Bookr that were loaded dynamically using the REST API.

Before we move onto the activity for this chapter, we will talk about some considerations for other JavaScript frameworks when working with Django.

THE VERBATIM TEMPLATE TAG

We have seen that when using React, we can use JSX interpolation values in Django templates. This is because JSX uses single braces to interpolate values, and Django uses double braces. As long as there are spaces between the JSX and Django braces, it should work fine.

Other frameworks, such as Vue, also use double braces for variable interpolation. What that means is if you had a Vue component's HTML in your template, you might try to interpolate a value like this:

```
<h1>Hello, {{ name }}!</h1>
```

Of course, when Django renders the template, it will interpolate the **name** value before the Vue framework gets a chance to render.

We can use the **verbatim** template tag to have Django output the data exactly as it appears in the template, without performing any rendering or variable interpolation. Using it with the previous example is simple:

```
{% verbatim %}
<h1>Hello, {{ name }}!</h1>
{% endverbatim %}
```

Now when Django renders the template, the HTML between the template tags will be output exactly as it is written, allowing Vue (or another framework) to take over and interpolate the variables itself. Many other frameworks separate their templates into their own files, which should not conflict with Django's templates.

There are many JavaScript frameworks available, and which one you ultimately decide to use will depend on your own opinion or what your company/team uses. If you do run into conflicts, the solution will depend on your particular framework. The examples in this section should help lead you in the right direction.

We have now covered most things you will need to integrate React (or other JavaScript frameworks) with Django. In the next activity, you will implement these learnings to fetch the most recent reviews on Bookr.

ACTIVITY 16.01: REVIEWS PREVIEW

In this activity, we will update the Bookr main page to fetch the six most recent reviews and display them. The user will be able to click buttons to go forward to the next six reviews, and then back to the previous ones.

These steps will help you complete the activity:

1. First, we can clean up some code from previous exercises. You can take backups of these files to preserve them for later reference if you like. Alternatively, you can use the GitHub versions too, for future reference. Delete the **react_example** view, **react-example** URL, **react-example.html** template, and **react-example.js** file.

2. Create a **recent-reviews.js** static file.

3. Create two components, a **ReviewDisplay** component that displays the data for a single review, and a **RecentReviews** component that handles fetching the review data and displaying a list of **ReviewDisplay** components.

    First, create the **ReviewDisplay** class. In its constructor, you should read the **review** being passed in through the **props** and assign it to the state.

4. The **render** method of **ReviewDisplay** should return JSX HTML like this:

```
<div className="col mb-4">
<div className="card">
<div className="card-body">
<h5 className="card-title">{ BOOK_TITLE }
<strong>({ REVIEW_RATING })</strong>
</h5>
<h6 className="card-subtitle mb-2 text-muted">CREATOR_EMAIL</h6>
<p className="card-text">REVIEW_CONTENT</p>
</div>
<div className="card-footer">
<a href={'/books/' + BOOK_ID` + '/' } className="card-link">
  View Book</a>
</div>
</div>
</div>
```

However, you should replace the **BOOK_TITLE**, **REVIEW_RATING**, **CREATOR_EMAIL**, **REVIEW_CONTENT**, and **BOOK_ID** placeholders with their proper values from the **review** that the component has fetched.

> **NOTE**
>
> Note that when working with JSX and React, the **class** of an element is set with the **className** attribute, not **class**. When it's rendered as HTML, it becomes **class**.

5. Create another React component called **RecentReviews**. Its **constructor** method should set up the **state** with the following keys/values:

   reviews: **[]** (empty list)

   currentUrl: **props.url**

   nextUrl: **null**

   previousUrl: **null**

   loading: **false**

6. Implement a method to download the reviews from the REST API. Call it **fetchReviews**. It should return immediately if **state.loading** is **true**. Then, it should set the **loading** property of **state** to **true**.

7. Implement **fetch** in the same way as you did in *Exercise 16.04, Fetching and Rendering Books*. It should follow the same pattern of requesting **state.currentUrl** and then getting the JSON data from the response. Then, set the following values in **state**:

   loading: **false**

   reviews: **data.results**

   nextUrl: **data.next**

   previousUrl: **data.previous**

8. Implement a **componentDidMount** method. This is a method that is called when React has loaded the component onto the page. It should call the **fetchReviews** method.

9. Create a **loadNext** method. If the **nextUrl** in **state** is null, it should return immediately. Otherwise, it should set **state.currentUrl** to **state. nextUrl**, then call **fetchReviews**.

10. Similarly, create a **loadPrevious** method; however, this should set **state. currentUrl** to **state.previousUrl**.

11. Implement the render method. If the state is loading, then it should return the text **Loading**... inside an **<h5>** element.

12. Create two variables to store the **previousButton** and **nextButton** HTML. They both should have the **btn btn-secondary** class and the next button should also have the **float-right** class. They should have **onClick** attributes set to call the **loadPrevious** or **loadNext** methods. They should have their **disabled** attributes set to **true** if the respective **previousUrl** or **nextUrl** attributes are **null**. The button text should be *Previous* or *Next*.

13. Iterate over the reviews using the **map** method and store the result to a variable. Each **review** should be represented by a **ReviewDisplay** component with the attribute **key** set to the review's **pk** and **review** set to the **Review** class. If there are no reviews (**reviews.length === 0**), then the variable instead should be an **<h5>** element with the content *No reviews to display*.

14. Finally, return all the content wrapped in **<div>** elements, like this:

```
<div>
<div className="row row-cols-1 row-cols-sm-2 row-cols-md-3">
     { reviewItems }
</div>
<div>
     {previousButton}
     {nextButton}
</div>
</div>
```

The **className** we are using here will display each review preview in one, two, or three columns depending on the screen size.

15. Next, edit **base.html**. You will add all the new content inside the **content** block so that it will not be displayed on the non-main pages that override this block. Add an **<h4>** element with the content **Recent Reviews**.

16. Add a **<div>** element for React to render into. Make sure you give it a unique **id**.

17. Include the **<script>** tags to include React, React DOM, Babel, and the **recent-reviews.js** file. These four tags should be similar to what you had in *Exercise 16.04, Fetching and Rendering Books*.

18. The last thing to add is another **<script>** tag containing the **ReactDOM. render** call code. The root component being rendered is **RecentReviews**. It should have a **url** attribute set to the value **url="{% url 'api:review-list' %}?limit=6"**. This does a URL lookup for **ReviewViewSet** and then appends a page size argument of **6**, limiting the number of reviews that are retrieved to a maximum of **6**.

Once you have completed these steps, you should be able to navigate to **http://127.0.0.1:8000/** (the main Bookr page) and see a page like this:

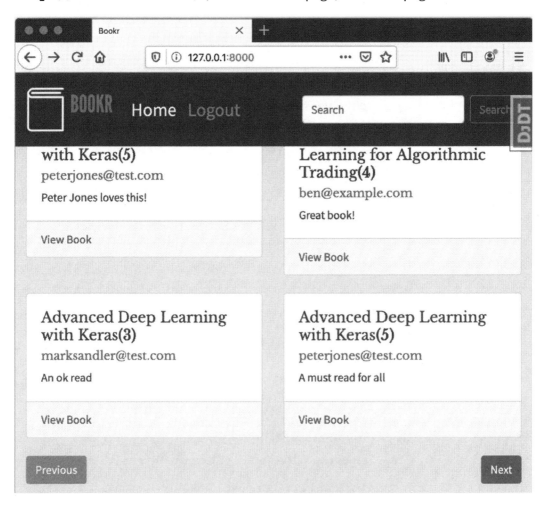

Figure 16.19: Completed reviews preview

In the screenshot, the page has been scrolled to show the **Previous/Next** buttons. Notice the **Previous** button is disabled because we are on the first page.

If you click **Next**, you should see the next page of reviews. If you click **Next** enough times (depending on how many reviews you have), you will eventually reach the last page and then the **Next** button will be disabled:

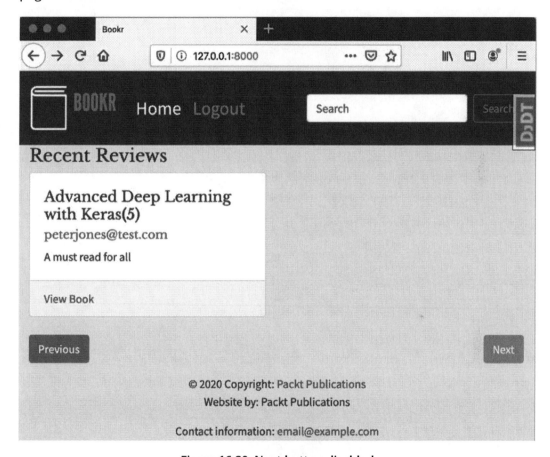

Figure 16.20: Next button disabled

If you have no reviews, then you should see the message **No reviews to display**:

Figure 16.21: No reviews to display. text

While the page is loading the reviews, you should see the text **Loading**...; however, it will probably only display for a split second since the data is being loaded off your own computer:

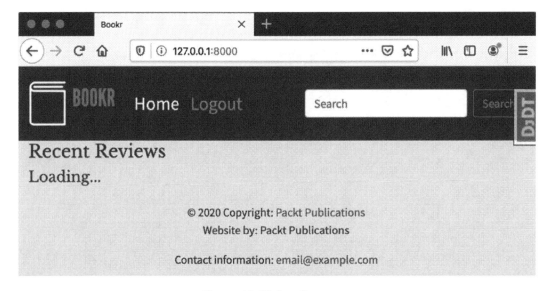

Figure 16.22: Loading text

> **NOTE**
>
> The solution to this activity can be found at http://packt.live/2Nh1NTJ.

SUMMARY

In this chapter, we introduced JavaScript frameworks and described how they work with Django to enhance templates and add interactivity. We introduced the JavaScript language and covered some of its main features, variable types, and classes. We then introduced the concepts behind React and how it builds HTML by using components. We built a React component using just JavaScript and the `React.createElement` function. After that, we introduced JSX and saw how it made the development of components easier, by letting you directly write HTML in your React components. The concepts of **promises** and the `fetch` function were introduced, and we saw how to get data from a REST API using `fetch`. The chapter finished with an exercise that retrieved reviews from Bookr using the REST API and rendered them to the page in an interactive component.

In the next chapter, we will look at how to deploy our Django project to a production web server. You can download the chapter from the GitHub repository for this book at http://packt.live/2Kx6FmR.

INDEX